YOUR COMPLETE 2025 PERSONAL HOROSCOPE

Monthly Astrological Prediction Forecast Readings of Every Zodiac Astrology Sun Star Signs- Love, Romance, Money, Finances, Career, Health, Spirituality.

Iris Quinn

Alpha Zuriel Publishing

Your Complete 2025 Personal Horoscope/ Iris Quinn. -- 1st ed.

"Astrology is a language. If you understand this language, the sky speaks to you."
— IRIS QUINN

CONTENTS

CHAPTER ONE

INTRODUCTION

Astrology, a celestial language as old as time itself, has captivated the hearts and minds of people across cultures and centuries. It is an ancient practice that seeks to unravel the mysteries of the cosmos and shed light on the intricate tapestry of human existence. Astrology is rooted in the belief that the positions and movements of celestial bodies, such as the sun, moon, planets, and stars, hold a profound influence over our lives, shaping our personalities, relationships, and destinies.

The origins of astrology can be traced back to the ancient civilizations of Mesopotamia, Egypt, and Greece, where the night sky served as a vast canvas upon which the stories of gods and mortals were written. These early stargazers observed the rhythmic dance of the heavens and sought to find meaning and guidance in the patterns they discerned. Over time, astrology evolved into a complex system of interpretation, with each celestial body and zodiac sign associated with specific traits, elements, and energies.

At the heart of astrology lies the zodiac, an imaginary belt in the sky divided into twelve equal parts, each represented by a unique constellation. The twelve zodiac signs—Aries, Taurus, Gemini, Cancer, Leo, Virgo, Libra, Scorpio, Sagittarius, Capricorn, Aquarius, and Pisces—form the foundation of astrological interpretation. Each sign embodies a distinct set of characteristics, strengths, weaknesses, and potentials, which are believed to be imprinted upon a person at the moment of their birth.

Beyond the zodiac signs, astrology also takes into account the positions and aspects of the planets, luminaries (sun and moon), and other celestial points. The planets are seen as the active forces that shape our experiences and growth, each with its own symbolic meaning and area of influence. The sun, often referred to as the "ruler of the zodiac," represents our core identity, vitality, and creative expression. The moon, on the other hand, governs our emotions, intuition, and subconscious realms. The interplay between these celestial bodies and their positions in relation to one another creates a dynamic and ever-changing cosmic dance that mirrors the complexities of human life.

Astrologers employ various tools and techniques to interpret this celestial symphony, chief among them being the natal chart. A natal chart is a snapshot of the sky at the precise moment of an individual's birth, capturing the positions of the planets, signs, and houses. It serves as a cosmic blueprint, offering insight into a person's innate qualities, challenges, and potentials. By studying the natal chart, astrologers can unlock the secrets of the soul and provide guidance for personal growth, self-understanding, and navigating life's many challenges and opportunities.

In addition to natal astrology, there are many other branches and techniques within the astrological tradition. Transits, for example, involve the current positions of the planets and how they interact with an individual's natal chart, indicating periods of change, growth, and opportunity. Synastry, or relationship astrology, explores the compatibility and dynamics between two individuals by comparing their natal charts. Horary astrology seeks to answer specific questions by casting a chart for the moment the question is asked, while electional astrology helps determine auspicious times for important events or undertakings.

While astrology has faced skepticism and criticism from the scientific community, it remains a powerful tool for self-discovery, personal growth, and finding meaning in the vast expanse of the universe. It offers a framework for understanding the cycles and seasons of our lives, the challenges we face, and the opportunities for transformation that await us. Whether one views astrology as a form of divination, a psychological tool, or a symbolic language, its enduring popularity is a testament to the human desire to connect with something greater than ourselves and to find our place in the grand cosmic narrative.

As we embark on this astrological voyage, let us briefly explore these foundational elements before delving into the intriguing realm of your 2025 Horoscope.

Glossary of Astrological Terms

The Planets:

In astrology, the planets are considered the main actors in the cosmic play, each with its own unique energy, symbolism, and influence on human life. The ten celestial bodies recognized in modern astrology are the Sun, Moon, Mercury, Venus, Mars, Jupiter, Saturn, Uranus, Neptune, and Pluto. Each planet represents a specific set of qualities, drives, and life themes that shape our experiences and growth.

The Sun: The Sun is the center of our solar system and the most important celestial body in astrology. It represents our core identity, vitality, creative self-expression, and life purpose. The Sun's position in our natal chart indicates our innate qualities, strengths, and areas of greatest potential.

The Moon: The Moon governs our emotional nature, instinctual responses, and subconscious patterns. It represents our inner world, memories, and the ways we nurture ourselves and others. The Moon's position in our natal chart reveals our emotional needs, family dynamics, and the ways we find comfort and security.

Mercury: Mercury is the planet of communication, learning, and mental processes. It governs our thoughts, perceptions, and the ways we gather and share information. Mercury's position in our natal chart indicates our communication style, learning preferences, and intellectual interests.

Venus: Venus is the planet of love, beauty, and harmony. It represents our values, relationships, and the ways we experience pleasure and attraction. Venus's position in our natal chart reveals our approach to love, our aesthetic sensibilities, and the ways we create balance and harmony in our lives.

Mars: Mars is the planet of action, assertion, and desire. It represents our energy, passion, and the ways we pursue our goals and desires. Mars's position in our natal chart indicates our assertiveness, courage, and the ways we handle conflict and competition.

Jupiter: Jupiter is the planet of expansion, growth, and abundance. It represents our beliefs, philosophies, and the ways we seek meaning and purpose in life. Jupiter's position in our natal chart reveals our areas of greatest opportunity, our capacity for faith and optimism, and the ways we experience luck and success.

Saturn: Saturn is the planet of structure, responsibility, and limitation. It represents our challenges, fears, and the ways we learn discipline and mastery. Saturn's position in our natal chart indicates our areas of greatest challenge, our sense of duty and responsibility, and the ways we build structure and security in our lives.

Uranus: Uranus is the planet of revolution, innovation, and change. It represents our urge for freedom, individuality, and the ways we break from tradition and convention. Uranus's position in our natal chart reveals our areas of greatest originality, our capacity for sudden insight and change, and the ways we experience liberation and awakening.

Neptune: Neptune is the planet of imagination, spirituality, and transcendence. It represents our dreams, intuition, and the ways we connect with the divine and the collective unconscious. Neptune's position in our natal chart indicates our areas of greatest creativity, our spiritual yearnings, and the ways we experience unity and oneness.

Pluto: Pluto is the planet of transformation, power, and regeneration. It represents our deepest fears, obsessions, and the ways we experience death and rebirth. Pluto's position in our natal chart reveals our areas of greatest intensity, our capacity for profound change and healing, and the ways we confront the shadow side of life.

Chiron: Chiron is a minor planet or asteroid that is often included in modern astrological interpretations. Known as the "wounded healer," Chiron represents our deepest wounds, our capacity for empathy and healing, and the ways we turn our pain into wisdom and service to others. Chiron's position in our natal chart indicates our areas of greatest vulnerability and potential for healing and growth.

The Elements:

In astrology, the twelve zodiac signs are divided into four elements: Fire, Earth, Air, and Water. Each element represents a fundamental quality of energy and consciousness that shapes our personality and life experiences.

Fire Signs (Aries, Leo, Sagittarius): Fire signs are passionate, energetic, and creative. They represent the spark of life, the urge for self-expression, and the quest for meaning and purpose. Fire signs are associated with qualities such as courage, enthusiasm, and inspiration.

Earth Signs (Taurus, Virgo, Capricorn): Earth signs are practical, grounded, and reliable. They represent the material world, the need for stability and security, and the ability to manifest ideas into reality. Earth signs are associated with qualities such as perseverance, responsibility, and practicality.

Air Signs (Gemini, Libra, Aquarius): Air signs are intellectual, communicative, and social. They represent the realm of ideas, the power of the mind, and the need for connection and exchange. Air signs are associated with qualities such as curiosity, adaptability, and innovation.

Water Signs (Cancer, Scorpio, Pisces): Water signs are emotional, intuitive, and empathetic. They represent the inner world of feelings, the capacity for deep connection and understanding, and the ability to flow with the tides of life. Water signs are associated with qualities such as sensitivity, compassion, and imagination.

The Houses:

In astrology, the twelve houses of the zodiac represent different areas of life experience. Each house is associated with specific themes, activities, and relationships that shape our journey through life.

1st House: The first house represents our sense of self, our appearance, and the ways we initiate and assert ourselves in the world.

2nd House: The second house represents our values, resources, and the ways we experience abundance and security.

3rd House: The third house represents our communication style, our learning processes, and our relationships with siblings and neighbors.

4th House: The fourth house represents our home life, family dynamics, and the ways we create emotional security and belonging.

5th House: The fifth house represents our creativity, self-expression, and the ways we experience joy, romance, and playfulness.

6th House: The sixth house represents our daily routines, work life, and the ways we maintain health and well-being.

7th House: The seventh house represents our partnerships, relationships, and the ways we experience balance and harmony with others.

8th House: The eighth house represents our experiences of death, rebirth, and transformation, as well as our shared resources and intimate connections.

9th House: The ninth house represents our quest for meaning, our philosophies and beliefs, and the ways we expand our horizons through travel, education, and spirituality.

10th House: The tenth house represents our career, public image, and the ways we achieve recognition and success in the world.

11th House: The eleventh house represents our friendships, social networks, and the ways we contribute to and benefit from community and collective endeavors.

12th House: The twelfth house represents our inner world, our subconscious patterns, and the ways we experience solitude, surrender, and spiritual connection.

The Aspects:

In astrology, aspects refer to the angular relationships between planets in a natal chart. These relationships are believed to indicate the ways in which the energies of the planets interact and influence each other, creating patterns of harmony, tension, or dynamic exchange.

Conjunction: A conjunction occurs when two or more planets are in the same sign and degree, blending their energies and qualities in a unified expression.

Opposition: An opposition occurs when two planets are 180 degrees apart, creating a dynamic of tension, balance, and integration between opposing forces.

Square: A square occurs when two planets are 90 degrees apart, creating a dynamic of challenge, conflict, and the need for effort and growth.

Trine: A trine occurs when two planets are 120 degrees apart, creating a dynamic of harmony, flow, and natural talent or ability.

Sextile: A sextile occurs when two planets are 60 degrees apart, creating a dynamic of opportunity, cooperation, and creative potential.

The Qualities:

In astrology, the twelve zodiac signs are also divided into three qualities or modalities: Cardinal, Fixed, and Mutable. Each quality represents a mode of expression and a way of responding to life's challenges and opportunities.

Cardinal Signs (Aries, Cancer, Libra, Capricorn): Cardinal signs are initiators, leaders, and agents of change. They represent the urge to take action, to start new projects, and to pioneer new directions in life.

Fixed Signs (Taurus, Leo, Scorpio, Aquarius): Fixed signs are stabilizers, organizers, and sustainers. They represent the ability to commit, to maintain focus and determination, and to bring projects to completion.

Mutable Signs (Gemini, Virgo, Sagittarius, Pisces): Mutable signs are adapters, communicators, and integrators. They represent the ability to be flexible, to gather and synthesize information, and to navigate change and transition with ease.

Grand Square:

A Grand Square, also known as a Grand Cross, is a powerful and dynamic configuration in a natal chart, formed when four planets are in square aspect to each other, creating a cross-like pattern. This configuration represents a significant life challenge or crisis that requires the individual to confront and integrate opposing forces and energies in order to achieve balance, growth, and transformation.

Karma:

In astrology, karma refers to the belief that our past actions and choices, both in this life and in previous lifetimes, have a significant impact on our current experiences and relationships. The placement of the Moon's Nodes (the North Node and the South Node) in the natal chart is often interpreted as indicating the individual's karmic path, with the South Node representing past patterns and the North Node representing the direction of growth and evolution.

Natal:

In astrology, the term "natal" refers to the moment of an individual's birth and the astrological chart that is calculated for that precise time and location. The natal chart, also known as a birth chart, is a snapshot of the heavens at the moment of birth, showing the positions of the planets, signs, and houses. The natal chart is the foundation of astrological interpretation, providing insight into an individual's personality, strengths, challenges, and life path.

Retrogrades:

In astrology, a planet is said to be retrograde when it appears to be moving backward in the sky from Earth's perspective. During a retrograde period, the energy and influence of the planet is believed to be turned inward, requiring reflection, reassessment, and the resolution of past issues. Each planet has its own retrograde cycle, with Mercury being the most well-known and frequent, occurring three to four times a year.

Transits:

In astrology, transits refer to the current positions of the planets and their angular relationships to the positions of the planets in an individual's natal chart. Transits are used to forecast current and future trends, opportunities, and challenges in an individual's life. As the transiting planets move through the zodiac, they activate different areas of the natal chart, triggering specific themes and experiences related to the houses and planets involved.

By understanding these fundamental concepts and components of astrology, we can begin to explore the rich and complex language of the stars and its profound insights into human life and experience. The interplay of planets, signs, houses, and aspects in the natal chart creates a unique cosmic signature that reflects the individual's innate qualities, potentials, and life journey. As we move through the transits and cycles of time, we are invited to engage with these energies consciously, to embrace the opportunities for growth and transformation, and to align ourselves with the greater wisdom and purpose of the universe.

CHAPTER TWO

GENERAL ASTROLOGY FOR 2025

Let's now look at the general astrology of 2025. This is significant transits that affect everyone, from a holistic perspective.

THE YEAR OF THE WOOD SNAKE 2025.

2025 is the Year of the Wood Snake in the Chinese zodiac. The Snake is a symbol of wisdom, intuition, and transformation. In Chinese astrology, the Wood element represents growth, creativity, and new beginnings. The combination of the Snake and Wood elements in 2025 suggests a year of profound changes, both on a personal and global scale, with an emphasis on adaptability, innovation, and spiritual growth.

Symbolism:
The Snake is the sixth animal in the Chinese zodiac and is associated with intelligence, sophistication, and mystery. In ancient Chinese philosophy, the Snake represents the concept of yin, the feminine principle of receptivity, intuition, and hidden knowledge. The Wood element adds a layer of flexibility, creativity, and growth to the Snake's energy, suggesting a year of significant transformations and new opportunities.

The Snake is also linked to the concept of rebirth and shedding one's skin, symbolizing the process of letting go of old patterns and embracing change. This theme of transformation will be prominent in 2025, as individuals and societies navigate the challenges and opportunities presented by the rapidly evolving world.

Economic Trends:
The Year of the Wood Snake is likely to bring significant shifts in the global economy. The Snake's energy favors strategic thinking, long-term planning, and calculated risks, while the Wood element encourages innovation and growth. This combination suggests that businesses and individuals who adapt to changing circumstances and invest in sustainable, forward-thinking projects are likely to thrive.

The technology sector, particularly in green energy, biotech, and artificial intelligence, is expected to experience significant growth in 2025. The Wood Snake's influence may also lead to increased investment in infrastructure projects, such as transportation and renewable energy, as governments and private sector entities seek to create jobs and stimulate economic recovery in the wake of the global pandemic.

However, the Snake's tendency towards secrecy and hidden agendas may also lead to increased scrutiny of financial institutions and multinational corporations. Transparency and accountability will be key themes in the economic landscape of 2025, as the public demands greater oversight and regulation of powerful entities.

Social and Cultural Impact:

The Year of the Wood Snake is likely to bring significant social and cultural shifts, as individuals and communities grapple with the ongoing effects of the global pandemic, climate change, and social inequality. The Snake's energy encourages introspection and self-reflection, while the Wood element promotes growth and new beginnings. This combination suggests that 2025 will be a year of profound personal and collective transformation, as people seek to redefine their values, relationships, and ways of living.

The Snake's association with hidden knowledge and intuition may also lead to a resurgence of interest in ancient wisdom traditions, alternative healing practices, and spirituality. The Wood element's influence may encourage the growth of eco-conscious communities, sustainable living initiatives, and a renewed appreciation for nature and the environment.

However, the Snake's tendency towards secrecy and mistrust may also exacerbate social tensions and political polarization. The challenge for individuals and societies in 2025 will be to find common ground, build bridges, and work together towards shared goals, despite differences in beliefs and backgrounds.

Technological Innovations:

The Year of the Wood Snake is likely to bring significant advancements in technology, particularly in the fields of artificial intelligence, biotechnology, and green energy. The Snake's intelligence and strategic thinking, combined with the Wood element's creativity and innovation, suggest that 2025 will be a year of groundbreaking discoveries and inventions.

In the field of artificial intelligence, we can expect to see significant progress in natural language processing, computer vision, and machine learning. These advancements may lead to the development of more sophisticated virtual assistants, personalized learning algorithms, and intelligent automation systems that can streamline business processes and improve efficiency.

In biotechnology, the Year of the Wood Snake may bring breakthroughs in personalized medicine, gene editing, and regenerative therapies. The Snake's association with rebirth and transformation, combined with the Wood element's focus on growth and healing, suggest that 2025 will be a year of significant progress in the fight against chronic diseases and age-related conditions.

The green energy sector is also expected to experience significant growth in 2025, as governments and private sector entities invest in renewable energy projects, such as solar, wind, and hydro power. The Wood Snake's influence may also lead to the development of more efficient energy storage systems, smart grid technologies, and sustainable transportation solutions.

Global Politics:

The Year of the Wood Snake is likely to bring significant shifts in global politics, as nations grapple with the ongoing effects of the global pandemic, climate change, and social inequality. The Snake's strategic thinking and long-term planning, combined with the Wood element's focus on growth and new beginnings, suggest that 2025 will be a year of significant diplomatic breakthroughs and international cooperation.

However, the Snake's tendency towards secrecy and hidden agendas may also lead to increased tensions and conflicts between nations, particularly in the realm of trade, technology, and geopolitical influence. The challenge for global leaders in 2025 will be to find common ground, build trust, and work together towards shared goals, despite differences in ideology and interests.

The Year of the Wood Snake may also bring increased attention to issues of social and environmental justice, as activists and grassroots movements push for greater accountability and transparency from governments and corporations. The Wood element's influence may encourage the growth of international coalitions and partnerships focused on addressing climate change, poverty, and human rights abuses.

Personal Growth and Relationships:

The Year of the Wood Snake is likely to be a transformative year for personal growth and relationships. The Snake's energy encourages introspection, self-reflection, and the shedding of old patterns and beliefs that no longer serve us. The Wood element adds a layer of creativity, flexibility, and growth to this process, suggesting that 2025 will be a year of significant personal breakthroughs and new beginnings.

In the realm of relationships, the Year of the Wood Snake may bring increased focus on authenticity, vulnerability, and deep connection. The Snake's association with hidden knowledge and intuition may lead to greater self-awareness and empathy in interpersonal interactions, while the Wood element's influence may encourage the growth of supportive, nurturing relationships based on mutual trust and respect.

However, the Snake's tendency towards secrecy and mistrust may also lead to challenges in relationships, particularly if there are unresolved issues or power imbalances at play. The key to navigating these challenges in 2025 will be open communication, honesty, and a willingness to confront difficult truths with compassion and understanding.

The Year of the Wood Snake may also bring increased focus on personal development and learning, as individuals seek to acquire new skills, knowledge, and experiences that align with their values and passions. The Wood element's influence may encourage the pursuit of creative hobbies, artistic expression, and holistic well-being practices, such as yoga, meditation, and nature-based therapies.

Spirituality and Self-Discovery:

The Year of the Wood Snake is likely to be a year of profound spiritual growth and self-discovery. The Snake's association with hidden knowledge, intuition, and transformation, combined with the Wood element's focus on growth and new beginnings, suggest that 2025 will be a year of significant breakthroughs in personal and collective consciousness.

The Snake's energy encourages us to shed our old skin and embrace change, letting go of limiting beliefs, patterns, and identities that no longer serve our highest good. The Wood element's influence may lead to a resurgence of interest in ancient wisdom traditions, alternative healing practices, and eco-spirituality, as individuals seek to reconnect with nature and the divine feminine.

The Year of the Wood Snake may also bring increased focus on the importance of mindfulness, self-care, and inner work. The Snake's tendency towards introspection and self-reflection may lead to greater awareness of our thoughts, emotions, and behaviors, and a desire to cultivate greater self-compassion, resilience, and emotional intelligence.

However, the Snake's association with secrecy and hidden knowledge may also lead to challenges in the realm of spirituality and self-discovery. The key to navigating these challenges in 2025 will be discernment, critical thinking, and a willingness to question our assumptions and beliefs, while remaining open to new perspectives and experiences.

Health and Wellness:

The Year of the Wood Snake is likely to bring increased focus on holistic health and wellness, as individuals seek to cultivate greater balance, vitality, and resilience in the face of global challenges. The Snake's association with transformation and rebirth, combined with the Wood element's focus on growth and healing, suggest that 2025 will be a year of significant advancements in integrative medicine, mind-body therapies, and preventative healthcare.

The Snake's energy encourages us to tune into our bodies' wisdom and intuition, and to address the root causes of illness and imbalance, rather than simply treating symptoms. The Wood element's influence may lead to a resurgence of interest in herbal medicine, acupuncture, and other traditional healing modalities, as well as a greater emphasis on nutrition, exercise, and stress management as key components of overall health and well-being.

The Year of the Wood Snake may also bring increased focus on mental health and emotional well-being, as individuals seek to cultivate greater resilience, adaptability, and inner peace in the face of life's challenges. The Snake's tendency towards introspection and self-reflection may lead to greater awareness of the impact of trauma, stress, and unresolved emotions on our physical and mental health, and a desire to seek out effective therapies and support systems.

However, the Snake's association with secrecy and hidden knowledge may also lead to challenges in the realm of health and wellness, such as the spread of misinformation, or the exploitation of vulnerable individuals by unscrupulous practitioners. The key to navigating these challenges in 2025 will be critical thinking, research, and a willingness to seek out reputable sources of information and support.

Education and Learning:
The Year of the Wood Snake is likely to bring significant shifts in the realm of education and learning, as individuals and institutions grapple with the ongoing effects of the global pandemic, technological disruption, and changing social and economic realities. The Snake's strategic thinking and adaptability, combined with the Wood element's focus on growth and innovation, suggest that 2025 will be a year of significant experimentation and transformation in the way we teach, learn, and acquire new skills and knowledge.

The Snake's energy encourages us to be lifelong learners, constantly seeking out new opportunities for growth and development, both personally and professionally. The Wood element's influence may lead to a resurgence of interest in experiential learning, project-based education, and interdisciplinary studies, as individuals seek to cultivate a more holistic, integrative approach to knowledge and problem-solving.

The Year of the Wood Snake may also bring increased focus on the importance of emotional intelligence, creativity, and critical thinking skills in education and the workplace. The Snake's tendency towards introspection and self-reflection may lead to greater emphasis on self-awareness, empathy, and effective communication as key competencies for success in the 21st century.

However, the Snake's association with secrecy and hidden knowledge may also lead to challenges in the realm of education and learning, such as the spread of misinformation, or the exploitation of students by for-profit institutions. The key to navigating these challenges in 2025 will be transparency, accountability, and a commitment to ethical, student-centered practices in education and training.

Environmental Considerations:
The Year of the Wood Snake is likely to bring increased focus on environmental sustainability and the urgent need for collective action to address climate change and ecological degradation. The Snake's association with transformation and rebirth, combined with the Wood element's focus on growth and harmony with nature, suggest that 2025 will be a year of significant progress in the transition towards a more sustainable, regenerative economy and way of life.

The Snake's energy encourages us to shed our old skin and embrace change, letting go of unsustainable practices, technologies, and systems that are harming the planet and its inhabitants. The Wood element's influence may lead to a resurgence of interest in renewable energy, circular economy models, and nature-based solutions, as individuals and organizations seek to align their activities with the principles of ecology and regeneration.

The Year of the Wood Snake may also bring increased focus on the importance of biodiversity conservation, sustainable land management, and the rights of indigenous peoples and local communities as stewards of the Earth's natural heritage. The Snake's tendency towards hidden knowledge and intuition may lead to greater appreciation for traditional ecological knowledge and the wisdom of indigenous cultures in guiding our relationship with the natural world.

However, the Snake's association with secrecy and hidden agendas may also lead to challenges in the realm of environmental action, such as the influence of powerful vested interests, or the spread of misinformation and denial about the severity of the ecological crisis. The key to navigating these challenges in 2025 will be transparency, accountability, and a commitment to science-based, collaborative approaches to environmental problem-solving.

In conclusion, the Year of the Wood Snake in 2025 is likely to be a year of profound transformation, innovation, and growth, both on a personal and collective level. The Snake's energy of wisdom, intuition, and adaptability, combined with the Wood element's focus on creativity, vitality, and harmony with nature, suggest that this will be a year of significant breakthroughs and new beginnings in many areas of life, from technology and education to health and spirituality.

However, the Snake's tendency towards secrecy and hidden knowledge may also lead to challenges and obstacles, particularly in the realms of politics, economics, and social justice. The key to navigating these challenges in 2025 will be to cultivate greater self-awareness, empathy, and discernment, while remaining open to new perspectives and experiences, and working collaboratively towards shared goals and values.

Ultimately, the Year of the Wood Snake invites us to shed our old skin and embrace the process of transformation and growth, both individually and collectively. By tapping into the wisdom and creativity of the Snake, and the vitality and resilience of the Wood element, we can navigate the challenges and opportunities of this pivotal year with grace, compassion, and a renewed sense of purpose and possibility.

2025 ASTROLOGY PREDICTIONS

2025 will be an astrologically transformative and significant year, colored by major planetary shifts, powerful eclipses, and important aspects between the outer planets. The cosmic energies this year will catalyze profound changes on both the individual and collective levels.

The year kicks off with Venus entering Pisces on January 2, bringing a dreamy, compassionate and imaginative energy to relationships and creative pursuits. Mercury shifts into Aquarius on the 27th, stimulating innovative ideas and encouraging humanitarian efforts.

Late January through February sees Saturn forming significant aspects to Pluto and Chiron, which will be a major theme throughout the year. This represents an opportunity for deep healing, maturation and confronting issues of power and control vs. cooperation and higher purpose. The Aquarius New Moon on January 29 plants potent seeds for envisioning a new paradigm.

March is an intense month, with Saturn moving into Pisces on the 24th, beginning a new 2.5 year cycle of learning spiritual lessons, dissolving boundaries and refining our ideals. The Aries New Moon on the 29th is a Partial Solar Eclipse, giving an energetic push towards courageous new beginnings. However, it occurs near the South Node, so we must release baggage from the past in order to surge ahead.

April features a powerful Total Lunar Eclipse in Libra on the 12th, exposing imbalances in relationships and highlighting the need for greater harmony, equality and social justice. Pluto stations retrograde on May 4th, beginning a 5-month phase of deconstructing and regenerating outdated power structures. The Scorpio Full Moon on May 12 intensifies the purging process.

Late May brings a significant shift as Saturn dips into Aries from May 24 to July 13. This will give us a preview of its full transit through Aries starting in 2026, initiating a phase of asserting boundaries, pioneering leadership and claiming personal sovereignty.

June is a pivotal month with Jupiter entering Cancer on the 9th, bringing expansion to home, family and emotional connection over the next year. The Saturn-Neptune square on June 18-19 can bring disillusionment but also the opportunity to align our dreams and ideals with concrete reality. The Cancer New Moon on June 25 supports setting intentions for more nurturing, security and receptivity.

July starts off with a New Moon in Cancer on July 1, further emphasizing themes of the home, family roots, and emotional needs. On July 4, Venus enters Gemini, lightening the mood and bringing a more social, communicative energy to relationships.

The pace accelerates with Mercury turning retrograde in Leo from July 18 to August 11, which will be a time to slow down, reflect and reevaluate creative projects and self-expression. The Full Moon Total Lunar Eclipse in Aquarius on August 7 can bring sudden revelations and shifts in group dynamics.

Mid-August brings a series of planetary stations, with Ceres turning retrograde in Aries on the 11th, encouraging reflection on how we nurture ourselves and others. Jupiter stations retrograde in Cancer on August 23, giving us four months to refine our emotional, domestic and familial growth. The Leo New Moon on the 24th supports reconnecting with our inner child and individual creative spark.

September features a New Moon Partial Solar Eclipse in Virgo on the 21st near the equinox, which will provide a burst of focused, pragmatic energy for improving daily routines, work and health. Venus enters Libra on October 13, returning our focus to relationships, harmony and social connection. The Sun's entry into Scorpio on October 22 and New Moon in Scorpio on October 21 take us into the depths of power, passion and transformation.

In November, Jupiter ends its retrograde phase and resumes direct motion on November 11, bringing renewed growth and optimism. The Taurus Full Moon on November 5 helps stabilize and ground the changes that have been unfolding. Mercury starts its last retrograde cycle of the year on November 9 in Sagittarius, turning our attention back to meaning, truth and belief systems.

December opens with Neptune direct in Pisces squared by the Gemini Full Moon on December 4. This can bring a crisis of faith but also the chance for spiritual breakthroughs and creative inspiration. The Capricorn Solar Eclipse on December 19 sets the stage for ambitious new beginnings as we approach 2026. Venus and the Sun entering Capricorn on the 24th and 21st enhance the hardworking, goal-oriented energies. The Cancer Full Moon on December 27 provides emotional sustenance for the journey ahead.

In summary, 2025 will be a year of bridging the ideal and the real, the spiritual and the material. We'll be challenged to mature and take responsibility, while also opening our hearts and imaginations. Waves of change will catalyze both personal and collective transformation. Staying grounded, adaptable and true to our core purpose will help us make the most of this powerful year of change and growth.

CHAPTER THREE

ARIES 2025 HOROSCOPE

Overview Aries 2025 (March 21 - April 19)

2025 promises to be a year of transformative growth, self-discovery, and new beginnings for those born under the sign of Aries. As the celestial bodies dance through the heavens, they will bring a mix of challenges and opportunities that will shape your journey throughout the year.

The year begins with Mars, your ruling planet, in the sign of Cancer. This placement suggests a strong focus on home, family, and emotional security in the first part of the year. You may find yourself drawn to nurturing your close relationships, creating a comfortable living space, and exploring your inner world of feelings and intuition. This is a time to build a strong foundation for the growth and changes to come.

In mid-January, Uranus will turn direct in your 2nd house of values and resources, bringing a fresh perspective on your financial situation and your sense of self-worth. This is a time to break free from limiting beliefs and embrace new opportunities for abundance and prosperity. Trust your unique talents and skills, and be open to unconventional ways of earning and managing your resources.

As the year progresses, a significant shift occurs in March when Saturn moves into your sign, Aries. This transit, which will last until May 2025, marks the beginning of a new 30-year cycle of growth and maturity. Saturn's influence will challenge you to take responsibility for your life, to set clear goals and boundaries, and to develop the discipline and perseverance needed to achieve your dreams. This is a time to confront your fears, learn from your mistakes, and build a strong sense of self-reliance and integrity.

The Aries New Moon on March 29 brings a powerful opportunity for new beginnings and fresh starts. This is a time to set intentions for the year ahead, to clarify your vision and purpose, and to take bold action towards your goals. The influence of Saturn will ensure that your efforts are grounded, realistic, and sustainable over the long term.

In mid-April, Jupiter will form a square aspect to Pluto, highlighting the need for deep transformation and renewal in your life. This transit may bring up issues of power, control, and hidden shadows that need to be confronted and healed. Trust in the process of growth and change, and be willing to let go of what no longer serves you. This is a time to embrace your inner strength and resilience, and to trust in the wisdom of the universe.

As the year progresses, the North Node will shift into your 12th house of spirituality and inner growth, while the South Node will move into your 6th house of health and service. This suggests a powerful opportunity for emotional healing, spiritual awakening, and the release of past patterns and traumas. You may find yourself drawn to practices such as meditation, therapy, or creative expression as a way to connect with your inner world and find a deeper sense of meaning and purpose.

In late April, Pluto will turn retrograde in your 11th house of friendships and social groups, bringing a period of reflection and re-evaluation in your connections with others. This is a time to assess the quality and authenticity of your relationships, and to let go of any connections that are draining or toxic. Focus on building a supportive network of like-minded individuals who share your values and aspirations.

The mid-year period brings a series of powerful eclipses that will accelerate your growth and transformation. The Total Lunar Eclipse in Virgo on March 14 will highlight the need for self-care, health, and service in your life. This is a time to focus on your physical and emotional well-being, and to find ways to contribute your unique gifts and talents to the world. The Partial Solar Eclipse in Aries on March 29 will bring a powerful opportunity for new beginnings and self-discovery. Trust your instincts and take bold action towards your goals, even if it means stepping outside your comfort zone.

In mid-June, Saturn will briefly shift into Aries, giving you a preview of the growth and challenges to come. This is a time to take stock of your life, to assess your strengths and weaknesses, and to start putting in place the structures and discipline needed for long-term success. Focus on building a strong foundation for the future, and trust that your efforts will pay off in the long run.

The second half of the year brings a focus on relationships, creativity, and self-expression. Venus, the planet of love and beauty, will spend an extended period in your 5th house of romance and creativity, bringing opportunities for joy, passion, and artistic pursuits. This is a time to let your unique light shine, to express your authentic self, and to attract love and abundance into your life.

In late September, Mars will shift into your 7th house of partnerships, bringing a dynamic and passionate energy to your closest relationships. This is a time to assert your needs and desires, to communicate openly and honestly with your loved ones, and to work together towards common goals. Be mindful of potential conflicts or power struggles, and strive to find a balance between your own needs and the needs of others.

The Partial Solar Eclipse in Virgo on September 21 will bring a powerful opportunity for growth and transformation in your daily routines, health, and work life. This is a time to let go of old habits and patterns that no longer serve you, and to embrace a more holistic and mindful approach to your well-being. Trust in the power of small, consistent steps towards your goals, and be open to new opportunities for learning and growth.

As the year comes to a close, Jupiter will turn direct in your 4th house of home and family, bringing a sense of expansion and optimism to your personal life. This is a time to celebrate your achievements, to enjoy the fruits of your labors, and to deepen your connections with loved ones. Trust in the journey of growth and self-discovery, and know that you have the inner strength and wisdom to navigate whatever challenges may come your way.

Throughout the year, the influence of Chiron in your 12th house of spirituality and inner growth will continue to bring opportunities for deep healing and transformation. This is a time to confront your wounds and shadows, to embrace your vulnerability and sensitivity, and to find a deeper sense of compassion and understanding for yourself and others. Trust in the power of surrender and faith, and know that your struggles and challenges are ultimately serving your highest growth and evolution.

Overall, 2025 is a year of powerful growth, transformation, and self-discovery for Aries. With Saturn and the eclipses bringing challenges and opportunities for maturity and responsibility, and with Jupiter and Venus bringing expansion and joy in your personal life, this is a time to embrace your unique path and purpose with courage and confidence. Trust in the journey, stay true to yourself, and know that the universe is conspiring in your favor. With an open heart and a willingness to learn and grow, you have the power to create a life of deep meaning, fulfillment, and purpose.

January 2025

Overview Horoscope for the Month:

Welcome to January 2025, Aries! This month is all about new beginnings, self-reflection, and setting the stage for an incredible year ahead. With Mars, your ruling planet, entering the nurturing sign of Cancer on January 6th, you may find yourself feeling more introspective and focused on your emotional well-being. This is a time to connect with your inner world, to reflect on your past experiences, and to set intentions for the future that align with your deepest desires and values.

The New Moon in Aquarius on January 29th brings a powerful opportunity for fresh starts and new perspectives. This is a time to embrace your unique qualities, to think outside the box, and to connect with like-minded individuals who share your vision for a better world. Trust in the power of your own creativity and innovation, and don't be afraid to take bold steps towards your dreams.

Love:

In love, January 2025 is a month of emotional depth and intimacy. With Mars in Cancer, you may find yourself craving a deeper sense of connection and security in your relationships. This is a time to open your heart, to express your feelings with vulnerability and authenticity, and to create a safe and nurturing space for love to flourish.

If you're in a committed relationship, take time to connect with your partner on a soul level. Share your hopes, fears, and dreams, and listen with empathy and understanding. This is a time to strengthen your bond through acts of love, kindness, and mutual support.

If you're single, you may find yourself drawn to people who offer emotional stability and comfort. Look for partners who share your values of honesty, loyalty, and emotional intelligence. Don't be afraid to take things slow and build a strong foundation of trust and friendship before diving into a romantic relationship.

Career:

In your career, January 2025 is a month of reflection, planning, and laying the groundwork for future success. With Mars in Cancer, you may feel a strong desire to create a work environment that feels supportive, nurturing, and emotionally fulfilling. This is a time to reflect on your career goals and values, and to make sure that your work aligns with your deepest sense of purpose and meaning.

Take time to review your past accomplishments and challenges, and identify areas where you can improve and grow. Set clear intentions for the year ahead, and break them down into manageable steps that you can take each day, week, and month.

If you're considering a career change or starting a new business, the New Moon in Aquarius on January 29th is a powerful time to take action. Trust in your unique talents and skills, and don't be afraid to think outside the box and try something new. Surround yourself with supportive colleagues and mentors who believe in your vision and can help you navigate any challenges that arise.

Finances:

In finances, January 2025 is a month of security, stability, and long-term planning. With Mars in Cancer, you may feel a strong desire to create a sense of financial safety and comfort for yourself and your loved ones. This is a time to review your budget, to identify areas where you can save and invest, and to make sure that your financial decisions align with your values and goals.

Take time to reflect on your relationship with money, and identify any limiting beliefs or patterns that may be holding you back from abundance and prosperity. Practice gratitude for the resources and opportunities that you already have, and trust that the universe will continue to support you as you work towards your financial goals.

If you're considering making a major purchase or investment, do your research and seek the advice of trusted financial advisors. Make sure that any decisions you make are grounded in your long-term vision for financial security and stability.

Health:

In health, January 2025 is a month of self-care, nurturing, and emotional well-being. With Mars in Cancer, you may feel a strong desire to create a sense of comfort and safety in your physical and emotional body. This is a time to listen to your body's needs and rhythms, and to prioritize activities that bring you a sense of peace, relaxation, and rejuvenation.

Take time to engage in gentle exercise, such as yoga, walking, or swimming, that helps you feel grounded and centered. Nourish your body with healthy, whole foods that support your immune system and energy levels. Make sure to get plenty of rest and sleep, and create a bedtime routine that helps you unwind and release any stress or tension from the day.

On an emotional level, practice self-compassion and kindness towards yourself. Acknowledge any feelings of anxiety, fear, or uncertainty that may arise, and offer yourself the same love and support that you would offer a dear friend. Seek out activities that bring you joy, creativity, and a sense of connection to something greater than yourself.

Travel:

In travel, January 2025 may bring opportunities for short trips or staycations that allow you to reconnect with your roots and nurture your emotional well-being. With Mars in Cancer, you may feel a strong desire to spend time with family and loved ones, to visit places that hold special meaning and memories, and to create a sense of comfort and belonging wherever you go.

If you do decide to travel, choose destinations that offer a sense of peace, beauty, and emotional resonance. Consider booking a cozy cabin in the woods, a seaside retreat, or a spa weekend that allows you to unwind and recharge.

If travel isn't possible or practical, find ways to bring a sense of adventure and exploration into your daily life. Try a new recipe from a favorite cuisine, explore a nearby park or nature trail, or curl up with a good book that transports you to another time and place.

Insight from the Stars:

The celestial energies of January 2025 remind you of the power of emotional intelligence, intuition, and inner wisdom. With Mars in Cancer, you are being called to connect with your deepest feelings and desires, to trust in the guidance of your heart, and to create a life that feels authentic, meaningful, and emotionally fulfilling.

The New Moon in Aquarius on January 29th invites you to embrace your unique qualities and perspectives, to connect with like-minded individuals who share your vision for a better world, and to take bold steps towards your dreams and goals. Trust in the power of your own creativity, innovation, and inner knowing, and don't be afraid to think outside the box and try something new.

Remember that you are a powerful creator and manifester, and that your thoughts, emotions, and actions have the power to shape your reality and bring your deepest desires to life. Stay open to the guidance and support of the universe, and trust that everything is unfolding in perfect timing and alignment with your highest good.

Best Days of the Month:

January 2nd: Venus enters Pisces, bringing a dreamy, romantic, and imaginative energy to your love life and creative pursuits.

January 11th: The True Node enters Pisces, highlighting your spiritual growth and soul's evolution.

January 21st: Mercury enters Aquarius, bringing fresh ideas and innovative thinking to your communication and mental processes.

January 29th: The New Moon in Aquarius invites you to embrace your unique qualities, connect with like-minded individuals, and take bold steps towards your dreams and goals.

January 30th: Uranus turns direct in Taurus, bringing sudden insights, breakthroughs, and positive changes to your financial situation and values.

February 2025

Overview Horoscope for the Month:

February 2025 is a month of passion, creativity, and self-expression for you, Aries. With Venus entering your sign on February 4th, you'll feel a powerful surge of confidence, charisma, and magnetism. This is a time to shine your light brightly, to pursue your deepest desires and passions, and to make bold moves towards your dreams and goals.

The Full Moon in Leo on February 12th illuminates your 5th house of romance, creativity, and self-expression. This is a time to celebrate your unique talents and gifts, to let your inner child out to play, and to take center stage in your own life story. Trust in the power of your own creativity and joy, and don't be afraid to take risks and put yourself out there.

At the same time, the presence of Saturn, Uranus, and Pluto in your 11th, 12th, and 10th houses respectively suggests that February 2025 is also a month of deep inner work and transformation. You may find yourself grappling with issues of power, control, and surrender, as you learn to let go of old patterns and beliefs that no longer serve you. Trust in the process of growth and evolution, and know that the challenges you face are ultimately serving your highest good.

Love:

In love, February 2025 is a month of passion, romance, and self-love. With Venus in your sign from February 4th to March 1st, you'll feel more attractive, desirable, and confident than ever before. This is a time to embrace your sensual nature, to express your love and affection freely, and to attract partners who appreciate and adore you for who you truly are.

If you're single, you may find yourself suddenly surrounded by potential suitors and admirers. Don't be afraid to take the lead in pursuing your romantic interests, but also make sure to take time to get to know someone before diving in too deep. Look for partners who share your values, passions, and sense of adventure, and who support and encourage your personal growth and evolution.

If you're in a committed relationship, February 2025 is a time to reignite the spark of passion and romance. Plan special date nights, surprise your partner with thoughtful gestures and gifts, and make time for intimate conversations and physical affection. At the same time, be mindful of any power struggles or control issues that may arise, and work to communicate openly and honestly with your partner to find a resolution.

Career:

In your career, February 2025 is a month of creativity, innovation, and leadership. With Mars entering Leo on February 7th, you'll feel a powerful drive to take charge of your professional life and make your mark on the world. This is a time to showcase your unique talents and skills, to take on new challenges and responsibilities, and to pursue your passions with courage and enthusiasm.

At the same time, the presence of Saturn in your 11th house of networking and community suggests that success in your career may come through collaboration and teamwork. Look for opportunities to connect with like-minded individuals who share your vision and values, and be open to feedback and support from mentors and colleagues.

If you're an entrepreneur or business owner, February 2025 is a time to take bold risks and pursue new opportunities for growth and expansion. Trust in your instincts and creativity, and don't be afraid to think outside the box and try something new. Just make sure to do your due diligence and research before making any major investments or decisions.

Finances:

In finances, February 2025 is a month of abundance, prosperity, and manifestation. With Jupiter in your 2nd house of money and resources, you may find yourself suddenly blessed with unexpected windfalls, bonuses, or opportunities for financial growth. This is a time to embrace a mindset of abundance and gratitude, and to trust that the universe is conspiring to support your material needs and desires.

At the same time, the presence of Uranus in your 2nd house suggests that your financial situation may be somewhat unpredictable or unstable. Be open to new sources of income and revenue streams, but also make sure to have a solid plan in place for saving and budgeting. Avoid impulsive purchases or risky investments, and focus on building a strong foundation of financial security and stability.

If you're struggling with debt or financial stress, February 2025 is a time to seek out support and guidance from trusted advisors or professionals. Don't be afraid to ask for help or to negotiate payment plans or settlements that work for your unique situation. Remember that your self-worth is not tied to your bank account balance, and that true abundance comes from a place of inner peace and contentment.

Health:

In health, February 2025 is a month of vitality, energy, and self-care. With the Sun in your sign until February 18th, you'll feel a powerful sense of aliveness and enthusiasm for life. This is a time to focus on building strength, endurance, and resilience, both physically and emotionally.

Make time for regular exercise and physical activity, whether it's hitting the gym, going for a run, or trying a new yoga or dance class. Nourish your body with whole, nutrient-dense foods that support your energy levels and immune system, and make sure to stay hydrated and well-rested.

At the same time, be mindful of any tendencies towards burnout or overexertion. With Mars in Leo, you may feel a strong drive to push yourself to the limit, but it's important to listen to your body's signals and take breaks when needed. Practice self-compassion and kindness towards yourself, and remember that true health is about balance and harmony, not perfection.

Travel:

In travel, February 2025 may bring opportunities for short trips or weekend getaways that feed your sense of adventure and curiosity. With Venus in your sign, you may feel a strong desire to explore new places, try new things, and connect with new people. This is a time to indulge your wanderlust and follow your heart wherever it leads you.

Consider planning a spontaneous road trip with friends or loved ones, or booking a last-minute flight to a destination that's been on your bucket list. Look for experiences that allow you to step outside your comfort zone and challenge yourself in new ways, whether it's trying a new cuisine, learning a new language, or embarking on a wild outdoor adventure.

At the same time, be mindful of any travel restrictions or safety concerns related to the ongoing pandemic. Make sure to do your research and follow all necessary precautions and guidelines to ensure a safe and enjoyable trip.

Insight from the Stars:

The celestial energies of February 2025 remind you of the power of self-love, creativity, and authenticity. With Venus in your sign, you are being called to embrace your unique beauty, talents, and desires, and to express yourself freely and joyfully in all areas of your life. Trust in the power of your own magnetism and charisma, and know that you have the ability to attract abundance, love, and success simply by being true to yourself.

At the same time, the presence of Saturn, Uranus, and Pluto in your chart suggests that February 2025 is also a time of deep inner work and transformation. You may find yourself grappling with issues of power, control, and surrender, as you learn to let go of old patterns and beliefs that no longer serve you. Trust in the process of growth and evolution, and know that the challenges you face are ultimately serving your highest good.

Remember that you are a powerful creator and manifester, and that your thoughts, words, and actions have the power to shape your reality. Stay focused on your dreams and goals, surround yourself with positive and supportive people, and trust that the universe is conspiring in your favor. With an open heart and a willingness to embrace change and growth, February 2025 can be a month of incredible joy, abundance, and self-discovery for you, Aries.

Best Days of the Month:

February 4th: Venus enters Aries, bringing a surge of confidence, charisma, and magnetism to your love life and creative pursuits.

February 7th: Mars enters Leo, igniting your passion, creativity, and leadership skills in your career and public life.

February 12th: The Full Moon in Leo illuminates your 5th house of romance, creativity, and self-expression, inviting you to celebrate your unique talents and gifts.

February 19th: Jupiter sextile Chiron, bringing opportunities for healing, growth, and self-discovery in your financial and personal life.

February 23rd: Mars direct in Cancer, ending its retrograde period and bringing forward momentum and clarity to your home and family life.

March 2025

Overview Horoscope for the Month:

Aries, March 2025 is a pivotal month for you, filled with powerful astrological alignments that will shape the course of your journey for years to come. The headline event is Saturn's entry into your sign on March 24th, marking the beginning of a new 28-year cycle of growth, responsibility, and maturation. This is a time to step into your power, to take ownership of your life path, and to build the structures and foundations that will support your long-term success and fulfillment.

At the same time, the New Moon in your sign on March 29th brings a potent opportunity for new beginnings and fresh starts. This is a time to set clear intentions for the future you want to create, to take bold action towards your goals and dreams, and to trust in the power of your own creativity and resilience.

The presence of Jupiter, Uranus, and Neptune in your 12th house of spirituality and unconscious mind suggests that March 2025 is also a month of deep inner work and transformation. You may find yourself grappling with issues of surrender, faith, and divine guidance, as you learn to let go of control and trust in the unfolding of your soul's journey. Be open to messages and insights from your dreams, intuition, and synchronicities, and trust that the universe is conspiring to support your highest good.

Love:

In love, March 2025 is a month of depth, intimacy, and emotional healing. With Venus moving through your 12th house of spirituality and unconscious patterns until March 27th, you may find yourself drawn to explore the hidden depths of your own psyche and the psyche of your partner. This is a time to face your fears and vulnerabilities, to let go of old wounds and traumas, and to open your heart to a deeper level of love and connection.

If you're in a committed relationship, March 2025 is a powerful time to work on issues of trust, communication, and emotional intimacy. Be willing to have difficult conversations, to express your needs and desires honestly, and to listen to your partner with empathy and understanding. Remember that true love is not about perfection, but about growth, healing, and mutual support.

If you're single, March 2025 may bring a soulmate connection or a deep spiritual bond with someone who shares your values and vision. Be open to unconventional or unexpected ways of meeting people, and trust your intuition when it comes to matters of the heart. At the same time, make sure to do your inner work and heal any past wounds or patterns that may be blocking your ability to give and receive love fully.

Career:

In your career, March 2025 is a month of hard work, discipline, and long-term planning. With Saturn entering your sign on March 24th, you're being called to take your professional life to the next level and to build a legacy that reflects your true values and purpose. This is a time to set clear goals and benchmarks, to develop your skills and expertise, and to take on new challenges and responsibilities with courage and determination.

At the same time, the presence of Uranus and Neptune in your 12th house of spirituality and unconscious mind suggests that your career path may be influenced by a higher calling or a sense of divine purpose. You may find yourself drawn to work that allows you to make a positive impact on the world, to serve others with compassion and empathy, or to express your unique gifts and talents in a way that feels authentic and meaningful.

If you're an entrepreneur or business owner, March 2025 is a time to focus on building strong foundations and systems that will support your long-term growth and success. Be willing to put in the hard work and effort required to manifest your vision, but also make sure to take care of your own well-being and energy levels along the way.

Finances:

In finances, March 2025 is a month of responsibility, discipline, and long-term planning. With Saturn entering your sign, you're being called to take a serious look at your financial situation and to make any necessary changes or adjustments to ensure your long-term security and stability. This may involve creating a budget, paying off debt, or investing in your future through savings, retirement accounts, or real estate.

At the same time, the presence of Jupiter and Neptune in your 12th house of spirituality and unconscious mind suggests that your relationship with money may be influenced by deeper issues of self-worth, abundance, and divine providence. You may find yourself grappling with feelings of scarcity or lack, or questioning your own deserving of financial success and prosperity.

To navigate these challenges, focus on cultivating a mindset of abundance and gratitude, and trust that the universe will provide for your needs as you align your actions with your highest values and purpose. Be open to unexpected sources of income or financial blessings, but also make sure to do your due diligence and research before making any major financial decisions.

Health:

In health, March 2025 is a month of vitality, resilience, and self-care. With the Sun in your sign until March 20th, you'll feel a powerful sense of energy and enthusiasm for life. This is a time to focus on building strength, endurance, and immunity, both physically and emotionally.

Make time for regular exercise and movement, whether it's hitting the gym, going for a run, or practicing yoga or martial arts. Nourish your body with whole, nutrient-dense foods that support your energy levels and overall well-being, and make sure to stay hydrated and well-rested.

At the same time, be mindful of any tendencies towards overwork or self-neglect. With Saturn entering your sign, you may feel a strong drive to push yourself to the limit, but it's important to listen to your body's signals and take breaks when needed. Practice self-compassion and kindness towards yourself, and remember that true health is about balance, harmony, and self-love.

Travel:

In travel, March 2025 may bring opportunities for spiritual pilgrimages, retreats, or journeys of self-discovery. With Jupiter, Uranus, and Neptune in your 12th house of spirituality and unconscious mind, you may feel a strong desire to explore new dimensions of reality, to connect with higher realms of consciousness, or to seek out wisdom and guidance from teachers, healers, or spiritual communities.

Consider planning a trip to a sacred site or power spot, such as a temple, ashram, or natural wonder. Look for experiences that allow you to tap into your inner wisdom, to release old patterns and beliefs, and to open your heart and mind to new possibilities and perspectives.

At the same time, be mindful of any tendencies towards escapism or avoidance. While travel can be a powerful tool for growth and transformation, it's important to make sure that you're not using it as a way to run away from your responsibilities or challenges. Make sure to ground yourself in practical reality, and to integrate any insights or experiences you gain on your journey into your daily life and relationships.

Insight from the Stars:

The celestial energies of March 2025 remind you of the power of surrender, faith, and divine guidance. With Saturn entering your sign and the New Moon in Aries, you are being called to step into your power, to take responsibility for your life path, and to build the structures and foundations that will support your long-term success and fulfillment. At the same time, the presence of Jupiter, Uranus, and Neptune in your 12th house invites you to let go of control, to trust in the unfolding of your soul's journey, and to open yourself to the wisdom and guidance of the universe.

Remember that you are a spiritual being having a human experience, and that your challenges and obstacles are ultimately serving your highest growth and evolution. Stay connected to your inner truth, surround yourself with love and support, and trust that everything is happening for your highest good. With courage, faith, and a willingness to embrace change and growth, March 2025 can be a month of incredible transformation, healing, and awakening for you, Aries.

Best Days of the Month:

March 14th: The Full Moon in Virgo illuminates your 6th house of health, work, and service, bringing a sense of clarity and purpose to your daily routines and responsibilities.

March 24th: Saturn enters Aries, marking the beginning of a new 28-year cycle of growth, responsibility, and maturation in your life path and identity.

March 27th: Venus enters Aries, bringing a surge of confidence, charisma, and magnetism to your love life and creative pursuits.

March 29th: The New Moon in Aries brings a powerful opportunity for new beginnings, fresh starts, and bold action towards your goals and dreams.

March 30th: Neptune enters Aries, inviting you to open yourself to new dimensions of spirituality, creativity, and imagination in your life path and identity.

April 2025

Overview Horoscope for the Month:

Aries, April 2025 is a month of intensity, transformation, and rebirth for you. The cosmic energies are calling you to dive deep into your psyche, to confront your shadows and fears, and to emerge stronger, wiser, and more authentic than ever before. With the Sun, Mercury, and Venus all moving through your sign for much of the month, you'll feel a powerful sense of vitality, clarity, and magnetism. This is a time to take bold action towards your goals and dreams, to express yourself with confidence and creativity, and to trust in the power of your own unique path.

At the same time, the presence of Pluto, Jupiter, and Chiron in your 12th, 11th, and 1st houses respectively suggests that April 2025 is also a month of deep healing, spiritual growth, and personal evolution. You may find yourself grappling with issues of power, control, and surrender, as you learn to let go of old patterns and beliefs that no longer serve you. Be open to insights and breakthroughs that come through dreams, synchronicities, and moments of divine guidance, and trust that the challenges you face are ultimately serving your highest good.

The headline event of the month is the powerful Total Lunar Eclipse in Libra on April 12th, which will illuminate your 7th house of partnerships and relationships. This is a time to face the truth about your connections with others, to release any toxic or imbalanced dynamics, and to cultivate a greater sense of harmony, equality, and mutual respect in your relationships. Be willing to have difficult conversations, to set clear boundaries, and to make any necessary changes or adjustments to ensure that your partnerships are aligned with your highest values and goals.

Love:

In love, April 2025 is a month of passion, intensity, and deep emotional connection. With Venus moving through your sign until April 30th, you'll feel a powerful sense of magnetism and allure, attracting admirers and potential partners like bees to honey. This is a time to embrace your sensual nature, to express your desires and needs with confidence, and to explore new dimensions of intimacy and pleasure in your relationships.

If you're in a committed partnership, the Total Lunar Eclipse in Libra on April 12th may bring some intense revelations or challenges to the surface. You may find yourself confronting issues of power, control, or co-dependency, or feeling a need for greater autonomy and freedom in your relationship. Be willing to have honest conversations with your partner, to listen with empathy and understanding, and to work together to find solutions that honor both of your needs and desires.

If you're single, April 2025 may bring some intense and transformative connections into your life. You may find yourself attracted to someone who challenges you to grow and evolve, or who mirrors back to you the parts of yourself that you need to heal or integrate. Be open to the lessons and opportunities that arise, but also make sure to maintain healthy boundaries and to prioritize your own self-care and well-being.

Career:

In your career, April 2025 is a month of ambition, leadership, and personal power. With the Sun, Mercury, and Venus all moving through your sign, you'll feel a strong drive to take charge of your professional life and to make your mark on the world. This is a time to showcase your unique talents and skills, to take on new challenges and responsibilities, and to pursue your goals with confidence and determination.

At the same time, the presence of Pluto in your 12th house of spirituality and unconscious mind suggests that your career path may be undergoing a deep transformation or rebirth. You may find yourself questioning your true purpose or calling, or feeling a need to align your work with your deepest values and beliefs. Trust your intuition and inner guidance as you navigate these changes, and be open to new opportunities and directions that may arise.

If you're an entrepreneur or business owner, April 2025 is a powerful time to take your venture to the next level. Be willing to take calculated risks, to innovate and experiment, and to trust in your own vision and leadership. At the same time, make sure to build strong partnerships and collaborations that can support your growth and success, and to cultivate a sense of integrity and purpose in all of your business dealings.

Finances:

In finances, April 2025 is a month of abundance, prosperity, and personal power. With Jupiter in your 11th house of hopes, dreams, and community, you may find yourself attracting new opportunities for financial growth and success through your network and connections. This is a time to think big, to pursue your wildest dreams and aspirations, and to trust in the power of synchronicity and divine timing.

At the same time, the presence of Chiron in your 1st house of self and identity suggests that your relationship with money and abundance may be undergoing a deep healing or transformation. You may find yourself confronting old wounds or beliefs around worthiness, scarcity, or financial insecurity, and learning to cultivate a greater sense of self-love and self-worth. Remember that true abundance comes from within, and that your value is not determined by your bank balance or material possessions.

To navigate these energies, focus on cultivating a mindset of gratitude and sufficiency, and on aligning your financial goals with your deepest values and purpose. Be open to unexpected sources of income or support, but also make sure to do your due diligence and research before making any major financial decisions. Trust that the universe will provide for your needs as you stay true to your path and purpose.

Health:

In health, April 2025 is a month of vitality, resilience, and deep healing. With the Sun, Mercury, and Venus all moving through your sign, you'll feel a powerful sense of energy and enthusiasm for life. This is a time to focus on building strength, endurance, and immunity, both physically and emotionally.

Make time for regular exercise and movement, whether it's through high-intensity workouts, yoga, or dance. Nourish your body with whole, nutrient-dense foods that support your energy levels and overall well-being, and make sure to stay hydrated and well-rested.

At the same time, the presence of Chiron in your 1st house of self and identity suggests that April 2025 may bring some deep healing or transformation around your relationship with your body and your sense of self-worth. You may find yourself confronting old wounds or traumas, or learning to love and accept yourself more fully. Be gentle and compassionate with yourself during this process, and seek out the support and guidance of trusted healers or therapists if needed.

Travel:

In travel, April 2025 may bring some unexpected or transformative journeys that challenge you to grow and evolve. With Uranus in your 2nd house of values and resources, you may find yourself drawn to travel experiences that shake up your sense of security or comfort, or that invite you to question your assumptions and beliefs. This could be anything from a solo backpacking trip through a foreign country to a spiritual retreat or workshop that pushes you out of your comfort zone.

At the same time, the presence of Saturn in your 12th house of spirituality and unconscious mind suggests that any travel experiences you undertake in April 2025 may have a deep spiritual or transformative purpose. You may find yourself drawn to sacred sites or power spots, or seeking out wisdom and guidance from teachers or mentors who can help you navigate your inner journey.

Whatever form your travels take, be open to the lessons and opportunities that arise, and trust that they are ultimately serving your highest growth and evolution. Make sure to take care of your physical and emotional well-being during your journeys, and to integrate any insights or experiences you gain into your daily life and relationships.

Insight from the Stars:

The celestial energies of April 2025 remind you of the power of transformation, healing, and personal evolution. With the Sun, Mercury, and Venus all moving through your sign, you are being called to step into your full power and potential, to express yourself with confidence and authenticity, and to trust in the unique path that is unfolding before you. At the same time, the presence of Pluto, Jupiter, and Chiron in your chart invites you to dive deep into your psyche, to confront your shadows and fears, and to emerge stronger, wiser, and more whole.

Remember that growth and transformation often involve discomfort and uncertainty, but that these challenges are ultimately serving your highest good. Stay connected to your inner truth, surround yourself with love and support, and trust that the universe is conspiring in your favor. With courage, faith, and a willingness to embrace change, April 2025 can be a month of incredible breakthroughs, healing, and personal power for you, Aries.

Best Days of the Month:

April 4th: Saturn sextiles Uranus, bringing opportunities for innovation, change, and breakthrough in your career and financial life.

April 12th: The Total Lunar Eclipse in Libra illuminates your 7th house of partnerships and relationships, inviting you to release old patterns and cultivate greater harmony and balance in your connections with others.

April 16th: Mercury enters your sign, bringing clarity, communication, and mental acuity to your personal goals and self-expression.

April 21st: Venus enters your 2nd house of values and resources, attracting abundance, prosperity, and sensual pleasure into your life.

April 30th: The New Moon Solar Eclipse in Taurus activates your 2nd house of values and resources, planting powerful seeds for financial growth and material success in the months to come.

May 2025

Overview Horoscope for the Month:

Aries, May 2025 is a month of new beginnings, fresh starts, and exciting opportunities for you. The cosmic energies are urging you to take bold steps forward, to embrace your unique talents and abilities, and to trust in the power of your own creativity and innovation. With the Sun moving through your 2nd house of values and resources for much of the month, you'll feel a strong desire to build a solid foundation for your future, to cultivate a sense of security and abundance, and to align your actions with your deepest desires and goals.

The headline event of the month is Saturn's entry into your sign on May 24th, which will mark the beginning of a new 2.5-year cycle of growth, responsibility, and personal mastery. This is a time to take a serious look at your life path and purpose, to set clear boundaries and commitments, and to develop the discipline and perseverance needed to achieve your long-term goals. While this transit may bring some challenges and obstacles, it is ultimately an opportunity to step into your full power and potential, and to create a life that is truly authentic and fulfilling.

At the same time, the presence of Jupiter, Uranus, and Pluto in your 11th, 2nd, and 12th houses respectively suggests that May 2025 is also a month of unexpected blessings, sudden breakthroughs, and deep personal transformation. You may find yourself attracting new opportunities for growth and expansion through your social networks and connections, or experiencing sudden shifts in your values and priorities that lead you towards a more authentic and empowered way of being. Trust in the wisdom of the universe, and be open to the magic and synchronicity that is all around you.

Love:

In love, May 2025 is a month of sensuality, intimacy, and deep emotional connection. With Venus moving through your 2nd house of values and resources until May 19th, you'll feel a strong desire to build a sense of security and stability in your relationships, and to express your affection and desire through tangible gestures and gifts. This is a time to indulge in the pleasures of the senses, to explore new dimensions of physical and emotional intimacy, and to cultivate a deeper sense of self-worth and deserving in your connections with others.

If you're in a committed partnership, May 2025 is a powerful time to deepen your bond and commitment to one another. Take time to express your appreciation and gratitude for your partner, to listen with empathy and understanding, and to find new ways to support and nurture one another's growth and evolution. Be willing to have honest conversations about your needs and desires, and to make any necessary adjustments to ensure that your relationship is built on a foundation of trust, respect, and mutual fulfillment.

If you're single, May 2025 may bring some exciting new prospects for romance and connection. With Jupiter in your 11th house of social networks and community, you may find yourself meeting someone special through a friend or group activity, or attracting admirers who share your values and interests. Be open to the possibilities that arise, but also make sure to take your time and really get to know someone before diving in too deep. Trust your intuition and inner guidance, and prioritize your own self-care and well-being in any new connections that form.

Career:

In your career, May 2025 is a month of innovation, creativity, and personal empowerment. With the Sun and Mercury moving through your 2nd house of values and resources, you'll feel a strong drive to align your work with your deepest passions and priorities, and to build a sense of financial security and abundance through your professional pursuits. This is a time to showcase your unique talents and abilities, to take on new challenges and responsibilities, and to trust in your own vision and leadership.

At the same time, the presence of Uranus in your 2nd house suggests that May 2025 may bring some unexpected shifts or disruptions in your career path or financial situation. You may find yourself feeling a need for greater freedom and autonomy in your work, or experiencing sudden opportunities for growth and change that require you to think outside the box and take some risks. Trust your intuition and inner guidance as you navigate these shifts, and be open to new possibilities and directions that may arise.

If you're an entrepreneur or business owner, May 2025 is a powerful time to launch new projects or initiatives, to expand your reach and influence, and to cultivate a sense of purpose and mission in your work. Be willing to take calculated risks, to innovate and experiment, and to surround yourself with supportive and inspiring collaborators who share your vision and values.

Finances:

In finances, May 2025 is a month of abundance, prosperity, and personal empowerment. With the Sun, Mercury, and Venus all moving through your 2nd house of values and resources, you'll feel a strong desire to build a solid foundation for your financial future, to cultivate a sense of security and stability, and to align your spending and earning with your deepest desires and goals. This is a time to take a serious look at your budget and financial plan, to make any necessary adjustments or improvements, and to trust in your own ability to attract and manifest the resources you need to thrive.

At the same time, the presence of Uranus in your 2nd house suggests that May 2025 may bring some unexpected windfalls or opportunities for financial growth and expansion. You may find yourself attracting new sources of income or investment, or experiencing sudden shifts in your values and priorities that lead you towards a more authentic and empowered relationship with money. Trust in the wisdom of the universe, and be open to the magic and synchronicity that is all around you.

To navigate these energies, focus on cultivating a mindset of abundance and gratitude, and on aligning your financial goals with your deepest values and purpose. Be willing to take calculated risks and try new approaches, but also make sure to do your due diligence and research before making any major financial decisions. Remember that true wealth comes from within, and that your value and worth are not determined by your bank balance or material possessions.

Health:

In health, May 2025 is a month of vitality, resilience, and personal empowerment. With the Sun and Mercury moving through your 2nd house of values and resources, you'll feel a strong desire to prioritize your physical and emotional well-being, to cultivate a sense of self-care and self-love, and to align your lifestyle and habits with your deepest desires and goals. This is a time to focus on building strength, endurance, and immunity, both physically and emotionally.

Make time for regular exercise and movement, whether it's through high-intensity workouts, yoga, or dance. Nourish your body with whole, nutrient-dense foods that support your energy levels and overall well-being, and make sure to stay hydrated and well-rested.

At the same time, the presence of Chiron in your 1st house of self and identity suggests that May 2025 may bring some deep healing or transformation around your relationship with your body and your sense of self-worth. You may find yourself confronting old wounds or traumas, or learning to love and accept yourself more fully. Be gentle and compassionate with yourself during this process, and seek out the support and guidance of trusted healers or therapists if needed.

Travel:

In travel, May 2025 may bring some exciting opportunities for adventure, exploration, and personal growth. With Jupiter in your 11th house of social networks and community, you may find yourself attracted to group travel experiences or trips that allow you to connect with like-minded individuals and expand your horizons. This could be anything from a yoga retreat or spiritual pilgrimage to a cultural immersion program or volunteer project.

At the same time, the presence of Saturn in your 12th house of spirituality and inner wisdom suggests that any travel experiences you undertake in May 2025 may have a deep transformative or healing purpose. You may find yourself drawn to sacred sites or power spots, or seeking out experiences that challenge you to confront your fears and limitations and step into your full potential.

Whatever form your travels take, be open to the lessons and opportunities that arise, and trust that they are ultimately serving your highest growth and evolution. Make sure to take care of your physical and emotional well-being during your journeys, and to integrate any insights or experiences you gain into your daily life and relationships.

Insight from the Stars:

The celestial energies of May 2025 remind you of the power of personal empowerment, creativity, and self-love. With the Sun, Mercury, and Venus all moving through your 2nd house of values and resources, you are being called to align your actions and choices with your deepest desires and goals, to cultivate a sense of security and abundance, and to trust in your own unique talents and abilities. At the same time, the presence of Saturn, Jupiter, and Uranus in your chart invites you to take responsibility for your life path and purpose, to embrace unexpected opportunities for growth and change, and to step into your full power and potential.

Remember that true wealth and success come from within, and that your value and worth are not determined by external factors or validation. Stay connected to your inner truth, surround yourself with love and support, and trust that the universe is conspiring in your favor. With courage, creativity, and a willingness to embrace your authentic self, May 2025 can be a month of incredible breakthroughs, abundance, and personal empowerment for you, Aries.

Best Days of the Month:

May 4th: The First Quarter Moon in Leo activates your 5th house of creativity, self-expression, and joy, inspiring you to let your unique light shine and pursue your passions with confidence and enthusiasm.

May 12th: The Full Moon in Scorpio illuminates your 8th house of intimacy, transformation, and shared resources, inviting you to deepen your emotional and financial connections and release any patterns or beliefs that are holding you back.

May 18th: Jupiter forms a powerful square to the True Node, bringing opportunities for growth, expansion, and alignment with your soul's purpose and destiny.

May 24th: Saturn enters your sign, marking the beginning of a new 2.5-year cycle of personal growth, responsibility, and mastery.

May 26th: The New Moon in Gemini activates your 3rd house of communication, learning, and social connections, planting powerful seeds for new ideas, projects, and relationships in the months to come.

June 2025

Overview Horoscope for the Month:

Aries, June 2025 is a month of emotional depth, personal growth, and powerful transformations for you. The cosmic energies are calling you to dive deep into your inner world, to confront your fears and vulnerabilities, and to emerge with a greater sense of self-awareness, emotional intelligence, and spiritual wisdom. With the Sun moving through your 4th house of home, family, and emotional foundations for much of the month, you'll feel a strong desire to create a sense of safety, security, and belonging in your personal life, and to nurture your closest relationships with love, care, and attention.

The headline event of the month is Jupiter's entry into Cancer on June 9th, which will bring a powerful wave of expansion, growth, and abundance to your home and family life over the next year. This is a time to focus on creating a warm, welcoming, and nurturing environment in your living space, and to cultivate deeper emotional connections with your loved ones. You may find yourself feeling more sensitive, intuitive, and empathetic than usual, and may be drawn to explore your ancestral roots, family history, or cultural heritage in a deeper way.

At the same time, the presence of Saturn, Neptune, and Pluto in your 1st, 12th, and 11th houses respectively suggests that June 2025 is also a month of intense personal growth, spiritual awakening, and social transformation. You may find yourself grappling with issues of identity, purpose, and authenticity, and may be called to let go of old patterns, beliefs, or relationships that no longer serve your highest good. Trust in the wisdom of your inner guidance, and be open to the profound shifts and changes that are unfolding in your life.

Love:

In love, June 2025 is a month of emotional intimacy, vulnerability, and deep soul connections. With Venus moving through your 4th house of home and family from June 6th to July 4th, you'll feel a strong desire to create a sense of comfort, security, and emotional safety in your romantic relationships. This is a time to prioritize quality time with your loved ones, to express your affection and care through nurturing gestures and heartfelt communication, and to cultivate a deeper sense of trust, understanding, and emotional bonding.

If you're in a committed partnership, June 2025 is a powerful time to deepen your emotional and spiritual connection with your partner. Take time to share your deepest fears, hopes, and dreams with one another, and to offer each other unconditional love, support, and acceptance. You may find yourselves exploring new levels of intimacy and vulnerability together, and may be called to confront and heal any old wounds or patterns that are holding you back from fully opening your hearts to each other.

If you're single, June 2025 may bring some profound soul connections and romantic opportunities your way. With Jupiter moving into your 4th house of home and family, you may find yourself attracted to someone who feels like "home" to you, someone with whom you can create a deep emotional and spiritual bond. Be open to the possibilities that arise, but also make sure to take your time and really tune into your own emotional needs and desires. Trust your intuition and inner guidance, and prioritize your own self-care and emotional well-being in any new connections that form.

Career:

In your career, June 2025 is a month of personal empowerment, authentic expression, and meaningful work. With Mars moving through your 6th house of daily work and service from June 17th to July 18th, you'll feel a strong drive to align your professional pursuits with your deepest values, passions, and sense of purpose. This is a time to focus on developing your skills, talents, and expertise in a way that feels authentic and fulfilling to you, and to seek out work opportunities that allow you to make a positive difference in the world.

At the same time, the presence of Saturn in your 1st house of self and identity suggests that June 2025 may bring some challenges or obstacles in your career path that require you to step up, take responsibility, and assert your personal authority and leadership. You may find yourself grappling with issues of self-doubt, imposter syndrome, or external criticism, and may be called to develop greater self-confidence, discipline, and resilience in the face of adversity. Trust in your own unique gifts and abilities, and be willing to put in the hard work and effort required to achieve your professional goals and aspirations.

Finances:

In finances, June 2025 is a month of abundance, prosperity, and positive change. With Jupiter moving into your 4th house of home and family on June 9th, you may find yourself experiencing a significant increase in your financial resources, whether through a raise, promotion, inheritance, or other unexpected windfall. This is a time to focus on creating a sense of security, stability, and long-term prosperity in your financial life, and to make wise investments and financial decisions that support your personal and family goals.

At the same time, the presence of Uranus in your 2nd house of money and resources suggests that June 2025 may bring some unexpected shifts or disruptions in your financial situation that require you to think outside the box and adapt to changing circumstances. You may find yourself exploring new sources of income, developing innovative financial strategies, or letting go of old patterns or beliefs around money that no longer serve you. Trust in the wisdom of the universe, and be open to the new opportunities and possibilities that are emerging in your financial life.

Health:

In health, June 2025 is a month of emotional healing, self-care, and inner transformation. With the Sun moving through your 4th house of home and family, you may find yourself feeling more sensitive, introspective, and emotionally vulnerable than usual. This is a time to prioritize your emotional well-being, to practice self-compassion and self-acceptance, and to seek out the support and guidance of trusted healers, therapists, or loved ones as needed.

At the same time, the presence of Neptune in your 12th house of spirituality and inner wisdom suggests that June 2025 may bring some profound spiritual insights, intuitive messages, or healing experiences that help you to release old emotional wounds, traumas, or patterns. You may find yourself drawn to practices such as meditation, yoga, energy healing, or psychotherapy as ways to access your inner guidance, process your emotions, and cultivate greater inner peace and wholeness.

Travel:

In travel, June 2025 may bring some opportunities for emotional healing, family bonding, and ancestral connection. With Jupiter moving into your 4th house of home and family, you may find yourself drawn to travel experiences that allow you to explore your roots, connect with your cultural heritage, or deepen your emotional bonds with loved ones. This could be anything from a family reunion or genealogy trip to a pilgrimage to a sacred site or ancestral homeland.

At the same time, the presence of Saturn in your 1st house of self and identity suggests that any travel experiences you undertake in June 2025 may require you to step out of your comfort zone, take on new responsibilities, or confront personal challenges or fears. You may find yourself called to embark on a solo journey of self-discovery, or to take on a leadership role in a group travel experience. Trust in your own inner strength and resilience, and be open to the profound growth and transformation that can come from stepping into the unknown.

Insight from the Stars:

The celestial energies of June 2025 remind you of the power of emotional intelligence, spiritual wisdom, and personal transformation. With the Sun moving through your 4th house of home and family, and Jupiter entering Cancer, you are being called to cultivate a deeper sense of emotional safety, security, and belonging in your personal life, and to nurture your closest relationships with love, care, and attention. At the same time, the presence of Saturn, Neptune, and Pluto in your chart invites you to confront your fears and vulnerabilities, to let go of old patterns and beliefs that no longer serve you, and to step into your full power and potential as a spiritual being having a human experience.

Remember that growth and transformation often require us to face our shadows and embrace our deepest truths, even when it feels uncomfortable or challenging. Trust in the wisdom of your inner guidance, surround yourself with love and support, and know that the universe is always conspiring in your favor. With courage, compassion, and a willingness to dive deep, June 2025 can be a month of profound emotional healing, spiritual awakening, and personal empowerment for you, Aries.

Best Days of the Month:

June 4th: The First Quarter Moon in Virgo activates your 6th house of daily work and service, inspiring you to get organized, focus on your health and well-being, and align your actions with your highest values and sense of purpose.

June 11th: The Full Moon in Sagittarius illuminates your 9th house of travel, education, and spiritual growth, bringing opportunities for expansion, adventure, and profound insights and revelations.

June 18th: Saturn forms a powerful trine to the True Node, aligning your personal growth and evolution with your soul's path and purpose.

June 21st: The Sun enters Cancer, marking the Summer Solstice and activating your 4th house of home, family, and emotional foundations. This is a powerful time for setting intentions, creating sacred space, and nurturing your closest relationships.

June 25th: The New Moon in Cancer brings a fresh start and new beginnings to your home and family life, planting powerful seeds for emotional healing, personal growth, and deepening connections with loved ones.

July 2025

Overview Horoscope for the Month:

Aries, July 2025 is a month of passion, creativity, and self-expression for you. The cosmic energies are urging you to step into the spotlight, to embrace your unique talents and abilities, and to let your light shine brightly in the world. With the Sun moving through your 5th house of romance, creativity, and self-expression for much of the month, you'll feel a strong desire to pursue your passions, to take risks and try new things, and to express yourself with confidence, authenticity, and joy.

The headline event of the month is the New Moon in Cancer on July 1st, which will bring a powerful new beginning to your home and family life. This is a time to set intentions for creating a nurturing, supportive, and emotionally fulfilling home environment, and to deepen your connections with loved ones. You may find yourself feeling more sensitive, intuitive, and empathetic than usual, and may be called to explore your ancestral roots, family history, or cultural heritage in a deeper way.

At the same time, the presence of Saturn, Uranus, and Neptune in your 1st, 2nd, and 12th houses respectively suggests that July 2025 is also a month of personal growth, financial innovation, and spiritual awakening. You may find yourself grappling with issues of identity, values, and purpose, and may be called to let go of old patterns, beliefs, or limitations that no longer serve your highest good. Trust in the wisdom of your inner guidance and be open to the profound shifts and changes that are unfolding in your life.

Love:

In love, July 2025 is a month of passion, romance, and heart-opening experiences. With Venus moving through your 5th house of love and creativity from July 4th to July 30th, you'll feel a strong desire to express your affection, desire, and appreciation for your loved ones in creative, playful, and spontaneous ways. This is a time to prioritize pleasure, joy, and fun in your romantic relationships, and to explore new ways of connecting with your partner on a deeper level.

If you're in a committed partnership, July 2025 is a powerful time to reignite the spark of passion and excitement in your relationship. Plan special date nights, surprise your partner with thoughtful gestures and gifts, and make time for intimate conversations and shared experiences. You may find yourselves exploring new hobbies, interests, or creative projects together, and may be called to take risks and try new things in the name of love and growth.

If you're single, July 2025 may bring some exciting romantic opportunities and heart-opening experiences your way. With the Sun and Venus activating your 5th house of romance and creativity, you may find yourself attracting admirers left and right, and may be called to express your unique charm, charisma, and magnetism in bold, confident ways. Be open to the possibilities that arise, but also make sure to stay true to your own desires, values, and boundaries. Trust your intuition and inner guidance, and prioritize your own self-love and self-care in any new connections that form.

Career:

In your career, July 2025 is a month of leadership, innovation, and personal empowerment. With Mars moving through your 7th house of partnerships and collaborations from July 18th to August 27th, you'll feel a strong drive to connect with others, to build strategic alliances and partnerships, and to assert your personal power and influence in your professional life. This is a time to focus on developing your leadership skills, to take on new challenges and responsibilities, and to seek out opportunities for growth, advancement, and success.

At the same time, the presence of Uranus in your 2nd house of money and resources suggests that July 2025 may bring some unexpected shifts or disruptions in your financial situation or career path. You may find yourself exploring new sources of income, developing innovative business strategies, or letting go of old patterns or beliefs around money and success that no longer serve you. Trust in the wisdom of the universe, and be open to the new opportunities and possibilities that are emerging in your professional life.

Finances:

In finances, July 2025 is a month of abundance, prosperity, and positive change. With Jupiter in your 4th house of home and family, you may find yourself experiencing a significant increase in your financial resources, whether through a raise, promotion, inheritance, or other unexpected windfall. This is a time to focus on creating a sense of security, stability, and long-term prosperity in your financial life, and to make wise investments and financial decisions that support your personal and family goals.

At the same time, the presence of Uranus in your 2nd house of money and resources suggests that July 2025 may bring some unexpected shifts or disruptions in your financial situation that require you to think outside the box and adapt to changing circumstances. You may find yourself exploring new sources of income, developing innovative financial strategies, or letting go of old patterns or beliefs around money that no longer serve you. Trust in the wisdom of the universe, and be open to the new opportunities and possibilities that are emerging in your financial life.

Health:

In health, July 2025 is a month of vitality, self-care, and inner healing. With the Sun moving through your 5th house of joy, creativity, and self-expression, you may find yourself feeling more energized, enthusiastic, and alive than usual. This is a time to prioritize your physical health and well-being, to engage in activities that bring you pleasure and fulfillment, and to express yourself with confidence, authenticity, and joy.

At the same time, the presence of Chiron in your 1st house of self and identity suggests that July 2025 may bring some opportunities for deep inner healing and personal growth. You may find yourself confronting old wounds, traumas, or patterns that have been holding you back from living your best life, and may be called to develop greater self-awareness, self-compassion, and self-acceptance. Trust in the wisdom of your body and your inner guidance, and seek out the support and guidance of trusted healers, therapists, or loved ones as needed.

Travel:

In travel, July 2025 may bring some exciting opportunities for adventure, creativity, and personal growth. With the Sun and Venus activating your 5th house of joy, creativity, and self-expression, you may find yourself drawn to travel experiences that allow you to explore your passions, express your unique talents and abilities, and connect with like-minded individuals. This could be anything from a creative retreat or workshop to a fun-filled vacation with loved ones.

At the same time, the presence of Saturn in your 1st house of self and identity suggests that any travel experiences you undertake in July 2025 may require you to step out of your comfort zone, take on new responsibilities, or confront personal challenges or fears. You may find yourself called to embark on a solo journey of self-discovery, or to take on a leadership role in a group travel experience. Trust in your own inner strength and resilience, and be open to the profound growth and transformation that can come from stepping into the unknown.

Insight from the Stars:

The celestial energies of July 2025 remind you of the power of passion, creativity, and personal empowerment. With the Sun and Venus moving through your 5th house of romance, creativity, and self-expression, you are being called to embrace your unique talents and abilities, to pursue your passions with confidence and joy, and to let your light shine brightly in the world. At the same time, the presence of Saturn, Uranus, and Neptune in your chart invites you to take responsibility for your life path and purpose, to embrace unexpected opportunities for growth and change, and to trust in the wisdom of your inner guidance and spiritual awakening.

Remember that true success and fulfillment come from living in alignment with your deepest values, desires, and authentic self. Trust in the journey of your own becoming, surround yourself with love and support, and know that the universe is always conspiring in your favor. With courage, creativity, and a willingness to take risks and try new things, July 2025 can be a month of incredible joy, passion, and personal growth for you, Aries.

Best Days of the Month:

July 1st: The New Moon in Cancer brings a powerful new beginning to your home and family life, setting the stage for emotional healing, deepening connections, and creating a nurturing, supportive environment.

July 10th: The Full Moon in Capricorn illuminates your 10th house of career and public reputation, bringing opportunities for recognition, advancement, and success in your professional life.

July 19th: Jupiter forms a powerful trine to Chiron, bringing opportunities for deep inner healing, personal growth, and spiritual awakening.

July 22nd: The Sun enters Leo, activating your 5th house of romance, creativity, and self-expression. This is a powerful time for pursuing your passions, expressing your unique talents and abilities, and letting your light shine brightly in the world.

July 30th: Venus enters Virgo, bringing a grounded, practical energy to your relationships and financial life, and helping you to focus on the details and make wise, discerning choices.

August 2025

Overview Horoscope for the Month:

Aries, August 2025 is a month of transformation, self-discovery, and personal growth for you. The cosmic energies are inviting you to dive deep into your inner world, to confront your fears and shadows, and to emerge with a greater sense of self-awareness, authenticity, and purpose. With the Sun moving through your 6th house of health, work, and daily routines for much of the month, you'll feel a strong desire to get organized, to focus on your well-being and self-care, and to align your actions with your highest values and goals.

The headline event of the month is the New Moon in Leo on August 24th, which will bring a powerful new beginning to your creativity, self-expression, and romantic life. This is a time to set intentions for pursuing your passions, expressing your unique talents and abilities, and letting your light shine brightly in the world. You may find yourself feeling more confident, charismatic, and magnetic than usual, and may be called to take risks and try new things in the name of love, joy, and personal growth.

At the same time, the presence of Uranus, Neptune, and Pluto in your 2nd, 12th, and 11th houses respectively suggests that August 2025 is also a month of financial innovation, spiritual awakening, and social transformation. You may find yourself grappling with issues of values, resources, and shared power, and may be called to let go of old patterns, beliefs, or relationships that no longer serve your highest good. Trust in the wisdom of your inner guidance, and be open to the profound shifts and changes that are unfolding in your life.

Love:

In love, August 2025 is a month of depth, intimacy, and emotional healing. With Venus moving through your 6th house of health and service from August 19th to September 13th, you may find yourself drawn to relationships that offer a sense of grounding, stability, and mutual support. This is a time to focus on the practical, everyday aspects of love and partnership, and to show your affection and care through acts of service, kindness, and devotion.

If you're in a committed relationship, August 2025 is a powerful time to deepen your emotional and spiritual connection with your partner. Take time to have honest, vulnerable conversations about your needs, desires, and challenges, and to offer each other unconditional love and support. You may find yourselves working through old wounds or patterns together, and may be called to let go of any resentments, grudges, or unhealthy dynamics that are holding you back from true intimacy and trust.

If you're single, August 2025 may bring some unexpected romantic opportunities and soul connections your way. With Uranus activating your 2nd house of values and self-worth, you may find yourself attracted to someone who challenges your beliefs about love, relationships, and personal power. Be open to the possibilities that arise, but also make sure to stay true to your own needs, boundaries, and desires. Trust your intuition and inner guidance, and prioritize your own self-love and self-care in any new connections that form.

Career:

In your career, August 2025 is a month of hard work, discipline, and personal growth. With the Sun and Mercury activating your 6th house of daily work and service, you'll feel a strong drive to get organized, to focus on the details and practicalities of your job, and to develop your skills and expertise in a meaningful way. This is a time to take on new responsibilities, to seek out opportunities for learning and growth, and to align your professional pursuits with your highest values and sense of purpose.

At the same time, the presence of Jupiter and Chiron in your 4th and 1st houses respectively suggests that August 2025 may bring some opportunities for career advancement or recognition through your personal connections, family, or home life. You may find yourself called to take on a leadership role in your community, to start a home-based business, or to pursue a career path that allows you to nurture and support others in a meaningful way. Trust in your own unique gifts and talents, and be willing to put in the hard work and dedication required to achieve your goals.

Finances:

In finances, August 2025 is a month of innovation, transformation, and unexpected opportunities. With Uranus activating your 2nd house of money and resources, you may find yourself exploring new sources of income, developing innovative financial strategies, or letting go of old patterns or beliefs around money and success that no longer serve you. This is a time to think outside the box, to take calculated risks, and to trust in the wisdom of the universe to provide for your needs and desires.

At the same time, the presence of Neptune and Pluto in your 12th and 11th houses respectively suggests that August 2025 may bring some challenges or obstacles related to shared resources, debts, or financial partnerships. You may find yourself grappling with issues of power, control, or trust in your financial dealings, and may be called to confront any fears or shadows around money, security, or self-worth. Trust in your own inner guidance and resources, and seek out the support and guidance of trusted advisors or professionals as needed.

Health:

In health, August 2025 is a month of self-care, discipline, and personal growth. With the Sun and Mercury activating your 6th house of health and daily routines, you'll feel a strong desire to focus on your physical, mental, and emotional well-being. This is a time to develop healthy habits and practices, to prioritize self-care and stress management, and to align your lifestyle with your highest values and goals.

At the same time, the presence of Chiron in your 1st house of self and identity suggests that August 2025 may bring some opportunities for deep inner healing and personal growth. You may find yourself confronting old wounds, traumas, or patterns that have been holding you back from living your best life, and may be called to develop greater self-awareness, self-compassion, and self-acceptance. Trust in the wisdom of your body and your inner guidance, and seek out the support and guidance of trusted healers, therapists, or loved ones as needed.

Travel:

In travel, August 2025 may bring some opportunities for personal growth, spiritual awakening, and inner exploration. With Neptune activating your 12th house of spirituality and unconscious mind, you may find yourself drawn to travel experiences that allow you to connect with your inner wisdom, explore your dreams and intuition, and tap into the collective unconscious. This could be anything from a meditation retreat or yoga workshop to a solo journey of self-discovery in a far-off land.

At the same time, the presence of Pluto in your 11th house of friendships and social groups suggests that any travel experiences you undertake in August 2025 may be influenced by your relationships and connections with others. You may find yourself called to travel with a group of like-minded individuals, to explore issues of power and shared resources in your social circles, or to confront any challenges or obstacles related to group dynamics or shared goals. Trust in your own inner strength and resilience, and be open to the profound growth and transformation that can come from stepping outside your comfort zone.

Insight from the Stars:

The celestial energies of August 2025 remind you of the power of self-discovery, personal growth, and inner transformation. With the Sun and Mercury activating your 6th house of health, work, and daily routines, you are being called to focus on the practical, everyday aspects of your life, and to align your actions with your highest values and goals. At the same time, the presence of Uranus, Neptune, and Pluto in your chart invites you to embrace unexpected opportunities for change and growth, to trust in the wisdom of your inner guidance and spiritual awakening, and to let go of any patterns, beliefs, or relationships that no longer serve your highest good.

Remember that true success and fulfillment come from living in alignment with your deepest truth, authenticity, and purpose. Trust in the journey of your own becoming, surround yourself with love and support, and know that the universe is always conspiring in your favor. With courage, discipline, and a willingness to dive deep into your inner world, August 2025 can be a month of incredible growth, healing, and personal transformation for you, Aries.

Best Days of the Month:

August 7th: The Full Moon in Aquarius illuminates your 11th house of friendships, social groups, and hopes and dreams, bringing opportunities for collaboration, networking, and manifesting your vision for the future.

August 11th: Mercury turns direct in your 5th house of creativity and self-expression, bringing clarity and forward momentum to your passion projects and artistic pursuits.

August 23rd: Jupiter turns retrograde in your 4th house of home and family, inviting you to reflect on your emotional foundations, ancestral roots, and inner sense of belonging.

August 24th: The New Moon in Leo brings a powerful new beginning to your creativity, self-expression, and romantic life, setting the stage for passion, joy, and personal growth in the month ahead.

August 28th: Uranus forms a harmonious sextile with Neptune, bringing unexpected opportunities for spiritual growth, creative inspiration, and inner awakening.

September 2025

Overview Horoscope for the Month:

Aries, September 2025 is a month of balance, harmony, and personal growth for you. The cosmic energies are inviting you to find a sense of equilibrium in your life, to cultivate meaningful relationships and partnerships, and to align your actions with your highest values and goals. With the Sun moving through your 7th house of relationships and partnerships for much of the month, you'll feel a strong desire to connect with others, to collaborate and cooperate, and to find a sense of mutual support and understanding in your interactions.

The headline event of the month is the Partial Solar Eclipse in Virgo on September 21st, which will bring a powerful new beginning to your health, work, and daily routines. This is a time to set intentions for developing healthy habits and practices, for aligning your lifestyle with your highest values and goals, and for finding a sense of purpose and meaning in your everyday life. You may find yourself feeling more focused, disciplined, and motivated than usual, and may be called to take practical steps towards improving your physical, mental, and emotional well-being.

At the same time, the presence of Saturn, Uranus, and Neptune in your 12th, 2nd, and 12th houses respectively suggests that September 2025 is also a month of spiritual growth, financial innovation, and inner transformation. You may find yourself grappling with issues of faith, surrender, and letting go, and may be called to trust in the wisdom of the universe and the unfolding of your soul's journey. Trust in your own inner guidance, and be open to the profound shifts and changes that are taking place within you and around you.

Love:

In love, September 2025 is a month of balance, harmony, and emotional connection. With Venus moving through your 7th house of relationships and partnerships from September 13th to October 8th, you'll feel a strong desire to cultivate meaningful connections with others, to find a sense of mutual understanding and support, and to express your affection and appreciation in loving, harmonious ways. This is a time to prioritize your relationships, to invest time and energy into nurturing your connections, and to find a sense of beauty, pleasure, and joy in your interactions with others.

If you're in a committed relationship, September 2025 is a powerful time to deepen your emotional and spiritual bond with your partner. Take time to have heartfelt conversations, to express your needs and desires openly and honestly, and to find ways to support and encourage each other's growth and well-being. You may find yourselves exploring new levels of intimacy and vulnerability together, and may be called to let go of any patterns or dynamics that are no longer serving your relationship.

If you're single, September 2025 may bring some beautiful opportunities for connection and romance your way. With the Sun and Venus activating your 7th house of relationships and partnerships, you may find yourself attracting people who share your values, interests, and desires for mutual growth and support. Be open to the possibilities that arise, but also make sure to stay true to your own needs and boundaries. Trust your intuition and inner guidance, and prioritize your own self-love and self-care in any new connections that form.

Career:

In your career, September 2025 is a month of collaboration, teamwork, and personal growth. With Mars moving through your 10th house of career and public reputation from September 22nd to November 4th, you'll feel a strong drive to take on new challenges and responsibilities, to assert your leadership and expertise, and to make a meaningful impact in your professional life. This is a time to focus on your long-term goals and aspirations, to seek out opportunities for advancement and recognition, and to align your actions with your highest values and sense of purpose.

At the same time, the presence of the Partial Solar Eclipse in Virgo on September 21st suggests that September 2025 may bring some powerful new beginnings and opportunities for growth in your work life. You may find yourself called to take on a new role or project, to develop new skills or expertise, or to find ways to streamline your workflow and increase your efficiency and productivity. Trust in your own unique gifts and talents, and be willing to put in the hard work and dedication required to achieve your goals.

Finances:

In finances, September 2025 is a month of innovation, transformation, and unexpected opportunities. With Uranus continuing to activate your 2nd house of money and resources, you may find yourself exploring new sources of income, developing innovative financial strategies, or letting go of old patterns or beliefs around money and success that no longer serve you. This is a time to think outside the box, to take calculated risks, and to trust in the wisdom of the universe to provide for your needs and desires.

At the same time, the presence of Saturn in your 12th house of spirituality and unconscious mind suggests that September 2025 may bring some deeper lessons and insights around your relationship with money and abundance. You may find yourself grappling with issues of faith, surrender, and letting go, and may be called to trust in the universe to provide for your needs in unexpected ways. Remember that true wealth and abundance come from within, and that your value and worth are not defined by your material possessions or financial status.

Health:

In health, September 2025 is a month of vitality, discipline, and personal growth. With the Partial Solar Eclipse in Virgo activating your 6th house of health and daily routines, you'll feel a strong desire to focus on your physical, mental, and emotional well-being. This is a time to develop healthy habits and practices, to prioritize self-care and stress management, and to align your lifestyle with your highest values and goals.

At the same time, the presence of Chiron in your 1st house of self and identity suggests that September 2025 may bring some opportunities for deep inner healing and personal growth. You may find yourself confronting old wounds, traumas, or patterns that have been holding you back from living your best life, and may be called to develop greater self-awareness, self-compassion, and self-acceptance. Trust in the wisdom of your body and your inner guidance, and seek out the support and guidance of trusted healers, therapists, or loved ones as needed.

Travel:

In travel, September 2025 may bring some opportunities for personal growth, spiritual awakening, and inner exploration. With Neptune continuing to activate your 12th house of spirituality and unconscious mind, you may find yourself drawn to travel experiences that allow you to connect with your inner wisdom, explore your dreams and intuition, and tap into the collective unconscious. This could be anything from a meditation retreat or yoga workshop to a solo journey of self-discovery in a far-off land.

At the same time, the presence of Saturn in your 12th house of spirituality and unconscious mind suggests that any travel experiences you undertake in September 2025 may require you to confront your fears, limitations, and shadows. You may find yourself called to let go of old patterns or beliefs that are no longer serving you, to surrender to the unknown, and to trust in the wisdom of the universe to guide you towards your highest good. Trust in your own inner strength and resilience, and be open to the profound growth and transformation that can come from stepping outside your comfort zone.

Insight from the Stars:

The celestial energies of September 2025 remind you of the power of balance, harmony, and personal growth. With the Sun and Venus activating your 7th house of relationships and partnerships, you are being called to cultivate meaningful connections with others, to find a sense of mutual understanding and support, and to align your actions with your highest values and goals. At the same time, the presence of the Partial Solar Eclipse in Virgo, along with Saturn, Uranus, and Neptune in your chart, invites you to embrace opportunities for deep inner healing, spiritual growth, and personal transformation.

Remember that true success and fulfillment come from living in alignment with your deepest truth, authenticity, and purpose. Trust in the journey of your own becoming, surround yourself with love and support, and know that the universe is always conspiring in your favor. With courage, discipline, and a willingness to find balance and harmony in all areas of your life, September 2025 can be a month of incredible growth, healing, and personal transformation for you, Aries.

Best Days of the Month:

September 3rd: Jupiter forms a harmonious trine with the North Node, bringing opportunities for spiritual growth, personal expansion, and alignment with your soul's purpose and destiny.

September 7th: The Full Moon in Pisces illuminates your 12th house of spirituality, surrender, and inner wisdom, inviting you to let go of control, trust in the universe, and connect with your deepest intuition and guidance.

September 21st: The Partial Solar Eclipse in Virgo activates your 6th house of health, work, and daily routines, bringing powerful new beginnings and opportunities for growth and transformation in these areas of your life.

September 27th: Mercury turns direct in your 7th house of relationships and partnerships, bringing clarity, understanding, and forward momentum to your connections with others.

September 29th: The New Moon in Libra brings a fresh start and new opportunities for balance, harmony, and growth in your relationships and social interactions.

October 2025

Overview Horoscope for the Month:

Aries, October 2025 is a month of depth, intensity, and personal transformation for you. The cosmic energies are inviting you to dive deep into your psyche, to confront your fears and shadows, and to emerge with a greater sense of self-awareness, personal power, and emotional resilience. With the Sun moving through your 8th house of intimacy, shared resources, and personal transformation for much of the month, you'll feel a strong desire to explore the hidden depths of your soul, to let go of old patterns and beliefs that no longer serve you, and to embrace the process of death and rebirth in all areas of your life.

The headline event of the month is the New Moon in Libra on October 21st, which will bring a powerful new beginning to your relationships, partnerships, and social interactions. This is a time to set intentions for creating more balance, harmony, and mutual understanding in your connections with others, and to cultivate a greater sense of love, beauty, and grace in your life. You may find yourself feeling more diplomatic, charming, and attractive than usual, and may be called to use your social skills and influence to create positive change in the world around you.

At the same time, the presence of Pluto in your 11th house of friendships, social groups, and hopes and dreams suggests that October 2025 is also a month of intense social transformation and power struggles. You may find yourself grappling with issues of control, manipulation, and hidden agendas in your relationships and social interactions, and may be called to confront any patterns of codependency, enabling, or unhealthy power dynamics that are holding you back from true intimacy and connection. Trust in your own inner strength and wisdom, and be willing to let go of any relationships or social ties that are no longer aligned with your highest good.

Love:

In love, October 2025 is a month of intensity, passion, and emotional healing. With Venus moving through your 8th house of intimacy and shared resources from October 8th to November 7th, you'll feel a strong desire to explore the depths of your heart, to express your deepest feelings and desires, and to create a profound sense of emotional and spiritual connection with your partner. This is a time to let down your walls, to be vulnerable and authentic in your interactions, and to trust in the power of love to heal and transform even the deepest wounds and scars.

If you're in a committed relationship, October 2025 is a powerful time to deepen your emotional and physical intimacy with your partner. Take time to explore each other's hidden desires and fantasies, to share your deepest secrets and fears, and to offer each other unconditional love and support. You may find yourselves working through old traumas or patterns of codependency together, and may be called to let go of any power struggles or control issues that are holding you back from true intimacy and trust.

If you're single, October 2025 may bring some intense and transformative romantic experiences your way. With Pluto activating your 11th house of friendships and social groups, you may find yourself attracted to someone who challenges your beliefs about love, power, and personal freedom. Be open to the possibilities that arise, but also make sure to stay true to your own needs, boundaries, and desires. Trust your intuition and inner guidance, and prioritize your own self-love and self-care in any new connections that form.

Career:

In your career, October 2025 is a month of personal power, leadership, and transformation. With Mars moving through your 11th house of friendships, social groups, and hopes and dreams from November 4th to December 15th, you'll feel a strong drive to assert your influence and authority in your professional life, to take on new challenges and responsibilities, and to make a meaningful impact in the world around you. This is a time to focus on your long-term goals and aspirations, to seek out opportunities for growth and advancement, and to align your actions with your highest values and sense of purpose.

At the same time, the presence of Pluto in your 11th house of friendships and social groups suggests that October 2025 may bring some intense power struggles and transformations in your professional relationships and collaborations. You may find yourself grappling with issues of control, manipulation, and hidden agendas in your interactions with colleagues, clients, or business partners, and may be called to confront any patterns of enabling, codependency, or unhealthy power dynamics that are holding you back from true success and fulfillment. Trust in your own inner strength and wisdom, and be willing to let go of any professional ties or relationships that are no longer aligned with your highest good.

Finances:

In finances, October 2025 is a month of transformation, shared resources, and unexpected opportunities. With the Sun and Venus activating your 8th house of intimacy, shared resources, and personal transformation, you may find yourself exploring new sources of income or investment through partnerships, collaborations, or joint ventures. This is a time to think outside the box, to take calculated risks, and to trust in the wisdom of the universe to provide for your needs and desires in unexpected ways.

At the same time, the presence of Pluto in your 11th house of friendships and social groups suggests that October 2025 may bring some intense power struggles or transformations in your financial dealings with others. You may find yourself grappling with issues of control, manipulation, or hidden agendas in your financial partnerships or collaborations, and may be called to confront any patterns of enabling, codependency, or unhealthy power dynamics that are holding you back from true financial freedom and abundance. Remember that true wealth and prosperity come from within, and that your value and worth are not defined by your material possessions or financial status.

Health:

In health, October 2025 is a month of deep healing, transformation, and personal growth. With the Sun and Venus activating your 8th house of intimacy, shared resources, and personal transformation, you may find yourself exploring new forms of healing or therapy that allow you to release old traumas, patterns, or beliefs that are holding you back from optimal health and well-being. This is a time to prioritize self-care and self-love, to listen to the wisdom of your body and intuition, and to trust in the power of your own inner healing and resilience.

At the same time, the presence of Chiron in your 1st house of self and identity suggests that October 2025 may bring some opportunities for deep inner healing and personal growth. You may find yourself confronting old wounds, traumas, or patterns that have been holding you back from living your best life, and may be called to develop greater self-awareness, self-compassion, and self-acceptance. Trust in the wisdom of your body and your inner guidance, and seek out the support and guidance of trusted healers, therapists, or loved ones as needed.

Travel:

In travel, October 2025 may bring some opportunities for personal growth, spiritual awakening, and inner exploration. With Neptune continuing to activate your 12th house of spirituality and unconscious mind, you may find yourself drawn to travel experiences that allow you to connect with your inner wisdom, explore your dreams and intuition, and tap into the collective unconscious. This could be anything from a meditation retreat or yoga workshop to a solo journey of self-discovery in a far-off land.

At the same time, the presence of Pluto in your 11th house of friendships and social groups suggests that any travel experiences you undertake in October 2025 may be influenced by your relationships and connections with others. You may find yourself called to travel with a group of like-minded individuals, to explore issues of power and shared resources in your social circles, or to confront any challenges or obstacles related to group dynamics or shared goals. Trust in your own inner strength and resilience, and be open to the profound growth and transformation that can come from stepping outside your comfort zone.

Insight from the Stars:

The celestial energies of October 2025 remind you of the power of depth, intensity, and personal transformation. With the Sun and Venus activating your 8th house of intimacy, shared resources, and personal transformation, you are being called to dive deep into your psyche, to confront your fears and shadows, and to embrace the process of death and rebirth in all areas of your life. At the same time, the presence of Pluto in your 11th house of friendships and social groups invites you to explore issues of power, control, and hidden agendas in your relationships and interactions with others, and to let go of any patterns or dynamics that are no longer serving your highest good.

Remember that true growth and transformation often require us to face our deepest fears and vulnerabilities, and to surrender to the wisdom and guidance of the universe. Trust in your own inner strength and resilience, surround yourself with love and support, and know that the challenges and obstacles you face are ultimately serving your highest evolution and awakening. With courage, self-awareness, and a willingness to embrace the unknown, October 2025 can be a month of incredible depth, healing, and personal transformation for you, Aries.

Best Days of the Month:

October 13th: Venus enters Scorpio, bringing a deep, intense, and transformative energy to your relationships, intimacy, and shared resources.

October 13th: Pluto turns direct in your 11th house of friendships and social groups, bringing a sense of empowerment, transformation, and forward momentum to your social interactions and collaborations.

October 21st: The New Moon in Libra activates your 7th house of relationships and partnerships, bringing powerful new beginnings and opportunities for balance, harmony, and growth in your connections with others.

October 22nd: The Sun enters Scorpio, marking the beginning of a month-long period of depth, intensity, and personal transformation in all areas of your life.

October 22nd: Neptune turns direct in your 12th house of spirituality and unconscious mind, bringing a sense of clarity, inspiration, and spiritual awakening to your inner world and intuitive guidance.

.

November 2025

Overview Horoscope for the Month:

Aries, November 2025 is a month of expansion, adventure, and personal growth for you. The cosmic energies are inviting you to broaden your horizons, to explore new ideas and possibilities, and to embrace a more optimistic and philosophical approach to life. With the Sun moving through your 9th house of higher learning, travel, and spirituality for much of the month, you'll feel a strong desire to seek out new experiences, to expand your knowledge and understanding of the world, and to connect with a sense of meaning and purpose that transcends your everyday reality.

The headline event of the month is the Full Moon in Taurus on November 5th, which will bring a powerful culmination and release to your financial and material affairs. This is a time to celebrate your achievements and successes, to appreciate the abundance and prosperity in your life, and to let go of any limiting beliefs or patterns around money and self-worth that are holding you back from true fulfillment and joy. You may find yourself feeling more grounded, sensual, and self-indulgent than usual, and may be called to enjoy the simple pleasures and comforts of life with gratitude and presence.

At the same time, the retrograde cycles of Mercury and Juno throughout the month suggest that November 2025 is also a time of deep reflection, introspection, and inner growth. You may find yourself revisiting old ideas, beliefs, or commitments, and may be called to reassess your values, priorities, and long-term goals in light of your changing circumstances and evolving sense of self. Trust in the wisdom of your inner guidance, and be open to the insights and revelations that emerge from your deepest contemplation and self-inquiry.

Love:

In love, November 2025 is a month of adventure, exploration, and spiritual connection. With Venus moving through your 9th house of higher learning, travel, and spirituality from November 7th to December 3rd, you'll feel a strong desire to expand your horizons, to seek out new experiences and perspectives, and to connect with your partner on a deeper level of meaning and purpose. This is a time to explore new ideas and philosophies together, to travel to exotic or inspiring locations, and to cultivate a sense of wonder, awe, and reverence for the mysteries of life and love.

If you're in a committed relationship, November 2025 is a powerful time to deepen your emotional and spiritual bond with your partner. Take time to share your hopes, dreams, and aspirations with each other, to explore new forms of intimacy and connection, and to support each other's growth and evolution with love, compassion, and understanding. You may find yourselves exploring issues of faith, belief, and higher purpose together, and may be called to align your relationship with a sense of shared mission and destiny.

If you're single, November 2025 may bring some exciting and expansive romantic opportunities your way. With Jupiter and Chiron activating your 1st and 12th houses respectively, you may find yourself attracted to someone who challenges your beliefs, expands your consciousness, and helps you to heal old wounds and traumas related to love and intimacy. Be open to the possibilities that arise, but also make sure to stay true to your own needs, values, and boundaries. Trust your intuition and inner guidance, and prioritize your own self-love and self-care in any new connections that form.

Career:

In your career, November 2025 is a month of growth, learning, and personal development. With Mars moving through your 12th house of spirituality, surrender, and inner wisdom from December 15th to January 27th, you may find yourself feeling a strong urge to align your work with a sense of higher purpose, to let go of any ego-driven desires or attachments, and to trust in the wisdom of the universe to guide you towards your true calling and destiny. This is a time to focus on developing your inner resources, to cultivate a sense of humility, compassion, and service in your professional life, and to seek out opportunities for growth and learning that expand your consciousness and deepen your sense of meaning and purpose.

At the same time, the retrograde cycle of Mercury in your 9th house of higher learning and travel from November 9th to November 29th suggests that November 2025 may bring some delays, challenges, or miscommunications related to your educational or professional pursuits. You may find yourself revisiting old ideas, beliefs, or plans, and may be called to reassess your long-term goals and strategies in light of changing circumstances or new information. Trust in the wisdom of your inner guidance, and be open to the insights and revelations that emerge from your deepest reflection and self-inquiry.

Finances:

In finances, November 2025 is a month of abundance, prosperity, and positive change. With the Full Moon in Taurus on November 5th activating your 2nd house of money, resources, and self-worth, you may find yourself experiencing a powerful culmination or release related to your financial situation. This is a time to celebrate your achievements and successes, to appreciate the abundance and prosperity in your life, and to let go of any limiting beliefs or patterns around money and self-worth that are holding you back from true fulfillment and joy.

At the same time, the presence of Uranus and the North Node in your 2nd house of money and resources suggests that November 2025 may bring some unexpected opportunities or changes related to your financial situation. You may find yourself attracted to new sources of income, innovative investment strategies, or unconventional ways of generating wealth and abundance. Trust in the wisdom of the universe to provide for your needs and desires, and be open to the possibilities that arise in your financial life.

Health:

In health, November 2025 is a month of vitality, resilience, and inner growth. With the Sun moving through your 9th house of higher learning, travel, and spirituality, you may find yourself feeling a strong desire to expand your consciousness, to explore new forms of healing and self-care, and to cultivate a sense of meaning and purpose that transcends your physical reality. This is a time to prioritize your mental, emotional, and spiritual well-being, to seek out experiences and practices that uplift and inspire you, and to trust in the wisdom of your body and inner guidance to lead you towards optimal health and vitality.

At the same time, the presence of Chiron in your 12th house of spirituality, surrender, and inner wisdom suggests that November 2025 may bring some opportunities for deep healing and personal growth related to your physical and emotional health. You may find yourself confronting old wounds, traumas, or patterns that have been holding you back from living your best life, and may be called to develop greater self-awareness, self-compassion, and self-acceptance. Trust in the wisdom of your body and your inner guidance, and seek out the support and guidance of trusted healers, therapists, or loved ones as needed.

Travel:

In travel, November 2025 may bring some exciting opportunities for adventure, exploration, and personal growth. With Venus activating your 9th house of travel, higher learning, and spirituality, you may find yourself drawn to travel experiences that allow you to expand your horizons, explore new cultures and ideas, and connect with a sense of meaning and purpose that transcends your everyday reality. This could be anything from a long-distance trip to a foreign country, to a spiritual pilgrimage or retreat, to an educational program or workshop that deepens your knowledge and understanding of the world.

At the same time, the retrograde cycle of Mercury in your 9th house of travel and higher learning from November 9th to November 29th suggests that any travel experiences you undertake in November 2025 may require extra planning, flexibility, and patience. You may find yourself dealing with delays, cancellations, or miscommunications related to your travel plans, and may be called to reassess your itinerary or expectations in light of changing circumstances or new information. Trust in the wisdom of the universe to guide you towards the experiences and opportunities that are most aligned with your highest good, and be open to the profound growth and transformation that can come from stepping outside your comfort zone.

Insight from the Stars:

The celestial energies of November 2025 remind you of the power of expansion, adventure, and personal growth. With the Sun and Venus activating your 9th house of higher learning, travel, and spirituality, you are being called to broaden your horizons, to explore new ideas and possibilities, and to embrace a more optimistic and philosophical approach to life. At the same time, the retrograde cycles of Mercury and Juno throughout the month invite you to reflect deeply on your values, priorities, and long-term goals, and to align your actions and choices with your highest truth and purpose.

Remember that true growth and evolution often require us to step outside our comfort zone, to confront our fears and limitations, and to embrace the unknown with faith, courage, and an open heart. Trust in your own inner wisdom and resilience, surround yourself with love and support, and know that the challenges and obstacles you face are ultimately serving your highest good and awakening. With curiosity, enthusiasm, and a willingness to embrace the adventure of life, November 2025 can be a month of incredible expansion, meaning, and personal growth for you, Aries.

Best Days of the Month:

November 4th: Mars enters Sagittarius, bringing a bold, adventurous, and expansive energy to your actions, pursuits, and personal growth.

November 5th: The Full Moon in Taurus illuminates your 2nd house of money, resources, and self-worth, bringing a powerful culmination and release to your financial and material affairs.

November 7th: Pluto trines the North Node, bringing opportunities for deep transformation, empowerment, and alignment with your soul's path and purpose.

November 27th: Saturn turns direct in your 12th house of spirituality, surrender, and inner wisdom, bringing a sense of clarity, structure, and forward momentum to your inner growth and spiritual development.

November 30th: Venus enters Capricorn, bringing a grounded, practical, and ambitious energy to your relationships, values, and long-term goals.

December 2025

Overview Horoscope for the Month:

Aries, December 2025 is a month of intensity, transformation, and personal power for you. The cosmic energies are inviting you to dive deep into your psyche, to confront your fears and shadows, and to emerge with a greater sense of self-mastery, emotional resilience, and spiritual wisdom. With the Sun moving through your 10th house of career, public reputation, and long-term goals for much of the month, you'll feel a strong desire to take charge of your life direction, to assert your leadership and authority, and to make a meaningful impact in the world around you.

The headline event of the month is the Solar Eclipse in Sagittarius on December 19th, which will bring a powerful new beginning and fresh start to your 9th house of higher learning, travel, and spiritual growth. This is a time to set intentions for expanding your horizons, exploring new ideas and possibilities, and aligning your actions with a sense of meaning and purpose that transcends your everyday reality. You may find yourself feeling more optimistic, adventurous, and philosophical than usual, and may be called to take bold steps towards your dreams and aspirations with faith, courage, and enthusiasm.

At the same time, the direct stations of Neptune and Chiron in your 12th and 1st houses respectively suggest that December 2025 is also a month of deep spiritual awakening, emotional healing, and personal growth. You may find yourself experiencing profound insights, revelations, and breakthroughs related to your innermost fears, wounds, and desires, and may be called to surrender to a higher power or divine plan that is guiding your life journey. Trust in the wisdom of your inner guidance, and be open to the miracles and synchronicities that are unfolding in your life.

Love:

In love, December 2025 is a month of intensity, passion, and emotional depth. With Venus moving through your 10th house of career and public reputation from December 3rd to December 28th, you may find yourself attracted to someone who shares your ambition, success, and status, or who challenges you to step into your power and authority in your romantic life. This is a time to express your love and desire with confidence, charisma, and authenticity, and to create a relationship dynamic that supports your long-term goals and aspirations.

If you're in a committed relationship, December 2025 is a powerful time to deepen your emotional and spiritual connection with your partner. Take time to share your deepest fears, vulnerabilities, and dreams with each other, and to offer each other unconditional love, support, and acceptance. You may find yourselves working through issues of power, control, and intimacy together, and may be called to let go of any ego-driven patterns or defenses that are holding you back from true love and connection.

If you're single, December 2025 may bring some intense and transformative romantic experiences your way. With Pluto activating your 11th house of friendships and social groups, you may find yourself attracted to someone who challenges your beliefs about love, relationships, and personal freedom. Be open to the possibilities that arise, but also make sure to stay true to your own needs, boundaries, and desires. Trust your intuition and inner guidance, and prioritize your own self-love and self-care in any new connections that form.

Career:

In your career, December 2025 is a month of ambition, success, and personal power. With the Sun and Venus activating your 10th house of career and public reputation, you'll feel a strong drive to take charge of your professional life, to assert your leadership and expertise, and to make a meaningful impact in your field or industry. This is a time to focus on your long-term goals and aspirations, to seek out opportunities for growth and advancement, and to showcase your unique talents and abilities with confidence and charisma.

At the same time, the Solar Eclipse in Sagittarius on December 19th suggests that December 2025 may bring some powerful new beginnings and fresh starts related to your career path or life direction. You may find yourself inspired to pursue a new career opportunity, to launch a new project or business venture, or to take a bold leap of faith towards your dreams and aspirations. Trust in the wisdom of the universe to guide you towards your highest good, and be open to the possibilities and opportunities that are unfolding in your professional life.

Finances:

In finances, December 2025 is a month of abundance, prosperity, and personal power. With Jupiter activating your 10th house of career and public reputation, you may find yourself experiencing a significant increase in your income, resources, or financial opportunities related to your professional pursuits. This is a time to focus on your long-term financial goals and strategies, to make wise investments and decisions that support your success and security, and to trust in the abundance and prosperity that is flowing into your life.

At the same time, the presence of Pluto in your 11th house of friendships and social groups suggests that December 2025 may bring some intense power dynamics or transformations related to your financial partnerships or collaborations. You may find yourself grappling with issues of trust, control, or shared resources in your financial dealings with others, and may be called to assert your own needs and boundaries with clarity and confidence. Remember that true wealth and abundance come from within, and that your value and worth are not defined by external factors or validation.

Health:

In health, December 2025 is a month of vitality, resilience, and inner growth. With the Sun and Venus activating your 10th house of career and public reputation, you may find yourself feeling more energized, confident, and motivated than usual. This is a time to prioritize your physical health and well-being, to engage in activities that boost your energy and vitality, and to create a sense of balance and harmony between your professional and personal life.

At the same time, the direct stations of Neptune and Chiron in your 12th and 1st houses respectively suggest that December 2025 may bring some powerful opportunities for spiritual healing, emotional release, and personal growth. You may find yourself experiencing profound insights, revelations, or breakthroughs related to your innermost fears, wounds, or desires, and may be called to develop greater self-awareness, self-compassion, and self-acceptance. Trust in the wisdom of your body and your inner guidance, and seek out the support and guidance of trusted healers, therapists, or loved ones as needed.

Travel:

In travel, December 2025 may bring some exciting opportunities for adventure, exploration, and personal growth. With the Solar Eclipse in Sagittarius activating your 9th house of travel, higher learning, and spiritual growth, you may find yourself drawn to travel experiences that allow you to expand your horizons, explore new cultures and ideas, and connect with a sense of meaning and purpose that transcends your everyday reality. This could be anything from a long-distance trip to a foreign country, to a spiritual pilgrimage or retreat, to an educational program or workshop that deepens your knowledge and understanding of the world.

At the same time, the presence of Saturn in your 12th house of spirituality, surrender, and inner wisdom suggests that any travel experiences you undertake in December 2025 may require you to confront your fears, limitations, or unconscious patterns, and to surrender to a higher power or divine plan that is guiding your journey. Trust in the wisdom of the universe to lead you towards the experiences and opportunities that are most aligned with your highest good, and be open to the profound growth and transformation that can come from stepping outside your comfort zone.

Insight from the Stars:

The celestial energies of December 2025 remind you of the power of intensity, transformation, and personal growth. With the Sun and Venus activating your 10th house of career and public reputation, you are being called to step into your leadership, authority, and personal power, and to make a meaningful impact in the world around you. At the same time, the Solar Eclipse in Sagittarius and the direct stations of Neptune and Chiron invite you to expand your consciousness, heal your deepest wounds, and align your actions with a higher purpose and spiritual vision.

Remember that true success and fulfillment come from living in alignment with your deepest truth, authenticity, and inner wisdom. Trust in the journey of your own becoming, surround yourself with love and support, and know that the challenges and opportunities you face are ultimately serving your highest growth and evolution. With courage, self-awareness, and a willingness to embrace the intensity of life, December 2025 can be a month of incredible transformation, empowerment, and personal mastery for you, Aries.

Best Days of the Month:

December 4th: The Full Moon in Gemini illuminates your 3rd house of communication, learning, and social connections, bringing opportunities for intellectual stimulation, creative expression, and joyful interactions with others.

December 19th: The Solar Eclipse in Sagittarius brings a powerful new beginning and fresh start to your 9th house of travel, higher learning, and spiritual growth, inviting you to expand your horizons and align your actions with a higher purpose and vision.

December 21st: Jupiter enters Aquarius, bringing a wave of innovation, progress, and humanitarian energy to your 11th house of friendships, social groups, and community involvement.

December 24th: Venus enters Aquarius, bringing a unconventional, independent, and forward-thinking energy to your relationships, creativity, and self-expression.

December 27th: Mercury turns direct in your 9th house of travel, higher learning, and spiritual growth, bringing clarity, understanding, and forward momentum to your ideas, plans, and aspirations.

TAURUS 2025 HOROSCOPE

Overview Taurus 2025

(April 20 - May 20)

2025 is poised to be a year of significant change, growth, and self-discovery for those born under the steadfast sign of Taurus. As the planets traverse the celestial landscape, they will bring a dynamic mix of challenges and opportunities that will shape your journey throughout the year, encouraging you to embrace transformation while staying grounded in your values and sense of security.

The year commences with a powerful planetary concentration in the Fire signs, igniting your passion for exploration and personal development. Jupiter, the planet of expansion and growth, spends the first half of the year in your 3rd House of communication, short trips, learning, and skills. This is a fantastic time to broaden your horizons through education, workshops, or online courses. Engage in stimulating conversations with siblings, neighbors, or colleagues, and remain open to fresh ideas and perspectives. Your curiosity and desire for knowledge will be at an all-time high, so embrace this opportunity to enhance your skills and expand your mindset.

However, on June 9, Jupiter shifts gears and enters Cancer, your 4th House of home, family, and emotional foundations. This transition brings a more nurturing and protective energy to your domestic life and inner world. You may feel a strong urge to create a comfortable and secure living space, spend quality time with loved ones, and explore your emotional roots. This is an excellent time to focus on home improvement projects, family bonding, and strengthening your sense of belonging.

As Jupiter moves through Cancer, it will form challenging square aspects to Saturn in Aries (June 15) and Neptune in Aries (June 18), both in your 12th House of spirituality, solitude, and endings. These transits may bring up deep-seated fears, doubts, or limiting beliefs that need to be confronted and released. You may experience a period of introspection and soul-searching as you grapple with questions of faith, purpose, and surrender. Lean into your Taurean strength and practicality to find grounding during these times of uncertainty. Remember that growth often involves letting go of what no longer serves you to make space for new beginnings.

The Lunar Nodes, powerful points of destiny and growth, will spend the year moving through Aries and Libra, activating your 12th and 6th Houses. The North Node in Libra invites you to cultivate more balance, harmony, and cooperation in your daily routines and work life. Focus on creating a healthy work-life balance, nurturing supportive relationships with colleagues, and finding joy in service to others. The South Node in Aries may challenge you to release the need for constant self-reliance and control, learning to trust in the flow of life and accept help when needed.

Eclipses will play a pivotal role in your journey this year, particularly those occurring in Taurus and Scorpio, your 1st and 7th Houses of self and partnerships. Lunar eclipses in Scorpio on May 13 and November 7 may bring significant shifts or endings in your closest relationships, both personal and professional. Use these intense energies to dive deep into your emotional depths, exploring issues of intimacy, power, and shared resources. Be willing to confront any shadows or imbalances in your partnerships, working towards greater authenticity and transformation.

Solar eclipses in Taurus on October 21 and April 29 will shine a powerful spotlight on your sense of self, personal identity, and unique path forward. These cosmic wildcards may bring unexpected opportunities for growth, change, and new beginnings. Embrace the chance to reinvent yourself, make bold moves, and step into your power. Trust your inner compass and let your values guide you through any upheavals or uncertainties.

A major astrological event occurs on March 23 when Saturn, the planet of structure, responsibility, and maturity, enters Aries, your 12th House of spirituality and inner work. This transit, lasting until 2026, marks the beginning of a profound journey of self-reflection, healing, and letting go. Saturn will challenge you to confront your deepest fears, doubts, and limiting patterns, inviting you to do the hard work of self-mastery and spiritual growth. While this transit may feel isolating or challenging at times, it is a powerful opportunity to build a solid foundation of inner strength, resilience, and self-awareness. Embrace solitude, meditation, and therapeutic practices to navigate this transformative period.

Another significant shift takes place on March 23 when Pluto, the planet of power, transformation, and rebirth, moves into Aquarius, your 10th House of career and public image. This transit, lasting until 2044, will bring a profound restructuring of your professional life and long-term goals. You may feel called to step into a leadership role, make bold career moves, or align your work with your deepest passions and values. Pluto will challenge you to confront any power dynamics or hidden agendas in your professional life, inviting you to claim your authority and make a meaningful impact in the world. Trust the process of destruction and regeneration, knowing that what falls away is making space for a more authentic and empowered version of yourself to emerge.

Your ruling planet Venus will have an eventful year, starting with an extended visit to Aries, your 12th House of spirituality and transcendence. From July 22 to September 3, Venus will be retrograde in this sensitive sector, inviting you to dive deep into your inner world and explore your hidden desires, fears, and creative potential. This is a profound time for healing, forgiveness, and letting go of the past. You may feel a strong urge to retreat, reflect, and connect with your intuition. Trust the messages and insights that arise during this period, as they will guide you towards greater self-love, compassion, and spiritual growth.

On June 21, a powerful Venus-Mars conjunction at the last degree of Aries will bring a potent opportunity for release, transformation, and new beginnings. This cosmic reset button will help you break free from old patterns, wounds, and limitations, paving the way for a more authentic and empowered expression of yourself. Embrace the energy of courage, passion, and self-assertion, and trust that you have the strength to move forward with clarity and purpose.

After this intense period of inner work, Venus will grace your sign from September 3 to October 8, bringing a much-needed dose of self-love, beauty, and pleasure. This is a wonderful time to focus on self-care, pampering, and expressing your unique style and creativity. You may also experience a surge of romantic interest or opportunities for financial abundance. Embrace the energy of self-worth, value, and deserving, knowing that you are worthy of love, respect, and success.

In the second half of the year, the astrological focus shifts to the nurturing and intuitive Water signs. Jupiter's entry into Cancer on May 18 will bring a renewed sense of emotional connection, security, and belonging. This is a wonderful time to deepen your bonds with family, explore your ancestral roots, and create a nurturing home environment. You may also feel a strong urge to explore your creativity, intuition, and emotional intelligence. Trust your instincts and let your heart guide you towards experiences and relationships that feel nourishing and supportive.

Mars, the planet of action, energy, and desire, will tour nostalgic Cancer from August 23 to October 15, activating your 4th House of home, family, and emotional foundations. This transit may bring up old memories, patterns, or family dynamics that need to be addressed and healed. You may feel more sensitive, moody, or protective during this time, so be sure to prioritize self-care and set healthy boundaries with loved ones. Channel any excess energy into home improvement projects, cooking, or nurturing your inner child.

As Mars moves into Scorpio, your 7th House of partnerships, from October 15 to January 9, 2025, you can expect a surge of passion, intensity, and transformation in your closest relationships. This is a powerful time to confront any issues of power, control, or intimacy in your partnerships, working towards greater depth, honesty, and mutual empowerment. You may also feel a strong urge to collaborate with others on shared goals or projects, pooling your resources and talents for maximum impact. Just be mindful of potential conflicts or power struggles, and strive to find a balance between asserting your needs and considering the needs of others.

On the financial front, 2025 looks to be a promising year for Taureans, with Jupiter bringing opportunities for growth, expansion, and abundance. If you are self-employed or in a creative field, the first half of the year is particularly favorable for marketing your skills, attracting new clients, or launching innovative projects. Your natural Taurean gifts of practicality, perseverance, and financial savvy will serve you well, especially in the latter part of the year when many planets cluster in grounded Earth signs. Focus on creating a solid budget, saving for the future, and investing in your long-term security and stability.

As the year comes to a close, you can look back on 2025 as a year of profound growth, transformation, and self-discovery. While change and uncertainty may have felt uncomfortable at times for your stability-loving sign, trust that the challenges you've faced have served to strengthen your resilience, adaptability, and inner power.

You've learned to embrace change as an opportunity for growth, to trust your instincts and values, and to let go of what no longer serves you. As you move forward into 2026 and beyond, know that you have the inner resources, wisdom, and courage to create a life that is truly authentic, meaningful, and fulfilling. Keep shining your unique light, Taurus, and trust that the universe is guiding you towards your highest good. Here's to a year of growth, abundance, and joyful self-discovery!

January 2025

Overview Horoscope for the Month:

Welcome to January 2025, Taurus! This month marks the beginning of a transformative year filled with opportunities for personal growth, emotional healing, and spiritual awakening. With a powerful stellium of planets in Capricorn activating your 9th house of higher learning, travel, and philosophy, you are being called to expand your horizons, challenge your beliefs, and seek new adventures that broaden your perspective on life.

The New Moon in Aquarius on January 29th falls in your 10th house of career and public image, bringing fresh energy and innovative ideas to your professional life. This is a time to step outside your comfort zone, embrace your unique talents and skills, and make bold moves towards your long-term goals and aspirations.

Love:

In love, January 2025 is a month of deep emotional connection and spiritual intimacy. With Venus, your ruling planet, entering dreamy Pisces on January 2nd, you may find yourself craving a soul-level bond with your partner or seeking a relationship that transcends the physical realm. This is a time to open your heart, express your feelings with vulnerability and authenticity, and create a safe space for love to flourish.

If you're in a committed relationship, take time to connect with your partner through shared spiritual practices, such as meditation, yoga, or dream work. Explore the deeper meaning and purpose of your union, and find ways to support each other's personal and spiritual growth.

If you're single, you may find yourself attracted to people who share your values, beliefs, and spiritual path. Look for partners who inspire you to be your best self, who challenge you to grow and evolve, and who offer emotional depth and understanding. Trust your intuition and let your heart guide you towards meaningful connections.

Career:

In your career, January 2025 is a month of ambition, achievement, and public recognition. With a powerful stellium of planets in Capricorn activating your 10th house of career and public image, you are being called to step into your power, claim your authority, and make your mark in the world. This is a time to set clear goals, create a strategic plan, and take practical steps towards your long-term vision of success.

The New Moon in Aquarius on January 29th brings fresh energy and innovative ideas to your professional life. Trust your unique talents and skills, and don't be afraid to think outside the box and try new approaches. Network with like-minded individuals who share your vision and values, and seek out mentors who can guide you towards your highest potential.

If you're considering a career change or starting a new business, do your research and make sure that your plans are grounded in reality. Focus on building a strong foundation of skills, experience, and relationships that can support you in the long run.

Finances:

In finances, January 2025 is a month of practicality, responsibility, and long-term planning. With Saturn, the planet of structure and discipline, traveling through your 8th house of shared resources and investments, you are being called to take a serious look at your financial situation and make wise choices that support your long-term security and stability.

Review your budget, identify areas where you can save and invest, and make sure that your financial decisions align with your values and goals. If you have any debts or financial obligations, create a realistic plan to pay them off and free yourself from unnecessary burdens.

Consider seeking the advice of a financial planner or advisor who can help you navigate any challenges and make the most of your resources. Trust your own judgment and instincts, and don't be afraid to make necessary changes or adjustments to your financial strategy.

Health:

In health, January 2025 is a month of vitality, resilience, and inner strength. With Mars, the planet of energy and action, entering nurturing Cancer on January 6th, you may find yourself feeling more introspective and focused on your emotional well-being. This is a time to listen to your body's needs and rhythms, and to prioritize activities that bring you a sense of comfort, security, and inner peace.

Take time to engage in gentle exercise, such as yoga, walking, or swimming, that helps you feel grounded and centered. Nourish your body with healthy, whole foods that support your immune system and energy levels. Make sure to get plenty of rest and sleep, and create a bedtime routine that helps you unwind and release any stress or tension from the day.

On an emotional level, practice self-compassion and kindness towards yourself. Acknowledge any feelings of anxiety, fear, or uncertainty that may arise, and offer yourself the same love and support that you would offer a dear friend. Seek out activities that bring you joy, creativity, and a sense of connection to something greater than yourself.

Travel:

In travel, January 2025 may bring opportunities for long-distance journeys or spiritual pilgrimages that expand your mind, heart, and soul. With a powerful stellium of planets in Capricorn activating your 9th house of travel, higher learning, and philosophy, you are being called to step outside your comfort zone and explore new horizons that broaden your perspective on life.

Consider booking a trip to a place that holds deep spiritual significance for you, such as a sacred site, a retreat center, or a natural wonder that inspires awe and reverence. Seek out experiences that challenge your beliefs, open your mind to new ideas and cultures, and deepen your connection to the greater mysteries of life.

If travel isn't possible or practical, find ways to bring a sense of adventure and exploration into your daily life. Enroll in a course or workshop that expands your knowledge and skills, read books or watch documentaries that introduce you to new concepts and perspectives, or engage in spiritual practices that help you connect with a higher power or purpose.

Insights from the Stars:

The celestial energies of January 2025 remind you of the power of faith, surrender, and spiritual growth. With Venus in Pisces activating your 11th house of hopes, wishes, and community, you are being called to connect with like-minded souls who share your vision of a better world and support you on your path of personal and collective evolution.

The New Moon in Aquarius on January 29th invites you to embrace your unique talents and skills, to think outside the box and innovate in your career and public life, and to trust in the power of your own creativity and vision. Let go of any limiting beliefs or fears that may be holding you back, and have faith in your ability to manifest your dreams and goals.

Remember that you are a powerful creator and co-creator, and that your thoughts, emotions, and actions have the power to shape your reality and contribute to the greater good. Stay open to the guidance and support of the universe, and trust that everything is unfolding in perfect timing and alignment with your highest purpose and potential.

Best Days of the Month:

January 2nd: Venus enters Pisces, bringing a dreamy, romantic, and imaginative energy to your friendships, social life, and community involvement.

January 6th: Mars enters Cancer, activating your 3rd house of communication, learning, and short trips. This is a great time to express your feelings, learn new skills, and explore your local environment

January 11th: The True Node enters Pisces, highlighting your spiritual growth, soul's evolution, and connection to a higher purpose or calling.

January 29th: The New Moon in Aquarius invites you to embrace your unique talents and skills, innovate in your career and public life, and connect with like-minded individuals who share your vision and values

January 30th: Uranus turns direct in Taurus, bringing sudden insights, breakthroughs, and positive changes to your sense of self, identity, and personal freedom. Trust your instincts and let your authentic self shine.

February 2025

Overview Horoscope for the Month:

Welcome to February 2025, Taurus! This month promises to be a time of deep emotional healing, spiritual growth, and positive change. With the Sun traveling through your 10th house of career and public image for most of the month, you are being called to step into your power, claim your authority, and make your mark in the world. Trust in your unique talents and abilities, and don't be afraid to take bold steps towards your long-term goals and aspirations.

The Full Moon in Leo on February 12th illuminates your 4th house of home, family, and emotional foundations. This is a time to nurture your closest relationships, create a safe and comfortable living space, and connect with your roots and inner sense of security. Let go of any past wounds or patterns that may be holding you back, and embrace the healing power of love, forgiveness, and self-acceptance.

Love:

In love, February 2025 is a month of passion, creativity, and self-expression. With Venus, your ruling planet, entering fiery Aries on February 4th, you may find yourself feeling more bold, assertive, and confident in your romantic pursuits. This is a time to take the lead in your relationships, express your desires with clarity and conviction, and attract partners who appreciate your unique qualities and strengths.

If you're in a committed relationship, take time to reignite the spark of passion and adventure with your partner. Plan a special date or getaway that allows you to break free from your usual routines and explore new experiences together. Be open and honest about your needs and desires, and work together to create a dynamic of mutual respect, support, and growth.

If you're single, you may find yourself attracted to people who are confident, independent, and unafraid to take risks. Look for partners who inspire you to be your best self, who challenge you to step outside your comfort zone, and who appreciate your unique talents and abilities. Trust your instincts and let your heart guide you towards meaningful connections.

Career:

In your career, February 2025 is a month of recognition, achievement, and positive change. With the Sun illuminating your 10th house of career and public image, you are being called to step into the spotlight and showcase your unique talents and abilities. This is a time to take on new challenges, pursue your long-term goals with passion and determination, and make your mark in your chosen field.

The Full Moon in Leo on February 12th brings a sense of completion and culmination to your professional endeavors. Trust in the work you've put in, and be open to receiving recognition and rewards for your efforts. If you've been considering a career change or starting a new business, this is a powerful time to take action and manifest your vision into reality.

Seek out mentors, colleagues, and collaborators who share your values and support your growth. Network with like-minded individuals who can offer guidance, resources, and opportunities for advancement. Stay focused on your long-term goals, and don't be afraid to take calculated risks that align with your authentic self and purpose.

Finances:

In finances, February 2025 is a month of abundance, prosperity, and positive change. With Jupiter, the planet of expansion and abundance, traveling through your 2nd house of money and resources, you are being called to embrace a mindset of abundance and trust in the flow of the universe. This is a time to release any fears or limiting beliefs around scarcity or lack, and to open yourself up to new opportunities for income and wealth.

Review your budget, identify areas where you can save and invest, and make sure that your financial decisions align with your values and long-term goals. Consider seeking the advice of a financial planner or advisor who can help you create a strategy for growth and stability. Trust your own judgment and instincts, and be open to unexpected sources of income or support.

On a deeper level, reflect on your relationship with money and abundance. What beliefs or patterns may be holding you back from experiencing true prosperity and fulfillment? How can you cultivate a sense of gratitude, generosity, and trust in the universe? Remember that you are a powerful creator and co-creator, and that your thoughts and actions have the power to shape your financial reality.

Health:

In health, February 2025 is a month of vitality, resilience, and inner growth. With Mars, the planet of energy and action, traveling through your 3rd house of communication and learning, you may find yourself feeling more curious, expressive, and mentally active. This is a time to feed your mind with new ideas and perspectives, engage in stimulating conversations and debates, and explore new ways of thinking and communicating.

Take time to engage in activities that challenge your mind and keep you mentally sharp, such as reading, writing, or learning a new skill. Be open to different viewpoints and opinions, and practice active listening and empathy in your interactions with others. At the same time, be mindful of your words and the impact they can have on others. Speak from a place of kindness, compassion, and understanding.

On a physical level, make sure to get plenty of rest and exercise to support your immune system and overall well-being. Consider incorporating more plant-based foods into your diet, and limit your intake of processed or inflammatory foods. Take breaks throughout the day to stretch, breathe deeply, and connect with your body's natural rhythms and needs.

Travel:

In travel, February 2025 may bring opportunities for short trips or adventures that feed your mind and soul. With Mars activating your 3rd house of communication and learning, you may find yourself drawn to destinations that offer intellectual stimulation, cultural enrichment, or new experiences. Consider booking a trip to a museum, art gallery, or historical site that piques your curiosity and expands your knowledge.

If travel isn't possible or practical, find ways to bring a sense of adventure and exploration into your daily life. Take a different route to work, try a new restaurant or cuisine, or attend a local event or workshop that introduces you to new ideas and perspectives. Be open to serendipity and spontaneity, and trust that the universe will bring you the experiences and connections you need for your growth and evolution.

Insights from the Stars:

The celestial energies of February 2025 remind you of the power of authenticity, self-expression, and positive change. With Venus in Aries activating your 12th house of spirituality and inner growth, you are being called to connect with your deepest desires, fears, and dreams. This is a time to release any masks or facades you may be wearing, and to embrace your true self with courage and vulnerability.

The Full Moon in Leo on February 12th illuminates your 4th house of home, family, and emotional foundations. Trust in the healing power of love, forgiveness, and self-acceptance, and let go of any past wounds or patterns that may be holding you back. Surround yourself with people who support and inspire you, and create a living space that reflects your authentic self and values.

Remember that you are a powerful creator and co-creator, and that your thoughts, emotions, and actions have the power to shape your reality and contribute to the greater good. Stay open to the guidance and support of the universe, and trust that everything is unfolding in perfect timing and alignment with your highest purpose and potential.

Best Days of the Month:

February 4th: Venus enters Aries, bringing a bold, passionate, and confident energy to your spiritual growth and inner transformation.

February 5th: The First Quarter Moon in Taurus invites you to take practical steps towards your long-term goals and aspirations, and to trust in your own judgment and instincts.

February 12th: The Full Moon in Leo illuminates your home, family, and emotional foundations, bringing a sense of completion and culmination to your personal life and relationships.

February 16th: Pallas enters Aquarius, activating your 10th house of career and public image. This is a great time to bring innovative ideas and strategic thinking to your professional pursuits.

February 27th: The New Moon in Pisces invites you to connect with your intuition, imagination, and spiritual purpose. Set intentions for healing, growth, and positive change in all areas of your life.

March 2025

Overview Horoscope for the Month:

Welcome to March 2025, Taurus! This month promises to be a time of profound transformation, spiritual awakening, and new beginnings. The astrological energies align to support your journey inward, encouraging you to confront your fears, release limiting patterns, and connect with your soul's true purpose. Embrace the opportunities for self-discovery and trust in the wisdom of the universe as you navigate this powerful time.

March 2025 is a significant month for you, Taurus, as Saturn enters your 12th house of spirituality and inner growth on the 1st. This transit, lasting until 2026, marks the beginning of a profound journey of self-reflection, healing, and letting go. You are called to do the deep inner work of confronting your fears, releasing old patterns and beliefs, and connecting with your soul's true calling. Embrace solitude, introspection, and self-reflection, trusting in the guidance of the universe.

The New Moon in Aries on March 29th falls in your 12th house, amplifying the themes of spiritual awakening and emotional release. Set intentions for healing, forgiveness, and inner peace, knowing that the universe supports you in your growth and transformation.

Love:

In love, March 2025 emphasizes the importance of emotional depth, vulnerability, and spiritual intimacy. With Venus, your ruling planet, in sensitive Pisces for most of the month, you may crave a soul-level connection with your partner or seek a relationship that transcends the superficial. Open your heart, express your feelings authentically, and create a safe space for love to flourish.

For committed Taureans, focus on strengthening your bond through shared spiritual practices, deep conversations, and acts of compassion. Single Taureans may find themselves attracted to individuals who share their values, offer emotional understanding, and inspire personal growth. Trust your intuition and let your heart guide you toward meaningful connections.

Career:

Your career sector is influenced by Saturn's transit through your 12th house, prompting a period of introspection, reflection, and inner growth. You may question your current path or seek a deeper sense of purpose and meaning in your professional life. Reassess your goals, values, and priorities, ensuring that your work aligns with your authentic self and soul's calling.

Trust that the universe is guiding you toward your highest potential, even if the path is not always clear. Seek guidance from mentors or spiritual advisors who can support you in your journey of self-discovery and transformation.

Finances:

In finances, March 2025 is a month of spiritual abundance, trust, and surrender. With Venus and Jupiter activating your 12th house, you are called to release fears or limiting beliefs around money and embrace a mindset of gratitude and faith. Trust in the flow and provision of the universe, knowing that you will always be supported.

Review your budget, identify areas where you can give back or share your resources, and ensure that your financial decisions align with your spiritual values. Consider setting aside a portion of your income for charitable donations or tithing, trusting that the more you give, the more you will receive.

Health:

Your physical and emotional well-being are highlighted this month, as the cosmic energies support your journey of spiritual healing, self-care, and inner peace. With the Sun in Pisces illuminating your 12th house, honor your body's natural rhythms and prioritize activities that bring you calm, relaxation, and renewal.

Engage in gentle, restorative practices like yoga, meditation, or aromatherapy, and surround yourself with soothing environments. Nourish your body with whole, natural foods, and limit exposure to stress and negativity. Practice self-compassion, forgiveness, and acceptance, allowing yourself to process emotions in healthy ways.

Travel:

March 2025 may bring opportunities for spiritual retreats, pilgrimages, or journeys of self-discovery. With Saturn in your 12th house, you may feel called to visit sacred sites, connect with nature, or explore new spiritual practices and traditions. Consider planning a trip to a destination that holds deep meaning and significance for you.

If travel is not possible, find ways to bring a sense of adventure and exploration into your daily life. Take walks in nature, visit local spiritual centers, or attend workshops that introduce you to new ideas and perspectives. Remain open to synchronicity and divine guidance, trusting in the experiences and connections that arise.

Insights from the Stars:

The celestial energies of March 2025 remind you of the power of surrender, faith, and inner wisdom. Saturn's entry into your 12th house calls you to let go of control, trust in the greater plan of the universe, and connect with your deepest truth and purpose. Embrace the unknown, face your fears and shadows, and allow yourself to be transformed by the power of divine love and grace.

The New Moon in Aries on March 29th brings a powerful opportunity for healing, forgiveness, and new beginnings in your spiritual life. Set intentions for inner peace, emotional release, and positive change, knowing that the universe supports you every step of the way. Remember that you are a divine being of light and love, and your soul's purpose is to shine your unique gifts in service to the world.

Best Days of the Month:

March 1st: Saturn enters Aries, activating your 12th house of spirituality and inner growth. A powerful time for self-reflection, introspection, and inner transformation begins.

March 6th: The First Quarter Moon in Gemini invites you to communicate your feelings and ideas authentically, seeking new perspectives that support your growth.

March 14th: The Full Moon in Virgo brings a powerful opportunity for healing, self-care, and service. Trust your intuition and find ways to share your gifts with the world.

March 20th: The Sun enters Aries, marking the beginning of the astrological new year and a cycle of growth and transformation. Set intentions for the year ahead, trusting in the power of new beginnings.

March 29th: The New Moon in Aries falls in your 12th house, bringing a potent time for healing, forgiveness, and spiritual awakening. Set intentions for inner peace, emotional release, and positive change, trusting in the universe's guidance and support.

April 2025

Overview Horoscope for the Month:

Welcome to April 2025, Taurus! This month promises to be a time of powerful transformation, new beginnings, and personal growth. With the Sun traveling through your 12th house of spirituality and inner work for most of the month, you are being called to connect with your deepest self, release old patterns and beliefs, and embrace a new level of self-awareness and inner wisdom. This is a time to trust in the power of surrender, faith, and divine timing, and to allow yourself to be guided by your intuition and higher purpose.

The New Moon Solar Eclipse in Taurus on April 29th falls in your 1st house of self and identity, bringing a powerful opportunity for personal transformation, self-discovery, and new beginnings. Set intentions for the next six months and beyond, and trust that the universe is supporting you in creating a life that aligns with your authentic self and soul's purpose.

Love:

In matters of the heart, April 2025 emphasizes the importance of emotional intimacy, vulnerability, and spiritual connection. With Venus, your ruling planet, in sensitive Pisces until the 12th, you may find yourself craving a deep, soulful bond with your partner or seeking a relationship that transcends the superficial. Open your heart, express your feelings with authenticity, and create a safe space for love to blossom.

As Venus moves into fiery Aries on the 30th, you may experience a shift towards a more passionate, assertive, and independent approach to love. Embrace this energy to express your desires, set clear boundaries, and attract relationships that honor your individuality and strength.

Career:

In your career, April 2025 is a month of inner growth, self-reflection, and spiritual alignment. With the Sun traveling through your 12th house of spirituality and inner work, you may find yourself questioning your current path or seeking a deeper sense of purpose and meaning in your professional life. This is a time to reassess your goals, values, and priorities, and to make sure that your work aligns with your authentic self and soul's calling.

Take time to reflect on your strengths, weaknesses, and areas for growth, and be willing to let go of any limiting beliefs or patterns that may be holding you back. Seek out mentors, coaches, or spiritual guides who can support you in your journey of self-discovery and transformation. Trust that the universe is guiding you towards your highest potential and purpose, even if the path is not always clear or easy.

If you're considering a career change or starting a new business, the New Moon Solar Eclipse in Taurus on April 29th is a powerful time to set intentions and take action towards your dreams. Trust in your unique talents and abilities, and don't be afraid to take risks or step outside your comfort zone. Remember that your work is a reflection of your soul's purpose, and that you have the power to create a life and career that brings you joy, fulfillment, and abundance.

Finances:

In finances, April 2025 is a month of spiritual abundance, trust, and surrender. With Venus traveling through your 12th house of spirituality and inner growth for the first part of the month, you are being called to release any fears or limiting beliefs around money and abundance, and to trust in the flow and provision of the universe. This is a time to cultivate a mindset of gratitude, generosity, and faith, and to open yourself up to unexpected sources of income and support.

Review your budget, identify areas where you can give back or share your resources with others, and make sure that your financial decisions align with your spiritual values and beliefs. Consider setting aside a portion of your income for charitable donations, tithing, or other forms of giving that bring you joy and fulfillment. Trust that the more you give, the more you will receive, and that the universe will always provide for your needs and desires.

On a deeper level, reflect on your relationship with money and abundance, and any past wounds or traumas that may be blocking your flow of wealth and prosperity. Practice forgiveness, release, and self-love, and affirm your worthiness and deserving of all good things. Remember that true abundance comes from within, and that your inner state of being is the foundation for your external reality.

Health:

Your physical and emotional well-being are highlighted this month, as the cosmic energies support your journey of healing, release, and inner peace. With the Sun and Mercury in your 12th house, prioritize activities that promote relaxation, introspection, and spiritual connection, such as meditation, yoga, or energy healing.

Pay attention to any physical symptoms or emotional discomfort that may arise, as they may be messages from your body and soul guiding you towards greater self-care and balance. Practice self-compassion, forgiveness, and acceptance, and seek support from trusted healers or therapists if needed.

Travel:

In travel, April 2025 may bring opportunities for spiritual retreats, pilgrimages, or journeys of self-discovery. With the Sun traveling through your 12th house of spirituality and inner work, you may feel called to visit sacred sites, connect with nature, or explore new spiritual practices and traditions. Consider booking a trip to a place that holds deep meaning and significance for you, such as a monastery, ashram, or natural wonder.

If travel isn't possible or practical, find ways to bring a sense of adventure and exploration into your daily life. Take a nature walk, visit a local temple or church, or attend a spiritual workshop or event that introduces you to new ideas and perspectives. Be open to synchronicity and divine guidance, and trust that the universe will bring you the experiences and connections you need for your growth and evolution.

Insights from the Stars:

The celestial energies of April 2025 remind you of the power of surrender, faith, and inner wisdom. With the Sun traveling through your 12th house of spirituality and inner work, you are being called to let go of control, trust in the greater plan of the universe, and connect with your deepest truth and purpose. This is a time to embrace the unknown, face your fears and shadows, and allow yourself to be transformed by the power of divine love and grace.

The New Moon Solar Eclipse in Taurus on April 29th brings a powerful opportunity for personal transformation, self-discovery, and new beginnings. Set intentions for the next six months and beyond, and trust that the universe is supporting you in creating a life that aligns with your authentic self and soul's purpose. Remember that you are a divine being of light and love, and that your journey is unfolding in perfect timing and alignment with your highest good.

Best Days of the Month:

April 4th: Saturn sextile Uranus, bringing a harmonious blend of structure and innovation, tradition and progress. This is a great time to make positive changes in your life that align with your long-term goals and aspirations.

April 7th: Mercury goes direct in Pisces, bringing clarity and forward momentum to your communication, ideas, and plans. Trust your intuition and inner guidance, and express yourself with authenticity and compassion.

April 12th: The Full Moon in Libra illuminates your 6th house of health, work, and service, bringing a sense of balance and harmony to your daily routines and relationships. Focus on self-care, collaboration, and finding joy in the present moment.

April 21st: Saturn conjunct the True Node, bringing a powerful opportunity for spiritual growth, karmic healing, and alignment with your soul's purpose. Trust in the wisdom of the universe, and let go of any obstacles or limitations that are holding you back.

April 29th: The New Moon Solar Eclipse in Taurus falls in your 1st house of self and identity, bringing a powerful opportunity for personal transformation, self-discovery, and new beginnings. Set intentions for the next six months and beyond, and trust in the power of your own strength, beauty, and worth.

May 2025

Overview Horoscope for the Month:

Taurus, May 2025 is a month of profound change, growth, and new beginnings for you. The astrological energies are intense and transformative, with a series of powerful planetary alignments and eclipses shaking up the status quo and calling you to step into your power and purpose. This is a time to let go of the past, embrace the present, and trust in the unfolding of your future.

The month begins with the Sun in your sign, illuminating your 1st house of self and identity. This is your time to shine, Taurus, and to celebrate your unique gifts, talents, and qualities. You may feel a renewed sense of confidence, vitality, and purpose, and a desire to express yourself more fully and authentically in the world.

However, the Full Moon Lunar Eclipse in Scorpio on May 13th will bring intense emotions and revelations to the surface, particularly in your 7th house of partnerships and relationships. This eclipse will challenge you to confront any fears, secrets, or power dynamics that may be holding you back from true intimacy and connection. It's time to let go of any toxic patterns or relationships that no longer serve your highest good, and to open yourself up to deeper levels of trust, vulnerability, and transformation.

Love:

In love, May 2025 is a month of passion, intensity, and transformation. With Venus, your ruling planet, traveling through fiery Aries for most of the month, you may feel a renewed sense of desire, confidence, and assertiveness in your romantic life. This is a time to take the lead in your relationships, express your needs and desires openly and honestly, and attract partners who appreciate your strength and independence.

If you're in a committed relationship, the Full Moon Lunar Eclipse in Scorpio on May 13th will bring any underlying issues or power struggles to the surface. This is an opportunity to have deep, honest conversations with your partner about your fears, desires, and boundaries, and to work together to create a more authentic and intimate connection. Be willing to let go of any expectations or attachments that may be holding you back from true love and vulnerability.

If you're single, this eclipse may bring unexpected encounters or revelations that challenge your beliefs about love and relationships. Stay open to new possibilities and perspectives, and trust that the universe is guiding you towards the right person at the right time. Focus on healing any past wounds or traumas, and cultivating a deep sense of self-love and self-worth.

Career:

In your career, May 2025 is a month of ambition, innovation, and breakthrough. With Mars, the planet of action and energy, traveling through your 10th house of career and public image for most of the month, you may feel a renewed sense of drive, determination, and leadership in your professional life. This is a time to take bold steps towards your goals and dreams, and to assert your unique talents and abilities in the world.

However, the Full Moon Lunar Eclipse in Scorpio on May 13th may bring unexpected changes or challenges to your career path or public reputation. This eclipse will expose any hidden agendas, power struggles, or fears that may be holding you back from true success and fulfillment. It's time to let go of any limiting beliefs or patterns, and to trust in your own inner guidance and intuition.

Stay open to new opportunities and collaborations that align with your values and purpose, and be willing to take calculated risks and think outside the box. You may need to confront any fears or doubts that arise, and to trust in your own resilience and adaptability. Remember that your career is a reflection of your soul's journey, and that every challenge is an opportunity for growth and transformation.

Finances:

In finances, May 2025 is a month of abundance, prosperity, and breakthrough. With Venus traveling through your 2nd house of money and resources for the first part of the month, you may experience unexpected windfalls, opportunities, or insights that help you to manifest your financial goals and dreams. This is a time to trust in the flow and abundance of the universe, and to cultivate a mindset of gratitude, generosity, and positive expectation.

However, the Full Moon Lunar Eclipse in Scorpio on May 13th may bring any hidden fears, blocks, or power struggles around money and resources to the surface. This eclipse will challenge you to confront any limiting beliefs or patterns that may be holding you back from true financial freedom and empowerment. It's time to let go of any scarcity mentality or attachment to material possessions, and to focus on creating a sense of inner wealth and fulfillment.

Review your budget, investments, and financial plans, and make any necessary adjustments or changes that align with your values and goals. Consider seeking the guidance of a trusted financial advisor or mentor who can help you to navigate any challenges or opportunities that arise. Remember that your relationship with money is a reflection of your relationship with yourself, and that true abundance comes from within.

Health:

In health, May 2025 is a month of vitality, resilience, and transformation. With the Sun traveling through your sign for most of the month, you may feel a renewed sense of energy, strength, and well-being. This is a time to prioritize your physical, mental, and emotional health, and to cultivate daily practices and habits that support your overall vitality and resilience.

However, the Full Moon Lunar Eclipse in Scorpio on May 13th may bring any hidden fears, traumas, or blocks around your health and well-being to the surface. This eclipse will challenge you to confront any self-sabotaging behaviors or patterns that may be holding you back from true healing and transformation. It's time to let go of any unhealthy attachments or addictions, and to focus on creating a sense of inner peace and balance.

Take time to rest, recharge, and listen to your body's needs and signals. Engage in activities that bring you joy, relaxation, and a sense of connection to your inner self, such as meditation, yoga, or spending time in nature. Nourish your body with healthy, whole foods, and limit your exposure to toxins, stress, and negative influences.

Travel:

In travel, May 2025 may bring unexpected opportunities for adventure, exploration, and personal growth. With Mars traveling through your 9th house of travel, higher education, and philosophy for most of the month, you may feel a strong desire to expand your horizons, learn new things, and experience different cultures and perspectives.

Consider taking a trip or enrolling in a course or workshop that aligns with your interests and passions. This is a time to step outside your comfort zone, challenge your assumptions and beliefs, and open yourself up to new ideas and possibilities.

However, the Full Moon Lunar Eclipse in Scorpio on May 13th may bring any hidden fears, anxieties, or power struggles around travel and exploration to the surface. This eclipse will challenge you to confront any limiting beliefs or patterns that may be holding you back from true freedom and adventure. It's time to let go of any attachments to safety or security, and to trust in the journey of your soul.

Insights from the Stars:

The celestial energies of May 2025 remind you of the power of transformation, authenticity, and self-mastery. With the Sun illuminating your sign, and the Full Moon Lunar Eclipse in Scorpio activating your 7th house of partnerships and relationships, you are being called to step into your full power and potential, and to let go of any masks, illusions, or limitations that no longer serve your highest good.

This is a time to embrace your shadow, face your fears, and trust in the wisdom and guidance of the universe. You are a powerful creator and manifester, and your thoughts, beliefs, and actions have the power to shape your reality and attract your deepest desires and dreams.

Stay open to the unexpected, and trust that every challenge or setback is an opportunity for growth, learning, and transformation. Remember that you are a divine being of love and light, and that your soul's journey is unfolding in perfect timing and alignment with your highest good.

Best Days of the Month:

May 1st: Uranus sextile the True Node, bringing unexpected insights, breakthroughs, and opportunities for growth and change. Trust your intuition and be open to new possibilities and perspectives.

May 4th: The First Quarter Moon in Leo invites you to take bold steps towards your goals and dreams, and to express your unique creativity and passion in the world.

May 13th: The Full Moon Lunar Eclipse in Scorpio brings intense emotions and transformative energies to your relationships and partnerships. Let go of any toxic patterns or attachments, and open yourself up to deeper levels of intimacy, vulnerability, and connection.

May 18th: Jupiter sextile Chiron and square the True Node, bringing opportunities for healing, growth, and alignment with your soul's purpose. Trust in the wisdom of your wounds, and let go of any limiting beliefs or patterns that no longer serve you.

May 25th: The New Moon in Gemini invites you to set intentions around communication, learning, and self-expression. Trust in the power of your voice and your ideas, and be open to new perspectives and possibilities.

June 2025

Overview Horoscope for the Month:

Taurus, June 2025 is a month of emotional depth, spiritual growth, and personal empowerment for you. The astrological energies are intense and transformative, with a series of powerful planetary alignments and eclipses inviting you to dive deep into your inner world, confront your shadows, and emerge with a renewed sense of purpose and passion.

The month begins with Venus, your ruling planet, entering your sign on June 6th, bringing a heightened sense of beauty, sensuality, and self-worth to your life. This is a time to celebrate your unique qualities and talents, and to attract abundance, love, and joy into your world. However, Venus will also form a challenging square aspect to Saturn in Pisces on June 12th, asking you to confront any fears, doubts, or limitations that may be holding you back from true intimacy and connection.

The New Moon in Gemini on June 25th will activate your 2nd house of money, resources, and self-worth, inviting you to set powerful intentions around abundance, prosperity, and financial freedom. This is a time to trust in your own value and worth, and to cultivate a mindset of gratitude, generosity, and positive expectation.

Love:

In love, June 2025 is a month of emotional intensity, spiritual growth, and deep connection. With Venus traveling through your sign for most of the month, you may feel a heightened sense of magnetism, charm, and desirability. This is a time to express your love and affection openly and authentically, and to attract partners who appreciate your unique qualities and talents.

If you're in a committed relationship, the Venus-Saturn square on June 12th may bring any underlying fears, doubts, or limitations to the surface. This is an opportunity to have honest, vulnerable conversations with your partner about your needs, desires, and boundaries, and to work together to create a more authentic and intimate connection. Be willing to let go of any expectations or attachments that may be holding you back from true love and vulnerability.

If you're single, the New Moon in Gemini on June 25th may bring unexpected opportunities for love and romance. Stay open to new possibilities and perspectives, and trust that the universe is guiding you towards the right person at the right time. Focus on cultivating a deep sense of self-love and self-worth, and on attracting partners who reflect your highest values and desires.

Career:

In your career, June 2025 is a month of innovation, collaboration, and personal growth. With Mars, the planet of action and energy, traveling through your 11th house of groups, friends, and community for most of the month, you may feel a strong desire to connect with like-minded individuals, join forces with others, and make a positive impact in the world.

This is a time to network, collaborate, and share your ideas and talents with others. You may be invited to join a new team, organization, or project that aligns with your values and goals. Be open to new opportunities and perspectives, and trust that the universe is guiding you towards your highest potential and purpose.

However, the Venus-Saturn square on June 12th may bring any underlying fears, doubts, or limitations around your career and public image to the surface. This is an opportunity to confront any self-sabotaging behaviors or patterns, and to cultivate a deeper sense of self-trust and self-confidence. Remember that your worth and value are not defined by external validation or success, but by your own inner sense of purpose and integrity.

Finances:

In finances, June 2025 is a month of abundance, prosperity, and personal growth. With Venus traveling through your sign for most of the month, you may experience a heightened sense of self-worth, value, and deserving. This is a time to trust in your own talents and abilities, and to attract financial opportunities and resources that align with your highest values and goals.

The New Moon in Gemini on June 25th will activate your 2nd house of money, resources, and self-worth, inviting you to set powerful intentions around abundance, prosperity, and financial freedom. This is a time to cultivate a mindset of gratitude, generosity, and positive expectation, and to trust that the universe is always providing for your needs and desires.

However, the Venus-Saturn square on June 12th may bring any underlying fears, doubts, or limitations around money and security to the surface. This is an opportunity to confront any scarcity mentality or limiting beliefs, and to cultivate a deeper sense of trust and faith in the abundance of the universe. Remember that your true wealth and security come from within, and that you are always supported and provided for by a loving and benevolent universe.

Health:

In health, June 2025 is a month of vitality, resilience, and personal growth. With Venus traveling through your sign for most of the month, you may feel a heightened sense of physical vitality, sensuality, and well-being. This is a time to prioritize your self-care and self-love, and to cultivate daily practices and habits that support your overall health and happiness.

Take time to rest, recharge, and listen to your body's needs and signals. Engage in activities that bring you joy, relaxation, and a sense of connection to your inner self, such as massage, yoga, or spending time in nature. Nourish your body with healthy, whole foods, and limit your exposure to toxins, stress, and negative influences.

However, the Venus-Saturn square on June 12th may bring any underlying fears, doubts, or limitations around your health and well-being to the surface. This is an opportunity to confront any self-sabotaging behaviors or patterns, and to cultivate a deeper sense of self-compassion and self-acceptance. Remember that your body is a sacred temple, and that you deserve to treat yourself with love, kindness, and respect.

Travel:

In travel, June 2025 may bring unexpected opportunities for adventure, exploration, and personal growth. With Mars traveling through your 11th house of groups, friends, and community for most of the month, you may feel a strong desire to connect with others, explore new places and cultures, and expand your horizons.

Consider taking a trip with friends or joining a group tour or retreat that aligns with your interests and passions. This is a time to step outside your comfort zone, challenge your assumptions and beliefs, and open yourself up to new ideas and possibilities.

However, the Venus-Saturn square on June 12th may bring any underlying fears, doubts, or limitations around travel and exploration to the surface. This is an opportunity to confront any limiting beliefs or patterns that may be holding you back from true freedom and adventure. Remember that growth and expansion often require stepping into the unknown, and that every challenge is an opportunity for learning and transformation.

Insights from the Stars:

The celestial energies of June 2025 remind you of the power of self-love, self-worth, and personal empowerment. With Venus traveling through your sign, and the New Moon in Gemini activating your 2nd house of money, resources, and self-worth, you are being called to celebrate your unique qualities and talents, and to trust in your own value and deserving.

This is a time to let go of any limiting beliefs or patterns that may be holding you back from true abundance, joy, and fulfillment. You are a powerful creator and manifester, and your thoughts, beliefs, and actions have the power to shape your reality and attract your deepest desires and dreams.

Stay open to the unexpected, and trust that every challenge or setback is an opportunity for growth, learning, and transformation. Remember that you are a divine being of love and light, and that your soul's journey is unfolding in perfect timing and alignment with your highest good.

Best Days of the Month:

June 1st: Jupiter biquintile Pluto, bringing opportunities for deep transformation, healing, and personal growth. Trust in the wisdom of your soul, and be open to new possibilities and perspectives.

June 4th: Saturn sextile Uranus, bringing a harmonious blend of stability and change, tradition and innovation. This is a time to make positive changes in your life that align with your highest values and goals.

June 11th: The Full Moon in Sagittarius illuminates your 8th house of intimacy, shared resources, and personal transformation. Let go of any fears or limitations that may be holding you back from true connection and abundance.

June 21st: The Sun enters Cancer, marking the Summer Solstice and a powerful time of spiritual growth and emotional healing. Nurture yourself and your loved ones, and trust in the wisdom of your heart.

June 25th: The New Moon in Gemini activates your 2nd house of money, resources, and self-worth. Set powerful intentions around abundance, prosperity, and financial freedom, and trust in your own value and deserving.

July 2025

Overview Horoscope for the Month:

Taurus, July 2025 is a month of personal growth, spiritual awakening, and positive change for you. The astrological energies are dynamic and transformative, with a series of powerful planetary alignments and eclipses inviting you to step into your power, embrace your authentic self, and create a life that aligns with your deepest values and desires.

The month begins with Mars, the planet of action and energy, entering Leo on July 18th, activating your 4th house of home, family, and emotional foundations. This transit will bring a renewed sense of passion, creativity, and self-expression to your personal life, and may inspire you to make positive changes in your living space or family dynamics.

The Full Moon in Capricorn on July 10th will illuminate your 9th house of travel, higher education, and spiritual growth, inviting you to expand your horizons, seek new adventures, and connect with your higher purpose. This is a time to let go of any limiting beliefs or patterns that may be holding you back from true freedom and fulfillment, and to trust in the wisdom and guidance of the universe.

Love:

In love, July 2025 is a month of passion, romance, and emotional depth. With Venus, your ruling planet, traveling through Cancer for most of the month, you may feel a strong desire for intimacy, security, and emotional connection in your relationships. This is a time to nurture your loved ones, express your feelings openly and authentically, and create a safe and supportive space for love to flourish.

If you're in a committed relationship, the Full Moon in Capricorn on July 10th may bring a renewed sense of commitment, stability, and long-term vision to your partnership. This is a time to discuss your shared goals and dreams, and to make plans for the future that align with your deepest values and desires. Be willing to compromise and find a balance between your individual needs and the needs of the relationship.

If you're single, the Mars-Venus conjunction in Leo on July 21st may bring exciting opportunities for romance and passion. This is a time to express your unique qualities and talents, and to attract partners who appreciate and celebrate your authentic self. Focus on cultivating a deep sense of self-love and self-worth, and trust that the universe will bring you the right person at the right time.

Career:

In your career, July 2025 is a month of ambition, leadership, and positive change. With the Sun traveling through your 3rd house of communication, learning, and networking for most of the month, you may feel a strong desire to share your ideas, skills, and talents with others, and to make a positive impact in your community or industry.

This is a time to network, collaborate, and seek out new opportunities for growth and advancement. You may be invited to speak, write, or teach about your area of expertise, or to take on a leadership role in a project or organization that aligns with your values and goals.

However, the Full Moon in Capricorn on July 10th may bring any underlying fears, doubts, or limitations around your career and public image to the surface. This is an opportunity to confront any self-sabotaging behaviors or patterns, and to cultivate a deeper sense of self-trust and self-confidence. Remember that your worth and value are not defined by external validation or success, but by your own inner sense of purpose and integrity.

Finances:

In finances, July 2025 is a month of abundance, prosperity, and positive change. With Venus traveling through your 3rd house of communication and networking for most of the month, you may experience unexpected opportunities for financial growth and success through your connections and interactions with others.

This is a time to share your ideas, skills, and talents with the world, and to attract abundance and prosperity through your unique gifts and contributions. Trust in your own value and worth, and be open to receiving support, resources, and opportunities from unexpected sources.

However, the Full Moon in Capricorn on July 10th may bring any underlying fears, doubts, or limitations around money and security to the surface. This is an opportunity to confront any scarcity mentality or limiting beliefs, and to cultivate a deeper sense of trust and faith in the abundance of the universe. Remember that your true wealth and security come from within, and that you are always supported and provided for by a loving and benevolent universe.

Health:

In health, July 2025 is a month of vitality, resilience, and emotional healing. With Mars entering Leo on July 18th, activating your 4th house of home, family, and emotional foundations, you may feel a renewed sense of energy, passion, and creativity in your personal life. This is a time to prioritize your self-care and self-expression, and to cultivate daily practices and habits that support your physical, emotional, and spiritual well-being.

Take time to rest, recharge, and listen to your body's needs and signals. Engage in activities that bring you joy, relaxation, and a sense of connection to your inner child, such as dancing, singing, or playing. Nourish your body with healthy, whole foods, and limit your exposure to toxins, stress, and negative influences.

However, the Full Moon in Capricorn on July 10th may bring any underlying fears, doubts, or limitations around your health and well-being to the surface. This is an opportunity to confront any self-sabotaging behaviors or patterns, and to cultivate a deeper sense of self-compassion and self-acceptance. Remember that your body is a sacred temple, and that you deserve to treat yourself with love, kindness, and respect.

Travel:

In travel, July 2025 may bring exciting opportunities for adventure, exploration, and personal growth. With the Full Moon in Capricorn on July 10th illuminating your 9th house of travel, higher education, and spiritual growth, you may feel a strong desire to expand your horizons, seek new experiences, and connect with your higher purpose.

Consider taking a trip or enrolling in a course or workshop that aligns with your interests and passions. This is a time to step outside your comfort zone, challenge your assumptions and beliefs, and open yourself up to new ideas and possibilities.

However, the Full Moon in Capricorn may also bring any underlying fears, doubts, or limitations around travel and exploration to the surface. This is an opportunity to confront any limiting beliefs or patterns that may be holding you back from true freedom and adventure. Remember that growth and expansion often require stepping into the unknown, and that every challenge is an opportunity for learning and transformation.

Insights from the Stars:

The celestial energies of July 2025 remind you of the power of self-expression, creativity, and emotional healing. With Mars entering Leo, activating your 4th house of home, family, and emotional foundations, and Venus traveling through Cancer, your 3rd house of communication and connection, you are being called to express your authentic self, nurture your loved ones, and create a life that aligns with your deepest values and desires.

This is a time to let go of any masks, facades, or limitations that may be holding you back from true joy, fulfillment, and self-realization. You are a powerful creator and manifester, and your thoughts, beliefs, and actions have the power to shape your reality and attract your deepest desires and dreams.

Stay open to the unexpected, and trust that every challenge or setback is an opportunity for growth, learning, and transformation. Remember that you are a divine being of love and light, and that your soul's journey is unfolding in perfect timing and alignment with your highest good.

Best Days of the Month:

July 1st: The Sun conjunct Mercury, bringing clarity, insight, and positive communication to your interactions and relationships. This is a great time to share your ideas, express your feelings, and connect with others.

July 10th: The Full Moon in Capricorn illuminates your 9th house of travel, higher education, and spiritual growth. Let go of any limiting beliefs or patterns that may be holding you back from true freedom and fulfillment, and trust in the wisdom and guidance of the universe.

July 18th: Mars enters Leo, activating your 4th house of home, family, and emotional foundations. This is a time to express your passion, creativity, and self-expression in your personal life, and to make positive changes in your living space or family dynamics.

July 22nd: The Sun enters Leo, marking the beginning of a new cycle of creativity, self-expression, and personal growth. Celebrate your unique qualities and talents, and trust in your own inner light and power.

July 30th: The New Moon in Leo invites you to set powerful intentions around your personal goals, desires, and self-expression. Trust in your own worth and value, and take bold steps towards creating a life that aligns with your authentic self and purpose.

August 2025

Overview Horoscope for the Month:

Taurus, August 2025 is a month of self-discovery, spiritual growth, and personal empowerment for you. The astrological energies are intense and transformative, with a series of powerful planetary alignments and eclipses inviting you to dive deep into your inner world, confront your shadows, and emerge with a renewed sense of purpose and passion.

The month begins with Venus, your ruling planet, entering Leo on August 25th, activating your 4th house of home, family, and emotional foundations. This transit will bring a heightened sense of creativity, self-expression, and joy to your personal life, and may inspire you to make positive changes in your living space or family dynamics.

The Full Moon in Aquarius on August 9th will illuminate your 10th house of career, public image, and long-term goals, inviting you to reassess your professional path, let go of any limiting beliefs or patterns, and align your work with your authentic self and purpose. This is a time to trust in your unique talents and abilities, and to make bold moves towards your dreams and aspirations.

Love:

In love, August 2025 is a month of emotional depth, vulnerability, and transformation. With Venus traveling through Cancer for most of the month, you may feel a strong desire for intimacy, security, and emotional connection in your relationships. This is a time to nurture your loved ones, express your feelings openly and authentically, and create a safe and supportive space for love to flourish.

If you're in a committed relationship, the Full Moon in Aquarius on August 9th may bring unexpected insights or revelations about your partnership. This is an opportunity to have honest, open conversations with your partner about your needs, desires, and long-term goals, and to make any necessary changes or adjustments to your relationship dynamics. Be willing to let go of any expectations or attachments that may be holding you back from true intimacy and growth.

If you're single, the Venus-Pluto opposition on August 26th may bring intense feelings of desire, passion, and transformation to your love life. This is a time to confront any fears or shadows around intimacy and vulnerability, and to attract partners who reflect your deepest values and desires. Focus on cultivating a deep sense of self-love and self-worth, and trust that the universe will bring you the right person at the right time.

Career:

In your career, August 2025 is a month of innovation, leadership, and positive change. With the Full Moon in Aquarius on August 9th illuminating your 10th house of career, public image, and long-term goals, you may feel a strong desire to make a meaningful impact in your work, and to align your professional path with your authentic self and purpose.

This is a time to reassess your career goals, let go of any limiting beliefs or patterns, and take bold steps towards your dreams and aspirations. You may be recognized for your unique talents and contributions, or offered new opportunities for growth and advancement. Trust in your own worth and value, and don't be afraid to take risks or think outside the box.

However, the Venus-Pluto opposition on August 26th may bring any underlying fears, doubts, or power struggles in your career to the surface. This is an opportunity to confront any self-sabotaging behaviors or patterns, and to cultivate a deeper sense of self-trust and self-confidence. Remember that your worth and value are not defined by external validation or success, but by your own inner sense of purpose and integrity.

Finances:

In finances, August 2025 is a month of abundance, prosperity, and positive change. With Venus traveling through your 4th house of home and family for most of the month, you may experience unexpected opportunities for financial growth and success through your personal connections and relationships.

This is a time to trust in the abundance and support of the universe, and to attract wealth and resources through your unique gifts and contributions. Focus on cultivating a mindset of gratitude, generosity, and positive expectation, and be open to receiving blessings and opportunities from unexpected sources.

However, the Full Moon in Aquarius on August 9th may bring any underlying fears, doubts, or limitations around money and security to the surface. This is an opportunity to confront any scarcity mentality or limiting beliefs, and to cultivate a deeper sense of trust and faith in the abundance of the universe. Remember that your true wealth and security come from within, and that you are always supported and provided for by a loving and benevolent universe.

Health:

In health, August 2025 is a month of vitality, resilience, and emotional healing. With Mars traveling through Virgo for most of the month, activating your 5th house of creativity, self-expression, and joy, you may feel a renewed sense of energy, passion, and enthusiasm for life. This is a time to prioritize your self-care and self-love, and to cultivate daily practices and habits that support your physical, emotional, and spiritual well-being.

Take time to rest, recharge, and listen to your body's needs and signals. Engage in activities that bring you pleasure, relaxation, and a sense of connection to your inner child, such as art, music, or play. Nourish your body with healthy, whole foods, and limit your exposure to toxins, stress, and negative influences.

However, the Full Moon in Aquarius on August 9th may bring any underlying fears, doubts, or limitations around your health and well-being to the surface. This is an opportunity to confront any self-sabotaging behaviors or patterns, and to cultivate a deeper sense of self-compassion and self-acceptance. Remember that your body is a sacred temple, and that you deserve to treat yourself with love, kindness, and respect.

Travel:

In travel, August 2025 may bring opportunities for personal growth, self-discovery, and spiritual awakening. With the Sun traveling through your 5th house of creativity, self-expression, and joy for most of the month, you may feel a strong desire to explore new places, try new things, and connect with your inner child.

Consider taking a trip or enrolling in a workshop or retreat that aligns with your interests and passions. This is a time to step outside your comfort zone, challenge your assumptions and beliefs, and open yourself up to new ideas and possibilities.

However, the Full Moon in Aquarius on August 9th may bring any underlying fears, doubts, or limitations around travel and exploration to the surface. This is an opportunity to confront any limiting beliefs or patterns that may be holding you back from true freedom and adventure. Remember that growth and expansion often require stepping into the unknown, and that every challenge is an opportunity for learning and transformation.

Insights from the Stars:

The celestial energies of August 2025 remind you of the power of self-love, self-expression, and personal transformation. With Venus traveling through your 4th house of home and family, and Mars activating your 5th house of creativity and joy, you are being called to connect with your inner child, express your authentic self, and create a life that aligns with your deepest values and desires.

This is a time to let go of any masks, facades, or limitations that may be holding you back from true happiness, fulfillment, and self-realization. You are a powerful creator and manifester, and your thoughts, beliefs, and actions have the power to shape your reality and attract your deepest desires and dreams.

Stay open to the unexpected, and trust that every challenge or setback is an opportunity for growth, learning, and transformation. Remember that you are a divine being of love and light, and that your soul's journey is unfolding in perfect timing and alignment with your highest good.

Best Days of the Month:

August 3rd: Uranus quintile True Node, bringing unexpected insights, breakthroughs, and opportunities for growth and change. Trust your intuition and be open to new possibilities and perspectives.

August 11th: Mercury goes direct in Leo, bringing clarity, insight, and forward momentum to your communication, ideas, and plans. Express yourself with confidence and authenticity, and trust in the power of your voice and vision.

August 16th: The Last Quarter Moon in Taurus illuminates your 1st house of self and identity, inviting you to let go of any limiting beliefs or patterns that may be holding you back from true self-expression and personal growth. Embrace your unique qualities and talents, and trust in your own worth and value.

August 23rd: The New Moon in Virgo activates your 5th house of creativity, self-expression, and joy, inviting you to set powerful intentions around your personal goals, desires, and passions. Trust in the power of play, pleasure, and self-love, and take bold steps towards creating a life that brings you joy and fulfillment.

August 28th: Uranus sextile Neptune, bringing a harmonious blend of innovation and inspiration, practicality and spirituality. This is a great time to connect with your higher purpose, trust in the wisdom of the universe, and make positive changes in your life that align with your deepest values and dreams.

September 2025

Overview Horoscope for the Month:

Taurus, September 2025 is a month of introspection, spiritual growth, and personal transformation for you. The astrological energies are intense and profound, with a series of powerful planetary alignments and eclipses inviting you to go within, connect with your inner wisdom, and align your life with your deepest values and purpose.

The month begins with Saturn, the planet of structure, responsibility, and karmic lessons, entering Pisces on September 1st, activating your 11th house of friends, groups, and social causes. This transit, which will last until 2028, will bring a heightened sense of duty, commitment, and purpose to your social life and community involvement, and may challenge you to let go of any superficial connections or activities that no longer serve your highest good.

The Full Moon Total Lunar Eclipse in Pisces on September 7th will illuminate your 11th house, bringing powerful insights, revelations, and shifts in your friendships, networks, and long-term goals. This is a time to trust in the wisdom of the universe, surrender to the flow of life, and allow any necessary endings or beginnings to unfold in divine timing.

Love:

In love, September 2025 is a month of emotional depth, spiritual connection, and karmic healing. With Venus, your ruling planet, traveling through Virgo for most of the month, you may feel a strong desire for authenticity, purity, and service in your relationships. This is a time to focus on the practical details of love, and to cultivate a sense of devotion, humility, and unconditional acceptance towards yourself and others.

If you're in a committed relationship, the Saturn-Neptune conjunction on September 8th may bring a powerful opportunity for spiritual growth, emotional healing, and karmic resolution in your partnership. This is a time to let go of any illusions, expectations, or attachments that may be holding you back from true intimacy and connection, and to trust in the divine plan for your relationship. Be willing to do the inner work of forgiveness, compassion, and unconditional love, and to support each other's soul growth and evolution.

If you're single, the New Moon Partial Solar Eclipse in Virgo on September 21st may bring unexpected opportunities for love and romance through your work, health, or service to others. This is a time to focus on cultivating a deep sense of self-love, self-care, and self-respect, and to attract partners who reflect your highest values and aspirations. Trust in the wisdom of your heart, and be open to the magic and synchronicity of the universe.

Career:

In your career, September 2025 is a month of purpose, service, and spiritual alignment. With Mars, the planet of action and drive, entering Scorpio on September 22nd, activating your 7th house of partnerships and collaboration, you may feel a strong desire to join forces with others, create powerful alliances, and make a meaningful impact in your work and community.

This is a time to focus on the deeper purpose and meaning of your career, and to align your professional path with your soul's mission and values. You may be called to take on a leadership role, mentor others, or use your skills and talents to serve a higher cause. Trust in your unique gifts and contributions, and don't be afraid to take bold steps towards your dreams and aspirations.

However, the Full Moon Total Lunar Eclipse in Pisces on September 7th may bring any underlying fears, doubts, or limitations in your career to the surface. This is an opportunity to confront any self-sabotaging behaviors or patterns, and to cultivate a deeper sense of trust, faith, and surrender in your professional journey. Remember that your true success and fulfillment come from living in alignment with your soul's purpose, and that every challenge is an opportunity for growth and transformation.

Finances:

In finances, September 2025 is a month of abundance, prosperity, and spiritual alignment. With Venus traveling through your 6th house of work, health, and service for most of the month, you may experience unexpected opportunities for financial growth and success through your practical skills, dedication, and commitment to excellence.

This is a time to focus on the deeper meaning and purpose of money, and to align your financial goals with your spiritual values and aspirations. Trust in the abundance and support of the universe, and be open to receiving blessings and opportunities from unexpected sources. Focus on cultivating a mindset of gratitude, generosity, and positive expectation, and be willing to share your resources and talents with others in need.

However, the Full Moon Total Lunar Eclipse in Pisces on September 7th may bring any underlying fears, doubts, or limitations around money and security to the surface. This is an opportunity to confront any scarcity mentality or limiting beliefs, and to cultivate a deeper sense of trust and faith in the divine plan for your life. Remember that your true wealth and security come from within, and that you are always supported and provided for by a loving and benevolent universe.

Health:

In health, September 2025 is a month of balance, purification, and spiritual alignment. With the Sun traveling through Virgo for most of the month, activating your 5th house of joy, creativity, and self-expression, you may feel a strong desire to prioritize your physical, emotional, and spiritual well-being, and to cultivate daily practices and habits that support your vitality, resilience, and inner peace.

This is a time to focus on the mind-body-spirit connection, and to align your health and wellness goals with your deepest values and aspirations. Take time to rest, recharge, and listen to your body's wisdom and guidance. Engage in activities that bring you joy, pleasure, and a sense of connection to your inner child, such as dance, art, or nature. Nourish your body with clean, wholesome foods, and limit your exposure to toxins, stress, and negative influences.

However, the Full Moon Total Lunar Eclipse in Pisces on September 7th may bring any underlying fears, doubts, or limitations around your health and well-being to the surface. This is an opportunity to confront any self-sabotaging behaviors or patterns, and to cultivate a deeper sense of self-compassion, self-acceptance, and self-love. Remember that your body is a sacred temple, and that you deserve to treat yourself with kindness, respect, and reverence.

Travel:

In travel, September 2025 may bring opportunities for spiritual growth, personal transformation, and karmic healing. With Saturn entering Pisces on September 1st, activating your 11th house of friends, groups, and social causes, you may feel a strong desire to travel with like-minded individuals, join a spiritual community or retreat, or engage in a humanitarian mission or service project.

This is a time to focus on the deeper meaning and purpose of your travels, and to align your adventures with your soul's journey and evolution. Consider taking a pilgrimage to a sacred site, attending a transformational workshop or conference, or immersing yourself in a foreign culture or way of life that expands your perspective and challenges your assumptions.

However, the Full Moon Total Lunar Eclipse in Pisces on September 7th may bring any underlying fears, doubts, or limitations around travel and exploration to the surface. This is an opportunity to confront any limiting beliefs or patterns that may be holding you back from true freedom and adventure, and to cultivate a deeper sense of trust, faith, and surrender in the journey of life. Remember that every experience, whether pleasant or challenging, is an opportunity for growth, learning, and transformation.

Insights from the Stars:

The celestial energies of September 2025 remind you of the power of surrender, faith, and spiritual alignment. With Saturn entering Pisces, activating your 11th house of friends, groups, and social causes, and the Full Moon Total Lunar Eclipse illuminating this same area of your chart, you are being called to let go of any superficial connections or activities that no longer serve your highest good, and to align your social life and community involvement with your soul's purpose and values.

This is a time to trust in the wisdom and guidance of the universe, and to allow any necessary endings or beginnings to unfold in divine timing. You are a powerful co-creator and manifestor, and your thoughts, beliefs, and actions have the power to shape your reality and attract your deepest desires and dreams. Stay open to the magic and synchronicity of life, and trust that every challenge or setback is an opportunity for growth, healing, and transformation.

Remember that you are a divine being of love and light, and that your soul's journey is unfolding in perfect harmony with the greater plan of the universe. Embrace your unique gifts and talents, and trust in your ability to make a positive difference in the world, one person and one moment at a time.

Best Days of the Month:

September 3rd: Jupiter trine True Node, bringing opportunities for spiritual growth, karmic healing, and alignment with your soul's purpose. Trust in the wisdom and guidance of the universe, and be open to new possibilities and perspectives.

September 7th: The Full Moon Total Lunar Eclipse in Pisces illuminates your 11th house of friends, groups, and social causes, bringing powerful insights, revelations, and shifts in your social life and community involvement. Let go of any superficial connections or activities that no longer serve your highest good, and trust in the divine plan for your life.

September 18th: Mercury enters Libra, activating your 6th house of work, health, and service. This is a great time to focus on the practical details of your life, communicate your needs and boundaries clearly, and cultivate a sense of balance, harmony, and cooperation in your daily routines and relationships.

September 21st: The New Moon Partial Solar Eclipse in Virgo activates your 5th house of joy, creativity, and self-expression, inviting you to set powerful intentions around your personal goals, desires, and passions. Trust in the power of play, pleasure, and self-love, and take bold steps towards creating a life that brings you happiness and fulfillment.

September 29th: Venus enters Libra, bringing a harmonious and balanced energy to your work, health, and service sector. Focus on creating beauty, peace, and harmony in your daily life, and cultivate a sense of gratitude, grace, and diplomacy in your interactions with others.

October 2025

Overview Horoscope for the Month:

Taurus, October 2025 is a month of new beginnings, personal growth, and spiritual awakening for you. The astrological energies are intense and transformative, with a series of powerful planetary alignments and eclipses inviting you to embrace change, let go of the past, and step into your highest potential and purpose.

The month begins with Venus, your ruling planet, entering Scorpio on October 6th, activating your 7th house of partnerships, relationships, and self-awareness. This transit will bring a heightened sense of intensity, depth, and passion to your connections with others, and may challenge you to confront any fears, shadows, or power dynamics that may be holding you back from true intimacy and authenticity.

The New Moon Partial Solar Eclipse in Libra on October 21st will illuminate your 6th house of work, health, and service, bringing powerful opportunities for new beginnings, fresh starts, and positive changes in your daily routines, habits, and lifestyle. This is a time to set clear intentions, take inspired action, and trust in the unfolding of your path and purpose.

Love:

In love, October 2025 is a month of intensity, transformation, and spiritual growth. With Venus traveling through Scorpio for most of the month, you may feel a strong desire for deep connection, emotional honesty, and soul-level intimacy in your relationships. This is a time to dive beneath the surface, explore your desires and fears, and cultivate a sense of trust, vulnerability, and empowerment in your interactions with others.

If you're in a committed relationship, the Venus-Uranus opposition on October 11th may bring unexpected insights, revelations, or shifts in your partnership. This is an opportunity to break free from any limiting patterns or dynamics, and to embrace a new level of freedom, individuality, and authenticity in your connection. Be willing to have honest conversations, take risks, and explore new ways of relating that honor both your needs and your partner's.

If you're single, the New Moon Partial Solar Eclipse in Libra on October 21st may bring powerful opportunities for new love, romance, and self-discovery. This is a time to focus on cultivating a deep sense of self-love, self-respect, and self-awareness, and to attract partners who reflect your highest values and aspirations. Trust in the wisdom of your heart, and be open to the magic and synchronicity of the universe.

Career:

In your career, October 2025 is a month of innovation, collaboration, and positive change. With Mercury, the planet of communication and learning, entering Scorpio on October 6th, activating your 7th house of partnerships and cooperation, you may feel a strong desire to join forces with others, share your ideas and insights, and create powerful alliances and networks in your professional life.

This is a time to focus on the deeper purpose and meaning of your work, and to align your career path with your soul's mission and values. You may be called to take on a leadership role, mentor others, or use your skills and talents to make a positive impact in your industry or community. Trust in your unique gifts and contributions, and don't be afraid to take bold steps towards your dreams and aspirations.

However, the Full Moon in Aries on October 6th may bring any underlying fears, doubts, or limitations in your career to the surface. This is an opportunity to confront any self-sabotaging behaviors or patterns, and to cultivate a deeper sense of courage, confidence, and self-belief in your professional journey. Remember that your true success and fulfillment come from living in alignment with your soul's purpose, and that every challenge is an opportunity for growth and transformation.

Finances:

In finances, October 2025 is a month of abundance, prosperity, and spiritual alignment. With Jupiter, the planet of expansion and abundance, traveling through your 3rd house of communication, learning, and self-expression for most of the month, you may experience unexpected opportunities for financial growth and success through your ideas, insights, and creative talents.

This is a time to focus on the power of your thoughts, words, and beliefs, and to align your financial goals with your spiritual values and aspirations. Trust in the abundance and support of the universe, and be open to receiving blessings and opportunities from unexpected sources. Focus on cultivating a mindset of gratitude, generosity, and positive expectation, and be willing to share your resources and talents with others in need.

However, the Full Moon in Aries on October 6th may bring any underlying fears, doubts, or limitations around money and security to the surface. This is an opportunity to confront any scarcity mentality or limiting beliefs, and to cultivate a deeper sense of trust and faith in the divine plan for your life. Remember that your true wealth and security come from within, and that you are always supported and provided for by a loving and benevolent universe.

Health:

In health, October 2025 is a month of transformation, healing, and spiritual growth. With Pluto, the planet of power and regeneration, turning direct in your 9th house of higher wisdom, beliefs, and personal growth on October 13th, you may feel a strong desire to deepen your understanding of yourself, your purpose, and your place in the world, and to release any limiting patterns or behaviors that may be holding you back from optimal health and well-being.

This is a time to focus on the mind-body-spirit connection, and to align your health and wellness goals with your deepest values and aspirations. Take time to rest, recharge, and listen to your body's wisdom and guidance. Engage in activities that bring you a sense of peace, clarity, and inner strength, such as meditation, yoga, or energy healing. Nourish your body with clean, wholesome foods, and limit your exposure to toxins, stress, and negative influences.

However, the New Moon Partial Solar Eclipse in Libra on October 21st may bring powerful opportunities for new beginnings and positive changes in your daily routines, habits, and lifestyle. This is a time to set clear intentions, take inspired action, and trust in the unfolding of your path and purpose. Remember that your health and well-being are a reflection of your inner state of being, and that true healing comes from aligning your mind, body, and spirit with the wisdom and guidance of the universe.

Travel:

In travel, October 2025 may bring opportunities for personal growth, self-discovery, and spiritual awakening. With Mars, the planet of action and adventure, entering Sagittarius on October 29th, activating your 8th house of transformation, intimacy, and shared resources, you may feel a strong desire to explore new horizons, challenge your comfort zone, and deepen your understanding of yourself and others.

This is a time to focus on the deeper meaning and purpose of your travels, and to align your adventures with your soul's journey and evolution. Consider taking a trip that allows you to connect with your inner wisdom, explore your shadows and fears, and cultivate a sense of trust, surrender, and empowerment. This could be a solo journey, a couple's retreat, or a group adventure that challenges you to grow and transform in powerful ways.

However, the Full Moon in Aries on October 6th may bring any underlying fears, doubts, or limitations around travel and exploration to the surface. This is an opportunity to confront any limiting beliefs or patterns that may be holding you back from true freedom and adventure, and to cultivate a deeper sense of courage, confidence, and self-belief in the journey of life. Remember that every experience, whether pleasant or challenging, is an opportunity for growth, learning, and transformation.

Insights from the Stars:

The celestial energies of October 2025 remind you of the power of transformation, authenticity, and spiritual growth. With Venus entering Scorpio, activating your 7th house of partnerships and self-awareness, and the New Moon Partial Solar Eclipse illuminating your 6th house of work, health, and service, you are being called to embrace change, let go of the past, and step into your highest potential and purpose.

This is a time to trust in the wisdom and guidance of the universe, and to allow any necessary endings or beginnings to unfold in divine timing. You are a powerful co-creator and manifestor, and your thoughts, beliefs, and actions have the power to shape your reality and attract your deepest desires and dreams. Stay open to the magic and synchronicity of life, and trust that every challenge or setback is an opportunity for growth, healing, and transformation.

Remember that you are a divine being of love and light, and that your soul's journey is unfolding in perfect harmony with the greater plan of the universe. Embrace your unique gifts and talents, and trust in your ability to make a positive difference in the world, one person and one moment at a time.

Best Days of the Month:

October 7th: Mars enters Scorpio, activating your 7th house of partnerships and self-awareness. This is a great time to focus on deepening your connections with others, exploring your desires and fears, and cultivating a sense of trust, vulnerability, and empowerment in your relationships.

October 13th: Pluto turns direct in your 9th house of higher wisdom, beliefs, and personal growth. This is a powerful time for spiritual awakening, inner transformation, and the release of any limiting patterns or behaviors that may be holding you back from your highest potential and purpose.

October 16th: The Last Quarter Moon in Cancer illuminates your 3rd house of communication, learning, and self-expression, inviting you to share your ideas and insights with others, explore new ways of thinking and being, and cultivate a sense of emotional intelligence and empathy in your interactions.

October 21st: The New Moon Partial Solar Eclipse in Libra activates your 6th house of work, health, and service, bringing powerful opportunities for new beginnings, fresh starts, and positive changes in your daily routines, habits, and lifestyle. Set clear intentions, take inspired action, and trust in the unfolding of your path and purpose.

October 29th: Mars enters Sagittarius, activating your 8th house of transformation, intimacy, and shared resources. This is a great time to explore new horizons, challenge your comfort zone, and deepen your understanding of yourself and others through travel, adventure, and personal growth.

November 2025

Overview Horoscope for the Month:

Welcome to November 2025, Taurus! This month promises to be a time of profound transformation, inner growth, and new beginnings. The astrological energies align to support your journey of self-discovery, urging you to embrace change, let go of old patterns, and trust in the unfolding of your unique path. With a powerful stellium of planets in Scorpio activating your 7th house of partnerships and relationships, you are called to dive deep into the realm of intimacy, vulnerability, and emotional authenticity.

November 2025 is a pivotal month for you, Taurus, as it marks a significant turning point in your personal and relational growth. The Sun, Mercury, and Venus all travel through the intense and transformative sign of Scorpio, illuminating your 7th house of one-on-one partnerships, marriage, and interpersonal dynamics. This cosmic alignment invites you to confront the shadows, fears, and power struggles that may be holding you back from true intimacy and connection, and to embrace the healing power of vulnerability, trust, and emotional honesty.

The New Moon in Scorpio on November 20th brings a potent opportunity for new beginnings, fresh starts, and deepening commitments in your closest relationships. Set intentions for the kind of partnerships you wish to attract or nurture, focusing on the qualities of authenticity, depth, and soul-level connection.

Love:

In matters of the heart, November 2025 emphasizes the importance of emotional intensity, psychological depth, and transformative intimacy. With Venus, your ruling planet, in the mysterious and magnetic sign of Scorpio until the 30th, you may find yourself craving a soul-level bond with your partner, one that goes beyond surface-level attraction and into the realm of deep, raw, and vulnerable connection. This is a time to confront any fears, secrets, or power dynamics that may be blocking the flow of love and trust in your relationships, and to cultivate a space of safety, honesty, and emotional authenticity.

For single Taureans, the New Moon in Scorpio on November 20th brings a powerful opportunity to set intentions for the kind of partner and relationship you truly desire. Focus on the qualities of depth, intensity, and emotional connection, and trust that the universe will guide you towards individuals who resonate with your soul's yearnings. Be open to unexpected encounters and connections, as they may hold the key to profound growth and transformation.

For Taureans in committed relationships, this month invites you to take your connection to a deeper, more intimate level. The Full Moon in Taurus on November 5th illuminates your 1st house of self, identity, and personal desires, urging you to assert your needs, boundaries, and authentic self-expression within the context of your partnership. Have honest, vulnerable conversations with your partner about your fears, desires, and dreams, and work together to create a dynamic of mutual support, empowerment, and growth.

Career:

Your career sector is activated this month, Taurus, with Mars, the planet of action and ambition, traveling through the expansive and visionary sign of Sagittarius. This cosmic placement ignites your 8th house of shared resources, investments, and transformative power, urging you to take bold steps towards your long-term goals and aspirations. Trust your instincts and intuition when it comes to making strategic moves or taking calculated risks in your professional life, as they may lead to significant breakthroughs and opportunities for growth.

The New Moon in Scorpio on November 20th may bring unexpected shifts or changes in your work partnerships or collaborations. Embrace the transformative power of letting go of what no longer serves your highest good, and trust that any endings or new beginnings are ultimately guiding you towards your true path and purpose.

Finances:

November 2025 brings a focus on joint finances, shared resources, and the psychological dynamics of money and power. With the Sun, Mercury, and Venus activating your 8th house of investments, debts, and other people's resources, you are called to confront any fears, shadows, or limiting beliefs around financial intimacy and interdependence. This is a time to have honest, transparent conversations with your partner or trusted advisors about your financial goals, needs, and strategies, and to cultivate a mindset of abundance, trust, and mutual support.

The Full Moon in Taurus on November 5th may bring a culmination or turning point in your personal financial situation, urging you to assert your values, needs, and desires when it comes to money and material security. Trust your instincts and practical wisdom when making financial decisions, and remember that true wealth and abundance come from a place of inner worth and self-sufficiency.

Health:

Your physical and emotional well-being are highlighted this month, Taurus, as the intense and transformative energies of Scorpio activate your 7th house of one-on-one relationships and interpersonal dynamics. This cosmic placement may bring up deep-seated emotions, fears, or patterns related to intimacy, vulnerability, and power dynamics, urging you to confront and heal any wounds or blocks that may be impacting your overall health and vitality.

Make time for self-care practices that support your emotional and psychological well-being, such as therapy, journaling, or deep conversations with trusted friends and loved ones. Focus on cultivating a sense of inner balance, resilience, and emotional authenticity, and trust that any challenges or discomforts that arise are ultimately guiding you towards greater wholeness and healing.

Travel:

November 2025 may bring opportunities for transformative travel experiences or journeys of self-discovery, Taurus. With Mars, the planet of action and adventure, in the expansive and philosophical sign of Sagittarius, you may feel called to explore new horizons, both literally and figuratively. Consider planning a trip or retreat that allows you to dive deep into your psyche, confront your fears and shadows, and emerge with a renewed sense of purpose and perspective.

If physical travel is not possible, consider embarking on an inner journey through practices such as meditation, dream work, or shamanic journeying. Trust that any insights, revelations, or breakthroughs that arise are ultimately guiding you towards greater self-awareness, growth, and transformation.

Insights from the Stars:

The celestial energies of November 2025 remind you of the power of vulnerability, authenticity, and emotional depth, Taurus. As you navigate the intense and transformative energies of Scorpio, trust that you are being called to confront your shadows, heal your wounds, and emerge with a renewed sense of strength, resilience, and self-awareness.

Remember that true intimacy and connection require a willingness to be seen, heard, and accepted in all of your raw, messy, and beautiful humanity. Embrace the power of vulnerability, trust, and emotional honesty, and know that you are worthy of love, respect, and belonging, just as you are.

Best Days of the Month:

November 5th: The Full Moon in your sign illuminates your 1st house of self, identity, and personal desires, urging you to assert your needs, boundaries, and authentic self-expression.

November 9th: Mercury stations retrograde in Scorpio, inviting you to reflect on your communication patterns, relationship dynamics, and emotional needs.

November 20th: The New Moon in Scorpio brings a powerful opportunity for new beginnings, fresh starts, and deepening commitments in your closest relationships.

November 23rd: Jupiter stations direct in Taurus, ending its retrograde phase and bringing renewed opportunities for growth, expansion, and abundance in your personal and professional life.

November 30th: Venus enters Sagittarius, igniting your 8th house of intimacy, shared resources, and transformative power, and bringing a sense of adventure, optimism, and growth to your relationships and financial dealings.

December 2025

Overview Horoscope for the Month:

Welcome to December 2025, Taurus! This month promises to be a time of inner reflection, spiritual growth, and profound transformation. As the year comes to a close, the astrological energies align to support your journey of self-discovery, urging you to connect with your deepest truths, release old patterns and beliefs, and embrace the power of new beginnings. With a strong emphasis on your 8th house of intimacy, shared resources, and personal transformation, you are called to dive deep into the realms of vulnerability, trust, and emotional authenticity.

December 2025 is a significant month for you, Taurus, as it marks the beginning of a powerful new cycle of growth and self-discovery. The Sun's transit through the philosophical and expansive sign of Sagittarius until the 21st illuminates your 8th house of deep emotional connections, psychological healing, and spiritual transformation. This cosmic placement invites you to confront your fears, shadows, and limiting beliefs, and to embrace the power of surrender, faith, and inner wisdom.

The New Moon in Sagittarius on December 19th brings a potent opportunity for setting intentions, planting seeds, and embarking on a new journey of personal and spiritual growth. Focus on the areas of your life where you wish to experience greater depth, meaning, and purpose, and trust that the universe will guide you towards the resources, support, and opportunities you need to thrive.

Love:

In matters of the heart, December 2025 emphasizes the importance of emotional intimacy, vulnerability, and spiritual connection. With Venus, your ruling planet, traveling through the intense and passionate sign of Scorpio until the 24th, you may find yourself craving a deep, soulful bond with your partner, one that goes beyond surface-level attraction and into the realm of raw, honest, and transformative love. This is a time to confront any fears, secrets, or power dynamics that may be blocking the flow of trust and intimacy in your relationships, and to cultivate a space of safety, acceptance, and emotional authenticity.

For single Taureans, the New Moon in Sagittarius on December 19th brings a powerful opportunity to set intentions for the kind of partner and relationship you truly desire. Focus on the qualities of depth, meaning, and spiritual connection, and trust that the universe will guide you towards individuals who resonate with your soul's yearnings. Be open to unexpected encounters and connections, as they may hold the key to profound growth and transformation.

For Taureans in committed relationships, this month invites you to take your connection to a deeper, more intimate level. The Full Moon in Gemini on December 4th illuminates your 2nd house of values, self-worth, and material resources, urging you to examine your beliefs and patterns around love, money, and security. Have honest, vulnerable conversations with your partner about your needs, desires, and fears, and work together to create a dynamic of mutual support, empowerment, and growth.

Career:

Your career sector is activated this month, Taurus, with Mars, the planet of action and ambition, entering the disciplined and pragmatic sign of Capricorn on the 15th. This cosmic placement ignites your 9th house of higher education, long-distance travel, and personal growth, urging you to expand your horizons, take on new challenges, and pursue your long-term goals with determination and focus. Trust your instincts and practical wisdom when it comes to making strategic moves or taking calculated risks in your professional life, as they may lead to significant breakthroughs and opportunities for advancement.

The New Moon in Sagittarius on December 19th may bring unexpected shifts or changes in your work environment or job responsibilities. Embrace the power of adaptability, flexibility, and positive thinking, and trust that any endings or new beginnings are ultimately guiding you towards your true path and purpose.

Finances:

December 2025 brings a focus on shared finances, investments, and the psychological dynamics of money and power. With Venus, your ruling planet, traveling through the intense and transformative sign of Scorpio until the 24th, you are called to confront any fears, shadows, or limiting beliefs around financial intimacy and interdependence. This is a time to have honest, transparent conversations with your partner or trusted advisors about your financial goals, needs, and strategies, and to cultivate a mindset of abundance, trust, and mutual support.

The Full Moon in Gemini on December 4th may bring a culmination or turning point in your personal financial situation, urging you to communicate your values, needs, and desires when it comes to money and material security. Trust your instincts and practical wisdom when making financial decisions, and remember that true wealth and abundance come from a place of inner worth and self-sufficiency.

Health:

Your physical and emotional well-being are highlighted this month, Taurus, as the intense and transformative energies of Scorpio and Sagittarius activate your 8th house of deep emotional healing and spiritual growth. This cosmic placement may bring up deep-seated emotions, fears, or patterns related to intimacy, vulnerability, and power dynamics, urging you to confront and heal any wounds or blocks that may be impacting your overall health and vitality.

Make time for self-care practices that support your emotional and psychological well-being, such as therapy, journaling, or deep conversations with trusted friends and loved ones. Focus on cultivating a sense of inner balance, resilience, and emotional authenticity, and trust that any challenges or discomforts that arise are ultimately guiding you towards greater wholeness and healing.

Travel:

December 2025 may bring opportunities for transformative travel experiences or journeys of self-discovery, Taurus. With Mars, the planet of action and adventure, entering the disciplined and pragmatic sign of Capricorn on the 15th, you may feel called to explore new horizons, both literally and figuratively. Consider planning a trip or retreat that allows you to expand your mind, challenge your assumptions, and connect with your higher purpose and spiritual path.

If physical travel is not possible, consider embarking on an inner journey through practices such as meditation, yoga, or philosophical study. Trust that any insights, revelations, or breakthroughs that arise are ultimately guiding you towards greater self-awareness, growth, and transformation.

Insights from the Stars:

The celestial energies of December 2025 remind you of the power of surrender, faith, and inner wisdom, Taurus. As you navigate the intense and transformative energies of Scorpio and Sagittarius, trust that you are being called to let go of control, embrace the unknown, and connect with your deepest truths and highest potential.

Remember that true growth and transformation often require a willingness to step outside of your comfort zone, confront your fears and shadows, and trust in the journey of your soul. Embrace the power of vulnerability, authenticity, and emotional depth, and know that you are supported and guided by the universe every step of the way.

Best Days of the Month:

December 4th: The Full Moon in Gemini illuminates your 2nd house of values, self-worth, and material resources, urging you to communicate your needs, desires, and boundaries in your personal and financial relationships.

December 12th: Mercury enters Capricorn, bringing a sense of focus, discipline, and practicality to your thoughts, communications, and long-term planning.

December 19th: The New Moon in Sagittarius brings a powerful opportunity for setting intentions, planting seeds, and embarking on a new journey of personal and spiritual growth.

December 24th: Venus enters Capricorn, igniting your 9th house of higher education, long-distance travel, and personal growth, and bringing a sense of commitment, responsibility, and long-term vision to your relationships and creative pursuits.

December 29th: Jupiter squares Chiron, inviting you to confront and heal any wounds or blocks related to your sense of self-worth, security, and belonging, and to embrace the power of self-acceptance, compassion, and inner wisdom.

GEMINI 2025 HOROSCOPE

Overview Gemini 2025

(May 21 - June 20)

Welcome, dear Gemini, to your astrological journey through 2025! As the cosmic winds shift and the planets dance through the heavens, this year promises to be a dynamic and transformative time filled with opportunities for growth, expansion, and a deepening of your connections with others. In this horoscope, we'll explore the celestial influences that will shape your experiences, challenges, and triumphs over the next twelve months.

The year begins with Saturn, the Lord of Karma, firmly entrenched in the sign of Pisces, activating your 12th house of spirituality, inner growth, and unconscious patterns. This placement suggests that the first few months of 2025 may involve deep introspection, soul-searching, and a need to confront your shadows and release any outdated beliefs or traumas that have been holding you back. Trust in the process of surrender and letting go, as this is ultimately paving the way for profound personal transformation.

On January 27th, Mercury, your ruling planet, enters Aquarius, igniting your 11th house of community, friendships, and social networks. This is a time when you may find yourself drawn to connecting with like-minded individuals, joining groups or organizations that align with your values and interests, and exploring unconventional ways of expressing your unique ideas and perspectives. Be open to new perspectives and ways of thinking, as these connections could prove catalytic in broadening your horizons.

The New Moon in Aquarius on January 29th presents a powerful opportunity for setting intentions related to your social circles, humanitarian interests, and long-term aspirations. This lunation is further amplified by the direct station of Uranus on January 30th, the planet of innovation and rebellion in your 9th house of higher learning, philosophy, and adventure. Trust your intuitive flashes of insight and be willing to embrace change and new experiences that expand your worldview.

As we move into February, Venus, the planet of love and beauty, enters your sign on the 8th, bringing a delightful boost of charm, social grace, and personal magnetism. This is an excellent time to put yourself out there, connect with others, and let your unique personality shine. However, be mindful of potential indecisiveness or a tendency to spread yourself too thin, as these are classic Gemini pitfalls.

The Full Moon in Leo on February 12th activates your 3rd house of communication, local community, and daily routines. This lunation could bring a heightened need for self-expression, as well as potential tensions or conflicts in your immediate environment. Use this energy wisely by channeling it into creative projects, writing, or taking a course to expand your intellectual horizons.

On March 3rd, Mercury enters Aries, igniting your 10th house of career, public image, and life direction. This is an excellent time to assert yourself professionally, to communicate your ideas and goals with clarity and conviction, and to take bold steps towards advancing your ambitions. However, be mindful of potential impulsivity or a tendency to come across as overly aggressive or confrontational.

The Aries New Moon on March 29th, accompanied by a Partial Solar Eclipse, presents a powerful opportunity for new beginnings in your professional life and public standing. This is a time to set clear intentions for your long-term goals and to take decisive action towards manifesting your aspirations. The influence of Saturn in your 12th house will ensure that your efforts are grounded, realistic, and aligned with your deeper values and purpose.

As we move into April, Jupiter, the planet of expansion and abundance, forms a challenging square aspect to Pluto in your 8th house of shared resources, intimacy, and transformation. This transit could bring up issues related to power dynamics, control, and a need for deep psychological healing and renewal. Trust in the process of growth and change, and be willing to let go of what no longer serves you, even if it feels uncomfortable or challenging.

On May 20th, the Sun enters your sign, marking the beginning of your astrological new year. This is a time of heightened energy, confidence, and a desire for new experiences and personal growth. The New Moon in Gemini on May 26th presents an excellent opportunity to set intentions for the year ahead, to clarify your vision and goals, and to take bold action towards manifesting your dreams and aspirations.

However, the influence of Saturn in your 12th house suggests that you may need to confront some inner demons, limiting beliefs, or past traumas before you can fully embrace your personal power and potential. Trust in the process of inner work and soul-searching, and be willing to let go of anything that no longer serves your highest good.

In mid-June, Jupiter, the planet of expansion and abundance, enters your 7th house of partnerships, highlighting the importance of close relationships and collaborations in your life during this time. This transit could bring new romantic connections, business partnerships, or a deepening of existing bonds. However, with Jupiter squaring Saturn in Aries, there may also be challenges or tensions related to balancing your personal needs with those of others.

The Lunar Eclipse in Sagittarius on June 11th activates your 9th house of higher learning, philosophy, and adventure, presenting an opportunity for profound growth and transformation in these areas of your life. Be open to new ideas, experiences, and ways of expanding your worldview, even if it means stepping outside your comfort zone.

As we move into the second half of the year, Mars, the planet of passion and assertion, enters your 4th house of home and family on July 16th. This could bring a heightened focus on domestic matters, emotional security, and nurturing your closest bonds. However, with Mars squaring Saturn in Aries, there may also be potential conflicts or power struggles within your personal life that need to be addressed and resolved.

The Lunar Eclipse in Aquarius on August 9th activates your 11th house of community, friendships, and social networks, potentially bringing shifts or changes within your social circles. Be mindful of any connections or group dynamics that no longer align with your values or aspirations, and be willing to let go of what no longer serves your growth and evolution.

On September 22nd, the Sun enters Libra, activating your 7th house of partnerships and close relationships. This is an excellent time to focus on strengthening your bonds with others, to communicate openly and honestly, and to find a balance between your needs and those of your loved ones.

The Partial Solar Eclipse in Virgo on September 21st occurs in your 6th house of health, daily routines, and service, presenting an opportunity for profound growth and transformation in these areas of your life. Trust in the power of small, consistent steps towards creating greater balance, wellness, and a sense of contribution to the world around you.

As we move into the final months of the year, Venus, the planet of love and beauty, enters your 7th house of partnerships on November 6th, bringing a heightened focus on close relationships and social connections. This could be an excellent time for deepening existing bonds or attracting new romantic or business partnerships into your life.

On December 21st, Jupiter, the planet of expansion and abundance, turns retrograde in your 7th house of partnerships, potentially bringing a period of reflection and re-evaluation in your closest connections. Use this time to assess the quality and authenticity of your relationships, and to let go of any dynamics or patterns that are no longer serving your growth and evolution.

Throughout the year, the influence of Chiron, the "Wounded Healer," in your 10th house of career and public image will continue to bring opportunities for deep healing and integration of your unique talents, gifts, and life purpose. Trust in your ability to overcome any challenges or perceived limitations, and to share your authentic self with the world in a way that inspires and uplifts others.

Overall, 2025 promises to be a dynamic and transformative year for Gemini, with opportunities for growth, expansion, and a deepening of your connections with others. While there may be challenges and periods of introspection or upheaval, trust in the process and in your ability to adapt and evolve. Embrace the shifts and changes that come your way, and use your versatile and adaptable nature to navigate the cosmic currents with grace and wisdom. With an open mind and a willingness to learn and grow, you have the power to create a life that is truly aligned with your highest potential and purpose.

January 2025

Overview Horoscope for the Month:

Welcome to the start of 2025, dear Gemini! January brings an exciting blend of energies that will set the tone for your year ahead. With five planets in Capricorn activating your 9th house of philosophy, travel, and higher learning, you'll feel an insatiable thirst for exploring new horizons – both intellectually and physically. However, the influence of taskmaster Saturn in your 12th house of spirituality suggests you'll need to find balance between your adventurous spirit and a commitment to inner work.

Love:

The potent Capricorn energy this month puts relationships with a serious, pragmatic spin for you air signs. If you're in a committed partnership, January is ideal for having honest discussions about the future and ensuring you're on the same page about big goals. Single Geminis may be attracted to potential mates who exhibit maturity and ambition. However, with Venus retrograding mid-month, be cautious about diving into new entanglements too quickly. This is a better period for focusing on self-love.

Career:

With six planets traveling through your 9th house of career at various points, January's astrology is extremely favorable for professional progress and recognition. You may receive opportunities to expand your role, start a new business venture, publish writing, or take on higher learning. However, Saturn's presence suggests any endeavors begun now will require serious commitment and hard work to flourish over time. Be pragmatic, but seize chances to elevate your platform.

Finances:

Thanks to Saturn's grounding influence, January's earthy Capricorn emphasis helps stabilize your finances, Gemini. You'll feel motivated to budget wisely, cut frivolous expenses, and map out a long-term plan for building security. Income could increase from a successful career venture, but avoid overspending or making risky investments while Venus retrogrades after the 15th. Cultivate patience and focus on saving wherever able.

Health:

With Jupiter continuing its journey through your 6th house of health and routines, you'll begin 2025 feeling energized and eager to adopt positive lifestyle changes. The Capricorn influence helps you commit to new regimens like exercising regularly, eating more wholesome meals, and reining in any overindulgent habits. However, don't become so strict and disciplined that you burn yourself out. Balance hard work with adequate rest and relaxation too.

Travel:

Thanks to the stellium (cluster of planets) in your 9th house of travel and exploration, you'll be bitten by an intense case of wanderlust in January! Getaways near and far are highlighted, perhaps manifesting as an impromptu weekend road trip with friends, booking an international adventure, or even just immersing yourself in cultures different than your own locally. Embrace any opportunities to stretch your horizons.

Insights from the Stars:

The key theme for you this January revolves around balance, Gemini. With the cluster of pragmatic earth energy in your philosophical 9th house, you'll feel an acute sense of commitment and dedication to expanding your knowledge and life experiences. Yet Saturn's influence in your spiritual 12th house reminds you that inner reflection and finding your center is just as vital. Look for ways to fuse mental stimulation with emotional depth this month.

Best Days:

January 2nd: New Moon in Capricorn – Set grounded intentions for study, travel, or a publishing pursuit.

January 6th: Mercury conjunct Venus – Express affection and discuss the future with loved ones.

January 17th: Sun sextile Jupiter – A wonderful day for optimism, learning, and personal growth.

January 22nd: Mars trine Uranus – Original ideas and innovative collaborations are favored.

January 28th: Mercury sextile Saturn – Put practical, disciplined effort into a cherished goal.

February 2025

Overview Horoscope for the Month:

February brings a lively, social energy for you, Gemini! With Venus entering your sign on the 8th and a Full Moon lighting up your 11th house of friendships and group activities on the 12th, your calendar will be fully booked with gatherings, meetings, and opportunities to mingle. However, taskmaster Saturn reminds you not to overcommit yourself - prioritize quality connections over shallow socializing. The playful Aquarius energies also encourage you to embrace your quirky, unconventional side this month.

Love:

When the love planet Venus blows into Gemini on February 8th, your powers of attraction and flirtation will be in full bloom! You'll radiate confidence and charm that draws admiring glances from potential suitors. If you're already coupled up, this transit adds zest and excitement to the relationship. However, with Mars squaring Pluto mid-month, there could be some intensity or power struggles, so stay mindful of each other's boundaries. For singles, the Full Moon on the 12th could spark a new romantic connection through your friend group.

Career:

While the social focus of February may be a welcome break from your workaholic tendencies, this doesn't mean your professional life will be stagnant. In fact, with the Sun, Mercury, and Saturn all moving through your 10th house of career achievements and public image at some point during the month, you'll be motivated to put your best foot forward. Keep networking and promoting your skills and talents - these efforts could pay off in exciting ways down the road when Jupiter lucks comes later in the year.

Finances:

Thanks to Venus' influence over your income sector, you could enjoy a lucrative financial month in February if you're open to moneymaking opportunities. However, steer clear of impulsive spending or falling for get-rich-quick schemes around the 19th when Venus squares dreamy Neptune. Instead, focus on budgeting and investing wisely, asking friends or mentors for guidance if needed. Avoid loaning money or taking on new debts during this period too.

Health:

With the warm sun beaming through your wellness sector for the first three weeks of February, this month ushers in an excellent window to reinvigorate your self-care routines. You'll feel naturally inspired to move your body through dance, yoga, sports, or simply long walks in nature. Embrace activities that bring you joy and keep your mind engaged. The Full Moon on the 12th could bring a health matter to light that needs addressing, so stay attuned to your intuition.

Travel:

If you've been craving a getaway, Gemini, this could be an ideal month to treat yourself to a rejuvenating adventure! With Venus activating your wanderlust sector from the 8th onward, you'll be eager broaden your horizons through mind-expanding experiences and exposure to different cultures or philosophies. A weekend road trip with friends or a spontaneous booking to an off-the-beaten path destination could be in the cards. Embrace your spirit of curiosity!

Insights from the Stars:

The key theme of this February's astrology is all about connecting - with others, with new ideas and experiences, and with your authentic self. With planets illuminating your social sectors, there will be endless opportunities to network, collaborate, and open yourself up to new communities or ways of thinking. However, don't lose yourself in the process of giving to others. Saturn's influence reminds you to stay grounded and nurture your independence as well.

Best Days:

February 5th: First Quarter Moon - Initiate a social plan, group activity or launch event.

February 8th: Venus enters Gemini - Your powers of charm and attraction are amplified!

February 12th: Full Moon in Leo - A romantic connection could take the next step.

February 16th: Mercury sextile Jupiter - Fantastic for learning, writing or taking a short trip.

February 22nd: Sun enters Pisces - Tune into your intuition and embrace your imaginative side.

March 2025

Overview Horoscope for the Month:

March brings a powerful wave of energy that will catalyze profound shifts and new beginnings for you, dear Gemini. With the looming Aries New Moon and Solar Eclipse on the 29th activating your 12th house of spirituality, you'll be pushed to confront your shadows, release old patterns, and undergo an inner metamorphosis. However, this process won't be easy with stern Saturn continuing its journey through this psychologically complex sector of your chart. Prepare for a month of deep soul-searching and introspection.

Love:

Your love life takes on a more intense, psychologically-charged tone in March thanks to Venus' placement in Taurus and your 8th house of intimacy and transformation at the start of the month. Existing partnerships could feel the urge to evolve to a deeper level of transparency, vulnerability and merging of souls. For singles, you may be attracting people who almost seem like "twin flame" connections - familiar souls who stir up your subconscious longings and fears. The New Moon/Solar Eclipse on the 29th instigates major relationship shifts or beginnings/endings related to intimacy.

Career:

With six planets gathering in fellow air sign Aquarius and your 11th house of groups, associations, and future visions, you'll find your attention pulled toward more aspirational, unconventional pursuits this month. Your creative ideas and innovative thinking will be valued, so find ways to network, connect with like-minded teams and causes, and showcase your visionary talents. If traditional career paths feel stifling now, don't fret - a Soul-directed reinvention might be inevitable after the Aries Eclipse.

Finances:

While the financial outlook for March isn't entirely clear for you, Gemini, you'd be wise to scrutinize any shared resources, debts, inheritances or taxes you're dealing with. With the self-protective Aries New Moon spotlighting your 12th house of subconscious patterns and karmic baggage, there could be outdated attitudes or deep wounds sabotaging your ability to cultivate abundance and security. Begin healing your relationship with money consciously or energetically. Avoid entering into financial entanglements without careful consideration.

Health:

Your personal health and wellbeing takes center stage at this month's Aries New Moon and Solar Eclipse, asking you to look at any unhealthy patterns, compulsions or limiting beliefs that are undermining your vitality.

With penetrating Pluto involved, you could have a profound psychological awakening around a chronic health condition, addiction, or the roots of self-destructive tendencies. However unpleasant this process is, facing your shadows head-on can catalyze profound healing and transformation. Adopt a self-nurturing mindset and be compassionate with yourself.

Travel:

With so much inward-directed energy swirling in March, international travel or adventure is less prioritized now. However, you could find yourself being pulled toward locales or activities that get you more deeply in touch with your spirituality, intuition, and subconscious psyche. Consider booking a vision quest, shamanic ritual, or meditative retreat close to home. You'll crave time and space away from worldly distractions to do the soul work that this potent astrology is demanding.

Insights from the Stars:

The key theme that the stars are illuminating for you this March is all about profound rebirth and transformation, Gemini. You're being pushed through an intense spiritual/psychological rebirth canal and a shedding of your old, outdated identity. It won't be pleasant, but this process is actually heavenly choreographed to set you free from self-limiting patterns that have been deeply ingrained in your subconscious. Call on your courage and take this awakening process with vulnerability and compassion for yourself.

Best Days:

March 6th: First Quarter Moon - Initiate a research project, group plan, or network.

March 14th: Full Moon in Virgo - An epiphany or realization around health and routines.

March 20th: Sun enters Aries - Set intentions around your spiritual growth.

March 25th: Mercury enters Aries - Your mental energy finds clarity of purpose.

March 29th: Aries New Moon & Solar Eclipse - An unmissable rebirth catalyst!.

April 2025

Overview Horoscope for the Month:

April begins on an introspective, spiritual note for you, Gemini, as the reverberations of March's powerful Aries New Moon and Solar Eclipse continue rippling through your psyche. The first three weeks of the month see the Sun, Mercury, and Venus all journeying through Aries and your 12th house of inner realms, ensuring your subconscious mind remains front and center. However, by the 19th when the Sun enters Taurus, you'll start regaining your typical energetic zest. Prepare for a month of profound awakenings balanced with renewed vitality.

Love:

Your love life could feel rather intense and psychologically probing in early April while Venus continues her journey through Aries and your 8th house of intimacy and merging. Existing partnerships may undergo a deep "soul-rebirthing" process, catalyzing greater transparency, vulnerability and shedding of protective barriers. If you're single, you could attract whirlwind attractions that feel fated or revelatory, dredging up subconscious attractions and fears. After the 21st when Venus enters Taurus though, the romantic vibe turns sweeter and more sensual. Nurture connections built on simple pleasures.

Career:

With go-getter Mars spending the entire month in your home and family sector, your attention in April turns inward to tending to domestic priorities, innerwork and releasing psychological baggage. While this transitional period may slow your external career momentum, it's providing fertile soil to realign your professional direction with your soul's deeper truth. If you've felt out of sync in your job, this month's energies awaken insights around your greater calling. After the 24th when Pluto ends its yearly retrograde, you'll feel more empowered to actualize these new visions.

Finances:

While the first three weeks of April may not be the most auspicious for major financial initiatives, you can use this time to do some serious reassessment and value-clarification around money. With the Sun, Mercury and Venus all activating your 12th house of psyche patterns, take time to examine how your ingrained attitudes, fears and definitions of self-worth may be influencing your ability to attract wealth. Work on dissolving scarcity mindsets and recalibrating your relationship to abundance. After the 21st, earnings could increase from new professional endeavors.

Health:

Your health & wellness routines remain a major focus throughout April's journey of self-discovery and awakening. With Mars continuing its transit of your domestic 4th house all month, you'll feel pulled to nurture your vitality through home-cooked meals, restorative practices, and soothing activities in your living space. The New Moon on the 19th provides a fertile seedtime for new exercise, diet or sleep regimens. Prioritize reducing stress and nourishing embodied self-love. An emotional or psychological unblocking could catalyze profound physical healing.

Travel:

With so much introspective planetary energy illuminating your psyche in April, international travel or adventure is less prioritized now. However, you could find yourself pulled to locales or activities closer to home that facilitate a process of deep inner exploration. A solo retreat, spiritual workshop or reconnection with nature could be appealing as you navigate the soul-discovery process this month's energies are catalyzing. Wait until May to make travel plans further afield.

Insights from the Stars:

The key theme the stars are shining down on you this April is all about navigating a profound spiritual awakening and rebirth, dear Gemini. You're being initiated through an intense metamorphosis, shedding your old identity and self-limiting patterns. While this process can feel disorienting and even painful at times, it's ultimately heavenly choreographed to liberate you to actualize your greatest potential. Call on your dual capacities for intellectual objectivity and emotional vulnerability as you work to integrate these transformative energies.

Best Days:

April 1st: Mars trine Pluto - Powerful drive and ability to face your shadows.

April 6th: Venus trine Saturn - Excellent for solidifying a commitment or financial establishment.

April 8th: Mercury conjunct Jupiter - Fantastic for learning, writing, or philosophical/spiritual exploration.

April 19th: Taurus New Moon - Seed new intentions around self-nurturing and values.

April 26th: Sun conjunct Uranus - Breakthroughs, surprises and awakened insights!.

May 2025

Overview Horoscope for the Month:

May brings a welcome breath of fresh, revitalizing energy for you after April's inward-turning journey, dear Gemini. With the Sun entering your sign on the 20th, you'll be reenergized and eager to put yourself out into the world in a bigger way. The Gemini New Moon on the 26th provides rocket fuel for personal reinvention and new beginnings aligned with the awakened version of yourself that's been emerging. However, with stern taskmaster Saturn still trekking through your spirit sector, maintaining humility and doing the inner work can't be avoided either.

Love:

Your love life lights up this month with relationship planets Venus and Mars activating your partnership sectors. If you're in a committed relationship, you'll feel inspired to reinvigorate the spark and collaborate more as a team on shared goals after May 7th when Venus enters Gemini. For singles, expect your powers of attraction and magnetism to go into high gear, especially after the New Moon on the 26th - get out and mingle! However, power struggles or control issues in relationships could flare with Mars squaring Saturn around mid-month. Approach dynamics mindfully.

Career:

With the confident Sun surging through your career and public image sector until the 20th, you'll make a striking professional impression at the start of May. This is a powerful window to step into greater leadership, launch a business venture, or put yourself out there in a bigger way through your work. After the 20th when the Sun enters Gemini though, your focus turns more toward personal passion projects, restarts, and redefining yourself on a broader level. This energy carries through in June, so no need to rush!

Finances:

Money matters take an innovative turn this month as multiple planets activate the financial areas of your chart. You could have an unexpected income boost from a new job, business idea or lucrative personal project after the 20th. The key is channeling that monetary energy into establishing stronger long-term security rather than impulse spending. With Saturn in your spiritual money sector all year, the stars are reminding you to align any wealth pursuits with your integrity and soul purpose. Avoid any get-rich-quick schemes.

Health:

With action planet Mars firing up your health and routine sector from May 11th until July, you'll have an extra reserve of energy to devote to fitness goals, dietary upgrades and lifestyle optimization. Consider trying a new workout regimen, sport or movement practice that keeps you physically and mentally engaged. You could make excellent progress now, as long as you remain consistent and disciplined. Your mental health gets a welcome boost after the 20th when your ruler Mercury enters Gemini, encouraging open communication and intellectual stimulation.

Travel:

Geminis will be seized by an acute case of wanderlust as the second half of May unfolds! With the Sun arriving in your sign on the 20th, followed by the Gemini New Moon on the 26th, you'll be craving freedom, adventure, and novel experiences that feed your curiosity. Whether it's a quick weekend jaunt, buying plane tickets for an international getaway, or simply immersing in a local subculture, you'll want a change of scenery. Open yourself up to wherever the winds may blow, as spontaneity is favored.

Insights from the Stars:

The key astrological theme for you this month, Gemini, is all about rebirth and reinvention. After April's journey of deep self-discovery, the universe is gifting you a window to emerge as your brilliantly actualized, authentic self. The Gemini New Moon on May 26th is an especially fertile launchpad for any fresh personal starts or pivotal new directions you feel called toward. However, Saturn's presence ensures this won't be an overnight makeover - you must approach this renaissance intentionally and with humble commitment. Have patience and faith in the process unfolding for you.

Best Days:

May 4th: First Quarter Moon - Take an inventive idea to the next level.

May 11th: Mars enters Aries - Fantastic energy for tackling a new fitness pursuit or project.

May 19th: Full Moon in Scorpio - Embrace pleasure, sensuality, and following your heart's desires.

May 20th: Sun enters Gemini - Happy Solar Return! Celebrate your beautiful self.

May 26th: Gemini New Moon - An auspicious rebirth! Initiate exciting new intentions.

June 2025

Overview Horoscope for the Month:

June brings an electrifying burst of energy into your world, Gemini! With the Sun still blazing through your sign until the 20th, you'll be overflowing with confidence, charisma and a zest for adventure. This is a fabulous month to initiate important personal projects, makeover your image, and put yourself out into the world in an unmistakable way. However, with Venus and Mars squaring off against strict Saturn mid-month, you may face some tests around staying disciplined and overcoming impatience. But you've got this!

Love:

Your romantic life is alight with excitement and possibility in June thanks to passionate Venus touring Gemini until the 26th. If you're in a committed relationship, this is a fabulous transit for reinvigorating the spark and keeping that "dating phase" magic alive through romantic gestures, heartfelt communication, and sexy spontaneity. For singles, your planetary ruler bestows you with magnetic powers of attraction - just watch that you don't come across as too flirtatious or noncommittal with crushes. The Full Moon on the 11th brings a potential relationship turning point or revelation.

Career:

With the confident Sun still illuminating your skills and talents until the 20th, June is an excellent month to showcase what you have to offer in your professional life, Gemini. This could look like pitching an innovative idea to a superior, signing up for a high-exposure speaking engagement or promotion, or taking bold steps toward entrepreneurship. While you may face delays or structural limitations around the 16th when Mars squares Saturn, don't get deterred. Those challenges are simply stoking your resilience. Approach your ambitions with pragmatism and you'll thrive.

Finances:

Thanks to your planetary ruler, messenger Mercury, cruising through your income sector from the 8th onward this month, you should enjoy a lucrative financial period if you keep putting yourself out there. However, avoid the temptation to wildly overspend while indulgent Venus occupies your sign too! Instead, focus on responsible management of cash flow and investments. The Full Moon in Sagittarius on the 11th could bring a money revelation around beliefs, debts or values that need readjustment to increase abundance. Stay focused and keep an open mind.

Health:

You should be feeling energized and eager to move your body this June, Gemini! With Mars firing up your vitality sector from the 11th on, you'll have plenty of motivation to experiment with new fitness routines, sports, or physical challenges that keep you mentally engaged too. Think outside the box - activities like rock climbing, martial arts, or dance could be appealing ways to cross-train. However, around the 16th when the flames of Mars clash with rigid Saturn, be cautious of overzealousness or injury risk by overdoing it. Moderation is wise.

Travel:

Thanks to June's lively, free-spirited vibes, you'll be absolutely champing at the bit for new experiences and adventures that feed your curiosity! Any opportunity to get out and explore new locations and subcultures will be utterly irresistible for you. Whether it's a quick weekend road trip, finally booking those plane tickets to a bucket list destination, or diving deep into an ethnic cultural immersion locally, change up your scenery in whatever way sings to your wanderlust. Spontaneity is preferred over meticulously planning every move.

Insights from the Stars:

The key astrological theme for you this month, Gemini, is all about joyfully and authentically expressing your unique, multi-faceted self out in the world. After a period of intense reinvention, you're being gifted cosmic encouragement to emerge from your cocoon as the brilliant butterfly you're becoming. Flaunt your colors, spread your wings and take up space without apologies! However, the influence of Saturn will require you to keep an eye on maintaining discipline, humility and pragmatism too. Approach your passions and personal goals with integrity and staying power.

Best Days:

June 2nd: Gemini New Moon - Set exciting new intentions around creativity and authenticity!

June 9th: Venus trine Saturn - Excellent for solidifying a commitment or financial investment.

June 11th: Full Moon in Sagittarius - An epiphany around your belief systems and philosophies.

June 16th: Mars square Saturn - Exercise patience; don't force matters or overdo it.

June 20th: Sun enters Cancer - Embrace your emotional, nurturing side for balance.

July 2025

Overview Horoscope for the Month:

After the high-energy expressive vibes of June, July brings a more introspective but equally dynamic tone for you, Gemini. With the Sun entering the nurturing waters of Cancer on the 20th, you'll be pulled to tend to your home/family life and tend to your deeper emotional needs. However, with Mars continuing its feisty tour of your sign until the 16th, you'll still be radiating confidence and assertiveness too. Finding the right equilibrium between putting yourself out there and carving out quieter spaces for restoration will be key.

Love:

Romance is set to sizzle for you in the first half of July, thanks to passionate Mars touring Gemini until the 16th. If you're coupled up, this transit encourages reinvigorating the spark through spontaneous dates, new adventures, and daring communication. However, be mindful of conflicts or ego battles around this period as the warrior planet can make folks headstrong. For Geminis still riding solo, this Mars power provides charisma to attract exciting connections - just don't come on too strong! After the 16th, you may feel a pull inward to nest with your sweetie.

Career:

While your professional momentum may have slowed slightly after June's charged energies, you can still make excellent progress this July if you remain strategic. With Mars in your sign until the 16th, you'll want to seize any opportunities to assert yourself, pitch bold ideas, and step into greater leadership. However, the influence of structured Saturn cautions against impulsive rashness. After the 16th when the red planet exits Gemini, you'll feel more motivated to work behind-the-scenes on achieving work/life balance. The Leo New Moon on the 24th presents a fertile fresh start.

Finances:

Money matters take an intriguing turn this July as Venus, the planet of wealth, spends an extended journey in your domestic sector. This influence from the 31st onward highlights potential income streams connected to your home, family business or property investments/assets. However, you may also be tempted toward overspending or emotional purchases tied to nostaligia or desiring more comforts/luxuries. When the willful Leo New Moon arrives on the 24th, reassess aligning your resources with what you truly value on a soul level. Release outdated scarcity mindsets.

Health:

With fiery Mars amping up your energy levels until the 16th, July provides an excellent window to establish health routines and regimens that truly stick. Consider trying fresh fitness formats like martial arts disciplines, dance, or outdoor sports that get you focused but keep your mental stimulation engaged too. After mid-month when the red planet exits your sign, you'll crave finding a balance between physical activity and restorative, bodywork practices. Draw boundaries against burnout or over-depletion by tuning into your body's needs.

Travel:

While your interstellar Gemini wanderlust may not be as vocal this July, you can still tap into that spontaneous, freedom-loving spirit through adventures closer to home. Weekend road trips or staycations that temporarily shift your environment could prove restorative and perspective-refreshing. After mid-month when the Sun enters your domestic 4th house, you might find more contentment in cozying up and nesting in familiar spaces too. However, avoid the temptation to fully hibernate! Stay open to inspiration from the local world around you.

Insights from the Stars:

The key astrological theme for you this July is all about achieving integration between your reflective, inwardly-focused needs and your dazzling, expressive exterior. The first half of the month provides a window to confidently assert yourself, take up space, and boldly showcase your talents and voice out in the world. However, after mid-month, you'll feel an intuitive pull to slow down, tend to your roots, and center back into your emotional foundations. Striking this equilibrium between extroverted action and soulful presence will be an empowering practice in self-nurturing.

Best Days:

July 4th: Venus enters Gemini - Love planet boosts your magnetic charisma and powers of attraction!

July 7th: Uranus enters Gemini - An awakening and reinvention of your identity and self-expression.

July 10th: Full Moon in Capricorn - Embrace maturity and find the courage to own your achievements.

July 16th: Mars enters Leo - Fantastic energy for pouring your heart into passion projects and creative self-expression.

July 24th: New Moon in Leo - Seed new intentions around joy, pleasure, and reclaiming your playful spirit..

August 2025

Overview Horoscope for the Month:

August brings a dynamic but balancing set of energies for you to navigate, Gemini. With the Sun still blazing through fiery Leo until the 22nd, the first three weeks emphasize expressing yourself boldly, pursuing passion projects, and finding fulfillment through creative self-love. However, when the Sun shifts into your humble 6th house of work and habits on the 22nd, you'll need to temper that verve with diligent efforts and routine. Finding the sweet spot that synthesizes fun with productivity will be key.

Love:

Thanks to your ruling planet Mercury joining the intimacy-seeking Scorpio crew this month, your love life takes on deeper, more psychologically-merging tones in August. If you're partnered up, this astro-weather facilitates bonding through vulnerable sharing, exploring spiritual or esoteric interests together, and reaching new levels of erotic closeness. For single Geminis, you may find yourself attracted to connections that feel fated or catalyze core psychological work - be discerning! The Full Moon on the 9th could bring a relationship epiphany.

Career:

While the career spotlight likely won't be shining as brightly on you in August compared to earlier this year, you can still make steady progress behind-the-scenes. With energizer Mars continuing its tour of Leo until the 27th, you'll be motivated to pour passion into personal projects, creative pursuits or work that allows for self-expression. However, after the 22nd when the Sun enters Virgo, adopting humble diligence towards advancing more traditional ambitions becomes favorable again too. Seek inspiration but remain pragmatic.

Finances:

Thanks to the fortunate trine between expansive Jupiter in your partnership sector and transformative Pluto in your shared resources zone on the 19th, you could experience an earnings boost or lucrative collaborative endeavor in August. However, with Mercury touring your 8th house of psychological merging, you may also need to examine ingrained attitudes or fears around money, power or self-worth. Empowering wealth affirmations or healing work could unlock more flow. After the 22nd, get meticulous about budgeting.

Health:

With the confident Sun beaming through your vitality sector until the 22nd, the first three weeks of August provide an energizing window for establishing exercise routines or exploring new physical pursuits that get your blood pumping. Movement disciplines that incorporate mental focus and a spiritual element like yoga, martial arts or dance could be appealing paths. After the 22nd though, you'll want to adopt a more realistic, regulated approach to self-care - think practical nutrition upgrades, consistent practices, and better work/life boundaries.

Travel:

Early August could find you seized by a bout of wanderlust, thanks to radiant solar energies activating your passion for adventure and novel experiences! If you can swing taking an impromptu trip - whether a weekend jaunt or finally booking those international plane tickets you've been dreaming of - this spirited astrology will certainly fuel it. However, after the 22nd when the travel well gets replenished and you shift into more diligent, practical mode, your urge to break from the daily grind may wane. Channel inspiration through staycations.

Insights from the Stars:

The key theme that the cosmic forces are illuminating for you this August is all about balancing celebratory self-expression with humble integration, Gemini. The first three weeks provide a window to boldly put yourself out into the world, lean into your fiery willpower, and find avenues for passion, pleasure and joy. However, from the 22nd onward, you'll need to temper that verve by committing to routines, responsible actions, and doing the daily "unsexy" work needed to move your lofty visions into sustainable reality. Approach this equilibrium with patience and self-love.

Best Days:

August 1st: Venus trine Jupiter - Excellent for attracting abundance, socializing or creative collaborations.

August 6th: Mars enters Libra - Your partnerships could use an infusion of dynamism and mutual understanding.

August 9th: Full Moon in Aquarius - An epiphany around your social circles, future visions or sense of belonging.

August 14th: Mercury conjunct Venus - Express your affections and connect through communication.

August 23rd: New Moon in Virgo - Set new routines, habits and self-care intentions with pragmatic optimism..

September 2025

Overview Horoscope for the Month:

September brings a grounding but also deeply transformative energy into your life, Gemini. With six planets traveling through the pragmatic earth sign Virgo until the 22nd, the first three weeks emphasize getting organized, establishing routines, and taking a systematic approach to any ambitions or pursuits. However, two powerhouse lunations - a Full Moon Total Lunar Eclipse in Pisces and a Partial Solar Eclipse in Virgo - ensure the month won't be lacking intensity! Prepare for profound awakenings and rebirths amidst the practical efforts.

Love:

Your platonic relationships and social connections take center stage in the first half of September, thanks to relationship planets Venus and Mars touring airy Libra. You'll feel energized to network, collaborate with like-minded others, and reinvigorate your sense of belonging in your communities. For singles, this could spark a romantic attraction through your friend group! However, the Pisces Lunar Eclipse on the 7th may bring a relationship epiphany, ending or spiritual awakening that reshapes your heart's perspective. After the 22nd, your focus shifts to merging intimately.

Career:

With the nitty-gritty Sun, Mercury, and your co-rulers Venus and Mars all touring your 6th house of work, habits and routines until the 22nd, September provides an extremely favorable window for buckling down to accomplish practical, sustainable ambitions. Whether it's launching a job search, systematizing your business operations, or upgrading your skills, you'll find it easier to establish consistent disciplines and do the "unsexy" prep needed. The Solar Eclipse on the 21st presents an opportunity to reinvent your daily responsibilities and lifestyle rhythms.

Finances:

Financially, the first three weeks of September favor prudent management, accounting for your income streams, and establishing organized budgets or savings goals. However, watch for compulsive overspending from the 7th to the 14th with the potent Eclipse AND retrograde station of wealth planet Venus. After the 22nd when Venus retrogrades into Virgo, you can efficiently revisit investments or monetary systems for recalibration if needed. The bigger theme this month is realigning your resources with your core values and ethics.

Health:

What an ideal astrological month for establishing wellness routines and exploring holistic healing modalities, Gemini! With the Sun, motivating Mars, intellectual Mercury and embodiment mentor Venus all touring the health-conscious Virgo realms of your chart, you'll find it infinitely easier to get into a productive groove around exercise, nutrition upgrades, and addressing any physical or psychological blockages through bodywork or therapy. Stay consistent and make incremental improvements over perfection. The Virgo Eclipse on the 21st spotlights potential lifestyle reinventions.

Travel:

With the majority of this month's planetary energy turned so inwardly towards work, routines, and psychological integration, international travel or far-flung adventures feel less emphasized for you in September, Gemini. However, that doesn't mean you can't still scratch your insatiable wanderlust itch through nearby explorations close to home! Local road trips, neighborhood immersions, or even just exploring the hidden enclaves within your city could provide perspective-refreshing shifts in scenery. Indulge your curiosity through wisdom teachings or cultural studies too.

Insights from the Stars:

The key astrological theme illuminating your journey through September is all about integration, Gemini - harmonizing your lofty visions, aspirations and sense of purpose with the humble day-to-day efforts, discipline and self-work necessary to achieve true, sustainable success. The lunar eclipses this month will be shaking up your internal and external worlds, catalyzing profound personal awakenings and reinventions. Approach this intensity without resistance, staying grounded in consistent practices and pragmatic optimism. Profound growth lives on the other side.

Best Days:

September 2nd: Mercury enters Virgo - Fantastic for buckling down on a research or work project.

September 7th: Full Moon Total Lunar Eclipse in Pisces - A deeply psychologically and spiritually awakening internal rebirth.

September 14th: Venus Retrograde - Reexamine your values, resources, self-worth and receptivity to abundance.

September 19th: Venus enters Virgo - Beautify your routines and find the pleasures in discipline.

September 21st: Partial Solar Eclipse in Virgo - Powerful new lifestyle and work reinvention launchpad!

October 2025

Overview Horoscope for the Month:

October brings an intense but fertile period of renewal and reinvention for you, Gemini. With the month beginning in the wake of September's eclipses, you'll still be riding the waves of profound personal awakenings and metamorphoses. The first three weeks see the Sun, Mercury, and your co-rulers Venus and Mars all clustered in passionate Scorpio, shining a light on your needs for depth, intimacy and soul-fueling transformation. Prepare to do some deep-diving! However, shifting energy arrives on the 22nd when the Sun enters truth-seeking Sagittarius, stoking your curiosity for exploration and expanded horizons again.

Love:

Your closest partnerships and one-on-one bonds take on deeper emotional intensity in October, thanks to the Scorpio stellium accentuating your 8th house of intimacy and psychological merging. Existing relationships could reach new levels of transparency, vulnerability and physical closeness, which can feel both exhilarating and confronting. For singles, you may find yourself magnetically drawn to soul-mate connections or people who stir your subconscious longings/shadows. Stay mindful of power dynamics. After the 19th when relationship planet Venus turns direct, situations become clearer.

Career:

While you may not necessarily make huge external career strides in October, the astrological emphasis is on doing some seriously deep internal work around your ambitions, future vision and integrity. With transformative Pluto and the Sun spotlighting your 9th house of life philosophies, you'll be pushed to clarify your spiritual calling and identify any outdated beliefs or toxic patterns sabotaging your success. Release rigidity and embrace fluidity. After the 22nd, you regain visionary clarity.

Finances:

The theme of reinvention extends to your financial situation this October too, Gemini. With Venus retrograding through your sectors of values, self-worth and shared resources until the 19th, you'll be pushed to look at deep-rooted attitudes, fears or relational/karmic patterns influencing your relationship to money, ownership or power dynamics. From shadow work springs tremendous empowerment though! After the 19th, renewed flow arrives if you've been willing to do the healing. Avoid financial risks before then.

Health:

October's astrological emphasis is very much centered in the psychological/spiritual realms for you, Gemini, which makes it an ideal period for exploring therapeutic, cathartic or consciousness-expanding practices related to your wellbeing. With powerful Scorpio planets illuminating your 8th house of shared vulnerabilities, you could experience profound breakthroughs through modalities like shadow work, intimacy counselling, breathwork or inner child healing. Be fearless in facing any compulsions or taboo issues. After the 22nd, a renewed zest for physical vitality arrives.

Travel:

With so many planets travelling through the psychologically penetrating realms of Scorpio until the 22nd, you may have decreased motivation for international travel or adventure in October, Gemini. However, that doesn't mean you can't seek out closer-to-home shifts in perspective through local immersions, workshops or communities aligned with your soul's deeper interests. Things like shamanic rituals, esoteric studies or cultural events that take you inward could prove transformative. After the 22nd when wanderlust returns, start planning grander getaways.

Insights from the Stars:

The key astrological theme illuminating your journey in October is all about letting go, embracing rebirth, and becoming a deeper, more authentic version of yourself, Gemini. After September catalyzed profound awakenings, you now must follow through by going inward to reckon with your shadow elements, release toxic patterns, and identify your true spiritual callings. It may feel intense, but this metamorphosis is divinely-orchestrated to liberate you onto your highest path. Approach this rebirth with courage, vulnerability and trust in the process. Tremendous growth lives on the other side.

Best Days:

October 6th: Mercury enters Scorpio - Penetrating insights and depth of focus.

October 13th: Full Moon in Aries - Could reignite passion for a project or provoke confrontations that inspire empowerment.

October 19th: Venus Direct in Scorpio - Renewing flow in your relationships, values and self-worth.

October 22nd: Sun enters Sagittarius - Reclaiming optimism, adventure and hunger to expand your horizons.

October 29th: New Moon in Scorpio - Potent for personal reinvention aligned with your integrity.

Overview Horoscope for the Month:

After the intense psycho-spiritual excavations of October, November brings a well-timed atmospheric shift providing room for optimism, exploration and regaining your celebratory spirit, Gemini. With the Sun moved into truth-seeking Sagittarius until the 21st, the first three weeks of the month emphasize broadening your horizons through cultural expansions, philosophical learning and globetrotting adventures. However, the final week provides a grounding reminder to keep one foot on Earth as the Sun enters pragmatic Capricorn. Finding the balance between wanderlust and diligent goal-setting will be key this November.

Love:

Thanks to your co-rulers Venus and Mars touring Sagittarius together from the 16th onward, your one-on-one partnerships and romantic connections get infused with a spirited, uplifting energy this month! Couples will feel inspired to grow together through new experiences, intellectual stimulation and following their mutual curiosities. For singles, cross-cultural connections or walks of life/perspectives that excite your wanderlust could lead to passionate attractions. However, watch for potential conflicts around each other's ideologies or ethics with Venus squaring progressive Uranus.

Career:

While your professional ambitions likely won't steal the spotlight this November, you can expect opportunities for learning, teaching, publishing or pitching ideas that help expand your audience or platform in some way. With Mars also activating your 9th house of higher mind expansion, you'll have the energetic courage to take more daring, unconventional or innovative risks in sharing your knowledge or leadership skills. Aim to inspire others while also approaching your goals with realistic optimism.

Finances:

After the heavy financial shake-ups and value work of the past two months, November's planetary placements could bring more flow, Gemini. However, it won't come without some effort or mindset repatterning on your part. With Venus touring your resources sector after the 16th and then activating your income zone in early December, this is an ideal period for updating your budget, releasing mindsets of scarcity, and opening the channel to greater abundance through practices of gratitude, ethical giving and redefining your beliefs around wealth. Prosperity is an inside job!

Health:

With warrior Mars charging through your health sector from November 16th to January, you'll have an extra dose of motivational fire to dive into physical upgrades or fitness pursuits during the final months of 2025. Consider taking up a new athletic passion like martial arts, rock climbing or dance genres that blend movement with mental engagement. You'll thrive by combining metabolic conditioning with the intellectual stimulation your curious sign craves. Just be mindful of burnout or injuries by over-exerting. Feed your sense of adventure while finding joy in the process.

Travel:

Thanks to the energizing influence of globetrotting Sagittarius activating your zones of exploration and adventure this month, your itch for novel experiences and nomadic freedom will be roaring loudly! If you have the opportunity to sate your curiosities through international travel or cultural immersions, November provides prime energy for setting off on epic journeys. Even smaller, spontaneous getaways that temporarily shift your scenery can provide perspective-refreshing respites now. Stay open to surprise detours or serendipitous encounters that inspire growth.

Insights from the Stars:

The key astrological energy illuminating your path through November is all about striking the ideal balance between broadening your experiential horizons and pragmatically laying the groundwork for sustainable success, Gemini. The first three weeks provide an opportune window for adventure, learning, teaching, and following the trail of your expanding philosophies and world views. However, after the 21st, the cosmic tides turn towards manifesting those visions into concrete form through consistent effort and structural strategies. Follow your inspiration while keeping optimism rooted in realism.

Best Days:

November 4th: New Moon in Scorpio - Seed intentions around intimacy, vulnerability and reclaiming your authentic personal power.

November 7th: Venus enters Sagittarius - A breath of life in your relationships and financial flow.

November 16th: Mars enters Sagittarius - Finding courage to take leaps of faith and explore new territory.

November 19th: Full Moon in Taurus - A revelation around income, values or self-worth upgrades.

November 21st: Sun enters Capricorn - Regain pragmatism while still channeling your wonder for the world.

December 2025

Overview Horoscope for the Month:

As the year winds down, December brings a balancing mix of wanderlust and pragmatic energy for you to navigate, Gemini. With the Sun still touring expansive Sagittarius until the 21st, the first three weeks will keep beckoning you to explore new horizons through travel, cross-cultural connections, and mind-expanding philosophies. However, once the solstice arrives and the Sun shifts into hardworking Capricorn, you'll need to apply disciplined efforts towards tangible goals and responsibilities too. Finding the equilibrium between free-spirited curiosity and level-headed ambition will be key.

Love:

Your partnerships get infused with an adventurous, spontaneous vibe for the first half of December thanks to passionate Mars touring fire sign Sagittarius. Couples will feel inspired to break out of ruts by discovering new cultural experiences, intellectual stimulation or outdoor thrills together. For singles, fateful attractions could arrive through travel, higher learning or people who awaken your philosophical curiosities. However, watch for belief conflicts or competitiveness once Mars enters Capricorn. Lead with empathy, not egos.

Career:

With the career-focused Capricorn zone of your chart majorly lit up from December 21st onward, you can expect the final weeks of 2025 to kick your professional efforts into high gear! This grounding, pragmatic influence helps you realign with structuring disciplined routines, consistent hustle towards tangible goals, and embracing greater leaderships responsibilities or public visibility. However, it will require focus, commitment and patience - skills you possess but that the free-spirited Sagittarius vibes earlier in the month could throw off. Stay balanced.

Finances:

Thanks to sweet-talking Venus touring your income sector for the first half of December, you could receive a welcome monetary boost from your work, business endeavors or lucrative personal projects/skills. However, once Venus shifts into Capricorn on the 24th, you'll need to channel that financial flow responsibly through budgeting discipline, long-term investments or practices that increase security. Look for novel revenue streams too through monetizing an expertise. Balancing optimism with pragmatic stewardship is wise now.

Health:

With energetic Mars continuing its journey through your wellness realms until mid-January, you'll have an abundance of physical vitality and stamina this December to devote to fitness goals, athletic pursuits or nutritional upgrades. However, the battle will be in balancing activity with rest/rejuvenation. Through the 19th, your sense of adventure could lead you to favor thrilling new movement disciplines like rock-climbing but at risk of overdoing it. After the 21st though, consistency and sustainable routines become easier with grounded Capricorn's influence. Pace yourself.

Travel:

If you've been craving far-flung exploration and opportunities to indulge your wanderlust in 2025, the first three weeks of December serve it up deliciously, Gemini! With the radiant Sagittarius influence stimulating your curiosity until the 21st, you'll be utterly inspired to book that long-awaited international adventure, cross-cultural study program or epic road trip you've been dreaming about. However, the tides turn towards the year's end when Saturn and Capricorn's energy pulls you back towards tending to home/family obligations or diligently laying foundations before pursuing escapades.

Insights from the Stars:

The key astrological force shaping your journey this December is all about harmonizing your dualistic capacities for freedom and structure, curiosity and pragmatism, Gemini. The month begins with an invigorating breath of wanderlust, spontaneity and appetite for new experiences that awaken your spirit. However, by the solstice, you'll be pulled to regain your footing through disciplined routines, consistent efforts towards tangible goals, and establishing a stronger work/life balance. Rather than resisting either drive, see if you can create harmony between the two so neither overpowers the other.

Best Days:

December 4th: Full Moon in Gemini - An empowering opportunity to re-embrace and celebrate your multifaceted self!

December 7th: Mercury enters Sagittarius - Fantastic for learning, traveling or widening your perspective through studies.

December 11th: Mars conjunct Neptune - Inspired spiritual quests, travel plans or artistic pursuits emerge!

December 19th: Mars enters Capricorn - Your determination and disciplined efforts get a powerful boost of dynamic energy.

December 22nd: Jupiter Direct - Growth and abundance opportunities open again after a period of realignment.

CANCER 2025 HOROSCOPE

Overview Cancer 2025

(June 21 - July 22)

Welcome, dear Cancers, to an astrological year that promises to be a profound journey of spiritual awakening, emotional healing, and a deepening connection to your innermost truths. As the celestial bodies dance their cosmic rhythms, they will illuminate both challenges and opportunities that will shape your evolution toward greater authenticity, inner peace, and soul-aligned manifestation. Prepare to dive deep into the depths of your psyche and shed the layers that have been obscuring your radiant essence.

The year begins with Mars transiting through the mystical waters of Pisces, amplifying your sensitivities and drawing you inward to explore your subconscious realms. This emerges as a fertile time for engaging with spiritual practices, artistic expression, or anything that facilitates a deeper attunement with your intuitive wisdom. Embrace solitude, ritual, and trust the signs and symbols that arise from your dreams and imagination.

A pivotal shift occurs on January 11th when the karmic North Node ingresses into Pisces, orchestrating an 18-month cycle centered on your spiritual unfoldment. This transit presents a powerful invitation to release any limiting beliefs, ancestral patterns or past life imprints that have disconnected you from your soul's essential nature. Modalities like past life regression, shamanic journeying or creative visualization could aid in integrating soul fragments. Stay open to profound awakenings.

On March 1st, stern taskmaster Saturn enters Aries, amplifying your 10th house of public image, career mastery and life's purpose. For the next few months until May, you'll face tests that require increased discipline, focus and confronting fears/limitations around visibility and authority. Any lingering insecurities or impostor complexes will get triggered to be healed. Trust that these hurdles are helping build the resilience and gravitas needed to fully step onto your soul's stage.

The Aries New Moon on March 29th, electrified by a Partial Solar Eclipse, provides rocket fuel for pivotal new beginnings in your professional and public realms. But with pragmatic Saturn's influence, your efforts must be grounded in sustainable strategies and diligent commitments. This eclipse marks the emergence of a new you that is ready to lead, be seen and share your authentic gifts fearlessly with the world.

In mid-April, expansive Jupiter's challenging square to transformative Pluto illuminates potent psychological shadows and power dynamics needing to be reckoned with in your closest unions. Toxic patterns of control, repression or subconscious sabotage get exposed, catalyzing profound emotional renewal and liberation within your bonds. For some, this could initiate relationship endings if necessary for growth. For others, a soul-rebirthing recommitment. Stay open to the lessons and prepare to do the deeper work.

June brings an exhilarating but also potentially volatile energy as your ruling planet Mars barrels into your sign on the 17th, stoking your courage, passion and personal willpower for the first time in two years. While this transit amplifies your charisma and capacity for bold self-expression, it also increases propensity for conflicts, power struggles and reactive outbursts you'll need to temper. Channel this forceful fire sign energy into assertive goal-setting and courageous authenticity, but avoid burning bridges selfishly.

The Lunar Eclipse in Sagittarius on June 11th shines a spotlight on your 9th house of wisdom, growth experiences and worldly exploration. An awakening around your personal philosophies, belief structures or perspectives on "truth" could rock your world, setting you on an expanded trajectory to broaden your horizons through travel, cross-cultural immersion or higher learning. Be open to exploring new teachings and leaving your comfort zones. Unexpected journeys await!

The season of Cancer arrives on June 20th with the Solstice, kicking off your personal New Year energy! At this auspicious time, take stock of the profound shifts that have already occurred and set empowered intentions for the continued rebirth and reclamation of your sovereignty in the months ahead. The New Moon in your sign on June 26th provides cosmic fertile ground for these new beginnings, whether personal evolutions or launches of important initiatives.

July 16th brings sweet relief from the intense activations of the first half of the year as abundant Jupiter finally shifts into Cancer and your 4th house of home, family and emotional foundations. For the next 12 months, you'll experience expansive blessings in nurturing your deepest feelings of safety, belonging and inner contentment. This is a beautiful year for strengthening family bonds, creating your dream living space, and establishing roots that allow you to blossom into your most authentic self. Make your home a sanctuary.

The second half of 2025 requires your focus and determination as Saturn finally arrives at his destination in Aries and your 10th house of worldly domain. From August through 2028, you'll face an extended period of being tested around commitment to your ambitions and long-term goals. Structures and diligence will need to be constructed to support the public emergence and visibility your soul's work requires. Know that these challenges, while demanding, are ultimately fortifying your force of character as a respected master at the height of your craft or calling.

September brings more evolutionary shifts and reinventions as the Virgo New Moon on the 22nd arrives accompanied by a Partial Solar Eclipse in your 5th house of creativity, joy and self-expression. With catalytic

Pluto involved, you may experience sudden awakenings or breakdowns around how you've been self-censoring your authenticity and playing it "safe" with sharing your full truth. This cosmic rebirthing sets you on a raw, courageous path of unapologetically creating from your heart's inspiration and no longer suppressing your passions for anyone's approval. Flow your art, speak your poetry, birth your unique creations without fear!

This theme of authenticity and celebrating your life force currents extends into your relationships as well, with passionate Mars entering your partnership sector on September 22nd. You may experience a rekindling of romantic sparks and creative collaborations that feel energizing and liberating. For some, this initiates new attractions that help you embody your sensual essence. However, watch for power dynamics or ego conflicts arising that require clear boundaries and vulnerability. Lead with the radiant heart you've reclaimed.

The year begins winding down in October with expansive Jupiter entering your communication sector on the 21st, blessing you with inspiration, optimism and new avenues for sharing your ideas/philosophies more widely. Higher learning curriculums, writing/media projects or publication endeavors get green-lit during this transit into mid-2026. Share your unique voice and watch your reach organically grow.

Anchor into your personal power, wisdom and emotional mastery as the astrological year concludes in December with a Capricorn New Moon Solar Eclipse in your 8th house of intimacy, shared resources and psycho-spiritual rebirth. This potent lunation shines a light on any remnant self-sabotaging patterns of disempowerment, lack mentality or limiting beliefs around your Divine deservingness of sovereignty. With Pluto involved, emotional catharsis unlocks profound awakenings and richer capacities for vulnerability and tantric merging—whether figuratively with the Beloved Self, or literally with others. Own your depth, radiance and multitudes, honorable Cancer. You've reclaimed your majesty.

This year, the planets are conspiring to purify you of layers of conditioning and programming that have obscured the magnitude of your luminous, feeling, psychically potent essence. While intense internal and external shake-ups will feel confronting at times, trust these are necessary initiations into a more authentic, self-actualized version of your soul's intentions. Embrace solitude when you need it, but know your sensitivity is also a source of profound strength to be shared with the world. Allow the currents of 2025 to awaken you to the depths of your being, so that from these cleansed roots, you can more radiantly embody and manifest your soul's wisdom out into sacred form. The journey inward ultimately births the beauty outward.

January 2025

Overview Horoscope for the Month:

As we ring in the new year, the celestial energies are beckoning you inward, dear Cancer. With a powerful lineup of planets traveling through the deep, transformative waters of Pisces, January 2025 emerges as a time for profound introspection, emotional release, and a return to your intuitive roots. While the external world may seem hushed, a rich inner awakening is stirring that will ultimately rebirth you with greater sensitivity and connection to your soul's truth. Prepare to go within and listen.

Love:

Your romantic partnerships take on an intense, soul-merging tone this January thanks to Venus and Mars transiting through Pisces and igniting your 8th house of intimacy and psychic bonding. Existing bonds will feel driven to explore deeper levels of erotic communion, emotional transparency, and shared vulnerability. For singles, attractions could feel fated or catalytic for core psychological work and profound awakenings. However, power dynamics or shadow projections in relationships may also get triggered now, requiring you to strengthen self-awareness. Lead with your heart's wisdom.

Career:

While your external career goals may not be the major focus this month, Cancer, January's cosmic energies are offering you opportunities to realign your professional path with greater authenticity and purpose. With taskmaster Saturn still trekking through your public sector until May, you'll continue being pushed to show up with maturity and personal authority. However, the Pisces planets are also illuminating blind spots or misalignments between your worldly ambitions and your innermost values. Get clear now on the "why" fueling your work to manifest increased soul-fulfillment moving forward.

Finances:

The Capricorn energies of the past few months brought a pragmatic focus on budgets, financial strategy, and building material security, dear Cancer. In January though, the celestial tides turn more toward assessing your ingrained beliefs, attachments, and shadows related to abundance, self-worth, and wealth consciousness. With transformative Pluto traveling with the Sun, this is an incredibly fertile period for doing the inner work to heal your relationship to money, releasing fears or limiting patterns that block greater prosperity. Trust this psycho-spiritual excavation process, however intense.

Health:

With outgoing Mars touring your restful 12th house this January, you'll likely be craving extended time and space to nurture your spiritual and emotional wellbeing. Take advantage of this cosmic pause by immersing yourself in restorative practices that soothe your sensitive soul - things like meditation, breathwork, artistic expression or spiritual studies. Nourish yourself with solitude, gentle bodywork, and honoring any feelings that need to be felt and released. As the first month of the year, this is a beautiful reset for your mental, physical and psychic self-care.

Travel:

With so much inward-turning, psychological energy swirling this month, international travel or worldly adventures feel less emphasized in January, dear Cancer. However, you may feel drawn to taking rejuvenating solo retreats or pilgrimages to sacred sites that replenish your spiritual wellspring. Locations near bodies of water could feel especially cathartic, as could any place that facilitates solitude, ritual, and deepening your mystical studies or connections. For now, look for inspiration closer to home before venturing afar later in 2025.

Insights from the Stars:

The key astrological forces illuminating your journey through January are all about diving inward to access the wisdom of your subconscious, dear Cancer. This is a potent period for psychological and spiritual rebirth where you'll be pushed to confront any shadows, attachments or fears that have disconnected you from your sensitivity and authentic self-expression. While this process could feel intense or disorienting at times, trust that it's divinely choreographed to purify you down to your truth. Embrace solitude and trust the signs from your dreams and visions. Tremendous growth lives in surrendering to your intuition.

Best Days:

January 6th: Mars sextile Uranus - Seize this energy for assertion, innovation, and following your personal freedom!

January 14th: Venus sextile Uranus - Your powers of attraction, joy and magnetism get amplified. Socialize!

January 18th: Mercury conjunct Pluto - Fantastic for delving into psychological depths through research or conversations.

January 23rd: New Moon in Aquarius - This group-oriented lunation provides fertile soil for social initiatives or original collaborations.

January 30th: Uranus stations direct - Clarity and momentum returns after periods of reassessment. Stay open-minded..

February 2025

Overview Horoscope for the Month:

February brings a powerful convergence of planetary energies that will catalyze major shifts and transformations in your life, dear Cancer. The first half of the month is marked by a buildup of intensity, with Mars retrograding back into your sign on the 6th. This cosmic backspin will prompt you to revisit unfinished emotional business and reclaim your personal power. Simultaneously, revolutionary Uranus forms a potent alignment with the karmic North Node on the 7th, electrifying your spiritual axis. Profound awakenings are imminent!

The Full Moon Lunar Eclipse in Leo on the 12th is a game-changer. Monumental events surrounding relationships, creative expression, and your ability to shine could dramatically reshape your life's trajectory. Have courage and embrace the inevitable metamorphosis. The second half of February brings welcome relief as Mars turns direct on the 23rd, helping you reassert your drive. Anchor into your truth as the New Moon in Pisces (27th) opens a fertile cycle for planting intention seeds.

Love:
Your love life takes a radical turn this month as dynamic forces conspire to obliterate stale relating patterns. If coupled, Venus's lengthy journey through fiery Aries could inflame passions deliciously or problematically, depending on how consciously you wield this potent erotic energy. Power struggles and control issues may erupt, teaching you invaluable lessons about balancing autonomy and intimacy. An openness to transform your union is required.

For singles, this month's cosmic turbulence could abruptly sever karmic ties, making room for a soul-shaking connection. Be vigilant for someone who magnetically draws you out of your defensive shell. Just ensure you aren't being lured by an unhealthy rescuer-fixer dynamic. Above all, February demands you love yourself unconditionally through this molting process.

Career:
The first three weeks of February are best reserved for introspection regarding your professional trajectory, rather than outward-directed ambition. With Mars backspinning through your sign until the 23rd, you may struggle with waning motivation and self-doubt. Use this pause pragmatically to realign with your truest values and rework unsatisfying lifestyle patterns.

After Mars turns direct on the 23rd, you'll regain clarity and forward momentum. The potent Pisces New Moon (27th) opens an auspicious two-week period for planting seeds, be they job applications, business proposals, or creative projects expressing your talents. Have faith that the universe is conspiring to illuminate an authentic path aligned with your soul's purpose.

Finances:

Financial tensions could escalate to a breaking point in February, presenting you with radical choices to stabilize your economic foundation. An opportune Jupiter-Pluto alignment on the 17th brings the potential for a lucrative investment or strategy to increase prosperity. However, you may also be challenged to confront self-limiting attitudes impacting your abundance.

The Full Moon Lunar Eclipse (12th) could expose monetary vulnerabilities within a partnership that require you to rebalance the giving and receiving scales. Approaching issues of shared resources from a space of wisdom rather than fear will be a potent money magnet. As the month concludes, find inspired ways to monetize your passions and you'll attract abundance.

Health:

Take radical preventative self-care measures in February as this month's astrological intensity places considerable strain on your body's energetic reserves. With Mars retrograding through your sign until the 23rd, you'll need to consciously conserve vitality by resting deeply, staying hydrated, and simplifying your schedule. Meditative practices like yin yoga can counter excess cardinal fire and settle unrested minds.

The Pisces New Moon (27th) begins a fertile cycle for overhauling unhealthy lifestyle habits. Start a detoxifying cleanse, explore alternative therapies, or reduce your exposure to environmental toxins. Listen to your body's wisdom - it's communicating crucial messages about restoring equilibrium. Above all, treat yourself with infinite compassion as you shed old skins.

Travel:

Travel could figure prominently for you this month, whether literal or philosophical journeying. The Full Moon Eclipse on the 12th may open surprising gateways to venture abroad for personal or professional reasons, perhaps unexpectedly. Wherever you roam, step fully into the unfamiliar with a spirit of adventure.

For those staying closer to home, February's metamorphic energies make local exploration equally enriching. Wander alone in nature and study your reactions to the changing scenery. Be open to synchronicities illuminating your life's path. Above all, embrace an attitude of pilgrimage and sacred wonderment - the entire world is a classroom revealing vital lessons.

Insights from the Stars:

The cosmic skyscape in February imparts the wisdom that rebirth can only arise through the courageous release of all that no longer serves your highest evolution. You are being initiated into deeper self-mastery and spiritual authenticity, however disruptive or uncomfortable the metamorphic process may feel. Trust that you are being stripped of inessential baggage so your most brilliant light can shine forth unobstructed.

This is a prolific time for planting seeds, so visualize your soul's most cherished dreams with laser-focused intention. What you emanate now has incredible gestative power to bloom exponentially when properly nourished. Perhaps most importantly, remember you are never alone on this journey - unseen cosmic forces are offering protection, direction and abiding love.

Best Days of the Month:

February 7th: Uranus conjoins the North Node, catalyzing lightning-bolt revelations and spiritual awakenings.

February 12th: The Full Moon/Lunar Eclipse in Leo brings cathartic releases and dramatic plot twists in your life story. Surrender to the emotional depths.

February 17th: A Jupiter-Pluto alignment brings opportunities for financial breakthroughs and increased prosperity.

February 23rd: Mars turns direct in your sign after a lengthy retrograde, helping you regain confidence, courage and forward momentum.

February 27th: The New Moon in Pisces opens a fertile new cycle for planting intentions and manifesting your inspired visions into reality.

March 2025

Overview Horoscope for the Month:

March opens up a cosmic gateway into new beginnings and fresh energy for you, Cancer. After an intense February, you'll feel a welcome reprieve as the Sun enters Aries on the 20th, kicking off the astrological new year in your relationship sector. This sparks a revival in your one-on-one connections and important partnerships. The New Moon in Aries on the 29th marks a powerful rebirth for how you relate. If coupled, renew your commitment to cooperation and compromise. If single, prepare for magnetic connections that reflect your evolving values.

Love:

Your love life undergoes a delicious reawakening this month as romantic potential fills the air. Venus, the planet of love, shifts into Aries on the 30th, activating passion and desire in your relationships. If involved, this cosmic honeymoon phase helps reignite the spark, but be mindful of old attachment patterns resurfacing. For singles, you'll feel an urge to merge coming on strong - just be discerning about who you choose to entangle with.

An exciting development arrives when lusty Mars enters Leo on the 18th, heating up your intimacy sector for the next six weeks. Creative expressions of affection and sexuality are favored now. Just watch for melodrama or power struggles that could accompany this fiery transit.

Career:

Your professional life is cosmically activated this month as the Aries New Moon on the 29th opens an auspicious new career cycle! The next two weeks are prime for launching enterprises, updating your resume/portfolio, or applying for new positions. Stay motivated, as opportunities are presenting themselves for you to make an impact.

However, with Mars transiting your privacy sector until the 18th, you may struggle with waning ambition or distractions on the home front. Save outward-directed efforts for after mid-month when you'll receive a welcome boost of energy for going after your goals with full force.

Finances:

Financial matters stabilize for you in March after any upheavals in February. An auspicious Jupiter-Chiron alignment on the 18th helps resolve monetary blocks or brings opportunities for increasing your prosperity. If debt has been weighing you down, this cosmic bonus helps you gain traction on a payment plan.

Stay attentive around the Full Moon on the 14th, which could expose vulnerabilities around shared resources that require renegotiation within a partnership. In general, this month is favorable for reviewing your cash flow and making thoughtful adjustments to build greater security.

Health:

With March's planets traveling through grounded earth signs, you'll be supported in establishing sustainable self-care routines this month. The first half finds potent Mars visiting your private sector, signaling your body requires extended rest and rejuvenation. Don't overtax your energy reserves now - schedule plenty of downtime.

As Mars moves into Leo mid-month, your vitality and motivation soar! Engage your creativity through dance, outdoor activities, or vibrant exercise that suits your current fitness level. The earthy Aries New Moon on the 29th is perfect for planting seeds like a new workout regimen or meal plan that supports your holistic well-being.

Travel:

March isn't the most auspicious month for taking extended journeys, with the planets focusing your gaze inward. However, the Full Moon in earthy Virgo on the 14th could bring an opportunity to visit nearby nature locales that help ground and recenter you. Solo hikes or beach strolls are favored now to reconnect with your elemental roots.

If traveling for business, the lunar eclipse on the 14th may unexpectedly require a work-related trip that ultimately expands your perspectives in positive ways. Just be sure to build in enough personal time to counterbalance heavy demands. An open mind and heart allows wisdom to flow from unexpected sources.

Insights from the Stars:

The star wisdom this month reminds you that your perspective creates your reality, beloved Cancer. As the feisty Aries energies pour into your relationships, remain mindful of where you're projecting old stories or limiting assumptions onto others. Choose to meet connections from a refreshed, receptive state and watch how dynamics beautifully transform and realign.

With six planets touring earthy Taurus and Virgo in March, you're also being encouraged to root more deeply into your body and surrounding environment. Replenish your spiritual and energetic stores by reverencing Mother Earth's tangible abundance. Savor nourishing flavors, sensual textures, euphonic sounds - open all your senses to receiving the divine generosity of nature's blessings.

Best Days of the Month:

March 6th: First Quarter Moon in Gemini - Edifying discussions and short trips satisfy your curiosity.

March 14th: Full Moon Lunar Eclipse in Virgo - A release around work or health, with positive developments despite any initial chaos.

March 18th: Jupiter sextile Chiron - Lady Luck smiles upon you, helping you resolve financial/mindset blocks.

March 20th: Sun enters Aries - A whole new personal cycle dawns, revitalizing you with fresh spirit!

March 29th: New Moon in Aries - An auspicious window opens for planting seeds of intention in your relationships.

April 2025

Overview Horoscope for the Month:

April kicks off with potent cosmic energy activating your sectors of daily work, wellness routines, and small services to others. You'll be motivated to tackle any lingering tasks or chores around the home while also focusing on self-improvement. The New Moon in Aries on the 29th provides a fertile reboot for establishing productive habits and schedules. Just watch for moodiness or impatience during the first half of the month while fiery Mars travels through your privacy zone.

The fortunate trine between Jupiter and the karmic North Node on April 17th brings blessings through your social networks. Existing connections could lead to fortunate new opportunities blossoming. Prioritize circulating with those who inspire your highest vision. You're magnetic this month for attracting helpful people and fortuitous circumstances aligned with your soul's evolution.

Love:

April's planetary energy is largely focused on more pragmatic domestic and work matters rather than romance - but that doesn't mean your love life will be dull! In fact, this month provides some sweet surprises on the relationship front.

If coupled, the playful Aries New Moon (29th) helps reignite the fun, passion and laughter you first fell in love over. It's the perfect time for a spontaneous weekend getaway or any break from routine that allows you to reconnect as lovers. For singles, exciting introductions through friends, local networks or group activities are likely from mid-month onward once Mars fires up your social sector on the 18th. Be open to sparks flying when you least expect it!

Career:

Your work and life routines receive a cosmic reboot this April that allows you to hit refresh with increased energy, discipline and enthusiasm. The Aries New Moon in your six sector of habits on the 29th launches a fertile cycle for establishing better patterns around self-care, schedules and any job searching. With six planets touring earthy Taurus, you'll have abundant stamina and patience for making gradual, sustainable progress.

Expansion arrives around the 17th when the North Node aligns with expansive Jupiter. An opportunity to increase your income or launch an entrepreneurial venture may present itself during this auspicious window. Don't hesitate to showcase your skills and what you can offer prospective employers or clients. This month helps you assert your true worth in the workplace.

Finances:

Financial themes take a more positive turn this month after any February turbulence was cleared out by last month's eclipses. As disciplined Mars tours your resources sector until April 18th, you'll have increased motivation for budgeting, paying off debt, or carefully tracking where your money goes. This pragmatic cosmic helper can yield powerful results with a bit of strategy.

Once Mars fires up your income sector after the 18th, you could see new money-making opportunities developing, especially through social networking. The abundant North Node further amplifies your prosperity prospects, so continue showing up authentically and self-promoting your value. Positive returns are likely with concerted effort.

Health:

Make self-care routines a top priority this April while the Sun, Mercury, Venus and the karmic lunar nodes activate your wellness sector! You'll feel potently inspired and motivated to adopt positive new habits around diet, fitness, work-life balance or other lifestyle adjustments that enhance your vitality. Don't overcommit, but choose one achievable new regimen to build into your schedule.

The New Moon on the 29th is fertile for beginning a new program, treatment protocol, or different approach to managing any chronic health conditions. If the seeds you plant are nurtured consistently, you'll see wonderful results ripening by late spring! Just don't neglect sufficient rest and solitude time amidst all this productive bustle.

Travel:

Travel isn't particularly highlighted for you this month, Cancer darling. The planets are keeping your gaze directed more inwardly towards local surroundings and home atmospherics. However, the Jupiter-North Node trine on the 17th could bring global connections or mind-expanding exposures through social circles and community networks.

If you do find yourself venturing farther afield, you'll likely derive the most satisfaction from casual day trips, solo sojourns or impromptu excursions with minimal advance planning. An open, spontaneous attitude allows you to make the most of unexpected encounters or chance discoveries during transit. No complex itineraries required - just remain effortlessly engaged with the world around you.

Insights from the Stars:

April's celestial wisdom encourages you to make yourself, your self-care routines and immediate environments top priority right now. The earthy Taurus emphasis gracing the skies says, "if you focus on creating solid foundations in all aspects of your daily existence, the rest will follow." When you establish life-enhancing daily patterns early in Spring's fertile cycle, greater ease and flow will naturally emerge as a result.

So take time to make your living spaces feel grounded and nurturing. Eat nourishing whole foods and notice how your energy increases. Trade mindless digital distractions for embodied activities that engage your senses. Get plenty of high-quality sleep too. These simple adjustments, however incremental they feel, can powerfully uplift your quality of life! Also watch for opportunities arriving through your circles near month's end - embrace what wants to grow through you.

Best Days of the Month:

April 13th: Mars trines Pluto - You feel empowered pursuing your desires with unstoppable determination.

April 17th: Jupiter trine North Node - An incredibly fortunate transit presenting golden opportunities via social connections.

April 18th: Mars enters Virgo - Your energy and ambition receive a delicious reboot after waning in recent weeks. Excitingly productive times ahead!

April 23rd: Sun enters Taurus - You're reinvigorated to establish a stable, prosperous and simple lifestyle amidst life's complexities. Grounded routines restore equilibrium.

April 29th: New Moon in Aries - The perfect launchpad for making a fresh start with habits, self-care, work or wellness pursuits..

May 2025

Overview Horoscope for the Month:

May brings positive momentum and pragmatic progress after April's earthy restart, dear Cancer. The first half of the month is highly productive as motivating Mars tours your work and health sector. Coupled with abundant planetary energy in grounded Taurus, you'll feel inspired to improve routines, organize your environments, and establish sensible foundations. Just don't become overly rigid - leave room for spontaneity!

Relief and celebration arrive in the second half of May as the Sun enters lively Gemini on the 20th, kicking off your personal annual rebirth! The New Moon in Gemini on the 26th marks an especially fertile cycle for new beginnings linked to your self-expression, self-confidence and independence. Step into the spotlight and let your unique voice shine without apology.

Love:

Relationships take on a lighter, more fun-loving quality this month as amorous Venus ingresses into versatile Gemini on June 6th. If coupled, this sweet transit helps playfulness, laughter and easy communication flow more freely between you and your partner. Take a weekend trip together or find new ways to inject spontaneity into your shared routines.

For singles, exciting new flirtations and connections seem to spark out of nowhere once the Sun shifts into your sign on the 20th. Let your natural charisma and confidence shine and romance will be hard to avoid! Just be mindful of potential melodrama or mixed signals once messenger Mercury turns retrograde mid-June.

Career:

Work matters continue commanding center-stage in the first three weeks of May as dynamic Mars tours your sixth house of daily effort and organization. Your stamina and tolerance for detailed, meticulous tasks runs especially high during this cycle, so tackle any outstanding administrative duties or health checks. Just avoid being an overzealous perfectionist - some imperfections add character!

The arrival of the Gemini New Moon on the 26th brings a joyful creative rebirth that could unlock innovative ideas for earning additional income through your natural talents and communication skills. An Etsy store, boutique consulting services, or social media opportunities are just a few options to explore further. Let playfulness guide your moneymaking mindset right now.

Finances:

Financial streams should begin stabilizing this May as your planetary ruler, the Moon, forms supportive alignments with abundant Jupiter (18th) and Pluto (30th). If monetary tension or shortages have been creating anxiety, these transits provide much-needed breathing room, potentially through new income sources, debt restructuring or shedding financial drains.

The caveat is that Mercury, which oversees commerce and transactions, will turn retrograde from May 29th through June 22nd. During this signal scrambler, avoid major purchases or investments if possible and carefully review all documents before signing. Once the coast is clear in late June, you can revise budgets and payment plans with greater clarity.

Health:

Take full advantage of May's earthy, sensual Taurus vitality by engaging in physical activities that delight your senses. Time in nature hiking, cycling or tending a garden are favored for releasing any pent-up mental tensions stored in your body. The arrival of the Gemini New Moon cycle on the 25th also marks an ideal time for making sustainable dietary shifts or establishing new fitness goals - perhaps one focused on improved mobility and breathing?

If you've been managing chronic health issues, this is a great month for exploring complementary or alternative treatments. But avoid making any big changes or decisions until Mercury's retrograde clears in late June. For now, simply gather information and get in touch with your body's messaging without overthinking.

Travel:

Travel is looking fortuitous for you this May, Cancer! Especially around the Jupiter-Moon trine (18th) and expansive Gemini New Moon cycle kicking off on the 25th. These transits bring blessings toward fun adventures, wanderlust cravings and opportunities to experience new cultures, whether locally or abroad.

Solo road trips or overnight getaways are best when you can leave spontaneously without strict scheduling. Trying something completely different from your regular routines - perhaps an immersive learning experience, retreat or cultural activity - helps you shift out of overthinking mode. The more open you can remain, the more synchronous magic moments will unfold!

Insights from the Stars:

The celestial insights this May remind you of the power in using your innate sensitivity as a sacred asset, rather than a burden. When you trust the messages your intuition and emotions are sending, infinite wisdom becomes available that the rational mind alone cannot access. This is your spiritual intelligence emerging, helping you navigate life's adventures with greater clarity and self-trust.

So breathe deeply, observe your feelings with neutral compassion, and allow yourself to experience the richness of every sense perception as it arises. The world reflects the beauty, wildness and mystery you can embrace within yourself. Shed what feels confining, and delight in embodying your unique self in joyful, playful ways. Rebirth is yours in May!

Best Days of the Month:

May 2nd: Mars trine Pluto - You feel spiritually empowered and confident to follow your instincts.

May 18th: Jupiter sextile Moon - Great good fortune arrives through networks, education, publishing or travel. An auspicious day for launches!

May 20th: Sun enters Gemini - Your personal annual rebirth begins! The month ahead is filled with spontaneity, playfulness and reawakening.

May 25th: Mars enters Leo - Your confidence, romantic desirability and creative courage is stoked for the next two months.

May 26th: New Moon in Gemini - This fertile two-week cycle kickstarts a renaissance in how you share your authentic voice and gifts.

June 2025

Overview Horoscope for the Month:

June brings an electrifying start to your personal renaissance, dear Cancer! The month begins with motivating Mars igniting your passion projects and romantic flair as it tours fiery Leo. This cosmic power injection has you radiating confidence and charisma. Just watch for flare-ups of drama or impatience once Mercury turns retrograde mid-month.

The Full Moon Lunar Eclipse on June 11th precipitates jarring events or startling revelations around your home, family or living situation that demand your full attention. Though potentially disruptive, this lunation is clearing the way for vital changes and rebirths ahead. Trust the bigger picture unfolding.

The solstice on June 20th sees the Sun entering your sign, marking your astrological new year! Set fresh intentions under the potent Cancer New Moon on the 25th. This is an epic time of rebirth, recalibration and remembering who you were born to become.

Love:

Sparks are destined to fly in your love life this June with several astrological hotspots activating your romantic sectors! In the first half, audacious Mars tours Leo, firing up your charisma and sexual magnetism. If coupled, this transit brings a resurgence of passion and playfulness. For singles, your confidence and desirability are running extremely high.

The caveat arrives when communication planet Mercury turns retrograde on June 9th until July 7th. Old relationship dynamics or past lovers could resurface now, requiring you to gain closure before moving forward. Stay self-aware about projecting melodramatic stories onto your partner too. The Lunar Eclipse on the 11th provides radical liberation from whatever has been sabotaging intimacy.

Career:

Your professional life receives an adrenaline boost early in June as lusty Mars travels through your fulfillment sector until the 17th. During this cycle, don't be afraid to assert your talents and capabilities. An unapologetic attitude and aura of charisma and ease will draw promising opportunities your way.

However, do review any important documents carefully after the 9th when messenger Mercury turns retrograde. There may be delays, misunderstandings or revisions required in contracts, negotiations or creative projects. After the 22nd, these frustrations should clear up - but maintain patience in the meantime.

The Cancer New Moon on June 25th marks the perfect yearly moment for recalibrating your career goals and updating your personal brand/mission. How do you most want to shine?

Finances:

With abundant cosmic activity lighting up your earned income sector, making money is highlighted this month! Early June could bring exciting new moneymaking avenues through your charisma, talents or creative skills as bold Mars blazes through until the 17th. Don't hesitate to showcase what you uniquely offer.

However, cosmic keystones of financial astrology - Venus and Mercury - will both be retrograde from June 3rd through July. This could invite money delays, confusion or temporary cash crunches that require extra patience and care with spending decisions. Review documents cautiously and be willing to revise plans as needed. This retrograde will clear beautifully for positive forward movement by late July.

Health:

Make caring for your body and overall vitality a top priority this June, dear Cancer! With the first three weeks activating your health and routine sector, you're being cosmically guided to take ownership of any self-care regimens or medical treatments requiring more disciplined follow-through. The results will be worth your consistent efforts!

Keep in mind that messenger Mercury will be reversing through this same area from June 16th through July, so stay open to new information that may prompt course adjustments. If you've been on the fence about trying a new modality or approach, this retrograde is fantastic for researching alternatives. Above all, nourish yourself and trust your body's wisdom.

Travel:

Unexpected travel opportunities could manifest for you from mid-June onward, whether or international voyages or unplanned staycations! With the Lunar Eclipse arriving on the 11th these trips, while potentially chaotic, are meant to awaken you to new realities. Adopt a flexible, open-hearted mindset when journeying so the universe can shower you with delightful surprises.

After the 20th when the Sun shifts into your sign, any trips are highly favored as they'll reconnect you with your truest self and soul's compass. Book spontaneously if you can or take a local excursion somewhere providing freedom and perspective-broadening. Solo adventures work best for getting centered before your big rebirth ahead.

Insights from the Stars:

This June's cosmic wisdom reminds you that rebirth is an ongoing process of spiraling ever closer to your most authentic embodied self-expression. Each year you shed old skins that no longer serve your spirit's evolution and enter fresh cycles of metamorphosis.

The Cancer New Moon on the 25th marks an especially powerful inception point for consciously embracing the core of who you've always been underneath any labels, roles or limiting stories. Emerge fully this month as your spectacular sovereign self without apologies! Let all that makes you uniquely you shine forth brilliantly like a radiant, living work of sacred art.

Best Days in June:

June 2nd: First Quarter Moon in Virgo - Energy is high for launching a new health, work or organizational regimen.

June 9th: Mercury Retrograde begins - Temporarily pause on major launches as delays or revisions may be necessary. Great for rest/introspection.

June 11th: Full Moon/Lunar Eclipse in Sagittarius - Major shakeups and disruptive events occur around home/family. Embrace the necessary transformation.

June 15th: Jupiter square Saturn - Conflicts in beliefs/philosophies require compromise and expanded perspectives.

June 20th: Sun enters Cancer - Happy Solstice and astrological new year! A beautiful rebirth commences.

June 25th: New Moon in Cancer - Make a cosmic wish for your heart's deepest desires! An incredibly fertile cycle for reinvention dawns.

July 2025

Overview Horoscope for the Month:

July marks the heart of your astrological season, providing a fertile window for reinvention and rebirth, dear Cancer. The month begins with Mercury still retrograde until the 7th, so simply allow the first week to complete any unfinished private processing before you launch bold new initiatives. After the 9th, you'll feel increasingly energized to step into the spotlight and shine!

An exciting highlight arrives on the 7th when revolutionary Uranus ingresses into Gemini, your solar house of self-expression, communication and daily routines. For the next seven years, radical awakenings and unexpected liberations will spark across these life areas - just go with the thrilling flow. The New Moon in Leo on July 24th is an ideal launchpad for creative projects synthesizing the old with the new you.

Love:

Your romantic life promises excitement and potential game-changing plot twists in July! The month begins with amorous Venus still backspinning until the 4th, bringing the possibility of reunions or second chances with past lovers. If it's meant to be, it will feel fated - but don't force anything artificial.

From mid-month onward, once love planet Venus enters Leo, passion and charisma are running extremely high. You'll be oozing magnetic radiance and desirous of fun, romance and embodying your sensual self. Just watch for melodrama or control power struggles once Venus opposes rigid Saturn on the 30th. Singles could attract intense attractions that might be karmic initiations worth exploring.

Career:

July's astrology doesn't provide an incredibly auspicious climate for outward-directed ambition, as the cosmos are focused more on your inner processes. However, you'll find inspired motivation for creative pursuits, intellectual or literary projects, and generally allowing your unique self-expression to flow freely.

The career breakthrough you've been waiting for may arrive unexpectedly after Uranus' ingress into Gemini on the 7th radically shifts your daily work patterns, routines and approach to service. Innovative new roles that allow more independence could start rolling in if you stay alert to signals from the universe.

Finances:

Financial themes could require adjustment or recalibration early in July while Mercury is retrograde until the 7th. Rather than pushing ahead with new monetary plans, use this first week to complete outstanding taxes, invoices or budget revisions so your slate is clean after the 9th.

From there, take advantage of several astrological hot spots this month reigniting your money-making magnetism! The New Moon in Leo on the 24th marks the beginning of an incredibly fertile season for manifesting lucrative offers and prosperous opportunities through talents, creativity and authenticity. Have the courage to share your gifts with the world, and the universe will reward you generously.

Health:

With the Sun and New Moon igniting your sign in July, this month provides a powerful window for hitting the reset button on any health matters and self-care routines that feel outdated or stagnant. Take this annual period to assess what is and isn't serving your vitality, then make appropriate adjustments.

Small changes to diet, fitness, rest patterns and the home environment you dwell in can yield significant long-term results. Listen to your body's intuitive guidance and invest time in therapies and modalities that restore your luminous glow from the inside out. A disciplined approach embracing realistic micro-steps is best.

Travel:

July's planetary climate creates an ambient atmosphere supporting casual day trips and impromptu wanderings close to home rather than extended journeys. However, any sojourns near water - beaches, lakes, rivers - are highly favored and could help open you to spontaneous self-realizations, creative downloads and spiritual awakenings.

When Uranus enters Gemini on the 7th, get ready for a turn of unexpected events and opportunities for travel coming your way! Exciting international connections, conference speaking opportunities or learning adventures could start popping up in the coming months through your work and routines. Resolve to stay open-hearted and embrace any opportunities to expand your vision.

Insights from the Stars:

This July's star wisdom reminds you that freedom is an inside job. Any feelings of restlessness, boredom or existential dissatisfaction you're experiencing are your soul's gentle prompts to peel off another illusory layer and express your truth more radically.

With Uranus revolutionizing your self-expression sector from the 7th onward, you're being catalyzed to embrace profound authenticity on an entirely new level. So observe the impulse for change without judging yourself - these are sacred stirrings encouraging you to metamorphose into your highest embodiment. Let inspiration flow through the cracks and surprise yourself by living ever more uninhibited.

Best Days of the Month:

July 7th: Uranus enters Gemini - A radically awakened new chapter commences around communications, local environments and routines.

July 13th: Ceres Retrograde in Aries - Reexamine patterns of self-nurturance and boundaries with family.

July 19th: Jupiter quintile Chiron - Tremendous healing and resolution around core wounds or blocks is possible. Embrace miracles!

July 24th: New Moon in Leo - The seeds you plant today have incredible gestational power. Wishes around creativity, fertility and courage bear luxuriant fruit.

July 30th: Venus opposes Saturn - Commitment issues may feel heightened, but this transit helps separate the wheat from the chaff in relationships.

August 2025

Overview Horoscope for the Month:

August brings thrilling plot twists and unexpected course corrections for you, dear Cancer! The month begins with the skies electrified by July's ingress of radically awakening Uranus into Gemini, governing your daily routines, mindset and immediate surroundings. Disruptions to your usual rhythms should be embraced as cosmic wake-up calls jolting you into greater presence.

The Leo New Moon on July 24th launched you into an extremely fertile season for creative self-expression, romantic possibilities and courageous life reinvention that peaks around the 22nd. Don't shrink from the spotlight - this is your time to shine! Just prepare for intensity when passionate Mars opposes Pluto on the 6th, which could provoke power struggles.

An especially auspicious career opening manifests near the 11th when structured Saturn forms an incredibly stabilizing trine to Uranus. An innovative work opportunity allowing more autonomy may arrive, perfectly synthesizing your evolving values with pragmatic responsibilities.

Love:

Your romantic life is absolutely sizzling throughout August's fiery Leo season! In the first half of the month, red-hot Mars blazes through your partnership sector until the 17th, catalyzing chemistry, attraction and potential power struggles with your significant other or potential paramours. Just know that any relational intensity you're experiencing is forging deeper intimacy if navigated consciously.

From the 17th onward, once audacious Mars enters Virgo, you'll find your libido running very high, with potential for secret attractions or tantalizing flirtations. Coupled Crabs should schedule ample private couple time to thoroughly indulge these erotic stirrings! However you experience the romantic renaissance this month, open yourself to magical reconnection.

Career:

With expansive Jupiter touring your success sector for the past year, opportunities for career growth and achievement have been consistently opening for you. This month, the planet of miracles forms two incredibly auspicious alignments - a trine to Chiron on August 3rd and a fortuitous sextile to Uranus on August 28th. These cosmic boosts illuminate your most authentic, soul-aligned professional path with unusual clarity.

The Saturn-Uranus trine on the 11th could bring an innovative new position, entrepreneurial idea or exciting partnership that allows you more freedom while still providing necessary structure. Be willing to embrace disruption to your usual routines - the shake-ups serve your overall evolution. Finances, responsibilities and creative expression are beautifully synthesized near month's end.

Finances:

August helps you stabilize financial foundations while also encouraging fiscal expansion through creative talents and entrepreneurship. In the first half, prudent Saturn's trine to Uranus could bring an influx of income through digitally-linked businesses or monetization of your unique skills and interests.

After the 23rd, the Sun's entry into Virgo turns your focus towards practical budgeting and rebalancing your net worth. This monthly money review is assisted by grounded, analytical Virgo energy helping you precisely allocate funds as needed while also looking for lucrative new income streams. What innovative earnings concepts can you monetize?

Health:

Your body's health is being cosmically spotlighted in August, providing important revelations and potential course adjustments or beginnings of new regimens. As go-getter Mars tours your wellness sector until the 17th, you'll feel inspired to adopt more vigorous physical routines that push you slightly outside your comfort zone. Just avoid burnout or injury from overexertion.

The New Moon in Virgo on the 23rd marks an ideal two-week phase for establishing new, sustainable lifestyle habits - perhaps an anti-inflammatory meal plan or mobility program to increase flexibility? Work with your body's wisdom and be willing to implement the changes your vitality is requiring. Nurturing self-care yields radiant results!

Travel:

Opportunities for adventure, mind-expanding cultural immersions and exciting getaways abound this month! The first two weeks are perfect for impromptu road trips or weekend excursions close to home but still imbued with spontaneity and magic. An open, playful spirit is the ideal travel mindset now.

From mid-month onward, once Mars enters Virgo, you may feel the call towards more enriching educational or consciousness-expanding voyages. Learning opportunities through workshops, retreats or intensives could arise unexpectedly - say yes! Broadening your perspectives releases you from limiting mindsets and introduces solutions beyond your previous imaginings.

Insights from the Stars:

This August's star wisdom reveals that your creative courage and self-expression are meant to be this season's headliners! Any inhibitions, plays for validation or attachments to societal approval systems are falling away so you can more freely embody the radiant artist you were born to become.
Paradoxically, it's by choosing to walk your own unconventional path - rocking the traditional career/lifestyle boat and embracing taboo subjects - that you discover your truest power and soul's purpose. Particularly when Uranus opposes the Sun mid-month, you'll feel cosmic prompts to liberate your voice in ways that may startle others but catalyze positive change. Stay spiritually inspired and let inspiration soar!

Best Days of the Month:

August 3rd: Jupiter trine Chiron - Tremendous healing, teaching and prosperity expands your influence in beautiful ways.

August 6th: Mars opposes Pluto - Heightened intensity demands radical authenticity and conscious power.

August 11th: Saturn trine Uranus - An innovative new path/opportunity opens for more autonomy and freedom within structure.

August 22nd: Mercury enters Libra - Lovely relationship renewals, creative inspiration and poetry flow abundantly.

August 23rd: New Moon in Virgo - Fertile seeds for upgrading health, work and self-care regimens are planted now.

August 28th: Jupiter sextile Uranus - Lightning bolt epiphanies and exciting changes arrive related to life philosophies or travel.

September 2025

Overview for the Month:

September is going to be an intense ride for you, Cancer! The first half of the month is turbo-charged by fiery Mars blazing through the area of your chart that rules your daily routines, work, and health. This extra cosmic energy will help motivate you to make some serious positive changes to your lifestyle and habits.

However, things get even more dramatic mid-month as we build up to the potent Virgo New Moon on September 21st, which also features a partial solar eclipse! This super-charged lunation is activating your spirituality sector, giving you a cosmic green light to purge any destructive patterns or negative mental programming that's still holding you back. As unsettling as this process may feel, trust that it's part of your personal rebirth.

The intensity keeps rising after September 22nd when go-getter Mars moves into the relationship area of your chart for the next six weeks. Your closest partnerships and situationships will likely become mirrors, reflecting back to you how courageous (or fear-based) you're being. Radical honesty with yourself and others is required.

Love:

Your love life could get spicy in the first few weeks while passionate Mars tours Virgo! Couples should make plenty of private time to thoroughly explore intimacy and release any pent-up sexual energy – this cosmic energy is meant to be expressed. For singles, you may find yourself attracting exciting new prospects, but look beneath the surface. Are they really seeking connection, or just projecting fantasies?

After mid-month when Mars shifts into Libra, any power struggles or control issues within committed relationships will absolutely come to a head. While these tensions may be uncomfortable, they're helping to reshape your relating patterns for more conscious partnerships. Don't avoid the hard talks – they're necessary for real growth.

Career:

With structured Saturn spending its final weeks in a spiritual sector of your chart, you may find yourself questioning your core dreams and beliefs about your greater purpose. September's intensity could feel profoundly unsettling at times as you let go of any outdated or limited visions that no longer resonate.

The Virgo Solar Eclipse on September 21st marks a powerful reboot for your daily work, services to others, and overall physical vitality. From this point forward, your tasks and output gain deeper meaning when linked to some higher mission. Though delays or changes may be frustrating now, the detours are ultimately adjusting your trajectory to your most impactful role. Stay open!

Finances:

September's cosmic commotion will likely bring some financial shake-ups that require you to be flexible and responsive. In the beginning of the month while Saturn is still touring Pisces, focus on reviewing any debts, investments or long-term savings strategies. Listen to your intuition over just numbers on a spreadsheet.

From September 3rd onward, the karmic North Node shifts into steady Taurus, helping you stabilize your foundations like home and income-generating assets. Patience and consistent effort yield rewards now. The end of September is an especially fertile time for manifesting lucrative business breakthroughs if you're willing to take calculated risks aligned with your higher purpose.

Health:

With fiery Mars charging through the health and routine area of your chart for the first three weeks, you'll likely feel extra motivated to adopt some new exercise, diet or self-care program that challenges you in a good way. Pick one goal that feels sustainable and pour your energy into it!

The Virgo New Moon Eclipse on September 21st kicks off a powerful new cycle for upgrading your preventative wellness practices from a holistic mind-body-spirit approach. If you've been dealing with any chronic issues, this is the time to explore complementary therapies or look at root causes. Be patient and trust that any lifestyle upgrades begun now will have long-lasting benefits.

Travel:

With go-getter Mars firing up the domestic area of your chart until September 22nd, you may feel more inspired to stick close to home this month and get productive around the house. However, any impromptu regional trips that do come up around the 21st's eclipse could bring some unexpected shakeups or detours involving friends and family. Stay flexible!

After Mars moves into your partnership sector on the 22nd, an adventurous vacation with your spouse or closest friend could be exactly what you need to help expand your perspectives. Being immersed in unfamiliar environments centered around consciousness-expanding experiences or relationships is ideal. Remember, any travel for you right now is helping you transcend limited self-beliefs, so stay open!

Insights from the Stars:

The key cosmic lesson this September is about awakening through the purging process, dear Cancer. The universe is sending some major wake-up calls designed to help shed old layers of self-deception, limiting beliefs, and fears around intimacy, purpose and authentic self-expression. While this stripping phase may feel chaotic and unsettling, try to view it from a higher lens of ultimate liberation.

The more you can embrace the dissolution and "liquefying" of your old stuck identities, the more brilliantly your true radiant essence can shine forth. Call on your bravery when the cosmos gets rocky – your personal rebirth is both necessary and inevitable. You're becoming free on the deepest soul levels.

Best Days:

Sept 3rd - True Node enters Taurus, kicking off an 18-month cycle for stabilizing your values and self-worth.

Sept 7th - Lunar Eclipse ushering in releases around your daily work, service, or health routines. Embrace change.

Sept 17th - Mars trine Pluto gives you incredible willpower and courage to pursue your heart's desires.

Sept 21st - Virgo New Moon/Solar Eclipse initiating a fertile new cycle for remaking your vitality and identity.

Sept 23rd - When Mercury enters Libra, communication and social connections will start flowing more harmoniously.

Sept 29th - Mars trine Saturn helps you take calculated risks and make bold new commitments that change the game.

October 2025

Overview for the Month:

Buckle up, Cancer, because October is going to be an intense, transformational ride! The month kicks off with go-getter Mars still blazing through the relationship area of your chart, forming a fiery square to intense Pluto on the 4th. Any toxic power dynamics or deep-rooted issues in your closest partnerships will absolutely demand to be dealt with - no more bypassing or avoiding.

However, your ability to embrace rebirth and reinvent yourself gets majorly amplified after October 24th when taskmaster Saturn moves into Aries and the most personal sector of your chart. For the next 2.5 years, this planet is going to be stripping away anything inauthentic so that your most resilient, true self can finally emerge. While this process will inevitably feel unsettling at times, trust that it's restructuring you for an incredible evolution.

Emotional breakdowns are likely around the 26th when love planet Venus opposites shocking Uranus, shaking up your relationships and finances. But these destabilizing events are ultimately paving the way for the Scorpio New Moon Ecplise on October 27th to initiate a brand new 6-month cycle of profound personal rebirth and transformation. Get ready!

Love Life:

The romantic tensions keep rising throughout October while fiery Mars battles it out with powerful Pluto (4th) and then forms a challenging square to structure planet Saturn (23rd). If there's any unfinished baggage, manipulation games or control issues playing out in your closest partnerships, they're going to reach a breaking point now. You'll have to decide whether to make soul-level, permanent changes or consciously walk away.

That said, a surprising breath of fresh air arrives mid-month when Mars links up with revolutionary Uranus on the 17th, potentially introducing exciting new relationship prospects or alternative relating models you could explore. Stay open-minded and non-judgmental about whatever excites your spirit! Just watch for disruptive plot twists and breakdowns around month's end when Venus clashes with Uranus - these are ultimately catalyzing positive growth.

Career:

October kicks off a profoundly pivotal 2.5-year career cycle with structured Saturn's ingress into Aries and your identity sector on the 24th. For the next few years, this planet will be overhauling your self-concept and dismantling any professional paths, goals or work that's misaligned with your soul's truth. While feeling disoriented at times is inevitable, these mini-destructions create space for rebuilding a fully authentic vocation.

Luckily, the Scorpio New Moon Solar Eclipse on the 27th marks the start of a fertile new 6-month cycle of reinvention linked to your self-worth, income streams and confidence in sharing your unique gifts. As layers of outdated identities peel away, you'll start attracting career opportunities that are a true soul-level match. Follow any unconventional callings now without self-doubt.

Finances:

You'll receive more than one wake-up call around money matters this October, requiring you to stabilize your foundations but also embrace innovative income streams that feel spiritually-aligned. First, on the 17th, prosperous Jupiter clashes intensely with transformative Pluto, amplifying the consequences of any overspending, debt accumulation or financial recklessness.

However, abundance breakthroughs are very possible when the karmic North Node aligns with Jupiter later in the month, showering you with blessings and prosperity through your social networks or community engagement. Just steer clear of any risky money moves around the 26th's Venus-Uranus clash, which could bring some chaotic cash crunches. Be patient - the bigger picture is unfolding positively.

Health:

With powerhouse Saturn entering one of the health zones in your chart on October 24th, tuning into your body's needs and establishing consistent self-care rituals becomes an absolute cosmic priority for the next 2.5 years. Any unhealthy imbalances or lifestyle ruts you've been in will inevitably be destabilized now, pushing you to get proactive through positive new routines, treatments or modalities.

The Scorpio Solar Eclipse on the 27th clears the way for an especially fertile mind-body rebirth cycle to begin in November/December. This lunation is nudging you to approach your vitality from a holistic perspective, exploring modalities that honor the whole human being rather than just symptoms. Consider reviving some ancient or ancestral wisdom about natural living too.

Travel:

Expect the unexpected when it comes to travel this October! Any trips that do manifest - whether planned in advance or highly spontaneous - are absolutely guaranteed to shake up your perspectives and deliver eye-opening revelations that catapult your personal growth.

Your craving for adventure and mind-expanding journeys intensifies from mid-month onward once Mars links up with revolutionary Uranus on the 17th. Whether it's an off-the-beaten-track bucket list destination, a rustic retreat or consciousness-centered intensive, being immersed in new cultural scenery will powerfully inspire you on many levels. Don't hesitate to pack your bags and go wherever calls you boldly!

Insights from the stars:

The big cosmic lesson radiating through the stars this October centers around authenticity and self-actualization being the keys to your ultimate freedom and liberation, dear Crab. Over these next few years, Saturn's influence in your identity sector will inevitably cause any self-limiting identities, values or paths that don't resonate with your soul's truth to shatter and collapse.

While these seeds of ego-dissolution may feel incredibly disruptive across your personal or professional life, it's vital to zoom out and view everything through a higher lens of spiritual awakening. You're being divinely broken down so that you can fully rebirth into the most luminous version of your authentic self. Summon your courage through the chaos, stay spiritually inspired, and prepare yourself to radically embody who you were born to become!

Best Days of the Month:

October 4th - Mars-Pluto square reigniting intensity around intimacy, boundaries and power dynamics demanding change.

October 13th - Aries Full Moon marking a culmination or revelation around identities, independence and life direction.

October 17th - Jupiter-Pluto square and Mars-Uranus trine presenting game-changing opportunities for reinvention/expansion if you take calculated risks.

October 24th - Saturn's powerful ingress into Aries kicks off a 2.5-year cycle overhauling your purpose, identity and lifecourse.

October 27th - Scorpio New Moon/Solar Eclipse catalyzing a 6-month rebirth process linked to your confidence and ability to monetize your unique gifts and talents.

November 2025

Overview for the Month:

November promises to be a pivotal month of profound inner shift and outer restructuring for you, Cancer. The intensity from October's eclipses and planetary ingresses continues building, ultimately culminating in a cosmic reckoning of sorts by month's end. Stay centered and trust that these turbulence are serving your greater awakening and evolution.

The first three weeks bring a slowed, introspective pace as messenger Mercury turns retrograde on November 9th. Use this signal scrambler for productive rest, reflection and tying up any loose ends. By the 20th, you'll feel immense motivation returning for manifesting positive changes on the material plane.

An especially accelerated period arrives on November 27th when warrior planet Mars forms an electrifying alignment with engineering Saturn. This cosmic power couple inspires you to take calculated risks and make bold commitments aligned with your soul's truth. Monumental transformation and quantum leaps are absolutely inevitable now!

Love:

Your love life is likely to be a source of significant growth and possible turbulence this November. If in an existing partnership, simmering tensions, resentments or control dynamics that have been brewing could reach a breaking point during the first half of the month as Mercury revisits this area of your chart. Have courage to confront lingering issues once and for all - true vulnerability and transparency are required for lasting change.

If single, your romantic resilience may feel tested as the month unfolds. However, by November's final weeks, a profound clarity and inner resetting emerges that magnetizes your future soulmate or conscious collaborators. You're evolving beyond any prior relating limitations now.

Career:

With Mercury backspinning until November 29th, this isn't an ideal cycle for outward-directed ambition, big launches or self-promotion - at least not until the second half of December after the retrograde dust settles. In the meantime, use this sleepy professional time for introspection, reassessment and tying up any loose administrative ends.

However, a hugely promising new direction begins illuminating for you around November 27th's potent Mars-Saturn alignment, which highlights hidden opportunities in your career and sense of purpose. An innovative self-employment role, leadership position or entrepreneurial collaboration could manifest, finally synthesizing your kaleidoscope of talents and spiritual beliefs into an authentic, lucrative role.

Finances:

November's planetary skies bring some turbulence and restructuring to your financial foundations, requiring patience and trust in the bigger picture unfolding. The first half of the month sees Mercury reversing through the money zones of your chart, potentially creating cash flow squeezes, payment delays or adjustments required to budgets and investments. Avoid major purchases if possible until after December 9th when the retrograde concludes.

Around the 7th, your prosperity could receive a welcome boost through expanded social networks, publishing opportunities or possibly an inheritance. Just be cautious with any risky ventures around the Lunar Eclipse on November 19th, as hidden financial vulnerabilities may suddenly be exposed within a business or partnership.

Health:

Your physical vitality becomes replenished this November after several months of potential depletion or burnout. The first three weeks of the month are ideal for engaging in self-care practices, establishing sustainable exercise routines and easing back into wellness regimes. With Mercury retrograde through this sector until Thanksgiving, you may need to research alternative therapies or mindset shifts to support your holistic well-being.

After the 20th, you'll feel an undeniable surge in vigor and motivation to implement positive lifestyle upgrades, new diets or workout programs. An auspicious healing window opens in early December, so be patient about making any major health overhauls now - simply set the philosophical foundation and establish productive daily habits.

Travel:

The cosmic winds are not particularly favoring adventurous journeys or exploration in November, dear Crab. The first three weeks see Mercury reversing through the wanderlust zone of your chart, increasing the potential for miscommunications, delays and general chaos when traveling - you may need to reschedule any trips planned for this cycle.

However, the end of November ushers in an electrifying Mars-Saturn alignment that could deliver unexpected opportunities for travel connected to business or entrepreneurial themes in early 2023. Remain open to attending conferences, educational retreats or other "working vacations" that expose you to expansive personal and professional growth. This window is about expanding your vision of what is truly possible.

Insights from the Stars:

The key cosmic insight radiating through November's stars reveals the profound inner metamorphosis occurring within you, Cancer. Any stubborn self-limiting beliefs, fears or outdated attachments obstructing your path will absolutely reach a breaking point under this month's astrological heat, forcing you to transmute them into higher states of consciousness.

Rather than clinging to stories of victimhood, you're being spiritually awakened to recognize your own divine power to reshape reality through focused intention, thoughts and emotions. As chaotic as November's intensities may feel, try to align with the unstoppable, self-sovereignty emerging within your soul! The universe is conspiring to liberate you into your full authentic potency.

Best Days of the Month:

November 7th: North Node aligns with Jupiter - opportunities for income growth and expansion through social networks, education or publishing.

November 9th: Mercury Retrograde begins - delays, revisions and miscommunications around career, routine and self-care become activated. Rest and reflect.

November 19th: Full Moon Lunar Eclipse - exposing hidden financial vulnerabilities or imbalances within a business/partnership. Adjust accordingly.

November 20th: Sun enters Sagittarius - Your vital energies receive a welcome boost after last month's potential depletion.

November 27th: Mars-Saturn alignment - An electrifying catalyst for calculated risk-taking and making bold, life-restructuring commitments aligned with your highest truth.

December 2025

Overview for the Month:

The year is winding down but the intensity certainly isn't letting up for you this December, Cancer! The first three weeks bring a welcome slowdown, helping you catch your breath after last month's cosmic chaos and intensity. Use this grounding period to reflect, rest and realign before an incredibly fertile new annual cycle kicks off around the 21st.

You'll start to feel your vital life force returning as the Sun enters Capricorn on the 21st, aligning with the Solstice and activating your personal rebirth. The New Moon in Capricorn two days later marks an extraordinary window for resetting intentions and planting seeds for manifestation in 2026. Give yourself permission to boldly dream into the grandest visions for your becoming!

While the holidays could stir up some sentimental visitors from your past, maintain your center as you approach this threshold initiation. You're being divinely guided to shed any remaining limiting attachments so you can finally emerge as the fully empowered sovereign you were born to become.

Love Life:

Your romantic connections and partnerships continue undergoing major transformations in December, as the month's astrology contains both significant blessings and potential disruptions. If in a committed relationship, challenges that surfaced in November could reach a make-or-break climax early in the month. Have courage to either recommit on an entirely new level of intimacy, truth and transparency, or lovingly part ways.

For singles, December could see you attracting thrilling new amours and flirtations, but be discerning about motivations. Is this potential suitor aligned with your values and evolution? Pleasure-seeking connections without depth may disappoint. Your resilience will be tested to see how grounded you are in self-love.

By the Solstice on the 21st, an attitude of romantic renewal and passion blossoms! Singles will magnetize soulmate connections attuned to their rebirth, while couples experience psychic rejoining through vulnerability and mutual surrender. Follow the currents of love consciously unfolding.

Career:

After November's potential stagnation or uncertainties in your professional life, December delivers a breath of revitalizing fresh air for manifesting breakthroughs! The first three weeks are perfect for resting and resetting so you can clarify your vision. Then from the 21st onward, you'll feel unstoppable motivation and enthusiasm.

The New Moon on the 23rd marks an ideal time to take action steps towards manifesting an authentic vocation in alignment with your reawakened passion and soul's purpose. Any innovative entrepreneurial ideas, indie creative projects or leadership roles helping uplift humanity are destined to thrive. Focus on demonstrating your unique value and gifts.

However, you could also encounter obstructive egos or power struggles with colleagues or partners this month who aren't aligned with your mission. Stay impeccable in your integrity and witness jealousy or dismissiveness with compassion. Rise above any naysayers.

Finances:

The financial sectors of your chart receive multiple cosmic boosts this December that could yield exciting windfalls or income surges in 2026. However, you'll first need to get a bit more rigorous about examining your financial foundations and making adjustments early in the month.

Around the 7th, review any blind spots in your budgets, investments or revenue streams. With structured Saturn touring your money zone for the next few years, building sustainable practices around earning and allocating your resources is required for growth. Cosmic helpers like the Capricorn New Moon on the 23rd magnetize powerful opportunities to monetize your offerings and talents. Invest in your worth!

Health:

Your physical vitality makes a strong resurgence throughout December after any potential depletion or imbalances late last year. The first three weeks provide a sweet spot for resting, turning within and attuning to your body's wisdom without outer pressures. Take some rejuvenating solo time in nature to decompress and recenter.

After the 21st, you'll feel powerfully motivated to upgrade lifestyle habits and daily routines around diet, fitness, sleep and stress management. The New Moon on the 23rd launches an especially fertile new cycle for embracing mind-body modalities that honor your holistic wellbeing. What new rituals feel energetically aligned?

Travel:

With go-getter Mars touring the wanderlust sector of your chart from mid-month onward, you'll likely feel an inexorable pull to seek scenery and environments beyond your usual stomping grounds. This cosmic helper provides tremendous courage, momentum and virility for epic adventures to destinations that help expand your perspectives!

Use the slower first three weeks to plan out any bucket list journeys you're feeling inspired to embark upon in 2026. Whether an international pilgrimage, conscious retreat or exploration of sacred sites closer to home - you're being divinely guided to step outside your comfort zones. Where is your soul calling you to explore? Book those flights!

Insights from the Stars:

The key celestial insight woven through December's skies is one of profound individual empowerment and sovereignty through self-trust. Any lingering attachments to disempowering narratives, limiting beliefs, or approval seeking from external sources is cosmic completion -you're outgrowing the old entirely.

As the calendar year draws to a close, you're experiencing an extraordinary soul-level rebirth and the births of an entirely new relating to yourself, your purpose and untamed authenticity. Your words, presence, and quality of love you radiate are destined to move worlds if you simply surrender attachments to the known and remain open to the surprising awe your future holds. Trust your process. Magic is upon you.

Best Days of the Month:

December 3rd: Gemini Full Moon - Epiphanies and possible reunions around communications, mindset or local communities. Revelations abound.

December 7th: Mercury Direct - The cosmic messenger finally goes direct after an extended retrograde period, clearing the path forward. Review your budgets/investments.

December 14th: Venus enters Aquarius - Your social connections and networks become activated for positive synchronicity and expansion. Say "yes!"

December 21st: Sun enters Capricorn/Solstice - The start of an incredibly auspicious new annual cycle for you. Rebirth is initiated!

December 23rd: New Moon in Capricorn - This is your cosmic launchpad for planting seeds of new intentions and embodying your grandest, most authentic visions for 2026.

LEO 2025 HOROSCOPE

Overview Leo 2025

(July 23 - August 22)

The year 2025 promises to be a significant one for Leos, with various planetary transits and celestial events influencing different aspects of your life. Let's dive into the details and explore what the stars have in store for you.

The year begins with Mars entering Leo on April 18th, bringing a surge of energy, passion, and motivation. This is an excellent time to take initiative, start new projects, and assert yourself in your personal and professional life. With Mars in your sign until June 17th, you'll have the drive and confidence to pursue your goals and make your mark on the world.

In mid-June, Saturn briefly shifts into Aries, activating your 9th house of higher learning, philosophy, and spiritual growth. This transit may bring challenges or responsibilities related to your beliefs, education, or long-distance connections. It's essential to remain disciplined and committed to your personal growth during this time.

On July 22nd, the Sun, your ruling planet, enters your sign, marking the beginning of your birthday season. This is a time to celebrate your unique qualities, recharge your batteries, and set intentions for the year ahead. Embrace your creativity, leadership skills, and zest for life during this empowering period.

The Partial Solar Eclipse in Virgo on September 21st will occur in your 2nd house of finances and material resources. This eclipse may bring changes or new opportunities related to your income, possessions, or self-worth. It's a great time to reassess your values, set financial goals, and make practical plans for the future.

In late September, Mars enters Libra, your 3rd house of communication and learning. This transit can bring increased mental energy, curiosity, and a desire to connect with others. It's an excellent time to network, learn new skills, and express your ideas with confidence and clarity.

On October 22nd, the Sun enters Scorpio, highlighting your 4th house of home, family, and emotional foundation. This is a time to focus on your inner world, nurture your close relationships, and create a supportive and nurturing living space. Honor your emotional needs and prioritize self-care during this introspective period.

In mid-November, Venus enters Sagittarius, activating your 5th house of romance, creativity, and self-expression. This transit brings a playful, adventurous, and optimistic energy to your love life and artistic pursuits. It's a great time to take risks, try new things, and enjoy the pleasures of life.

As the year comes to a close, Jupiter enters Cancer on December 9th, bringing a 12-month cycle of growth, expansion, and opportunities in your 12th house of spirituality, intuition, and inner growth. This transit encourages you to connect with your higher self, explore your subconscious mind, and cultivate a deeper sense of peace and purpose.

Throughout the year, the Saturn-Neptune square will continue to influence your 9th and 12th houses, emphasizing the need for a balance between structure and flow, reality and imagination, in your spiritual and philosophical pursuits. Trust your intuition, stay open to new perspectives, and be willing to let go of limiting beliefs that no longer serve you.

In conclusion, 2025 is a year of personal growth, self-discovery, and new beginnings for Leo. With Mars and the Sun energizing your sign, you'll have the confidence and motivation to pursue your passions and make your dreams a reality. The eclipses and planetary transits will bring changes and opportunities in various areas of your life, from finances and relationships to education and spirituality. Stay true to yourself, embrace your unique qualities, and trust in the journey ahead. The stars are aligned in your favor, Leo, so make the most of this transformative and empowering year!

January 2025

Overview Horoscope for the Month:

January 2025 is a month of fresh starts and new adventures for you, Leo! The year kicks off with Mars, the planet of action and passion, shifting into caring Cancer on the 6th, activating your 12th house of spirituality, solitude and inner growth. You may feel a strong pull to slow down, tune into your intuition, and engage in deep self-reflection. Honor this introspective energy by creating space for meditation, journaling, or creative pursuits that allow you to process emotions and connect with your higher self.

The Full Moon in fellow fire sign Aries on the 13th illuminates your 9th house of travel, higher education and personal growth. You could have a sudden epiphany about a topic you're passionate about learning more or receive an exciting opportunity to broaden your horizons through a trip or new experience. Let your natural curiosity and zest for life be your guide.

Love & Relationships:

With Venus dancing through dreamy Pisces until the 26th, love takes on an ethereal, romantic quality for you this month, Leo. If you're coupled, prioritize quality time with your partner doing activities that inspire you and spark your shared sense of wonder, like attending a poetry reading or trying a new cuisine. You're craving soul-level connection, so don't shy away from intimate conversations about your hopes, dreams and desires.

For single Leos, the stars suggest keeping an open mind and heart. You could meet someone special while exploring a new spiritual practice or creative hobby. Focus more on the feeling of the connection versus surface-level compatibility. Trust what lights you up inside.

When Venus moves into bold Aries on the 27th, the vibe shifts to become more flirty, direct and adventurous. Take the lead in love and don't be afraid to make the first move if you feel a spark. Embrace your confident, charismatic Leo nature!

Career:

Professional matters take a backseat to your personal life and inner world for much of the month, Leo. You'll be more focused on tying up loose ends and completing projects already underway versus pushing ahead on new initiatives. The Capricorn New Moon on the 29th activates your 6th house of work, health and daily routines, providing supportive energy for implementing positive new habits and getting organized. Set realistic goals and break them down into manageable steps.

Your keen intuition can be an asset in business dealings - pay attention to those gut feelings, especially around the Aries Full Moon on the 13th. Behind the scenes research, strategic planning and refining your long-term vision are favored. Be patient and trust that your hard work will pay off in perfect timing.

Finances:

Mercury's retrograde through Capricorn until the 17th could bring some delays or mix-ups in financial matters. Double check statements, be extra clear in money-related communication, and avoid making major purchases or investments if possible. Stick to your budget as best you can.

The second half of January looks more promising for your cash flow. You could receive a bonus, raise or another source of unexpected income around the Aquarius New Moon on the 29th. Focus on the big picture in regards to your finances and be open to innovative money-making ideas. Joining forces with a partner or group could prove profitable.

Health & Wellness:

Make your physical, mental and emotional well-being a top priority this month, Leo. With Mars in Cancer highlighting your 12th house of rest and healing until mid-April, honor your body's need for downtime and lean into activities that soothe your soul. Gentle movement like yin yoga, time in nature, and creative expression can be especially therapeutic.

You're also more attuned to the mind-body-spirit connection now. Consider exploring holistic healing modalities or spiritually-uplifting practices to support your vitality. Getting a massage, acupuncture treatment or energy work session could provide a much needed recharge.

Travel:

Your appetite for new experiences and adventures comes alive at the Aries Full Moon on the 13th. Plan a weekend trip or book a faraway journey to a destination that's been calling to you. Get off the beaten path and allow space for magic and synchronicity. Solo travel is especially appealing as it offers a chance to fully immerse yourself in a foreign culture and connect with your own rhythms.

If international travel isn't possible, feed your wanderlust through armchair travel - read travelogues set in exotic locales, take a foreign language class, or cook up cuisine from your dream destination. The journey is just as much internal as external this month. Let a shift in perspective be your passport to a wider world.

Insights from the Stars:

January's astrology invites you to balance the dynamic tension between rest and action, Leo. Prioritize solitude and self-care as much as possible, especially while Mars travels through Cancer, but trust your instincts around the Aries Full Moon to take a bold leap of faith. Your curiosity and optimism are your biggest strengths - harness them in service of personal growth and the greater good.

You're learning to honor your sensitivity as a superpower versus a weakness. Embrace your softer side and allow yourself to feel all the feels. Your vulnerability and innate creativity are immensely healing for yourself and others. Let your light shine from the inside out and watch how much more magnetic you become. The world needs your unique leo magic now more than ever.

Best Days of the Month:

January 7th: Venus sextile Jupiter. Luck and opportunity are on your side, especially in love and creativity. Indulge in pleasure, pampering and play. Your natural charisma and joie de vivre attract abundance.

January 13th: Full Moon in Aries. Follow your passions down an exciting new path. You're ready for an adventure of the mind, body or soul. Take a risk, travel or expand your knowledge. Freedom is your keyword.

January 22nd: Sun enters Aquarius. Focus on partnerships of all kinds and let your quirks and unique personality shine. Brainstorm brilliant ideas with friends and colleagues. Your social life brings exciting surprises.

January 27th: Venus enters Aries. Turn up the heat on passion projects and pursue what lights you up. Romance takes on a fun, flirty vibe and you're eager to make bold moves. Lead with your heart.

February 2025

Overview Horoscope for the Month:

February 2025 is a dynamic and transformative month for you, Leo! The cosmos are conspiring to help you break free from limitation and chart a bold new course for your future. The month kicks off with a potent Full Moon in your sign on the 12th, putting your desires, creativity and self-expression in the spotlight. Trust your instincts and let your authentic self shine - the world needs your unique light and leadership now more than ever.

Mars, the planet of action and ambition, stations direct in Cancer on the 23rd, ending a two month retrograde that had you focused on internal processing versus external progress. You're feeling re-energized and ready to put insights gained around your subconscious patterns and emotional needs into tangible practice. Courage and confidence are your superpowers as the month comes to a close.

Love:

With Venus gracing your 8th house of intimacy and transformation for most of February, relationships take on a deep, soulful quality. You're craving connection that goes beyond the superficial and aren't afraid to have the hard conversations in service of mutual healing and growth. This is an excellent time to address any issues around vulnerability, trust or power dynamics with a partner. For single Leos, an intense attraction could lead to a profound soul connection. Stay open to the magic and synchronicity of the universe playing matchmaker.

Communication planet Mercury moves through your 7th house of partnership from the 14th onward, making it easier to express your needs and listen intently to a loved one. You're able to strike the delicate balance between asserting your individuality and honoring your partner's desires. Shared adventures, stimulating conversation and playful flirtation keep the sparks flying.

Career:

The Aquarius Sun illuminates your 7th house of one-on-one partnerships until the 18th, making this an ideal time for collaborations and joint ventures. Teaming up with a colleague or mentor whose skills complement your own can help you make major strides towards a cherished goal. Your ability to network and connect with influential people is heightened - don't be afraid to reach out and ask for support or opportunities.

The Leo Full Moon on the 12th brings a career matter to fruition or sheds light on your professional path forward. Trust your creativity and unique self-expression to set you apart from the crowd. You're ready to step into the spotlight and take on more responsibility or a leadership role. Just be sure any attention you attract is coming from a place of authenticity versus ego.

Finances:

Money matters get a cosmic boost this month, Leo, thanks to abundant Jupiter moving through your 8th house of shared resources and investments. An inheritance, loan, bonus, tax refund or partner's financial windfall could bless your bank account in unexpected ways. Stay open to receiving and practice gratitude for the abundance flowing your way.

With Venus activating your 8th house until the 27th, it's the perfect time to review or renegotiate joint financial agreements like mortgages, loans or investments. If debt has been an issue, you've got cosmic support to create a repayment plan and stick to it. Combine your creativity and passion with practical planning to manifest prosperity on your own terms.

Health:

Mars retrograde in your 12th house of rest and healing until the 23rd continues to emphasize the mind-body-spirit connection, Leo. Honor your need for extra downtime and make space for activities that soothe and replenish your soul. Journaling, meditation, therapy and creative pursuits can be especially cathartic for processing any heavy emotions that arise.

When Mars stations direct on the 23rd, you may feel a surge of energy and renewed motivation to pursue your wellness goals. Channel this fiery momentum into establishing sustainable self-care routines that support your physical vitality. Get your sweat on with a dance or kickboxing class or take your workouts outdoors to connect with nature's rejuvenating vibes.

Travel:

Your thirst for adventure and new experiences is ignited at the Leo Full Moon on the 12th. Plan a solo getaway or book a bucket-list trip that pushes you outside your comfort zone. You're in the mood to take risks, mingle with fascinating people and immerse yourself in foreign cultures. Let your curiosity be your guide.

If long distance travel isn't possible, embrace the power of your imagination as a portal to far-off lands. Read travel memoirs, watch foreign films, take an online class in art history or mythology. Feed your wanderlust from the inside out. A weekend road trip or staycation that takes you off the beaten path could quench your thirst for excitement closer to home.

Insights from the Stars:

February's astro-weather is all about claiming your sovereignty and stepping into your power, Leo. You're being called to shed layers of conditioning and limitation in order to express your most authentic, radiant self. Let go of any masks or personas you've been hiding behind and dare to be unapologetically you. Your vulnerability is your strength.

This is also a powerful month for healing and transformation, particularly around relationships and shared resources. Invite more depth, intimacy and trust into your partnerships by fearlessly communicating your needs and holding space for others to do the same. You're ready to break free from patterns of codependency or self-sabotage in order to manifest soul-nourishing connections.

Best Days of the Month:

February 12th: Full Moon in Leo. All eyes are on you as you take a bold leap towards a cherished dream. Trust your instincts and creative vision to guide you. Your charisma and star power are undeniable.

February 16th: Sun sextile Uranus. Expect the unexpected in the best possible way. Exciting opportunities arise that align with your authentic self. Embrace your inner rebel and make a break from the status quo.

February 19th: Venus sextile Uranus. Surprises and serendipity light up your love life and creativity. An unconventional attraction or innovative idea sets your heart on fire. Embrace the magic of the moment.

February 23rd: Mars stations direct in Cancer. After two months of introspection, you're ready to charge ahead on passion projects and personal goals. Trust your instincts and channel your emotions into purposeful action. Your persistence pays off.

February 27th: Venus enters Aries. Romance takes on an adventurous, spontaneous vibe. You're feeling bold and brave in matters of the heart. Take the lead in love and be direct about your desires. Your confidence is a major turn-on.

March 2025

Overview Horoscope for the Month:

March 2025 is a month of major transitions and new beginnings for you, Leo! The headline news is Saturn, the planet of structure and responsibility, moving into your 9th house of travel, higher education and personal growth on the 24th, where it will stay until February 2028. You're entering a phase of life where you're called to expand your horizons - literally and figuratively - and commit to a path of study or experience that stretches you beyond your comfort zone. Embrace the journey of becoming the most authentic, wise and world-ready version of yourself.

The Aries New Moon on the 29th is also a potent cosmic reset that lands in your 9th house, bringing fresh opportunities for travel, learning and optimistic risk-taking. Set intentions around a bucket-list trip, enrolling in a degree program, or embarking on an entrepreneurial venture. Trust that the universe is conspiring to support your boldest, most courageous moves.

Love:

With Venus in dreamy Pisces activating your 8th house of intimacy and transformation until the 27th, your relationships take on a deeply spiritual, soulful tone this month. You're craving connection that goes beyond the superficial and taps into the realm of unconditional love and acceptance. This is a powerful time for healing any wounds around vulnerability, trust or self-worth that may be blocking you from fully giving and receiving love.

If you're coupled, prioritize quality time with your partner that nourishes your mind, body and soul. A couples' retreat, tantric workshop or shared spiritual practice can deepen your bond. For single Leos, an attraction that feels fated or karmic could sweep you off your feet. Stay open to the magic of divine timing and soul contracts. When Venus moves into Aries on the 27th, your confidence and charisma are amplified. Take the lead in love and be direct about your desires.

Career:

With the Sun illuminating your 8th house of shared resources and investments until the 20th, much of your professional focus is on maximizing joint ventures and collaborations. Teaming up with a business partner, mentor or financial advisor whose skills complement your own can help you make major strides towards a long-term goal. Don't be afraid to ask for support or delegate tasks that fall outside your zone of genius.

The Aries New Moon on the 29th is a powerful time for planting seeds of intention around your career dreams and aspirations. Think big picture and let your entrepreneurial spirit soar. You're ready to take a bold leap of faith towards a path that aligns with your purpose and passions. Trust your instincts and let your unique creative vision be your guide.

Finances:

Money matters continue to be blessed by abundant Jupiter moving through your 8th house of shared resources and investments this month. An unexpected windfall, inheritance, or partner's financial success could boost your bottom line. Stay open to receiving and practice gratitude for the prosperity flowing your way.

With Venus also gracing your 8th house until the 27th, it's an ideal time to review and renegotiate any joint financial agreements, such as loans, mortgages, or investments. If debt has been an issue, you have cosmic support to create a practical repayment plan. Combine your creativity and passion with strategic planning to manifest abundance on your own terms.

Health:

Mars, the planet of energy and action, continues its journey through your 12th house of rest and healing until mid-April, emphasizing the mind-body-spirit connection. Make space for activities that soothe your soul and replenish your energy reserves, such as meditation, yoga, or creative pursuits. If you've been burning the candle at both ends, this is your cosmic cue to slow down and prioritize self-care.

The Aries New Moon on the 29th is a powerful time for setting intentions around your wellness goals and routines. Let go of any self-defeating habits or beliefs that are holding you back and embrace a fresh start. Commit to nourishing your body with wholesome foods, regular movement, and plenty of rest. Remember, your physical vitality is the foundation for everything else in your life.

Travel:

Your wanderlust is ignited this month, Leo, thanks to Saturn's ingress into your 9th house of travel and adventure on the 24th. You're entering a three-year phase where exploring new horizons - both literally and figuratively - is a key theme. Start planning that bucket-list trip or international move you've been dreaming of. Immersing yourself in foreign cultures and perspectives can be incredibly enriching for your personal growth.

If long-distance travel isn't possible just yet, consider signing up for a workshop or retreat that expands your mind and worldview. Even armchair travel, such as reading travelogues or watching documentaries about far-flung places, can satisfy your craving for adventure. The journey is just as much internal as external.

Insights from the Stars:

March's astrology is all about embracing change and stepping into your power, Leo. You're being called to shed limiting beliefs and patterns that are keeping you stuck in your comfort zone. Saturn's move into your 9th house on the 24th is a cosmic push to take responsibility for your personal growth and commit to a path of lifelong learning. Embrace the discomfort of being a beginner and trust that every challenge is an opportunity to expand your wisdom and resilience.

This is also a potent month for healing and transformation, particularly around themes of intimacy, vulnerability, and shared resources. Let go of any fears or defenses that are blocking you from fully giving and receiving love. You're worthy of soul-deep connection and abundant support. Open your heart and trust that the universe has your back.

Best Days of the Month:

March 11th: Jupiter sextile Uranus. Unexpected opportunities and serendipitous encounters abound. Stay open to the magic of synchronicity and be ready to pivot in a new direction. Your unique skills and quirks are your superpowers.

March 14th: Full Moon in Virgo. A work project or health matter comes to fruition. Celebrate your progress and release any perfectionist tendencies. Your dedication and attention to detail pay off.

March 24th: Saturn enters Aries. Commit to a path of study, travel, or personal growth that stretches you beyond your comfort zone. Embrace the journey of becoming the wise, world-ready version of yourself. Patience and persistence are key.

March 29th: New Moon in Aries. Set intentions for bold new beginnings and adventurous pursuits. Take a leap of faith towards your dreams and trust that the universe will catch you. Your courage and confidence are magnets for success..

April 2025

Overview Horoscope for the Month:

April 2025 is a month of dynamic change and personal growth for you, Leo! The headline news is Pluto, the planet of power and transformation, beginning its 20-year journey through your 7th house of partnership on the 4th. You're entering a long-term cycle where your closest relationships will undergo a profound metamorphosis. This is a time to confront any fears or patterns around intimacy, trust, and shared power that may be holding you back from soul-deep connection. Embrace the journey of learning to love fearlessly and authentically.

The Aries New Moon on the 27th is a powerful cosmic reset that lands in your 9th house of travel, higher education, and personal growth. Set intentions around expanding your horizons through a new course of study, entrepreneurial venture, or bucket-list adventure. Trust your boldest, most visionary ideas and take a leap of faith towards your dreams.

Love:

With the Sun illuminating your 9th house of adventure and higher learning until the 19th, your romantic life takes on an exploratory, philosophical tone. You're attracted to partners who can engage you in stimulating conversation and broaden your perspective. If you're coupled, plan a trip or take a class together that pushes you both outside your comfort zone. The shared experience of learning and growing together can deepen your bond.

Venus, the planet of love and pleasure, graces your 10th house of career and public image from the 30th onwards, bringing a charming, magnetic quality to your professional relationships. Your creative talents and unique self-expression are your superpowers in the workplace. Don't be afraid to showcase your skills and advocate for your worth. A office romance or creative collaboration could also blossom.

Career:

With Mars, the planet of ambition and action, charging through your sign from the 18th onwards, your career goals get a major boost of momentum. You're feeling confident, courageous, and ready to take on new challenges. Trust your instincts and be proactive in pursuing opportunities that align with your passions and purpose. Your leadership skills and entrepreneurial spirit are in the spotlight.

The Taurus New Moon on the 27th is a powerful time for setting intentions around your professional dreams and aspirations. What legacy do you want to leave in the world? Clarify your long-term vision and take practical steps towards making it a reality. Your persistence and determination will pay off.

Finances:

With Pluto beginning its transformative journey through your 7th house of partnership on the 4th, your financial landscape may undergo some shifts in the coming years. This is a time to confront any fears or power struggles around money and shared resources. If you're in a committed relationship, have an honest conversation

YOUR COMPLETE PERSONAL HOROSCOPE 2025· 181

with your partner about your values and goals. You may need to renegotiate joint financial agreements or create a new budget that works for both of you.

The Aries New Moon on the 27th is a powerful time for setting intentions around abundance and prosperity. Trust that the universe will provide for your needs as you pursue your passions and purpose. Stay open to unexpected sources of income or financial opportunities. Your creativity and innovation are your greatest assets.

Health:

With Mars moving into your sign on the 18th, your physical energy and vitality get a major boost. You're feeling motivated to start a new fitness routine or take on a challenging athletic pursuit. Channel your competitive spirit into reaching your wellness goals, but be mindful not to push yourself too hard too fast. Listen to your body's signals and prioritize rest and recovery.

The Taurus New Moon on the 27th is a powerful time for setting intentions around self-care and nourishment. Commit to healthy habits that support your overall well-being, such as eating whole foods, staying hydrated, and getting plenty of sleep. Indulge your senses with a spa day or nature retreat. When you feel good in your body, everything else in your life flows more smoothly.

Travel:

Your wanderlust is ignited this month, Leo, thanks to the Sun in adventurous Aries activating your 9th house of travel and expansion until the 19th. You're craving new experiences and perspectives that push you outside your comfort zone. Plan a solo trip or book a group tour to a destination that's been on your bucket list. Immersing yourself in foreign cultures and landscapes can be incredibly enriching for your personal growth.

If long-distance travel isn't possible just yet, consider signing up for a workshop or retreat that expands your mind and worldview. Even armchair travel, such as reading travelogues or watching documentaries about far-flung places, can satisfy your craving for adventure. The journey is just as much internal as external.

Insights from the Stars:

April's astrology is all about embracing change and stepping into your power, Leo. Pluto's move into your 7th house of partnership on the 4th is a cosmic push to confront any fears or patterns that may be blocking you from soul-deep intimacy and connection. Trust that the universe is guiding you towards relationships that support your highest growth and evolution. Let go of any masks or defenses and allow yourself to be seen and loved fully.

This is also a potent month for expanding your horizons and taking bold leaps of faith towards your dreams. The Aries New Moon on the 27th is a powerful portal for setting intentions around travel, education, and personal growth. Trust your vision and let your passions be your compass. You have the courage and confidence to navigate any challenges that come your way.

Best Days of the Month:

April 4th: Saturn sextile Uranus. Unexpected opportunities and innovative solutions arise. Embrace change and think outside the box. Your unique perspective is your superpower.

April 12th: Full Moon in Libra. A relationship matter comes to a head. Seek balance and compromise. Lead with compassion and strive for win-win solutions.

April 18th: Mars enters Leo. Your energy, confidence, and charisma are off the charts. Take bold action towards your goals and passions. Your leadership skills are in high demand.

April 27th: New Moon in Taurus. Set intentions for financial abundance and material security. Clarify your values and commit to practical steps towards your long-term goals. Trust that you have everything you need to thrive.

Overview Horoscope for the Month:

May 2025 is a month of exciting opportunities and personal growth for you, Leo! The headline news is Jupiter, the planet of expansion and abundance, forming a supportive sextile aspect to Chiron, the asteroid of healing and wholeness, in your 9th house of travel, higher education, and personal growth on the 18th. This cosmic alignment brings a powerful opportunity to stretch beyond your comfort zone and embrace experiences that support your highest evolution. Trust that the universe is conspiring to help you grow and thrive.

The Gemini New Moon on the 26th is a potent time for setting intentions around communication, learning, and self-expression. You're feeling curious, adaptable, and ready to explore new ideas and perspectives. Embrace your inner student and let your natural charisma shine in social situations. Your unique voice has the power to inspire and uplift others.

Love:

With Venus, the planet of love and pleasure, gracing your 11th house of friendship and community from the 4th onwards, your social life is buzzing with activity. You're feeling popular, magnetic, and ready to connect with like-minded individuals who share your passions and values. Attend events or join groups that align with your interests and let your natural charm and warmth attract new connections.

If you're single, a friendship could blossom into something more romantic around the Gemini New Moon on the 26th. Keep an open mind and heart, and let your playful, flirtatious side shine. If you're coupled, prioritize quality time with your partner doing activities that bring you both joy and laughter. A double date or group outing can refresh your bond.

Career:

With Mars, the planet of ambition and action, charging through your sign all month, your career goals are infused with extra momentum and drive. You're feeling confident, assertive, and ready to take on new challenges in the workplace. Trust your instincts and be proactive in pursuing opportunities that align with your passions and purpose. Your leadership skills and creative vision are your superpowers.

The Gemini New Moon on the 26th is a powerful time for networking and pitching your ideas to others. Your communication skills are in the spotlight, so don't be afraid to speak up and share your unique perspective. A brainstorming session or collaboration with colleagues could lead to a breakthrough.

Finances:

The Scorpio Full Moon on the 12th illuminates your 4th house of home and family, bringing a financial matter to a head. You may need to have an honest conversation with loved ones about your budget, shared resources, or long-term security goals. Trust your intuition and be open to innovative solutions. A home-based business or real estate opportunity could also arise.

With Jupiter and Chiron aligning in your 9th house of expansion and growth on the 18th, you're being called to invest in experiences that stretch you beyond your comfort zone. Consider taking a course or workshop that enhances your skills and increases your earning potential. Trust that the universe will provide for your needs as you pursue your passions and purpose.

Health:

With Mars energizing your sign all month, you're feeling motivated to prioritize your physical health and well-being. Channel your competitive spirit into setting and achieving fitness goals, such as training for a race or trying a new sport. Just be mindful not to push yourself too hard too fast. Listen to your body's signals and incorporate plenty of rest and recovery time into your routine.

The Gemini New Moon on the 26th is a potent time for setting intentions around mental health and self-care. Commit to practices that calm your mind and soothe your nervous system, such as meditation, journaling, or spending time in nature. Engage your curiosity and learn something new that stimulates your intellect. When you feel mentally and emotionally balanced, your physical health flourishes.

Travel:

Your wanderlust reaches a fever pitch this month, Leo, thanks to Jupiter and Chiron aligning in your 9th house of travel and adventure on the 18th. You're craving experiences that expand your horizons and push you outside your comfort zone. Consider booking a trip to a destination that's been on your bucket list or signing up for a study abroad program. Immersing yourself in foreign cultures and perspectives can be incredibly enriching for your personal growth.

If long-distance travel isn't possible right now, seek out opportunities for adventure closer to home. Take a weekend road trip to a nearby town or explore a new neighborhood in your city. Even small shifts in your daily routine can satisfy your craving for novelty and excitement.

Insights from the Stars:

May's astrology is all about embracing growth and stepping into your power, Leo. Jupiter and Chiron's alignment in your 9th house on the 18th is a cosmic invitation to heal any wounds around your sense of purpose and direction. Trust that your unique path is unfolding exactly as it's meant to, even if it looks different than you expected. Let go of any limiting beliefs or fears that are holding you back from pursuing your passions wholeheartedly.

This is also a potent month for expanding your social circle and collaborating with others who share your values and vision. The Gemini New Moon on the 26th is a powerful portal for setting intentions around community, networking, and self-expression. Your voice has the power to inspire and uplift others, so don't be afraid to speak your truth and share your gifts with the world.

Best Days of the Month:

May 4th: Venus enters Gemini. Your social life is buzzing with activity and connection. Attend events or join groups that align with your passions and let your natural charm shine.

May 12th: Full Moon in Scorpio. A financial or family matter comes to a head. Trust your intuition and be open to innovative solutions. A home-based business or real estate opportunity could arise.

May 18th: Jupiter sextile Chiron. Healing and growth opportunities abound, especially around travel, education, and personal development. Invest in experiences that stretch you beyond your comfort zone.

May 26th: New Moon in Gemini. Set intentions around communication, learning, and self-expression. Your unique voice has the power to inspire and uplift others. Embrace your inner student and let your curiosity lead the way.

June 2025

Overview Horoscope for the Month:

June 2025 is a month of exciting opportunities and personal growth for you, Leo! The headline news is Mars, the planet of action and ambition, moving into your sign on the 17th, where it will stay until late July. This cosmic alignment brings a powerful boost of energy, confidence, and motivation to pursue your goals and desires. You're feeling bold, courageous, and ready to take on new challenges. Trust your instincts and let your natural leadership skills shine.

The Gemini New Moon on the 25th is a potent time for setting intentions around communication, learning, and self-expression. You're feeling curious, adaptable, and eager to explore new ideas and perspectives. Embrace your inner student and let your unique voice be heard. Your words have the power to inspire and uplift others.

Love:

With Venus, the planet of love and pleasure, dancing through your 11th house of friendship and community until the 6th, your social life is buzzing with activity. You're feeling popular, magnetic, and ready to connect with like-minded individuals who share your passions and values. Attend events or join groups that align with your interests and let your natural charm and warmth attract new connections.

When Venus moves into your 12th house of spirituality and inner growth on the 6th, your focus shifts to more introspective pursuits. This is a time to nurture your relationship with yourself and explore the depths of your emotional world. If you're in a committed partnership, prioritize intimate, one-on-one time with your loved one. Heart-to-heart conversations can deepen your bond.

Career:

With Mars charging through your 12th house of behind-the-scenes work until the 17th, much of your professional focus is on tying up loose ends and completing projects that have been on the back burner. Trust your intuition and listen to your inner guidance when making career decisions. Your dreams and subconscious mind hold clues to your true path and purpose.

When Mars moves into your sign on the 17th, your career goals get a major boost of momentum and drive. You're feeling confident, assertive, and ready to take on new challenges in the workplace. Trust your instincts and be proactive in pursuing opportunities that align with your passions and talents. Your leadership skills and creative vision are your superpowers.

Finances:

The Sagittarius Full Moon on the 11th illuminates your 5th house of creativity, self-expression, and play, bringing a financial matter to a head. You may receive recognition or compensation for a creative project or hobby that you're passionate about. Trust your unique talents and let your authentic self shine. Your joy and enthusiasm are your greatest assets.

With Mars moving through your 12th house of hidden resources until the 17th, you may uncover new sources of income or financial support that you weren't previously aware of. Keep an open mind and be receptive to unexpected opportunities. A generous gift or act of kindness from someone in your network could also boost your bottom line.

Health:

With Mars energizing your 12th house of rest and renewal until the 17th, your physical and emotional well-being are in the spotlight. This is a time to prioritize self-care and listen to your body's signals. If you've been burning the candle at both ends, use this opportunity to slow down and recharge your batteries. Engage in activities that bring you a sense of peace and relaxation, such as meditation, yoga, or spending time in nature.

When Mars moves into your sign on the 17th, you'll feel a surge of energy and motivation to pursue your fitness goals. Channel your competitive spirit into trying a new sport or physical activity that challenges you. Just be mindful not to push yourself too hard too fast. Incorporate plenty of rest and recovery time into your routine to avoid burnout.

Travel:

Your wanderlust is activated this month, Leo, thanks to the Sagittarius Full Moon on the 11th illuminating your 5th house of adventure and play. You're craving new experiences and perspectives that expand your horizons and bring you joy. Consider planning a weekend getaway or booking a trip to a destination that's been on your bucket list. Immersing yourself in different cultures and landscapes can be incredibly enriching for your personal growth.

If long-distance travel isn't possible right now, seek out opportunities for exploration and discovery closer to home. Visit a new park or nature reserve, try a foreign cuisine restaurant, or attend a cultural event that broadens your worldview. Even small shifts in your daily routine can satisfy your craving for novelty and excitement.

Insights from the Stars:

June's astrology is all about embracing your authentic self and stepping into your power, Leo. Mars' move into your sign on the 17th is a cosmic invitation to be bold, courageous, and unapologetically you. Trust your instincts and let your unique light shine bright. You have the strength and resilience to overcome any obstacle and achieve your dreams.

This is also a potent month for self-discovery and inner growth. The Gemini New Moon on the 25th is a powerful portal for setting intentions around self-awareness, emotional healing, and spiritual awakening. Take time to reflect on your journey so far and release any limiting beliefs or patterns that are holding you back. You're ready to step into a new chapter of your life with greater wisdom, compassion, and authenticity.

Best Days of the Month:

June 4th: Venus enters Cancer. Your social life takes on a nurturing, emotional tone. Prioritize quality time with loved ones and engage in activities that make you feel safe and supported.

June 11th: Full Moon in Sagittarius. A creative project or passion comes to fruition. Trust your unique talents and let your joy and enthusiasm shine. An adventure or trip could also be on the horizon.

June 17th: Mars enters Leo. Your energy, confidence, and motivation are off the charts. Take bold action towards your goals and dreams. Your leadership skills and creative vision are your superpowers.

June 25th: New Moon in Gemini. Set intentions around communication, learning, and self-expression. Embrace your curiosity and let your unique voice be heard. Your words have the power to inspire and uplift others..

July 2025

Overview Horoscope for the Month:

July 2025 is a month of personal growth, self-discovery, and new beginnings for you, Leo! With the Sun, your ruling planet, moving through your sign from the 22nd onwards, you're feeling confident, radiant, and ready to shine your unique light in the world. This is a powerful time to set intentions for the year ahead and take bold action towards your dreams and goals. Trust your instincts and let your natural leadership skills guide the way.

The Leo New Moon on the 24th is a potent cosmic reset that marks the beginning of a new chapter in your personal journey. Set intentions around self-love, creative expression, and authentic living. You're ready to let go of old patterns and beliefs that no longer serve you and step into a more empowered version of yourself. Embrace your inner fire and let your passions be your compass.

Love:

With Venus, the planet of love and pleasure, dancing through your sign from the 25th onwards, your romantic life is infused with extra magnetism and charm. If you're single, this is a wonderful time to put yourself out there and attract new love into your life. Trust your natural charisma and let your authentic self shine. If you're in a committed partnership, prioritize quality time with your loved one doing activities that bring you both joy and laughter. Reignite the spark of passion and playfulness in your connection.

The Leo New Moon on the 24th is a powerful portal for setting intentions around love and relationships. Get clear on the qualities and values you desire in a partner and visualize yourself in a healthy, happy, and fulfilling union. Release any past hurts or resentments that may be blocking you from fully opening your heart. You're worthy of deep, soulful love.

Career:

With Mars, the planet of ambition and drive, charging through your sign all month, your career goals are infused with extra momentum and confidence. You're feeling assertive, proactive, and ready to take on new challenges in the workplace. Trust your creative vision and leadership skills to guide you towards success. This is a fantastic time to launch a new project, pitch your ideas to higher-ups, or take on additional responsibilities that showcase your talents.

The Leo New Moon on the 24th is a potent time for setting intentions around your professional path and purpose. Get clear on your long-term goals and take practical steps towards making them a reality. Believe in yourself and your ability to make a positive impact in the world. Your unique gifts and passions are your greatest assets.

Finances:

The Aquarius Full Moon on the 10th illuminates your 7th house of partnerships and shared resources, bringing a financial matter to a head. If you're in a committed relationship, you may need to have an honest conversation with your partner about your budget, investments, or long-term security goals. Work together to find solutions that feel fair and balanced for both of you. If you're single, this is a good time to review any joint financial agreements or debts and make sure they align with your values and priorities.

With Mars energizing your sign all month, you may feel more motivated to take charge of your finances and pursue new income streams. Trust your entrepreneurial spirit and think outside the box when it comes to generating wealth. Your creativity and innovation are your superpowers.

Health:

With the Sun shining in your sign from the 22nd onwards, you're feeling energized, vital, and ready to prioritize your physical and emotional well-being. This is a wonderful time to start a new fitness routine or health regimen that aligns with your goals and values. Listen to your body's signals and honor its needs for rest, nourishment, and movement. Incorporate activities that bring you joy and make you feel alive, such as dancing, swimming, or hiking in nature.

The Leo New Moon on the 24th is a powerful portal for setting intentions around self-care and personal growth. Commit to practices that support your mental, emotional, and spiritual well-being, such as meditation, journaling, or therapy. Surround yourself with people and environments that uplift and inspire you. When you feel good in your mind, body, and soul, you radiate a magnetic energy that attracts abundance in all areas of your life.

Travel:

Your wanderlust is activated this month, Leo, thanks to the Sun moving through your sign from the 22nd onwards. You're craving new experiences and adventures that expand your horizons and ignite your passion for life. Consider planning a trip to a destination that's been on your bucket list or signing up for a workshop or retreat that supports your personal growth. Immersing yourself in different cultures and perspectives can be incredibly enriching for your mind and soul.

If long-distance travel isn't possible right now, find ways to infuse your daily life with a sense of exploration and discovery. Visit a new neighborhood in your city, try a foreign cuisine restaurant, or attend a cultural event that broadens your worldview. Even small shifts in your routine can satisfy your craving for novelty and excitement.

Insights from the Stars:

July's astrology is all about embracing your authentic self and stepping into your power, Leo. The Sun's move through your sign from the 22nd onwards is a cosmic invitation to celebrate your unique qualities and share your gifts with the world. Let go of any masks or personas that you've been hiding behind and allow yourself to be seen and loved for who you truly are. Your vulnerability is your strength.

The Leo New Moon on the 24th is a powerful portal for setting intentions around self-love, creative expression, and personal growth. Trust that you have everything you need within you to create a life that feels joyful, fulfilling, and abundant. Surround yourself with people and experiences that uplift and inspire you. You're ready to let your inner light shine bright and illuminate the path ahead.

Best Days of the Month:

July 7th: Uranus enters Gemini. Expect the unexpected in your social life and community. Embrace new friendships and connections that challenge you to think outside the box. Your unique perspective is your superpower.

July 10th: Full Moon in Aquarius. A partnership or financial matter comes to a head. Work together to find solutions that feel fair and balanced for all involved. Trust your intuition and be open to innovative ideas.

July 22nd: Sun enters Leo. Happy birthday season, Leo! You're feeling confident, radiant, and ready to shine your unique light in the world. Set intentions for the year ahead and take bold action towards your dreams.

July 24th: New Moon in Leo. A powerful cosmic reset that marks the beginning of a new chapter in your personal journey. Set intentions around self-love, creative expression, and authentic living. Embrace your inner fire and let your passions be your compass.

August 2025

Overview Horoscope for the Month:

August 2025 is a month of personal growth, self-discovery, and new beginnings for you, Leo! With the Sun, your ruling planet, shining in your sign until the 22nd, you're feeling confident, radiant, and ready to take on the world. This is a powerful time to celebrate your unique qualities and share your gifts with others. Trust your instincts and let your natural leadership skills guide the way.

The Aquarius Full Moon on the 9th illuminates your 7th house of partnerships and one-on-one relationships, bringing a significant connection to a turning point. You may need to have an honest conversation with a loved one about your needs, desires, and boundaries. Work together to find solutions that honor both of your individuality and support your growth as a team. If you're single, this could mark the beginning of a new romance or friendship that challenges you to expand your perspective and embrace your authentic self.

Love:

With Venus, the planet of love and pleasure, dancing through your sign from the 13th onwards, your romantic life is infused with extra magnetism and charm. If you're single, this is a wonderful time to put yourself out there and attract new love into your life. Trust your natural charisma and let your authentic self shine. If you're in a committed partnership, prioritize quality time with your loved one doing activities that bring you both joy and excitement. Plan a spontaneous date night or weekend getaway to reignite the spark of passion and adventure in your connection.

Mercury, the planet of communication, will be retrograde in your sign from the 18th onwards, inviting you to reflect on your thoughts, words, and self-expression. This is a good time to review any important conversations or agreements with loved ones and make sure you're on the same page. Be patient with misunderstandings and take time to clarify your intentions. Trust that any challenges are ultimately serving your growth and evolution as a partner and individual.

Career:

With Mars, the planet of ambition and drive, charging through your 2nd house of income and resources until the 22nd, you're feeling motivated to take charge of your finances and pursue new opportunities for growth and abundance. Trust your skills, talents, and value in the workplace. If you've been considering asking for a raise or promotion, this is a favorable time to advocate for yourself and negotiate better terms. You have the power to create the professional life you desire.

When the Sun moves into Virgo on the 22nd, the focus shifts to your 2nd house of money and material resources. This is a good time to review your budget, streamline your expenses, and set clear financial goals for the future. Look for ways to maximize your earning potential and invest in your long-term security. Your hard work and dedication will pay off.

Finances:

The Aquarius Full Moon on the 9th illuminates your 7th house of partnerships and shared resources, bringing a financial matter to a head. If you're in a committed relationship, you may need to have an honest conversation with your partner about your budget, investments, or long-term security goals. Work together to find solutions that feel fair and balanced for both of you. If you're single, this is a good time to review any joint financial agreements or debts and make sure they align with your values and priorities.

With Mars energizing your 2nd house of income and resources until the 22nd, you may feel more motivated to take charge of your finances and pursue new streams of revenue. Trust your entrepreneurial spirit and think outside the box when it comes to generating wealth. Your creativity and innovation are your superpowers.

Health:

With the Sun shining in your sign until the 22nd, you're feeling energized, vital, and ready to prioritize your physical and emotional well-being. This is a wonderful time to continue any fitness routines or health regimens that you started last month. Listen to your body's signals and honor its needs for rest, nourishment, and movement. Incorporate activities that bring you joy and make you feel empowered, such as dancing, swimming, or martial arts.

When Mars moves into Virgo on the 22nd, you may feel a surge of motivation to get organized and streamline your daily routines. This is a good time to declutter your space, both physically and mentally, and make room for new, healthy habits. Focus on small, consistent actions that support your overall well-being, such as eating nourishing foods, staying hydrated, and getting enough sleep. Remember, self-care is not a luxury, but a necessity for your vitality and success.

Travel:

Your wanderlust continues to be activated this month, Leo, thanks to the Sun shining in your sign until the 22nd. You're craving new experiences and adventures that expand your horizons and ignite your passion for life. If you have the opportunity to travel, consider destinations that offer a mix of excitement and relaxation, such as a tropical beach resort or a city with a vibrant cultural scene. Immersing yourself in different environments and perspectives can be incredibly rejuvenating for your mind and soul.

If travel isn't possible right now, find ways to infuse your daily life with a sense of exploration and discovery. Take a day trip to a nearby town or nature reserve, sign up for a class or workshop that teaches you a new skill, or host a foreign movie night with friends. Even small shifts in your routine can satisfy your craving for novelty and excitement.

Insights from the Stars:

August's astrology is all about embracing your authentic self and stepping into your power, Leo. The Sun's journey through your sign until the 22nd is a cosmic invitation to celebrate your unique qualities and share your gifts with the world. Let go of any fears or doubts that may be holding you back from shining your light fully. You are worthy of love, success, and abundance just as you are.

The Aquarius Full Moon on the 9th is a powerful portal for releasing any limiting beliefs or patterns in your relationships that no longer serve your highest good. Trust that by being true to yourself and communicating your needs openly and honestly, you create space for more fulfilling and supportive connections to blossom. Remember, your vulnerability is your strength.

Best Days of the Month:

August 9th: Full Moon in Aquarius. A significant partnership reaches a turning point. Have an honest conversation about your needs, desires, and boundaries. Work together to find solutions that honor both of your individuality and support your growth as a team.

August 13th: Venus enters Leo. Your magnetism and charm are off the charts. If single, put yourself out there and attract new love into your life. If coupled, prioritize quality time with your partner doing activities that bring you both joy and excitement.

August 22nd: Sun enters Virgo / Mars enters Virgo. The focus shifts to your daily routines, health, and work life. Get organized, streamline your schedule, and prioritize self-care. Your hard work and dedication will pay off.

August 23rd: New Moon in Virgo. Set intentions around your physical and mental well-being, as well as your professional goals. Focus on small, consistent actions that support your overall vitality and success. Trust that you have the power to create the life you desire.

Overview Horoscope for the Month:

September 2025 is a month of personal growth, self-reflection, and new beginnings for you, Leo. With the Sun shining in your 2nd house of values, finances, and self-worth until the 22nd, you're being called to reassess your priorities and align your resources with your authentic desires. This is a powerful time to get clear on what truly matters to you and make choices that support your long-term security and happiness.

The Pisces Full Moon on the 7th illuminates your 8th house of intimacy, shared resources, and emotional depth, bringing a significant relationship or financial matter to a turning point. You may need to have an honest conversation with a loved one or business partner about your needs, boundaries, and expectations. Trust your intuition and be open to the transformative power of vulnerability and surrender.

Love:

With Venus, the planet of love and relationships, dancing through your sign until the 19th, your magnetism and charm are off the charts. If you're single, this is a wonderful time to put yourself out there and attract new love into your life. Trust your natural charisma and let your authentic self shine. If you're in a committed partnership, prioritize quality time with your loved one doing activities that bring you both joy and pleasure. Plan a romantic date night or surprise your partner with a thoughtful gesture that shows how much you care.

When Venus moves into Virgo on the 19th, the focus shifts to your 2nd house of values and self-worth. This is a good time to reflect on what you need to feel secure, loved, and appreciated in your relationships. Be honest with yourself and your partner about your emotional and material needs. Work together to create a solid foundation of trust, respect, and mutual support.

Career:

With Mars, the planet of ambition and drive, charging through your 3rd house of communication and ideas from the 22nd onwards, you're feeling motivated to share your thoughts, skills, and expertise with others. This is a fantastic time to network, collaborate, and pitch your ideas to colleagues or clients. Trust your creativity and innovative thinking to help you stand out from the crowd.

The Virgo New Moon on the 21st is a powerful portal for setting intentions around your professional goals and aspirations. Get clear on what you want to achieve in the coming months and take practical steps towards making it a reality. Focus on honing your skills, streamlining your workflow, and delivering high-quality results. Your hard work and dedication will pay off in the form of recognition, rewards, and new opportunities for growth.

Finances:

The Pisces Full Moon on the 7th illuminates your 8th house of shared resources and financial partnerships, bringing a money matter to a head. If you've been considering making a significant investment or negotiating a business deal, this is a good time to trust your intuition and make a decision that aligns with your long-term goals and values. Be open to creative solutions and unexpected sources of support.

With the Sun shining in your 2nd house of income and material security until the 22nd, you're being called to take a closer look at your budget, spending habits, and financial goals. Look for ways to increase your earning potential, save more money, and invest in your future. Remember, your self-worth is not defined by your bank account balance. Focus on cultivating a sense of abundance and gratitude for all the blessings in your life.

Health:

With Mars energizing your 3rd house of communication and mental activity from the 22nd onwards, you may feel a surge of restless energy and a desire to learn, explore, and express yourself. This is a good time to channel your curiosity and enthusiasm into activities that stimulate your mind and keep you physically active, such as hiking, dancing, or trying a new hobby.

The Virgo New Moon on the 21st is a powerful portal for setting intentions around your physical and mental well-being. Focus on creating healthy habits and routines that support your overall vitality and resilience, such as eating nourishing foods, staying hydrated, and getting enough rest. Make time for self-care practices that help you manage stress and maintain a positive outlook, such as meditation, journaling, or spending time in nature.

Travel:

With the Sun shining in your 2nd house of material security and comfort until the 22nd, you may be more inclined to plan a vacation that offers a mix of luxury and relaxation. Consider booking a stay at a high-end resort or spa where you can indulge in pampering treatments, delicious meals, and beautiful surroundings. This is a good time to treat yourself to a little extra TLC and enjoy the fruits of your labors.

When Mars moves into your 3rd house of short trips and local adventures on the 22nd, you may feel a surge of wanderlust and a desire to explore your own backyard. Take a day trip to a nearby town or city, go on a scenic drive, or visit a local attraction that you've always wanted to see. Engaging with your immediate environment can be just as enriching as traveling to far-off destinations.

Insights from the Stars:

September's astrology is all about aligning your resources with your values and cultivating a sense of security and self-worth, Leo. The Sun's journey through your 2nd house until the 22nd is a cosmic invitation to reassess your priorities and make choices that support your long-term happiness and well-being. Let go of any limiting beliefs or habits that are holding you back from feeling abundant, worthy, and fulfilled.

The Pisces Full Moon on the 7th is a powerful portal for releasing any fears, doubts, or emotional baggage that may be blocking your ability to fully trust and surrender in your relationships and financial partnerships. Remember, vulnerability is a strength, not a weakness. By being open and honest about your needs and desires, you create space for deeper intimacy, understanding, and growth.

Best Days of the Month:

September 7th: Full Moon in Pisces. A significant relationship or financial matter reaches a turning point. Trust your intuition and be open to the transformative power of vulnerability and surrender.

September 19th: Venus enters Virgo. The focus shifts to your values, self-worth, and material security. Reflect on what you need to feel loved, appreciated, and abundant in your relationships and finances.

September 21st: New Moon in Virgo. Set intentions around your professional goals, health habits, and personal growth. Focus on creating routines and systems that support your overall vitality, productivity, and success.

September 22nd: Sun enters Libra / Mars enters Scorpio. The energy shifts towards your relationships, communication skills, and mental activity. Collaborate with others, express your ideas, and explore new avenues for learning and growth.

October 2025

Overview Horoscope for the Month:

October 2025 is a month of transformation, self-discovery, and new beginnings for you, Leo. With the Sun shining in your 4th house of home, family, and emotional foundations until the 22nd, you're being called to focus on your inner world and create a sense of security and belonging within yourself. This is a powerful time to connect with your roots, honor your feelings, and cultivate a nurturing environment that supports your growth and well-being.

The Aries Full Moon on the 6th illuminates your 9th house of travel, higher education, and personal growth, bringing a significant opportunity or challenge related to your beliefs, adventures, or long-term goals. You may feel a strong urge to break free from your comfort zone and explore new horizons, both literally and figuratively. Trust your instincts and be open to the transformative power of stepping into the unknown.

Love:

With Venus, the planet of love and relationships, dancing through your 3rd house of communication and social connections until the 13th, you're feeling more expressive, curious, and open to meeting new people. This is a great time to network, flirt, and engage in lively conversations with friends, colleagues, and potential love interests. If you're single, you may find yourself attracted to someone who stimulates your mind and makes you laugh. If you're in a committed partnership, prioritize quality time with your loved one doing activities that allow you to learn and grow together, such as taking a class or exploring a new hobby.

When Venus moves into your 4th house of home and family on the 13th, the focus shifts to creating a warm, welcoming, and harmonious environment in your personal life. This is a good time to spend quality time with loved ones, decorate your living space, or host a cozy gathering at home. If there have been any tensions or conflicts in your relationships, this is an opportunity to lead with compassion, understanding, and a willingness to compromise.

Career:

With Mars, the planet of ambition and action, charging through your 4th house of home and family all month, you may feel a strong urge to take charge of your personal life and create a solid foundation for your long-term security and success. This is a great time to assess your work-life balance, set boundaries around your time and energy, and make any necessary changes to your living situation or family dynamics. Trust your instincts and be proactive in creating a supportive environment that allows you to thrive both personally and professionally.

The Libra New Moon on the 21st is a powerful portal for setting intentions around your career goals, public image, and leadership skills. Take some time to reflect on what you want to achieve in the coming months and years, and visualize yourself embodying the qualities of a confident, capable, and inspiring leader. Focus on building strong relationships with colleagues, clients, and mentors who share your values and vision for success.

Finances:

The Aries Full Moon on the 6th illuminates your 9th house of long-term goals and big-picture thinking, bringing a financial opportunity or challenge related to your investments, education, or entrepreneurial ventures. Trust your instincts and be open to taking calculated risks that align with your values and vision for the future. If you've been considering making a major purchase or investment, this is a good time to do your research and seek the advice of trusted experts.

With Venus gracing your 4th house of home and family from the 13th onwards, you may feel inspired to beautify your living space or invest in your long-term security and comfort. This is a good time to review your budget, save money for a rainy day, and make any necessary repairs or upgrades to your home. Remember, your financial well-being is closely tied to your emotional well-being, so focus on creating a sense of abundance, gratitude, and peace in your personal life.

Health:

With the Sun illuminating your 4th house of emotional foundations until the 22nd, you may feel a strong urge to prioritize your mental and emotional well-being this month. This is a great time to focus on self-care practices that help you feel grounded, nurtured, and at peace, such as meditation, therapy, or spending time in nature. If you've been feeling overwhelmed or stressed lately, give yourself permission to slow down, rest, and recharge your batteries.

When the Sun moves into your 5th house of creativity, self-expression, and joy on the 22nd, you may feel a surge of energy and inspiration to pursue activities that light you up from the inside out. This is a great time to engage in hobbies or projects that allow you to express your unique talents and passions, such as art, music, dance, or writing. Remember, play is just as important as work when it comes to maintaining a healthy, balanced lifestyle.

Travel:

The Aries Full Moon on the 6th illuminates your 9th house of travel, adventure, and higher learning, bringing a significant opportunity or challenge related to your desire for exploration and growth. If you've been feeling restless or stuck in a rut lately, this is a great time to plan a trip or embark on a new course of study that expands your horizons and challenges you to step outside your comfort zone. Trust your instincts and be open to the transformative power of immersing yourself in new cultures, ideas, and experiences.

With Mars energizing your 4th house of home and family all month, you may also feel inspired to explore your own backyard and connect with your local community. This is a great time to take a staycation, visit a nearby park or museum, or attend a cultural event that allows you to appreciate the beauty and diversity of your hometown. Remember, sometimes the greatest adventures are the ones that happen closest to home.

Insights from the Stars:

October's astrology is all about creating a strong foundation for your long-term security, happiness, and growth, Leo. The Sun's journey through your 4th house until the 22nd is a cosmic invitation to connect with your roots, honor your emotions, and cultivate a sense of belonging within yourself and your relationships. Trust that by tending to your inner world and personal life, you're laying the groundwork for greater success and fulfillment in all areas of your life.

The Aries Full Moon on the 6th is a powerful portal for releasing any fears, doubts, or limiting beliefs that may be holding you back from pursuing your dreams and reaching your full potential. Remember, growth often involves discomfort and uncertainty, but the rewards are always worth the risk. Trust your instincts, believe in yourself, and take a leap of faith towards the life you truly desire.

Best Days of the Month:

October 6th: Full Moon in Aries. A significant opportunity or challenge related to travel, education, or personal growth arises. Trust your instincts and be open to stepping outside your comfort zone.

October 13th: Venus enters Libra. The focus shifts to creating harmony, beauty, and balance in your home and family life. Prioritize quality time with loved ones and make your living space a sanctuary.

October 21st: New Moon in Libra. Set intentions around your career goals, public image, and leadership skills. Visualize yourself embodying the qualities of a confident, capable, and inspiring leader.

October 22nd: Sun enters Scorpio. The energy shifts towards creativity, self-expression, and joy. Pursue activities that light you up from the inside out and allow you to express your unique talents and passions..

November 2025

Overview Horoscope for the Month:

November 2025 is a month of creativity, self-expression, and new beginnings for you, Leo. With the Sun shining in your 5th house of romance, joy, and creativity until the 21st, you're being called to embrace your inner child and let your unique light shine brightly. This is a powerful time to pursue your passions, take risks, and express yourself authentically and unapologetically.

The Taurus Full Moon on the 5th illuminates your 10th house of career, reputation, and public image, bringing a significant achievement, challenge, or turning point related to your professional goals and aspirations. You may receive recognition for your hard work and dedication, or feel called to make a bold move in your career that aligns with your true purpose and values. Trust your instincts and be open to the transformative power of stepping into your leadership potential.

Love:

With Venus, the planet of love and relationships, dancing through your 5th house of romance and creativity until the 30th, you're feeling more magnetic, confident, and expressive in your love life. If you're single, this is an excellent time to put yourself out there and attract a partner who appreciates your unique qualities and talents. Be open to playful, spontaneous connections that bring you joy and laughter. If you're in a committed relationship, prioritize fun, passion, and creativity in your interactions with your loved one. Plan a romantic date night, share your hopes and dreams, or work on a creative project together.

Mars, the planet of desire and action, will be charging through your 5th house of romance and self-expression from the 4th onwards, adding even more fire and intensity to your love life. You may feel a strong urge to take the lead in your relationships and go after what you want with confidence and enthusiasm. Just be mindful of coming on too strong or being overly impulsive in your actions. Balance your passion with patience and sensitivity to your partner's needs and feelings.

Career:

The Taurus Full Moon on the 5th illuminates your 10th house of career, reputation, and public image, bringing a significant achievement, challenge, or turning point related to your professional goals and aspirations. You may receive recognition for your hard work and dedication, or feel called to make a bold move in your career that aligns with your true purpose and values. Trust your instincts and be open to the transformative power of stepping into your leadership potential.

With Mars energizing your 5th house of creativity and self-expression from the 4th onwards, you may feel a surge of inspiration and motivation to pursue projects or ideas that showcase your unique talents and skills. This is an excellent time to take risks, think outside the box, and bring your creative vision to life. Just be mindful of overextending yourself or taking on more than you can realistically handle. Focus on quality over quantity and trust that your efforts will pay off in the long run.

Finances:

The Taurus Full Moon on the 5th illuminates your 10th house of career and public image, bringing a financial opportunity or challenge related to your professional goals and aspirations. You may receive a raise, bonus, or new source of income as a result of your hard work and dedication. Alternatively, you may need to reassess your budget or financial priorities to ensure that they align with your long-term goals and values. Trust your instincts and be open to creative solutions and new possibilities for abundance.

With Venus gracing your 5th house of joy and creativity until the 30th, you may feel inspired to invest in experiences or pursuits that bring you pleasure and fulfillment. This is a great time to treat yourself to a hobby or activity that you love, or to splurge on a special item or experience that makes you feel pampered and appreciated. Just be mindful of overspending or indulging in impulsive purchases. Balance your desire for enjoyment with a sense of responsibility and moderation.

Health:

With the Sun illuminating your 5th house of joy and self-expression until the 21st, you may feel a strong urge to prioritize activities and experiences that make you feel alive, energized, and fulfilled. This is a great time to engage in physical activities that you enjoy, such as dancing, sports, or outdoor adventures. You may also feel inspired to express yourself creatively through art, music, or writing as a way to release stress and emotions.

When the Sun moves into your 6th house of health and wellness on the 21st, the focus shifts to creating healthy habits and routines that support your overall well-being. This is a great time to reassess your diet, exercise regimen, and self-care practices to ensure that they are nourishing and sustainable. You may also feel called to be of service to others in some way, such as volunteering for a cause you care about or offering your skills and talents to help someone in need.

Travel:

With Mars energizing your 5th house of adventure and self-expression from the 4th onwards, you may feel a strong urge to travel and explore new horizons this month. This is an excellent time to plan a trip or vacation that allows you to step outside your comfort zone and experience new cultures, ideas, and experiences. You may also feel inspired to take a creative or educational journey, such as attending a workshop or retreat that helps you develop your talents and passions.

If long-distance travel is not possible at this time, consider exploring your local area with a sense of curiosity and wonder. Visit a new neighborhood, try a new restaurant or activity, or attend a cultural event that broadens your perspective and ignites your imagination. Remember, adventure can be found anywhere if you approach life with an open heart and mind.

Insights from the Stars:

November's astrology is all about embracing your inner child, expressing your unique creativity, and taking bold steps towards your dreams and desires, Leo. The Sun's journey through your 5th house until the 21st is a cosmic invitation to let your light shine brightly and unapologetically. Trust that by following your joy and passion, you are aligning with your true purpose and potential.

The Taurus Full Moon on the 5th is a powerful portal for manifesting your professional goals and aspirations, and for stepping into your leadership potential. Remember, success is not just about achieving external recognition or rewards, but about living in alignment with your authentic values and purpose. Trust your instincts, stay grounded in your truth, and be open to the transformative power of embracing your calling.

Best Days of the Month:

November 5th: Full Moon in Taurus. A significant achievement, challenge, or turning point related to your career and public image arises. Trust your instincts and be open to stepping into your leadership potential.

November 4th: Mars enters Sagittarius. The energy shifts towards adventure, exploration, and personal growth. Take risks, expand your horizons, and pursue experiences that ignite your passion and curiosity.

November 21st: Sun enters Sagittarius. The focus shifts to health, wellness, and service. Create healthy habits and routines that support your overall well-being, and find ways to be of service to others.

November 30th: Venus enters Capricorn. Your love life takes on a more serious, committed tone. Focus on building strong, stable relationships based on mutual respect, trust, and shared values..

December 2025

Overview Horoscope for the Month:

December 2025 is a month of introspection, transformation, and new beginnings for you, Leo. With the Sun shining in your 6th house of health, wellness, and service until the 21st, you're being called to focus on your daily routines, habits, and practices that support your overall well-being. This is a powerful time to reassess your priorities, let go of what no longer serves you, and create a strong foundation for your personal and professional growth.

The Gemini Full Moon on the 4th illuminates your 11th house of friendships, community, and future vision, bringing a significant realization, opportunity, or turning point related to your social connections and long-term goals. You may feel a strong urge to connect with like-minded individuals who share your values and aspirations, or to take a bold step towards manifesting your dreams and ideals. Trust your intuition and be open to the transformative power of collaboration and innovation.

Love:

With Venus, the planet of love and relationships, dancing through your 6th house of service and daily routines until the 24th, you may find yourself drawn to partnerships that are grounded in practicality, stability, and mutual support. This is a great time to focus on the daily habits and rituals that nurture your closest relationships, such as cooking meals together, running errands, or tackling household projects. If you're single, you may feel attracted to someone who shares your values and work ethic, or who inspires you to be your best self.

When Venus moves into your 7th house of partnerships on the 24th, the focus shifts to creating harmony, balance, and beauty in your one-on-one relationships. This is a wonderful time to deepen your connection with your significant other through heartfelt conversations, shared adventures, and acts of love and appreciation. If you're single, you may feel ready to attract a soulmate connection or take a existing relationship to the next level. Trust your heart and be open to the magic of love and romance.

Career:

With Mars, the planet of ambition and drive, energizing your 6th house of work and service all month, you may feel a strong urge to take charge of your professional life and make meaningful contributions to your community or industry. This is an excellent time to tackle projects that require focus, discipline, and attention to detail, or to take on a leadership role that allows you to mentor or guide others. Just be mindful of overextending yourself or taking on more than you can realistically handle. Balance your desire to be of service with a commitment to self-care and boundary-setting.

The Capricorn New Moon on the 19th is a powerful portal for setting intentions related to your career, reputation, and public image. Take some time to reflect on your long-term goals and aspirations, and visualize yourself achieving success and fulfillment in your chosen path. Focus on building strong relationships with colleagues, clients, and mentors who support your growth and development, and trust that your hard work and dedication will pay off in the long run.

Finances:

The Gemini Full Moon on the 4th illuminates your 11th house of hopes, dreams, and community, bringing a financial opportunity or challenge related to your long-term goals and aspirations. You may receive unexpected support or resources from a friend, group, or organization that shares your values and vision. Alternatively, you may need to reassess your budget or financial priorities to ensure that they align with your true purpose and passions. Trust your intuition and be open to creative solutions and new possibilities for abundance.

With Venus gracing your 6th house of work and service until the 24th, you may find opportunities to increase your income or receive recognition for your skills and talents in the workplace. This is a great time to focus on developing your expertise, networking with colleagues, and taking on projects that showcase your value and contributions. Just be mindful of overworking yourself or neglecting your personal life in the pursuit of financial gain. Balance your desire for success with a commitment to self-care and enjoyment.

Health:

With the Sun illuminating your 6th house of health and wellness until the 21st, you're being called to prioritize your physical, mental, and emotional well-being this month. This is an excellent time to reassess your self-care practices, diet, exercise routine, and stress management techniques to ensure that they are nourishing and sustainable. You may feel inspired to try a new healing modality, such as acupuncture or massage, or to incorporate more mindfulness and relaxation into your daily life.

When the Sun moves into your 7th house of partnerships on the 21st, the focus shifts to creating balance and harmony in your relationships. This is a great time to prioritize quality time with loved ones, engage in activities that bring you closer together, and practice the art of compromise and communication. Remember, taking care of yourself is not selfish, but rather a necessary foundation for being able to show up fully and authentically in your relationships.

Travel:

With Mars energizing your 6th house of work and service all month, you may find yourself traveling for business or professional development purposes. This is an excellent time to attend conferences, workshops, or training programs that help you expand your skills and knowledge in your field. You may also feel called to take a service-oriented trip, such as volunteering for a cause you care about or participating in a community project.

If personal travel is on your agenda, consider destinations that offer a blend of relaxation, adventure, and cultural enrichment. You may be drawn to places that have a strong connection to nature, spirituality, or history, or that allow you to immerse yourself in new experiences and perspectives. Trust your intuition and be open to the transformative power of stepping outside your comfort zone and embracing the unknown.

Insights from the Stars:

December's astrology is all about creating a strong foundation for your personal and professional growth, Leo. The Sun's journey through your 6th house until the 21st is a cosmic invitation to get grounded in your daily routines, habits, and practices that support your overall well-being. Trust that by taking care of the details and practicalities of life, you are setting yourself up for long-term success and fulfillment.

The Gemini Full Moon on the 4th is a powerful portal for manifesting your hopes, dreams, and ideals, and for connecting with like-minded individuals who share your vision and values. Remember, you are not alone on your journey, and there is strength and magic in collaboration and community. Trust your intuition, speak your truth, and be open to the transformative power of innovation and imagination.

Best Days of the Month:

December 4th: Full Moon in Gemini. A significant realization, opportunity, or turning point related to your friendships, community, and future vision arises. Trust your intuition and be open to the power of collaboration and innovation.

December 19th: New Moon in Capricorn. Set intentions related to your career, reputation, and public image. Focus on building strong relationships and trust that your hard work and dedication will pay off.

December 21st: Sun enters Capricorn. The focus shifts to partnerships, balance, and harmony. Prioritize quality time with loved ones and practice the art of compromise and communication.

December 24th: Venus enters Aquarius. Your love life takes on a more unconventional, adventurous tone. Be open to new experiences and perspectives in your relationships, and trust the magic of serendipity and synchronicity.

VIRGO 2025 HOROSCOPE

Overview Virgo 2025

(August 23 - September 22)

As the celestial dance of 2025 unfolds, those born under the sign of Virgo are set to embark on a transformative journey of self-discovery, growth, and spiritual awakening. The cosmic energies align to create a powerful year filled with opportunities for profound personal development and the manifestation of your deepest desires.

The year commences with Mars, the planet of action and assertiveness, entering your 12th house of spirituality and inner growth on June 17th. This transit marks the beginning of a significant period of introspection, self-reflection, and emotional processing. You may find yourself drawn to practices such as meditation, therapy, or creative expression as a means to explore your subconscious mind, heal past wounds, and connect with your higher self. Embrace this time as an opportunity to release old patterns, fears, and limiting beliefs that have been holding you back. By doing so, you create space for new insights, inspiration, and personal breakthroughs to emerge.

On July 18th, Mercury, your ruling planet, will turn retrograde in your 1st house of self and identity. This cosmic event initiates a period of deep self-inquiry and re-evaluation of your personal goals, values, and authentic self-expression. Use this time to reflect on your progress, refine your communication skills, and make any necessary adjustments to your plans or routines. Be patient with yourself during this process, as it may take time to gain clarity and make decisions that align with your true path forward.

The Full Moon in Virgo on September 7th is a pivotal moment for your personal growth and emotional well-being. Occurring in your 1st house of self and identity, this lunation illuminates your unique qualities, strengths, and areas for improvement. Trust your instincts during this time, as they will guide you towards the changes and releases necessary for your highest good. Honor your feelings, practice self-compassion, and be willing to let go of any habits, relationships, or beliefs that no longer serve your evolution. This is a powerful opportunity to embrace your authentic self and step into a new chapter of self-love and self-acceptance.

On September 21st, a transformative Partial Solar Eclipse will occur in your sign, Virgo, bringing a major turning point and fresh start in your personal life. This eclipse, located in your 1st house of self and identity, marks a significant shift in your self-perception, personal goals, and life direction. Embrace this powerful energy to set bold intentions, take courageous action, and align yourself with your true purpose and desires. Trust that the universe is supporting you in this process of rebirth and renewal, and have faith in your ability to create the life you truly want to live.

In the following months, the North Node, a point of spiritual growth and karmic evolution, will shift into your 9th house of higher learning, belief systems, and personal philosophy. Simultaneously, the South Node, representing past patterns and release, will move into your 3rd house of communication, learning, and immediate environment. This significant transit, lasting until July 2026, will bring profound opportunities for growth and expansion through travel, education, and spiritual exploration. You may feel called to broaden your horizons, challenge your existing beliefs, and seek out new experiences that deepen your understanding of yourself and the world around you. At the same time, you may need to release outdated ideas, thought patterns, or communication styles that no longer align with your evolving truth. Trust in the wisdom of your journey, and be open to the lessons and insights that come your way.

On October 22nd, Venus, the planet of love, beauty, and value, will enter your 2nd house of finances, resources, and self-worth. This transit brings a focus on your relationship with money, material comfort, and personal values. Use this time to reflect on your financial goals, cultivate a mindset of abundance, and attract more beauty, pleasure, and prosperity into your life. Remember that your self-worth is not defined by external factors, but rather by your inner sense of value and purpose. Embrace your unique gifts and talents, and trust in your ability to create a life of abundance and fulfillment.

As the year comes to a close, Jupiter, the planet of expansion, growth, and opportunity, will turn direct in your 10th house of career and public image on November 11th. This transit brings a sense of optimism, success, and recognition in your professional life. Trust in your skills and abilities, seize new opportunities for growth and advancement, and let your unique talents shine. This is a time to dream big, set ambitious goals, and take bold steps towards your desired outcomes. Remember that your hard work and dedication will pay off, and that the universe is conspiring in your favor.

Throughout the year, Saturn, the planet of structure, responsibility, and life lessons, will continue its transit through your 7th house of partnerships and committed relationships. This transit, which lasts until May 2025, will bring significant growth, challenges, and opportunities in your one-on-one connections. You may find yourself attracted to more mature, committed partnerships that challenge you to grow and evolve. At the same time, you may need to address any fears, insecurities, or power dynamics that arise in your relationships. Use this time to build stronger foundations of trust, respect, and mutual support with your loved ones. Set clear boundaries, communicate openly and honestly, and take responsibility for your own growth and happiness within your partnerships.

Additionally, the influence of Uranus, the planet of change, innovation, and awakening, will continue to bring sudden insights, breakthroughs, and shifts in your 9th house of higher learning and belief systems. This transit, which lasts until April 2026, will challenge you to break free from limiting beliefs, explore new ideas and perspectives, and embrace your unique path and purpose. Stay open to the unexpected, trust your intuition, and be willing to let go of any outdated ways of thinking or being that no longer serve your highest good. Remember that change, even when uncomfortable, is necessary for your growth and liberation.

As a Virgo, your natural gifts of practicality, discernment, and service will be powerful tools for navigating the ups and downs of this transformative year. Trust in your ability to analyze situations, find solutions, and create order out of chaos. At the same time, remember to balance your logical mind with your intuitive heart, and to make space for rest, play, and self-care amidst your responsibilities and goals.

Throughout the year, prioritize practices that nourish your mind, body, and soul, such as journaling, nature walks, or creative hobbies. Surround yourself with supportive, inspiring people who appreciate and encourage your authentic self-expression. And most importantly, trust in the wisdom of your own inner voice, even when it challenges you to step outside of your comfort zone.

2025 is a year of profound growth, self-discovery, and spiritual awakening for you, dear Virgo. Embrace the journey with courage, curiosity, and compassion, knowing that every challenge and opportunity is guiding you towards your highest potential and purpose. Trust in the love and support of the universe, and know that you have the strength, resilience, and wisdom to create a life of deep meaning, joy, and fulfillment.

Remember, your greatest power lies in your ability to align your thoughts, words, and actions with your authentic truth and purpose. By staying true to yourself, honoring your unique path, and serving others with your natural gifts and talents, you will create ripples of positive change in your own life and in the world around you.

So embrace the transformative power of this year, dear Virgo, and trust that you are exactly where you need to be. Your authentic light is needed in the world, and your greatest growth and success lie ahead. Stay open, stay curious, and stay true to your heart's deepest desires. The universe is conspiring in your favor, and the best is yet to come!

January 2025

Overview Horoscope for the Month:

Welcome to January 2025, Virgo! This month promises to be a time of new beginnings, personal growth, and exciting opportunities. With the Sun traveling through your 5th house of creativity, self-expression, and romance for most of the month, you may find yourself feeling more confident, playful, and eager to take risks and try new things.

The New Moon in Aquarius on January 29th falls in your 6th house of health, work, and daily routines, bringing a fresh start and new opportunities for self-improvement and positive change. Set intentions for better self-care, improved work-life balance, and a more organized and efficient daily life.

Love:

In love, January 2025 is a month of passion, romance, and self-expression. With Venus entering your 7th house of partnerships on January 2nd, you may find yourself attracted to people who inspire you intellectually and creatively, and who share your values and ideals. If you're in a committed relationship, this is a great time to deepen your connection through shared activities, meaningful conversations, and acts of love and appreciation.

If you're single, you may find yourself drawn to people who are unique, unconventional, and authentic. Be open to new experiences and don't be afraid to express your true self and desires. Trust your intuition and let your heart guide you towards meaningful connections.

Career:

In your career, January 2025 is a month of innovation, collaboration, and networking. With Mercury entering your 6th house of work and service on January 8th, you may find yourself drawn to projects and opportunities that allow you to use your skills and talents in new and creative ways. This is a great time to brainstorm ideas, seek out new knowledge and insights, and connect with colleagues and mentors who can support your growth and success.

If you're considering a career change or starting a new business, the New Moon in Aquarius on January 29th is a powerful time to set intentions and take action towards your goals. Trust in your unique strengths and abilities, and don't be afraid to think outside the box and take calculated risks.

Finances:

In finances, January 2025 is a month of abundance, prosperity, and smart money management. With Mars entering your 8th house of shared resources and investments on January 6th, you may find yourself motivated to take charge of your financial future and make positive changes in your spending and saving habits. Review your budget, identify areas where you can cut back or invest more wisely, and consider seeking out the advice of a financial expert or advisor.

On a deeper level, reflect on your relationship with money and abundance, and any limiting beliefs or patterns that may be holding you back. Practice gratitude, generosity, and trust in the universe's ability to provide for your needs and desires.

- Health:

In health, January 2025 is a month of self-care, wellness, and positive habits. With the New Moon in Aquarius falling in your 6th house of health and daily routines on January 29th, this is a powerful time to set intentions for better self-care, improved nutrition, and regular exercise. Consider trying a new fitness class or wellness practice that aligns with your interests and goals, and make sure to prioritize rest, relaxation, and stress management.

On an emotional level, practice self-compassion, mindfulness, and positive self-talk, and surround yourself with supportive and uplifting people who inspire you to be your best self. Remember that true health and well-being come from a holistic approach that nourishes your mind, body, and spirit.

Travel:

In travel, January 2025 may bring opportunities for short trips, weekend getaways, or adventures close to home. With the Sun and Venus activating your 5th house of creativity and play, you may feel drawn to destinations that offer artistic and cultural experiences, such as museums, galleries, or live performances. Consider planning a trip with friends or loved ones who share your interests and passions, and make sure to leave room for spontaneity and fun.

If travel isn't possible or practical, find ways to bring a sense of adventure and exploration into your daily life. Try a new restaurant, take a different route to work, or explore a new neighborhood or park in your area. Be open to new experiences and perspectives, and trust that the universe will bring you the opportunities and connections you need for your growth and happiness.

Insights from the Stars:

The celestial energies of January 2025 remind you of the power of self-expression, creativity, and authenticity. With the Sun and Venus activating your 5th house of joy and romance, you are being called to let your unique light shine and share your gifts and talents with the world. Trust in your natural abilities and passions, and don't be afraid to take risks and try new things.

The New Moon in Aquarius on January 29th brings a powerful opportunity for positive change and growth in your daily life and routines. Set intentions for better self-care, improved work-life balance, and a more organized and efficient approach to your responsibilities. Remember that small, consistent steps can lead to big results over time.

Best Days of the Month:

January 2nd: Venus enters Pisces, activating your 7th house of partnerships and relationships. This is a great time to deepen your connections with loved ones and express your affection and appreciation.

January 6th: The First Quarter Moon in Aries invites you to take bold action towards your goals and desires, and to trust in your natural leadership and initiative.

January 13th: The Full Moon in Cancer brings a powerful opportunity for emotional healing, self-care, and nurturing your inner world. Take time to rest, reflect, and connect with your feelings and intuition.

January 19th: The Sun enters Aquarius, marking the beginning of a new cycle of innovation, collaboration, and social awareness. Embrace your unique individuality and find ways to make a positive difference in your community and the world.

January 29th: The New Moon in Aquarius falls in your 6th house of health, work, and daily routines, bringing a fresh start and new opportunities for self-improvement and positive change. Set intentions for better self-care, improved work-life balance, and a more organized and efficient daily life.

February 2025

Overview Horoscope for the Month:

Welcome to February 2025, Virgo! This month promises to be a time of deep emotional healing, spiritual growth, and meaningful connections. With the Sun traveling through your 7th house of partnerships and relationships for most of the month, you may find yourself focusing more on your closest bonds and seeking out deeper levels of intimacy and understanding.

The Full Moon in Leo on February 12th falls in your 12th house of spirituality, inner wisdom, and healing, bringing a powerful opportunity for emotional release, forgiveness, and transformation. Trust in the wisdom of your heart and allow yourself to let go of any past wounds or limiting beliefs that may be holding you back.

Love:

In love, February 2025 is a month of emotional depth, vulnerability, and spiritual connection. With Venus entering your 8th house of intimacy and transformation on February 2nd, you may find yourself craving a deeper level of closeness and authenticity in your romantic relationships. If you're in a committed partnership, this is a great time to have honest conversations about your fears, desires, and dreams, and to support each other's personal and spiritual growth.

If you're single, you may find yourself attracted to people who are emotionally mature, psychologically profound, and spiritually attuned. Be open to connections that challenge you to grow and evolve, and trust your intuition when it comes to matters of the heart.

Career:

In your career, February 2025 is a month of collaboration, teamwork, and shared success. With Mercury entering your 7th house of partnerships on February 14th, you may find yourself working closely with colleagues, clients, or business partners on projects that require cooperation and communication. This is a great time to network, build alliances, and seek out mentors or advisors who can support your professional growth and development.

If you're considering a career change or starting a new business venture, the New Moon in Pisces on February 27th is a powerful time to set intentions and take action towards your dreams. Trust in the power of your intuition and imagination, and don't be afraid to think big and aim high.

Finances:

In finances, February 2025 is a month of shared resources, investments, and long-term planning. With Mars traveling through your 8th house of joint finances and inheritances for most of the month, you may find yourself focusing more on your financial partnerships, such as with a spouse, business partner, or financial advisor. Review your budget, make sure you're on the same page with your partner about your financial goals and priorities, and consider seeking out professional advice or guidance if needed.

On a deeper level, reflect on your relationship with money and abundance, and any fears or limiting beliefs that may be holding you back from true prosperity. Practice gratitude, generosity, and trust in the universe's ability to provide for your needs and desires.

Health:

In health, February 2025 is a month of emotional healing, self-care, and inner peace. With the Full Moon in Leo falling in your 12th house of spirituality and healing on February 12th, this is a powerful time to release any past traumas, wounds, or negative patterns that may be affecting your physical and emotional well-being. Consider trying a new therapy or healing modality, such as acupuncture, reiki, or hypnotherapy, and make sure to prioritize rest, relaxation, and stress management.

On a physical level, focus on nourishing your body with whole, natural foods, staying hydrated, and getting plenty of fresh air and exercise. Listen to your body's wisdom and trust in its ability to heal and regenerate itself.

Travel:

In travel, February 2025 may bring opportunities for romantic getaways, spiritual retreats, or trips that focus on deepening your connections with loved ones. With Venus activating your 8th house of intimacy and transformation, you may feel drawn to destinations that offer a sense of privacy, beauty, and emotional depth, such as a secluded beach, a cozy cabin in the woods, or a luxurious spa resort.

If travel isn't possible or practical, find ways to bring a sense of adventure and exploration into your daily life. Try a new cuisine, learn a new language or skill, or explore a new hobby or interest that allows you to express your creativity and passions.

Insights from the Stars:

The celestial energies of February 2025 remind you of the power of vulnerability, authenticity, and emotional healing. With the Sun and Mercury activating your 7th house of partnerships and relationships, you are being called to open your heart, speak your truth, and seek out deeper levels of connection and understanding with others.

The Full Moon in Leo on February 12th brings a powerful opportunity for spiritual growth, inner wisdom, and emotional release. Trust in the guidance of your intuition and allow yourself to let go of any past wounds or limiting beliefs that may be holding you back from your highest potential and purpose.

Best Days of the Month:

February 5th: The First Quarter Moon in Taurus invites you to focus on your values, resources, and self-worth, and to take practical steps towards your goals and desires.

February 12th: The Full Moon in Leo falls in your 12th house of spirituality, inner wisdom, and healing, bringing a powerful opportunity for emotional release, forgiveness, and transformation.

February 18th: The Sun enters Pisces, marking the beginning of a new cycle of spiritual growth, creativity, and intuitive wisdom. Trust in the power of your imagination and allow yourself to dream big and aim high.

February 27th: The New Moon in Pisces falls in your 7th house of partnerships and relationships, bringing a fresh start and new opportunities for connection, collaboration, and mutual understanding. Set intentions for deeper intimacy, authenticity, and spiritual growth in your closest bonds.

March 2025

Overview Horoscope for the Month:

Welcome to March 2025, Virgo! This month promises to be a time of profound transformation, self-discovery, and new beginnings. With Saturn entering your 7th house of partnerships and relationships on March 7th, you may find yourself focusing more on the quality and integrity of your closest bonds, and seeking out connections that support your personal and spiritual growth.

The New Moon in Aries on March 29th falls in your 8th house of intimacy, shared resources, and transformation, bringing a powerful opportunity for deep emotional healing, financial breakthroughs, and positive change. Set intentions for greater vulnerability, trust, and abundance in your life, and trust in the power of surrender and letting go.

Love:

In love, March 2025 is a month of commitment, responsibility, and emotional maturity. With Saturn entering your 7th house of partnerships on March 7th, you may find yourself taking a more serious and realistic approach to your romantic relationships, and seeking out connections that are built on a foundation of trust, respect, and mutual support. If you're in a committed partnership, this is a great time to have honest conversations about your goals, values, and expectations, and to work together to create a stronger and more stable bond.

If you're single, you may find yourself attracted to people who are reliable, responsible, and emotionally mature. Be open to connections that challenge you to grow and evolve, but also make sure to set clear boundaries and take things slow. Trust in the power of divine timing and allow your relationships to unfold naturally.

Career:

In your career, March 2025 is a month of hard work, discipline, and long-term planning. With Saturn entering your 7th house of partnerships and public relations on March 7th, you may find yourself taking on more responsibility and leadership in your professional life, and seeking out collaborations and alliances that can help you achieve your goals. This is a great time to focus on building your reputation, developing your skills and expertise, and creating a solid foundation for future success.

If you're considering a career change or starting a new business venture, the New Moon in Aries on March 29th is a powerful time to set intentions and take bold action towards your dreams. Trust in your natural talents and abilities, and don't be afraid to take calculated risks and step outside your comfort zone.

Finances:

In finances, March 2025 is a month of shared resources, long-term investments, and financial responsibility. With Saturn entering your 8th house of joint finances and inheritances on March 7th, you may find yourself taking a more serious and realistic approach to your financial partnerships and obligations. Review your budget, make sure you're on track with your long-term financial goals, and consider seeking out professional advice or guidance if needed.

On a deeper level, reflect on your relationship with money and abundance, and any fears or limiting beliefs that may be holding you back from true prosperity. Practice gratitude, generosity, and trust in the universe's ability to provide for your needs and desires, but also make sure to take practical steps towards financial security and stability.

Health:

In health, March 2025 is a month of self-discipline, structure, and healthy habits. With Saturn entering your 6th house of health and wellness on March 7th, you may find yourself taking a more serious and committed approach to your physical and emotional well-being. Consider starting a new exercise routine, meal plan, or self-care practice that aligns with your long-term health goals, and make sure to prioritize rest, relaxation, and stress management.

On an emotional level, practice self-compassion, mindfulness, and positive self-talk, and surround yourself with supportive and uplifting people who inspire you to be your best self. Remember that true health and well-being come from a holistic approach that nourishes your mind, body, and spirit.

Travel:

In travel, March 2025 may bring opportunities for business trips, educational pursuits, or adventures that challenge you to step outside your comfort zone. With Saturn activating your 9th house of higher learning and exploration, you may feel drawn to destinations that offer a sense of structure, discipline, and personal growth, such as a language immersion program, a yoga retreat, or a historical site.

If travel isn't possible or practical, find ways to bring a sense of adventure and exploration into your daily life. Take a class or workshop that expands your knowledge and skills, volunteer for a cause that aligns with your values, or explore a new neighborhood or cultural event in your area.

Insights from the Stars:

The celestial energies of March 2025 remind you of the power of commitment, responsibility, and personal growth. With Saturn entering your 7th house of partnerships and relationships, you are being called to take a more serious and realistic approach to your closest bonds, and to seek out connections that support your long-term goals and values.

The New Moon in Aries on March 29th brings a powerful opportunity for deep emotional healing, financial breakthroughs, and positive change in your life. Trust in the power of surrender and letting go, and allow yourself to release any past wounds, limiting beliefs, or unhealthy attachments that may be holding you back from your highest potential and purpose.

Best Days of the Month:

March 6th: The First Quarter Moon in Gemini invites you to focus on your goals, plans, and communication skills, and to take practical steps towards your dreams and aspirations.

March 14th: The Full Moon in Virgo falls in your 1st house of self and identity, bringing a powerful opportunity for personal growth, self-awareness, and emotional healing. Trust in your natural talents and abilities, and allow yourself to shine your unique light in the world.

March 20th: The Sun enters Aries, marking the beginning of a new astrological year and a fresh start in your 8th house of intimacy, shared resources, and transformation. Embrace the power of new beginnings and allow yourself to release any past baggage or limitations.

March 29th: The New Moon in Aries falls in your 8th house of intimacy, shared resources, and transformation, bringing a powerful opportunity for deep emotional healing, financial breakthroughs, and positive change. Set intentions for greater vulnerability, trust, and abundance in your life, and trust in the power of surrender and letting go.

April 2025

Overview Horoscope for the Month:

Welcome to April 2025, Virgo! This month promises to be a time of adventure, personal growth, and expanding your horizons. With the Sun traveling through your 9th house of higher learning, travel, and spirituality for most of the month, you may find yourself seeking out new experiences, knowledge, and wisdom that broaden your perspective and enrich your life.

The Full Moon in Libra on April 12th falls in your 2nd house of values, finances, and self-worth, bringing a powerful opportunity for abundance, prosperity, and positive change in your material world. Trust in your natural talents and abilities, and allow yourself to receive the blessings and opportunities that come your way.

Love:

In love, April 2025 is a month of exploration, freedom, and open-mindedness. With Venus entering your 9th house of adventure and higher learning on April 30th, you may find yourself attracted to people who are intellectually stimulating, culturally diverse, and spiritually evolved. If you're in a committed partnership, this is a great time to plan a romantic getaway, take a class or workshop together, or explore new ways of connecting and communicating with each other.

If you're single, you may find yourself drawn to people who are adventurous, independent, and open-minded. Be open to connections that challenge you to grow and evolve, but also make sure to maintain your own sense of freedom and autonomy. Trust in the power of divine timing and allow your relationships to unfold naturally.

Career:

In your career, April 2025 is a month of innovation, creativity, and thinking outside the box. With Mercury entering your 10th house of career and public reputation on April 16th, you may find yourself taking on new projects, roles, or responsibilities that showcase your unique talents and abilities. This is a great time to network, collaborate with others, and seek out opportunities that align with your long-term goals and aspirations.

If you're considering a career change or starting a new business venture, the New Moon in Taurus on April 27th is a powerful time to set intentions and take practical steps towards your dreams. Trust in your natural skills and abilities, and don't be afraid to take calculated risks and try new things.

Finances:

In finances, April 2025 is a month of abundance, prosperity, and positive change. With the Full Moon in Libra falling in your 2nd house of values and finances on April 12th, you may find yourself receiving unexpected blessings, opportunities, or financial windfalls. Make sure to stay grounded and practical in your approach to money, and consider seeking out professional advice or guidance if needed.

On a deeper level, reflect on your relationship with money and abundance, and any fears or limiting beliefs that may be holding you back from true prosperity. Practice gratitude, generosity, and trust in the universe's ability to provide for your needs and desires, and allow yourself to receive the blessings and opportunities that come your way.

Health:

In health, April 2025 is a month of vitality, energy, and positive habits. With Mars entering your 6th house of health and wellness on April 18th, you may find yourself feeling more motivated and energized to take care of your physical and emotional well-being. Consider trying a new exercise routine, healthy eating plan, or self-care practice that aligns with your long-term health goals, and make sure to prioritize rest, relaxation, and stress management.

On an emotional level, practice self-love, self-acceptance, and positive self-talk, and surround yourself with supportive and uplifting people who inspire you to be your best self. Remember that true health and well-being come from a holistic approach that nourishes your mind, body, and spirit.

Travel:

In travel, April 2025 may bring opportunities for long-distance trips, cultural experiences, or adventures that expand your mind and broaden your horizons. With the Sun activating your 9th house of travel and higher learning, you may feel drawn to destinations that offer a sense of freedom, exploration, and personal growth, such as a foreign country, a spiritual retreat, or a natural wonder.

If travel isn't possible or practical, find ways to bring a sense of adventure and exploration into your daily life. Take a virtual tour of a museum or art gallery, learn a new language or skill online, or explore a new hobby or interest that allows you to express your creativity and curiosity.

Insights from the Stars:

The celestial energies of April 2025 remind you of the power of adventure, personal growth, and expanding your horizons. With the Sun and Venus activating your 9th house of higher learning and spirituality, you are being called to seek out new experiences, knowledge, and wisdom that broaden your perspective and enrich your life.

The Full Moon in Libra on April 12th brings a powerful opportunity for abundance, prosperity, and positive change in your material world. Trust in your natural talents and abilities, and allow yourself to receive the blessings and opportunities that come your way.

Best Days of the Month:

April 4th: The First Quarter Moon in Cancer invites you to focus on your emotional needs, family connections, and inner world, and to take practical steps towards creating a sense of safety, security, and belonging.

April 12th: The Full Moon in Libra falls in your 2nd house of values, finances, and self-worth, bringing a powerful opportunity for abundance, prosperity, and positive change in your material world. Trust in your natural talents and abilities, and allow yourself to receive the blessings and opportunities that come your way.

April 19th: The Sun enters Taurus, marking the beginning of a new cycle of stability, security, and grounded energy in your 9th house of travel, higher learning, and spirituality. Embrace the power of practical wisdom and allow yourself to build a strong foundation for your personal and spiritual growth.

April 27th: The New Moon in Taurus falls in your 9th house of travel, higher learning, and spirituality, bringing a powerful opportunity for adventure, personal growth, and expanding your horizons. Set intentions for new experiences, knowledge, and wisdom that broaden your perspective and enrich your life, and trust in the power of practical action and grounded energy.

May 2025

Overview Horoscope for the Month:

Welcome to May 2025, Virgo! This month promises to be a time of career advancement, public recognition, and personal achievement. With the Sun traveling through your 10th house of career and public reputation for most of the month, you may find yourself in the spotlight and receiving praise and opportunities for your hard work and dedication.

The Full Moon in Scorpio on May 12th falls in your 3rd house of communication, learning, and self-expression, bringing a powerful opportunity for deep conversations, intellectual breakthroughs, and positive change in your mental world. Trust in your natural intelligence and curiosity, and allow yourself to explore new ideas and perspectives that expand your mind and enrich your life.

Love:

In love, May 2025 is a month of passion, intensity, and deep connection. With Venus entering your 10th house of career and public reputation on May 4th, you may find yourself attracted to people who are ambitious, successful, and confident. If you're in a committed partnership, this is a great time to support each other's goals and dreams, and to celebrate each other's achievements and successes.

If you're single, you may find yourself drawn to people who are powerful, charismatic, and intellectually stimulating. Be open to connections that challenge you to grow and evolve, but also make sure to maintain your own sense of independence and autonomy. Trust in the power of divine timing and allow your relationships to unfold naturally.

Career:

In your career, May 2025 is a month of success, recognition, and advancement. With the Sun and Venus activating your 10th house of career and public reputation, you may find yourself receiving praise, promotions, or opportunities that showcase your unique talents and abilities. This is a great time to take on leadership roles, pursue your long-term goals, and make a positive impact in your field or industry.

If you're considering a career change or starting a new business venture, the New Moon in Gemini on May 26th is a powerful time to set intentions and take practical steps towards your dreams. Trust in your natural skills and abilities, and don't be afraid to network, collaborate, and seek out mentors or advisors who can support your success.

Finances:

In finances, May 2025 is a month of stability, security, and long-term planning. With Saturn entering your 8th house of shared resources and investments on May 24th, you may find yourself taking a more serious and responsible approach to your financial partnerships and obligations. Make sure to review your budget, savings, and investments, and consider seeking out professional advice or guidance if needed.

On a deeper level, reflect on your relationship with money and abundance, and any fears or limiting beliefs that may be holding you back from true prosperity. Practice gratitude, generosity, and trust in the universe's ability to provide for your needs and desires, and allow yourself to build a strong foundation for your long-term financial success.

Health:

In health, May 2025 is a month of balance, harmony, and self-care. With the Full Moon in Scorpio falling in your 3rd house of communication and mental well-being on May 12th, you may find yourself feeling more introspective, emotional, and sensitive than usual. Make sure to prioritize rest, relaxation, and stress management, and consider trying a new therapy or healing modality that supports your emotional and mental health.

On a physical level, focus on maintaining a balanced and healthy lifestyle, with regular exercise, nutritious meals, and plenty of water and sleep. Listen to your body's wisdom and trust in its ability to heal and regenerate itself, and don't be afraid to seek out professional help or guidance if needed.

Travel:

In travel, May 2025 may bring opportunities for business trips, professional development, or adventures that align with your career goals and aspirations. With the Sun and Venus activating your 10th house of career and public reputation, you may feel drawn to destinations that offer a sense of prestige, sophistication, and success, such as a major city, a luxurious resort, or a professional conference or event.

If travel isn't possible or practical, find ways to bring a sense of adventure and exploration into your daily life. Take a virtual tour of a famous landmark or museum, attend a webinar or online course that enhances your skills and knowledge, or explore a new neighborhood or cultural event in your area.

Insights from the Stars:

The celestial energies of May 2025 remind you of the power of success, recognition, and personal achievement. With the Sun and Venus activating your 10th house of career and public reputation, you are being called to step into your power, pursue your goals and dreams, and make a positive impact in the world.

The Full Moon in Scorpio on May 12th brings a powerful opportunity for deep conversations, intellectual breakthroughs, and positive change in your mental world. Trust in your natural intelligence and curiosity, and allow yourself to explore new ideas and perspectives that expand your mind and enrich your life.

Best Days of the Month:

May 4th: The First Quarter Moon in Leo invites you to focus on your creative pursuits, self-expression, and inner child, and to take practical steps towards bringing more joy, passion, and play into your life.

May 12th: The Full Moon in Scorpio falls in your 3rd house of communication, learning, and self-expression, bringing a powerful opportunity for deep conversations, intellectual breakthroughs, and positive change in your mental world. Trust in your natural intelligence and curiosity, and allow yourself to explore new ideas and perspectives that expand your mind and enrich your life.

May 20th: The Sun enters Gemini, marking the beginning of a new cycle of communication, learning, and social connection in your 10th house of career and public reputation. Embrace the power of networking, collaboration, and intellectual stimulation, and allow yourself to shine your unique light in the world.

May 26th: The New Moon in Gemini falls in your 10th house of career and public reputation, bringing a powerful opportunity for success, recognition, and personal achievement. Set intentions for your long-term goals and aspirations, and trust in the power of communication, curiosity, and intellectual growth to support your success and fulfillment.

Overview Horoscope for the Month:

Welcome to June 2025, Virgo! This month promises to be a time of social connection, community involvement, and humanitarian pursuits. With the Sun traveling through your 11th house of friendships, groups, and social causes for most of the month, you may find yourself drawn to activities and experiences that allow you to make a positive impact in the world and connect with like-minded individuals who share your values and vision.

The Full Moon in Sagittarius on June 11th falls in your 4th house of home, family, and emotional foundations, bringing a powerful opportunity for healing, nurturing, and positive change in your personal life. Trust in the power of love, compassion, and emotional authenticity, and allow yourself to create a sense of safety, security, and belonging in your relationships and environment.

Love:

In love, June 2025 is a month of friendship, camaraderie, and shared interests. With Venus entering your 11th house of social connections and community on June 6th, you may find yourself attracted to people who are socially conscious, intellectually curious, and emotionally intelligent. If you're in a committed partnership, this is a great time to connect with your partner through shared activities, hobbies, or causes that align with your values and passions.

If you're single, you may find yourself drawn to people who are independent, unconventional, and open-minded. Be open to connections that challenge you to grow and evolve, but also make sure to maintain your own sense of individuality and autonomy. Trust in the power of divine timing and allow your relationships to unfold naturally.

Career:

In your career, June 2025 is a month of collaboration, innovation, and social impact. With Mercury entering your 11th house of groups and networking on June 8th, you may find yourself working on projects or initiatives that involve teamwork, creativity, and forward-thinking ideas. This is a great time to network, brainstorm, and seek out opportunities that align with your long-term goals and aspirations.

If you're considering a career change or starting a new business venture, the New Moon in Cancer on June 25th is a powerful time to set intentions and take practical steps towards your dreams. Trust in your natural skills and abilities, and don't be afraid to seek out mentors, advisors, or collaborators who can support your success and growth.

Finances:

In finances, June 2025 is a month of abundance, prosperity, and positive change. With Jupiter entering your 11th house of community and social connections on June 9th, you may find yourself receiving unexpected blessings, opportunities, or financial support from your network or community. Make sure to stay open to new possibilities and ideas, and consider seeking out professional advice or guidance if needed.

On a deeper level, reflect on your relationship with money and abundance, and any fears or limiting beliefs that may be holding you back from true prosperity. Practice gratitude, generosity, and trust in the universe's ability to provide for your needs and desires, and allow yourself to receive the blessings and opportunities that come your way.

Health:

In health, June 2025 is a month of vitality, energy, and positive habits. With Mars entering your 1st house of self and physical identity on June 17th, you may find yourself feeling more motivated and energized to take care of your physical and emotional well-being. Consider trying a new exercise routine, healthy eating plan, or self-care practice that aligns with your long-term health goals, and make sure to prioritize rest, relaxation, and stress management.

On an emotional level, practice self-love, self-acceptance, and positive self-talk, and surround yourself with supportive and uplifting people who inspire you to be your best self. Remember that true health and well-being come from a holistic approach that nourishes your mind, body, and spirit.

Travel:

In travel, June 2025 may bring opportunities for group trips, social gatherings, or adventures that align with your humanitarian or philanthropic interests. With the Sun activating your 11th house of community and social causes, you may feel drawn to destinations that offer a sense of purpose, connection, and social impact, such as a volunteer project, a cultural exchange, or an eco-friendly retreat.

If travel isn't possible or practical, find ways to bring a sense of adventure and exploration into your daily life. Join a local community group or organization that aligns with your values and interests, attend a social event or gathering that expands your network and horizons, or explore a new hobby or activity that allows you to express your creativity and passion.

Insights from the Stars:

The celestial energies of June 2025 remind you of the power of community, connection, and social impact. With the Sun and Venus activating your 11th house of friendships, groups, and humanitarian pursuits, you are being called to share your gifts and talents with the world, and to make a positive difference in the lives of others.

The Full Moon in Sagittarius on June 11th brings a powerful opportunity for healing, nurturing, and positive change in your personal life. Trust in the power of love, compassion, and emotional authenticity, and allow yourself to create a sense of safety, security, and belonging in your relationships and environment.

Best Days of the Month:

June 2nd: The First Quarter Moon in Virgo invites you to focus on your personal goals, self-improvement, and daily routines, and to take practical steps towards creating a sense of order, efficiency, and well-being in your life.

June 11th: The Full Moon in Sagittarius falls in your 4th house of home, family, and emotional foundations, bringing a powerful opportunity for healing, nurturing, and positive change in your personal life. Trust in the power of love, compassion, and emotional authenticity, and allow yourself to create a sense of safety, security, and belonging in your relationships and environment.

June 20th: The Sun enters Cancer, marking the beginning of a new cycle of emotional connection, nurturing, and personal growth in your 11th house of friendships, groups, and social causes. Embrace the power of vulnerability, empathy, and compassion, and allow yourself to create meaningful and supportive connections with others.

June 25th: The New Moon in Cancer falls in your 11th house of friendships, groups, and social causes, bringing a powerful opportunity for community involvement, humanitarian pursuits, and positive social change. Set intentions for creating a sense of belonging, purpose, and connection in your life, and trust in the power of emotional authenticity and compassion to support your growth and fulfillment.

July 2025

Overview Horoscope for the Month:

Welcome to July 2025, Virgo! This month promises to be a time of spiritual growth, inner reflection, and emotional healing. With the Sun traveling through your 12th house of spirituality, solitude, and subconscious mind for most of the month, you may find yourself drawn to activities and experiences that allow you to connect with your inner wisdom, explore your deepest emotions, and release any past wounds or limiting beliefs that may be holding you back.

The Full Moon in Capricorn on July 10th falls in your 5th house of creativity, self-expression, and joy, bringing a powerful opportunity for personal fulfillment, artistic inspiration, and positive change in your life. Trust in the power of your unique talents and abilities, and allow yourself to express your authentic self with confidence and enthusiasm.

Love:

In love, July 2025 is a month of emotional intimacy, vulnerability, and spiritual connection. With Venus entering your 12th house of spirituality and unconditional love on July 30th, you may find yourself attracted to people who are compassionate, intuitive, and spiritually attuned. If you're in a committed partnership, this is a great time to deepen your emotional bond, share your innermost feelings and desires, and explore the spiritual dimensions of your relationship.

If you're single, you may find yourself drawn to people who are introspective, empathetic, and emotionally mature. Be open to connections that challenge you to grow and evolve, but also make sure to maintain healthy boundaries and take time for self-care and inner reflection. Trust in the power of divine timing and allow your relationships to unfold naturally.

Career:

In your career, July 2025 is a month of introspection, reflection, and inner guidance. With Mercury entering your 12th house of spirituality and intuition on July 26th, you may find yourself seeking a deeper sense of purpose and meaning in your work. This is a great time to reassess your goals and priorities, explore new possibilities and directions, and trust in the wisdom of your inner voice.

If you're considering a career change or starting a new business venture, the New Moon in Leo on July 24th is a powerful time to set intentions and take practical steps towards your dreams. Trust in your natural skills and abilities, and don't be afraid to seek out mentors, advisors, or collaborators who can support your success and growth.

Finances:

In finances, July 2025 is a month of abundance, prosperity, and positive change. With Jupiter activating your 12th house of spirituality and inner wisdom for most of the month, you may find yourself receiving unexpected blessings, opportunities, or financial support from unexpected sources. Make sure to stay open to new possibilities and ideas, and consider seeking out professional advice or guidance if needed.

On a deeper level, reflect on your relationship with money and abundance, and any fears or limiting beliefs that may be holding you back from true prosperity. Practice gratitude, generosity, and trust in the universe's ability to provide for your needs and desires, and allow yourself to receive the blessings and opportunities that come your way.

Health:

In health, July 2025 is a month of emotional healing, self-care, and inner peace. With the Sun activating your 12th house of spirituality and subconscious mind, you may find yourself feeling more introspective, sensitive, and emotionally aware than usual. Make sure to prioritize rest, relaxation, and stress management, and consider trying a new therapy or healing modality that supports your emotional and spiritual well-being.

On a physical level, focus on maintaining a balanced and healthy lifestyle, with regular exercise, nutritious meals, and plenty of water and sleep. Listen to your body's wisdom and trust in its ability to heal and regenerate itself, and don't be afraid to seek out professional help or guidance if needed.

Travel:

In travel, July 2025 may bring opportunities for spiritual retreats, solo journeys, or adventures that allow you to connect with your inner world and explore new dimensions of consciousness. With the Sun activating your 12th house of spirituality and solitude, you may feel drawn to destinations that offer a sense of peace, tranquility, and inner reflection, such as a secluded beach, a meditation center, or a sacred pilgrimage site.

If travel isn't possible or practical, find ways to bring a sense of adventure and exploration into your daily life. Create a sacred space in your home for meditation, journaling, or creative expression, attend a spiritual workshop or retreat online, or explore a new practice or modality that allows you to connect with your inner wisdom and divine guidance.

Insights from the Stars:

The celestial energies of July 2025 remind you of the power of introspection, intuition, and emotional healing. With the Sun and Mercury activating your 12th house of spirituality, solitude, and subconscious mind, you are being called to connect with your inner wisdom, explore your deepest emotions, and release any past wounds or limiting beliefs that may be holding you back.

The Full Moon in Capricorn on July 10th brings a powerful opportunity for personal fulfillment, artistic inspiration, and positive change in your life. Trust in the power of your unique talents and abilities, and allow yourself to express your authentic self with confidence and enthusiasm.

Best Days of the Month:

July 2nd: The First Quarter Moon in Libra invites you to focus on your relationships, partnerships, and social connections, and to take practical steps towards creating a sense of balance, harmony, and cooperation in your life.

July 10th: The Full Moon in Capricorn falls in your 5th house of creativity, self-expression, and joy, bringing a powerful opportunity for personal fulfillment, artistic inspiration, and positive change in your life. Trust in the power of your unique talents and abilities, and allow yourself to express your authentic self with confidence and enthusiasm.

July 22nd: The Sun enters Leo, marking the beginning of a new cycle of creativity, self-expression, and personal growth in your 12th house of spirituality, solitude, and subconscious mind. Embrace the power of your inner child, authentic self, and divine guidance, and allow yourself to shine your unique light in the world.

July 24th: The New Moon in Leo falls in your 12th house of spirituality, solitude, and subconscious mind, bringing a powerful opportunity for emotional healing, inner reflection, and spiritual growth. Set intentions for connecting with your inner wisdom, exploring your deepest emotions, and releasing any past wounds or limiting beliefs that may be holding you back, and trust in the power of your intuition and divine guidance to support your growth and fulfillment.

August 2025

Overview Horoscope for the Month:

Welcome to August 2025, Virgo! This month promises to be a time of new beginnings, self-discovery, and personal growth. With the Sun traveling through your 1st house of self, identity, and personal goals for most of the month, you may find yourself feeling more confident, energized, and motivated to pursue your dreams and aspirations. This is a great time to focus on your own needs and desires, set new intentions and goals, and take bold steps towards creating the life you want to live.

The New Moon in Virgo on August 23rd falls in your 1st house of self, bringing a powerful opportunity for self-reflection, personal development, and positive change in your life. Trust in your natural talents and abilities, and allow yourself to embrace your unique qualities and strengths with pride and enthusiasm.

Love:

In love, August 2025 is a month of passion, romance, and self-expression. With Venus entering your 1st house of self and personal desires on August 25th, you may find yourself feeling more attractive, confident, and magnetic than usual. If you're in a committed partnership, this is a great time to express your love and affection, plan special dates or activities, and deepen your emotional and physical intimacy with your partner.

If you're single, you may find yourself drawn to people who appreciate and admire your unique qualities and strengths. Be open to new connections and experiences, but also make sure to prioritize your own needs and desires. Trust in the power of your own worth and value, and allow yourself to attract relationships that support your growth and happiness.

Career:

In your career, August 2025 is a month of initiative, leadership, and personal achievement. With Mercury entering your 1st house of self and personal goals on September 2nd, you may find yourself feeling more focused, articulate, and motivated to pursue your career aspirations. This is a great time to take on new projects or responsibilities, showcase your skills and talents, and seek out opportunities for growth and advancement.

If you're considering a career change or starting a new business venture, the New Moon in Virgo on August 23rd is a powerful time to set intentions and take practical steps towards your dreams. Trust in your natural abilities and strengths, and don't be afraid to take calculated risks and put yourself out there.

Finances:

In finances, August 2025 is a month of personal responsibility, practicality, and long-term planning. With the Sun and Mercury activating your 1st house of self and personal resources, you may find yourself taking a more proactive and disciplined approach to your finances. This is a great time to review your budget, set financial goals, and make wise investments or purchases that align with your values and priorities.

On a deeper level, reflect on your relationship with money and abundance, and any beliefs or patterns that may be limiting your financial success. Practice gratitude, generosity, and self-worth, and allow yourself to receive the abundance and prosperity that you deserve.

Health:

In health, August 2025 is a month of vitality, self-care, and positive habits. With Mars entering your 1st house of self and physical vitality on August 21st, you may find yourself feeling more energetic, motivated, and proactive about your health and well-being. This is a great time to start a new fitness routine, healthy eating plan, or self-care practice that supports your physical, mental, and emotional health.

On a spiritual level, focus on cultivating a positive mindset, practicing self-love and self-acceptance, and connecting with your inner wisdom and guidance. Listen to your body's needs and trust in its natural ability to heal and thrive, and don't be afraid to seek out professional help or support if needed.

Travel:

In travel, August 2025 may bring opportunities for solo trips, personal retreats, or adventures that allow you to explore new aspects of yourself and your world. With the Sun and Venus activating your 1st house of self and personal identity, you may feel drawn to destinations that offer a sense of freedom, independence, and self-discovery, such as a solo backpacking trip, a personal growth workshop, or a cultural immersion experience.

If travel isn't possible or practical, find ways to bring a sense of adventure and exploration into your daily life. Try a new hobby or activity that challenges you to step outside your comfort zone, explore a new part of your city or town, or connect with people from different backgrounds and cultures.

Insights from the Stars:

The celestial energies of August 2025 remind you of the power of self-discovery, personal growth, and new beginnings. With the Sun, Mercury, and Venus activating your 1st house of self, identity, and personal goals, you are being called to embrace your unique qualities and strengths, pursue your dreams and aspirations, and take bold steps towards creating the life you want to live.

The New Moon in Virgo on August 23rd brings a powerful opportunity for self-reflection, personal development, and positive change in your life. Trust in your natural talents and abilities, and allow yourself to embrace your authentic self with pride and enthusiasm.

Best Days of the Month:

August 1st: The First Quarter Moon in Scorpio invites you to focus on your personal power, shared resources, and emotional depth, and to take practical steps towards creating a sense of intimacy, trust, and transformation in your life.

August 9th: The Full Moon in Aquarius falls in your 6th house of work, health, and daily routines, bringing a powerful opportunity for innovation, collaboration, and positive change in your everyday life. Trust in the power of your unique skills and talents, and allow yourself to embrace new ideas and approaches that support your well-being and success.

August 22nd: The Sun enters Virgo, marking the beginning of a new cycle of self-discovery, personal growth, and positive change in your 1st house of self, identity, and personal goals. Embrace the power of your own worth and value, and allow yourself to shine your unique light in the world.

August 23rd: The New Moon in Virgo falls in your 1st house of self, bringing a powerful opportunity for self-reflection, personal development, and new beginnings. Set intentions for embracing your authentic self, pursuing your dreams and aspirations, and taking bold steps towards creating the life you want to live, and trust in the power of your own talents and abilities to support your growth and fulfillment.

September 2025

Overview Horoscope for the Month:

Welcome to September 2025, Virgo! This month promises to be a time of practical progress, self-improvement, and personal growth. With the Sun traveling through your 2nd house of finances, resources, and self-worth for most of the month, you may find yourself focusing on your material world, working to build a sense of security and abundance, and developing a stronger sense of self-value and self-esteem.

The Full Moon in Pisces on September 7th falls in your 7th house of partnerships and relationships, bringing a powerful opportunity for emotional connection, spiritual intimacy, and positive change in your closest bonds. Trust in the power of vulnerability, compassion, and unconditional love, and allow yourself to deepen your connections with others and with your own heart.

Love:

In love, September 2025 is a month of commitment, devotion, and emotional depth. With Venus entering your 2nd house of love and romance on September 19th, you may find yourself feeling more grounded, sensual, and appreciative of the simple pleasures and comforts of love. If you're in a committed partnership, this is a great time to express your affection and appreciation through tangible acts of love and service, such as cooking a special meal, giving a thoughtful gift, or planning a cozy date night at home.

If you're single, you may find yourself attracted to people who are reliable, stable, and emotionally mature. Be open to connections that offer a sense of comfort, security, and mutual respect, but also make sure to prioritize your own needs and desires. Trust in the power of your own worth and value, and allow yourself to attract relationships that support your growth and happiness.

Career:

In your career, September 2025 is a month of hard work, discipline, and practical progress. With Mars entering your 2nd house of finances and resources on September 22nd, you may find yourself feeling more motivated, ambitious, and focused on your professional goals and aspirations. This is a great time to take on new projects or responsibilities, develop your skills and talents, and seek out opportunities for growth and advancement.

If you're considering a career change or starting a new business venture, the New Moon in Virgo on September 21st is a powerful time to set intentions and take practical steps towards your dreams. Trust in your natural abilities and strengths, and don't be afraid to put in the hard work and effort required to achieve your goals.

Finances:

In finances, September 2025 is a month of abundance, prosperity, and positive change. With the Sun and Mercury activating your 2nd house of finances and resources, you may find yourself feeling more optimistic, resourceful, and proactive about your financial situation. This is a great time to review your budget, set financial goals, and make wise investments or purchases that align with your values and priorities.

On a deeper level, reflect on your relationship with money and abundance, and any beliefs or patterns that may be limiting your financial success. Practice gratitude, generosity, and self-worth, and allow yourself to receive the abundance and prosperity that you deserve.

Health:

In health, September 2025 is a month of balance, self-care, and positive habits. With the Full Moon in Pisces falling in your 7th house of partnerships and balance on September 7th, you may find yourself feeling more sensitive, intuitive, and in need of emotional support and connection. This is a great time to prioritize your own self-care and well-being, while also reaching out to others for love and support.

On a physical level, focus on maintaining a balanced and healthy lifestyle, with regular exercise, nutritious meals, and plenty of rest and relaxation. Listen to your body's needs and trust in its natural wisdom and healing abilities, and don't be afraid to seek out professional help or guidance if needed.

Travel:

In travel, September 2025 may bring opportunities for short trips, weekend getaways, or adventures that allow you to explore new places and experiences close to home. With the Sun and Mercury activating your 2nd house of comfort and security, you may feel drawn to destinations that offer a sense of familiarity, relaxation, and simple pleasures, such as a cozy bed and breakfast, a scenic nature retreat, or a local cultural event.

If travel isn't possible or practical, find ways to bring a sense of adventure and exploration into your daily life. Try a new restaurant or cuisine, explore a new park or nature trail, or connect with friends and loved ones for a fun and memorable outing.

Insights from the Stars:

The celestial energies of September 2025 remind you of the power of practical progress, self-improvement, and personal growth. With the Sun, Mercury, and Venus activating your 2nd house of finances, resources, and self-worth, you are being called to focus on your material world, build a sense of security and abundance, and develop a stronger sense of self-value and self-esteem.

The Full Moon in Pisces on September 7th brings a powerful opportunity for emotional connection, spiritual intimacy, and positive change in your closest relationships. Trust in the power of vulnerability, compassion, and unconditional love, and allow yourself to deepen your connections with others and with your own heart.

Best Days of the Month:

September 1st: The First Quarter Moon in Sagittarius invites you to focus on your personal growth, higher learning, and spiritual beliefs, and to take practical steps towards expanding your mind, exploring new ideas, and discovering your own truth and wisdom.

September 7th: The Full Moon in Pisces falls in your 7th house of partnerships and relationships, bringing a powerful opportunity for emotional connection, spiritual intimacy, and positive change in your closest bonds. Trust in the power of vulnerability, compassion, and unconditional love, and allow yourself to deepen your connections with others and with your own heart.

September 21st: The New Moon in Virgo falls in your 1st house of self, bringing a powerful opportunity for self-reflection, personal development, and new beginnings. Set intentions for embracing your authentic self, pursuing your dreams and aspirations, and taking bold steps towards creating the life you want to live, and trust in the power of your own talents and abilities to support your growth and fulfillment.

September 22nd: The Sun enters Libra, marking the beginning of a new cycle of balance, harmony, and social connection in your 2nd house of finances, resources, and self-worth. Embrace the power of cooperation, diplomacy, and mutual support, and allow yourself to create a sense of abundance and prosperity in your life.

October 2025

Overview Horoscope for the Month:

Welcome to October 2025, Virgo! This month brings a focus on your personal growth, self-expression, and relationships. The Sun starts the month in your 2nd house of finances and self-worth, encouraging you to reassess your values and build a stronger sense of security. As the Sun moves into your 3rd house of communication on October 22nd, you may find yourself more curious, expressive, and eager to learn new things.

The Full Moon in Aries on October 6th illuminates your 8th house of intimacy and transformation, bringing hidden emotions to the surface and encouraging you to let go of what no longer serves you. Embrace this opportunity for deep healing and personal growth.

Love:

In love, October 2025 brings a mix of passion and practicality. Venus enters your 2nd house of values and self-worth on October 13th, encouraging you to focus on building stable, secure relationships based on mutual respect and shared values. If you're single, you may find yourself attracted to grounded, reliable partners who appreciate your intelligence and wit.

For those in committed partnerships, the New Moon in Libra on October 21st activates your 2nd house of finances and resources, making it an excellent time to discuss shared goals and make plans for your future together.

Career:

Your career sector is activated this month, with Mercury entering your 10th house of public reputation on October 6th. This is an excellent time to network, communicate your ideas, and showcase your skills. You may find yourself taking on new responsibilities or receiving recognition for your hard work.

The New Moon in Libra on October 21st falls in your 2nd house of finances, signaling a fresh start in your earning potential or a new income stream. Trust your abilities and don't be afraid to negotiate for what you're worth.

Finances:

October 2025 brings a strong focus on your financial sector, with the Sun, Mercury, and the New Moon activating your 2nd house of money and resources. This is an excellent time to review your budget, set financial goals, and make practical plans for your future security.

The Full Moon in Aries on October 6th illuminates your 8th house of shared resources and investments, which may bring financial matters to a head. Be open to transforming your relationship with money and letting go of any limiting beliefs or habits.

Health:

Your health sector is highlighted this month, with Mars entering your 6th house of wellness on October 22nd. This can bring a burst of energy and motivation to prioritize your physical and mental well-being. Consider starting a new exercise routine or healthy eating plan, and make sure to manage stress through self-care practices like meditation or yoga.

The Full Moon in Aries on October 6th activates your 8th house of emotional healing, making it an excellent time to release pent-up feelings and practice forgiveness, both for yourself and others.

Travel:

Short trips and local adventures are favored this month, with the Sun moving through your 3rd house of travel and communication from October 22nd onwards. This is an excellent time to explore your surroundings, visit nearby places of interest, or connect with siblings or neighbors.

If planning a longer journey, the New Moon in Libra on October 21st can be a good time to set intentions and make travel plans, especially if they involve a partner or loved one.

Insights from the Stars:

October 2025 is a month of personal growth and transformation for you, Virgo. The Full Moon in Aries on October 6th brings powerful insights and healing opportunities, while the New Moon in Libra on October 21st signals a fresh start in your financial sector.

Jupiter's presence in your 11th house of friendships and community throughout the month suggests that connecting with others and pursuing your dreams can lead to exciting opportunities and personal fulfillment. Trust in the power of collaboration and shared vision.

Best Days of the Month:

October 6th: The Full Moon in Aries illuminates your 8th house of intimacy and transformation, bringing hidden emotions to the surface and encouraging deep healing.

October 13th: Venus enters your 2nd house of finances and self-worth, attracting abundance and encouraging you to value yourself and your resources.

October 21st: The New Moon in Libra falls in your 2nd house of money and possessions, signaling a fresh start in your earning potential or financial planning.

October 22nd: The Sun enters Scorpio and your 3rd house of communication and learning, sparking your curiosity and desire to connect with others.

October 29th: Mercury enters Sagittarius and your 4th house of home and family, facilitating open communication and understanding with loved ones..

November 2025

Overview Horoscope for the Month:

Welcome to November 2025, Virgo! This month promises to be a time of introspection, emotional healing, and personal transformation. With the Sun traveling through your 4th house of home, family, and inner foundations for most of the month, you may find yourself focusing on your personal life, nurturing your close relationships, and creating a sense of safety and belonging in your domestic environment.

The Full Moon in Taurus on November 5th falls in your 9th house of higher learning, travel, and spiritual growth, bringing a powerful opportunity for expanding your horizons, exploring new ideas and philosophies, and connecting with your inner wisdom and truth. Trust in the power of your own beliefs and experiences, and allow yourself to learn and grow in ways that feel authentic and meaningful to you.

Love:

In love, November 2025 is a month of emotional intimacy, vulnerability, and deep connection. With Venus entering your 4th house of home and family on November 6th, you may find yourself feeling more nurturing, compassionate, and focused on creating a loving and harmonious atmosphere in your personal relationships. If you're in a committed partnership, this is a great time to spend quality time together, share your feelings and needs openly, and work on creating a strong foundation of trust and support.

If you're single, you may find yourself attracted to people who are emotionally mature, nurturing, and family-oriented. Be open to connections that offer a sense of comfort, security, and shared values, but also make sure to honor your own needs for independence and personal growth. Trust in the power of your own inner wisdom and intuition, and allow yourself to attract relationships that support your highest good and happiness.

Career:

In your career, November 2025 is a month of hard work, discipline, and practical progress. With Mars entering your 6th house of work and daily routines on November 4th, you may find yourself feeling more focused, energized, and motivated to tackle your professional responsibilities and goals. This is a great time to take on new projects, develop your skills and expertise, and seek out opportunities for growth and advancement in your field.

If you're considering a career change or starting a new business venture, the New Moon in Scorpio on November 20th is a powerful time to set intentions and take bold steps towards your dreams. Trust in your natural talents and abilities, and don't be afraid to embrace your unique vision and leadership potential.

Finances:

In finances, November 2025 is a month of stability, security, and long-term planning. With the Sun and Mercury activating your 4th house of home and family, you may find yourself focusing on creating a strong financial foundation for yourself and your loved ones. This is a great time to review your budget, make smart investments, and plan for your future financial goals and needs.

On a deeper level, reflect on your relationship with money and security, and any fears or limiting beliefs that may be holding you back from true abundance and prosperity. Practice gratitude, generosity, and trust in the universe's ability to provide for your needs, and allow yourself to receive the blessings and opportunities that come your way.

Health:

In health, November 2025 is a month of self-care, balance, and emotional well-being. With the Full Moon in Taurus falling in your 9th house of higher learning and spiritual growth on November 5th, you may find yourself feeling more introspective, philosophical, and in need of inner peace and harmony. This is a great time to prioritize your mental and emotional health, practice stress-reduction techniques, and seek out activities that bring you a sense of meaning and purpose.

On a physical level, focus on maintaining a balanced and healthy lifestyle, with regular exercise, nutritious meals, and plenty of rest and relaxation. Listen to your body's needs and trust in its natural wisdom and healing abilities, and don't be afraid to seek out professional help or guidance if needed.

Travel:

In travel, November 2025 may bring opportunities for long-distance trips, cultural experiences, or adventures that expand your mind and broaden your horizons. With the Full Moon in Taurus activating your 9th house of travel and higher learning on November 5th, you may feel drawn to destinations that offer a sense of beauty, luxury, and sensual pleasure, such as a scenic resort, a world-class museum, or a gourmet food tour.

If travel isn't possible or practical, find ways to bring a sense of adventure and exploration into your daily life. Take a class or workshop that introduces you to new ideas and perspectives, read a book or watch a documentary that expands your knowledge and understanding, or connect with people from different cultures and backgrounds to broaden your worldview.

Insights from the Stars:

The celestial energies of November 2025 remind you of the power of emotional healing, inner wisdom, and personal transformation. With the Sun, Mercury, and Venus activating your 4th house of home, family, and inner foundations, you are being called to nurture your close relationships, create a sense of safety and belonging in your personal life, and connect with your deepest feelings and needs.

The Full Moon in Taurus on November 5th brings a powerful opportunity for expanding your horizons, exploring new ideas and philosophies, and connecting with your inner wisdom and truth. Trust in the power of your own beliefs and experiences, and allow yourself to learn and grow in ways that feel authentic and meaningful to you.

Best Days of the Month:

November 4th: Mars enters Sagittarius and your 4th house of home and family, bringing energy and motivation to your personal life and domestic projects.

November 5th: The Full Moon in Taurus illuminates your 9th house of travel, higher learning, and spiritual growth, encouraging you to expand your horizons and seek new experiences.

November 6th: Venus enters Scorpio and your 3rd house of communication and learning, enhancing your ability to express yourself with depth and passion.

November 20th: The New Moon in Scorpio falls in your 3rd house of communication and ideas, signaling a fresh start in your thinking, writing, or networking activities.

November 28th: The First Quarter Moon in Pisces activates your 7th house of partnerships and relationships, supporting collaboration, compromise, and mutual understanding.

December 2025

Overview Horoscope for the Month:

Hey there, Virgo! December 2025 is all about spreading your wings and embracing new adventures. The Sun is shining bright in your 4th house of home and family as the month begins, so you might be feeling extra cozy and domestic. But don't get too comfy, because on December 21st, the Sun moves into your 5th house of creativity, romance, and self-expression, urging you to let your inner child out to play.

The New Moon in Sagittarius on December 19th is a cosmic invitation to set intentions around expanding your horizons, whether that means planning a trip, starting a new hobby, or taking a leap of faith in love. Trust your instincts and don't be afraid to color outside the lines.

Love:

'Tis the season for love, Virgo! With Venus gracing your 5th house of romance from December 24th, you'll be feeling extra flirty and magnetic. If you're single, this is an amazing time to put yourself out there and attract someone who appreciates your unique brand of charm. Coupled up? Plan some fun date nights and focus on keeping the spark alive.

The Full Moon in Gemini on December 4th lights up your 10th house of career and public image, so don't be surprised if your love life and professional life start to intertwine. Just make sure to maintain healthy boundaries and communicate openly with your partner.

Career:

December 2025 is all about shaking things up in your career, Virgo. With Mercury entering your 5th house of creativity on January 1st, you'll be bursting with innovative ideas and the confidence to pitch them to higher-ups. Don't be afraid to take some calculated risks and think outside the box.

The New Moon in Sagittarius on December 19th is a great time to set intentions around expanding your skill set or exploring new career paths. Trust that the universe has your back and is guiding you towards your true calling.

Finances:

Your financial sector is looking stable and secure this month, Virgo. The Sun in your 4th house of home and family until December 21st suggests that you'll be focusing on creating a solid foundation for yourself and your loved ones. This could mean investing in property, saving for a rainy day, or simply being more mindful of your spending habits.

The Full Moon in Gemini on December 4th illuminates your 10th house of career and public image, which could bring some unexpected financial opportunities or rewards for your hard work. Just make sure to read the fine print and don't overextend yourself.

Health:

Your health and wellness are in the spotlight this month, Virgo. With Mars traveling through your 6th house of health and daily routines for most of December, you'll have the energy and motivation to prioritize self-care and make positive lifestyle changes. This could mean starting a new exercise routine, trying out a new diet, or simply making more time for rest and relaxation.

The New Moon in Sagittarius on December 19th is a great time to set intentions around improving your physical, mental, and emotional well-being. Remember to be patient with yourself and celebrate your progress, no matter how small.

Travel:

Adventure is calling your name this month, Virgo! With the Sun moving into your 5th house of fun and play on December 21st, you'll be itching to explore new horizons and experience life to the fullest. This could mean planning a weekend getaway, booking a vacation for the new year, or simply being more spontaneous in your daily life.

The Full Moon in Gemini on December 4th illuminates your 10th house of career and public image, which could bring some travel opportunities related to work or networking. Just make sure to double-check your itinerary and pack accordingly.

Insights from the Stars:

December 2025 is a month of joy, creativity, and self-expression for you, Virgo. The universe is urging you to let your inner child out to play and embrace your unique quirks and talents. Don't be afraid to take some risks and trust that the universe has your back.

At the same time, the Full Moon in Gemini on December 4th reminds you to stay grounded and focused on your long-term goals, especially when it comes to your career and public image. Strike a balance between having fun and being responsible, and remember that it's okay to ask for help when you need it.

Best Days of the Month:

December 4th: The Full Moon in Gemini lights up your 10th house of career and public image, bringing recognition and rewards for your hard work.

December 19th: The New Moon in Sagittarius falls in your 4th house of home and family, making it a great time to set intentions around creating a cozy and nurturing space for yourself and your loved ones.

December 21st: The Sun enters Capricorn and your 5th house of creativity, romance, and self-expression, urging you to let loose and have some fun.

December 24th: Venus enters Capricorn and your 5th house of love and pleasure, making it an ideal time for flirting, dating, and enjoying life's simple joys.

December 27th: The First Quarter Moon in Aries activates your 8th house of intimacy and transformation, supporting deep emotional connections and personal growth.

LIBRA 2025 HOROSCOPE

Overview Libra 2025

(September 23 - October 22)

Dear Libra, 2025 is set to be a year of significant personal growth, transformative relationships, and a deepening connection to your authentic self. The celestial bodies are aligning in ways that will support you in expanding your horizons, both internally and externally. Let's take a closer look at the key astrological events that will shape your journey over the coming year.

The year begins with Mars, the planet of action and desire, in your 10th house of career and public image. This placement suggests that you'll be feeling ambitious and driven to make progress in your professional life. You may find yourself taking on new responsibilities or leadership roles, and your efforts are likely to be recognized and rewarded. However, with Mars forming a challenging square aspect to Chiron in your 7th house of relationships in late February, you may need to navigate some tension between your personal and professional commitments. Be mindful of any tendencies to overwork or neglect your emotional needs during this time.

As we move into March, a significant shift occurs when Saturn, the planet of structure and responsibility, enters your 7th house of partnerships. This transit, which will last until 2025, marks the beginning of a new cycle in your closest relationships. Saturn's influence will encourage you to take a serious look at the health and sustainability of your partnerships, both romantic and business. You may find yourself making long-term commitments or ending relationships that are no longer serving your growth. This is a time to build relationships on a foundation of mutual respect, trust, and shared values.

The Aries New Moon on March 29 falls in your 7th house, bringing a powerful opportunity to set intentions for the kind of relationships you want to attract and nurture in the coming year. This is a time to get clear on your needs and boundaries, and to communicate them openly and honestly with your partner(s). The influence of Saturn will ensure that any new connections formed during this time have the potential for long-term stability and growth.

In mid-April, Jupiter, the planet of expansion and growth, will form a square aspect to Pluto in your 4th house of home and family. This transit may bring up deep-seated emotional patterns or family dynamics that need to be addressed and healed. You may find yourself confronting issues of power, control, or manipulation in your close relationships. Trust in the process of transformation, and be willing to let go of any unhealthy attachments or beliefs that are holding you back. This is a time to create a solid foundation of love and security within yourself, so that you can show up more fully and authentically in your relationships.

As the North Node shifts into your 9th house of travel, education, and spiritual growth in April, you'll feel called to broaden your horizons and explore new ideas and experiences. This is a powerful time for learning, both about yourself and the world around you. Consider taking a course, embarking on a long-distance trip, or diving into a spiritual or philosophical practice that resonates with you. The South Node's presence in your 3rd house suggests that you may need to let go of limiting beliefs or thought patterns that are keeping you stuck in old ways of perceiving yourself and others.

The mid-year period is marked by a series of powerful eclipses that will accelerate your growth and bring significant changes to your relationships and sense of self. The Lunar Eclipse in Virgo on September 7 falls in your 12th house of spirituality and inner work, highlighting the need for emotional healing and release. You may find yourself confronting hidden fears, anxieties or self-defeating patterns during this time. Be gentle with yourself, and trust that any challenges that arise are ultimately serving your highest good.

The Solar Eclipse in Libra on October 21 is a particularly significant event for you, as it falls in your 1st house of self and identity. This eclipse marks a powerful new beginning in your personal growth and self-expression. You may find yourself letting go of old identities or roles that no longer align with your authentic self, and stepping into a new phase of confidence and self-assurance. Trust your intuition, and don't be afraid to take bold steps towards creating the life and relationships you truly desire.

As we move into the final months of the year, Venus, your ruling planet, will spend an extended period of time in your 9th house of travel and adventure. This placement suggests that you may find yourself drawn to new experiences and connections that expand your perspective and sense of what's possible. If you're single, you may attract a partner from a different cultural background or with a strong philosophical or spiritual bent. If you're in a relationship, you may find yourself growing and learning together through shared adventures and intellectual pursuits.

The year comes to a close with a powerful Full Moon in your sign on March 14, 2026. This lunation highlights the transformative growth you've undergone over the past year, and illuminates the path forward for your continued evolution. Trust in the journey, Libra, and know that you have all the inner resources and wisdom you need to create a life and relationships that truly fulfill and inspire you.

Throughout the year, remember to stay true to your core Libran values of balance, harmony, and partnership. Your natural gifts of diplomacy, fairness, and aesthetic sensibility will serve you well in navigating any challenges that arise. Above all, trust in the power of love and connection to guide you towards your highest good.

January 2025

Overview Horoscope for the Month:

Welcome to January 2025, Libra! This month promises to be a time of new beginnings, personal growth, and exciting opportunities. With Mars entering your 4th house of home and family on January 6th, you may feel a strong urge to nest, redecorate, or spend quality time with loved ones. This is a great time to focus on creating a nurturing and supportive environment that reflects your personal style and values.

The Full Moon in Cancer on January 13th illuminates your 10th house of career and public reputation, bringing recognition and rewards for your hard work and dedication. Trust that your efforts are being noticed and appreciated, and don't be afraid to step into the spotlight and claim your power.

Love:

In love, January 2025 is a month of deepening intimacy, emotional connection, and heart-centered communication. With Venus, your ruling planet, entering sensitive Pisces on January 2nd, you may find yourself craving a soulful and romantic connection with your partner or potential love interest. This is a time to open your heart, express your feelings with authenticity and vulnerability, and create a safe space for love to flourish.

If you're in a committed relationship, take time to nurture your bond through shared activities, deep conversations, and physical affection. Plan a cozy date night at home, write love letters to each other, or surprise your partner with a thoughtful gesture that shows how much you care. Be willing to listen with an open heart and mind, and prioritize quality time together.

If you're single, you may find yourself attracted to people who share your values, interests, and emotional depth. Trust your intuition and let your heart guide you towards meaningful connections. Be open to meeting someone through shared social circles, online dating, or serendipitous encounters. Remember that true love starts with self-love, so focus on cultivating a positive and compassionate relationship with yourself first and foremost.

Career:

In your career, January 2025 is a month of innovation, collaboration, and creative problem-solving. With Mercury entering Aquarius on January 8th, you may find yourself drawn to unconventional ideas and approaches that challenge the status quo. This is a great time to brainstorm with colleagues, network with like-minded professionals, and explore new ways of doing things.

The Full Moon on January 13th highlights your achievements and success in your career, bringing recognition and rewards for your hard work and dedication. Trust that your unique talents and contributions are valued and appreciated, and don't be afraid to step into leadership roles or take on new responsibilities.

If you're considering a career change or starting a new business venture, the New Moon in Aquarius on January 29th is an auspicious time to set intentions and take action towards your goals. Trust in your vision and abilities, and surround yourself with supportive and inspiring people who believe in your potential.

Finances:

In finances, January 2025 is a month of abundance, growth, and positive change. With Venus and Jupiter aligning in your 6th house of work and daily routines, you may find opportunities for increased income, bonuses, or financial rewards through your job or business. This is a great time to focus on maximizing your earning potential and creating a solid foundation for long-term financial stability.

Review your budget, identify areas where you can save or invest, and make sure that your financial decisions align with your values and priorities. Consider working with a financial planner or advisor to create a personalized strategy for building wealth and achieving your long-term goals.

On a deeper level, reflect on your relationship with money and abundance, and any limiting beliefs or patterns that may be holding you back. Practice gratitude, generosity, and positive affirmations around your finances, and trust that the universe is conspiring to support your highest good.

Health:

In health, January 2025 is a month of vitality, self-care, and mind-body balance. With Mars energizing your 4th house of home and emotional wellbeing, you may feel a strong desire to create a healthy and nurturing environment that supports your physical and mental health. This is a great time to declutter your space, upgrade your home gym or yoga studio, or invest in high-quality self-care products and tools.

Make sure to prioritize rest, relaxation, and stress management, especially around the Full Moon on January 13th when emotions may be heightened. Practice mindfulness, meditation, or deep breathing exercises to calm your mind and body, and engage in activities that bring you joy and rejuvenation.

On a physical level, focus on nourishing your body with whole, nutrient-dense foods, staying hydrated, and getting plenty of fresh air and exercise. Consider trying a new fitness class or outdoor activity that challenges you and boosts your energy levels. Remember that true health starts from the inside out, so prioritize your emotional and spiritual wellbeing just as much as your physical health.

Travel:

January 2025 may not be the best month for long-distance travel, Libra, with Mars and Mercury both in more inward-focused signs. However, this is a great time for short trips, weekend getaways, or staycations that allow you to recharge and reconnect with yourself and loved ones.

Consider planning a cozy cabin retreat, spa weekend, or nature hike that immerses you in beauty and tranquility. If you do need to travel for work or personal reasons, make sure to prioritize self-care and rest, and create a grounding routine that helps you stay centered and balanced on the go.

Insights from the Stars:

The celestial energies of January 2025 remind you of the power of emotional intelligence, empathy, and heart-centered communication. With Venus and Jupiter aligning in sensitive Pisces, you are being called to lead with love, compassion, and understanding in all your interactions and relationships. Trust your intuition and let your heart be your guide, even in challenging or uncertain situations.

The Full Moon in Cancer on January 13th illuminates your deepest feelings, needs, and desires, and invites you to honor your emotional truth and vulnerability. Don't be afraid to express your authentic self and ask for the support and nurturing you need from others. Remember that your sensitivity is a superpower, not a weakness, and that your ability to connect deeply with others is a gift to be cherished.

Best Days of the Month:

January 6th: Mars enters your 4th house of home and family, energizing your domestic life and emotional bonds.

January 13th: Full Moon in Cancer illuminates your 10th house of career and public reputation, bringing recognition and rewards.

January 27th: Mercury enters Aquarius, sparking innovative ideas and collaborative opportunities in your work and creative projects.

January 29th: New Moon in Aquarius, inviting you to set intentions and take action towards your dreams and aspirations.

February 2025

Overview Horoscope for the Month:

Welcome to February 2025, Libra! This month is all about deepening your connections, both with yourself and others. With the Sun in Aquarius illuminating your 5th house of romance, creativity, and self-expression for most of the month, you'll feel inspired to let your unique light shine and share your gifts with the world. Embrace your individuality and don't be afraid to stand out from the crowd.

The Full Moon in Leo on February 12th falls in your 11th house of friendships and community, highlighting the importance of your social networks and support systems. Surround yourself with people who uplift and inspire you, and be willing to lend a helping hand to those in need. Trust that the connections you make now will have a lasting impact on your life.

Love :

February 2025 is a month of passion, romance, and deepening intimacy for you, Libra. With Venus, your ruling planet, entering fiery Aries on February 4th, you may feel a strong urge to take the lead in your love life and go after what you want with confidence and enthusiasm. If you're single, this is a great time to put yourself out there and make the first move with someone you're attracted to. Trust your instincts and don't be afraid to take a risk.

If you're in a committed relationship, the Full Moon on February 12th invites you to celebrate your love and express your appreciation for your partner in a big, bold way. Plan a romantic getaway, write a heartfelt love letter, or surprise them with a thoughtful gift that shows how much you care. Remember that the key to a strong and lasting relationship is open communication, mutual respect, and a willingness to grow together.

Career:

In your career, February 2025 is a month of networking, collaboration, and innovative thinking. With Mercury entering Aquarius on February 3rd, you may find yourself drawn to unconventional ideas and approaches that challenge the status quo. This is a great time to brainstorm with colleagues, attend industry events, or take on a leadership role in a group project.

The New Moon in Pisces on February 27th falls in your 6th house of work and daily routines, inviting you to set intentions around creating more balance, harmony, and purpose in your professional life. Consider ways you can streamline your tasks, delegate responsibilities, or incorporate more self-care and mindfulness practices into your workday. Trust that when you prioritize your well-being, your productivity and success will naturally follow.

Finances:

In finances, February 2025 is a month of abundance, growth, and positive change. With Jupiter, the planet of expansion and opportunity, entering Taurus on February 11th, you may find new sources of income or financial support opening up to you. This is a great time to focus on building long-term wealth and security, whether through investments, savings, or a side hustle that aligns with your passions and values.

However, with Uranus squaring your ruling planet Venus on February 15th, there may be some unexpected expenses or financial curveballs that require you to think on your feet. Stay flexible, adaptable, and open to new solutions and strategies. Trust that any challenges that arise are ultimately helping you develop a stronger and more resilient relationship with money.

Health:

In health, February 2025 is a month of vitality, self-care, and mind-body balance. With the Sun energizing your 5th house of pleasure and play, you may feel a strong urge to engage in activities that bring you joy, laughter, and creative fulfillment. This is a great time to take up a new hobby, try a fun fitness class, or indulge in some pampering and relaxation.

However, with Mars entering Leo on February 16th, there may be a tendency to overdo it or push yourself too hard in the pursuit of your goals. Make sure to listen to your body's signals and prioritize rest and recovery when needed. Remember that true health is about finding a balance between effort and ease, discipline and self-compassion.

Travel:

February 2025 is a great month for short trips, weekend getaways, or adventures close to home that feed your soul and spark your curiosity. With the Sun in Aquarius, you may be drawn to unconventional or off-the-beaten-path destinations that offer a fresh perspective and a chance to break out of your comfort zone.

Consider planning a road trip with friends, attending a cultural event or festival, or exploring a new neighborhood or city that you've always been curious about. The key is to approach your travels with an open mind and a willingness to embrace the unexpected. Trust that the journey is just as important as the destination, and that every experience is an opportunity for growth and self-discovery.

Insights from the Stars:

The celestial energies of February 2025 remind you of the power of authenticity, creativity, and self-expression. With the Sun and Mercury both in Aquarius, you are being called to embrace your unique voice and vision, and share your gifts with the world in a way that feels true to you. Don't be afraid to stand out from the crowd or take a unconventional path – your individuality is your greatest strength and asset.

At the same time, the Full Moon in Leo on February 12th highlights the importance of community, collaboration, and shared joy. Remember that you don't have to go it alone – there is strength in numbers and support in connection. Surround yourself with people who inspire you, challenge you, and bring out the best in you. And don't forget to celebrate your successes and milestones along the way – life is meant to be enjoyed and savored, not just endured.

Best Days of the Month:

February 5th: First Quarter Moon in Taurus – A great day for indulging in sensual pleasures and enjoying the finer things in life.

February 12th: Full Moon in Leo – A time to celebrate your achievements, express your creativity, and let your light shine.

February 20th: Last Quarter Moon in Sagittarius – An opportunity to let go of limiting beliefs and embrace a more expansive, adventurous outlook on life.

February 27th: New Moon in Pisces – A powerful day for setting intentions around emotional healing, spiritual growth, and creative manifestation.

March 2025

Overview Horoscope for the Month:

Welcome to March 2025, Libra! This month is all about finding balance, harmony, and grace in the midst of change and transformation. With Saturn entering Aries on March 1st, you may feel a strong urge to take charge of your life and make bold moves towards your goals and dreams. Trust your instincts and don't be afraid to take calculated risks – the universe is supporting you every step of the way.

The New Moon in Aries on March 29th falls in your 7th house of partnerships and relationships, highlighting the importance of collaboration, compromise, and mutual support. Whether you're working on a creative project, building a business, or deepening a romantic connection, remember that you don't have to go it alone. Seek out people who share your values and vision, and be willing to give and receive help when needed.

Love:

March 2025 is a month of passion, intensity, and deep emotional connections for you, Libra. With Venus, your ruling planet, entering sensitive Pisces on March 2nd, you may find yourself craving more intimacy, romance, and spiritual connection in your relationships. This is a great time to open your heart, share your feelings, and explore the deeper meanings and purposes of your partnerships.

However, with Venus turning retrograde on March 1st, there may be some challenges or obstacles that arise in your love life. Old issues or unresolved conflicts may resurface, requiring you to confront them with honesty, compassion, and understanding. Remember that every challenge is an opportunity for growth and healing, and that the most meaningful relationships are often the ones that require the most work and dedication.

If you're single, the New Moon on March 29th may bring new opportunities for love and connection. Keep an open mind and heart, and don't be afraid to put yourself out there and take a chance on someone new. Trust that the universe is guiding you towards the right person at the right time.

Career:

In your career, March 2025 is a month of hard work, determination, and strategic planning. With Saturn entering your 6th house of daily routines and responsibilities, you may feel a strong urge to get organized, streamline your tasks, and create more structure and discipline in your work life. This is a great time to set clear goals, create a schedule, and break down big projects into manageable steps.

However, with Mercury turning retrograde on March 15th, there may be some delays, miscommunications, or technical difficulties that arise in your work. Stay flexible, adaptable, and patient, and don't be afraid to ask for help or clarification when needed. Remember that every setback is an opportunity to learn, grow, and refine your skills and strategies.

The Full Moon on March 14th falls in your 12th house of spirituality and inner wisdom, reminding you to trust your intuition and listen to your inner voice. If you're feeling stuck or unsure about your career path, take some time to meditate, journal, or seek guidance from a trusted mentor or advisor. Trust that the answers you seek are already within you, waiting to be discovered.

Finances:

In finances, March 2025 is a month of stability, security, and long-term planning. With Saturn entering your 6th house of daily routines and responsibilities, you may feel a strong urge to get your financial house in order, create a budget, and make smart investments for the future. This is a great time to review your spending habits, cut back on unnecessary expenses, and start saving for a rainy day.

However, with Jupiter squaring Chiron on March 18th, there may be some financial challenges or obstacles that arise, requiring you to confront your fears, doubts, or limiting beliefs around money. Remember that every challenge is an opportunity for growth and healing, and that true abundance comes from a place of inner peace, gratitude, and self-worth.

The New Moon on March 29th is a powerful time to set intentions around financial abundance, prosperity, and success. Visualize yourself living the life of your dreams, and take practical steps towards making that vision a reality. Trust that the universe is conspiring in your favor, and that every penny saved and invested is a seed planted for future growth and abundance.

Health:

In health, March 2025 is a month of self-care, self-love, and inner healing. With the Sun in Pisces for most of the month, you may feel more sensitive, intuitive, and emotionally vulnerable than usual. This is a great time to prioritize your mental and emotional well-being, and to engage in practices that bring you peace, comfort, and inner strength.

Consider starting a meditation practice, taking a yoga class, or spending time in nature to connect with your inner wisdom and find balance and harmony within yourself. Make sure to get plenty of rest, eat nourishing foods, and surround yourself with positive, uplifting people and environments.

However, with Mars entering Cancer on March 23rd, there may be some challenges or obstacles that arise in your physical health, requiring you to slow down, listen to your body, and make necessary adjustments to your lifestyle and habits. Remember that true health is about finding balance and moderation in all things, and that every challenge is an opportunity for growth, healing, and self-discovery.

Travel:

March 2025 may not be the best time for long-distance travel or big adventures, Libra, with Mercury and Venus both retrograde for much of the month. However, this is a great time for inner journeys, spiritual retreats, or creative staycations that allow you to explore your inner world and tap into your imagination and intuition.

Consider taking a solo trip to a peaceful, natural setting, attending a meditation or yoga retreat, or spending a weekend immersed in a creative project or hobby that brings you joy and fulfillment. The key is to approach your travels and adventures with a sense of curiosity, openness, and willingness to let go of expectations and embrace the unknown.

If you do need to travel for work or personal reasons, make sure to double-check your itinerary, allow extra time for delays or changes, and pack a sense of humor and flexibility along with your luggage. Remember that every journey, whether inner or outer, is an opportunity for growth, learning, and self-discovery.

Insights from the Stars:

The celestial energies of March 2025 remind you of the power of balance, harmony, and inner peace in the midst of change and transformation. With Saturn entering Aries and the New Moon in Aries on March 29th, you are being called to take bold, decisive action towards your goals and dreams, while also staying true to your values of fairness, justice, and cooperation.

Remember that true success and happiness come from a place of alignment, authenticity, and inner wholeness, not just external achievements or accolades. Trust your inner wisdom and intuition to guide you towards the right path, and don't be afraid to make necessary changes or adjustments along the way.

At the same time, the retrograde cycles of Venus and Mercury remind you of the importance of patience, reflection, and self-awareness in your relationships, communications, and inner world. Take time to review your past experiences, heal old wounds, and release any patterns or beliefs that no longer serve your highest good. Remember that every challenge is an opportunity for growth, learning, and self-discovery.

Best Days of the Month:

March 5th: First Quarter Moon in Gemini – A great day for learning, exploring new ideas, and connecting with like-minded people.

March 14th: Full Moon in Virgo – A powerful time for releasing old habits, patterns, or beliefs that no longer serve your health and well-being.

March 20th: Sun enters Aries – A fresh start and new beginnings in your relationships, partnerships, and creative endeavors.

March 29th: New Moon in Aries – A potent time for setting intentions, taking bold action, and planting seeds for future growth and success.

April 2025

Overview Horoscope for the Month:

April 2025 is a month of new beginnings, fresh starts, and exciting opportunities for you, Libra. With the Sun in Aries illuminating your 7th house of partnerships and relationships, you may find yourself focusing on collaboration, compromise, and mutual support in both your personal and professional life. The New Moon in Taurus on April 27th highlights your 8th house of intimacy, shared resources, and personal transformation, inviting you to deepen your connections and explore the hidden depths of your psyche.

Love:

In love, April 2025 brings a mix of passion, intensity, and emotional healing for you, Libra. Venus, your ruling planet, enters fiery Aries on April 4th, igniting your desire for adventure, excitement, and new experiences in your relationships. If you're single, this is a great time to put yourself out there and take a chance on someone who sparks your curiosity and enthusiasm. If you're in a committed partnership, use this energy to reignite the spark and explore new ways of connecting and expressing your love.

Career:

Your career sector is buzzing with activity this month, Libra, with Mercury entering Taurus on April 10th and Mars entering Leo on April 18th. This is a great time to focus on practical, tangible goals and take bold, confident steps towards your professional aspirations. Networking, self-promotion, and creative problem-solving are all highlighted, so don't be afraid to put yourself out there and showcase your unique talents and abilities.

Finances:

In finances, April 2025 is a month of stability, security, and long-term planning for you, Libra. With Saturn forming a supportive sextile to Uranus on April 4th, you may find innovative solutions to old financial challenges or receive unexpected windfalls or opportunities for growth. The New Moon on April 27th is a powerful time to set intentions around abundance, prosperity, and financial freedom, so be sure to clarify your goals and take practical steps towards making them a reality.

Health:

Your health sector is highlighted this month, Libra, with the Full Moon in Libra on April 12th illuminating your 1st house of self, body, and personal identity. This is a great time to focus on self-care, self-love, and physical wellness, and to release any habits, patterns, or beliefs that no longer serve your highest good. Consider starting a new exercise routine, trying a new healthy recipe, or incorporating more mindfulness and relaxation practices into your daily life.

Travel:

April 2025 may not be the best time for long-distance travel, Libra, with Mercury and Mars both in more practically-oriented signs. However, this is a great month for short trips, weekend getaways, or even virtual adventures that allow you to explore new ideas, cultures, and perspectives from the comfort of your own home. If you do need to travel for work or personal reasons, be sure to plan ahead, double-check your itinerary, and allow extra time for delays or unexpected changes.

Insights from the Stars:

The celestial energies of April 2025 remind you of the power of balance, harmony, and inner peace in the midst of change and growth. With the Sun in Aries and the New Moon in Taurus, you are being called to find a middle ground between assertiveness and receptivity, action and reflection, and individuality and partnership. Trust your inner wisdom to guide you towards the right path, and don't be afraid to ask for help or support when you need it.

Best Days of the Month:

April 5th: First Quarter Moon in Cancer – A great day for emotional connection, self-care, and nurturing your inner child.

April 12th: Full Moon in Libra – A powerful time for releasing old patterns, finding inner balance, and celebrating your unique beauty and grace.

April 20th: Sun enters Taurus – A time for grounding, stabilizing, and focusing on practical, tangible goals and aspirations.

April 27th: New Moon in Taurus – A potent time for setting intentions around abundance, prosperity, and personal transformation.

May 2025

Overview Horoscope for the Month:

May 2025 is a month of growth, expansion, and new opportunities for you, Libra. With the Sun in Taurus illuminating your 8th house of intimacy, shared resources, and personal transformation, you may find yourself focusing on deepening your connections, exploring your hidden depths, and embracing change and growth in all areas of your life. The New Moon in Gemini on May 26th highlights your 9th house of travel, education, and higher wisdom, inviting you to broaden your horizons and explore new ideas and perspectives.

Love:

In love, May 2025 brings a mix of sensuality, communication, and emotional depth for you, Libra. Venus, your ruling planet, enters sensual Taurus on May 6th, enhancing your desire for comfort, stability, and physical touch in your relationships. This is a great time to focus on building a strong foundation of trust, respect, and mutual understanding with your partner, and to explore new ways of expressing your love and affection. If you're single, be open to meeting someone who shares your values and desires for a committed, long-term relationship.

Career:

Your career sector is highlighted this month, Libra, with Mercury entering Gemini on May 25th and Mars entering Virgo on May 17th. This is a great time to focus on communication, networking, and skill-building in your professional life, and to take practical, detailed steps towards your long-term goals and aspirations. Don't be afraid to speak up, share your ideas, and collaborate with others who share your vision and work ethic. Trust your intuition and be open to unexpected opportunities for growth and advancement.

Finances:

In finances, May 2025 is a month of stability, security, and long-term planning for you, Libra. With Venus entering Taurus on May 6th, you may find yourself focusing on building a strong foundation of financial stability and abundance, and exploring new ways of earning, saving, and investing your resources. The New Moon on May 26th is a powerful time to set intentions around financial freedom, prosperity, and abundance, so be sure to clarify your goals and take practical steps towards making them a reality.

Health:

Your health sector is highlighted this month, Libra, with the Full Moon in Scorpio on May 12th illuminating your 2nd house of body, self-worth, and physical resources. This is a great time to focus on self-care, self-love, and emotional healing, and to release any toxic habits, patterns, or beliefs that no longer serve your highest good. Consider trying a new holistic health practice, such as acupuncture or aromatherapy, or incorporating more mindfulness and stress-reduction techniques into your daily routine.

Travel:

May 2025 is a great month for travel, education, and exploration for you, Libra, with the New Moon in Gemini on May 26th activating your 9th house of higher wisdom and foreign experiences. This is a wonderful time to plan a trip, take a course, or explore a new culture or perspective that expands your horizons and enriches your life. Be open to unexpected opportunities for growth and adventure, and trust that the universe is guiding you towards experiences that will deepen your understanding of yourself and the world around you.

Insights from the Stars:

The celestial energies of May 2025 remind you of the power of vulnerability, authenticity, and emotional intelligence in all areas of your life. With the Sun in Taurus and the Full Moon in Scorpio, you are being called to embrace your deepest feelings, desires, and fears, and to share them openly and honestly with others. Trust that your sensitivity and empathy are your greatest strengths, and that by being true to yourself and your emotions, you will attract the love, support, and abundance that you deserve.

Best Days of the Month:

May 4th: First Quarter Moon in Leo – A great day for creative self-expression, playfulness, and celebrating your unique talents and abilities.

May 12th: Full Moon in Scorpio – A powerful time for releasing old wounds, transforming negative patterns, and embracing your inner power and resilience.

May 20th: Sun enters Gemini – A time for learning, exploring, and connecting with others who share your curiosity and love of knowledge.

May 26th: New Moon in Gemini – A potent time for setting intentions around travel, education, and personal growth, and for planting seeds of new ideas and aspirations.

June 2025

Overview Horoscope for the Month:

June 2025 is a pivotal month for personal growth, self-discovery, and expanding your horizons, dear Libra. The Sun's journey through your 9th house of higher learning, adventure, and spirituality encourages you to step out of your comfort zone and embrace new experiences. You may feel a strong urge to travel, study, or explore different cultures and philosophies. Trust your intuition and follow your curiosity – the universe is guiding you towards opportunities for mind-expanding insights and meaningful connections.

The New Moon in Cancer on June 25th illuminates your 10th house of career and public reputation, planting seeds for fresh professional goals and initiatives. This is an auspicious time to set intentions related to your long-term aspirations, leadership roles, and public image. Trust your unique talents and abilities, and don't be afraid to step into the spotlight and showcase your achievements.

Love:

In matters of the heart, June 2025 begins with Venus, your ruling planet, dancing through playful, curious Gemini. Until June 6th, you may find yourself craving variety, intellectual stimulation, and flirtatious banter in your relationships. If single, this is a great time to meet new people through social events, online dating, or shared interests. Coupled Libras can reignite the spark by trying new activities together and engaging in witty, uplifting conversations.

From June 6th onwards, Venus shifts into your 10th house of public image, attracting admirers and opportunities through your career and professional networks. Your charm, diplomacy, and social graces will be on full display, making you a magnet for positive attention and influential connections. If attached, you and your partner may enjoy attending high-profile events or working towards shared goals in the public eye.

The Full Moon in Sagittarius on June 11th illuminates your 3rd house of communication, siblings, and local community. This lunation may bring important conversations, revelations, or emotional breakthroughs in your relationships with loved ones. Be open to expressing your truth and listening with empathy and understanding. Some Libras may also receive significant news or opportunities related to writing, teaching, or short trips.

Career:

Your career sector is poised for growth and expansion this month, thanks to Jupiter's influential presence in your 10th house until June 9th. This transit brings luck, optimism, and a sense of purpose to your professional pursuits. You may receive recognition for your hard work, attract mentors or influential allies, or be offered new roles or responsibilities that align with your long-term goals. Trust your vision and leadership abilities, and don't be afraid to take calculated risks or seize opportunities for advancement.

Mars, the planet of action and ambition, enters detail-oriented Virgo on June 17th, activating your 12th house of spirituality, solitude, and inner work. This transit encourages you to balance your outward success with inner reflection and self-care. Make time for meditation, journaling, or therapy to process any subconscious fears, doubts, or limiting beliefs that may be holding you back. By embracing your intuition and emotional intelligence, you can make more aligned, authentic choices in your career.

Finances:

With Saturn retrograde in your 6th house of daily work and financial management, June 2025 is an opportune time to review your budget, expenses, and long-term financial strategies. You may need to make some adjustments or cut back on unnecessary spending in order to prioritize your savings and investment goals. Focus on creating a sustainable, realistic plan for your money that aligns with your values and aspirations.

The First Quarter Moon in Virgo on June 2nd motivates you to take practical action steps towards your financial goals. Break down larger objectives into smaller, manageable tasks, and celebrate each milestone along the way. Consider seeking advice from a trusted financial advisor or mentor who can offer guidance and support tailored to your unique needs and circumstances.

Health:

This month, the Sun's journey through your 9th house of exploration and higher learning inspires you to nourish your mind, body, and spirit through diverse, enriching experiences. Engage in activities that expand your perspective and challenge you to grow, such as trying a new form of exercise, taking a workshop or class, or exploring holistic healing modalities. You may also benefit from spending time in nature, traveling to inspiring locations, or connecting with people from different cultures and backgrounds.

Mars' entry into Virgo on June 17th activates your 12th house of rest, solitude, and inner work. This transit reminds you to prioritize self-care, relaxation, and emotional processing. Make time for activities that help you unwind and recharge, such as taking a bath, practicing yoga or meditation, or engaging in creative hobbies. Pay attention to your dreams and intuition, as they may offer valuable insights and guidance for your well-being.

Travel:

The first three weeks of June are ideal for embarking on adventures and expanding your horizons, as the Sun illuminates your 9th house of long-distance travel and higher learning. If possible, plan a trip that combines cultural immersion, natural beauty, and personal growth. You may be drawn to destinations that offer opportunities for spiritual or philosophical exploration, such as retreats, workshops, or sacred sites.

If international travel is not feasible, consider exploring new experiences closer to home that broaden your mind and enrich your perspective. Attend a cultural festival, take a weekend road trip to a nearby town or natural wonder, or sign up for a course or workshop that intrigues you. The key is to approach your adventures with an open mind, a sense of curiosity, and a willingness to step outside your comfort zone.

Insights from the Stars:

June 2025 is a month of personal growth, self-discovery, and aligning with your higher purpose, dear Libra. The celestial energies encourage you to embrace your authentic self and share your unique gifts and insights with the world. Trust your intuition and let your inner compass guide you towards experiences and connections that resonate with your soul.

As you navigate the ups and downs of this transformative month, remember to balance your quest for outward success and achievement with inward reflection and self-care. By tending to your emotional and spiritual needs, you'll be better equipped to manifest your dreams and make a positive impact in your relationships and community.

Best Days of the Month:

June 2nd: First Quarter Moon in Virgo - A great day for tackling practical matters and taking action steps towards your goals.

June 11th: Full Moon in Sagittarius - An auspicious time for heart-to-heart conversations, emotional breakthroughs, and expressing your truth.

June 20th: Sun enters Cancer - The start of a new solar cycle that emphasizes your career, public image, and long-term aspirations.

June 25th: New Moon in Cancer - A powerful day for setting intentions related to your professional goals, leadership abilities, and public reputation.

July 2025

Overview Horoscope for the Month:

July 2025 spotlights your career, public image, and long-term goals, dear Libra. With the Sun illuminating your 10th house of professional achievements and aspirations, you'll have opportunities to showcase your talents, take on leadership roles, and make significant strides in your chosen field. Your hard work and dedication will be noticed and rewarded, leading to potential promotions, raises, or new job offers.

However, Mercury's retrograde through your 10th house from July 18th onwards may bring some challenges or delays in your career progress. Use this time to review, refine, and reassess your professional path, making sure it aligns with your authentic values and long-term vision. Be prepared for miscommunications or misunderstandings with colleagues or authority figures, and practice patience and diplomacy in your interactions.

The Leo New Moon on July 24th brings fresh energy and inspiration to your career sector, making it an auspicious time to set intentions and launch new projects or initiatives. Trust your creativity, leadership abilities, and unique self-expression to guide you towards success and fulfillment in your professional endeavors.

Love:

In matters of the heart, July 2025 emphasizes friendship, community, and shared ideals in your relationships. With Venus gracing your 11th house of social connections until July 30th, you may find yourself attracted to people who share your values, interests, and aspirations. If single, this is a wonderful time to expand your social circle, join groups or organizations aligned with your passions, and meet potential partners through your network.

If you're already in a committed relationship, this month encourages you and your partner to focus on your shared dreams and goals, and to support each other's individual growth and friendships. Attend events or activities together that inspire you both, and don't hesitate to lean on your mutual friends for advice or encouragement.

Mercury's retrograde through your 10th house of public image from July 18th onwards may bring some challenges or misunderstandings in your relationships, especially if work demands or career pressures create tension. Be mindful of your communication style and strive to express your needs and feelings with clarity and compassion. Make time for honest, open conversations with your partner, and be willing to compromise and find solutions that work for both of you.

Career:

Your career sector takes center stage this month, as the Sun travels through your 10th house of professional achievements and public reputation. This is a time to step into the spotlight, showcase your talents and accomplishments, and take on leadership roles or high-profile projects. Your hard work and dedication will be noticed and appreciated by superiors and colleagues, potentially leading to promotions, raises, or new opportunities for growth and advancement.

However, Mercury's retrograde through your 10th house from July 18th onwards may bring some challenges or setbacks in your career progress. Double-check important documents, emails, and communications for errors or misunderstandings, and be prepared for delays or last-minute changes in your schedule or projects. Use this time to review and refine your long-term goals and strategies, making sure they align with your authentic values and priorities.

Networking and collaboration will be key themes this month, as the Sun and Mercury highlight your 11th house of social connections and teamwork. Reach out to colleagues, mentors, or industry peers for advice, resources, or opportunities to work together on mutually beneficial projects. Attend conferences, workshops, or events that allow you to expand your professional circle and learn from experts in your field.

Finances:

With Saturn continuing its retrograde journey through your 5th house of creativity, self-expression, and risk-taking, July 2025 encourages you to reassess your financial strategies and investments. You may need to be more cautious or selective in your spending, avoiding impulsive purchases or speculative ventures that could deplete your resources. Focus on building a solid, sustainable foundation for your long-term financial security, and don't hesitate to seek advice from trusted professionals or mentors.

The Capricorn Full Moon on July 10th illuminates your 2nd house of income, values, and self-worth, bringing clarity and insight into your financial situation. This is a powerful time to release limiting beliefs or fears around money and abundance, and to align your spending and saving habits with your authentic priorities and goals. Celebrate your talents, skills, and unique contributions, and trust that you deserve to be fairly compensated for your efforts.

Health:

With Mars energizing your 12th house of rest, solitude, and inner work for most of the month, July 2025 emphasizes the importance of self-care, relaxation, and emotional well-being. You may feel a stronger need for alone time, introspection, and spiritual practices that help you connect with your intuition and process subconscious thoughts or feelings. Make space in your schedule for activities that promote inner peace and balance, such as meditation, yoga, journaling, or therapy.

Pay attention to your dreams, as they may offer valuable insights and guidance for your health and well-being. Keep a dream journal and explore any recurring themes or symbols that arise, as they may point to areas of your life that need attention or healing. If you're feeling overwhelmed or stressed, don't hesitate to reach out to trusted friends, family members, or professionals for support and guidance.

The Virgo New Moon on July 29th brings fresh energy and motivation to your health and wellness routines. Set intentions related to self-care, nutrition, exercise, and stress management, and take practical action steps towards your goals. This is a great time to start a new fitness regimen, try a healthy recipe, or implement daily habits that support your physical, mental, and emotional well-being.

Travel:

With the Sun focused on your 10th house of career and public responsibilities for most of the month, extensive travel plans may need to take a backseat to work demands and professional obligations. However, short trips or weekend getaways can still provide a refreshing break from your daily routine and help you recharge your batteries. If possible, combine business with pleasure by attending a conference or workshop in a new location, or by networking with colleagues or clients in a relaxed, informal setting.

If you do need to travel for work during Mercury retrograde from July 18th onwards, be sure to double-check your itinerary, reservations, and important documents for errors or changes. Allow extra time for delays or last-minute adjustments, and have backup plans in place in case of unexpected disruptions. Maintain a flexible, adaptable mindset, and use any downtime or detours as opportunities for reflection, self-discovery, or connecting with new people and experiences.

Insights from the Stars:

July 2025 is a month of balancing your professional ambitions with your personal well-being and relationships, dear Libra. The celestial energies encourage you to step into your power and leadership abilities, while also honoring your need for rest, introspection, and emotional processing. Trust your intuition and inner wisdom to guide you towards choices and actions that align with your authentic self and long-term vision.

Mercury retrograde reminds you to slow down, reflect, and communicate with clarity and compassion, especially in your career and public interactions. Use this time to review and refine your goals, strategies, and relationships, releasing what no longer serves your growth and making space for new opportunities and connections that resonate with your soul.

Remember that true success and fulfillment come from a place of inner peace, self-awareness, and alignment with your values. By tending to your emotional and spiritual needs, you'll be better equipped to manifest your dreams and make a positive impact in your career and community. Embrace your unique gifts and leadership style, and trust that the universe is supporting you every step of the way.

Best Days of the Month:

July 2nd: First Quarter Moon in Libra - A powerful day for setting intentions, asserting your needs and desires, and finding balance in your relationships.

July 10th: Full Moon in Capricorn - An auspicious time for releasing limiting beliefs around money and self-worth, and celebrating your talents and achievements.

July 22nd: Sun enters Leo - The start of a new solar cycle that emphasizes your friendships, social networks, and community involvement.

July 24th: New Moon in Leo - A great day for setting intentions related to your long-term goals, creative self-expression, and authentic leadership abilities..

August 2025

Overview Horoscope for the Month:

August 2025 brings a focus on friendships, community, and your hopes and dreams for the future, dear Libra. The Sun's journey through your 11th house of social connections and aspirations encourages you to nurture your relationships with like-minded individuals who share your values and goals. You may find yourself drawn to group activities, humanitarian causes, or innovative projects that allow you to make a positive impact on the world around you.

The New Moon in Leo on August 1st sets the stage for new beginnings and fresh starts in your social life and community involvement. Set intentions related to expanding your network, joining a club or organization that aligns with your interests, or collaborating with others on a creative or altruistic endeavor. Trust that the connections you make now will support your personal and professional growth in meaningful ways.

Love:

In matters of the heart, August 2025 emphasizes the importance of emotional intimacy, vulnerability, and deep connection. With Venus entering Cancer on July 30th and traveling through your 10th house of public image and reputation, you may find yourself attracted to partners who offer stability, security, and emotional support. If you're in a committed relationship, this is a wonderful time to prioritize quality time with your loved one, express your affection and appreciation, and work together towards shared goals and dreams.

If you're single and looking for love, you may find yourself drawn to people who are nurturing, compassionate, and family-oriented. Be open to meeting potential partners through your career or public life, as your natural charm and diplomacy will be on full display. However, be mindful of Mercury's retrograde through your 11th house of friendships from August 22nd to September 11th, as miscommunications or misunderstandings with friends or acquaintances could create tension in your love life.

The Full Moon in Aquarius on August 9th illuminates your 5th house of romance, creativity, and self-expression. This lunation may bring a culmination or turning point in a romantic relationship, creative project, or personal passion. Trust your heart and intuition to guide you towards authentic joy and fulfillment, and don't be afraid to let your unique light shine.

Career:

Your career and public life continue to be a major focus this month, with several planets activating your 10th house of professional achievements and ambitions. Mars, the planet of action and drive, enters your career sector on August 6th, giving you a boost of energy and motivation to pursue your goals and take on leadership roles. You may find yourself taking on new responsibilities, spearheading projects, or advocating for your ideas and vision with confidence and assertiveness.

However, with Mercury and the Sun both moving through your 11th house of networking and teamwork, it's important to balance your individual ambitions with the needs and contributions of your colleagues and collaborators. Seek out opportunities to work together towards common goals, and be open to feedback and input from others. Your ability to facilitate cooperation and harmony will be a valuable asset in any professional setting.

The New Moon in Leo on August 1st is a powerful time to set intentions related to your long-term career aspirations, public reputation, and leadership abilities. Visualize yourself achieving your dreams and making a positive impact in your field, and take practical action steps towards manifesting your vision. Trust that your unique talents and perspective are needed and appreciated, and don't be afraid to step into the spotlight and shine.

Finances:

With Venus, your ruling planet, moving through your 10th house of career and public status for most of the month, August 2025 brings opportunities for financial growth and abundance through your professional endeavors. You may receive recognition or rewards for your hard work and contributions, such as a raise, bonus, or lucrative new contract. Use your natural charm and diplomacy to negotiate favorable terms and advocate for your worth.

However, with Mercury retrograde in your 11th house of friendships and social connections from August 22nd to September 11th, be cautious about mixing business with pleasure or getting involved in financial arrangements with friends or acquaintances. Double-check any agreements or contracts for errors or misunderstandings, and be clear about your expectations and boundaries to avoid potential conflicts down the road.

The Full Moon in Aquarius on August 9th illuminates your 5th house of creativity, self-expression, and risk-taking. This lunation may bring a financial breakthrough or opportunity related to a creative project, hobby, or entrepreneurial venture. Trust your unique talents and vision, and be open to unconventional or innovative ways of generating income and abundance.

Health:

August 2025 emphasizes the importance of balance, self-care, and emotional well-being for your overall health and vitality. With the Sun and Mercury moving through your 11th house of friendships and community, you may find yourself drawn to group activities or social events that nourish your mind, body, and spirit. Seek out opportunities to connect with others who share your interests in wellness, spirituality, or personal growth, and don't hesitate to reach out for support when you need it.

At the same time, Mars' entry into your 10th house of career and public responsibilities on August 6th may bring a surge of energy and drive to your professional life. While this can be a great time to take on new challenges and pursue your ambitions, be mindful of overextending yourself or neglecting your self-care in the process. Make sure to prioritize rest, relaxation, and stress management techniques, such as meditation, deep breathing, or time in nature.

The New Moon in Leo on August 1st is a powerful time to set intentions related to your physical, emotional, and spiritual well-being. Consider starting a new self-care routine, joining a yoga or fitness class, or exploring holistic healing modalities that resonate with you. Trust your body's wisdom and intuition to guide you towards practices and habits that support your overall health and vitality.

Travel:

With the Sun and Mercury activating your 11th house of friendships, social connections, and group activities, August 2025 is a great time for travel or adventures with friends or like-minded individuals. You may feel drawn to attend a conference, workshop, or retreat that allows you to expand your knowledge, skills, or spiritual awareness while connecting with others who share your interests and values.

Short trips or weekend getaways with your social circle can also provide a refreshing break from your daily routine and responsibilities. Consider planning a group vacation or road trip to a destination that offers a mix of fun, relaxation, and personal growth. Be open to new experiences and perspectives, and use this time to strengthen your bonds and create lasting memories with your loved ones.

However, with Mercury retrograde in your 11th house from August 22nd to September 11th, be prepared for potential delays, miscommunications, or last-minute changes to your travel plans. Double-check your reservations, itinerary, and important documents, and have backup plans in place in case of unexpected disruptions. Maintain a flexible and adaptable mindset, and use any challenges or detours as opportunities for growth, learning, and self-discovery.

Insights from the Stars:

August 2025 is a month of balancing your individual aspirations with your social connections and community involvement, dear Libra. The celestial energies encourage you to embrace your unique talents and leadership abilities, while also nurturing your relationships with friends, colleagues, and like-minded individuals who support your growth and well-being.

Mercury's retrograde through your 11th house of friendships and social networks from August 22nd to September 11th reminds you to communicate with clarity, compassion, and integrity in all of your interactions. Be mindful of gossip, misunderstandings, or unresolved conflicts that could create tension or drama in your relationships. Use this time to review and refine your social commitments, releasing any connections or obligations that no longer align with your values and goals.

Trust that your authentic self-expression and unique perspective are valuable assets in any group or community setting. Don't be afraid to speak your truth, share your ideas, and advocate for causes that matter to you. At the same time, be open to feedback, collaboration, and compromise, recognizing that true progress and innovation often require a diversity of viewpoints and experiences.

Remember that your ultimate fulfillment and happiness come from a sense of connection, purpose, and alignment with your deepest values and aspirations. By nurturing your relationships, pursuing your passions, and making a positive impact in your community, you'll create a life that is rich in love, joy, and meaning.

Best Days of the Month:

August 1st: New Moon in Leo - A powerful day for setting intentions related to your friendships, social networks, and hopes and dreams for the future.

August 9th: Full Moon in Aquarius - An auspicious time for celebrating your creative talents, romantic connections, and personal passions.

August 13th: Venus conjunct the North Node - A day of karmic encounters, meaningful connections, and spiritual growth in your career and public life.

August 23rd: Sun enters Virgo - The start of a new solar cycle that emphasizes your inner world, spiritual growth, and emotional healing.

September 2025

September 2025 is a month of introspection, spiritual growth, and emotional healing for you, dear Libra. With the Sun journeying through your 12th house of inner work, solitude, and surrender, you may feel called to retreat from the busyness of everyday life and focus on your inner world. This is a time to release old patterns, wounds, or limiting beliefs that no longer serve your highest good, and to connect with your intuition, dreams, and subconscious mind.

The New Moon in Virgo on September 21st brings a powerful opportunity for new beginnings and fresh starts in your spiritual life and emotional well-being. Set intentions related to forgiveness, compassion, and unconditional love for yourself and others. Trust that the universe is supporting you in letting go of the past and embracing a more peaceful, fulfilling future.

Love:

In matters of the heart, September 2025 emphasizes the importance of vulnerability, empathy, and emotional intimacy. With Venus traveling through your 11th house of friendships and social connections until September 19th, you may find yourself drawn to people who share your values, interests, and hopes for the future. If you're single, this is a great time to meet potential partners through your network of friends, colleagues, or community groups. Be open to unconventional or unexpected connections that challenge and inspire you to grow.

If you're in a committed relationship, this month encourages you to deepen your emotional bond and spiritual connection with your partner. Make time for heart-to-heart conversations, shared adventures, and activities that nourish your soul. Be willing to be vulnerable and authentic with each other, and to offer support and understanding during times of stress or uncertainty.

The Full Moon in Pisces on September 7th illuminates your 6th house of daily work, health, and service. This lunation may bring a culmination or turning point in your job, wellness routine, or responsibilities to others. Trust your intuition and inner wisdom to guide you towards balance, harmony, and self-care. Release any perfectionist tendencies or self-criticisms, and embrace your human imperfections with compassion and grace.

Career:

Your career and public life may take a backseat to your inner world and emotional well-being this month, dear Libra. With the Sun and several other planets moving through your 12th house of solitude, spirituality, and closure, you may feel a need to step back from the spotlight and focus on your personal growth and healing. This is a time to reflect on your long-term goals, values, and purpose, and to release any outdated or unfulfilling commitments or responsibilities.

However, with Mars traveling through your 11th house of networking and teamwork for most of the month, you may still find opportunities for collaboration, innovation, and social impact in your professional life. Seek out like-minded colleagues or mentors who share your vision and values, and be open to unconventional or creative solutions to challenges or setbacks. Your ability to facilitate cooperation, harmony, and positive change will be a valuable asset in any work setting.

The New Moon in Virgo on September 21st is a powerful time to set intentions related to your spiritual growth, emotional healing, and inner peace. If you're feeling called to make a career change or transition, trust your intuition and take practical steps towards aligning your work with your soul's purpose. Remember that true success and fulfillment come from a place of authenticity, integrity, and service to others.

Finance:

With Venus, your ruling planet, moving through your 11th house of friendships and social connections until September 19th, September 2025 brings opportunities for financial growth and abundance through your network and community. You may receive valuable advice, resources, or referrals from friends, colleagues, or acquaintances who support your goals and aspirations. Be open to unexpected or unconventional sources of income or investment, and trust your intuition to guide you towards prosperity and success.

However, with the Sun and several other planets moving through your 12th house of hidden matters and unconscious patterns, it's important to be mindful of any self-sabotaging behaviors or limiting beliefs around money and abundance. Take time to reflect on your relationship with finances, and to release any fears, doubts, or insecurities that may be holding you back from experiencing true wealth and prosperity.

The Full Moon in Pisces on September 7th illuminates your 6th house of daily work, routines, and financial management. This lunation may bring a culmination or turning point in your budget, spending habits, or income streams. Trust your intuition and inner wisdom to guide you towards balance, simplicity, and sustainability in your financial life. Release any tendencies towards overspending, underearning, or self-sacrifice, and embrace a mindset of abundance, gratitude, and self-worth.

Health:

September 2025 emphasizes the importance of rest, relaxation, and emotional healing for your overall health and well-being. With the Sun and several other planets moving through your 12th house of solitude, spirituality, and surrender, you may feel a stronger need for alone time, introspection, and self-care. Make space in your schedule for activities that nourish your soul and help you connect with your inner wisdom, such as meditation, journaling, or creative expression.

Pay attention to your dreams and intuition, as they may offer valuable insights and guidance for your physical, emotional, and spiritual health. If you're feeling overwhelmed, anxious, or depressed, don't hesitate to reach out for support from trusted friends, family members, or professionals. Remember that seeking help is a sign of strength, not weakness, and that you deserve to prioritize your own healing and well-being.

The Full Moon in Pisces on September 7th illuminates your 6th house of health, wellness, and daily routines. This lunation may bring a culmination or turning point in your self-care practices, dietary habits, or exercise regimen. Trust your body's wisdom and intuition to guide you towards balance, vitality, and wholeness. Release any perfectionist tendencies or self-criticisms, and embrace a more compassionate, accepting approach to your physical and emotional needs.

Travel:

With the Sun and several other planets activating your 12th house of solitude, spirituality, and inner work, September 2025 may not be the most active month for travel or external adventures. However, this is an excellent time for inner journeys, spiritual retreats, or solo trips that allow you to connect with your deeper self and find peace and clarity amidst the chaos of everyday life.

If you do feel called to travel this month, consider destinations that offer opportunities for reflection, introspection, and emotional healing, such as a meditation retreat, yoga workshop, or nature getaway. Be open to synchronicities, coincidences, or unexpected detours that may lead you towards profound insights, encounters, or experiences.

Keep in mind that Mercury will be retrograde in your 12th house from September 21st to October 11th, which may bring some challenges or delays in your travel plans. Double-check your itinerary, reservations, and important documents, and have backup plans in place in case of last-minute changes or disruptions. Maintain a flexible, adaptable mindset, and use any obstacles or setbacks as opportunities for growth, learning, and self-discovery.

Insights from the Stars:

September 2025 is a month of deep introspection, emotional healing, and spiritual awakening for you, dear Libra. The celestial energies are inviting you to turn inward, to confront your shadows and wounds, and to embrace the transformative power of surrender, forgiveness, and unconditional love.

The Partial Solar Eclipse in Virgo on September 21st marks a powerful new beginning in your journey of self-discovery and inner growth. This eclipse may bring unexpected insights, revelations, or opportunities that challenge you to let go of old patterns, beliefs, or relationships that no longer serve your highest good. Trust that the universe is guiding you towards a more authentic, fulfilling path, even if it feels uncomfortable or uncertain at times.

Remember that true healing and transformation often require a willingness to sit with discomfort, to face our fears and vulnerabilities, and to trust in the wisdom of our own hearts. By embracing your sensitivity, intuition, and compassion, you'll be able to navigate the ups and downs of this profound inner journey with grace, resilience, and faith.

Best Days of the Month:

September 7th: Full Moon in Pisces - A powerful day for releasing emotional baggage, surrendering to the flow of life, and finding peace and closure in your work and health matters.

September 14th: Venus enters Libra - A time of increased charm, harmony, and ease in your relationships and social interactions.

September 21st: Partial Solar Eclipse in Virgo - A profound new beginning in your spiritual life, inner world, and emotional healing journey.

September 22nd: Sun enters Libra - The start of a new solar cycle that emphasizes your personal growth, self-expression, and individuality.

October 2025

Overview Horoscope for the Month:

October 2025 is a month of new beginnings, personal growth, and self-discovery for you, dear Libra. With the Sun traveling through your sign for most of the month, you'll feel a renewed sense of vitality, confidence, and purpose. This is a time to focus on your own needs, desires, and aspirations, and to take bold steps towards creating the life you truly want to live.

The New Moon in Libra on October 21st brings a powerful opportunity for fresh starts and new chapters in your personal journey. Set intentions related to your self-image, relationships, and long-term goals, and trust that the universe is supporting you in manifesting your dreams into reality. Embrace your unique qualities, talents, and perspectives, and don't be afraid to shine your light and express your authentic self to the world.

Love:

In matters of the heart, October 2025 emphasizes the importance of balance, harmony, and mutual understanding in your relationships. With Venus, your ruling planet, traveling through your sign from October 13th onwards, you'll exude an extra dose of charm, grace, and magnetism. If you're single, this is an excellent time to attract new love interests or romantic prospects who appreciate your intellect, wit, and style. Be open to unexpected encounters or connections that challenge and inspire you to grow.

If you're in a committed partnership, this month encourages you to focus on creating more equality, fairness, and reciprocity in your relationship. Have honest conversations with your partner about your needs, desires, and expectations, and be willing to listen to their perspective with an open mind and heart. Look for ways to compromise, collaborate, and support each other's individual growth and happiness.

The Full Moon in Aries on October 6th illuminates your 7th house of partnerships and one-on-one relationships. This lunation may bring a culmination, turning point, or revelation in your romantic life or business partnerships. Trust your intuition and inner wisdom to guide you towards connections that are aligned with your values, goals, and authentic self. Release any relationships or dynamics that are draining, toxic, or unfulfilling, and make space for new, healthy, and mutually beneficial partnerships to emerge.

Career:

Your career and professional life are highlighted this month, dear Libra, with several planets activating your 10th house of public image, achievement, and success. Mars, the planet of action and ambition, enters your career sector on October 22nd, giving you a boost of energy, confidence, and motivation to pursue your goals and take on new challenges. You may find yourself taking on leadership roles, spearheading projects, or advocating for your ideas and vision with passion and determination.

However, with Mercury retrograde in your sign from October 22nd to November 11th, it's important to be mindful of communication, negotiation, and decision-making in your career. Double-check emails, contracts, and important documents for errors or misunderstandings, and be prepared for delays, revisions, or unexpected changes in your plans or strategies. Use this time to review, refine, and reassess your professional path, making sure it aligns with your authentic values, talents, and aspirations.

The New Moon in Libra on October 21st is a powerful time to set intentions related to your career goals, public reputation, and long-term success. Visualize yourself achieving your dreams and making a positive impact in your field, and take practical action steps towards manifesting your vision. Trust that your unique skills, creativity, and leadership abilities are valued and needed in the world, and don't be afraid to take calculated risks or seize opportunities that align with your purpose and passions.

Finances:

With the Sun illuminating your 2nd house of money, resources, and self-worth for the first part of the month, October 2025 is a great time to focus on your financial goals, budgeting, and long-term security. Take stock of your income, expenses, and investments, and look for ways to increase your earning potential, reduce unnecessary spending, or build a more sustainable and abundant financial foundation.

The Full Moon in Aries on October 6th illuminates your 8th house of shared resources, debts, and investments. This lunation may bring a culmination, turning point, or revelation in your joint finances, taxes, or insurance matters. Trust your instincts and inner guidance to make wise, informed decisions that support your long-term financial well-being and independence. Release any fears, doubts, or limiting beliefs around money and abundance, and embrace a mindset of prosperity, gratitude, and self-worth.

With Venus, your ruling planet, traveling through your 2nd house of money and resources from October 13th onwards, you may attract new sources of income, financial opportunities, or material blessings. Be open to unexpected gifts, windfalls, or rewards for your talents and efforts, and trust that the universe is conspiring to support your financial growth and stability. Remember to balance your desire for luxury and pleasure with a sense of responsibility, moderation, and long-term planning.

Health:

October 2025 emphasizes the importance of self-care, balance, and inner harmony for your overall health and well-being. With the Sun traveling through your sign for most of the month, you may feel a renewed sense of vitality, energy, and motivation to prioritize your physical, emotional, and spiritual needs. Make time for activities that nourish your body, mind, and soul, such as exercise, meditation, creative expression, or spending time in nature.

However, with Mars entering your 10th house of career and public responsibilities on October 22nd, you may face increased demands, stress, or pressure in your professional life. Be mindful of overextending yourself or neglecting your self-care in the pursuit of success or recognition. Make sure to set healthy boundaries, delegate tasks, and take regular breaks to recharge your batteries and maintain your inner peace and equilibrium.

The New Moon in Libra on October 21st is a powerful time to set intentions related to your health, wellness, and self-care routines. Consider starting a new exercise regimen, healthy eating plan, or stress-management practice that supports your physical vitality and emotional resilience. Trust your body's wisdom and intuition to guide you towards habits and choices that promote balance, harmony, and holistic well-being.

Travel:

With the Sun illuminating your 1st house of self, identity, and personal goals for most of the month, October 2025 is an excellent time for solo travel, self-discovery journeys, or adventures that align with your authentic desires and aspirations. Consider taking a trip that allows you to explore new places, cultures, or experiences that expand your mind, heart, and horizons. Be open to synchronicities, coincidences, or unexpected detours that may lead you towards profound insights, encounters, or opportunities for growth and transformation.

However, with Mercury retrograde in your sign from October 22nd to November 11th, it's important to be extra cautious and prepared when traveling during this period. Double-check your itinerary, reservations, and important documents, and have backup plans in place in case of last-minute changes, delays, or disruptions. Maintain a flexible, adaptable mindset, and use any challenges or obstacles as opportunities for learning, problem-solving, and self-discovery.

If possible, plan your travel for the first part of the month, when the cosmic energies are more stable and supportive. The New Moon in Libra on October 21st is a great time to set intentions related to your travel goals, bucket list destinations, or personal growth aspirations. Trust that the journey is just as important as the destination, and that every experience is an opportunity to learn more about yourself, others, and the world around you.

Insights from the Stars:

October 2025 is a month of profound personal growth, self-discovery, and new beginnings for you, dear Libra. The celestial energies are inviting you to embrace your authentic self, to celebrate your unique qualities and talents, and to take bold steps towards creating the life you truly desire and deserve.

The New Moon in your sign on October 21st marks a powerful new chapter in your journey of self-realization and personal empowerment. This lunation may bring unexpected insights, opportunities, or encounters that challenge you to step out of your comfort zone, to confront your fears and limitations, and to trust in your own inner wisdom and strength. Remember that growth often requires discomfort, vulnerability, and a willingness to let go of what no longer serves your highest good.

At the same time, Mercury's retrograde through your sign from October 22nd to November 11th reminds you to be patient, reflective, and discerning in your communication, decisions, and actions. Use this time to review, refine, and reassess your personal goals, relationships, and self-image, making sure they align with your authentic values, needs, and aspirations. Trust that any delays, setbacks, or misunderstandings are ultimately serving your growth and evolution, even if they feel frustrating or confusing in the moment.

Remember that true happiness and fulfillment come from a place of inner balance, harmony, and self-love. By embracing your own unique journey, by cultivating gratitude and compassion for yourself and others, and by staying true to your heart's deepest desires and values, you'll be able to navigate the ups and downs of this transformative month with grace, resilience, and wisdom.

Best Days of the Month:

October 6th: Full Moon in Aries - A powerful day for releasing old patterns, fears, or limitations in your relationships and partnerships.

October 13th: Venus enters Libra - A time of increased charm, magnetism, and ease in your personal interactions and self-expression.

October 21st: New Moon in Libra - A profound new beginning in your journey of self-discovery, personal growth, and authentic living.

October 29th: Sun conjunct Mercury Retrograde - A day of heightened intuition, self-reflection, and inner wisdom..

November 2025

Overview Horoscope for the Month:

November 2025 is a month of deep introspection, emotional healing, and spiritual growth for you, dear Libra. With the Sun traveling through your 2nd house of values, resources, and self-worth for most of the month, you'll be called to examine your relationship with money, possessions, and your own sense of worthiness and deserving. This is a time to release any limiting beliefs, fears, or attachments that may be preventing you from experiencing true abundance, prosperity, and fulfillment.

The New Moon in Scorpio on November 20th brings a powerful opportunity for new beginnings and fresh starts in your financial life and material world. Set intentions related to increasing your income, building long-term security, and aligning your resources with your authentic values and priorities. Trust that the universe is supporting you in manifesting your needs and desires, and that you are worthy of experiencing comfort, stability, and success.

Love:

In matters of the heart, November 2025 emphasizes the importance of vulnerability, intimacy, and emotional depth in your relationships. With Venus, your ruling planet, traveling through your 2nd house of values and self-worth until November 30th, you may find yourself attracted to partners who offer stability, security, and a strong sense of commitment. If you're in a relationship, this is a great time to have honest conversations with your partner about your shared values, goals, and long-term vision for your life together.

However, with Mercury retrograde in your 2nd house until November 11th, there may be some challenges or misunderstandings around money, possessions, or differing values in your relationships. Be patient, compassionate, and willing to listen to your partner's perspective with an open mind and heart. Look for ways to compromise, collaborate, and find mutually beneficial solutions that honor both of your needs and desires.

The Full Moon in Taurus on November 5th illuminates your 8th house of intimacy, shared resources, and deep emotional connections. This lunation may bring a culmination, revelation, or turning point in your closest relationships, particularly around issues of trust, vulnerability, and power dynamics. Trust your intuition and inner wisdom to guide you towards connections that are authentic, supportive, and aligned with your highest good.

Career:

Your career and professional life continue to be a major focus this month, dear Libra, with several planets activating your 10th house of public image, achievement, and success. Mars, the planet of action and ambition, travels through your career sector all month, giving you extra energy, confidence, and motivation to pursue your goals and take on new challenges. You may find yourself taking on leadership roles, spearheading projects, or advocating for your ideas and vision with passion and determination.

However, with Mercury retrograde in your 2nd house of income and resources until November 11th, it's important to be mindful of financial negotiations, contracts, or business deals during this period. Double-check any agreements or documents for errors or misunderstandings, and be prepared for delays, revisions, or unexpected changes in your plans or strategies. Use this time to review, refine, and reassess your professional values, goals, and long-term financial security.

The New Moon in Scorpio on November 20th is a powerful time to set intentions related to your career aspirations, public reputation, and leadership abilities. Visualize yourself achieving your dreams and making a positive impact in your field, and take practical action steps towards manifesting your vision. Trust that your unique talents, skills, and experience are valuable assets that can help you navigate any challenges or obstacles that arise.

Finance:

With the Sun illuminating your 2nd house of money, resources, and self-worth for most of the month, November 2025 is an excellent time to focus on your financial goals, budgeting, and long-term prosperity. Take stock of your income, expenses, and investments, and look for ways to increase your earning potential, reduce unnecessary spending, or build a more sustainable and abundant financial foundation.

However, with Mercury retrograde in your 2nd house until November 11th, it's important to be extra cautious and mindful with your financial decisions and transactions during this period. Double-check bank statements, bills, and receipts for errors or discrepancies, and avoid making any major purchases or investments until after Mercury goes direct. Use this time to review, reassess, and refine your financial strategies, making sure they align with your authentic values and priorities.

The Full Moon in Taurus on November 5th illuminates your 8th house of shared resources, debts, and investments. This lunation may bring a culmination, revelation, or turning point in your joint finances, taxes, or insurance matters. Trust your instincts and inner guidance to make wise, informed decisions that support your long-term financial well-being and security. Release any fears, doubts, or limiting beliefs around money and abundance, and embrace a mindset of gratitude, sufficiency, and trust in the universe's support.

Health:

November 2025 emphasizes the importance of self-care, emotional healing, and inner balance for your overall health and well-being. With the Sun traveling through your 2nd house of physical and material comfort for most of the month, you may feel a stronger need to nourish your body with healthy food, adequate rest, and sensory pleasures that delight your senses. Make time for activities that bring you joy, relaxation, and a sense of groundedness, such as cooking, gardening, or receiving a massage.

However, with Mars traveling through your 10th house of career and public responsibilities all month, you may face increased demands, stress, or pressure in your professional life. Be mindful of overextending yourself or neglecting your self-care in the pursuit of success or recognition. Make sure to set healthy boundaries, delegate tasks, and take regular breaks to recharge your batteries and maintain your physical and emotional well-being.

The New Moon in Scorpio on November 20th is a powerful time to set intentions related to your physical and emotional health, self-care practices, and inner transformation. Consider starting a new wellness regimen, therapy or healing modality, or spiritual practice that supports your mind-body-spirit connection. Trust your intuition and inner wisdom to guide you towards habits and choices that promote deep healing, release, and renewal.

Travel:

With the Sun illuminating your 2nd house of personal resources and material comfort for most of the month, November 2025 may be a good time for short trips, weekend getaways, or travel experiences that allow you to indulge your senses and enjoy the finer things in life. Consider planning a luxurious spa retreat, a gourmet food tour, or a visit to a beautiful natural setting that helps you feel grounded, nourished, and rejuvenated.

However, with Mercury retrograde in your 2nd house until November 11th, it's important to be extra cautious and prepared when making travel plans or arrangements during this period. Double-check your itinerary, reservations, and important documents, and have backup plans in place in case of last-minute changes, delays, or disruptions. Maintain a flexible, adaptable mindset, and use any challenges or obstacles as opportunities for learning, problem-solving, and self-discovery.

If possible, plan your travel for the second half of the month, when the cosmic energies are more stable and supportive. The New Moon in Scorpio on November 20th is a great time to set intentions related to your travel goals, bucket list destinations, or personal growth aspirations. Trust that every journey, whether inner or outer, is an opportunity to deepen your self-awareness, expand your perspectives, and connect with the beauty and wisdom of the world around you.

Insights from the Stars:

November 2025 is a month of profound inner transformation, emotional healing, and spiritual growth for you, dear Libra. The celestial energies are inviting you to delve beneath the surface of your material reality, to confront your deepest fears, desires, and attachments, and to embrace the power of surrender, trust, and inner alchemy.

The New Moon in Scorpio on November 20th marks a powerful new beginning in your journey of self-discovery, financial empowerment, and emotional liberation. This lunation may bring unexpected insights, opportunities, or encounters that challenge you to let go of old patterns, beliefs, or relationships that no longer serve your highest good. Remember that true abundance and security come from a place of inner wholeness, self-love, and alignment with your authentic values and purpose.

At the same time, Mercury's retrograde through your 2nd house until November 11th reminds you to be patient, reflective, and discerning in your financial decisions, negotiations, and communications. Use this time to review, refine, and reassess your relationship with money, possessions, and your own sense of self-worth, making sure they align with your deepest needs, desires, and aspirations. Trust that any delays, setbacks, or misunderstandings are ultimately serving your growth and evolution, even if they feel frustrating or confusing in the moment.

Remember that true prosperity and fulfillment come from a place of inner balance, harmony, and connection to your authentic self. By embracing your own unique journey, by cultivating gratitude and compassion for yourself and others, and by staying true to your heart's deepest values and wisdom, you'll be able to navigate the ups and downs of this transformative month with grace, resilience, and trust in the universe's abundant support and love.

Best Days of the Month:

November 5th: Full Moon in Taurus - A powerful day for releasing old patterns, fears, or limitations around money, security, and self-worth.

November 11th: Mercury goes direct in Libra - A time of increased clarity, communication, and forward momentum in your personal and financial life.

November 20th: New Moon in Scorpio - A profound new beginning in your journey of emotional healing, financial empowerment, and spiritual transformation.

November 30th: Venus enters Sagittarius - A time of increased optimism, adventure, and expansiveness in your relationships and social connections.

December 2025

Overview Horoscope for the Month:

December 2025 is a month of expansive learning, personal growth, and spiritual exploration for you, dear Libra. With the Sun traveling through your 3rd house of communication, learning, and local community for most of the month, you'll feel a strong desire to expand your mind, connect with like-minded individuals, and explore new ideas and perspectives. This is a great time to take a class, attend a workshop, or engage in stimulating conversations and debates that challenge and inspire you.

The New Moon in Sagittarius on December 19th brings a powerful opportunity for new beginnings and fresh starts in your intellectual pursuits, social connections, and short-distance travel. Set intentions related to expressing your authentic voice, sharing your knowledge and wisdom, and building a supportive network of friends and colleagues. Trust that the universe is guiding you towards experiences and encounters that will help you grow, learn, and thrive.

Love:

In matters of the heart, December 2025 emphasizes the importance of open communication, intellectual compatibility, and shared adventures in your relationships. With Venus, your ruling planet, traveling through your 3rd house of communication and local community until December 24th, you may find yourself attracted to partners who stimulate your mind, make you laugh, and enjoy exploring new ideas and experiences together. If you're single, this is an excellent time to meet potential love interests through social events, online dating, or shared hobbies and interests.

If you're in a committed relationship, this month encourages you to prioritize quality time and meaningful conversations with your partner. Plan fun date nights, take a short trip together, or engage in activities that allow you to learn and grow as a couple. Be open to trying new things, expressing your thoughts and feelings honestly, and finding ways to keep the spark of curiosity and playfulness alive in your connection.

The Full Moon in Gemini on December 4th illuminates your 9th house of higher learning, travel, and spiritual growth. This lunation may bring a culmination, revelation, or turning point in your personal beliefs, philosophy, or long-distance relationships. Trust your intuition and inner wisdom to guide you towards experiences and connections that expand your horizons, deepen your faith, and align with your highest truth and purpose.

Career:

Your career and professional life take a backseat to your personal growth and intellectual pursuits this month, dear Libra. With the Sun and several other planets activating your 3rd house of communication, learning, and mental agility, you may find yourself more focused on developing new skills, networking with colleagues, or exploring creative projects and ideas. This is a great time to attend conferences, workshops, or training programs that enhance your knowledge and expertise in your field.

However, with Mars entering your 12th house of solitude, spirituality, and inner work on December 15th, you may also feel a stronger need for rest, reflection, and introspection in your work life. Take time to review your long-term goals, assess your current job satisfaction, and listen to your intuition about any changes or adjustments you may need to make in your career path. Trust that any challenges or obstacles that arise are ultimately guiding you towards a more authentic, fulfilling, and aligned professional journey.

The New Moon in Sagittarius on December 19th is a powerful time to set intentions related to your communication skills, intellectual growth, and ability to share your unique ideas and perspectives with others. Visualize yourself expressing your truth with clarity, confidence, and compassion, and take practical steps towards manifesting your vision. Remember that your voice and insights are valuable assets that can help you make a positive impact in your work and community.

Finances:

With the Sun illuminating your 3rd house of communication, learning, and short-distance travel for most of the month, December 2025 is a good time to focus on building your financial knowledge, skills, and resources. Consider taking a course or workshop on budgeting, investing, or entrepreneurship, or seeking advice from a trusted financial advisor or mentor. Look for ways to increase your income through freelance work, side hustles, or creative projects that align with your talents and passions.

The Full Moon in Gemini on December 4th illuminates your 9th house of higher education, travel, and personal growth. This lunation may bring a financial opportunity or breakthrough related to your studies, publishing, or international connections. Trust your instincts and inner guidance to make wise, informed decisions that support your long-term prosperity and abundance. Release any fears, doubts, or limiting beliefs around money and success, and embrace a mindset of curiosity, optimism, and faith in the universe's support.

With Venus, your ruling planet, traveling through your 3rd house of communication and commerce until December 24th, you may also attract financial opportunities or material blessings through your social connections, networking, or local community. Be open to unexpected gifts, favors, or introductions that can help you expand your resources and reach your goals. Remember to balance your desire for pleasure and indulgence with a sense of responsibility, moderation, and long-term planning.

Health and Well-being:

December 2025 emphasizes the importance of mental stimulation, physical activity, and social connection for your overall health and well-being. With the Sun traveling through your 3rd house of communication and local community for most of the month, you may feel a stronger desire to engage in activities that keep your mind sharp, your body active, and your social life vibrant. Consider joining a book club, taking a dance or fitness class, or volunteering for a cause that aligns with your values and interests.

However, with Mars entering your 12th house of solitude, spirituality, and inner work on December 15th, you may also feel a stronger need for rest, reflection, and emotional healing. Make time for activities that help you relax, recharge, and connect with your inner wisdom, such as meditation, journaling, or spending time in nature. Pay attention to your dreams, intuition, and physical sensations, as they may offer valuable insights and guidance for your health and well-being.

The New Moon in Sagittarius on December 19th is a powerful time to set intentions related to your physical vitality, mental clarity, and emotional resilience. Consider starting a new self-care practice, wellness routine, or holistic healing modality that supports your mind-body-spirit connection. Trust that by nurturing your own health and happiness, you'll be better able to show up fully and authentically in your relationships, work, and community.

Travel:

With the Sun illuminating your 3rd house of short-distance travel, learning, and exploration for most of the month, December 2025 is an excellent time for local adventures, weekend getaways, or educational trips that expand your mind and horizons. Consider visiting a nearby city or town you've never been to before, attending a cultural event or festival, or taking a road trip with friends or loved ones. Be open to spontaneous detours, unexpected encounters, and serendipitous opportunities for growth and discovery.

The Full Moon in Gemini on December 4th highlights your 9th house of long-distance travel, higher education, and spiritual growth. This lunation may bring a culmination, revelation, or turning point related to a travel plan, study program, or personal quest for meaning and purpose. Trust your intuition and inner compass to guide you towards experiences and destinations that align with your highest truth and aspirations. Release any fears, doubts, or limiting beliefs that may be holding you back from embracing new adventures and possibilities.

If possible, plan your travel for the first half of the month, when the cosmic energies are more supportive of movement, communication, and exploration. The New Moon in Sagittarius on December 19th is a great time to set intentions related to your travel goals, bucket list destinations, or personal growth aspirations. Remember that every journey, whether outer or inner, is an opportunity to learn more about yourself, others, and the world around you, and to expand your capacity for wonder, compassion, and joy.

Insights from the Stars:

December 2025 is a month of intellectual growth, spiritual exploration, and personal expansion for you, dear Libra. The celestial energies are inviting you to open your mind, embrace new perspectives and possibilities, and trust in the wisdom and guidance of the universe. With the Sun and several other planets activating your 3rd house of communication, learning, and local community, you have a powerful opportunity to share your unique voice, insights, and ideas with the world, and to connect with like-minded individuals who support your growth and evolution.

The New Moon in Sagittarius on December 19th marks a powerful new beginning in your journey of mental and spiritual exploration. This lunation may bring unexpected opportunities, encounters, or epiphanies that challenge you to expand your horizons, question your assumptions, and embrace a more adventurous, optimistic, and faith-filled approach to life. Remember that true wisdom and understanding come from a place of openness, curiosity, and willingness to learn from diverse sources and experiences.

At the same time, Mars' entry into your 12th house of solitude, spirituality, and inner work on December 15th reminds you to balance your outward pursuits with inward reflection and self-care. Use this time to listen to your intuition, process your emotions, and release any patterns, beliefs, or relationships that no longer serve your highest good. Trust that by honoring your own needs for rest, healing, and introspection, you'll be better able to show up fully and authentically in your relationships, work, and community.

Remember that true growth and fulfillment come from a place of alignment, authenticity, and connection to your deepest truth and purpose. By embracing your own unique journey, by cultivating a mindset of abundance, gratitude, and faith, and by staying open to the magic and mystery of the universe, you'll be able to navigate the ups and downs of this expansive month with grace, resilience, and joy.

Best Days of the Month:

December 4th: Full Moon in Gemini - A powerful day for releasing old patterns, beliefs, or limitations around learning, communication, and personal growth.

December 11th: Mercury enters Capricorn - A time of increased focus, discipline, and strategic thinking in your work, finances, and long-term goals.

December 19th: New Moon in Sagittarius - A profound new beginning in your journey of intellectual and spiritual expansion, travel, and higher education.

December 21st: Sun enters Capricorn - The start of a new solar cycle that emphasizes your home, family, and emotional foundations.

SCORPIO 2025 HOROSCOPE

Overview Scorpio 2025

(October 23 - November 21)

2025 is shaping up to be a transformative and empowering year for those born under the sign of Scorpio. As the celestial bodies weave their intricate dance, they will bring a mix of intense experiences, profound insights, and opportunities for growth and metamorphosis. Buckle up, Scorpio, because this year is going to be a wild ride!

The year kicks off with a powerful focus on your 3rd house of communication, learning, and local community. With Mars, your traditional ruling planet, spending an extended period in this sector, you'll be fired up and ready to speak your truth, learn new skills, and make your mark on the world around you. This is a fantastic time to take a course, start a blog, or get involved in your local community. Just be mindful of potential conflicts or misunderstandings, as Mars can sometimes bring a bit of a "my way or the highway" attitude.

But wait, there's more! In mid-January, Uranus, the planet of sudden change and innovation, will turn direct in your 7th house of partnerships. This could bring some exciting and unexpected developments in your closest relationships, whether romantic, business, or platonic. Be open to new ways of relating and collaborating, and don't be afraid to let go of connections that are no longer serving your highest good.

As the year progresses, a major shift occurs in March when Saturn, the planet of structure and responsibility, moves into your 6th house of health, work, and daily routines. This transit, which will last until 2025, is an opportunity to get serious about your well-being and your work life. It's time to establish healthy habits, set clear boundaries, and take charge of your schedule. Yes, it may require some discipline and hard work, but the rewards will be well worth it in the long run.

The Aries New Moon on March 29 falls in your 6th house, bringing a powerful opportunity to set intentions around your health, work, and daily habits. This is a great time to start a new exercise routine, revamp your diet, or tackle that big project at work. Just be sure to pace yourself and don't take on more than you can handle.

In mid-April, Jupiter, the planet of expansion and growth, will form a square aspect to Pluto, your modern ruling planet, in your 3rd house. This could bring some intense and transformative experiences related to communication, learning, or travel. You may find yourself questioning long-held beliefs or confronting hidden truths. Trust in the process of growth and evolution, even if it feels uncomfortable at times.

As the year progresses, the North Node, a point of destiny and soul growth, will shift into your 7th house of partnerships, while the South Node will move into your 1st house of self and identity. This suggests a powerful opportunity to learn and grow through your relationships with others, while also letting go of old patterns of self-reliance and independence. It's time to embrace vulnerability, intimacy, and collaboration, even if it feels scary at times.

In late April, Pluto will turn retrograde in your 3rd house, bringing a period of deep reflection and internal processing related to your thoughts, beliefs, and communication style. This is a time to dig deep and confront any fears, shadows, or limiting patterns that may be holding you back. Trust in the power of introspection and self-awareness to guide you towards greater clarity and authenticity.

The mid-year period brings a series of powerful eclipses that will accelerate your growth and transformation. The Total Lunar Eclipse in Virgo on March 14 will highlight the need for balance and integration between your individuality and your relationships. This is a time to assess the give-and-take in your partnerships and to make any necessary adjustments. The Partial Solar Eclipse in Aries on March 29 will bring a powerful opportunity to set intentions around your health, work, and daily routines. Trust your instincts and take bold action towards your goals.

In mid-June, Saturn will briefly shift into your 5th house of creativity, self-expression, and romance, giving you a preview of the growth and challenges to come in these areas. This is a time to take stock of your creative pursuits and your love life, and to start putting in place the structures and boundaries needed for long-term success and fulfillment.

The second half of the year brings a focus on your inner world, spirituality, and emotional healing. Jupiter, the planet of expansion and growth, will spend an extended period in your 8th house of deep transformation, intimacy, and shared resources. This is a powerful time for personal growth, therapy, and facing your deepest fears and desires. Trust in the process of death and rebirth, and know that the universe is supporting you every step of the way.

In late September, Mars, your traditional ruling planet, will shift into your 1st house of self and identity, bringing a surge of energy, confidence, and assertiveness. This is a fantastic time to take bold action towards your goals, to assert your needs and desires, and to make your mark on the world. Just be mindful of potential conflicts or power struggles, and strive to find a balance between your own needs and the needs of others.

The Partial Solar Eclipse in Virgo on September 21 will bring a powerful opportunity for healing and transformation in your 11th house of friendships, groups, and community. This is a time to let go of any toxic or draining social connections, and to embrace a more authentic and supportive network of like-minded individuals. Trust in the power of vulnerability and shared humanity to guide you towards greater connection and belonging.

As the year comes to a close, Jupiter will turn direct in your 8th house, bringing a sense of hope, faith, and optimism to your deepest emotional and spiritual journey. This is a time to trust in the process of growth and transformation, to embrace the unknown, and to have faith in your own resilience and strength. Know that the challenges and struggles you've faced this year have ultimately been serving your highest good and evolution.

Throughout the year, the influence of Neptune in your 5th house of creativity, romance, and self-expression will continue to bring a sense of magic, inspiration, and unconditional love to these areas of your life. This is a beautiful time to tap into your imagination, to express your unique talents and gifts, and to open your heart to the beauty and wonder of the world around you. Trust in the power of creativity and love to heal, transform, and uplift you.

In December, Venus will join Pluto in your 3rd house, intensifying your desire for deep, honest communication and intellectual stimulation in your relationships. The Capricorn New Moon on December 19 will bring a powerful opportunity to set intentions around your communication skills, learning, and local community involvement.

Overall, 2025 is a year of profound growth, transformation, and self-discovery for Scorpio. With Saturn and the eclipses bringing challenges and opportunities for discipline, responsibility, and emotional healing, and with Jupiter and Neptune bringing expansion, faith, and creativity, this is a time to embrace your deepest truths and your highest potential. Trust in the journey, stay true to yourself, and know that the universe is guiding you towards your ultimate destiny. With an open heart, a curious mind, and a willingness to face your fears, you have the power to create a life of profound meaning, love, and purpose. Here's to an incredible 2025, Scorpio!

January 2025

Overview Horoscope for the Month:

Scorpio, January 2025 is a month of profound transformation and new beginnings. As the year kicks off, you'll feel a powerful urge to shed old skin and embrace a new version of yourself. The celestial energies are aligned to support your growth and evolution, but it won't always be a smooth ride. Prepare for some intense soul-searching, deep healing, and major breakthroughs. Trust the journey and know that you are exactly where you need to be.

The month starts with a bang as Vesta, the asteroid of devotion and sacred service, enters your sign on January 2nd. This transit will amplify your natural intensity and passion, and call you to dedicate yourself to a higher purpose or cause. You may find yourself feeling more focused, disciplined, and committed to your goals and values. Use this energy to fuel your ambition and make a positive impact in the world.

On January 6th, Mars, your traditional ruling planet, stations retrograde in Cancer, your 9th house of travel, higher education, and spiritual growth. This transit, which lasts until February 23rd, will bring a period of reflection and re-evaluation around your beliefs, philosophies, and long-term goals. You may find yourself questioning your path or seeking a deeper meaning and purpose in life. Be open to new perspectives and insights, and trust that the universe is guiding you towards your highest truth.

The Full Moon in Cancer on January 13th will bring a powerful culmination or turning point in your spiritual journey or educational pursuits. You may receive important news or opportunities related to travel, publishing, or higher learning. Trust your intuition and be willing to take a leap of faith towards your dreams. Remember that growth often requires stepping outside your comfort zone.

Love:

In love, January 2025 is a month of deep intimacy, vulnerability, and emotional healing. With Venus, the planet of love and relationships, entering sensitive Pisces on January 2nd, you'll be craving a soul-level connection with your partner or seeking a relationship that transcends the physical realm. This is a time to open your heart, express your deepest feelings and desires, and create a safe space for love to flourish.

If you're in a committed relationship, take time to nurture your bond through shared activities that bring you closer together, such as a romantic getaway, couples' therapy, or spiritual practice. Be willing to be vulnerable and transparent about your fears, wounds, and dreams, and trust in the healing power of love and intimacy. Remember that true love requires both partners to show up fully and authentically.

If you're single, you may find yourself attracted to people who share your depth, intensity, and spiritual values. Look for partners who are willing to do the inner work of growth and transformation, and who appreciate your unique qualities and strengths. Trust your intuition and let your heart guide you towards meaningful connections. Remember that the most important relationship is the one you have with yourself.

Career:

In your career, January 2025 is a month of powerful new beginnings and opportunities for growth. With the New Moon in Aquarius on January 29th falling in your 4th house of home and family, you may be considering a major career change or relocating for work. Trust that the universe is guiding you towards your highest potential and purpose, even if the path is not always clear or easy.

Take time to reflect on your long-term goals and values, and make sure that your work aligns with your authentic self and soul's calling. If you're feeling unfulfilled or stuck in your current job, consider exploring new options or seeking out mentors who can support you in your professional development. Remember that your work is a reflection of your inner world, and that you have the power to create a career that brings you joy, fulfillment, and abundance.

Finances:

In finances, January 2025 is a month of unexpected windfalls and opportunities for growth. With Uranus, the planet of sudden change and innovation, turning direct in your 7th house of partnerships on January 30th, you may receive financial support or resources from a spouse, business partner, or collaborator. Be open to new ways of earning and managing money, and trust that the universe will provide for your needs and desires.

Review your budget and financial goals, and make sure that your spending aligns with your values and priorities. Consider investing in your personal and professional development, such as taking a course or hiring a coach, as this can pay off in the long run. Remember that true wealth comes from within, and that your inner state of abundance and gratitude is the foundation for your external reality.

Health:

In health, January 2025 is a month of deep healing, self-care, and inner transformation. With Mars, your traditional ruling planet, stationing retrograde in your 9th house of spirituality and higher learning, you may be called to explore alternative healing modalities or philosophies that support your well-being. Consider practices such as acupuncture, energy work, or shamanic journeying to help you release old patterns and traumas.

Take time to nurture your physical, emotional, and spiritual health through regular exercise, healthy eating, and stress management techniques. Make sure to get plenty of rest and sleep, and to create a daily routine that supports your overall well-being. Remember that true health comes from a holistic approach that addresses all aspects of your being.

Travel:

In travel, January 2025 may bring unexpected opportunities for adventure, learning, and personal growth. With Mars retrograde in your 9th house of travel and higher education, you may be called to revisit a place or culture that holds special meaning for you, or to explore new spiritual or philosophical traditions. Trust your intuition and be open to synchronicity and divine guidance.

If travel isn't possible or practical, find ways to bring a sense of adventure and exploration into your daily life. Take a class on a subject that fascinates you, attend a cultural event or festival, or connect with people from different backgrounds and perspectives. Remember that travel is not just about the destination, but about the journey of self-discovery and growth.

Insights from the Stars:

The celestial energies of January 2025 remind you of the power of surrender, trust, and inner transformation. With Mars retrograde in your 9th house of spirituality and higher learning, you are being called to let go of control, embrace the unknown, and allow yourself to be guided by a higher power or purpose. This is a time to face your fears, heal your wounds, and connect with your deepest truth and wisdom.

The Full Moon in Cancer on January 13th brings a powerful opportunity for emotional release, forgiveness, and new beginnings in your spiritual journey. Trust that the universe is supporting you every step of the way, and that your challenges and obstacles are ultimately serving your highest growth and evolution. Remember that you are a powerful creator and healer, and that your soul's purpose is to shine your light and love in the world.

Best Days of the Month:

January 2nd: Vesta enters Scorpio - A powerful time to dedicate yourself to a higher purpose or cause.

January 13th: Full Moon in Cancer - A culmination or turning point in your spiritual journey or educational pursuits.

January 19th: Sun enters Aquarius - A fresh start in your home and family life, with opportunities for innovation and change.

January 27th: Mercury enters Aquarius - Brilliant ideas and insights related to your home, family, or career.

January 29th: New Moon in Aquarius - A powerful new beginning in your home and family life, with opportunities for growth and transformation..

February 2025

Overview Horoscope for the Month:

Scorpio, February 2025 is a month of deep emotional healing, spiritual awakening, and powerful new beginnings. As the shortest month of the year, it packs a punch with intense celestial energies that will catalyze your growth and transformation. Prepare to dive deep into your psyche, confront your shadows, and emerge as a more authentic and empowered version of yourself. Trust the process and know that you have the strength and resilience to handle whatever comes your way.

The month starts with a bang as Venus, the planet of love and relationships, enters fiery Aries on February 4th. This transit will bring a burst of passion, confidence, and assertiveness to your love life and creative pursuits. You may find yourself feeling more bold, spontaneous, and eager to take risks in matters of the heart. Use this energy to express your desires, pursue your dreams, and let your unique light shine.

On February 12th, the Full Moon in Leo illuminates your 10th house of career and public reputation. This powerful lunation will bring a culmination or turning point in your professional life, with opportunities for recognition, advancement, and success. Trust your talents and abilities, and don't be afraid to step into the spotlight and claim your rightful place. Remember that your work is a reflection of your soul's purpose and that you have the power to make a positive impact in the world.

Love:

In love, February 2025 is a month of passion, adventure, and new beginnings. With Venus entering Aries on February 4th, you'll be feeling more confident, assertive, and eager to take the lead in your relationships. If you're single, this is a fantastic time to put yourself out there, flirt with potential partners, and explore new romantic possibilities. Be bold, be playful, and let your unique personality shine.

If you're in a committed relationship, use this energy to spice things up and bring more excitement and spontaneity to your love life. Plan a surprise date, try a new hobby or activity together, or express your desires and fantasies with honesty and vulnerability. Remember that true intimacy requires both partners to be open, authentic, and willing to take risks.

On February 14th, Mercury enters dreamy Pisces, bringing a more romantic, intuitive, and imaginative energy to your communication style. Use this transit to express your feelings through poetry, music, or art, and to connect with your partner on a deeper, more soulful level. Trust your intuition and let your heart guide you towards more meaningful and fulfilling connections.

Career:

In your career, February 2025 is a month of powerful new beginnings, opportunities for growth, and public recognition. With the Full Moon in Leo on February 12th illuminating your 10th house of career and reputation, you may receive a promotion, award, or other forms of acknowledgement for your hard work and talents. Trust that your efforts are being seen and appreciated, and that you are making a positive impact in your field.

Take time to reflect on your long-term career goals and aspirations, and make sure that your work aligns with your values, passions, and purpose. If you're feeling unfulfilled or stuck in your current job, consider exploring new options or seeking out mentors who can support you in your professional development. Remember that your career is a journey, not a destination, and that every experience is an opportunity for growth and learning.

Finances:

In finances, February 2025 is a month of abundance, prosperity, and new opportunities for growth. With Jupiter, the planet of expansion and abundance, forming a sextile aspect to Chiron in your 5th house of creativity and self-expression, you may receive financial rewards or opportunities related to your artistic talents or entrepreneurial ventures. Trust your unique gifts and abilities, and don't be afraid to put yourself out there and showcase your work.

Review your budget and financial goals, and make sure that your spending aligns with your values and priorities. Consider investing in your personal and professional development, such as taking a course or attending a workshop, as this can pay off in the long run. Remember that true wealth comes from a sense of inner abundance, gratitude, and purpose, and that money is simply a tool to support your dreams and aspirations.

Health:

In health, February 2025 is a month of deep emotional healing, self-care, and inner transformation. With Mars, your traditional ruling planet, finally turning direct in Cancer on February 23rd, you may feel a renewed sense of energy, vitality, and motivation to take care of your physical and emotional well-being. Use this transit to establish healthy habits, routines, and boundaries that support your overall health and happiness.

Take time to nurture your body, mind, and soul through regular exercise, healthy eating, and stress-management techniques. Consider practices such as yoga, meditation, or therapy to help you release old patterns, traumas, and negative beliefs that may be holding you back. Remember that true health comes from a holistic approach that addresses all aspects of your being, and that self-love and self-care are essential for your growth and evolution.

Travel:

In travel, February 2025 may bring opportunities for spiritual pilgrimages, retreats, or journeys of self-discovery. With Neptune forming a conjunction with the True Node in Pisces on February 7th, you may feel called to visit sacred sites, connect with nature, or explore new spiritual practices and traditions. Trust your intuition and be open to synchronicity and divine guidance.

If travel isn't possible or practical, find ways to bring a sense of adventure, exploration, and wonder into your daily life. Take a nature walk, visit a local museum or art gallery, or attend a cultural event or workshop that expands your horizons and perspective. Remember that travel is not just about the destination, but about the journey of inner growth, learning, and transformation.

Insights from the Stars:

The celestial energies of February 2025 remind you of the power of vulnerability, authenticity, and emotional healing. With the Full Moon in Leo illuminating your 10th house of career and public reputation, you are being called to step into your true power and purpose, and to let your unique light shine in the world. Trust that your challenges, setbacks, and obstacles are ultimately serving your highest growth and evolution, and that you have the strength, resilience, and wisdom to overcome any adversity.

On February 27th, Saturn forms a semi-sextile aspect to Chiron in your 5th house of creativity, self-expression, and romance. This transit will bring opportunities for deep healing, self-acceptance, and transformation in these areas of your life. Trust that your wounds, insecurities, and vulnerabilities are actually your greatest teachers and sources of strength, and that by embracing them with love and compassion, you can unlock your true potential and purpose.

Best Days of the Month:

February 4th: Venus enters Aries - A burst of passion, confidence, and assertiveness in your love life and creative pursuits.

February 12th: Full Moon in Leo - A powerful culmination or turning point in your career, with opportunities for recognition and success.

February 23rd: Mars turns direct in Cancer - A renewed sense of energy, vitality, and motivation to take care of your physical and emotional well-being.

February 27th: New Moon in Pisces - A fresh start in your creative, romantic, and spiritual life, with opportunities for healing and transformation.

February 28th: Mercury enters Aries - Bold, direct, and assertive communication in your relationships and professional life.

March 2025

Overview Horoscope for the Month:

Scorpio, March 2025 is a month of profound transformation, spiritual awakening, and powerful new beginnings. As the first month of spring, it brings a sense of renewal, rebirth, and growth that will catalyze your evolution and expansion. Prepare to shed old skin, release limiting patterns and beliefs, and embrace a new version of yourself that is more authentic, empowered, and aligned with your soul's purpose. Trust the journey and know that you are exactly where you need to be.

The month starts with a bang as Saturn, the planet of structure, responsibility, and karma, enters fiery Aries on March 24th. This major transit, which will last until May 2025, will bring a powerful new chapter in your life related to your work, health, and daily routines. You may feel called to take on more responsibility, discipline, and commitment in these areas, and to establish systems and structures that support your long-term goals and well-being. Embrace the challenge and know that your efforts will pay off in the long run.

On March 29th, the New Moon in Aries coincides with a powerful Partial Solar Eclipse, bringing a potent new beginning and fresh start in your 6th house of health, work, and service. This is a fantastic time to set intentions, launch new projects, or make positive changes in your lifestyle and habits. Trust your instincts and take bold action towards your goals, even if it means stepping outside your comfort zone. Remember that you have the strength, courage, and resilience to handle whatever comes your way.

Love:

In love, March 2025 is a month of deep emotional connections, spiritual intimacy, and powerful new beginnings. With Venus, the planet of love and relationships, traveling through sensitive Pisces for most of the month, you may find yourself craving a soul-level bond with your partner or seeking a relationship that transcends the physical realm. This is a time to open your heart, express your deepest feelings and desires, and create a safe space for love to flourish.

If you're in a committed relationship, take time to nurture your bond through shared activities that bring you closer together, such as a romantic getaway, couples' therapy, or spiritual practice. Be willing to be vulnerable and transparent about your fears, wounds, and dreams, and trust in the healing power of love and intimacy. Remember that true love requires both partners to show up fully and authentically.

If you're single, you may find yourself attracted to people who share your depth, intensity, and spiritual values. Look for partners who are willing to do the inner work of growth and transformation, and who appreciate your unique qualities and strengths. Trust your intuition and let your heart guide you towards meaningful connections. Remember that the most important relationship is the one you have with yourself.

Career:

In your career, March 2025 is a month of powerful new beginnings, opportunities for growth, and increased responsibility. With Saturn entering your 6th house of work and daily routines on March 24th, you may feel called to take on more leadership, discipline, and commitment in your job or business. This is a fantastic time to establish systems, structures, and routines that support your long-term goals and success. Trust your skills, talents, and experience, and don't be afraid to take on new challenges or responsibilities.

On March 29th, the New Moon in Aries and Partial Solar Eclipse in your 6th house of work and service brings a powerful fresh start and new beginning in your professional life. This is an excellent time to launch new projects, start a new job or business, or make positive changes in your work environment or habits. Trust your instincts and take bold action towards your goals, even if it means stepping outside your comfort zone. Remember that your work is a reflection of your soul's purpose and that you have the power to make a positive impact in the world.

Finances:

In finances, March 2025 is a month of new opportunities, increased discipline, and long-term planning. With Saturn entering your 6th house of work and daily routines on March 24th, you may feel called to take a more structured, responsible, and committed approach to your finances and resources. This is a fantastic time to create a budget, pay off debts, or start saving for the future. Trust that your efforts and discipline will pay off in the long run, and that you have the power to create financial stability and abundance.

On March 29th, the New Moon in Aries and Partial Solar Eclipse in your 6th house of work and service may bring unexpected financial opportunities or rewards related to your job or business. Be open to new ways of earning or managing money, and trust that the universe will provide for your needs and desires. Remember that true wealth comes from a sense of inner abundance, gratitude, and purpose, and that money is simply a tool to support your dreams and aspirations.

Health:

In health, March 2025 is a month of powerful new beginnings, increased discipline, and self-care. With Saturn entering your 6th house of health and well-being on March 24th, you may feel called to take a more structured, responsible, and committed approach to your physical, mental, and emotional health. This is a fantastic time to start a new exercise routine, healthy eating plan, or self-care practice that supports your long-term vitality and well-being. Trust that your efforts and discipline will pay off in the long run, and that you have the power to create a strong, healthy, and vibrant body, mind, and spirit.

On March 29th, the New Moon in Aries and Partial Solar Eclipse in your 6th house of health and well-being brings a powerful fresh start and new beginning in your self-care and wellness journey. This is an excellent time to make positive changes in your lifestyle, habits, and routines, and to prioritize your physical, mental, and emotional health. Trust your instincts and take bold action towards your wellness goals, even if it means stepping outside your comfort zone. Remember that true health comes from a holistic approach that addresses all aspects of your being, and that self-love and self-care are essential for your growth and evolution.

Travel:

In travel, March 2025 may bring unexpected opportunities for adventure, learning, and personal growth. With Neptune, the planet of spirituality and imagination, entering Aries on March 30th, you may feel called to explore new horizons, cultures, or spiritual practices that expand your perspective and awareness. Trust your intuition and be open to synchronicity and divine guidance.

If travel isn't possible or practical, find ways to bring a sense of adventure, exploration, and wonder into your daily life. Take a class on a subject that fascinates you, attend a cultural event or workshop, or connect with people from different backgrounds and walks of life. Remember that travel is not just about the destination, but about the journey of inner growth, learning, and transformation.

Insights from the Stars:

The celestial energies of March 2025 remind you of the power of discipline, commitment, and self-mastery. With Saturn entering your 6th house of work, health, and daily routines, you are being called to take responsibility for your life, to establish structures and systems that support your long-term goals and well-being, and to embrace the challenges and opportunities for growth and transformation. Trust that your efforts, discipline, and perseverance will pay off in the long run, and that you have the strength, resilience, and wisdom to overcome any obstacle or setback.

On March 29th, the New Moon in Aries and Partial Solar Eclipse in your 6th house of work, health, and service brings a powerful new beginning and fresh start in these areas of your life. Trust your instincts, take bold action towards your goals, and know that the universe is supporting you every step of the way. Remember that you are a powerful creator and manifestor, and that your thoughts, beliefs, and actions shape your reality. Embrace your inner warrior, leader, and healer, and know that you have the power to create a life of purpose, passion, and fulfillment.

Best Days of the Month:

March 6th: Mars enters Leo - A burst of creativity, passion, and self-expression in your career and public life.

March 14th: Full Moon in Virgo - A powerful culmination or turning point in your friendships, social networks, and community involvement.

March 24th: Saturn enters Aries - A major new chapter and fresh start in your work, health, and daily routines.

March 29th: New Moon in Aries and Partial Solar Eclipse - A potent new beginning and powerful fresh start in your work, health, and self-care journey.

March 30th: Neptune enters Aries - A spiritual awakening and new beginning in your work, health, and daily routines, with opportunities for growth and transformation.

Overview Horoscope for the Month:

Scorpio, April 2025 is a month of deep transformation, spiritual awakening, and powerful new beginnings. As the second month of spring, it brings a sense of renewal, growth, and expansion that will catalyze your evolution and self-discovery. Prepare to shed old patterns, beliefs, and limitations, and to embrace a new version of yourself that is more authentic, empowered, and aligned with your soul's purpose. Trust the journey and know that you are exactly where you need to be.

The month starts with a powerful astrological event as Saturn forms a sextile aspect to Uranus on April 4th. This rare and harmonious alignment between the planets of structure and innovation brings opportunities for positive change, progress, and breakthroughs in your life. You may feel a strong desire to break free from old routines, habits, or limitations, and to embrace new ways of living, working, and relating that are more authentic and fulfilling. Trust your intuition and be open to unexpected opportunities and synchronicities that align with your highest goals and aspirations.

On April 12th, the Full Moon in Libra illuminates your 12th house of spirituality, surrender, and inner growth. This powerful lunation brings a culmination or turning point in your spiritual journey, inviting you to release old patterns, wounds, or limitations that no longer serve your highest good. You may experience deep insights, revelations, or healing experiences that help you to let go of the past and embrace a new level of emotional freedom and inner peace. Trust the process of release and renewal, and know that you are supported by the universe every step of the way.

Love:

In love, April 2025 is a month of deep intimacy, emotional healing, and spiritual growth. With Venus, the planet of love and relationships, entering your opposite sign of Taurus on April 30th, you may feel a strong desire for stability, security, and commitment in your partnerships. This is a fantastic time to nurture your existing relationships with love, patience, and devotion, or to attract new connections that are grounded in shared values, mutual respect, and long-term compatibility. Trust your heart and be open to giving and receiving love in all its forms.

If you're in a committed relationship, take time to deepen your bond through shared activities that bring you closer together, such as a romantic getaway, couple's massage, or nature retreat. Be willing to communicate your needs, desires, and boundaries with honesty and vulnerability, and to listen to your partner with an open heart and mind. Remember that true intimacy requires both partners to show up fully and authentically, and to support each other's growth and evolution.

If you're single, you may attract people who share your values, interests, and spiritual path. Look for partners who are grounded, reliable, and committed to personal growth and self-discovery. Trust your intuition and take your time getting to know potential partners before jumping into a serious relationship. Remember that the most important relationship is the one you have with yourself, and that self-love and self-care are essential for attracting healthy, fulfilling connections.

Career:

In your career, April 2025 is a month of positive change, progress, and innovation. With Saturn forming a sextile aspect to Uranus on April 4th, you may experience unexpected opportunities, breakthroughs, or advancements in your work or business. This is a fantastic time to take risks, embrace new challenges, and think outside the box in your professional life. Trust your skills, talents, and unique perspective, and don't be afraid to stand out from the crowd or take a leadership role in your field.

On April 16th, Mercury enters Aries, bringing a burst of energy, confidence, and assertiveness to your communication and networking skills. Use this transit to pitch your ideas, promote your work, or connect with influential people in your industry. Remember that your voice and message have the power to inspire, motivate, and create positive change in the world.

Finances:

In finances, April 2025 is a month of abundance, prosperity, and positive change. With Jupiter, the planet of expansion and abundance, forming a sextile aspect to Chiron in your 6th house of work and service on April 18th, you may experience financial rewards, opportunities, or breakthroughs related to your job, business, or investments. Trust that your efforts, skills, and talents are being recognized and valued, and that the universe is conspiring to support your financial growth and success.

On April 21st, Saturn forms a conjunction with the True Node in your 5th house of creativity, self-expression, and joy. This powerful alignment invites you to align your financial goals and strategies with your authentic passions, talents, and purpose. You may feel called to invest in your creative projects, start a side hustle, or pursue a career that allows you to express your unique gifts and abilities. Trust that when you follow your heart and do what you love, abundance and prosperity will naturally flow into your life.

Health:

In health, April 2025 is a month of deep healing, self-care, and spiritual growth. With Mars, your traditional ruling planet, entering Leo on April 18th, you may feel a renewed sense of vitality, confidence, and motivation to take care of your physical, mental, and emotional well-being. Use this transit to establish healthy habits, routines, and practices that support your long-term health and happiness, such as regular exercise, nutritious eating, and stress-management techniques.

On April 12th, the Full Moon in Libra illuminates your 12th house of spirituality, surrender, and inner growth, inviting you to release old patterns, traumas, or limitations that may be affecting your health and well-being. You may experience deep insights, revelations, or healing experiences that help you to let go of the past and embrace a new level of emotional freedom and inner peace. Trust the process of release and renewal, and know that you are supported by the universe every step of the way.

Travel:

In travel, April 2025 may bring opportunities for spiritual pilgrimages, retreats, or journeys of self-discovery. With Venus entering Taurus on April 30th, you may feel called to visit beautiful, natural settings that allow you to reconnect with your senses, your body, and the earth. Consider taking a trip to a peaceful, serene location such as a mountain retreat, beach resort, or eco-lodge, where you can unplug from technology, slow down, and immerse yourself in the healing energy of nature.

If travel isn't possible or practical, find ways to bring a sense of beauty, pleasure, and relaxation into your daily life. Take a scenic drive, visit a local park or garden, or create a cozy, inviting space in your home that allows you to unwind and recharge. Remember that travel is not just about the destination, but about the journey of inner growth, self-discovery, and connection with the world around you.

Insights from the Stars:

The celestial energies of April 2025 remind you of the power of surrender, faith, and inner growth. With the Full Moon in Libra illuminating your 12th house of spirituality and surrender on April 12th, you are being called to let go of control, trust in the flow of life, and allow yourself to be guided by a higher power or purpose. This is a time to face your fears, heal your wounds, and connect with your deepest truth and wisdom.

On April 17th, Jupiter forms a sesquadrate aspect to Pluto in your 3rd house of communication and learning. This challenging alignment may bring up intense power struggles, conflicts, or confrontations in your relationships or interactions with others. You may need to stand up for your beliefs, values, or boundaries, or to speak truth to power in some way. Trust your intuition and inner strength, and know that your voice and message have the power to create positive change and transformation in the world.

Best Days of the Month:

April 4th: Saturn sextile Uranus - Positive change, progress, and innovation in your career, finances, and personal growth.

April 12th: Full Moon in Libra - A powerful culmination or turning point in your spiritual journey, with opportunities for deep healing, release, and renewal.

April 16th: Mercury enters Aries - A burst of energy, confidence, and assertiveness in your communication and networking skills.

April 18th: Jupiter sextile Chiron - Financial rewards, opportunities, or breakthroughs related to your job, business, or investments.

April 30th: Venus enters Taurus - A desire for stability, security, and commitment in your relationships, with opportunities for deep intimacy, emotional healing, and spiritual growth.

May 2025

Overview Horoscope for the Month:

Scorpio, May 2025 is a month of intense transformation, spiritual growth, and personal empowerment. As the final month of spring, it brings a sense of culmination, completion, and new beginnings that will catalyze your evolution and self-discovery. Prepare to shed old patterns, beliefs, and limitations that no longer serve your highest good, and to embrace a new level of authenticity, freedom, and alignment with your soul's purpose. Trust the journey and know that you are exactly where you need to be.

The month starts with a powerful astrological event as Saturn semi-squares Pluto on May 1st. This challenging alignment between the planets of structure and transformation may bring up intense power struggles, conflicts, or confrontations in your relationships, career, or personal life. You may need to confront deep-seated fears, shadows, or limitations that are holding you back from your full potential, or to make difficult choices and changes that align with your true values and desires. Trust your inner strength and resilience, and know that the challenges you face are ultimately serving your highest growth and evolution.

On May 12th, the Full Moon in Scorpio illuminates your 1st house of self, identity, and personal power. This powerful lunation brings a culmination or turning point in your journey of self-discovery and transformation, inviting you to claim your authentic truth, voice, and purpose in the world. You may experience deep insights, revelations, or breakthroughs that help you to let go of old patterns of self-doubt, fear, or limitation, and to embrace a new level of confidence, courage, and self-expression. Trust the process of rebirth and renewal, and know that you have the power to create a life that truly reflects your deepest passions, values, and desires.

Love:

In love, May 2025 is a month of deep intimacy, emotional healing, and spiritual growth. With Venus, the planet of love and relationships, entering your 8th house of deep bonding and transformation on May 11th, you may feel a strong desire for soul-level connections, vulnerability, and emotional intensity in your partnerships. This is a fantastic time to deepen your existing relationships with honesty, trust, and mutual support, or to attract new connections that are based on shared values, passions, and spiritual growth. Trust your heart and be open to giving and receiving love in all its forms, even if it means facing your fears or shadows in the process.

If you're in a committed relationship, take time to explore the deeper layers of your connection through intimate conversations, shared adventures, or spiritual practices. Be willing to be vulnerable and transparent about your fears, desires, and dreams, and to support your partner's growth and evolution with love, compassion, and understanding. Remember that true intimacy requires both partners to show up fully and authentically, and to create a safe space for emotional healing and transformation.

If you're single, you may attract people who share your depth, intensity, and spiritual values. Look for partners who are willing to do the inner work of growth and self-discovery, and who appreciate your unique gifts and strengths. Trust your intuition and take your time getting to know potential partners before jumping into a serious relationship. Remember that the most important relationship is the one you have with yourself, and that self-love and self-care are essential for attracting healthy, fulfilling connections.

Career:

In your career, May 2025 is a month of power, success, and personal achievement. With Jupiter, the planet of expansion and abundance, forming a biquintile aspect to Pluto in your 3rd house of communication and networking on May 30th, you may experience unexpected opportunities, breakthroughs, or recognition in your work or business. This is a fantastic time to showcase your unique talents, ideas, and leadership skills, and to take bold action towards your professional goals and aspirations. Trust that your efforts and dedication are being seen and valued, and that the universe is conspiring to support your success and fulfillment.

On May 18th, Jupiter forms a square aspect to the True Node in your 6th house of work, health, and service. This challenging alignment may bring up questions or doubts about your current path or purpose, or highlight areas where you need to make changes or adjustments to align with your true calling. Trust your inner guidance and be open to new opportunities or directions that feel authentic and meaningful to you. Remember that your work is a reflection of your soul's purpose, and that you have the power to create a career that truly reflects your passions, values, and unique gifts.

Finances:

In finances, May 2025 is a month of abundance, prosperity, and positive change. With Jupiter, the planet of expansion and abundance, forming a sextile aspect to Chiron in your 6th house of work and service on May 18th, you may experience financial rewards, opportunities, or breakthroughs related to your job, business, or investments. Trust that your efforts, skills, and talents are being recognized and valued, and that the universe is supporting your financial growth and success.

On May 24th, Saturn enters your 6th house of work, health, and daily routines, bringing a new level of structure, discipline, and responsibility to your financial life. This is a fantastic time to create a budget, set financial goals, and develop a long-term plan for wealth and abundance. You may need to make some sacrifices or adjustments in the short term, but trust that your efforts will pay off in the long run. Remember that true prosperity comes from aligning your finances with your values, purpose, and highest good.

Health:

In health, May 2025 is a month of deep healing, self-care, and spiritual growth. With the Full Moon in your sign on May 12th, you may experience a powerful release or breakthrough in your physical, emotional, or spiritual well-being. This is a fantastic time to let go of old patterns, habits, or beliefs that are no longer serving your highest good, and to embrace a new level of vitality, energy, and self-love. Trust the process of renewal and regeneration, and know that you have the power to create a healthy, vibrant, and fulfilling life.

On May 24th, Saturn enters your 6th house of health and daily routines, bringing a new level of structure, discipline, and commitment to your self-care practices. This is a fantastic time to establish healthy habits, routines, and rituals that support your long-term well-being, such as regular exercise, nutritious eating, and stress-management techniques. You may need to make some sacrifices or adjustments in the short term, but trust that your efforts will pay off in the long run. Remember that true health comes from aligning your mind, body, and spirit with your highest good and purpose.

Travel:

In travel, May 2025 may bring opportunities for deep transformation, spiritual growth, and personal empowerment. With Venus entering your 8th house of deep bonding and transformation on May 11th, you may feel called to explore hidden or mystical places that allow you to connect with your inner world and the mysteries of life. Consider taking a trip to a sacred site, ancient ruins, or a place of natural wonder, where you can immerse yourself in the energy of transformation and rebirth.

If travel isn't possible or practical, find ways to bring a sense of depth, intensity, and spiritual growth into your daily life. Explore your inner world through practices such as meditation, journaling, or dream work, or seek out experiences that challenge you to step outside your comfort zone and embrace new perspectives. Remember that travel is not just about the destination, but about the journey of self-discovery and transformation.

Insights from the Stars:

The celestial energies of May 2025 remind you of the power of surrender, trust, and inner transformation. With the Full Moon in your sign on May 12th, you are being called to let go of control, embrace the unknown, and allow yourself to be guided by your deepest truth and wisdom. This is a time to face your fears, heal your wounds, and connect with your authentic self and purpose.

On May 18th, Jupiter forms a square aspect to the True Node in your 6th house of work, health, and service. This challenging alignment may bring up questions or doubts about your current path or purpose, or highlight areas where you need to make changes or adjustments to align with your true calling. Trust your inner guidance and be open to new opportunities or directions that feel authentic and meaningful to you. Remember that your work is a reflection of your soul's purpose, and that you have the power to create a life that truly reflects your passions, values, and unique gifts.

Best Days of the Month:

May 1st: Saturn semi-square Pluto - Intense power struggles, conflicts, or confrontations that ultimately serve your highest growth and evolution.

May 12th: Full Moon in Scorpio - A powerful culmination or turning point in your journey of self-discovery and transformation.

May 18th: Jupiter sextile Chiron - Financial rewards, opportunities, or breakthroughs related to your job, business, or investments.

May 24th: Saturn enters 6th house - A new level of structure, discipline, and commitment to your work, health, and daily routines.

May 30th: Jupiter biquintile Pluto - Unexpected opportunities, breakthroughs, or recognition in your career or business.

June 2025

Overview Horoscope for the Month:

Scorpio, June 2025 is a month of deep introspection, emotional healing, and spiritual growth. As the first month of summer, it brings a sense of warmth, vitality, and inner illumination that will catalyze your evolution and self-discovery. Prepare to dive deep into your psyche, confront your shadows and fears, and emerge with a renewed sense of purpose, power, and alignment with your soul's path. Trust the journey and know that you are exactly where you need to be.

The month starts with a powerful astrological event as Jupiter, the planet of expansion and growth, squares Saturn, your traditional ruler, on June 15th. This challenging alignment between the planets of opportunity and restriction may bring up tensions or obstacles in your personal or professional life, particularly around issues of freedom, responsibility, and long-term goals. You may need to find a balance between your desire for growth and adventure, and your need for structure, discipline, and stability. Trust your inner wisdom and be open to making necessary adjustments or compromises that align with your highest good.

On June 25th, the New Moon in Cancer illuminates your 9th house of higher learning, travel, and spiritual growth. This powerful lunation brings a new beginning or fresh start in your journey of knowledge, wisdom, and self-discovery. You may feel called to expand your horizons, explore new cultures or philosophies, or deepen your spiritual practice. Trust your intuition and be open to new opportunities or experiences that broaden your perspective and enrich your understanding of yourself and the world.

Love:

In love, June 2025 is a month of emotional intimacy, vulnerability, and spiritual connection. With Venus, the planet of love and relationships, entering your 9th house of higher learning and spiritual growth on June 4th, you may feel a strong desire for a partnership that expands your mind, heart, and soul. This is a fantastic time to connect with someone who shares your values, beliefs, and thirst for knowledge, or to deepen your existing relationship through shared learning, travel, or spiritual practices. Trust your heart and be open to giving and receiving love in all its forms, even if it means stepping outside your comfort zone.

If you're in a committed relationship, take time to explore new ways of connecting and communicating with your partner, such as learning a new language together, taking a class or workshop, or embarking on a spiritual retreat. Be willing to be vulnerable and transparent about your hopes, fears, and dreams, and to support your partner's growth and evolution with love, compassion, and understanding. Remember that true intimacy requires both partners to show up fully and authentically, and to create a safe space for emotional and spiritual growth.

If you're single, you may attract people who share your intellectual curiosity, adventurous spirit, and spiritual values. Look for partners who inspire you to learn, grow, and expand your horizons, and who appreciate your unique gifts and strengths. Trust your intuition and take your time getting to know potential partners before jumping into a serious relationship. Remember that the most important relationship is the one you have with yourself, and that self-love and self-discovery are essential for attracting healthy, fulfilling connections.

Career:

In your career, June 2025 is a month of growth, learning, and new opportunities. With Mars, your traditional ruler, entering your 10th house of career and public reputation on June 17th, you may feel a strong drive to advance your professional goals, take on new challenges, and make your mark in the world. This is a fantastic time to assert your leadership skills, showcase your talents and expertise, and pursue opportunities that align with your passions and purpose. Trust that your efforts and dedication are being seen and valued, and that the universe is supporting your success and fulfillment.

On June 18th, Jupiter forms a quincunx aspect to Pluto in your 3rd house of communication and networking. This challenging alignment may bring up power struggles or conflicts in your professional relationships or interactions, particularly around issues of control, influence, or authority. You may need to navigate complex dynamics or negotiations with tact, diplomacy, and a clear sense of your own boundaries and values. Trust your inner strength and integrity, and be open to finding creative solutions or compromises that serve the highest good of all involved.

Finances:

In finances, June 2025 is a month of abundance, prosperity, and positive change. With Jupiter, the planet of expansion and abundance, entering your 10th house of career and public reputation on June 9th, you may experience financial rewards, opportunities, or breakthroughs related to your job, business, or investments. Trust that your efforts, skills, and talents are being recognized and valued, and that the universe is supporting your financial growth and success.

On June 15th, Jupiter squares Saturn in your 5th house of creativity, self-expression, and joy. This challenging alignment may bring up tensions or obstacles around your ability to manifest abundance through your unique gifts and talents, or to find a balance between work and play, responsibility and pleasure. You may need to make some sacrifices or adjustments in the short term, but trust that your efforts will pay off in the long run. Remember that true prosperity comes from aligning your finances with your values, purpose, and highest good.

Health:

In health, June 2025 is a month of vitality, energy, and inner growth. With the Sun, the planet of life force and vitality, entering your 9th house of higher learning and spiritual growth on June 20th, you may feel a renewed sense of purpose, passion, and inner illumination. This is a fantastic time to expand your knowledge and understanding of health and wellness, explore new healing modalities or practices, and connect with your inner wisdom and guidance. Trust that your body, mind, and spirit are always working towards balance, harmony, and wholeness.

On June 25th, the New Moon in Cancer falls in your 9th house, bringing a new beginning or fresh start in your journey of health and well-being. This is a fantastic time to set intentions around your physical, emotional, and spiritual health, and to take action towards your goals and desires. You may feel called to start a new exercise routine, change your diet or lifestyle, or explore alternative therapies or practices that support your overall vitality and resilience. Trust the process of growth and transformation, and know that you have the power to create a healthy, vibrant, and fulfilling life.

Travel:

In travel, June 2025 may bring opportunities for adventure, learning, and personal growth. With Venus entering your 9th house of travel and higher learning on June 4th, you may feel called to explore new cultures, landscapes, or experiences that expand your mind, heart, and soul. Consider taking a trip to a foreign country, enrolling in a study abroad program, or embarking on a spiritual pilgrimage that allows you to connect with your inner truth and wisdom.

If travel isn't possible or practical, find ways to bring a sense of adventure, curiosity, and growth into your daily life. Explore your local community or region with fresh eyes, attend cultural events or festivals, or connect with people from different backgrounds and perspectives. Remember that travel is not just about the destination, but about the journey of self-discovery and transformation.

Insights from the Stars:

The celestial energies of June 2025 remind you of the power of growth, learning, and inner illumination. With Jupiter entering your 10th house of career and public reputation on June 9th, you are being called to expand your vision, take risks, and pursue opportunities that align with your highest purpose and potential. This is a time to trust your inner guidance, embrace your unique gifts and talents, and shine your light in the world.

On June 18th, Jupiter forms a quincunx aspect to Pluto in your 3rd house of communication and networking. This challenging alignment may bring up power struggles or conflicts in your relationships or interactions, particularly around issues of control, influence, or authority. Trust your inner strength and integrity, and be open to finding creative solutions or compromises that serve the highest good of all involved. Remember that your words and ideas have the power to transform and heal, and that you are a catalyst for positive change in the world.

Best Days of the Month:

June 4th: Venus enters 9th house - A desire for a partnership that expands your mind, heart, and soul, and opportunities for travel, learning, and spiritual growth.

June 9th: Jupiter enters 10th house - Financial rewards, opportunities, or breakthroughs related to your career or public reputation.

June 17th: Mars enters 10th house - A strong drive to advance your professional goals, take on new challenges, and make your mark in the world.

June 20th: Sun enters 9th house - A renewed sense of purpose, passion, and inner illumination, and opportunities for growth and self-discovery.

June 25th: New Moon in Cancer - A new beginning or fresh start in your journey of higher learning, travel, and spiritual growth, and intentions for health and well-being.

July 2025

Overview Horoscope for the Month:

Scorpio, July 2025 is a month of emotional intensity, spiritual awakening, and personal transformation. As the peak of summer, it brings a sense of heat, passion, and inner fire that will catalyze your evolution and self-discovery. Prepare to face your deepest fears, desires, and shadows, and to emerge with a renewed sense of power, purpose, and alignment with your soul's path. Trust the journey and know that you are exactly where you need to be.

The month starts with a powerful astrological event as Uranus, the planet of sudden change and awakening, turns retrograde in your 7th house of partnerships on July 6th. This transit may bring unexpected shifts, challenges, or breakthroughs in your closest relationships, particularly around issues of freedom, individuality, and authenticity. You may need to confront patterns of codependency, power struggles, or limiting beliefs that are holding you back from true intimacy and connection. Trust your inner wisdom and be open to making necessary changes or adjustments that align with your highest good.

On July 10th, the Full Moon in Capricorn illuminates your 3rd house of communication, learning, and self-expression. This powerful lunation brings a culmination or turning point in your journey of knowledge, understanding, and mental growth. You may receive important news, insights, or realizations that shift your perspective and understanding of yourself and the world. Trust your intuition and be open to new ideas, conversations, or experiences that expand your mind and enrich your sense of purpose and meaning.

Love:

In love, July 2025 is a month of deep intimacy, emotional healing, and spiritual connection. With Venus, the planet of love and relationships, entering your 10th house of career and public reputation on July 30th, you may feel a strong desire for a partnership that supports your professional goals, ambitions, and sense of purpose. This is a fantastic time to connect with someone who shares your values, work ethic, and vision for the future, or to deepen your existing relationship through shared projects, goals, or public appearances. Trust your heart and be open to giving and receiving love in all its forms, even if it means stepping into the spotlight or taking on new responsibilities.

If you're in a committed relationship, take time to explore new ways of supporting and empowering each other, such as collaborating on a business venture, attending networking events together, or taking on a leadership role in your community. Be willing to be vulnerable and transparent about your hopes, fears, and dreams, and to support your partner's growth and success with love, encouragement, and practical assistance. Remember that true partnership requires both individuals to show up fully and authentically, and to create a safe space for emotional and practical support.

If you're single, you may attract people who share your ambition, drive, and sense of purpose. Look for partners who inspire you to reach for your goals, take risks, and make a positive impact in the world, and who appreciate your unique gifts and strengths. Trust your intuition and take your time getting to know potential partners before jumping into a serious relationship. Remember that the most important relationship is the one you have with yourself, and that self-love and self-respect are essential for attracting healthy, fulfilling connections.

Career:

In your career, July 2025 is a month of growth, success, and public recognition. With the Sun, the planet of vitality and self-expression, entering your 10th house of career and public reputation on July 22nd, you may feel a strong drive to advance your professional goals, take on new challenges, and make your mark in the world. This is a fantastic time to showcase your talents, expertise, and leadership skills, and to pursue opportunities that align with your passions and purpose. Trust that your efforts and dedication are being seen and valued, and that the universe is supporting your success and fulfillment.

On July 18th, Jupiter forms a square aspect to Chiron in your 6th house of work, health, and service. This challenging alignment may bring up wounds, insecurities, or limitations around your ability to manifest your true calling or to find a sense of meaning and purpose in your daily work. You may need to confront patterns of self-doubt, perfectionism, or people-pleasing that are holding you back from authentic self-expression and fulfillment. Trust your inner healing process and be open to finding creative solutions or adjustments that allow you to align your work with your highest values and aspirations.

Finances:

In finances, July 2025 is a month of abundance, prosperity, and positive change. With Venus, the planet of love and money, entering your 10th house of career and public reputation on July 30th, you may experience financial rewards, opportunities, or breakthroughs related to your professional achievements, status, or public image. Trust that your efforts, skills, and talents are being recognized and valued, and that the universe is supporting your financial growth and success.

On July 13th, Saturn, your traditional ruler, turns retrograde in your 5th house of creativity, self-expression, and joy. This transit may bring up challenges or limitations around your ability to manifest abundance through your unique gifts and talents, or to find a sense of play, pleasure, and fulfillment in your financial life. You may need to confront patterns of scarcity, self-doubt, or over-responsibility that are holding you back from true prosperity and joy. Trust your inner wisdom and be open to making necessary adjustments or sacrifices that align with your highest values and long-term goals.

Health:

In health, July 2025 is a month of deep healing, transformation, and inner growth. With Mars, the planet of energy and action, entering your 12th house of spirituality, surrender, and inner work on June 22nd, you may feel a strong drive to explore your inner world, confront your shadows and fears, and release old patterns and traumas that are holding you back from true health and wholeness. This is a fantastic time to engage in practices such as meditation, therapy, or energy healing that support your emotional, mental, and spiritual well-being.

On July 10th, the Full Moon in Capricorn falls in your 3rd house of communication, learning, and self-expression, bringing a culmination or turning point in your journey of self-discovery and mental growth. You may receive important insights, realizations, or messages that shift your perspective and understanding of your health and well-being. Trust your intuition and be open to new ideas, practices, or modalities that support your overall vitality and resilience. Remember that true health comes from a holistic approach that addresses all aspects of your being - physical, emotional, mental, and spiritual.

Travel:

In travel, July 2025 may bring opportunities for personal growth, self-discovery, and inner exploration. With Mars entering your 12th house of spirituality and inner work on June 22nd, you may feel called to embark on a journey of self-reflection, emotional healing, or spiritual awakening. Consider taking a solo retreat, attending a meditation or yoga workshop, or visiting a sacred site or natural wonder that allows you to connect with your inner wisdom and guidance.

If travel isn't possible or practical, find ways to bring a sense of inner exploration, self-discovery, and healing into your daily life. Engage in practices such as journaling, dream work, or creative expression that allow you to access your subconscious mind and inner world. Remember that travel is not just about the destination, but about the journey of self-discovery and transformation.

Insights from the Stars:

The celestial energies of July 2025 remind you of the power of emotional healing, spiritual awakening, and inner transformation. With Uranus turning retrograde in your 7th house of partnerships on July 6th, you are being called to confront patterns of codependency, power struggles, or limiting beliefs that are holding you back from true intimacy and connection. This is a time to trust your inner wisdom, embrace your individuality and authenticity, and make necessary changes or adjustments that align with your highest good.

On July 18th, Jupiter forms a square aspect to Chiron in your 6th house of work, health, and service. This challenging alignment may bring up wounds, insecurities, or limitations around your ability to manifest your true calling or to find a sense of meaning and purpose in your daily work. Trust your inner healing process and be open to finding creative solutions or adjustments that allow you to align your work with your highest values and aspirations. Remember that your challenges and struggles are ultimately serving your growth and evolution, and that you have the power to transform your pain into purpose and passion.

Best Days of the Month:

July 6th: Uranus turns retrograde in 7th house - Unexpected shifts, challenges, or breakthroughs in your closest relationships that serve your growth and awakening.

July 10th: Full Moon in Capricorn - A culmination or turning point in your journey of communication, learning, and self-expression, and insights for health and well-being.

July 22nd: Sun enters 10th house - A strong drive to advance your professional goals, take on new challenges, and make your mark in the world.

July 30th: Venus enters 10th house - Financial rewards, opportunities, or breakthroughs related to your career or public reputation, and a desire for a partnership that supports your professional goals and ambitions.

July 31st: Mercury enters 10th house - Clear communication, networking, and mental focus in your career and public life.

August 2025

Overview Horoscope for the Month:

Scorpio, August 2025 is a month of deep transformation, emotional healing, and spiritual growth. As the final month of summer, it brings a sense of culmination, completion, and new beginnings that will catalyze your evolution and self-discovery. Prepare to shed old patterns, beliefs, and limitations that no longer serve your highest good, and to embrace a new level of authenticity, freedom, and alignment with your soul's purpose. Trust the journey and know that you have the strength and resilience to handle whatever comes your way.

The month starts with a powerful astrological event as Saturn, your traditional ruler, forms a sextile aspect to Uranus on August 11th. This harmonious alignment between the planets of structure and innovation brings opportunities for positive change, progress, and breakthroughs in your personal and professional life. You may feel a strong desire to break free from old routines, habits, or limitations, and to embrace new ways of living, working, and relating that are more authentic and fulfilling. Trust your intuition and be open to unexpected opportunities and synchronicities that align with your highest goals and aspirations.

On August 9th, the Full Moon in Aquarius illuminates your 4th house of home, family, and emotional foundations. This powerful lunation brings a culmination or turning point in your journey of emotional healing, self-care, and inner growth. You may experience deep insights, revelations, or breakthroughs that help you to release old wounds, patterns, or family dynamics that are holding you back from true happiness and fulfillment. Trust the process of release and renewal, and know that you have the power to create a nurturing, supportive, and loving environment for yourself and your loved ones.

Love:

In love, August 2025 is a month of deep intimacy, emotional healing, and spiritual growth. With Venus, the planet of love and relationships, entering your 11th house of friendships and social connections on August 25th, you may feel a strong desire for partnerships that are based on shared values, ideals, and visions for the future. This is a fantastic time to connect with like-minded individuals who share your passions, interests, and goals, or to deepen your existing relationships through group activities, social events, or humanitarian causes. Trust your heart and be open to giving and receiving love in all its forms, even if it means stepping outside your comfort zone or taking risks.

If you're in a committed relationship, take time to explore new ways of connecting and communicating with your partner, such as joining a club or organization together, attending workshops or seminars, or volunteering for a cause that you both care about. Be willing to be vulnerable and transparent about your hopes, dreams, and ideals, and to support your partner's growth and evolution with love, encouragement, and understanding. Remember that true intimacy requires both partners to show up fully and authentically, and to create a safe space for emotional and spiritual growth.

If you're single, you may attract people who share your values, interests, and vision for the future. Look for partners who inspire you to be your best self, who challenge you to grow and evolve, and who appreciate your unique gifts and strengths. Trust your intuition and take your time getting to know potential partners before jumping into a serious relationship. Remember that the most important relationship is the one you have with yourself, and that self-love and self-acceptance are essential for attracting healthy, fulfilling connections.

Career:

In your career, August 2025 is a month of innovation, progress, and positive change. With Uranus, the planet of sudden change and innovation, forming a sextile aspect to Saturn on August 11th, you may experience unexpected opportunities, breakthroughs, or advancements in your work or business. This is a fantastic time to take risks, embrace new challenges, and think outside the box in your professional life. Trust your unique talents, skills, and perspective, and don't be afraid to stand out from the crowd or take a leadership role in your field.

On August 6th, Mars, your traditional ruler, enters your 12th house of spirituality, surrender, and inner growth. This transit may bring a period of introspection, reflection, and inner work in your professional life. You may feel called to explore your deeper purpose, values, and motivations, and to make sure that your work aligns with your spiritual path and highest good. Trust your intuition and be open to making necessary changes or adjustments that allow you to express your authentic self and make a positive impact in the world.

Finances:

In finances, August 2025 is a month of abundance, prosperity, and positive change. With Jupiter, the planet of expansion and abundance, forming a trine aspect to the True Node in your 6th house of work and service on September 3rd, you may experience financial rewards, opportunities, or breakthroughs related to your job, business, or investments. Trust that your efforts, skills, and talents are being recognized and valued, and that the universe is supporting your financial growth and success.

On August 11th, Ceres, the asteroid of nurturing and abundance, turns retrograde in your 6th house of work and health. This transit may bring a period of reflection and re-evaluation around your ability to manifest abundance through your daily work and routines, or to find a sense of purpose and fulfillment in your financial life. You may need to confront patterns of scarcity, self-doubt, or over-giving that are holding you back from true prosperity and self-care. Trust your inner wisdom and be open to making necessary adjustments or boundaries that align with your highest values and long-term goals.

Health:

In health, August 2025 is a month of deep healing, self-care, and inner transformation. With the Full Moon in Aquarius on August 9th illuminating your 4th house of home, family, and emotional foundations, you may experience a powerful release or breakthrough in your physical, emotional, or spiritual well-being. This is a fantastic time to let go of old patterns, habits, or beliefs that are no longer serving your highest good, and to embrace a new level of self-love, self-care, and inner peace. Trust the process of renewal and regeneration, and know that you have the power to create a healthy, vibrant, and fulfilling life.

On August 6th, Mars enters your 12th house of spirituality, surrender, and inner growth, bringing a period of introspection, reflection, and inner work in your health and well-being. You may feel called to explore alternative healing modalities, spiritual practices, or self-care routines that support your physical, emotional, and spiritual health. Trust your intuition and be open to making necessary changes or adjustments that allow you to align your mind, body, and spirit with your highest good and purpose.

Travel:

In travel, August 2025 may bring opportunities for social connections, group activities, and humanitarian causes. With Venus entering your 11th house of friendships and social networks on August 25th, you may feel called to travel with friends, join a club or organization, or participate in a service project or volunteer opportunity. Consider taking a trip with like-minded individuals who share your passions, interests, and vision for the future, or exploring new cultures and communities that align with your values and ideals.

If travel isn't possible or practical, find ways to bring a sense of connection, purpose, and social engagement into your daily life. Attend local events, workshops, or gatherings that allow you to meet new people, learn new skills, or make a positive impact in your community. Remember that travel is not just about the destination, but about the journey of self-discovery, growth, and connection with others.

Insights from the Stars:

The celestial energies of August 2025 remind you of the power of authenticity, innovation, and positive change. With Saturn forming a sextile aspect to Uranus on August 11th, you are being called to break free from old patterns, limitations, and structures that are holding you back from your true potential and purpose. This is a time to embrace your unique talents, perspective, and vision, and to trust that the universe is supporting your growth and evolution.

On August 28th, Uranus, the planet of sudden change and awakening, forms a sextile aspect to Neptune in your 5th house of creativity, self-expression, and joy. This harmonious alignment brings opportunities for spiritual growth, artistic inspiration, and unconditional love in your life. You may feel a strong desire to express your authentic self, explore your imagination and intuition, or connect with a higher power or purpose. Trust your inner guidance and be open to unexpected insights, synchronicities, or encounters that align with your highest good and soul's path.

Best Days of the Month:

August 9th: Full Moon in Aquarius - A powerful culmination or turning point in your journey of emotional healing, self-care, and inner growth.

August 11th: Saturn sextile Uranus - Positive change, progress, and breakthroughs in your personal and professional life, with opportunities for authenticity and innovation.

August 12th: Mercury turns direct - Clear communication, mental focus, and forward momentum in your career, public image, and long-term goals.

August 25th: Venus enters 11th house - Opportunities for social connections, group activities, and humanitarian causes, with a desire for partnerships based on shared values and visions.

August 28th: Uranus sextile Neptune - Spiritual growth, artistic inspiration, and unconditional love in your life, with opportunities for authentic self-expression and higher purpose.

September 2025

Overview Horoscope for the Month:

Scorpio, September 2025 is a month of profound transformation, spiritual awakening, and personal empowerment. As the first month of autumn, it brings a sense of change, letting go, and new beginnings that will catalyze your evolution and self-discovery. Prepare to shed old patterns, beliefs, and limitations that no longer serve your highest good, and to embrace a new level of authenticity, wisdom, and alignment with your soul's purpose. Trust the journey and know that you have the strength and resilience to handle whatever comes your way.

The month starts with a powerful astrological event as Mars, your traditional ruler, enters your sign on September 22nd. This transit, which lasts until November 4th, will bring a surge of energy, passion, and motivation to pursue your goals, assert your needs and desires, and make your mark on the world. You may feel more confident, courageous, and ready to take bold action towards your dreams and aspirations. Use this time to focus on your personal growth, self-discovery, and self-empowerment, and to let go of any fears, doubts, or limitations that have been holding you back.

On September 7th, the Full Moon in Pisces illuminates your 5th house of creativity, self-expression, and joy. This powerful lunation, which coincides with a Total Lunar Eclipse, brings a culmination or turning point in your journey of artistic pursuits, romantic relationships, and personal fulfillment. You may experience deep emotions, revelations, or breakthroughs that help you to release old patterns, wounds, or blocks that have been preventing you from fully expressing your authentic self and enjoying life to the fullest. Trust the process of release and renewal, and know that you have the power to create a life filled with love, passion, and purpose.

Love:

In love, September 2025 is a month of deep intimacy, emotional healing, and spiritual growth. With Venus, the planet of love and relationships, entering your 12th house of spirituality, surrender, and unconditional love on September 19th, you may feel a strong desire for a soul-level connection with your partner or a divine love that transcends the physical realm. This is a fantastic time to deepen your existing relationship through shared spiritual practices, emotional vulnerability, and acts of selfless service, or to attract a new partnership that is based on mutual growth, healing, and unconditional love. Trust your heart and be open to giving and receiving love in all its forms, even if it means facing your deepest fears, wounds, or shadows.

If you're in a committed relationship, take time to explore the deeper layers of your connection, such as your shared values, beliefs, and spiritual path. Be willing to be vulnerable and transparent about your hopes, fears, and dreams, and to support your partner's growth and healing with love, compassion, and understanding. Remember that true intimacy requires both partners to show up fully and authentically, and to create a safe space for emotional and spiritual growth.

If you're single, you may attract people who share your depth, sensitivity, and spiritual values. Look for partners who are willing to do the inner work of growth and transformation, and who appreciate your unique gifts and strengths. Trust your intuition and take your time getting to know potential partners before jumping into a serious relationship. Remember that the most important relationship is the one you have with yourself and the divine, and that self-love and spiritual connection are essential for attracting healthy, fulfilling partnerships.

Career:

In your career, September 2025 is a month of power, ambition, and personal achievement. With Mars entering your sign on September 22nd, you may feel a strong drive to pursue your professional goals, take on new challenges, and assert your leadership skills and expertise. This is a fantastic time to start a new project, launch a business venture, or go after a promotion or raise. Trust your instincts and be willing to take bold, decisive action towards your dreams and aspirations, even if it means stepping outside your comfort zone or taking risks.

On September 21st, the New Moon in Virgo coincides with a Partial Solar Eclipse, bringing a powerful new beginning or fresh start in your 11th house of friendships, networking, and community. This is an excellent time to expand your social connections, join a professional organization or group, or collaborate with like-minded individuals who share your values, interests, and goals. Trust that the universe is guiding you towards the right people and opportunities that will support your growth and success, and be open to giving and receiving help and support along the way.

Finances:

In finances, September 2025 is a month of abundance, prosperity, and positive change. With Jupiter, the planet of expansion and abundance, forming a trine aspect to the True Node in your 6th house of work and service on September 3rd, you may experience financial rewards, opportunities, or breakthroughs related to your job, business, or investments. Trust that your efforts, skills, and talents are being recognized and valued, and that the universe is supporting your financial growth and success.

On September 11th, Saturn, your traditional ruler, turns direct in your 4th house of home, family, and emotional foundations. This transit may bring a period of stability, structure, and long-term planning in your financial life, particularly related to real estate, property, or family investments. You may need to take a more disciplined, responsible approach to your finances, and to make sure that your spending and saving habits align with your values, goals, and long-term security. Trust your inner wisdom and be open to making necessary adjustments or sacrifices that will pay off in the long run.

Health:

In health, September 2025 is a month of deep healing, self-care, and inner transformation. With the Full Moon in Pisces on September 7th coinciding with a Total Lunar Eclipse in your 5th house of self-expression and joy, you may experience a powerful release or breakthrough in your physical, emotional, or spiritual well-being. This is a fantastic time to let go of old patterns, habits, or beliefs that are no longer serving your highest good, and to embrace a new level of self-love, creativity, and vitality. Trust the process of renewal and regeneration, and know that you have the power to create a healthy, vibrant, and fulfilling life.

On September 22nd, Mars enters your sign, bringing a surge of energy, motivation, and vitality to your health and well-being. Use this transit to establish healthy habits, routines, and self-care practices that support your physical, emotional, and spiritual health, such as regular exercise, nutritious eating, and stress-management techniques. Trust your body's innate wisdom and be open to making necessary changes or adjustments that allow you to feel your best and thrive.

Travel:

In travel, September 2025 may bring opportunities for spiritual pilgrimages, retreats, or soul-searching journeys. With Venus entering your 12th house of spirituality, surrender, and inner growth on September 19th, you may feel called to visit sacred sites, connect with nature, or explore new spiritual practices and traditions that deepen your connection with the divine and your inner wisdom. Consider taking a trip to a peaceful, serene location such as a monastery, ashram, or natural wonder, where you can unplug from the outside world and tune into your inner guidance and intuition.

If travel isn't possible or practical, find ways to bring a sense of inner exploration, self-discovery, and spiritual growth into your daily life. Engage in practices such as meditation, prayer, or dream work that allow you to access your subconscious mind and connect with a higher power or purpose. Remember that travel is not just about the destination, but about the journey of self-discovery, healing, and transformation.

Insights from the Stars:

The celestial energies of September 2025 remind you of the power of surrender, faith, and inner transformation. With the Full Moon in Pisces coinciding with a Total Lunar Eclipse in your 5th house of creativity, self-expression, and joy on September 7th, you are being called to let go of control, trust in the flow of life, and allow yourself to be guided by a higher power or purpose. This is a time to face your deepest fears, heal your deepest wounds, and connect with your authentic self and soul's calling.

On September 22nd, Mars enters your sign, bringing a powerful new beginning and fresh start in your personal growth, self-discovery, and self-empowerment. Trust your instincts, take bold action towards your goals, and know that the universe is supporting you every step of the way. Remember that you are a powerful creator and manifestor, and that your thoughts, beliefs, and actions shape your reality. Embrace your inner warrior, leader, and healer, and know that you have the power to transform your life and the world around you.

Best Days of the Month:

September 3rd: Jupiter trine True Node - Financial rewards, opportunities, or breakthroughs related to your job, business, or investments, with a sense of purpose and fulfillment.

September 7th: Full Moon in Pisces and Total Lunar Eclipse - A powerful culmination or turning point in your journey of creativity, self-expression, and joy, with opportunities for deep healing and transformation.

September 19th: Venus enters 12th house - Opportunities for spiritual growth, unconditional love, and soul-level connections in your relationships and inner life.

September 21st: New Moon in Virgo and Partial Solar Eclipse - A powerful new beginning or fresh start in your friendships, networking, and community involvement, with opportunities for collaboration and support.

September 22nd: Mars enters Scorpio - A surge of energy, passion, and motivation to pursue your personal goals, assert your needs and desires, and make your mark on the world, with opportunities for growth and empowerment.

October 2025

Overview Horoscope for the Month:

Scorpio, October 2025 is a month of intense transformation, deep healing, and personal empowerment. As the heart of autumn and your birthday season, it brings a sense of rebirth, renewal, and new beginnings that will catalyze your evolution and self-discovery. Prepare to shed old skin, confront your shadows and fears, and emerge as a more authentic, powerful, and aligned version of yourself. Trust the journey and know that you have the strength, wisdom, and resilience to handle whatever comes your way.

The month starts with a powerful astrological event as Pluto, your modern ruler, turns direct in your 3rd house of communication, learning, and self-expression on October 13th. This transit, which has been retrograde since May 4th, will bring a sense of forward momentum, clarity, and empowerment to your mental and verbal abilities. You may feel a strong urge to speak your truth, share your knowledge and ideas, and assert your voice and influence in the world. Use this time to actively pursue your intellectual interests, engage in meaningful conversations and debates, and express yourself with confidence, conviction, and authenticity.

On October 21st, the New Moon in Libra falls in your 12th house of spirituality, surrender, and inner growth. This powerful lunation brings a new beginning or fresh start in your journey of emotional healing, spiritual awakening, and self-discovery. You may feel called to retreat from the world, engage in solitary practices such as meditation or journaling, and connect with your inner guidance and intuition. Trust the process of release and renewal, and know that you are being supported by the universe in your path of growth and transformation.

Love:

In love, October 2025 is a month of deep intimacy, emotional healing, and spiritual growth. With Venus, the planet of love and relationships, entering your sign on November 6th, you may feel a strong desire for passionate, intense, and transformative connections that challenge you to grow, evolve, and express your authentic self. This is a fantastic time to deepen your existing relationship through honest communication, vulnerability, and shared experiences, or to attract a new partnership that is based on mutual respect, trust, and growth. Trust your heart and be open to giving and receiving love in all its forms, even if it means facing your fears, wounds, or shadows.

If you're in a committed relationship, take time to explore the deeper layers of your connection, such as your shared values, goals, and long-term vision. Be willing to have difficult conversations, work through conflicts or challenges, and support each other's individual growth and evolution. Remember that true intimacy requires both partners to show up fully and authentically, and to create a safe space for emotional and spiritual growth.

If you're single, you may attract people who share your depth, intensity, and desire for transformation. Look for partners who are willing to do the inner work of healing and growth, and who appreciate your unique gifts, strengths, and challenges. Trust your intuition and take your time getting to know potential partners before jumping into a serious relationship. Remember that the most important relationship is the one you have with yourself, and that self-love and self-acceptance are essential for attracting healthy, fulfilling partnerships.

Career:

In your career, October 2025 is a month of power, ambition, and personal achievement. With Mars, your traditional ruler, traveling through your sign for the entire month, you may feel a strong drive to pursue your professional goals, take on new challenges, and assert your leadership skills and expertise. This is a fantastic time to start a new project, launch a business venture, or go after a promotion or raise. Trust your instincts and be willing to take bold, decisive action towards your dreams and aspirations, even if it means stepping outside your comfort zone or taking risks.

On October 27th, Jupiter, the planet of expansion and abundance, turns direct in your 10th house of career and public reputation. This transit, which has been retrograde since November 11th, will bring a sense of forward momentum, growth, and opportunity to your professional life. You may receive recognition, rewards, or new opportunities that align with your skills, talents, and long-term goals. Trust that the universe is supporting your success and fulfillment, and be open to new paths or directions that feel authentic and meaningful to you.

Finances:

In finances, October 2025 is a month of abundance, prosperity, and positive change. With Venus, the planet of love and money, entering your sign on November 6th, you may experience a surge of financial opportunities, rewards, or windfalls that align with your values, desires, and personal power. This is a fantastic time to assert your worth, negotiate for what you want, and make financial decisions that support your long-term security and abundance. Trust your instincts and be open to new sources of income or investments that feel authentic and empowering to you.

On October 16th, Mercury, the planet of communication and commerce, enters your sign, bringing a sense of mental clarity, focus, and persuasion to your financial dealings. Use this transit to actively pursue your financial goals, communicate your needs and desires, and make strategic decisions that align with your values and priorities. Remember that true wealth comes from a sense of inner abundance, gratitude, and purpose, and that money is simply a tool to support your dreams and aspirations.

Health:

In health, October 2025 is a month of deep healing, self-care, and inner transformation. With the New Moon in Libra on October 21st falling in your 12th house of spirituality and inner growth, you may feel a strong urge to retreat from the world, rest and recharge, and connect with your inner guidance and intuition. This is a fantastic time to engage in practices such as meditation, yoga, or energy healing that support your physical, emotional, and spiritual well-being, and to release any patterns, habits, or beliefs that are no longer serving your highest good.

On October 6th, Mars, your traditional ruler, forms a sextile aspect to Uranus in your 6th house of health and daily routines. This harmonious alignment brings opportunities for positive change, innovation, and breakthroughs in your self-care practices and lifestyle choices. You may feel inspired to try new forms of exercise, nutrition, or alternative therapies that support your vitality, energy, and overall well-being. Trust your body's innate wisdom and be open to making necessary changes or adjustments that allow you to feel your best and thrive.

Travel:

In travel, October 2025 may bring opportunities for personal growth, self-discovery, and inner exploration. With the New Moon in Libra on October 21st falling in your 12th house of spirituality and inner growth, you may feel called to take a solo retreat, attend a workshop or seminar, or visit a sacred site or natural wonder that allows you to connect with your inner wisdom and guidance. Consider taking a trip that focuses on emotional healing, spiritual awakening, or creative expression, such as a yoga retreat, art workshop, or nature immersion.

If travel isn't possible or practical, find ways to bring a sense of inner exploration, self-discovery, and growth into your daily life. Engage in practices such as journaling, dream work, or creative visualization that allow you to access your subconscious mind and connect with your authentic self and desires. Remember that travel is not just about the destination, but about the journey of self-discovery, healing, and transformation.

Insights from the Stars:

The celestial energies of October 2025 remind you of the power of authenticity, self-expression, and personal transformation. With Pluto turning direct in your 3rd house of communication and learning on October 13th, you are being called to speak your truth, share your knowledge and ideas, and assert your voice and influence in the world. This is a time to actively pursue your intellectual interests, engage in meaningful conversations and debates, and express yourself with confidence, conviction, and authenticity.

On October 23rd, Mars, your traditional ruler, forms a square aspect to Pluto in your 3rd house, bringing intense power struggles, conflicts, or confrontations in your communication, learning, or self-expression. You may need to confront deep-seated fears, wounds, or limitations that are holding you back from fully expressing your authentic self and desires, or to engage in difficult conversations or negotiations that challenge your beliefs, values, or sense of power. Trust your inner strength and wisdom, and know that the challenges you face are ultimately serving your growth, healing, and transformation.

Best Days of the Month:

October 6th: Mars sextile Uranus - Opportunities for positive change, innovation, and breakthroughs in your health, self-care, and daily routines.

October 13th: Pluto turns direct in 3rd house - Forward momentum, clarity, and empowerment in your communication, learning, and self-expression.

October 16th: Mercury enters Scorpio - Mental clarity, focus, and persuasion in your personal goals, desires, and financial dealings.

October 21st: New Moon in Libra - A new beginning or fresh start in your journey of emotional healing, spiritual awakening, and self-discovery.

October 27th: Jupiter turns direct in 10th house - Forward momentum, growth, and opportunity in your career, public reputation, and long-term goals.

November 2025

Overview Horoscope for the Month:

Scorpio, November 2025 is a month of intense transformation, deep healing, and personal empowerment. As the final month of autumn and the peak of your birthday season, it brings a sense of culmination, completion, and new beginnings that will catalyze your evolution and self-discovery. Prepare to shed old patterns, beliefs, and limitations that no longer serve your highest good, and to embrace a new level of authenticity, power, and alignment with your soul's purpose. Trust the journey and know that you have the strength, wisdom, and resilience to handle whatever comes your way.

The month starts with a powerful astrological event as Venus, the planet of love and relationships, enters your sign on November 6th. This transit, which lasts until November 30th, will bring a surge of magnetic attraction, personal charisma, and romantic opportunities to your life. You may feel more confident, alluring, and ready to pursue your heart's desires and attract the love, pleasure, and abundance you deserve. Use this time to focus on your self-love, self-care, and self-expression, and to surround yourself with beauty, art, and sensual delights that nourish your soul.

On November 28th, the New Moon in Sagittarius falls in your 2nd house of values, resources, and self-worth. This powerful lunation brings a new beginning or fresh start in your journey of financial abundance, personal empowerment, and self-esteem. You may feel called to reassess your priorities, values, and beliefs around money and success, and to align your resources and talents with your authentic self and purpose. Trust the process of manifestation and attraction, and know that you have the power to create a life of prosperity, fulfillment, and joy.

Love:

In love, November 2025 is a month of deep intimacy, emotional healing, and spiritual growth. With Venus traveling through your sign for most of the month, you may feel a strong desire for passionate, intense, and transformative connections that challenge you to grow, evolve, and express your authentic self. This is a fantastic time to deepen your existing relationship through honest communication, vulnerability, and shared experiences, or to attract a new partnership that is based on mutual respect, trust, and growth. Trust your heart and be open to giving and receiving love in all its forms, even if it means facing your fears, wounds, or shadows.

If you're in a committed relationship, take time to explore the deeper layers of your connection, such as your shared values, goals, and long-term vision. Be willing to have difficult conversations, work through conflicts or challenges, and support each other's individual growth and evolution. Remember that true intimacy requires both partners to show up fully and authentically, and to create a safe space for emotional and spiritual growth.

If you're single, you may attract people who share your depth, intensity, and desire for transformation. Look for partners who are willing to do the inner work of healing and growth, and who appreciate your unique gifts, strengths, and challenges. Trust your intuition and take your time getting to know potential partners before jumping into a serious relationship. Remember that the most important relationship is the one you have with yourself, and that self-love and self-acceptance are essential for attracting healthy, fulfilling partnerships.

Career:

In your career, November 2025 is a month of success, recognition, and personal achievement. With Mars, your traditional ruler, traveling through your 2nd house of values and resources until November 4th, you may feel a strong drive to pursue your financial goals, assert your worth, and make strategic decisions that support your long-term security and success. This is a fantastic time to negotiate a raise or promotion, start a side hustle or business venture, or invest in your skills and talents. Trust your instincts and be willing to take bold, decisive action towards your dreams and aspirations, even if it means stepping outside your comfort zone or taking risks.

On November 9th, Mercury, the planet of communication and commerce, turns retrograde in your 2nd house of values and resources. This transit, which lasts until November 29th, may bring a period of reflection, re-evaluation, and inner growth around your financial beliefs, habits, and strategies. You may need to review your budget, investments, or spending patterns, and to make necessary adjustments or changes that align with your authentic values and priorities. Trust your inner wisdom and be open to new perspectives or insights that can help you create a more abundant, fulfilling, and purposeful financial life.

Finances:

In finances, November 2025 is a month of abundance, prosperity, and positive change. With the New Moon in Sagittarius on November 28th falling in your 2nd house of values and resources, you may experience a powerful new beginning or fresh start in your journey of financial empowerment, self-worth, and manifestation. This is a fantastic time to set intentions, affirm your abundance, and take inspired action towards your financial goals and dreams. Trust that the universe is conspiring to support your success and fulfillment, and be open to unexpected opportunities or synchronicities that align with your highest good.

On November 12th, Saturn, your traditional ruler, turns direct in your 4th house of home, family, and emotional foundations. This transit, which has been retrograde since July 13th, will bring a sense of stability, structure, and forward momentum to your financial life, particularly related to real estate, property, or family investments. You may need to take a more disciplined, responsible approach to your finances, and to make sure that your spending and saving habits align with your values, goals, and long-term security. Trust your inner wisdom and be open to making necessary adjustments or sacrifices that will pay off in the long run.

Health:

In health, November 2025 is a month of deep healing, self-care, and inner transformation. With Neptune, the planet of spirituality and unconditional love, traveling through your 5th house of creativity, joy, and self-expression, you may feel a strong urge to engage in practices that nourish your soul, uplift your spirit, and connect you with a sense of divine love and grace. This is a fantastic time to explore artistic pursuits, romantic adventures, or playful activities that bring you a sense of joy, wonder, and inspiration, and to release any patterns, habits, or beliefs that are blocking your natural vitality and radiance.

On November 7th, Pluto, your modern ruler, forms a semi-square aspect to the True Node in your 5th house of creativity and self-expression. This challenging alignment may bring up deep fears, wounds, or limitations around your ability to fully express your authentic self and desires, or to connect with a sense of purpose and meaning in your life. You may need to confront patterns of self-doubt, shame, or repression that are holding you back from your true potential and joy. Trust your inner strength and wisdom, and know that the challenges you face are ultimately serving your growth, healing, and transformation.

Travel:

In travel, November 2025 may bring opportunities for adventure, learning, and personal growth. With Venus traveling through your sign for most of the month, you may feel a strong desire to explore new places, cultures, or experiences that expand your mind, heart, and soul. Consider taking a trip that focuses on beauty, art, or sensual pleasures, such as a wine-tasting tour, art museum visit, or spa retreat. Trust your instincts and be open to spontaneous detours or surprises that can lead to unexpected delights and discoveries.

If travel isn't possible or practical, find ways to bring a sense of adventure, curiosity, and growth into your daily life. Explore your local community or region with fresh eyes, attend cultural events or workshops, or connect with people from different backgrounds and perspectives. Remember that travel is not just about the destination, but about the journey of self-discovery, learning, and transformation.

Insights from the Stars:

The celestial energies of November 2025 remind you of the power of self-love, self-worth, and personal empowerment. With Venus traveling through your sign for most of the month, you are being called to embrace your unique beauty, talents, and desires, and to attract the love, abundance, and joy you deserve. This is a time to focus on your self-care, self-expression, and self-acceptance, and to surround yourself with people, experiences, and environments that reflect your authentic self and values.

On November 17th, Jupiter, the planet of expansion and growth, forms a sesquadrate aspect to Pluto in your 3rd house of communication and learning. This challenging alignment may bring up intense power struggles, conflicts, or confrontations in your relationships, interactions, or intellectual pursuits. You may need to confront deep-seated fears, wounds, or limitations that are holding you back from fully expressing your truth and wisdom, or to engage in difficult conversations or negotiations that challenge your beliefs, values, or sense of authority. Trust your inner strength and integrity, and know that the challenges you face are ultimately serving your growth, healing, and transformation.

Best Days of the Month:

November 6th: Venus enters Scorpio - A surge of magnetic attraction, personal charisma, and romantic opportunities in your life, with a focus on self-love, self-care, and self-expression.

November 12th: Saturn turns direct in 4th house - Forward momentum, stability, and structure in your financial life, particularly related to real estate, property, or family investments.

November 25th: Venus conjunct Jupiter in Scorpio - Abundant blessings, opportunities, and positive energy in your love life, finances, and personal growth.

November 28th: New Moon in Sagittarius - A powerful new beginning or fresh start in your journey of financial empowerment, self-worth, and manifestation.

November 30th: Venus enters Sagittarius - Expansive, optimistic, and adventurous energy in your love life, creativity, and self-expression, with opportunities for travel, learning, and personal growth.

December 2025

Overview Horoscope for the Month:

Scorpio, December 2025 is a month of deep introspection, emotional healing, and spiritual growth. As the final month of the year, it brings a sense of closure, completion, and new beginnings that will catalyze your evolution and self-discovery. Prepare to dive deep into your psyche, confront your shadows and fears, and emerge with a renewed sense of purpose, power, and alignment with your soul's path. Trust the journey and know that you are exactly where you need to be.

The month starts with a powerful astrological event as Neptune, the planet of spirituality and transcendence, turns direct in your 5th house of creativity, self-expression, and joy on December 10th. This transit, which has been retrograde since July 4th, will bring a sense of clarity, inspiration, and forward momentum to your artistic pursuits, romantic life, and personal fulfillment. You may feel a strong urge to express your authentic self, explore your imagination and intuition, and connect with a higher power or purpose. Use this time to actively pursue your passions, nurture your inner child, and embrace the magic and wonder of life.

On December 19th, the New Moon in Sagittarius falls in your 2nd house of values, resources, and self-worth. This powerful lunation brings a new beginning or fresh start in your journey of financial abundance, personal empowerment, and self-esteem. You may feel called to reassess your priorities, values, and beliefs around money and success, and to align your resources and talents with your authentic self and purpose. Trust the process of manifestation and attraction, and know that you have the power to create a life of prosperity, fulfillment, and joy.

Love:

In love, December 2025 is a month of deep intimacy, emotional healing, and spiritual growth. With Venus, the planet of love and relationships, joining Pluto in your 3rd house of communication and self-expression, you may feel a strong desire for honest, authentic, and transformative connections that challenge you to grow, evolve, and express your truth. This is a fantastic time to have deep, meaningful conversations with your partner, to share your innermost thoughts and feelings, and to create a safe space for vulnerability and trust. Trust your heart and be open to giving and receiving love in all its forms, even if it means facing your fears, wounds, or shadows.

If you're in a committed relationship, take time to explore the power of words, both spoken and unspoken, in your connection. Be willing to listen deeply, communicate openly, and support each other's growth and healing through honest, compassionate dialogue. Remember that true intimacy requires both partners to show up fully and authentically, and to create a safe space for emotional and spiritual growth.

If you're single, you may attract people who share your depth, intensity, and desire for meaningful communication. Look for partners who are willing to engage in deep, authentic conversations, and who appreciate your unique perspective, insights, and wisdom. Trust your intuition and take your time getting to know potential partners before jumping into a serious relationship. Remember that the most important relationship is the one you have with yourself, and that self-love and self-acceptance are essential for attracting healthy, fulfilling partnerships.

Career:

In your career, December 2025 is a month of innovation, progress, and positive change. With Mars, your traditional ruler, entering Capricorn on December 15th, you may feel a strong drive to pursue your professional goals, take on new responsibilities, and assert your leadership skills and expertise. This is a fantastic time to focus on your long-term career vision, to set ambitious yet realistic goals, and to take practical, strategic action towards your dreams and aspirations. Trust your instincts and be willing to put in the hard work and dedication required for success, even if it means facing challenges or obstacles along the way.

On December 11th, Mercury, the planet of communication and commerce, enters Capricorn, bringing a sense of mental clarity, focus, and discipline to your professional endeavors. Use this transit to actively pursue your career goals, communicate your ideas and plans, and make strategic decisions that align with your values and priorities. Remember that success is not just about achieving external milestones, but also about finding a sense of purpose, fulfillment, and inner satisfaction in your work.

Finances:

In finances, December 2025 is a month of abundance, prosperity, and positive change. With the New Moon in Sagittarius on December 19th falling in your 2nd house of values and resources, you may experience a powerful new beginning or fresh start in your journey of financial empowerment, self-worth, and manifestation. This is a fantastic time to set intentions, affirm your abundance, and take inspired action towards your financial goals and dreams. Trust that the universe is conspiring to support your success and fulfillment, and be open to unexpected opportunities or synchronicities that align with your highest good.

On December 21st, Jupiter, the planet of expansion and abundance, forms a square aspect to Chiron in your 6th house of work, health, and service. This challenging alignment may bring up wounds, insecurities, or limitations around your ability to manifest abundance through your daily work and routines, or to find a sense of purpose and fulfillment in your financial life. You may need to confront patterns of self-doubt, scarcity, or over-giving that are holding you back from true prosperity and self-care. Trust your inner wisdom and be open to making necessary adjustments or boundaries that align with your highest values and long-term goals.

Health:

In health, December 2025 is a month of vitality, energy, and inner growth. With the Sun, the planet of life force and vitality, entering your 3rd house of communication and learning on December 21st, you may feel a renewed sense of curiosity, mental clarity, and desire for knowledge and understanding. This is a fantastic time to engage in practices that stimulate your mind, expand your perspective, and keep you mentally sharp and agile, such as reading, writing, or learning a new skill or language. Trust that your mind-body connection is a powerful tool for overall health and well-being.

On December 26th, Uranus, the planet of sudden change and innovation, turns direct in your 7th house of partnerships and one-on-one relationships. This transit may bring unexpected shifts, breakthroughs, or awakenings in your closest connections, particularly around issues of freedom, individuality, and authenticity. You may need to confront patterns of codependency, power struggles, or limiting beliefs that are holding you back from true intimacy and growth. Trust your inner wisdom and be open to making necessary changes or adjustments that allow you to express your true self and create relationships that support your highest good.

Travel:

In travel, December 2025 may bring opportunities for spiritual growth, inner exploration, and connection with nature. With Neptune turning direct in your 5th house of creativity and self-expression on December 10th, you may feel a strong urge to visit beautiful, inspiring places that allow you to tap into your imagination, intuition, and sense of wonder. Consider taking a trip to a serene, natural setting, such as a beach, forest, or mountain retreat, where you can unplug from technology, slow down, and immerse yourself in the healing energy of the earth.

If travel isn't possible or practical, find ways to bring a sense of beauty, inspiration, and spiritual connection into your daily life. Engage in creative activities that allow you to express your unique talents and gifts, spend time in nature or with animals, or seek out experiences that uplift your soul and remind you of the magic and mystery of life. Remember that travel is not just about the destination, but about the journey of self-discovery, healing, and transformation.

Insights from the Stars:

The celestial energies of December 2025 remind you of the power of communication, self-expression, and spiritual growth. With Venus joining Pluto in your 3rd house of communication and learning, you are being called to speak your truth, share your knowledge and wisdom, and engage in meaningful conversations and connections that support your growth and transformation. This is a time to actively pursue your intellectual and creative interests, to express yourself with confidence and authenticity, and to trust in the power of words to heal, inspire, and create positive change.

On December 28th, Mercury, the planet of communication and learning, enters Aquarius, bringing a sense of innovation, originality, and social awareness to your mental pursuits and interactions. You may feel a strong urge to connect with like-minded individuals who share your values, ideals, and vision for the future, or to use your voice and influence to make a positive impact in your community or the world at large. Trust your unique perspective and insights, and know that your ideas and contributions have the power to create meaningful change and progress.

Best Days of the Month:

December 10th: Neptune turns direct in 5th house - Forward momentum, clarity, and inspiration in your creativity, self-expression, and spiritual growth.

December 19th: New Moon in Sagittarius - A powerful new beginning or fresh start in your journey of financial empowerment, self-worth, and manifestation.

December 21st: Sun enters 3rd house - Renewed curiosity, mental clarity, and desire for knowledge and understanding in your communication and learning.

December 26th: Uranus turns direct in 7th house - Unexpected shifts, breakthroughs, or awakenings in your closest relationships that support your growth and authenticity.

December 28th: Mercury enters Aquarius - Innovative, original, and socially aware energy in your mental pursuits and interactions, with opportunities for positive change and progress.

SAGITTARIUS 2025 HOROSCOPE

Overview Sagittarius 2025

(November 22 - December 21)

2025 is a year of expansion, adventure, and personal growth for those born under the sign of Sagittarius. The celestial bodies will align to bring you opportunities to broaden your horizons, explore new frontiers, and discover your true potential. Embrace the journey with an open mind and a curious heart, and trust that the universe has your back.

The year begins with Jupiter, your ruling planet, in the sign of Gemini. This placement suggests a strong focus on learning, communication, and intellectual pursuits in the first part of the year. You may find yourself drawn to new ideas, perspectives, and experiences that challenge your beliefs and expand your mind. This is a time to feed your curiosity, to engage in stimulating conversations, and to seek out knowledge and wisdom wherever you can find it.

In early February, Jupiter will turn direct in your 7th house of partnerships, bringing a renewed sense of optimism and growth to your closest relationships. This is a time to deepen your connections with others, to seek out new collaborations and alliances, and to learn from the people around you. Be open to the insights and perspectives of others, and trust that the right people will come into your life at the right time.

As the year progresses, a significant shift occurs in April when Pluto turns retrograde in your 3rd house of communication and learning. This transit may bring up deep-seated fears or insecurities around your ability to express yourself and be heard. It's a time to confront any limiting beliefs or patterns that may be holding you back from speaking your truth and sharing your ideas with the world. Trust in the power of your voice and your unique perspective, and know that your words have the power to inspire and transform.

The Total Lunar Eclipse in Pisces on September 7 will bring a powerful opportunity for emotional healing and spiritual growth. This eclipse falls in your 4th house of home and family, highlighting the need for a strong foundation and a sense of belonging. It's a time to let go of any past wounds or traumas that may be holding you back, and to embrace a deeper sense of love, compassion, and understanding for yourself and your loved ones. Trust in the power of forgiveness and release, and know that you are worthy of the love and support you seek.

In mid-June, Saturn will briefly shift into Aries, activating your 5th house of creativity, self-expression, and romance. This transit may bring some challenges or obstacles to your creative pursuits or your love life, but it's also an opportunity to build a stronger foundation for long-term success and fulfillment. Focus on developing your skills, your discipline, and your commitment to your passions, and trust that your efforts will pay off in the long run.

The second half of the year brings a focus on career, public image, and personal achievement. Mars, the planet of action and ambition, will spend an extended period in your 10th house of career and public recognition, bringing a powerful drive and determination to succeed. This is a time to take bold action towards your goals, to assert your leadership and authority, and to make your mark on the world. Trust in your abilities and your unique talents, and know that you have what it takes to achieve your dreams.

In late October, Jupiter will turn retrograde in your 8th house of transformation and shared resources, bringing a period of reflection and re-evaluation around your deepest fears, desires, and motivations. This is a time to confront any shadows or hidden aspects of yourself that may be holding you back from true intimacy and connection with others. It's also an opportunity to reassess your financial situation and your relationship with money and resources. Trust in the power of honesty, vulnerability, and self-awareness, and know that the challenges you face are ultimately serving your highest growth and evolution.

As the year comes to a close, the Partial Solar Eclipse in Sagittarius on December 19 will bring a powerful opportunity for new beginnings and fresh starts. This eclipse falls in your 1st house of self and identity, highlighting the need for authentic self-expression and personal autonomy. It's a time to let go of any masks or facades you may have been wearing, and to embrace your true self with courage and confidence. Trust in the journey of self-discovery and know that you have the strength and resilience to handle whatever challenges may come your way.

Throughout the year, the influence of Neptune in your 4th house of home and family will continue to bring a sense of spiritual connection and emotional sensitivity to your personal life. This is a time to cultivate a deeper sense of inner peace and contentment, to create a nurturing and supportive environment for yourself and your loved ones, and to trust in the power of intuition and imagination. Know that your home is your sanctuary, and that you have the ability to create a life of beauty, meaning, and purpose.

Overall, 2025 is a year of growth, adventure, and self-discovery for Sagittarius. With Jupiter bringing opportunities for learning and expansion, and with Mars and the eclipses bringing powerful energy for personal achievement and transformation, this is a time to embrace your unique path and purpose with enthusiasm and optimism. Trust in the journey, stay true to your values and ideals, and know that the universe is guiding you towards your highest potential. With an open heart and a adventurous spirit, you have the power to create a life of boundless joy, freedom, and fulfillment.

January 2025

Overview Horoscope for the Month:

Sagittarius, get ready for an exhilarating start to 2025! January is brimming with opportunities for growth, adventure, and self-discovery. As the month begins, Mars, the planet of action and energy, is retrograde in your 8th house of transformation and shared resources. This cosmic influence may bring up deep-seated fears or blockages around intimacy, vulnerability, and financial matters. However, don't let this discourage you – it's an opportunity to face your shadows head-on and emerge stronger, wiser, and more empowered.

The Full Moon in Cancer on January 13th illuminates your 8th house, bringing emotional intensity and the potential for profound healing and release. Trust your intuition, express your feelings openly, and allow yourself to be vulnerable with those you trust. This is a time to let go of past wounds, toxic patterns, or unhealthy attachments, and to create space for new levels of intimacy and connection.

Love:

Single Sagittarians may find themselves drawn to people who challenge them to grow and evolve, both emotionally and spiritually. Look for partners who appreciate your adventurous spirit and philosophical nature, but who also encourage you to explore your depths and face your fears. If you're already in a committed relationship, use this month's energies to deepen your bond through honest communication, shared adventures, and emotional vulnerability.

Venus, the planet of love and relationships, spends most of January in freedom-loving Aquarius, activating your 3rd house of communication and learning. This is a wonderful time to express your feelings through writing, art, or creative pursuits, and to engage in stimulating conversations with your partner or love interest. Attend a workshop, take a class, or plan a weekend getaway that feeds your mutual curiosity and desire for knowledge.

Career:

With Mars retrograde in your 8th house, you may feel a temporary slowdown or setback in your career or financial matters. Don't let this discourage you – use this time to reassess your goals, values, and motivations, and to make sure that your work aligns with your deepest passions and purpose. If you're feeling stuck or unfulfilled in your current job, start exploring new opportunities or ways to bring more creativity and meaning to your work.

The New Moon in Aquarius on January 29th activates your 3rd house of communication and learning, making it an excellent time to network, pitch ideas, or start a new course of study. Trust your innovative ideas and unique perspective, and don't be afraid to think outside the box or take calculated risks. Your natural optimism and enthusiasm will attract supportive people and opportunities your way.

Finances:

With Mars retrograde in your 8th house of shared resources, you may need to reassess your financial partnerships, investments, or debts. Be cautious about taking on new financial obligations or making impulsive decisions, and take the time to review your budget, savings, and long-term goals. If you're feeling stressed or overwhelmed about money matters, seek the guidance of a trusted financial advisor or mentor.

The Full Moon in Cancer on January 13th may bring a financial matter to a head, requiring you to confront any fears or insecurities around abundance and security. Trust that you have the resilience and resourcefulness to overcome any challenges, and focus on cultivating a mindset of gratitude, faith, and positive expectation. Remember that true wealth comes from within, and that you have the power to create the life and legacy you desire.

Health:

January's energies may bring a heightened awareness of your physical, emotional, and spiritual well-being. With Mars retrograde in your 8th house, you may be more sensitive to stress, anxiety, or hidden fears. Make sure to prioritize self-care, rest, and relaxation, and to create a daily routine that supports your overall health and vitality.

The Full Moon in Cancer on January 13th may bring up intense emotions or buried traumas that need to be acknowledged and released. Consider working with a therapist, healer, or spiritual guide to help you process any deep-seated issues or patterns that are holding you back. Trust in the power of vulnerability, forgiveness, and self-love to facilitate profound healing and transformation.

Travel:

With Venus in Aquarius activating your 3rd house of short trips and local adventures, January is a great month for exploring your own backyard or taking a spontaneous weekend getaway. Look for destinations that feed your curiosity, creativity, and desire for novelty, such as a quirky museum, art gallery, or cultural event.

If you're planning a longer trip or international adventure, be sure to do your research and take any necessary precautions, as Mars retrograde in your 8th house may bring unexpected delays, changes, or challenges. Stay flexible, open-minded, and trust that any detours or obstacles are ultimately leading you towards a greater purpose or life lesson.

Insights from the Stars:

Sagittarius, January 2025 is a month of deep soul-searching, emotional healing, and personal transformation. The cosmic energies are inviting you to confront your fears, embrace your shadows, and let go of anything that is no longer serving your highest good. Trust that the challenges you face are ultimately leading you towards a greater sense of freedom, authenticity, and purpose.

Remember that true growth and evolution often require discomfort, vulnerability, and the willingness to step outside your comfort zone. Embrace the journey with an open heart and a curious mind, and trust that the universe is conspiring in your favor, even when things feel uncertain or overwhelming.

Best Days of the Month:

January 2nd: Venus enters Pisces, bringing a dreamy, romantic energy to your 4th house of home and family. Spend quality time with loved ones and create a cozy, nurturing space for yourself.

January 6th: Mars retrograde re-enters Cancer, activating your 8th house of transformation and shared resources. Use this time to confront any fears or blockages around intimacy, vulnerability, and financial matters.

January 13th: Full Moon in Cancer illuminates your 8th house, bringing emotional intensity and the potential for profound healing and release. Trust your intuition and allow yourself to be vulnerable with those you trust.

January 18th: Mercury enters Aquarius, activating your 3rd house of communication and learning. Express your ideas and opinions with confidence, and seek out stimulating conversations and intellectual pursuits.

January 29th: New Moon in Aquarius activates your 3rd house, making it an excellent time to network, pitch ideas, or start a new course of study. Trust your innovative ideas and take calculated risks towards your goals.

February 2025

Overview Horoscope for the Month:

Sagittarius, February 2025 is a month of exciting opportunities, personal growth, and spiritual exploration. As the month begins, Venus, the planet of love and beauty, enters your 5th house of romance, creativity, and self-expression. This cosmic influence is set to bring joy, passion, and inspiration to your life, encouraging you to embrace your unique talents and follow your heart's desires.

The Full Moon in Leo on February 12th illuminates your 9th house of adventure, higher learning, and personal philosophy. This powerful lunar event may bring a culmination or turning point in your studies, travels, or spiritual pursuits. Trust your intuition, expand your horizons, and be open to new experiences and perspectives that challenge and inspire you.

Love:

With Venus gracing your 5th house of romance and pleasure, February is a fantastic month for love and relationships. If you're single, you may find yourself attracted to creative, passionate, and expressive individuals who share your zest for life. Be bold, flirtatious, and authentic in your interactions, and trust that your natural charisma and enthusiasm will attract the right people and opportunities your way.

If you're already in a committed relationship, use this month's energies to inject more fun, spontaneity, and romance into your connection. Plan a special date night, surprise your partner with a heartfelt gesture, or explore a new hobby or creative project together. The key is to prioritize joy, playfulness, and mutual appreciation, and to let your love light shine bright.

Career:

February's celestial influences are set to bring exciting opportunities and breakthroughs in your career and professional life. With Mars, the planet of action and ambition, entering your 10th house of career and public reputation on February 23rd, you may find yourself in the spotlight or taking on new leadership roles and responsibilities.

Trust your instincts, showcase your unique talents and skills, and don't be afraid to take calculated risks or pursue unconventional paths. Your natural optimism, enthusiasm, and visionary thinking will be your greatest assets, attracting supportive people and opportunities your way. Stay focused on your long-term goals, but also be open to unexpected detours or synchronicities that may lead you in a new and exciting direction.

Finances:

With Venus in your 5th house of creativity and self-expression, February is an excellent month to explore new ways to increase your income through your passions and talents. Consider starting a side hustle, freelancing, or monetizing a hobby or creative project that brings you joy and fulfillment.

At the same time, be mindful of impulsive spending or financial risk-taking, especially around the Full Moon in Leo on February 12th. Stay grounded in your values and long-term goals, and seek the guidance of a trusted financial advisor or mentor if needed. Remember that true abundance comes from within, and that your worth is not defined by your material possessions or bank balance.

Health:

February's energies are set to bring a renewed focus on your physical, mental, and emotional well-being. With the Sun and Mercury moving through your 4th house of home and family, you may find yourself craving more rest, relaxation, and nurturing self-care. Make sure to prioritize downtime, spend quality time with loved ones, and create a peaceful, supportive environment that allows you to recharge and rejuvenate.

At the same time, the Full Moon in Leo on February 12th may bring a burst of energy, vitality, and inspiration. Use this lunar influence to recommit to your fitness goals, try a new wellness practice, or explore a mind-body-spirit modality that aligns with your personal philosophy and beliefs. Trust that by taking care of yourself on all levels, you'll be better equipped to show up fully in all areas of your life.

Travel:

With the Full Moon in Leo illuminating your 9th house of travel and adventure, February is an excellent month for exploring new horizons and expanding your worldview. If possible, plan a trip or getaway that allows you to immerse yourself in a different culture, learn something new, or challenge your comfort zone.

If travel isn't feasible, consider exploring your own backyard or local community with fresh eyes and an open mind. Attend a cultural event, try a new cuisine, or strike up a conversation with someone from a different background or perspective. The key is to embrace curiosity, diversity, and the joy of discovery, and to let your adventurous spirit soar.

Insights from the Stars:

Sagittarius, February 2025 is a month of personal empowerment, creative expression, and spiritual growth. The cosmic energies are inviting you to embrace your unique gifts, follow your passions, and trust in the unfolding of your life's journey. Remember that you are the co-creator of your reality, and that your thoughts, beliefs, and actions have the power to shape your world.

Stay open to the magic and synchronicity of the universe, and trust that everything is happening for your highest good and evolution. Embrace the journey with a sense of wonder, gratitude, and faith, and know that you are exactly where you need to be, learning and growing in perfect divine timing.

Best Days of the Month:

February 4th: Venus enters Aries, igniting your 5th house of romance, creativity, and self-expression. Embrace your passions, take bold risks, and let your unique light shine.

February 12th: Full Moon in Leo illuminates your 9th house of adventure, higher learning, and personal philosophy. Expand your horizons, seek new experiences, and trust your intuition.

February 16th: Mercury enters Pisces, activating your 4th house of home and family. Spend quality time with loved ones, create a nurturing space, and prioritize rest and relaxation.

February 18th: Sun enters Pisces, bringing a focus on your emotional and spiritual well-being. Practice self-care, connect with your inner wisdom, and trust the flow of life.

February 23rd: Mars enters Leo, energizing your 10th house of career and public reputation. Take bold action towards your goals, showcase your talents, and embrace your leadership potential..

March 2025

Overview Horoscope for the Month:

Sagittarius, March 2025 is a month of profound transformation, spiritual awakening, and new beginnings. As the month begins, Saturn, the planet of structure, responsibility, and life lessons, enters your 5th house of romance, creativity, and self-expression. This significant cosmic shift may bring a more serious, committed energy to your love life and creative pursuits, asking you to take a mature, realistic approach to your passions and desires.

The New Moon in Aries on March 29th falls in your 5th house, signaling a powerful opportunity to set intentions and plant seeds for new creative projects, romantic adventures, or personal growth. Trust your instincts, take bold action, and believe in your ability to manifest your dreams into reality.

Love:

With Saturn now in your 5th house of romance and pleasure, March is a month of deepening commitment, emotional maturity, and long-term vision in your love life. If you're single, you may find yourself attracted to people who are stable, responsible, and share your values and goals. Take your time getting to know potential partners, and don't be afraid to set clear boundaries and expectations in your interactions.

If you're already in a committed relationship, use this month's energies to strengthen your bond through open communication, shared responsibilities, and a focus on building a solid foundation for the future. You may need to have some serious conversations about your goals, dreams, and long-term compatibility, but trust that this process will ultimately bring you closer together and deepen your love and respect for one another.

Career:

March's celestial influences are set to bring significant changes and opportunities in your career and professional life. With Pluto, the planet of power, transformation, and rebirth, entering your 2nd house of money and resources on March 23rd, you may find yourself reevaluating your financial goals, values, and priorities.

This is a time to let go of any limiting beliefs or patterns around money and success, and to embrace a more empowered, abundant mindset. Trust your skills, talents, and unique perspective, and don't be afraid to take calculated risks or pursue unconventional paths. Remember that true wealth comes from living in alignment with your authentic self and purpose, and that you have the power to create the life and career you desire.

Finances:

With Pluto now in your 2nd house of money and resources, March is an excellent month to take a deep dive into your financial situation and make any necessary changes or adjustments. This is a time to get clear on your values and priorities, and to create a budget and financial plan that supports your long-term goals and dreams.

You may also find yourself attracted to new sources of income or investment opportunities that align with your passions and purpose. Trust your instincts, do your research, and seek the guidance of a trusted financial advisor or mentor if needed. Remember that true abundance comes from a mindset of gratitude, generosity, and faith, and that your worth is not defined by your material possessions or bank balance.

Health:

March's energies are set to bring a renewed focus on your physical, mental, and emotional well-being. With the Full Moon in Virgo on March 14th illuminating your 10th house of career and public reputation, you may find yourself feeling the effects of stress, overwork, or burnout. Make sure to prioritize self-care, rest, and relaxation, and to set clear boundaries around your time and energy.

At the same time, the New Moon in Aries on March 29th brings a powerful opportunity to recommit to your health and fitness goals. Use this lunar influence to start a new wellness practice, try a new form of exercise, or make positive changes to your diet and lifestyle. Trust that by taking care of yourself on all levels, you'll be better equipped to show up fully in all areas of your life.

Travel:

With Saturn now in your 5th house of adventure and exploration, March is an excellent month for planning a meaningful, purposeful trip or journey. Consider destinations that allow you to learn something new, challenge your comfort zone, or deepen your spiritual practice.

If travel isn't feasible, consider exploring your own backyard or local community with a fresh perspective and an open mind. Attend a workshop or retreat, volunteer for a cause you believe in, or connect with people from different cultures and backgrounds. The key is to embrace growth, learning, and the joy of discovery, and to let your adventurous spirit guide you towards new horizons.

Insights from the Stars:

Sagittarius, March 2025 is a month of profound transformation, personal growth, and spiritual awakening. The cosmic energies are inviting you to take a deep, honest look at your life, your relationships, and your path forward. Trust that the challenges and changes you face are ultimately leading you towards a more authentic, fulfilling, and purposeful existence.

Stay open to the wisdom and guidance of the universe, and trust that everything is happening for your highest good and evolution. Embrace the journey with a sense of curiosity, courage, and faith, and know that you have the strength, resilience, and inner resources to navigate any obstacles or setbacks that may arise.

Best Days of the Month:

March 7th: Saturn enters Pisces, bringing a serious, committed energy to your 4th house of home and family. Focus on creating a stable, secure foundation for yourself and your loved ones.

March 14th: Full Moon in Virgo illuminates your 10th house of career and public reputation. Celebrate your accomplishments, release any stress or burnout, and recommit to your professional goals and aspirations.

March 20th: Sun enters Aries, igniting your 5th house of romance, creativity, and self-expression. Embrace your passions, take bold risks, and let your unique light shine.

March 23rd: Pluto enters Aquarius, initiating a powerful transformation in your 2nd house of money and resources. Let go of limiting beliefs around abundance and success, and embrace a more empowered, abundant mindset.

March 29th: New Moon in Aries falls in your 5th house of romance, creativity, and self-expression. Set intentions and plant seeds for new creative projects, romantic adventures, or personal growth. Trust your instincts and take bold action towards your dreams.

April 2025

Overview Horoscope for the Month:

Sagittarius, April 2025 is a month of exciting opportunities, personal growth, and spiritual exploration. As the month begins, Jupiter, your ruling planet, forms a square aspect to Pluto, signaling a time of deep transformation and soul-searching. This cosmic influence may bring up hidden fears, desires, or patterns that need to be acknowledged and released, paving the way for a more authentic, empowered version of yourself to emerge.

The New Moon in Aries on April 27th falls in your 5th house of romance, creativity, and self-expression, bringing a powerful opportunity to set intentions and plant seeds for new creative projects, romantic adventures, or personal growth. Trust your instincts, take bold action, and believe in your ability to manifest your dreams into reality.

Love:

With Venus, the planet of love and relationships, moving through your 5th house of romance and pleasure for most of April, this is a month of passion, creativity, and self-expression in your love life. If you're single, you may find yourself attracted to people who share your sense of adventure, humor, and zest for life. Be bold, flirtatious, and authentic in your interactions, and trust that your natural charisma and enthusiasm will attract the right people and opportunities your way.

If you're already in a committed relationship, use this month's energies to inject more fun, spontaneity, and romance into your connection. Plan a surprise date, express your love and appreciation in creative ways, or explore a new hobby or activity together. The key is to prioritize joy, playfulness, and mutual growth, and to let your love light shine bright.

Career:

April's celestial influences are set to bring exciting opportunities and breakthroughs in your career and professional life. With Mars, the planet of action and ambition, moving through your 10th house of career and public reputation, you may find yourself taking on new leadership roles, pursuing ambitious goals, or receiving recognition for your hard work and talents.

At the same time, the square aspect between Jupiter and Pluto on April 17th may bring up power struggles, conflicts, or challenges in your work environment. Stay true to your values and integrity, and don't be afraid to speak up for yourself or advocate for what you believe in. Trust that any obstacles or setbacks are ultimately leading you towards a more aligned, authentic path forward.

Finances:

With the North Node moving into your 8th house of shared resources and investments on April 11th, April is an excellent month to reevaluate your financial partnerships, debts, and long-term financial goals. This is a time to get clear on your values and priorities, and to make any necessary changes or adjustments to your budget, savings, or investment strategy.

You may also find yourself attracted to new sources of income or financial opportunities that align with your passions and purpose. Trust your instincts, do your research, and seek the guidance of a trusted financial advisor or mentor if needed. Remember that true abundance comes from a mindset of gratitude, generosity, and faith, and that your worth is not defined by your material possessions or bank balance.

Health:

April's energies are set to bring a renewed focus on your physical, mental, and emotional well-being. With the Sun moving through your 6th house of health and wellness for most of the month, this is an excellent time to prioritize self-care, establish healthy routines, and make positive changes to your diet, exercise, and lifestyle habits.

The Full Moon in Libra on April 12th illuminates your 11th house of friendships and social connections, reminding you of the importance of community, support, and connection in your overall well-being. Reach out to loved ones, participate in group activities or causes that inspire you, and surround yourself with people who uplift and encourage you to be your best self.

Travel:

With Saturn now in your 5th house of adventure and exploration, April is an excellent month for planning a meaningful, purposeful trip or journey. Consider destinations that allow you to learn something new, challenge your comfort zone, or deepen your spiritual practice.

If travel isn't feasible, consider exploring your own backyard or local community with a fresh perspective and an open mind. Attend a workshop or retreat, volunteer for a cause you believe in, or connect with people from different cultures and backgrounds. The key is to embrace growth, learning, and the joy of discovery, and to let your adventurous spirit guide you towards new horizons.

Insights from the Stars:

Sagittarius, April 2025 is a month of personal growth, spiritual exploration, and alignment with your true path and purpose. The cosmic energies are inviting you to let go of any limiting beliefs, fears, or patterns that may be holding you back from living your best life. Trust that the challenges and changes you face are ultimately leading you towards a more authentic, fulfilling, and joyful existence.

Stay open to the wisdom and guidance of the universe, and trust that everything is happening for your highest good and evolution. Embrace the journey with a sense of curiosity, courage, and faith, and know that you have the strength, resilience, and inner resources to navigate any obstacles or setbacks that may arise.

Best Days of the Month:

April 4th: Saturn sextile Uranus brings a harmonious blend of stability and innovation to your life. Embrace change, take calculated risks, and trust in the power of your unique vision and perspective.

April 11th: Venus enters Aries, igniting your 5th house of romance, creativity, and self-expression. Embrace your passions, take bold risks, and let your unique light shine.

April 16th: Mercury enters Aries, enhancing your communication skills and mental agility. Express your ideas and opinions with confidence, and trust in the power of your voice and message.

April 20th: Sun enters Taurus, bringing a grounded, practical energy to your 6th house of health and wellness. Focus on establishing healthy routines, nourishing your body and mind, and finding balance and stability in your daily life.

April 27th: New Moon in Taurus falls in your 6th house of health and wellness. Set intentions and plant seeds for new healthy habits, self-care practices, or positive changes to your diet and lifestyle. Trust that small, consistent steps can lead to big, transformative results over time.

May 2025

Overview Horoscope for the Month:

Sagittarius, May 2025 is a month of powerful transformation, spiritual growth, and new beginnings. As the month begins, the North Node shifts into your 7th house of partnerships and relationships, signaling a time of significant growth and evolution in your connections with others. This cosmic influence may bring new people, opportunities, or challenges into your life that help you learn important lessons about love, collaboration, and compromise.

The New Moon in Taurus on May 26th falls in your 6th house of health, work, and daily routines, bringing a powerful opportunity to set intentions and make positive changes in these areas of your life. Trust your instincts, take practical steps towards your goals, and believe in your ability to create a more balanced, fulfilling, and productive existence.

Love:

With Venus, the planet of love and relationships, moving through your 7th house of partnerships for most of May, this is a month of deep connection, mutual growth, and shared purpose in your love life. If you're single, you may find yourself attracted to people who challenge you to grow, learn, and see things from a different perspective. Be open, honest, and authentic in your interactions, and trust that the right person will appreciate and value the real you.

If you're already in a committed relationship, use this month's energies to deepen your bond, communicate openly and honestly, and work together towards common goals and dreams. You may need to negotiate compromises, set clear boundaries, or address any imbalances or power struggles that arise. Remember that a healthy, loving relationship is built on a foundation of trust, respect, and mutual support.

Career:

May's celestial influences are set to bring exciting opportunities and breakthroughs in your career and professional life. With Mars, the planet of action and ambition, moving through your 10th house of career and public reputation until May 18th, you may find yourself taking on new challenges, pursuing ambitious goals, or receiving recognition for your hard work and talents.

At the same time, the North Node's shift into your 7th house of partnerships on May 11th may bring new collaborations, alliances, or mentors into your professional life. Be open to learning from others, sharing your skills and knowledge, and working together towards a common vision or purpose. Trust that the right people and opportunities will come into your life at the perfect time.

Finances:

With Jupiter, your ruling planet, forming a sextile aspect to Chiron in your 5th house of creativity and self-expression on May 18th, May is an excellent month to explore new ways to generate income or abundance through your unique talents and passions. This is a time to believe in yourself, take calculated risks, and trust in the power of your creative vision and entrepreneurial spirit.

At the same time, be mindful of any financial decisions or investments that seem too good to be true, especially around the time of the Full Moon in Scorpio on May 12th. Stay grounded in your values and long-term goals, and seek the guidance of a trusted financial advisor or mentor if needed. Remember that true wealth comes from living in alignment with your authentic self and purpose.

Health:

May's energies are set to bring a renewed focus on your physical, mental, and emotional well-being. With the Sun moving through your 6th house of health and wellness for most of the month, this is an excellent time to prioritize self-care, establish healthy routines, and make positive changes to your diet, exercise, and lifestyle habits.

The New Moon in Taurus on May 26th brings a powerful opportunity to set intentions and make a fresh start in these areas of your life. Consider trying a new workout routine, exploring holistic healing modalities, or making small, sustainable changes to your daily habits and routines. Remember that true health and vitality come from a balance of mind, body, and spirit.

Travel:

With Saturn now in your 5th house of adventure and exploration, May is an excellent month for planning a meaningful, purposeful trip or journey. Consider destinations that allow you to learn something new, challenge your comfort zone, or deepen your spiritual practice.

If travel isn't feasible, consider exploring your own backyard or local community with a fresh perspective and an open mind. Attend a workshop or retreat, volunteer for a cause you believe in, or connect with people from different cultures and backgrounds. The key is to embrace growth, learning, and the joy of discovery, and to let your adventurous spirit guide you towards new horizons.

Insights from the Stars:

Sagittarius, May 2025 is a month of powerful transformation, spiritual growth, and alignment with your true path and purpose. The cosmic energies are inviting you to let go of any limiting beliefs, fears, or patterns that may be holding you back from living your best life. Trust that the challenges and changes you face are ultimately leading you towards a more authentic, fulfilling, and joyful existence.

Stay open to the wisdom and guidance of the universe, and trust that everything is happening for your highest good and evolution. Embrace the journey with a sense of curiosity, courage, and faith, and know that you have the strength, resilience, and inner resources to navigate any obstacles or setbacks that may arise.

Best Days of the Month:

May 11th: The North Node shifts into your 7th house of partnerships and relationships, signaling a time of significant growth and evolution in your connections with others. Be open to new people, opportunities, or challenges that help you learn important lessons about love, collaboration, and compromise.

May 18th: Jupiter sextile Chiron in your 5th house of creativity and self-expression brings opportunities for healing, growth, and abundance through your unique talents and passions. Believe in yourself, take calculated risks, and trust in the power of your creative vision and entrepreneurial spirit.

May 20th: Sun enters Gemini, bringing a curious, adaptable energy to your 7th house of partnerships and relationships. Engage in open, honest communication with others, seek out new perspectives and ideas, and be willing to learn and grow together.

May 24th: Saturn enters Aries, bringing a serious, committed energy to your 5th house of creativity, self-expression, and romance. Take responsibility for your desires and passions, set clear goals and boundaries, and trust in the power of discipline and perseverance to manifest your dreams.

May 26th: New Moon in Taurus falls in your 6th house of health, work, and daily routines. Set intentions and make positive changes in these areas of your life, focusing on practical steps, sustainable habits, and a holistic approach to well-being. Trust that small, consistent efforts can lead to big, transformative results over time.

June 2025

Overview Horoscope for the Month:

Sagittarius, June 2025 is a month of exciting adventures, personal growth, and spiritual exploration. As the month begins, Jupiter, your ruling planet, enters your 7th house of partnerships and relationships, bringing new opportunities for connection, collaboration, and shared purpose. This cosmic influence may bring significant people or experiences into your life that expand your horizons, challenge your beliefs, and help you grow in ways you never thought possible.

The Full Moon in Sagittarius on June 11th falls in your 1st house of self and identity, bringing a powerful opportunity to celebrate your unique talents, passions, and purpose. This is a time to let your light shine bright, express your authentic self, and trust in the power of your vision and wisdom to guide you towards your highest path and potential.

Love:

With Venus, the planet of love and relationships, moving through your 8th house of intimacy and transformation for most of June, this is a month of deep emotional connection, vulnerability, and spiritual growth in your love life. If you're single, you may find yourself attracted to people who challenge you to confront your fears, heal your wounds, and embrace your shadows. Be open, honest, and authentic in your interactions, and trust that the right person will appreciate and value the depth and complexity of your soul.

If you're already in a committed relationship, use this month's energies to deepen your bond, communicate openly and honestly about your desires and fears, and support each other through any challenges or changes that arise. You may need to let go of old patterns, beliefs, or dynamics that no longer serve your highest good, and trust in the transformative power of love to help you grow and evolve together.

Career:

June's celestial influences are set to bring exciting opportunities and breakthroughs in your career and professional life. With Mars, the planet of action and ambition, moving into your 10th house of career and public reputation on June 17th, you may find yourself taking on new responsibilities, pursuing ambitious goals, or receiving recognition for your hard work and talents.

At the same time, the North Node's presence in your 7th house of partnerships may bring new collaborations, alliances, or mentors into your professional life. Be open to learning from others, sharing your skills and knowledge, and working together towards a common vision or purpose. Trust that the right people and opportunities will come into your life at the perfect time to help you achieve your dreams and goals.

Finances:

With Neptune, the planet of dreams and intuition, forming a conjunction with the North Node in your 7th house of partnerships on June 7th, June is an excellent month to explore new ways to generate income or abundance through collaboration, creativity, and spiritual alignment. This is a time to trust your intuition, follow your heart, and believe in the power of your unique vision and purpose to attract the resources and support you need.

At the same time, be mindful of any financial decisions or investments that seem too good to be true, especially around the time of the New Moon in Gemini on June 25th. Stay grounded in your values and long-term goals, and seek the guidance of a trusted financial advisor or mentor if needed. Remember that true wealth comes from living in alignment with your authentic self and purpose, and that abundance flows when you trust in the universe to provide for your needs.

Health:

June's energies are set to bring a renewed focus on your physical, mental, and emotional well-being. With the Sun moving through your 7th house of relationships for most of the month, this is an excellent time to prioritize self-care, establish healthy boundaries, and cultivate supportive, nurturing connections with others.

The Full Moon in Sagittarius on June 11th brings a powerful opportunity to release any stress, tension, or negative habits that may be holding you back from optimal health and vitality. Consider trying a new wellness practice, such as yoga, meditation, or energy healing, or making small, sustainable changes to your diet and lifestyle. Remember that true health and happiness come from a balance of mind, body, and spirit, and that self-love is the foundation of all healing and growth.

Travel:

With Jupiter, your ruling planet, now in your 7th house of partnerships and relationships, June is an excellent month for planning a meaningful, shared adventure or journey with someone you love and trust. Consider destinations that allow you to explore new cultures, expand your mind, or deepen your spiritual practice together.

If travel isn't feasible, consider exploring your own backyard or local community with a fresh perspective and an open heart. Attend a workshop or retreat, volunteer for a cause you believe in, or connect with people from different backgrounds and walks of life. The key is to embrace growth, learning, and the joy of discovery, and to let your adventurous spirit guide you towards new horizons and possibilities.

Insights from the Stars:

Sagittarius, June 2025 is a month of powerful transformation, spiritual growth, and alignment with your true path and purpose. The cosmic energies are inviting you to let go of any limiting beliefs, fears, or patterns that may be holding you back from living your best life. Trust that the challenges and changes you face are ultimately leading you towards a more authentic, fulfilling, and joyful existence.

Stay open to the wisdom and guidance of the universe, and trust that everything is happening for your highest good and evolution. Embrace the journey with a sense of curiosity, courage, and faith, and know that you have the strength, resilience, and inner resources to navigate any obstacles or setbacks that may arise.

Best Days of the Month:

June 4th: Pluto turns retrograde in your 3rd house of communication and learning, inviting you to reflect on your thoughts, beliefs, and perceptions. Be open to new ideas and perspectives, and trust in the power of your mind to create your reality.

June 9th: Jupiter enters Cancer, bringing a nurturing, supportive energy to your 8th house of intimacy, transformation, and shared resources. Trust in the power of love, vulnerability, and emotional honesty to help you grow and evolve in your closest relationships.

June 11th: Full Moon in Sagittarius falls in your 1st house of self and identity, bringing a powerful opportunity to celebrate your unique talents, passions, and purpose. Let your light shine bright, express your authentic self, and trust in the power of your vision and wisdom to guide you towards your highest path and potential.

June 18th: Jupiter sextile Chiron in your 5th house of creativity, self-expression, and romance, bringing opportunities for healing, growth, and abundance through your unique talents and passions. Believe in yourself, take calculated risks, and trust in the power of your creative vision and entrepreneurial spirit.

June 25th: New Moon in Cancer falls in your 8th house of intimacy, transformation, and shared resources. Set intentions and make positive changes in these areas of your life, focusing on emotional healing, vulnerability, and the power of love to transform and uplift. Trust that the universe is supporting you in letting go of what no longer serves you and embracing a more authentic, abundant life.

July 2025

Overview Horoscope for the Month:

Sagittarius, July 2025 is a month of personal growth, emotional healing, and spiritual awakening. As the month begins, Mars, the planet of action and ambition, enters your 9th house of adventure, higher learning, and personal philosophy. This cosmic influence may ignite a deep desire to explore new horizons, expand your mind, and discover your true purpose and path in life. Trust your intuition, follow your passions, and be open to unexpected opportunities and synchronicities that guide you towards your highest potential.

The Full Moon in Capricorn on July 10th falls in your 2nd house of values, finances, and self-worth, bringing a powerful opportunity to release any limiting beliefs or patterns around money and abundance. This is a time to align your resources and actions with your true values and priorities, and to trust in the universe to provide for your needs and desires. Believe in your own worth and value, and know that you are deserving of all the good things life has to offer.

Love:

With Venus, the planet of love and relationships, moving through your 9th house of adventure and expansion for most of July, this is a month of exciting romantic possibilities and spiritual growth in your love life. If you're single, you may find yourself attracted to people who share your love of learning, travel, and personal growth. Be open to meeting someone special while pursuing your passions or exploring new experiences, and trust that the right person will appreciate and support your adventurous spirit.

If you're already in a committed relationship, use this month's energies to deepen your connection through shared adventures, meaningful conversations, and spiritual practices. Plan a trip or retreat together, explore new ideas and philosophies, or simply make time to connect on a soul level. Remember that true love is a journey of growth, discovery, and mutual support, and that the challenges you face together can ultimately bring you closer and make your bond stronger.

Career:

July's celestial influences are set to bring exciting opportunities and breakthroughs in your career and professional life. With the Sun moving through your 8th house of transformation, power, and shared resources for most of the month, you may find yourself navigating complex dynamics or power struggles in your work environment. Trust your instincts, stand up for your values and beliefs, and be willing to let go of any situations or relationships that no longer serve your highest good.

At the same time, the New Moon in Leo on July 24th brings a powerful opportunity to set intentions and make a fresh start in your career and public image. Consider ways to showcase your unique talents and abilities, take on new leadership roles, or pursue a path that aligns with your true passions and purpose. Trust that your hard work and dedication will pay off, and that the universe is supporting you in manifesting your dreams and goals.

Finances:

With the Full Moon in Capricorn on July 10th falling in your 2nd house of values, finances, and self-worth, July is an excellent month to release any limiting beliefs or patterns around money and abundance. This is a time to get clear on your true values and priorities, and to align your resources and actions with what truly matters to you.

Consider creating a budget or financial plan that reflects your long-term goals and dreams, and be open to new sources of income or opportunities that align with your passions and purpose. Trust that the universe is always providing for your needs, and that abundance flows when you live in alignment with your authentic self and values.

Health:

July's energies are set to bring a renewed focus on your physical, mental, and emotional well-being. With Chiron, the wounded healer, moving through your 5th house of self-expression and creativity, this is an excellent time to explore holistic healing modalities that help you release past traumas, reconnect with your inner child, and express your true self.

Consider trying a new form of creative expression, such as art therapy, dance, or music, or engaging in activities that bring you joy and help you relax and recharge. Remember that true health and happiness come from a balance of mind, body, and spirit, and that self-love and self-care are essential for your overall well-being.

Travel:

With Mars now in your 9th house of adventure and exploration, July is an excellent month for planning a meaningful, transformative journey or experience. Consider destinations that allow you to immerse yourself in new cultures, learn something new, or challenge your comfort zone in a way that helps you grow and evolve.

If travel isn't feasible, consider exploring your own backyard or local community with a fresh perspective and an open mind. Attend a workshop or retreat, take a class or course that interests you, or connect with people from different backgrounds and walks of life. The key is to embrace growth, learning, and the joy of discovery, and to let your adventurous spirit guide you towards new horizons and possibilities.

Insights from the Stars:

Sagittarius, July 2025 is a month of powerful transformation, spiritual growth, and alignment with your true path and purpose. The cosmic energies are inviting you to let go of any limiting beliefs, fears, or patterns that may be holding you back from living your best life. Trust that the challenges and changes you face are ultimately leading you towards a more authentic, fulfilling, and joyful existence.

Stay open to the wisdom and guidance of the universe, and trust that everything is happening for your highest good and evolution. Embrace the journey with a sense of curiosity, courage, and faith, and know that you have the strength, resilience, and inner resources to navigate any obstacles or setbacks that may arise.

Best Days of the Month:

July 1st: Mars enters Leo, bringing a bold, confident energy to your 9th house of adventure, higher learning, and personal philosophy. Trust your instincts, follow your passions, and be open to unexpected opportunities and synchronicities that guide you towards your highest potential.

July 10th: Full Moon in Capricorn falls in your 2nd house of values, finances, and self-worth, bringing a powerful opportunity to release any limiting beliefs or patterns around money and abundance. Align your resources and actions with your true values and priorities, and trust in the universe to provide for your needs and desires.

July 18th: Jupiter sextile Chiron in your 5th house of creativity, self-expression, and romance, bringing opportunities for healing, growth, and abundance through your unique talents and passions. Believe in yourself, take calculated risks, and trust in the power of your creative vision and entrepreneurial spirit.

July 22nd: Sun enters Leo, bringing a confident, expressive energy to your 9th house of adventure, higher learning, and personal philosophy. Let your light shine bright, express your authentic self, and trust in the power of your vision and wisdom to guide you towards your highest path and potential.

July 24th: New Moon in Leo falls in your 9th house of adventure, higher learning, and personal philosophy. Set intentions and make positive changes in these areas of your life, focusing on personal growth, spiritual exploration, and the pursuit of your passions and dreams. Trust that the universe is supporting you in expanding your horizons and discovering your true purpose and path..

August 2025

Overview Horoscope for the Month:

Sagittarius, August 2025 is a month of deep introspection, emotional healing, and spiritual growth. As the month begins, Venus, the planet of love and relationships, enters your 10th house of career and public image, bringing opportunities for recognition, advancement, and harmonious connections in your professional life. At the same time, Mercury, the planet of communication and learning, goes retrograde in your 9th house of higher education, travel, and philosophy, inviting you to reflect on your beliefs, aspirations, and life direction.

The Full Moon in Aquarius on August 9th illuminates your 3rd house of communication, learning, and short trips, highlighting the need for open-mindedness, adaptability, and mental stimulation. Embrace your curiosity, seek out new ideas and perspectives, and trust in the power of your mind to expand your understanding of yourself and the world around you.

Love:

With Venus gracing your 10th house of career and public image for most of August, you may find your love life intertwined with your professional pursuits. If you're single, you may meet someone special through work or networking events, or find yourself attracted to someone who shares your ambitions and goals. Be open to unexpected connections and opportunities, but also be discerning about mixing business with pleasure.

If you're in a committed relationship, this month's energies can bring a renewed sense of purpose and partnership to your love life. Support each other's career aspirations, celebrate each other's successes, and find ways to balance your personal and professional responsibilities. Remember that true love is about growing and evolving together, and that the challenges you face can ultimately strengthen your bond and deepen your connection.

Career:

August's celestial influences are set to bring exciting opportunities and breakthroughs in your career and public life. With Venus in your 10th house and Jupiter, your ruling planet, in your 8th house of shared resources and power dynamics, you may find yourself negotiating important contracts, collaborations, or financial arrangements that can have a significant impact on your long-term success and security.

Trust your instincts, stand up for your values and beliefs, and be willing to take calculated risks to advance your goals and dreams. At the same time, be mindful of any power struggles or conflicts that may arise, and strive to maintain your integrity and professionalism in all your interactions. Remember that true success comes from alignment with your authentic self and purpose, and that the universe is supporting you in manifesting your highest potential.

Finances:

With the Sun moving through your 9th house of higher education, travel, and personal growth for most of August, this is an excellent time to invest in your own learning and development. Consider taking a course, attending a workshop or seminar, or pursuing a certification or degree that can enhance your skills and knowledge in your field.

At the same time, be mindful of any financial decisions or investments that may be influenced by Mercury's retrograde in your 9th house. Do your research, read the fine print, and seek the guidance of trusted advisors before committing to any long-term plans or agreements. Trust that the universe will provide for your needs and desires when you align your actions with your values and purpose.

Health:

August's energies are set to bring a renewed focus on your physical, mental, and emotional well-being. With Chiron, the wounded healer, moving through your 5th house of self-expression, creativity, and joy, this is an excellent time to explore holistic healing modalities that help you reconnect with your inner child, release past traumas, and express your authentic self.

Consider trying a new form of creative expression, such as art therapy, dance, or music, or engaging in activities that bring you pleasure and help you relax and recharge. At the same time, be mindful of any tendencies towards overindulgence or escapism, and strive to maintain a healthy balance of work and play, discipline and spontaneity. Remember that true health and happiness come from a wholistic approach to self-care and self-love.

Travel:

With Mercury retrograde in your 9th house of travel, higher education, and personal growth for most of August, this may not be the best time for long-distance trips or international adventures. If you do need to travel, be prepared for delays, cancellations, or unexpected changes in plans, and have a flexible mindset and backup options.

Instead, consider exploring your own backyard or local community with fresh eyes and an open mind. Take a day trip to a nearby town or attraction, attend a cultural event or festival, or simply spend time in nature, reconnecting with the beauty and wonder of the world around you. Remember that true adventure and growth can happen anywhere, anytime, when you approach life with curiosity, enthusiasm, and a willingness to learn and explore.

Insights from the Stars:

Sagittarius, August 2025 is a month of deep introspection, emotional healing, and spiritual growth. The cosmic energies are inviting you to reflect on your beliefs, aspirations, and life direction, and to make any necessary adjustments or course corrections to align with your authentic self and purpose.

Trust that the challenges and changes you face are ultimately leading you towards a more fulfilling, meaningful, and joyful existence. Stay open to the wisdom and guidance of the universe, and know that you have the strength, resilience, and inner resources to navigate any obstacles or setbacks that may arise. Remember that true success and happiness come from living in alignment with your values, passions, and purpose, and that the journey of growth and self-discovery is an ongoing adventure.

Best Days of the Month:

August 1st: Venus enters Virgo, bringing a practical, purposeful energy to your 10th house of career and public image. Focus on your long-term goals, attend to the details, and strive for excellence and efficiency in your professional pursuits.

August 9th: Full Moon in Aquarius illuminates your 3rd house of communication, learning, and short trips. Embrace your curiosity, seek out new ideas and perspectives, and trust in the power of your mind to expand your understanding of yourself and the world around you.

August 22nd: Sun enters Virgo, bringing a focused, analytical energy to your 10th house of career and public image. Set realistic goals, break them down into manageable steps, and take consistent action towards your aspirations and dreams.

August 23rd: New Moon in Virgo falls in your 10th house of career and public image, bringing a powerful opportunity to set intentions and make a fresh start in your professional life. Clarify your vision, align your actions with your values and purpose, and trust in the universe to support you in manifesting your highest potential.

August 28th: Venus trines Neptune in your 4th house of home, family, and emotional security, bringing a dreamy, romantic energy to your personal life. Connect with loved ones, create a nurturing and inspiring environment, and trust in the power of love, compassion, and creativity to heal and transform your relationships and your sense of belonging.

September 2025

Overview Horoscope for the Month:

Sagittarius, September 2025 is a month of new beginnings, personal growth, and spiritual awakening. As the month starts, Mars, the planet of action and ambition, enters your 11th house of friendships, community, and social activism. This cosmic influence may inspire you to connect with like-minded individuals, join a cause or movement that aligns with your values, or take on a leadership role in your social circle. Trust your instincts, follow your passions, and be open to collaboration and teamwork as you pursue your goals and dreams.

The Full Moon in Pisces on September 7th brings a powerful opportunity for emotional healing, forgiveness, and release. Falling in your 4th house of home, family, and emotional foundations, this lunation invites you to let go of any past wounds, resentments, or limiting patterns that may be holding you back from experiencing true intimacy, security, and belonging. Practice self-compassion, seek support from loved ones, and trust in the power of love and acceptance to transform your relationships and your sense of self.

Love:

With Venus, the planet of love and relationships, moving through your 11th house of friendships and community for most of September, you may find your love life intertwined with your social life and group activities. If you're single, you may meet someone special through a shared interest, hobby, or cause, or find yourself attracted to someone who shares your ideals and vision for the future. Be open to unconventional connections and unexpected opportunities, but also be discerning about who you let into your inner circle.

If you're in a committed relationship, this month's energies can bring a renewed sense of shared purpose and partnership to your love life. Work together towards a common goal, support each other's individuality and independence, and find ways to balance your personal and social responsibilities. Remember that true love is about acceptance, understanding, and growth, and that the challenges you face can ultimately strengthen your bond and deepen your connection.

Career:

September's celestial influences are set to bring exciting opportunities and breakthroughs in your career and professional life. With the Sun moving through your 10th house of career, reputation, and public image for most of the month, you may find yourself in the spotlight or taking on new roles and responsibilities that showcase your unique talents and abilities.

At the same time, Mercury, the planet of communication and learning, moves into your 11th house of networking and social connections on September 18th, highlighting the importance of building and maintaining professional relationships. Attend industry events, join a professional organization, or reach out to colleagues and mentors for advice and support. Remember that true success comes from collaboration, innovation, and a willingness to learn and grow.

Finances:

With the New Moon in Virgo on September 21st falling in your 10th house of career and public recognition, this is an excellent time to set intentions and make plans for your long-term financial goals and aspirations. Consider ways to increase your income, invest in your skills and education, or pursue a promotion or raise that reflects your value and contributions.

At the same time, be mindful of any tendencies towards overspending or financial risk-taking, especially around the time of the Full Moon in Pisces on September 7th. Practice gratitude for what you already have, focus on experiences rather than possessions, and trust that the universe will provide for your needs and desires when you align your actions with your values and purpose.

Health:

September's energies are set to bring a renewed focus on your physical, mental, and emotional well-being. With Chiron, the wounded healer, moving through your 5th house of self-expression, creativity, and joy, this is an excellent time to explore holistic healing modalities that help you reconnect with your inner child, release past traumas, and express your authentic self.

Consider trying a new form of creative expression, such as art therapy, dance, or music, or engaging in activities that bring you pleasure and help you relax and recharge. At the same time, be mindful of any tendencies towards overindulgence or escapism, and strive to maintain a healthy balance of work and play, discipline and spontaneity. Remember that true health and happiness come from a wholistic approach to self-care and self-love.

Travel:

With Jupiter, your ruling planet, now direct in your 9th house of travel, higher education, and personal growth, September is an excellent month for planning a meaningful, transformative journey or experience. Consider destinations that allow you to immerse yourself in new cultures, learn something new, or challenge your comfort zone in a way that helps you grow and evolve.

If travel isn't feasible, consider exploring your own backyard or local community with a fresh perspective and an open mind. Attend a workshop or retreat, take a class or course that interests you, or connect with people from different backgrounds and walks of life. The key is to embrace growth, learning, and the joy of discovery, and to let your adventurous spirit guide you towards new horizons and possibilities.

Insights from the Stars:

Sagittarius, September 2025 is a month of powerful transformation, spiritual growth, and alignment with your true path and purpose. The cosmic energies are inviting you to let go of any limiting beliefs, fears, or patterns that may be holding you back from living your best life. Trust that the challenges and changes you face are ultimately leading you towards a more authentic, fulfilling, and joyful existence.

Stay open to the wisdom and guidance of the universe, and trust that everything is happening for your highest good and evolution. Embrace the journey with a sense of curiosity, courage, and faith, and know that you have the strength, resilience, and inner resources to navigate any obstacles or setbacks that may arise.

Best Days of the Month:

September 7th: Full Moon in Pisces illuminates your 4th house of home, family, and emotional foundations. Release past wounds and practice self-compassion.

September 18th: Mercury enters Libra, activating your 11th house of friendships, networking, and social connections. Build and maintain professional relationships.

September 21st: New Moon in Virgo falls in your 10th house of career and public recognition. Set intentions for your long-term financial goals and aspirations.

September 22nd: Sun enters Libra, bringing a harmonious, balanced energy to your 11th house of friendships, community, and social activism. Connect with like-minded individuals and pursue your passions.

September 29th: Venus trines Saturn in your 3rd house of communication and learning, bringing a stabilizing, committed energy to your relationships and interactions. Have important conversations and make long-term plans.

October 2025

Overview Horoscope for the Month:

Sagittarius, October 2025 is a month of deep introspection, emotional healing, and spiritual growth. As the month begins, Venus, the planet of love and relationships, enters your 12th house of spirituality, solitude, and inner work. This cosmic influence invites you to retreat from the world, reflect on your values and beliefs, and connect with your inner wisdom and intuition. Trust the process of letting go, surrendering control, and allowing yourself to be guided by a higher power or purpose.

The Full Moon in Aries on October 6th illuminates your 5th house of romance, creativity, and self-expression, bringing a powerful opportunity to express your authentic self, pursue your passions, and let your light shine. Take a risk, follow your heart, and trust in the power of your unique talents and abilities to bring joy, inspiration, and meaning to your life and the lives of others.

Love:

With Venus moving through your 12th house of spirituality and inner work for most of October, your love life may take on a more introspective, intuitive, and unconditional quality. If you're single, you may find yourself attracted to someone who shares your spiritual values and beliefs, or who helps you connect with your higher self and purpose. Be open to the unexpected, trust your intuition, and allow yourself to be vulnerable and authentic in your interactions.

If you're in a committed relationship, this month's energies can bring a deeper level of intimacy, compassion, and unconditional love to your partnership. Practice forgiveness, let go of any past wounds or resentments, and focus on the present moment and the love that you share. Remember that true love is a spiritual journey of growth, healing, and self-discovery, and that the challenges you face can ultimately bring you closer to your authentic self and to each other.

Career:

October's celestial influences are set to bring exciting opportunities and breakthroughs in your career and professional life. With Mars, the planet of action and ambition, moving through your 10th house of career, reputation, and public image for most of the month, you may find yourself taking on new challenges, pursuing your goals with passion and determination, and making significant progress towards your long-term aspirations.

At the same time, the New Moon in Libra on October 21st falls in your 11th house of networking, community, and social connections, highlighting the importance of collaboration, teamwork, and shared values in your professional life. Seek out like-minded individuals and organizations that align with your vision and purpose, and be open to new ideas and perspectives that can help you grow and succeed. Remember that true success comes from being true to yourself and making a positive impact on the world around you.

Finances:

With Pluto, the planet of power, transformation, and rebirth, now direct in your 2nd house of money, resources, and self-worth, October is an excellent month for making positive changes and breakthroughs in your financial life. Consider ways to increase your income, invest in your skills and education, or pursue new opportunities that align with your values and passions.

At the same time, be mindful of any tendencies towards obsession, control, or power struggles around money and resources, especially around the time of the Full Moon in Aries on October 6th. Practice gratitude for what you already have, focus on experiences rather than possessions, and trust that the universe will provide for your needs and desires when you align your actions with your higher purpose and soul's calling.

Health:

October's energies are set to bring a renewed focus on your physical, mental, and emotional well-being. With the Sun moving through your 12th house of spirituality, solitude, and inner work for most of the month, this is an excellent time to prioritize self-care, rest, and relaxation, and to explore holistic healing modalities that help you connect with your inner wisdom and intuition.

Consider trying a new form of meditation, yoga, or energy healing, or engaging in activities that bring you peace, clarity, and inner calm. At the same time, be mindful of any tendencies towards escapism, addiction, or self-sabotage, and strive to maintain a healthy balance of introspection and action, solitude and connection. Remember that true health and happiness come from a wholistic approach to self-care and self-love, and that your inner world is just as important as your outer world.

Travel:

With Jupiter, your ruling planet, now retrograde in your 8th house of transformation, power, and shared resources, October may not be the best month for long-distance travel or adventurous journeys. Instead, consider taking a more introspective, transformative approach to your travels, such as attending a spiritual retreat, exploring your ancestral roots, or delving into the mysteries of life and death.

If travel isn't possible or practical, consider exploring your own inner landscape through journaling, dream work, or creative visualization. Trust that the answers and insights you seek are already within you, and that the journey of self-discovery and spiritual growth is the most important journey of all.

Insights from the Stars:

Sagittarius, October 2025 is a month of deep introspection, emotional healing, and spiritual growth. The cosmic energies are inviting you to let go of any limiting beliefs, fears, or patterns that may be holding you back from living your best life, and to connect with your inner wisdom, intuition, and higher purpose.

Trust that the challenges and changes you face are ultimately leading you towards a more authentic, fulfilling, and joyful existence, and that the universe is conspiring in your favor, even when things feel uncertain or overwhelming. Stay open to the guidance and support of your angels, guides, and higher self, and know that you are never alone on this journey of growth and self-discovery.

Best Days of the Month:

October 6th: Full Moon in Aries illuminates your 5th house of romance, creativity, and self-expression. Express your authentic self and pursue your passions.

October 13th: Pluto turns direct in your 2nd house of money, resources, and self-worth. Make positive changes and breakthroughs in your financial life.

October 21st: New Moon in Libra falls in your 11th house of networking, community, and social connections. Seek out like-minded individuals and organizations that align with your vision and purpose.

October 22nd: Sun enters Scorpio, bringing a deep, transformative energy to your 12th house of spirituality, solitude, and inner work. Explore your inner landscape and connect with your higher self.

October 29th: Mercury enters Sagittarius, activating your 1st house of self, identity, and personal goals. Communicate your ideas and aspirations with confidence and enthusiasm.

November 2025

Overview Horoscope for the Month:

Sagittarius, November 2025 is a month of deep introspection, spiritual growth, and new beginnings. As the month starts, the Sun is in your 12th house of spirituality, solitude, and inner work, inviting you to retreat from the world, reflect on your life, and connect with your inner wisdom and intuition. This is a time to let go of any past wounds, resentments, or limiting patterns, and to open yourself up to new possibilities, insights, and blessings.

The New Moon in Scorpio on November 20th falls in your 12th house, bringing a powerful opportunity to set intentions for your spiritual growth, emotional healing, and inner transformation. Trust the process of surrendering control, embracing change, and allowing yourself to be guided by a higher power or purpose.

Love:

With Venus, the planet of love and relationships, moving through your 1st house of self, identity, and personal goals for most of November, your love life is likely to be closely intertwined with your personal growth and self-discovery. If you're single, focus on loving and accepting yourself fully, cultivating a strong sense of self-worth and self-respect, and trusting that the right person will come into your life at the perfect time.

If you're in a relationship, use this month's energies to deepen your connection, communicate openly and honestly about your needs and desires, and support each other's individual journeys of growth and self-realization. Be willing to let go of any past hurts or resentments, and focus on creating a loving, compassionate, and authentic partnership.

Career:

November's celestial influences are set to bring exciting opportunities and breakthroughs in your career and professional life. With Mars, the planet of action and ambition, moving through your 11th house of networking, community, and social connections, focus on building and nurturing professional relationships, collaborating with like-minded individuals, and aligning your work with your values and vision for the future.

Trust your instincts, take calculated risks, and be open to new ideas and perspectives that can help you grow and succeed. At the same time, be mindful of any power struggles or conflicts that may arise, and strive to maintain your integrity and professionalism in all your interactions.

Finances:

With Jupiter, your ruling planet, now direct in your 8th house of transformation, power, and shared resources, November is an excellent month for making positive changes and breakthroughs in your financial life. Consider ways to increase your income, invest in your skills and education, or pursue new opportunities that align with your passions and purpose.

At the same time, be mindful of any tendencies towards overspending or financial risk-taking, especially around the time of the Full Moon in Taurus on November 5th. Practice gratitude for what you already have, focus on experiences rather than possessions, and trust that the universe will provide for your needs and desires when you align your actions with your values and intentions.

Health:

November's energies are set to bring a renewed focus on your physical, mental, and emotional well-being. With the Sun moving through your 12th house of spirituality, solitude, and inner work for most of the month, prioritize self-care, rest, and relaxation, and explore holistic healing modalities that help you connect with your inner wisdom and intuition.

Consider trying a new form of meditation, yoga, or energy healing, or engaging in activities that bring you peace, clarity, and inner calm. At the same time, be mindful of any tendencies towards escapism, addiction, or self-sabotage, and strive to maintain a healthy balance of introspection and action, solitude and connection.

Travel:

With the North Node now in your 6th house of work, health, and daily routines, November may be a good month for short trips or local adventures that help you break out of your comfort zone, explore new places and experiences, and gain fresh perspectives on your life and work.

Consider taking a day trip to a nearby town or natural wonder, attending a workshop or retreat that aligns with your interests and goals, or simply spending time in nature, reconnecting with the beauty and wisdom of the world around you. Trust your curiosity and sense of adventure, and be open to unexpected opportunities for growth and learning.

Insights from the Stars:

Sagittarius, November 2025 is a month of deep introspection, emotional healing, and spiritual growth. The cosmic energies are inviting you to let go of any limiting beliefs, fears, or patterns that may be holding you back from living your best life, and to connect with your inner wisdom, intuition, and higher purpose.

Trust that the challenges and changes you face are ultimately leading you towards a more authentic, fulfilling, and joyful existence, and that the universe is conspiring in your favor, even when things feel uncertain or overwhelming. Stay open to the guidance and support of your angels, guides, and higher self, and know that you are never alone on this journey of growth and self-discovery.

Best Days of the Month:

November 5th: Full Moon in Taurus illuminates your 6th house of work, health, and daily routines. Release any stress, tension, or unhealthy habits, and embrace a more balanced, grounded approach to your well-being.

November 7th: Venus enters Sagittarius, activating your 1st house of self, identity, and personal goals. Focus on self-love, self-acceptance, and personal growth, and let your unique light shine brightly in the world.

November 20th: New Moon in Scorpio falls in your 12th house of spirituality, solitude, and inner work. Set intentions for spiritual growth, emotional healing, and inner transformation, and trust the process of letting go and surrendering to a higher power.

November 21st: Sun enters Sagittarius, bringing a confident, optimistic energy to your 1st house of self, identity, and personal goals. Celebrate your unique talents and qualities, pursue your passions and dreams, and embrace the adventure of life.

November 28th: Mercury enters Sagittarius, enhancing your communication skills and mental agility. Express your ideas and opinions with clarity, enthusiasm, and conviction, and trust in the power of your voice and message to inspire and uplift others...

December 2025

Overview Horoscope for the Month:

Sagittarius, December 2025 is a month of celebration, reflection, and new beginnings. With the Sun in your sign for most of the month, you are likely to feel a renewed sense of energy, confidence, and enthusiasm for life. This is a time to embrace your unique talents and qualities, pursue your passions and goals, and let your light shine brightly in the world.

The New Moon in Sagittarius on December 19th brings a powerful opportunity to set intentions for the year ahead, clarify your vision and purpose, and take bold action towards your dreams. Trust your instincts, follow your heart, and believe in the power of your own potential and possibilities.

Love:

With Venus, the planet of love and relationships, moving through your 2nd house of values, resources, and self-worth for most of December, your love life is likely to be closely intertwined with your sense of security, stability, and personal values. If you're single, focus on building a strong foundation of self-love and self-respect, cultivating a sense of abundance and prosperity, and trusting that the right person will appreciate and value you for who you are.

If you're in a relationship, use this month's energies to deepen your commitment, express your love and appreciation through tangible actions and gestures, and create a shared vision for the future that aligns with both of your values and goals. Be willing to have honest conversations about money, resources, and long-term planning, and trust that your love can weather any challenges or changes that may arise.

Career:

December's celestial influences are set to bring exciting opportunities and breakthroughs in your career and professional life. With Mars, the planet of action and ambition, moving through your 12th house of spirituality, solitude, and inner work, focus on aligning your work with your higher purpose, trusting your intuition, and letting go of any limiting beliefs or patterns that may be holding you back from success and fulfillment.

Consider taking time for reflection, meditation, or journaling to gain clarity on your long-term goals and aspirations, and be open to unexpected insights or opportunities that may arise from your inner wisdom and guidance. At the same time, be mindful of any tendencies towards burnout, overwork, or self-sabotage, and strive to maintain a healthy balance of effort and ease, action and rest.

Finances:

With Jupiter, your ruling planet, now in your 9th house of travel, higher education, and personal growth, December is an excellent month for investing in your own learning and development, exploring new sources of income or wealth, and expanding your financial horizons.

Consider taking a course, attending a workshop or seminar, or pursuing a certification or degree that can enhance your skills and knowledge in your field. At the same time, be mindful of any tendencies towards overspending or financial risk-taking, especially around the time of the Full Moon in Gemini on December 4th. Stay grounded in your values and long-term goals, and trust that abundance flows when you align your actions with your authentic self and purpose.

Health:

December's energies are set to bring a renewed focus on your physical, mental, and emotional well-being. With the Sun in your sign for most of the month, prioritize self-care, joy, and vitality, and explore holistic healing modalities that help you feel your best and shine your brightest.

Consider trying a new form of exercise, such as dance, yoga, or martial arts, or making small, sustainable changes to your diet and lifestyle that support your overall health and happiness. At the same time, be mindful of any tendencies towards overindulgence or neglect, and strive to maintain a healthy balance of discipline and pleasure, effort and ease.

Travel:

With Mercury, the planet of communication and learning, moving through your 1st house of self, identity, and personal goals for most of December, this is an excellent month for short trips, local adventures, and intellectual pursuits that help you expand your mind, broaden your horizons, and gain new perspectives on yourself and the world around you.

Consider taking a weekend getaway to a nearby city or natural wonder, attending a cultural event or festival that sparks your curiosity and creativity, or simply spending time exploring your own neighborhood or community with fresh eyes and an open heart. Trust your sense of adventure and discovery, and be open to unexpected opportunities for growth, learning, and connection.

Insights from the Stars:

Sagittarius, December 2025 is a month of celebration, reflection, and new beginnings. The cosmic energies are inviting you to embrace your unique talents and qualities, pursue your passions and goals, and let your light shine brightly in the world.

Trust that you have the wisdom, courage, and resilience to navigate any challenges or changes that may arise, and that the universe is always supporting you on your path of growth and evolution. Stay open to the magic and synchronicity of life, and know that your dreams and desires are leading you towards your highest potential and purpose.

Best Days of the Month:

December 4th: Full Moon in Gemini illuminates your 7th house of partnerships and relationships. Celebrate your connections, communicate openly and honestly, and find a balance between your individual needs and the needs of others.

December 19th: New Moon in Sagittarius brings a powerful opportunity to set intentions for the year ahead, clarify your vision and purpose, and take bold action towards your dreams. Trust your instincts, follow your heart, and believe in the power of your own potential and possibilities.

December 21st: Sun enters Capricorn, bringing a grounded, practical energy to your 2nd house of values, resources, and self-worth. Focus on building a strong foundation for your goals and dreams, and trust that your efforts will pay off in the long run.

December 24th: Venus enters Capricorn, enhancing your sense of commitment, responsibility, and long-term planning in your relationships and financial life. Express your love and appreciation with tangible actions and gestures, and create a shared vision for the future that aligns with your values and goals.

December 29th: Mercury enters Capricorn, sharpening your mind and communication skills in matters of business, career, and practical planning. Trust your intelligence and expertise, and communicate your ideas with clarity, confidence, and conviction.[t].

CAPRICORN 2025 HOROSCOPE

Overview Capricorn 2025

(December 22 - January 19)

Dear Capricorn, 2025 is a year of metamorphosis and renewal for you as the celestial bodies align to support your growth, ambitions, and personal transformation. Prepare to shed old skin and emerge as a more empowered, wise, and authentic version of yourself.

The year begins with a powerful focus on your sign, as the Sun, Mercury, Venus and Pluto are all clustered in Capricorn in January. This stellium amplifies your natural traits of discipline, pragmatism and determination. You'll feel a strong drive to take charge of your life, set ambitious goals, and work diligently towards them. The Capricorn New Moon on January 29 is your cosmic invitation to clarify your intentions and lay the groundwork for the year ahead.

In early February, the conjunction of Saturn and Neptune in Pisces activates your 3rd house of communication, learning and daily environment. This dreamy yet disciplined influence encourages you to infuse more creativity, imagination and compassion into your interactions and thought patterns. It's a favorable time to take up a visionary project, immerse yourself in uplifting studies, or lend a helping hand in your local community.

The pace quickens in March as Mars enters your 6th house of work and wellness, followed by Saturn's ingress into fiery Aries. You'll feel energized to tackle your to-do list, implement healthy routines, and assert yourself in your job. However, Saturn will also square off with Pluto in your sign, demanding that you release any burdens or limits that hold you back from your full potential. It's time to reclaim your power and let your true self shine.

April and May bring opportunities to expand your horizons through travel, higher education, or philosophical pursuits as Jupiter tours your 9th house of wisdom and adventure. This is an auspicious time to broaden your mind, explore new frontiers, and align with your core beliefs. The Lunar Eclipse in Libra on April 12 illuminates your 10th house of career and public image, bringing recognition for your hard work or initiating a shift in your professional path. Trust your instincts and stay true to your values as you navigate any changes.

The middle of the year is marked by a period of introspection and emotional processing as the eclipses activate your 12th house of spirituality and unconscious patterns. The Solar Eclipse in Cancer on June 25 followed by the Lunar Eclipse in Capricorn on July 9 provide a cosmic cleanse, helping you release past traumas, limiting beliefs, and unhealthy attachments. Make space for solitude, self-care, and inner work during this cathartic time. Counseling, journaling, or energy healing can be especially beneficial to integrate any hidden shadows.

As the North Node shifts into Libra and your 10th house in mid-July, your soul's purpose becomes increasingly tied to your calling and contributions in the world. You're primed to step into a leadership role, receive well-deserved accolades, or align your path with humanitarian causes. Let your integrity, wisdom, and dedication to excellence be your guide.

August is a dynamic month as Mars and Venus join forces in your 8th house of intimacy, shared resources, and transformation. You may experience a deepening of a soul connection, explore uncharted depths of your psyche, or undergo a healing crisis that ultimately leads to empowerment. This is an intense time of facing your fears and desires head-on. Honest communication, vulnerability, and emotional alchemization are key.

Come September, the cosmic spotlight returns to your career sector, with a Partial Solar Eclipse in Virgo turbocharging your ambitions and inviting a bold leap towards your dreams. You have the grit, strategic know-how, and unwavering determination to reach new heights. Focus on mastery and respect for your craft. As Mercury stations retrograde in your 10th house, you'll have an opportunity to revise your professional plans and ensure they're built on a solid, intentional foundation.

The last quarter of 2025 emphasizes themes of community, friendship, and collaboration. You may join forces with an exciting new network, deepen your involvement in a humanitarian cause, or receive support from a tribe of kindred spirits. The key is to balance your signature self-reliance with the gifts of interdependence and collective action. Together, you can create remarkable positive change.

As the year comes to a close, Mercury and Venus return to your sign, blessing you with enhanced mental clarity and magnetic charm. You're integrating the immense growth you've undergone and feeling more self-assured than ever. The Capricorn New Moon on December 27 is a beautiful time for reflection and celebration. Take stock of how far you've come and set your sights on even loftier vistas for 2026. You're in the driver's seat of your destiny, Capricorn, and the road ahead is paved with endless possibilities. Trust your resilience, stay anchored in your integrity, and keep climbing towards your highest purpose. The stars are aligned in your favor.

January 2025

Overview Horoscope for the Month:

Happy New Year, Capricorn! January 2025 is set to be a transformative and empowering month for you, as the cosmos align to support your personal growth, ambitions, and new beginnings. With the Sun, Mercury, Venus, and Pluto all converging in your sign at the start of the year, you're feeling a strong sense of purpose, determination, and self-mastery. This is your time to take charge of your life, set clear intentions, and commit to the hard work and discipline required to manifest your goals. The Capricorn New Moon on January 29th serves as a powerful cosmic reset, inviting you to clarify your vision, plant the seeds of your deepest desires, and trust in your ability to create the life you truly want.

Love:

In matters of the heart, January 2025 promises a mix of intensity, passion, and transformation for you, dear Capricorn. The Venus-Pluto conjunction in your sign mid-month brings the potential for profound emotional connections, soulmate encounters, or the deepening of existing bonds. You're craving authentic, meaningful relationships that support your personal growth and empower you to be your best self. This is a time to get radically honest about your desires, needs, and deal-breakers in love. If you're single, you may find yourself magnetically drawn to someone who shares your values, challenges you to grow, and sees the depth of your soul. Trust your instincts and don't settle for anything less than the love you deserve. If you're in a committed partnership, use this potent energy to have vulnerable conversations, deepen your intimacy, and co-create a shared vision for your future together. Remember, true love is not about perfection, but about supporting each other's evolution with compassion, respect, and unwavering commitment.

Career:

Capricorn, your career is set to soar to new heights this month, as the powerful stellium in your sign propels you towards success, recognition, and leadership. You're feeling ambitious, focused, and ready to take on new challenges that showcase your talents and expertise. This is an excellent time to put yourself out there, network with influential people in your field, and make bold moves towards your professional goals. Trust your instincts and don't be afraid to take calculated risks – the universe is conspiring in your favor. Just remember to balance your drive with diplomacy, collaboration, and integrity. Your hard work and dedication will pay off, but make sure your actions align with your values and the greater good. A significant career milestone, promotion, or opportunity could manifest around the New Moon on January 29th. Stay open to the possibilities and know that you have what it takes to succeed.

Finances:

January 2025 is a fantastic month to get your financial house in order, Capricorn. With the Sun, Mercury, Venus, and Pluto all in your sign, you have the focus, discipline, and resourcefulness to create a solid plan for long-term abundance and security. Take some time to review your budget, set clear financial goals, and identify any areas where you can cut back on expenses or increase your income. Consider investing in your own skills, education, or personal development, as this will pay dividends in the long run. If you've been thinking about starting a side hustle or pursuing a new revenue stream, this is a great time to take action. Trust your instincts and don't be afraid to seek the advice of a financial expert or mentor. Remember, true wealth is not just about material possessions, but about feeling secure, empowered, and aligned with your values. Focus on cultivating a mindset of abundance, gratitude, and generosity, and trust that the universe will support you in creating the financial freedom you desire.

Health:

Capricorn, your health and well-being are in the cosmic spotlight this month, as the planets in your sign encourage you to prioritize self-care, personal growth, and mind-body-spirit alignment. This is an excellent time to recommit to your wellness goals, start a new exercise routine, or explore holistic healing modalities that support your physical, emotional, and spiritual health. With Mars in your 6th house of daily routines, you have the energy and discipline to establish healthy habits that nourish your body and soul. Just be mindful not to overdo it or put too much pressure on yourself – balance is key. Make sure to carve out time for rest, relaxation, and activities that bring you joy and peace. If you've been dealing with any chronic health issues, this is a good time to seek the guidance of a trusted medical professional or alternative healer. Remember, true wellness is about honoring your body's wisdom, listening to your intuition, and treating yourself with love and compassion.

Travel:

January 2025 may not be the most ideal time for long-distance travel, Capricorn, as your focus is more on personal goals, career advancement, and inner growth. However, if you do need to travel for work or other obligations, make sure to plan ahead, double-check all details, and be prepared for potential delays or changes in itinerary. This is a good time to research and book future trips that align with your long-term vision and aspirations. If you're feeling the need for a change of scenery or a mental escape, consider taking a short weekend getaway or exploring a new neighborhood in your city. The key is to find ways to expand your horizons, stimulate your mind, and feed your soul, even if you can't physically travel far. Remember, sometimes the greatest adventures and discoveries happen within, as you journey into the depths of your own psyche and spirituality.

Insights from the Stars:

Capricorn, the celestial energies of January 2025 are urging you to embrace your personal power, step into your authority, and claim your rightful place in the world. With Saturn, your ruling planet, in a supportive aspect to the Sun, Mercury, Venus, and Pluto in your sign, you have the cosmic green light to make your dreams a reality. Trust your inner wisdom, harness your ambition, and don't be afraid to shine your light unapologetically. You are a natural leader, with the discipline, integrity, and resilience to overcome any obstacle and achieve your highest potential. This is a time to let go of self-doubt, limiting beliefs, and the need for external validation. Remember, you are the architect of your own reality, and you have the power to create a life that aligns with your deepest values and desires. Embrace your authentic self, trust the journey, and know that the universe is conspiring in your favor.

Best Days of the Month:

January 6th: First Quarter Moon in Aries - A powerful day for taking bold action towards your goals and asserting your leadership skills.

January 13th: Full Moon in Cancer - An emotional time for nurturing your inner world, connecting with loved ones, and creating a sense of home and belonging.

January 21st: Last Quarter Moon in Libra - An opportunity to find balance, harmony, and reconciliation in your relationships and partnerships.

January 29th: New Moon in Capricorn - A potent portal for setting intentions, planting the seeds of your dreams, and recommitting to your personal growth and soul's purpose.

February 2025

Overview Horoscope for the Month:

Welcome to February 2025, Capricorn! This month is all about building on the momentum and breakthroughs you experienced in January, while also focusing on your financial security, personal values, and self-worth. With the Sun illuminating your 2nd house of material resources and possessions, you're called to create a stable foundation for your long-term goals and aspirations. The Full Moon in Leo on February 12th highlights your 8th house of intimacy, shared resources, and personal transformation, bringing powerful insights and revelations about your deepest bonds, psychological patterns, and the ways in which you merge your energy with others. Trust the process of growth and evolution, and know that you have the strength and resilience to face any challenges that may arise.

Love:

In matters of the heart, February 2025 is a month of deepening emotional connections, honest communication, and shared values for you, Capricorn. With Venus transiting your 3rd and 4th houses, you're attracted to partners who stimulate your mind, engage your curiosity, and make you feel emotionally safe and supported. This is a beautiful time to have heartfelt conversations with your loved ones, express your affection and appreciation, and create a nurturing environment for your relationships to thrive. If you're single, you may find yourself drawn to someone who shares your intellectual interests, family values, or cultural background. Take things slow and focus on building a strong foundation of friendship, trust, and mutual respect. If you're in a committed partnership, use this month to deepen your emotional intimacy, communicate your needs and desires openly, and find new ways to support each other's growth and happiness. Remember, true love is a journey of discovery, compromise, and unconditional acceptance.

Career:

Capricorn, your career sector is buzzing with activity and opportunity this month, as Mars energizes your 6th house of work, service, and daily routines. You're feeling motivated, productive, and ready to tackle any challenges that come your way. This is an excellent time to take on new projects, showcase your skills and expertise, and prove your value in the workplace. Your hard work, dedication, and attention to detail will not go unnoticed, and you may receive recognition, a promotion, or a lucrative job offer as a result. Just be mindful of taking on too much at once, as the temptation to overwork or burn yourself out may be strong. Remember to prioritize self-care, delegation, and work-life balance, and don't be afraid to ask for help or support when needed. Trust that your efforts will pay off in the long run, and that your career path is unfolding in perfect divine timing.

Finances:

February 2025 is a powerful month for manifestation, abundance, and financial growth, Capricorn. With the Sun spotlighting your 2nd house of money, possessions, and personal values, you're called to align your spending habits, income streams, and long-term financial goals with your authentic self and life purpose. This is a great time to review your budget, cut back on unnecessary expenses, and invest in your own skills, talents, and personal development. Look for ways to increase your earnings, such as asking for a raise, starting a side hustle, or exploring new revenue streams that align with your passions and expertise. The key is to cultivate a mindset of abundance, gratitude, and self-worth, and to trust that the universe will support you in creating the financial freedom and security you desire. Remember, true wealth is not just about material possessions, but about feeling fulfilled, empowered, and aligned with your deepest values and aspirations.

Health:

Capricorn, your health and well-being are in the cosmic spotlight this month, as the planets encourage you to prioritize self-care, mindfulness, and balance in your daily life. With Mars energizing your 6th house of health, fitness, and routine, you have the motivation and discipline to make positive lifestyle changes that support your physical, emotional, and mental well-being. This is a great time to start a new exercise regimen, explore nutritious meal planning, or incorporate stress-reducing practices like meditation, yoga, or nature walks into your daily schedule. Just be mindful not to overdo it or put too much pressure on yourself to achieve perfection. Remember, true wellness is about listening to your body's wisdom, honoring your unique needs and rhythms, and treating yourself with kindness and compassion. If you've been dealing with any chronic health issues, this is a good time to seek the guidance of a trusted medical professional or holistic healer, and to explore alternative or complementary therapies that resonate with you.

Travel:

February 2025 may bring some unexpected travel opportunities, Capricorn, particularly related to work, education, or personal growth. With Mercury transiting your 3rd house of communication, learning, and short trips, you may find yourself taking impromptu weekend getaways, attending workshops or conferences, or exploring new neighborhoods and communities in your local area. This is a great time to feed your curiosity, expand your mind, and connect with like-minded individuals who share your interests and passions. If you're planning a longer journey, make sure to do your research, read the fine print, and have a backup plan in case of any delays or unforeseen circumstances. Remember, travel is not just about reaching a destination, but about the experiences, insights, and personal growth you gain along the way. Embrace the spirit of adventure, stay open to serendipity, and trust that every journey, whether inner or outer, is an opportunity for self-discovery and transformation.

Insights from the Stars:

Capricorn, the celestial energies of February 2025 are reminding you of the power of authenticity, self-awareness, and emotional intelligence in creating a fulfilling and purposeful life. With Saturn, your ruling planet, in a harmonious aspect to the Sun, Mercury, and Venus this month, you have the wisdom, maturity, and discernment to make choices that align with your highest good and deepest values. Trust your inner guidance system, listen to your intuition, and don't be afraid to set healthy boundaries or say no to people, situations, or commitments that drain your energy or compromise your integrity. Remember, you are the master of your own destiny, and you have the power to create a reality that reflects your true essence and potential. Embrace your unique quirks, honor your sensitive nature, and know that your vulnerability is a strength, not a weakness. The more you can accept and love yourself unconditionally, the more you'll attract relationships, opportunities, and experiences that mirror your inner light and authenticity.

Best Days of the Month:

February 5th: First Quarter Moon in Taurus - A powerful day for manifestation, abundance, and grounding your dreams in practical action steps.

February 12th: Full Moon in Leo - A passionate and creative time for expressing your authentic self, celebrating your achievements, and letting your inner child come out to play.

February 20th: Last Quarter Moon in Sagittarius - An opportunity for release, closure, and tying up loose ends related to travel, education, or personal growth.

February 27th: New Moon in Pisces - A mystical portal for setting intentions, connecting with your spiritual essence, and surrendering to the flow of the universe.

March 2025

Overview Horoscope for the Month:

Welcome to March 2025, Capricorn! This month promises to be a time of profound transformation, self-discovery, and spiritual awakening. With Saturn, your ruling planet, entering Pisces and your 3rd house of communication, learning, and local community on March 1st, you're being called to expand your mind, challenge your beliefs, and connect with like-minded individuals who share your values and vision. The New Moon in Aries on March 29th falls in your 4th house of home, family, and emotional foundations, bringing powerful opportunities for healing, forgiveness, and new beginnings in your personal life. Trust the process of growth and evolution, and know that you have the strength, resilience, and wisdom to navigate any changes or challenges that may arise.

Love:

In matters of the heart, March 2025 is a month of deep emotional intimacy, spiritual connection, and unconditional love for you, Capricorn. With Venus, the planet of love and relationships, moving through your 4th house of home and family, you're called to create a nurturing, supportive, and loving environment for your closest bonds to thrive. This is a beautiful time to express your affection, appreciation, and vulnerability with your loved ones, and to prioritize quality time, shared experiences, and emotional connection in your relationships. If you're single, you may find yourself attracted to someone who feels like home, who understands your sensitive nature, and who supports your personal growth and healing journey. Trust your intuition, take things slow, and focus on building a strong foundation of trust, respect, and mutual care. If you're in a committed partnership, use this month to deepen your intimacy, communicate your needs and desires openly, and create a shared vision for your future together. Remember, true love is a sacred journey of the heart, and it requires patience, presence, and a willingness to grow and evolve together.

Career:

Capricorn, your career sector is undergoing a powerful transformation this month, as Saturn moves into your 3rd house of communication, learning, and networking. You're being called to expand your skillset, knowledge base, and professional connections, and to align your work with your authentic values and purpose. This is an excellent time to take a course, attend a workshop or conference, or seek out mentorship or guidance from experts in your field. Your ability to communicate effectively, think critically, and collaborate with others will be key to your success and advancement. Just be mindful of taking on too many projects or commitments at once, as the temptation to overextend yourself may be strong. Remember to prioritize balance, self-care, and meaningful work that truly resonates with your soul. Trust that your hard work, dedication, and integrity will pay off in the long run, and that your career path is unfolding in perfect divine timing.

Finances:

March 2025 is a month of financial planning, budgeting, and long-term investments for you, Capricorn. With the Sun illuminating your 3rd house of communication and commerce, you're called to educate yourself about money management, financial literacy, and wealth-building strategies. This is a great time to review your spending habits, create a realistic budget, and explore new ways to increase your income or diversify your revenue streams. Look for opportunities to monetize your skills, talents, and expertise, such as freelancing, consulting, or starting a side business. The key is to align your financial goals with your personal values and life purpose, and to make choices that support your long-term security and abundance. Remember, true wealth is not just about accumulating material possessions, but about feeling fulfilled, empowered, and aligned with your deepest desires and aspirations.

Health:

Capricorn, your health and well-being are in the cosmic spotlight this month, as the planets encourage you to prioritize self-care, mindfulness, and emotional healing. With Saturn moving into your 3rd house of communication and mental processing, you may find yourself dealing with anxious thoughts, self-doubt, or negative self-talk. This is a powerful opportunity to confront your inner critic, challenge your limiting beliefs, and develop a more compassionate and supportive relationship with yourself. Engage in practices that promote relaxation, stress relief, and mental clarity, such as meditation, journaling, or talk therapy. On a physical level, make sure to stay hydrated, eat nourishing foods, and get plenty of rest and exercise. If you've been dealing with any chronic health issues, this is a good time to seek the guidance of a trusted medical professional or holistic healer, and to explore alternative or complementary therapies that support your mind-body-spirit connection.

Travel:

March 2025 may bring some unexpected travel opportunities, Capricorn, particularly related to education, personal growth, or spiritual exploration. With Saturn moving into your 3rd house of short trips and local adventures, you may find yourself taking weekend getaways, exploring new neighborhoods or communities, or attending workshops or retreats that expand your mind and feed your soul. This is a great time to step out of your comfort zone, try new things, and connect with people from different backgrounds or cultures. If you're planning a longer journey, make sure to do your research, read reviews, and have a clear intention or purpose for your trip. Remember, travel is not just about escaping your everyday life, but about discovering new aspects of yourself, broadening your perspective, and finding meaning and connection in the world around you. Embrace the spirit of curiosity, stay open to synchronicity, and trust that every journey, whether inner or outer, is an opportunity for growth, healing, and transformation.

Insights from the Stars:

Capricorn, the celestial energies of March 2025 are inviting you to embrace your inner wisdom, trust your intuition, and align your actions with your soul's purpose. With Saturn, your ruling planet, moving into Pisces and your 3rd house of communication and learning, you're being called to expand your consciousness, challenge your assumptions, and seek out knowledge and experiences that truly resonate with your heart. This is a time to let go of rigid expectations, perfectionist tendencies, or the need to control every outcome, and to surrender to the flow of the universe. Remember, you are a spiritual being having a human experience, and every challenge, setback, or opportunity is a chance to learn, grow, and evolve. Trust that you have the strength, resilience, and inner guidance to navigate any changes or uncertainties that may arise, and that your soul is always leading you towards your highest good and deepest fulfillment.

Best Days of the Month:

March 6th: First Quarter Moon in Gemini - A great day for learning, networking, and sharing your ideas and insights with others.

March 14th: Full Moon in Virgo - A powerful time for releasing perfectionism, embracing self-acceptance, and finding beauty in the imperfections of life.

March 20th: Sun enters Aries - A new astrological year begins, bringing fresh energy, motivation, and opportunities for personal growth and self-discovery.

March 29th: New Moon in Aries - A potent portal for setting intentions, planting the seeds of your dreams, and taking bold action towards your goals and desires.

April 2025

Overview Horoscope for the Month:

Capricorn, April 2025 is a month of deep emotional healing, spiritual growth, and personal transformation. With the Sun illuminating your 4th house of home, family, and inner foundations, you're being called to nurture your roots, honor your sensitivity, and create a safe and sacred space for your soul to thrive. The Full Moon in Libra on April 12th highlights your 10th house of career, public image, and long-term goals, bringing powerful opportunities for recognition, advancement, and alignment with your true purpose. Trust the process of growth and evolution, and know that you have the strength, resilience, and wisdom to navigate any changes or challenges that may arise.

Love:

In matters of the heart, April 2025 is a month of emotional intimacy, vulnerability, and unconditional love for you, Capricorn. With Venus, the planet of love and relationships, moving through your 5th house of romance, creativity, and self-expression, you're being called to open your heart, take risks, and let your authentic self shine. This is a beautiful time to prioritize pleasure, passion, and playfulness in your relationships, and to express your affection and appreciation for your loved ones in creative and meaningful ways. If you're single, you may find yourself attracted to someone who shares your values, sparks your curiosity, and brings out the best in you. Trust your intuition, take things slow, and focus on building a strong foundation of friendship, respect, and mutual admiration. If you're in a committed partnership, use this month to deepen your emotional connection, communicate your needs and desires openly, and explore new ways to keep the spark alive. Remember, true love is a journey of the heart, and it requires patience, presence, and a willingness to grow and evolve together.

Career:

Capricorn, your career sector is in the cosmic spotlight this month, as the Full Moon in Libra on April 12th illuminates your 10th house of professional goals, public image, and long-term success. You may find yourself receiving recognition, rewards, or opportunities for advancement that align with your true purpose and values. This is a powerful time to reflect on your achievements, celebrate your progress, and set intentions for the next phase of your career journey. Just be mindful of any power struggles, conflicts, or ego-driven dynamics that may arise, as the Mars-Jupiter conjunction in your 6th house of work and service can heighten tensions and competitiveness. Remember to stay grounded, focused, and true to your integrity, and to prioritize collaboration, teamwork, and the greater good. Trust that your hard work, dedication, and expertise will be valued and rewarded in the long run, and that your career path is unfolding in perfect divine timing.

Finances:

April 2025 is a month of financial planning, budgeting, and long-term investments for you, Capricorn. With the Sun illuminating your 4th house of home and family, you may find yourself focusing on domestic expenses, such as home improvements, renovations, or real estate transactions. This is a great time to review your spending habits, create a realistic budget, and explore ways to increase your savings or invest in your future security. Look for opportunities to generate passive income, such as renting out a property, starting a home-based business, or investing in stocks or mutual funds. The key is to align your financial goals with your personal values and life purpose, and to make choices that support your long-term stability and abundance. Remember, true wealth is not just about accumulating material possessions, but about feeling emotionally fulfilled, spiritually connected, and aligned with your deepest desires and aspirations.

Health:

Capricorn, your health and well-being are undergoing a powerful transformation this month, as the planets encourage you to prioritize self-care, emotional healing, and mind-body-spirit integration. With Chiron, the wounded healer, activating your 4th house of inner foundations and family dynamics, you may find yourself confronting old wounds, traumas, or patterns that have been holding you back from true wellness and vitality. This is a potent opportunity to seek therapy, counseling, or alternative healing modalities that support your emotional and psychological growth. On a physical level, make sure to stay hydrated, eat nourishing foods, and engage in gentle exercise or movement practices that help you release stress and tension. If you've been dealing with any chronic health issues, this is a good time to explore holistic or integrative approaches that address the root causes, rather than just the symptoms. Remember, true healing is a journey of self-discovery, self-acceptance, and self-love, and it requires patience, compassion, and a willingness to let go of what no longer serves you.

Travel:

April 2025 may bring some unexpected travel opportunities, Capricorn, particularly related to family, ancestral roots, or emotional healing. With the North Node activating your 9th house of long-distance journeys, higher education, and spiritual growth, you may feel called to embark on a pilgrimage, retreat, or cultural immersion that expands your mind, opens your heart, and connects you with your soul's purpose. This is a great time to explore your heritage, learn about different philosophies or belief systems, and seek out experiences that challenge your assumptions and broaden your perspective. If you're planning a trip, make sure to do your research, read reviews, and have a clear intention or purpose for your journey. Remember, travel is not just about escaping your everyday life, but about discovering new aspects of yourself, deepening your connection with the world around you, and finding meaning and purpose in the grand adventure of life. Embrace the spirit of curiosity, stay open to synchronicity, and trust that every journey, whether inner or outer, is an opportunity for growth, healing, and transformation.

Insights from the Stars:

Capricorn, the celestial energies of April 2025 are inviting you to embrace your emotional depth, trust your intuition, and align your actions with your soul's purpose. With the Sun, Mercury, and Venus activating your 4th house of home, family, and inner foundations, you're being called to nurture your roots, honor your sensitivity, and create a safe and sacred space for your heart to heal and your spirit to soar. This is a time to let go of any masks, defenses, or barriers that have been keeping you from authentic connection and vulnerability, and to open yourself up to the transformative power of love, compassion, and self-acceptance. Remember, you are a divine being of light and love, and your deepest wounds and shadows are portals to your greatest strengths and gifts.

Trust that you have the courage, resilience, and inner guidance to navigate any changes or challenges that may arise, and that your soul is always leading you towards your highest good and deepest fulfillment.

Best Days of the Month:

April 4th: Saturn sextile Uranus - A powerful day for innovation, progress, and breaking free from limitations or obstacles.

April 12th: Full Moon in Libra - A potent portal for harmony, balance, and aligning your personal and professional goals with your highest values and aspirations.

April 16th: Mercury enters Aries - A great time for new ideas, fresh perspectives, and bold communication in your personal and professional life.

April 20th: Sun enters Taurus - A new solar cycle begins, bringing stability, security, and a focus on your material and emotional foundations.

May 2025

Overview Horoscope for the Month:

Capricorn, May 2025 is a month of personal growth, self-expression, and creative exploration. With the Sun illuminating your 5th house of romance, passion, and authenticity, you're being called to let your unique light shine, pursue your heart's desires, and take risks in the name of love and joy. The New Moon in Taurus on May 26th activates your 5th house as well, bringing powerful opportunities for new beginnings, fresh starts, and bold self-expression. Trust the process of growth and evolution, and know that you have the courage, resilience, and creativity to manifest your dreams and desires.

Love:

In matters of the heart, May 2025 is a month of passion, playfulness, and emotional authenticity for you, Capricorn. With Venus, the planet of love and relationships, moving through your 6th house of daily routines and service, you're being called to find beauty, pleasure, and connection in the simple, everyday moments of life. This is a beautiful time to express your affection and appreciation for your loved ones through acts of kindness, thoughtful gestures, and quality time together. If you're single, you may find yourself attracted to someone who shares your values, supports your goals, and brings a sense of stability and security to your life. Trust your intuition, take things slow, and focus on building a strong foundation of friendship, respect, and mutual care. If you're in a committed partnership, use this month to deepen your emotional intimacy, communicate your needs and desires openly, and find new ways to keep the spark of romance alive. Remember, true love is a journey of the heart, and it requires patience, presence, and a willingness to grow and evolve together.

Career:

Capricorn, your career sector is undergoing a powerful transformation this month, as the Lunar Eclipse in Scorpio on May 12th activates your 11th house of networking, teamwork, and long-term goals. You may find yourself letting go of old attachments, limitations, or collaborations that no longer align with your true purpose and values, and embracing new opportunities, connections, and visions for your professional future. This is a potent time to reflect on your achievements, reassess your priorities, and set intentions for the next phase of your career journey. Just be mindful of any power struggles, conflicts, or hidden agendas that may arise, as the eclipse energy can bring buried tensions or secrets to the surface. Remember to stay grounded, focused, and true to your integrity, and to prioritize transparency, fairness, and the greater good. Trust that your hard work, dedication, and expertise will be recognized and rewarded in divine timing, and that your career path is unfolding in perfect alignment with your soul's purpose.

YOUR COMPLETE PERSONAL HOROSCOPE 2025· 375

Finances:

May 2025 is a month of financial planning, budgeting, and long-term investments for you, Capricorn. With the Sun and New Moon activating your 5th house of creativity, self-expression, and entrepreneurship, you may find yourself exploring new ways to monetize your talents, skills, and passions. This is a great time to start a side hustle, launch a creative project, or invest in your own business or brand. Look for opportunities to generate multiple streams of income, such as selling your art or crafts online, offering freelance services, or teaching classes or workshops. The key is to align your financial goals with your personal values and life purpose, and to make choices that support your long-term security and abundance. Remember, true wealth is not just about accumulating material possessions, but about feeling creatively fulfilled, emotionally satisfied, and aligned with your deepest desires and aspirations.

Health:

Capricorn, your health and well-being are in the cosmic spotlight this month, as the planets encourage you to prioritize self-care, pleasure, and vitality. With Mars, the planet of action and energy, moving through your 8th house of transformation, intimacy, and deep healing, you may find yourself confronting old wounds, traumas, or patterns that have been holding you back from true wellness and aliveness. This is a potent opportunity to engage in deep emotional work, such as therapy, journaling, or shamanic healing, and to release any toxic habits, relationships, or beliefs that no longer serve your highest good. On a physical level, make sure to stay hydrated, eat nourishing foods, and engage in activities that bring you joy, pleasure, and a sense of flow. If you've been dealing with any chronic health issues, this is a good time to explore alternative or holistic approaches that address the mind-body-spirit connection, such as acupuncture, reiki, or energy healing. Remember, true healing is a journey of self-discovery, self-acceptance, and self-love, and it requires patience, compassion, and a willingness to embrace your shadows as well as your light.

Travel:

May 2025 may bring some exciting travel opportunities, Capricorn, particularly related to creativity, self-expression, or personal growth. With Jupiter, the planet of expansion and abundance, activating your 6th house of daily routines and work, you may find yourself taking a business trip, attending a conference or workshop, or exploring new ways to bring more adventure and inspiration into your everyday life. This is a great time to break out of your comfort zone, try new things, and seek out experiences that broaden your mind, open your heart, and feed your soul. If you're planning a vacation, consider destinations that offer a mix of relaxation, culture, and natural beauty, such as a yoga retreat in Bali, a art history tour in Italy, or a wilderness adventure in Costa Rica. Remember, travel is not just about escaping your everyday life, but about discovering new aspects of yourself, deepening your connection with the world around you, and finding meaning and purpose in the grand adventure of life. Embrace the spirit of curiosity, stay open to synchronicity, and trust that every journey, whether inner or outer, is an opportunity for growth, healing, and transformation.

Insights from the Stars:

Capricorn, the celestial energies of May 2025 are inviting you to embrace your creative power, trust your heart's desires, and align your actions with your soul's purpose. With the Sun, Mercury, and Venus activating your 5th house of self-expression, passion, and authenticity, you're being called to let your unique light shine, take risks in the name of love and joy, and pursue the dreams and desires that make you come alive. This is a time to let go of any self-doubt, fear, or limitations that have been holding you back from your true potential, and to embrace the magic, mystery, and adventure of life. Remember, you are a divine creator, with the power to manifest your reality through your thoughts, beliefs, and actions. Trust that the universe is always conspiring in your favor, and that your deepest desires are a reflection of your soul's purpose. Have faith in yourself, follow your bliss, and know that you are loved, supported, and guided every step of the way.

Best Days of the Month:

May 4th: Saturn sextile Uranus - A powerful day for innovation, progress, and breaking free from limitations or obstacles.

May 12th: Full Moon Lunar Eclipse in Scorpio - A potent portal for deep transformation, emotional healing, and releasing what no longer serves your highest good.

May 16th: Mercury enters Taurus - A great time for practical planning, financial management, and grounding your ideas in tangible reality.

May 26th: New Moon in Taurus - A beautiful opportunity for new beginnings, fresh starts, and planting the seeds of your dreams and desires.

June 2025

Overview Horoscope for the Month:

Welcome to June 2025, Capricorn! This month promises to be a time of personal growth, self-improvement, and service to others. With the Sun illuminating your 6th house of health, work, and daily routines, you're being called to focus on your well-being, productivity, and the ways in which you can make a positive impact in the world. The New Moon in Cancer on June 25th activates your 7th house of partnerships and relationships, bringing powerful opportunities for new beginnings, deepening connections, and aligning yourself with people who support your highest good. Trust the process of growth and evolution, and know that you have the discipline, dedication, and integrity to create a life of balance, purpose, and fulfillment.

Love:

In matters of the heart, June 2025 is a month of emotional intimacy, vulnerability, and compromise for you, Capricorn. With Venus, the planet of love and relationships, moving through your 7th house of partnerships, you're being called to focus on the needs, desires, and well-being of your significant other. This is a beautiful time to express your affection, appreciation, and support for your partner, and to find ways to deepen your connection through shared activities, meaningful conversations, and acts of kindness. If you're single, you may find yourself attracted to someone who is emotionally mature, reliable, and committed to personal growth. Trust your intuition, take things slow, and focus on building a strong foundation of friendship, trust, and mutual respect. Remember, true love is a journey of the heart, and it requires patience, presence, and a willingness to meet each other halfway.

Career:

Capricorn, your career sector is in the cosmic spotlight this month, as the Sun and Mercury activate your 6th house of work, service, and daily responsibilities. You may find yourself taking on new projects, learning new skills, or seeking ways to improve your efficiency and productivity in the workplace. This is a great time to focus on the details, organize your schedule, and streamline your processes to ensure maximum success and satisfaction. Just be mindful of any tendencies towards perfectionism, overwork, or self-criticism, as the Mars-Neptune square on June 18th can heighten feelings of confusion, doubt, or overwhelm. Remember to take breaks, prioritize self-care, and ask for help when needed. Trust that your hard work, dedication, and expertise will be recognized and rewarded in divine timing, and that your career path is unfolding in perfect alignment with your soul's purpose.

Finances:

June 2025 is a month of financial planning, budgeting, and practical decision-making for you, Capricorn. With the Sun and Mercury illuminating your 6th house of work and daily routines, you may find yourself focusing on ways to increase your income, reduce your expenses, or invest in your long-term security. This is a great time to review your spending habits, create a realistic budget, and explore opportunities for additional sources of income, such as freelance work, side hustles, or passive investments. The key is to align your financial goals with your personal values and life purpose, and to make choices that support your overall well-being and happiness. Remember, true wealth is not just about accumulating material possessions, but about feeling secure, empowered, and fulfilled in all areas of your life.

Health:

Capricorn, your health and well-being are in the cosmic spotlight this month, as the Sun, Mercury, and Venus activate your 6th house of health, fitness, and daily habits. You're being called to focus on your physical, mental, and emotional well-being, and to make choices that support your vitality, balance, and overall quality of life. This is a great time to start a new exercise routine, try a healthy diet, or engage in activities that bring you joy, relaxation, and stress relief. Just be mindful of any tendencies towards overindulgence, addiction, or escapism, as the Mars-Neptune square on June 18th can heighten feelings of temptation, confusion, or self-sabotage. Remember to listen to your body's wisdom, practice moderation, and seek support when needed. Trust that your commitment to self-care, self-love, and self-improvement will pay off in the long run, and that your health is your greatest wealth.

Travel:

June 2025 may bring some unexpected travel opportunities, Capricorn, particularly related to work, service, or personal growth. With Mars, the planet of action and energy, moving through your 9th house of adventure, higher learning, and spiritual seeking, you may find yourself taking a business trip, attending a conference or workshop, or exploring new ways to expand your mind, broaden your horizons, and deepen your connection with the world around you. This is a great time to step out of your comfort zone, try new things, and seek out experiences that challenge your assumptions, inspire your curiosity, and awaken your sense of wonder. If you're planning a vacation, consider destinations that offer a mix of relaxation, education, and cultural immersion, such as a language immersion program in Spain, a yoga teacher training in India, or a volunteer trip to a developing country. Remember, travel is not just about escaping your everyday life, but about discovering new aspects of yourself, learning from different perspectives, and finding meaning and purpose in the grand adventure of life.

Insights from the Stars:

Capricorn, the celestial energies of June 2025 are inviting you to embrace your inner wisdom, trust your intuition, and align your actions with your highest values and aspirations. With Saturn, your ruling planet, forming a supportive sextile to Uranus on June 4th, you have the opportunity to break free from old patterns, limitations, or fears, and to embrace a new level of innovation, progress, and personal freedom. This is a time to let go of any beliefs, habits, or relationships that no longer serve your growth and evolution, and to open yourself up to the infinite possibilities of the universe. Remember, you are a powerful creator, with the ability to manifest your dreams and desires through your thoughts, words, and actions. Trust that the challenges and opportunities you face are all part of your soul's journey, and that you have the strength, resilience, and wisdom to navigate them with grace and purpose. Have faith in yourself, stay true to your path, and know that you are divinely guided and supported every step of the way.

Best Days of the Month:

June 4th: Saturn sextile Uranus - A powerful day for innovation, progress, and breaking free from limitations or obstacles.

June 11th: Full Moon in Sagittarius - A beautiful time for expansion, exploration, and aligning your actions with your highest truth and wisdom.

June 18th: Jupiter sextile Chiron - A healing and transformative aspect that supports emotional healing, spiritual growth, and the resolution of past wounds or traumas.

June 25th: New Moon in Cancer - A potent portal for new beginnings, fresh starts, and setting intentions related to your relationships, emotional well-being, and inner sense of security.

July 2025

Overview Horoscope for the Month:

Capricorn, July 2025 is a month of personal growth, self-reflection, and inner transformation. With the Sun illuminating your 7th house of partnerships and relationships until July 22nd, you're being called to focus on the balance, harmony, and mutual support in your closest connections. The Full Moon in Capricorn on July 9th brings a powerful opportunity for self-realization, emotional authenticity, and the release of any patterns or beliefs that no longer serve your highest good. Trust the process of growth and evolution, and know that you have the wisdom, integrity, and resilience to create a life of purpose, fulfillment, and deep connection.

Love:

In matters of the heart, July 2025 is a month of emotional intimacy, vulnerability, and compromise for you, Capricorn. With Venus, the planet of love and relationships, moving through your 8th house of deep bonding and transformation, you're being called to explore the shadows, desires, and fears that shape your intimate connections. This is a profound time to have honest conversations with your partner about your needs, boundaries, and expectations, and to find ways to deepen your trust, commitment, and mutual understanding. If you're single, you may find yourself attracted to someone who challenges you to grow, heal, and embrace your authentic self. Trust your intuition, take your time, and focus on building a connection based on shared values, emotional maturity, and a willingness to do the inner work. Remember, true love is a journey of the soul, and it requires courage, compassion, and a commitment to your own personal evolution.

Career:

Capricorn, your career sector is undergoing a powerful transformation this month, as the Full Moon in your sign on July 9th illuminates your 10th house of public image, professional goals, and long-term success. You may find yourself reaching a significant milestone, receiving recognition for your hard work, or facing a critical decision that will shape the direction of your career path. This is a time to trust your inner guidance, stay true to your values, and make choices that align with your authentic purpose and passions. Just be mindful of any tendencies towards workaholism, perfectionism, or self-doubt, as the Sun-Pluto opposition on July 17th can heighten feelings of intensity, pressure, or power struggles. Remember to prioritize self-care, set healthy boundaries, and seek support when needed. Trust that your dedication, expertise, and integrity will be rewarded in divine timing, and that your career is an expression of your soul's unique gifts and talents.

Finances:

July 2025 is a month of financial planning, budgeting, and long-term strategizing for you, Capricorn. With Mercury, the planet of communication and commerce, moving through your 8th house of shared resources and investments, you may find yourself focusing on ways to increase your financial security, pay off debts, or create a more equitable distribution of wealth in your relationships. This is a great time to have honest conversations with your partner or family members about your financial goals, concerns, and expectations, and to explore ways to support each other's economic well-being. Just be mindful of any tendencies towards secrecy, control, or mistrust, as the Mercury-Pluto opposition on July 22nd can heighten feelings of suspicion, jealousy, or manipulation. Remember to practice transparency, fairness, and open communication in all your financial dealings, and to make choices that align with your values and long-term vision. Trust that your resourcefulness, practicality, and wise management will lead to greater abundance, stability, and peace of mind in the long run.

Health:

Capricorn, your health and well-being are in the cosmic spotlight this month, as the planets encourage you to focus on your emotional, psychological, and spiritual healing. With Chiron, the wounded healer, stationing retrograde in your 4th house of home, family, and inner foundations on July 30th, you may find yourself revisiting old wounds, traumas, or family patterns that have shaped your sense of safety, belonging, and self-worth. This is a profound opportunity to seek therapy, counseling, or alternative healing modalities that support your inner child, your emotional resilience, and your ability to create a nurturing and supportive environment for yourself and your loved ones. On a physical level, make sure to prioritize rest, relaxation, and stress management, as the Mars-Uranus square on July 7th can heighten feelings of tension, anxiety, or impulsivity. Remember to listen to your body's wisdom, practice self-compassion, and seek help when needed. Trust that your commitment to your own healing, growth, and self-love will ripple out to create more loving, authentic, and fulfilling relationships in all areas of your life.

Travel:

July 2025 may bring some unexpected travel opportunities, Capricorn, particularly related to personal growth, spiritual seeking, or emotional healing. With the North Node moving through your 9th house of adventure, higher learning, and foreign cultures, you may feel called to embark on a transformative journey, attend a life-changing workshop or retreat, or explore new ways of expanding your mind, heart, and soul. This is a powerful time to step out of your comfort zone, challenge your assumptions and beliefs, and open yourself up to the wisdom and beauty of different perspectives and ways of being. If you're planning a trip, consider destinations that offer a mix of natural wonder, cultural richness, and sacred sites, such as a meditation retreat in the mountains of Tibet, a shamanic journey in the Amazon rainforest, or a pilgrimage to the holy lands of Jerusalem. Remember, travel is not just about escaping your everyday life, but about discovering the depths of your own being, connecting with the greater web of life, and finding your place in the grand mystery of existence.

Insights from the Stars:

Capricorn, the celestial energies of July 2025 are inviting you to embrace your inner authority, trust your soul's wisdom, and align your actions with your deepest values and aspirations. With Saturn, your ruling planet, forming a supportive trine to the North Node on July 21st, you have the opportunity to step into your true power, leadership, and purpose, and to make choices that support your long-term growth, success, and fulfillment. This is a time to let go of any fears, doubts, or limitations that have held you back from claiming your rightful place in the world, and to embrace the unique gifts, talents, and experiences that make you who you are. Remember, you are a wise, capable, and resilient being, with the strength, integrity, and determination to overcome any obstacle and achieve any goal you set your mind to. Trust that the challenges and opportunities you face are all part of your soul's journey, and that you have the courage, grace, and support to navigate them with wisdom, compassion, and purpose. Have faith in yourself, stay true to your path, and know that you are a vital part of the greater tapestry of life, weaving your thread of love, light, and service into the world.

Best Days of the Month:

July 9th: Full Moon in Capricorn - A powerful day for self-realization, emotional authenticity, and releasing what no longer serves your highest good.

July 21st: Saturn trine North Node - A supportive aspect for stepping into your true power, leadership, and purpose, and making choices that align with your long-term growth and success.

July 23rd: Sun enters Leo - A time of creative self-expression, heart-centered living, and joyful celebration of your unique gifts and talents.

July 28th: Venus enters Virgo - A beautiful opportunity for practical acts of love and service, and for bringing more order, beauty, and efficiency to your relationships and daily life.

August 2025

Overview Horoscope for the Month:

Welcome to August 2025, Capricorn! This month promises to be a time of deep transformation, emotional healing, and spiritual growth. With the Sun illuminating your 8th house of intimacy, shared resources, and psychological depths, you're being called to confront your shadows, fears, and desires, and to embrace the power of vulnerability, trust, and surrender. The New Moon in Leo on July 24th and the Full Moon in Aquarius on August 9th bring powerful opportunities for letting go of old patterns, beliefs, and attachments, and for birthing a new version of yourself that is more authentic, compassionate, and aligned with your soul's purpose. Trust the process of death and rebirth, and know that you have the strength, courage, and resilience to navigate any challenges or changes that may arise.

Love:

In matters of the heart, August 2025 is a month of deep emotional connection, passionate intensity, and transformative healing for you, Capricorn. With Venus, the planet of love and relationships, moving through your 8th and 9th houses this month, you're being called to explore the depths of your desires, fears, and attachments, and to open yourself up to new ways of giving and receiving love. This is a powerful time to have honest conversations with your partner about your needs, boundaries, and expectations, and to find ways to deepen your intimacy, trust, and mutual understanding. If you're single, you may find yourself attracted to someone who challenges you to grow, heal, and embrace your authentic self. Trust your intuition, take your time, and focus on building a connection based on shared values, emotional maturity, and a willingness to do the inner work. Remember, true love is a journey of the soul, and it requires courage, compassion, and a commitment to your own personal evolution.

Career:

Capricorn, your career sector is undergoing a powerful transformation this month, as Mars and Venus join forces in your 8th house of shared resources, power dynamics, and deep psychological shifts. You may find yourself confronting old fears, doubts, or limitations that have held you back from fully expressing your talents, skills, and leadership potential. This is a time to trust your inner guidance, stay true to your values, and make bold moves that align with your authentic purpose and passions. Just be mindful of any tendencies towards control, manipulation, or self-sabotage, as the Mars-Venus conjunction can heighten feelings of intensity, desire, and competition. Remember to practice self-care, set healthy boundaries, and seek support when needed. Trust that your hard work, dedication, and integrity will be rewarded in divine timing, and that your career is an expression of your soul's unique gifts and purpose.

Finances:

August 2025 is a month of deep financial transformation, metaphorical death and rebirth, and the unleashing of your true abundance and prosperity, Capricorn. With the Sun, Mercury, and Venus activating your 8th house of shared resources, investments, and psychological blocks around money, you're being called to confront any fears, limiting beliefs, or unhealthy patterns that have prevented you from fully owning your worth and receiving the financial flow you deserve. This is a powerful time to do some deep inner work around your relationship with money, to release any guilt, shame, or scarcity mentality, and to embrace a new paradigm of sufficiency, gratitude, and generosity. You may also find yourself dealing with themes of inheritance, taxes, debts, or joint finances this month, which can bring up intense emotions or power struggles. Remember to practice clear communication, fair negotiation, and emotional maturity in all your financial dealings, and to make choices that align with your values and long-term vision. Trust that as you heal your relationship with money, you open yourself up to new streams of abundance, prosperity, and fulfillment.

Health:

Capricorn, your health and well-being are undergoing a deep transformation this month, as the planets encourage you to release old toxins, patterns, and limitations, and to embrace a new level of vitality, resilience, and wholeness. With the Sun, Mercury, and Venus activating your 8th house of deep healing, regeneration, and metamorphosis, you're being called to confront any physical, emotional, or spiritual imbalances that have been holding you back from optimal health and happiness. This is a powerful time to seek out alternative or holistic healing modalities, such as acupuncture, energy work, or psychotherapy, and to explore the mind-body-soul connection in your wellness journey. You may also find yourself dealing with themes of addiction, obsession, or compulsion this month, which can be challenging but also transformative. Remember to practice self-compassion, seek support when needed, and trust in your body's innate wisdom and resilience. As you release what no longer serves you, you create space for new levels of vitality, joy, and aliveness to emerge.

Travel:

August 2025 may bring some intense but transformative travel experiences for you, Capricorn, particularly related to deep healing, spiritual awakening, or emotional catharsis. With Mars and Venus joining forces in your 8th house of death, rebirth, and metamorphosis, you may feel called to embark on a journey that challenges you to confront your fears, shadows, and limiting beliefs, and to embrace a new level of courage, authenticity, and freedom. This could be a powerful time to attend a transformational workshop or retreat, to explore sacred sites or natural wonders that hold deep meaning for you, or to embark on a solo journey of self-discovery and soul-searching. Just be mindful of any tendencies towards recklessness, impulsivity, or escapism, as the Mars-Venus conjunction can heighten feelings of intensity, desire, and restlessness. Remember to practice self-care, set clear intentions, and trust in the journey, even if it feels uncomfortable or uncertain at times. Trust that every experience, whether challenging or blissful, is an opportunity for growth, healing, and awakening.

Insights from the Stars:

Capricorn, the celestial energies of August 2025 are inviting you to embrace the power of surrender, trust, and transformation. With the Sun, Mercury, and Venus activating your 8th house of death, rebirth, and deep psychological shifts, you're being called to let go of any old identities, patterns, or attachments that no longer serve your highest good, and to allow yourself to be transformed by the fires of change and growth. This is a time to trust in the intelligence of the universe, to surrender to the flow of life, and to have faith that every ending is also a new beginning. Remember that you are a resilient, powerful, and eternal being, with the strength, wisdom, and courage to navigate any challenges or transitions that may arise. Trust in your soul's journey, stay open to the mysteries and miracles of existence, and know that you are always guided, protected, and loved by the divine forces of the cosmos.

Best Days of the Month:

August 9th: Full Moon in Aquarius - A powerful day for releasing old patterns, beliefs, and limitations, and for embracing a new level of freedom, innovation, and authenticity.

August 11th: Mercury stations direct - A time for clarity, insight, and forward momentum, particularly related to communication, learning, and self-expression.

August 18th: Mars and Venus conjunct in Leo - A passionate, creative, and transformative aspect that heightens desire, courage, and self-expression, but also requires emotional maturity and healthy boundaries.

August 30th: Jupiter biquintile Pluto - A rare and powerful aspect that supports deep psychological healing, spiritual transformation, and the emergence of new levels of wisdom, power, and purpose..

September 2025

Overview Horoscope for the Month:

Capricorn, September 2025 is a month of expansion, growth, and new horizons. With the Sun illuminating your 9th house of adventure, higher learning, and spiritual seeking, you're being called to broaden your mind, explore new frontiers, and align your actions with your deepest truth and highest purpose. The New Moon in Virgo on September 21st brings a powerful opportunity to set intentions related to travel, education, publishing, or entrepreneurship, while the Full Moon in Pisces on September 7th invites you to release any fears, illusions, or limiting beliefs that have held you back from fully embodying your wisdom, faith, and creativity. Trust the journey of growth and evolution, and know that you have the vision, resilience, and determination to create a life of meaning, purpose, and endless possibility.

Love:

In matters of the heart, September 2025 is a month of adventure, romance, and spiritual connection for you, Capricorn. With Venus, the planet of love and relationships, moving through your 9th and 10th houses this month, you're being called to expand your horizons, explore new dimensions of love and intimacy, and align your partnerships with your highest values and aspirations. If you're single, you may find yourself attracted to someone who shares your love of learning, travel, or personal growth, and who inspires you to be your best self. Be open to long-distance connections, cross-cultural romances, or unconventional arrangements that challenge your assumptions and beliefs about love. If you're in a committed relationship, this is a beautiful time to plan a romantic getaway, take a class or workshop together, or explore new ways of deepening your emotional, intellectual, and spiritual bond. Remember, true love is an adventure of the heart, mind, and soul, and it requires courage, curiosity, and a willingness to step outside your comfort zone.

Career:

Capricorn, your career sector is on fire this month, as Mars enters your 10th house of public image, professional goals, and long-term success on September 22nd. You're feeling ambitious, driven, and ready to take bold action towards your dreams and aspirations. This is a powerful time to put yourself out there, showcase your talents and skills, and make moves that align with your authentic purpose and leadership potential. Just be mindful of any tendencies towards aggression, competitiveness, or burnout, as Mars can sometimes bring up feelings of anger, frustration, or impatience. Remember to practice self-care, collaborate with others, and balance your hard work with rest and play. Trust that your dedication, expertise, and integrity will be recognized and rewarded in divine timing, and that your career is a vehicle for expressing your unique gifts and making a positive impact in the world.

Finances:

September 2025 is a month of financial growth, expansion, and opportunity for you, Capricorn. With Jupiter, the planet of abundance and prosperity, moving through your 8th house of shared resources, investments, and deep psychological shifts, you're being called to embrace a new level of financial flow, collaboration, and empowerment. This is a powerful time to explore new streams of income, negotiate better deals or contracts, or invest in ventures that align with your values and long-term vision. You may also find yourself dealing with themes of inheritance, taxes, debts, or joint finances this month, which can bring up intense emotions or power dynamics. Remember to practice clear communication, fair negotiation, and emotional maturity in all your financial dealings, and to make choices that support your overall well-being and happiness. Trust that as you heal your relationship with money and embrace a mindset of abundance, you open yourself up to new levels of prosperity, fulfillment, and joy.

Health:

Capricorn, your health and well-being are in a state of expansion, growth, and vitality this month, as the planets encourage you to embrace a more holistic, adventurous, and spiritually aligned approach to wellness. With the Sun, Mercury, and Venus activating your 9th house of higher learning, travel, and personal growth, you're being called to explore new philosophies, practices, and experiences that support your physical, emotional, and spiritual health. This is a great time to try a new yoga or meditation class, experiment with international cuisines or healing modalities, or embark on a wellness retreat or pilgrimage that nourishes your body, mind, and soul. You may also find yourself drawn to studies or teachings that expand your understanding of health, healing, and the nature of reality. Remember to approach your wellness journey with a sense of curiosity, open-mindedness, and self-compassion, and to trust in the innate wisdom and intelligence of your body. As you align your lifestyle with your deepest values and highest truth, you create a foundation of vitality, resilience, and radiance that will serve you for years to come.

Travel:

September 2025 is a month of exciting travel opportunities and adventures for you, Capricorn, as the celestial energies align to support your exploration of new horizons, cultures, and ways of being. With the Sun, Mercury, and Venus illuminating your 9th house of foreign lands, higher education, and spiritual seeking, you may find yourself called to embark on a transformative journey that expands your mind, opens your heart, and enriches your soul. This could be a great time to plan a study abroad program, a volunteer trip, or a pilgrimage to a sacred site that holds deep meaning for you. You may also be drawn to travel experiences that challenge your assumptions, beliefs, and comfort zones, such as a wilderness adventure, a cultural immersion, or a spiritual retreat. Whatever form your travels take, approach them with a sense of curiosity, humility, and openness to the unknown. Trust that every encounter, whether challenging or blissful, is an opportunity for growth, learning, and self-discovery. As you explore the world around you, you also explore the depths of your own being, and discover new dimensions of your potential, purpose, and place in the greater web of life.

Insights from the Stars:

Capricorn, the celestial energies of September 2025 are inviting you to embrace the power of faith, wisdom, and alignment with your highest truth. With Jupiter, the planet of expansion and growth, moving through your 8th house of deep transformation and regeneration, you're being called to let go of any old beliefs, patterns, or limitations that have kept you from fully embodying your authentic self and living your soul's purpose. This is a time to trust in the intelligence of the universe, to surrender to the flow of life, and to have faith that every experience, whether challenging or blissful, is guiding you towards your highest good and greatest evolution. Remember that you are a wise, powerful, and eternal being, with access to infinite resources, guidance, and support from the divine realms. Trust in your own inner knowing, stay open to the signs and synchronicities of the universe, and know that you are always being led towards your deepest fulfillment and most radiant expression of your true self.

Best Days of the Month:

September 3rd: Jupiter trine North Node - A powerful aspect that supports spiritual growth, karmic healing, and alignment with your soul's purpose and path.

September 7th: Full Moon in Pisces - A mystical and emotionally charged lunation that invites deep release, surrender, and connection with the divine realms.

September 21st: New Moon in Virgo - A potent portal for setting intentions, refining your skills and routines, and aligning your actions with your highest values and goals.

September 22nd: Mars enters Capricorn - A dynamic and ambitious transit that empowers you to take bold action, assert your leadership, and make strides towards your long-term aspirations.

October 2025

Overview Horoscope for the Month:

Welcome to October 2025, Capricorn! This month promises to be a time of career advancement, public recognition, and personal transformation. With the Sun illuminating your 10th house of professional goals, ambition, and status until October 22nd, you're being called to step into your power, claim your authority, and make bold moves towards your long-term aspirations. The New Moon in Libra on October 21st brings a powerful opportunity to set intentions related to your career, reputation, and leadership potential, while the Full Moon in Aries on October 6th invites you to release any fears, doubts, or self-limiting beliefs that have held you back from fully expressing your unique talents and gifts. Trust the process of growth and evolution, and know that you have the strength, resilience, and determination to achieve your highest goals and make a positive impact in the world.

Love:

In matters of the heart, October 2025 is a month of depth, intensity, and transformation for you, Capricorn. With Venus, the planet of love and relationships, moving through your 10th and 11th houses this month, you're being called to align your partnerships with your deepest values, aspirations, and sense of purpose. If you're in a committed relationship, this is a powerful time to have honest conversations with your partner about your shared goals, dreams, and visions for the future. You may find yourselves working together on a project or cause that is meaningful to you both, or exploring new ways of supporting each other's growth and success. If you're single, you may find yourself attracted to someone who shares your ambition, integrity, and commitment to making a difference in the world. Be open to connections that challenge you to step into your power, express your authenticity, and embrace your unique path and purpose. Remember, true love is a sacred bond that empowers you to be your best self and make a positive impact in the world.

Career:

Capricorn, your career sector is on fire this month, as the Sun, Mercury, and Venus activate your 10th house of professional goals, public image, and long-term success. You're feeling focused, driven, and ready to take your work and leadership to the next level. This is a powerful time to put yourself out there, showcase your talents and accomplishments, and make bold moves towards your dreams and aspirations. You may find yourself in the spotlight, receiving recognition or rewards for your hard work and dedication, or being offered new opportunities or promotions that align with your long-term vision. Just be mindful of any tendencies towards workaholism, perfectionism, or self-doubt, as the Full Moon in Aries on October 6th can bring up fears or insecurities related to your worth and value. Remember to practice self-care, set healthy boundaries, and surround yourself with supportive people who believe in you and your potential. Trust that your passion, expertise, and commitment to excellence will take you far, and that your career is a vehicle for expressing your unique gifts and making a positive impact in the world.

Finances:

October 2025 is a month of financial growth, expansion, and opportunity for you, Capricorn. With Jupiter, the planet of abundance and prosperity, moving through your 9th house of higher learning, travel, and entrepreneurship, you're being called to explore new ways of generating income, building wealth, and aligning your resources with your values and vision. This is a powerful time to invest in your education, skills, or personal development, or to consider starting your own business or venture that allows you to share your knowledge and expertise with others. You may also find yourself attracted to financial opportunities or investments that have a global or philanthropic dimension, such as socially responsible funds, international trade, or eco-friendly enterprises. Remember to approach your financial decisions with a sense of integrity, wisdom, and long-term vision, and to trust your intuition and inner guidance when it comes to money matters. As you align your resources with your deepest values and highest aspirations, you create a foundation of abundance, prosperity, and purpose that will serve you for years to come.

Health:

Capricorn, your health and well-being are in a state of balance, vitality, and resilience this month, as the planets support your efforts to prioritize self-care, mindfulness, and holistic wellness. With Mars, the planet of energy and action, moving through your 12th house of rest, retreat, and spiritual healing, you're being called to slow down, turn inward, and listen to the wisdom of your body and soul. This is a powerful time to engage in practices that promote relaxation, stress relief, and inner peace, such as meditation, yoga, or nature walks. You may also find yourself drawn to alternative or complementary healing modalities that address the root causes of any physical or emotional imbalances, such as acupuncture, energy work, or herbal medicine. Remember to approach your health journey with a sense of compassion, patience, and trust in the innate intelligence of your body. As you honor your needs for rest, nourishment, and self-love, you create a foundation of vitality, harmony, and radiance that will support you in all areas of your life.

Travel:

October 2025 may bring some exciting travel opportunities and adventures related to your career, education, or personal growth, Capricorn. With Jupiter, the planet of expansion and exploration, moving through your 9th house of foreign lands, higher learning, and spiritual seeking, you may find yourself called to embark on a journey that broadens your mind, opens your heart, and expands your horizons. This could be a great time to attend a conference or workshop in your field, to study abroad or pursue an advanced degree, or to take a sabbatical or career break that allows you to explore new cultures, ideas, and ways of being. You may also be drawn to travel experiences that have a purpose or mission beyond mere pleasure or escape, such as a volunteer trip, a cultural exchange, or a pilgrimage to a sacred site. Whatever form your travels take, approach them with a sense of curiosity, openness, and willingness to learn and grow. Trust that every encounter, whether challenging or inspiring, is an opportunity for self-discovery, transformation, and alignment with your highest path and purpose.

Insights from the Stars:

Capricorn, the celestial energies of October 2025 are inviting you to embrace your power, purpose, and potential as a leader, change-maker, and visionary. With Saturn, your ruling planet, forming a supportive trine to the North Node in Aries on October 21st, you're being called to step into your authority, claim your destiny, and make bold moves towards your long-term goals and aspirations. This is a time to trust in your inner guidance, to align your actions with your deepest values and highest truth, and to have faith in the unfolding of your unique path and purpose. Remember that you are a wise, capable, and resilient being, with the strength, integrity, and determination to overcome any challenge and achieve any dream. Trust in the journey of your soul, stay open to the lessons and opportunities of each moment, and know that you are always being guided and supported by the loving intelligence of the universe.

Best Days of the Month:

October 6th: Full Moon in Aries - A powerful lunation that invites you to release fears, doubts, and self-limiting beliefs, and to embrace your courage, confidence, and authentic self-expression.

October 16th: Mercury enters Scorpio - A deep and transformative transit that supports honest communication, psychological insight, and the unveiling of hidden truths and desires.

October 21st: New Moon in Libra - A potent portal for setting intentions related to your career, reputation, and leadership potential, and for aligning your goals with your values and vision.

October 21st: Saturn trine North Node - A supportive aspect that empowers you to claim your authority, align with your destiny, and make bold moves towards your long-term aspirations and purpose.

November 2025

Overview Horoscope for the Month:

Capricorn, November 2025 is a month of social connection, humanitarian pursuits, and personal liberation. With the Sun illuminating your 11th house of friendships, community, and hopes and dreams, you're being called to expand your network, collaborate with like-minded individuals, and work towards a vision of a better world. The New Moon in Scorpio on November 20th brings a powerful opportunity to set intentions related to your social life, group activities, and collective endeavors, while the Full Moon in Taurus on November 5th invites you to release any attachments, possessions, or values that no longer serve your highest good. Trust the process of growth and evolution, and know that you have the wisdom, compassion, and innovative spirit to create positive change in your life and in the world.

Love:

In matters of the heart, November 2025 is a month of unconventional romance, emotional freedom, and authentic connection for you, Capricorn. With Venus, the planet of love and relationships, moving through your 11th and 12th houses this month, you're being called to embrace a more liberated, unconditional, and spiritual approach to love and intimacy. If you're in a committed relationship, this is a powerful time to break free from any patterns, roles, or expectations that have limited your growth and happiness as a couple. You may find yourselves exploring new ways of relating, communicating, and supporting each other's individuality and independence. If you're single, you may find yourself attracted to someone who is unique, progressive, and emotionally mature, and who shares your vision of a more just, compassionate, and awakened world. Be open to connections that challenge you to expand your mind, open your heart, and embrace your authentic self. Remember, true love is a sacred journey of two souls walking together, supporting each other's freedom, growth, and highest potential.

Career:

Capricorn, your career sector is undergoing a powerful transformation this month, as the planetary energies support your efforts to align your work with your deepest values, passions, and sense of purpose. With Mars, the planet of action and ambition, moving through your 12th house of spirituality, surrender, and inner wisdom, you're being called to let go of any goals, projects, or commitments that no longer resonate with your soul's calling. This is a time to trust your intuition, listen to your inner guidance, and make space for new opportunities and directions that feel more authentic and fulfilling. You may find yourself drawn to careers or ventures that have a humanitarian, creative, or spiritual dimension, such as social activism, the arts, or holistic healing. Remember to approach your professional path with a sense of detachment, flexibility, and openness to change, and to trust that the universe is guiding you towards your highest potential and purpose.

Finances:

November 2025 is a month of financial collaboration, innovation, and social responsibility for you, Capricorn. With Jupiter, the planet of abundance and expansion, moving through your 10th house of career and public reputation, you're being called to align your financial goals with your values, integrity, and desire to make a positive impact in the world. This is a powerful time to explore new income streams, partnerships, or investments that support your long-term vision and contribute to the greater good. You may find yourself attracted to socially conscious businesses, ethical investing, or philanthropic endeavors that allow you to use your resources to create positive change. Remember to approach your financial decisions with a sense of discernment, wisdom, and generosity, and to trust that the more you give, the more you receive. As you align your wealth with your highest purpose and values, you create a foundation of prosperity, fulfillment, and social impact that will benefit you and others for years to come.

Health:

Capricorn, your health and well-being are in a state of renewal, rejuvenation, and spiritual alignment this month, as the planets support your efforts to prioritize self-care, inner peace, and holistic healing. With the Sun and Mercury activating your 11th house of social connection and community, you may find yourself drawn to group activities, classes, or events that promote physical, emotional, and mental well-being, such as yoga retreats, meditation circles, or wellness workshops. You may also feel inspired to join or create a support group or community that shares your health goals and values, and that provides a sense of belonging, accountability, and motivation. Remember to approach your wellness journey with a sense of curiosity, experimentation, and self-compassion, and to listen to the unique needs and rhythms of your body, mind, and soul. As you nurture your own health and happiness, you become a beacon of inspiration and healing for others, and contribute to the collective well-being of your community and the world.

Travel:

November 2025 may bring some unexpected travel opportunities and adventures related to your social life, community involvement, or humanitarian pursuits, Capricorn. With Uranus, the planet of change and innovation, moving through your 5th house of creativity, self-expression, and adventure, you may find yourself called to embark on a journey that awakens your sense of wonder, joy, and spontaneity. This could be a great time to take a trip with friends or like-minded individuals, to attend a festival or conference that celebrates your passions and values, or to explore a destination that is known for its progressive culture, artistic scene, or natural beauty. You may also be drawn to travel experiences that have a social or environmental impact, such as a volunteer vacation, an eco-tour, or a cultural exchange program. Whatever form your travels take, approach them with a sense of openness, flexibility, and willingness to step outside your comfort zone. Trust that every encounter, whether planned or serendipitous, is an opportunity for growth, connection, and alignment with your highest path and purpose.

Insights from the Stars:

Capricorn, the celestial energies of November 2025 are inviting you to embrace your role as a visionary, change-maker, and leader in creating a more just, compassionate, and awakened world. With Pluto, the planet of power and transformation, stationed direct in your 2nd house of values, resources, and self-worth on October 13th, you're being called to align your personal desires and ambitions with your soul's deepest truth and purpose.

This is a time to let go of any fears, limitations, or attachments that have kept you from fully embodying your authentic power and potential, and to trust in the unfolding of your unique path and destiny. Remember that you are a wise, courageous, and resilient being, with the strength, integrity, and determination to overcome any obstacle and create positive change in your life and in the world. Trust in the journey of your soul, stay open to the lessons and opportunities of each moment, and know that you are always being guided and supported by the loving intelligence of the universe.

Best Days of the Month:

November 5th: Full Moon in Taurus - A powerful lunation that invites you to release attachments, possessions, and values that no longer serve your highest good, and to embrace a more liberated, authentic, and abundant way of being.

November 7th: Uranus sextile Neptune - A rare and transformative aspect that supports spiritual awakening, creative inspiration, and the dissolution of old patterns and beliefs that have limited your growth and happiness.

November 20th: New Moon in Scorpio - A potent portal for setting intentions related to your social life, group activities, and humanitarian pursuits, and for aligning your actions with your deepest values and highest vision.

November 27th: Saturn semi-sextile Chiron - A healing and empowering aspect that supports the integration of past wounds, the development of inner wisdom, and the alignment of your personal goals with your soul's purpose and path.

December 2025

Overview Horoscope for the Month:

Welcome to December 2025, Capricorn! This month promises to be a time of spiritual growth, inner reflection, and emotional healing. With the Sun illuminating your 12th house of solitude, surrender, and divine connection, you're being called to slow down, turn inward, and listen to the whispers of your soul. The New Moon in Sagittarius on December 19th brings a powerful opportunity to set intentions related to your spiritual practice, creative expression, and inner peace, while the Full Moon in Gemini on December 4th invites you to release any thoughts, beliefs, or communication patterns that no longer serve your highest good. Trust the process of letting go, and know that you have the wisdom, compassion, and faith to navigate any challenges or uncertainties that may arise.

Love:

In matters of the heart, December 2025 is a month of emotional depth, spiritual intimacy, and unconditional love for you, Capricorn. With Venus, the planet of love and relationships, moving through your 12th house of divine connection and universal love, you're being called to embrace a more compassionate, forgiving, and transcendent approach to your romantic life. If you're in a committed relationship, this is a powerful time to release any grudges, resentments, or expectations that have limited your ability to love and be loved fully. You may find yourselves exploring new ways of communicating, connecting, and supporting each other's spiritual growth and emotional healing. If you're single, you may find yourself attracted to someone who is kind, empathetic, and spiritually awake, and who shares your desire for a love that is pure, unconditional, and divinely guided. Be open to connections that challenge you to open your heart, forgive your past, and trust in the power of love to heal and transform. Remember, true love is a sacred gift from the universe, and it requires surrender, grace, and a willingness to love without conditions or expectations.

Career:

Capricorn, your career sector is undergoing a powerful transformation this month, as the planetary energies support your efforts to align your work with your soul's deepest calling and purpose. With Mars, the planet of action and ambition, moving through your 1st house of self and identity, you're being called to take bold steps towards your personal goals and aspirations, and to assert your unique talents, skills, and leadership potential. This is a time to trust your instincts, follow your passions, and make career choices that feel authentic, fulfilling, and aligned with your highest values and vision. You may find yourself drawn to careers or projects that have a creative, spiritual, or humanitarian dimension, such as the arts, philanthropy, or personal development. Remember to approach your professional path with a sense of courage, integrity, and self-belief, and to trust that the universe is guiding you towards your true purpose and potential.

Finances:

December 2025 is a month of financial healing, surrender, and divine providence for you, Capricorn. With the Sun and Mercury activating your 12th house of spirituality, letting go, and higher power, you're being called to release any fears, anxieties, or limiting beliefs around money and abundance, and to trust in the infinite supply and support of the universe. This is a powerful time to practice gratitude, generosity, and faith in the face of any financial challenges or uncertainties, and to believe that all your needs and desires will be met in perfect timing and divine order. You may find yourself attracted to philanthropic causes, charitable giving, or tithing as a way of aligning your resources with your spiritual values and beliefs. Remember to approach your financial life with a sense of surrender, trust, and inner peace, and to know that true wealth comes from within, and is measured by the love, joy, and fulfillment you experience in your life.

Health:

Capricorn, your health and well-being are in a state of healing, renewal, and spiritual alignment this month, as the planets support your efforts to prioritize self-care, emotional release, and inner peace. With Chiron, the wounded healer, stationed direct in your 4th house of home, family, and emotional foundations on December 30th, you're being called to address any past traumas, family patterns, or emotional wounds that have impacted your sense of safety, belonging, and self-worth. This is a powerful time to seek therapy, counseling, or alternative healing modalities that support your emotional and psychological well-being, and to create a nurturing and supportive environment for your mind, body, and soul. You may also find yourself drawn to practices that promote relaxation, stress relief, and inner calm, such as meditation, prayer, or spending time in nature. Remember to approach your healing journey with a sense of patience, self-compassion, and trust in the wisdom of your body and soul, and to know that you are always loved, supported, and guided by the universe.

Travel:

December 2025 may bring some profound travel experiences and opportunities related to your spiritual growth, creative expression, or emotional healing, Capricorn. With Neptune, the planet of imagination, inspiration, and divine connection, moving through your 3rd house of communication, learning, and short trips, you may find yourself called to embark on a journey that expands your mind, opens your heart, and awakens your sense of wonder and creativity. This could be a great time to attend a spiritual retreat, creative workshop, or healing seminar in a beautiful and inspiring location, or to take a short trip to a place that holds special meaning or significance for you. You may also be drawn to travel experiences that involve poetry, music, art, or other forms of creative expression, as a way of tapping into your inner muse and connecting with the divine. Whatever form your travels take, approach them with a sense of openness, surrender, and trust in the journey, and know that every experience is an opportunity for growth, healing, and alignment with your highest path and purpose.

Insights from the Stars:

Capricorn, the celestial energies of December 2025 are inviting you to embrace the power of surrender, faith, and divine connection. With Jupiter, the planet of expansion, wisdom, and higher truth, moving through your 12th house of spirituality, transcendence, and letting go, you're being called to release any attachments, expectations, or fears that have kept you from fully trusting in the wisdom and guidance of the universe. This is a time to deepen your spiritual practice, connect with your inner wisdom, and allow yourself to be guided by the loving intelligence of the cosmos. Remember that you are a divine being of light and love, with access to infinite grace, support, and protection from the unseen realms. Trust in the journey of your soul, stay open to the signs and synchronicities of the universe, and know that you are always being led towards your highest good and greatest purpose.

Best Days of the Month:

December 4th: Full Moon in Gemini - A powerful lunation that invites you to release any thoughts, beliefs, or communication patterns that no longer serve your highest good, and to embrace a more authentic, clear, and compassionate way of expressing yourself.

December 10th: Neptune Direct - A subtle but profound shift that supports spiritual awakening, creative inspiration, and the dissolving of illusions and limiting beliefs.

December 19th: New Moon in Sagittarius - A potent portal for setting intentions related to your spiritual growth, creative expression, and inner peace, and for aligning your actions with your deepest truth and highest wisdom.

December 30th: Chiron Direct - A healing and empowering shift that supports the integration of past wounds, the development of inner wisdom, and the alignment of your personal goals with your soul's purpose and path..

AQUARIUS 2025 HOROSCOPE

Overview Aquarius 2025

(January 20 - February 18)

Dear Aquarius, 2025 is shaping up to be a year of significant growth, change and opportunity for you. The celestial bodies are aligning in powerful ways that will encourage you to expand your horizons, question the status quo, and make your unique mark on the world. Let's dive into the key astrological influences that will be shaping your journey this year.

The year kicks off with Saturn, the planet of discipline and responsibility, moving into fiery Aries in late May. Saturn's transit through Aries will light a motivational fire within you to take charge of your life and boldly pursue your ambitions. You'll be called to step up, believe in yourself, and put in the hard work needed to manifest your goals and dreams. Challenges that arise will ultimately make you stronger and wiser.

Your modern ruler Uranus continues its long journey through steadfast Taurus for most of the year, shaking up your perspectives on finances, material security and self-worth. Uranus pushes you to break free from limiting beliefs and embrace your quirky, inventive side even when it comes to typically traditional areas like money and possessions. Sudden changes, windfalls or revelations could arise that overturn the status quo. Remain flexible and open to new, unconventional ways of creating stability.

In July, Uranus makes a brief foray into versatile Gemini before retrograding back into Taurus in November. During this window, your mind will be lit up with groundbreaking ideas and you'll be eager to learn, share knowledge, and engage with a diversity of people and perspectives. Information and communication could take some wild, unexpected turns. This is an exciting time to open your mind, think outside the box, and let your thoughts roam free. Writing, teaching, media projects and networking are favored.

All year, transformational Pluto continues to move through your sign of Aquarius, an on-and-off transit that lasts until 2043. In 2025, you'll be feeling Pluto's intensity as it pushes you to radically transform yourself from the inside out and step fully into your power. The old you is shedding away and a more authentic, soulful self is emerging. Embrace the metamorphosis, even if it feels uncomfortable at times. By claiming the parts of yourself you used to hide, you can inspire others to do the same and create meaningful change in the world.

Mark your calendar for March 14, August 28 and September 7, when Saturn and Neptune join up in imaginative, compassionate Pisces. Your practical and intuitive sides merge, enabling you to apply your Aquarian humanitarianism in grounded, tangible ways to support others. Your spiritual beliefs may undergo a restructuring and you could feel called to join a higher cause. Creative projects that have been incubating in your mind can now take form in the real world. Leading with love and weaving more magic into your daily life will be especially fulfilling.

Jupiter, the planet of luck and expansion, moves into caring Cancer on June 9, bringing blessings and abundance to your work life and encouraging a more emotionally fulfilling approach to your daily responsibilities and routines. Your nurturing instincts are heightened and you may feel called to adopt a healthier lifestyle or be of service to family and loved ones. This is a wonderful time to live and work in alignment with what feels most nourishing to your heart and soul. Let your feelings be your guide.

Love and relationships are due for some exciting changes starting August 25, when Venus moves into bold, passionate Leo for an extended four-month stay. If you're single, you could meet someone who rocks your world and isn't afraid to adore you openly. Existing partnerships will be infused with fresh energy, creativity and playfulness. You'll be feeling more outgoing, inspired and willing to take risks in matters of the heart. Expect the unexpected in romance and prepare for thrilling new adventures with your beloved.

Taskmaster Saturn shifts into Pisces on September 1, bringing more structure and discipline to your spiritual life, imagination, and desire to be of service over the next two years. You could dedicate yourself to a philanthropic mission, health-related field or an artistic pursuit that uplifts the soul. Your enhanced empathy and sensitivity means you may need to set better emotional boundaries with others. Developing a regular mindfulness practice can be very grounding and enlightening now.

The Super Full Moon in Aquarius on August 13 is your astrological New Year, a potent time for intention-setting and tapping into your deepest desires for personal and collective change. La Luna will be forming helpful trines to Mars and Jupiter, making this an extra fortuitous lunation for going after your dreams with courage and expanding your social reach for the greater good of all. Your popularity could skyrocket and exciting opportunities may arise, especially related to group projects, humanitarian causes and technology.

Mercury's retrograde through Scorpio from October 22 to November 18 provides an opportunity to go within, reflect on your inner journey, and integrate all the spiritual and emotional growth you've experienced this year. Meditation, therapy and keeping a journal can facilitate powerful healing and inner transformation. You may need to withdraw from superficial interactions to focus on what's really meaningful. Issues from the past could resurface for resolution. Honesty and vulnerability will set you free.

As the year winds down, a magical Total Solar Eclipse in Sagittarius on December 5 sets the stage for visionary ideas, broadened horizons, and wild leaps of faith in 2026. You're being cosmically called to share your brilliance on a grander scale and take a stand for truth and justice. Believe in your most revolutionary ideas and trust that you have the power to create a better world for the collective. It's time to set your inner rebel free!

Throughout 2025, your Aquarius soul is being activated to step more fully into your authentic self and share your innovative vision to uplift humanity. You're not here to fit in or maintain the status quo, but to shake up old paradigms and bring more freedom to all. Let your freak flag fly and boldly march to the beat of your own drum. The more you embrace your beautiful weirdness, the more you give others permission to do the same. You're the change-maker the world needs now.

It's a year to expect the unexpected, as Uranus and Pluto keep you on your toes and push you to transform from the inside out. Stay flexible, open-minded and willing to question everything. You're breaking new ground, within and without.

Your steadfast humanitarian spirit is needed more than ever to help steer the collective in a more enlightened direction. Continue using technology in ingenious ways to educate the masses and fight for the causes close to your heart. You have the power to revolutionize outdated systems and materialize a more utopian future for all beings. Dream big and be the change!

You've got this, Aquarius. Here's to a wild, transformative, liberating year ahead. May you fly your Aquarian freak flag high and shake up the world in the best possible ways. Stay weird, my friend!.

January 2025

Overview Horoscope for the Month:

Aquarius, January 2025 is a month of profound self-discovery, personal growth, and new beginnings. The month starts with a powerful conjunction between Venus and Pluto in your sign on the 2nd, intensifying your desire for deep, meaningful connections and personal transformation. This alignment encourages you to let go of old patterns and embrace your authentic self. The Full Moon in Cancer on the 13th illuminates your 6th house of daily routines, work, and health, prompting you to find a better balance between your responsibilities and self-care. The New Moon in your sign on the 29th marks a significant new chapter in your personal journey, urging you to set intentions that align with your deepest desires and aspirations. With Mercury entering your sign on the 27th, followed by the Sun on the 29th, you'll feel a surge of mental clarity and vitality, empowering you to communicate your ideas with confidence and take bold action towards your goals.

Love:

In matters of the heart, January 2025 brings intense and transformative energy for Aquarius. The Venus-Pluto conjunction in your sign on the 2nd sets the stage for profound emotional connections and soul-level bonding. This is a time to be vulnerable, authentic, and open to deep intimacy with your loved ones. If single, you may find yourself attracted to someone who challenges you to grow and evolve. The Full Moon in Cancer on the 13th highlights the need for nurturing and emotional security in your relationships. Make sure to communicate your needs openly and create a safe space for your partner to do the same. With Mercury and the Sun entering your sign later in the month, you'll have the courage and clarity to express your feelings and desires with confidence. The New Moon in your sign on the 29th is a powerful time to set intentions for love and partnership, focusing on the qualities and experiences you wish to attract.

Career:

Aquarius, your career sector is activated this month, with Mars moving through your 6th house of work and daily routines. This transit brings a surge of energy and motivation to tackle your professional tasks and responsibilities. You may find yourself taking on new projects or challenges that showcase your unique skills and talents. The Full Moon in Cancer on the 13th illuminates your work-life balance, reminding you to prioritize self-care and emotional well-being amidst your career pursuits. Trust your intuition when it comes to job-related decisions, and don't be afraid to ask for support when needed. The New Moon in your sign on the 29th is a powerful time to set intentions for your professional growth and success, focusing on the goals and aspirations that align with your authentic self. With Mercury and the Sun in your sign, you'll have the mental clarity and confidence to communicate your ideas and take bold action towards your dreams.

Finances:

In financial matters, January 2025 brings transformative energy and potential for growth. The Venus-Pluto conjunction in your sign on the 2nd may prompt you to reassess your values and priorities around money and resources. This is a time to let go of any limiting beliefs or patterns that have been holding you back from abundance and prosperity. Trust that by aligning your financial goals with your deepest values and desires, you'll attract the resources and opportunities you need to thrive. The Full Moon in Cancer on the 13th may bring a financial matter to a head, especially if it involves joint resources or investments. Be open to negotiation and compromise, and trust your intuition when it comes to money-related decisions. The New Moon in your sign on the 29th is a powerful time to set intentions for financial growth and stability, focusing on the beliefs and habits that support your long-term security and success.

Health :

When it comes to your physical and emotional well-being, January 2025 is a month of self-care, balance, and transformation. With Mars moving through your 6th house of health and daily routines, you'll have the energy and motivation to tackle any wellness goals or challenges that come your way. This is a great time to start a new fitness regimen, healthy eating plan, or self-care practice that aligns with your unique needs and preferences. The Full Moon in Cancer on the 13th reminds you to prioritize emotional nourishment and intuitive self-care, especially if you've been neglecting your own needs in favor of others. Make time for activities that soothe your soul and help you feel grounded and centered. The New Moon in your sign on the 29th is a powerful time to set intentions for your overall well-being, focusing on the habits and mindsets that support your physical, mental, and emotional health. Trust that by taking care of yourself first, you'll be better equipped to show up fully in all areas of your life.

Travel :

Aquarius, although January 2025 may not be the busiest month for long-distance travel, there are still opportunities for adventure and personal growth closer to home. The Full Moon in Cancer on the 13th may inspire a short trip or getaway that nurtures your soul and helps you connect with loved ones. Consider planning a cozy weekend retreat or visit to a nearby natural wonder that allows you to unplug and recharge. The New Moon in your sign on the 29th is a powerful time to set intentions for future travel and exploration, focusing on the experiences and destinations that align with your personal growth and aspirations. Trust that by staying open to new adventures and perspectives, you'll enrich your life in countless ways. With Mercury and the Sun in your sign later in the month, you may find yourself connecting with people from different cultures and backgrounds, expanding your worldview and sense of possibility.

Insights from the Stars:

January 2025 is a pivotal month for Aquarius, as you navigate the powerful energies of transformation, self-discovery, and new beginnings. The Venus-Pluto conjunction in your sign on the 2nd sets the stage for profound growth and evolution, urging you to let go of old patterns and embrace your authentic self. Trust that by facing your fears and shadows with courage and compassion, you'll emerge stronger, wiser, and more empowered. The Full Moon in Cancer on the 13th reminds you to prioritize emotional nourishment and self-care, even amidst the demands of daily life. Make space for intuition, vulnerability, and connection, and trust that your deepest needs will be met. The New Moon in your sign on the 29th is a cosmic invitation to set intentions that align with your highest vision and purpose, knowing that you have the power to create the life you truly desire. With Mercury and the Sun in your sign, you'll have the mental clarity, confidence, and vitality to communicate your ideas and take bold action towards your dreams. Remember that you are a unique and valuable member of the cosmic community, here to share your gifts and make a positive impact on the world. Trust the journey, Aquarius, and know that the universe is conspiring in your favor.

Best Days of the Month:

January 2nd: Venus conjunct Pluto in Aquarius - Profound transformation and deepening of relationships.

January 13th: Full Moon in Cancer - Emotional nourishment and intuitive self-care.

January 27th: Mercury enters Aquarius - Mental clarity and enhanced communication.

January 29th: New Moon in Aquarius - Powerful new beginnings and intention-setting.

January 30th: Uranus direct in Taurus - Breakthrough insights and innovative solutions..

February 2025

Overview Horoscope for the Month:

Aquarius, February 2025 is a month of deep introspection, spiritual growth, and emotional healing. With the Sun journeying through your 12th house of inner work and subconscious mind for most of the month, you're called to retreat from the world and focus on your inner landscape. This is a time to confront your fears, release old patterns and beliefs that no longer serve you, and connect with your intuition and higher self. Trust that taking a step back from the hustle and bustle will ultimately lead to greater clarity, purpose, and peace. The Leo Full Moon on February 12th illuminates your 7th house of partnerships, bringing important revelations and opportunities for growth in your closest relationships. Communicate from the heart and be open to seeing things from a different perspective. The Pisces New Moon on February 27th plants the seeds for a spiritual awakening and renewed faith in the universe's plan for you. Surrender to the flow and trust that you're exactly where you're meant to be.

Love:

In matters of the heart, February invites you to deepen your connection with your partner or love interest through vulnerability, empathy, and unconditional acceptance. With Venus gracing your 4th house of home and family for most of the month, you're in the mood to nest and nurture your closest bonds. Show your affection through cozy, intimate gestures like cooking a special meal, cuddling up for a movie marathon, or sharing heartfelt memories. If single, you may feel more introspective and focused on self-love rather than actively seeking a new relationship. Use this time to heal any past wounds and get clear on the qualities you desire in a future mate. When Venus shifts into bold Aries on the 4th, you'll be ready to put yourself out there and take a risk in romance. An intriguing admirer could catch your eye at a social event or online. Keep an open mind and let your heart lead the way.

Career:

Your professional life takes a backseat to inner growth and reflection for most of February, as the Sun illuminates your 12th house of spirituality and solitude. This is a time to reassess your career goals and make sure they align with your soul's purpose. If you've been feeling unfulfilled or burnt out at work, use this introspective period to explore new paths or ways to infuse more meaning into your current role. Trust your intuition and be open to unexpected opportunities that may arise, even if they seem unconventional at first. With Mercury spending an extended time in your sign this month, your innovative ideas and unique perspective are your greatest assets. Don't be afraid to pitch a creative solution or volunteer for a project that showcases your brilliance. Behind-the-scenes work and research will also pay off. The Pisces New Moon on the 27th is ideal for planting the seeds for a more spiritually fulfilling career path. Envision your ideal work life and take inspired action to make it a reality.

Finances:

Financially, February is a month of letting go and trusting in the universe's abundance. With the Sun and Mercury activating your 12th house of surrender and release, you're learning to detach from material concerns and focus on the intangible riches of the soul. This is a time to practice gratitude for all the blessings in your life, even if your bank account isn't as flush as you'd like. Trust that your needs will always be met and that the right resources will come to you at the perfect time. If you're feeling anxious about money, use this introspective period to examine your beliefs and patterns around wealth and prosperity. Are you holding onto a scarcity mindset or self-limiting doubts? Release what no longer serves you and affirm your worthiness to receive. The Pisces New Moon on the 27th is a powerful time to set intentions around financial peace and spiritual abundance. Visualize yourself living a life of ease, flow, and plenty. The universe is conspiring in your favor.

Health:

When it comes to wellness, February encourages you to prioritize rest, relaxation, and inner peace. With the Sun and Mercury moving through your 12th house of solitude and spiritual health, you may feel more introspective and in need of alone time to recharge. Honor your body's signals and create space for quiet reflection, meditation, or gentle movement like yoga or tai chi. This is a time to release stress, anxiety, and toxic energy that may be weighing on your physical and emotional well-being. Practice self-compassion and treat yourself with the same kindness and care you'd extend to a beloved friend. The Leo Full Moon on the 12th illuminates your 7th house of partnerships, reminding you to seek support from loved ones and lean on your tribe for encouragement and accountability. Joining a wellness-focused group or working with a holistic health practitioner can also provide valuable guidance and motivation. Trust that prioritizing your well-being is the ultimate act of self-love.

Travel:

Aquarius, although February may not be the most action-packed month for travel, it's an ideal time for a spiritual retreat or pilgrimage that allows you to connect with your inner wisdom and higher purpose. With the Sun and Mercury activating your 12th house of solitude and inner work, you may feel called to visit a sacred site, ashram, or meditation center that facilitates deep healing and transformation. Trust your intuition and let your soul guide you to the perfect destination. If a physical journey isn't possible, consider an armchair adventure through books, documentaries, or virtual tours that expand your consciousness and broaden your horizons. The Pisces New Moon on the 27th plants the seeds for a future travel experience that nourishes your mind, body, and spirit. Set intentions for the types of adventures you'd like to attract and trust that the universe will provide the perfect opportunities at the right time. In the meantime, focus on the inner journey of self-discovery and trust that the greatest adventures often lie within.

Insights from the Stars:

February 2025 is a pivotal month for your spiritual growth and emotional healing, Aquarius. You're being called to dive deep into your subconscious mind and confront any fears, doubts, or limiting beliefs that may be holding you back from living your most authentic, fulfilling life. This is a time to practice radical self-acceptance and trust in the universe's plan for you, even if the path ahead seems uncertain or challenging at times. Remember that your sensitivity and intuition are your greatest superpowers, and that your unique perspective is needed in the world. Don't be afraid to let your light shine and share your truth, even if it goes against the status quo. You have the power to inspire others and create positive change through your compassion, creativity, and vision. Trust that the inner work you do this month will lay the foundation for a more enlightened, purpose-driven future. The universe is conspiring in your favor, and your greatest breakthroughs are just around the corner. Keep the faith and keep shining your light, Aquarius. The world needs your magic now more than ever.

Best Days of the Month:

February 4th: Venus enters Aries - Bold moves in love and creativity pay off.

February 12th: Full Moon in Leo - A turning point in relationships that illuminates the importance of vulnerability and authenticity.

February 16th: Mercury enters Pisces - Your intuition and imagination are heightened, leading to inspired ideas and spiritual insights.

February 27th: New Moon in Pisces - Set intentions for emotional healing, spiritual growth, and creative expression.

February 27th: Saturn sextile Chiron - Opportunities for deep healing and transformation in your career and public image..

March 2025

Overview Horoscope for the Month:

Aquarius, March 2025 is a month of new beginnings, self-discovery, and spiritual awakening. With Saturn, the planet of structure and discipline, entering your sign on March 7th, you're embarking on a new 2.5-year cycle of personal growth and maturity. This is a time to take responsibility for your life, set clear goals and boundaries, and commit to the hard work necessary to achieve your dreams. Trust that the challenges and obstacles that arise are opportunities for growth and self-mastery. The Aries New Moon on March 29th falls in your 3rd house of communication and learning, marking a powerful new beginning in how you express yourself and share your ideas with the world. This is a time to speak your truth, learn new skills, and connect with like-minded individuals who share your vision for a better future. Stay open to new perspectives and be willing to adapt your plans as needed. The universe is guiding you towards your highest path and purpose.

Love:

In matters of the heart, March is a month of deep emotional connection and spiritual intimacy. With Venus, the planet of love and beauty, spending an extended time in dreamy Pisces, you're craving a soul-level bond with your partner or love interest. This is a time to open your heart, express your feelings with vulnerability and compassion, and create a safe space for love to flourish. If you're in a committed relationship, take time to connect with your partner through shared spiritual practices, such as meditation, prayer, or dream work. Explore the deeper meaning and purpose of your union, and find ways to support each other's personal and spiritual growth. If you're single, you may find yourself attracted to people who share your spiritual values and beliefs, and who offer emotional depth and understanding. Trust your intuition and let your heart guide you towards meaningful connections. The Aries New Moon on March 29th brings a fresh start in communication and intellectual stimulation. Engage in heartfelt conversations and let your curiosity lead you to new experiences and adventures in love.

Career:

Aquarius, your career sector is lit up this month, with the Sun illuminating your 2nd house of income and resources until March 20th, and Saturn entering your sign on March 7th. This is a time to take a practical, disciplined approach to your work and financial goals, and to commit to the long-term strategies necessary for success. With Saturn in your sign for the next 2.5 years, you're being called to step up as a leader and authority figure in your field. Trust your unique talents and abilities, and don't be afraid to take on new responsibilities or challenges that push you outside your comfort zone. This is a time to build a strong foundation for your career and create structures that will support your growth and advancement in the years to come. The Aries New Moon on March 29th brings a fresh start in communication and networking. Reach out to colleagues and mentors who can offer guidance and support, and be open to new ideas and opportunities that come your way. Your innovative thinking and unique perspective are your greatest assets in the workplace.

Finances:

In finances, March is a month of practical planning and long-term strategy. With Saturn entering your sign on March 7th, you're being called to take a disciplined, responsible approach to your money and resources. This is a time to create a solid budget, pay off debts, and invest in your future security. Trust that the hard work and sacrifices you make now will pay off in the long run. The Sun in your 2nd house of income and resources until March 20th highlights your earning potential and financial skills. Look for ways to increase your income through your unique talents and abilities, and don't be afraid to negotiate for what you're worth. The Aries New Moon on March 29th brings a fresh start in financial communication and education. Seek out resources and mentors who can help you develop your financial literacy and make informed decisions about your money. Remember that true wealth comes from living in alignment with your values and purpose, and that your greatest resource is your own inner wisdom and resilience.

Health:

When it comes to wellness, March is a month of spiritual healing and self-care. With Venus spending an extended time in Pisces, your 12th house of inner work and emotional processing, you may feel more sensitive and introspective than usual. Take time to rest, recharge, and connect with your inner world through practices like meditation, journaling, or creative expression. This is a time to release old emotional patterns and beliefs that no longer serve you, and to cultivate a deeper sense of self-love and acceptance. The Aries New Moon on March 29th brings a fresh start in mental health and communication. Seek out supportive friends, family members, or therapists who can offer a listening ear and guidance, and don't be afraid to ask for help when you need it. Remember that your emotional and spiritual well-being is just as important as your physical health, and that true healing comes from within.

Travel:

Aquarius, although March may not be the busiest month for travel, it's an ideal time for short trips and educational pursuits that expand your mind and feed your soul. The Aries New Moon on March 29th activates your 3rd house of learning and communication, making it a great time to take a workshop, attend a conference, or visit a nearby destination that sparks your curiosity. Look for opportunities to connect with like-minded individuals and explore new ideas and perspectives. If a physical journey isn't possible, consider armchair travel through books, documentaries, or virtual tours that broaden your horizons and inspire your imagination. Remember that the greatest adventures often come from stepping outside your comfort zone and embracing the unknown. Trust your intuition and let your thirst for knowledge guide you towards enriching experiences and encounters.

Insights from the Stars:

March 2025 is a pivotal month for your personal growth and spiritual evolution, Aquarius. With Saturn entering your sign on March 7th, you're embarking on a new cycle of self-mastery and discipline that will challenge you to take responsibility for your life and commit to your highest path and purpose. This is a time to confront your fears, limitations, and shadow side, and to cultivate the inner strength and resilience necessary to overcome obstacles and achieve your goals. Trust that the universe is guiding you towards your greatest potential, even when the path ahead seems uncertain or challenging. The Aries New Moon on March 29th brings a powerful opportunity for new beginnings and fresh starts in communication, learning, and self-expression. This is a time to speak your truth, share your unique ideas and perspectives, and connect with others who share your vision for a better world. Remember that your voice and your vision matter, and that you have the power to create positive change through your words and actions. Stay open to new experiences and opportunities, and trust that the universe is conspiring in your favor. Your greatest breakthroughs and transformations are yet to come.

Best Days of the Month:

March 7th: Saturn enters Aquarius - A new cycle of personal growth and self-mastery begins.

March 14th: Mars enters Leo - Confidence and creativity are heightened, making it a great time to pursue your passions and take bold action towards your goals.

March 17th: Venus enters Aries - A fresh start in love and relationships, with a focus on assertiveness, independence, and adventure.

March 21st: Aries New Moon - A powerful opportunity for new beginnings and fresh starts in communication, learning, and self-expression.

March 23rd: Pluto enters Aquarius - A long-term cycle of deep transformation and personal empowerment begins, inviting you to embrace your authentic self and create positive change in the world..

Overview Horoscope for the Month:

Aquarius, April 2025 brings a powerful mix of energies that will inspire you to embrace change, pursue your passions, and connect with others on a deeper level. The month begins with a potent Saturn-Uranus sextile on April 4th, highlighting the importance of balancing structure and innovation in your life. This is a time to break free from limiting patterns and beliefs while still maintaining a sense of stability and responsibility. Trust your intuition and be open to new opportunities that align with your authentic self. The Aries New Moon on April 4th falls in your 3rd house of communication and learning, marking a fresh start in how you express yourself and share your ideas with the world. Use this energetic boost to start a new project, learn a new skill, or connect with like-minded individuals who share your vision for the future. Later in the month, the Scorpio Full Moon on April 25th illuminates your 10th house of career and public image, bringing a culmination or turning point in your professional life. Trust that your hard work and dedication will pay off, and don't be afraid to step into the spotlight and claim your rightful place as a leader and visionary.

Love:

In matters of the heart, April 2025 is a month of deep emotional connection and transformation. With Venus entering passionate Aries on April 3rd, you're feeling more assertive and confident in your romantic pursuits. If you're single, this is a great time to put yourself out there and make the first move on someone who catches your eye. Be bold, be direct, and trust your instincts. If you're in a committed relationship, use this fiery energy to reignite the spark and bring more excitement and adventure into your love life. Plan a surprise date, try a new activity together, or simply express your affection in a more passionate and demonstrative way. The Scorpio Full Moon on April 25th may bring a revelation or turning point in your partnership, forcing you to confront any deep-seated fears or power struggles that have been holding you back. Use this intense energy to have an honest and vulnerable conversation with your partner, and be willing to let go of any patterns or dynamics that no longer serve your highest good. Remember that true intimacy requires trust, communication, and a willingness to grow and evolve together.

Career:

Aquarius, your career sector is on fire this month, with a series of powerful planetary alignments activating your 10th house of professional success and public recognition. The month begins with a potent Saturn-Uranus sextile on April 4th, highlighting the importance of finding a balance between tradition and innovation in your work. This is a time to take a structured and disciplined approach to your goals while still being open to new ideas and unconventional solutions. Trust your unique vision and don't be afraid to think outside the box, even if it means challenging the status quo. Mid-month, the Sun and Mercury move through your 4th house of home and family, reminding you to strike a healthy work-life balance and make time for self-care and personal nurturing. Remember that your professional success is directly tied to your emotional and physical well-being, so don't neglect your own needs in pursuit of your goals. The Scorpio Full Moon on April 25th brings a culmination or turning point in your career, perhaps in the form of a promotion, a new job offer, or a major project coming to fruition. Trust that your hard work and dedication will be recognized and rewarded, and don't be afraid to step into the spotlight and claim your rightful place as a leader and visionary in your field.

Finances:

In financial matters, April 2025 is a month of abundance and opportunity for Aquarius. With Jupiter, the planet of expansion and prosperity, moving through your 2nd house of income and resources, you're attracting wealth and abundance from a variety of sources. This is a great time to explore new revenue streams, negotiate a raise or promotion, or invest in your long-term financial security. Trust that the universe is conspiring in your favor and that your positive attitude and hard work will pay off in tangible ways. The Aries New Moon on April 4th brings a fresh start in financial communication and education, making it an ideal time to seek out mentors, take a course on money management, or start a side hustle that aligns with your passions and skills. Remember that true abundance comes from a mindset of gratitude and generosity, so be sure to share your blessings with others and give back to your community in whatever way you can. The more you give, the more you will receive.

Health:

When it comes to your physical and emotional well-being, April 2025 is a month of balance and self-care for Aquarius. With the Sun and Mercury moving through your 4th house of home and family mid-month, you're reminded of the importance of creating a nurturing and supportive environment for yourself. This is a great time to declutter your living space, make some cozy and comforting upgrades, or simply spend more time relaxing and recharging in the comfort of your own home. The Aries New Moon on April 4th brings a fresh start in mental health and communication, making it an ideal time to start a new self-care practice like meditation, journaling, or therapy. Remember that your emotional and psychological well-being is just as important as your physical health, so don't neglect your inner world in pursuit of external success. Later in the month, the Scorpio Full Moon on April 25th may bring some intense emotions or power struggles to the surface, forcing you to confront any deep-seated fears or unresolved traumas that have been holding you back. Use this intense energy to do some deep healing work, whether through therapy, energy work, or simply allowing yourself to feel and process your emotions in a healthy way. Trust that by facing your shadows and embracing your whole self, you will emerge stronger, wiser, and more resilient than ever before.

Travel:

Aquarius, although April 2025 may not be the busiest month for long-distance travel, there are still plenty of opportunities for adventure and exploration closer to home. The Aries New Moon on April 4th falls in your 3rd house of local travel and communication, making it a great time to plan a weekend getaway or day trip to somewhere new and exciting. Look for opportunities to explore your own backyard, whether through hiking, biking, or simply wandering around a new neighborhood or town. This is also a great time to connect with friends and loved ones who live nearby, perhaps by hosting a dinner party, game night, or outdoor picnic. Remember that adventure doesn't always have to involve grand gestures or exotic locations – sometimes the most meaningful experiences happen right in our own communities, with the people we care about most. Later in the month, the Scorpio Full Moon on April 25th may bring a sudden opportunity for travel or expansion, perhaps related to your career or public image. Trust your instincts and be open to new experiences, even if they push you outside your comfort zone. The greatest growth and transformation often happen when we're willing to take risks and embrace the unknown.

Insights from the Stars:

April 2025 is a powerful month of change, growth, and transformation for Aquarius. With Saturn and Uranus forming a supportive sextile on April 4th, you're being called to find a balance between structure and innovation, tradition and progress, in all areas of your life. This is a time to break free from limiting patterns and beliefs while still maintaining a sense of stability and responsibility. Trust your unique vision and don't be afraid to think outside the box, even if it means challenging the status quo. The Aries New Moon on April 4th brings a fresh start in communication, learning, and self-expression, urging you to speak your truth and share your ideas with the world. Remember that your voice matters and that you have the power to inspire and uplift others with your words and actions. Later in the month, the Scorpio Full Moon on April 25th brings a culmination or turning point in your career and public image, forcing you to confront any fears or power struggles that have been holding you back. Use this intense energy to do some deep inner work, letting go of any patterns or dynamics that no longer serve your highest good. Trust that by embracing your authentic self and stepping into your power, you will attract the success, recognition, and fulfillment you deserve. Stay true to your vision, Aquarius, and keep shining your unique light in the world. The universe is conspiring in your favor, and your greatest breakthroughs are yet to come.

Best Days of the Month:

April 4th: Saturn sextile Uranus & Aries New Moon - A powerful day for breaking free from limiting patterns and embracing innovative new beginnings in communication and self-expression.

April 17th: Jupiter sesquiquadrate Pluto - An opportunity to transform your financial mindset and attract greater abundance and prosperity.

April 21st: Saturn conjunct North Node - A karmic alignment that brings fated opportunities for growth, success, and fulfillment in your career and life path.

April 25th: Scorpio Full Moon - A culmination or turning point in your career and public image, forcing you to confront fears and step into your power as a leader and visionary.

April 27th: Saturn semi-sextile Chiron - A healing influence that helps you overcome past wounds and insecurities, especially related to your sense of authority and responsibility in the world..

May 2025

Overview Horoscope for the Month:

Aquarius, May 2025 is a month of intense spiritual growth, emotional healing, and personal transformation. The month begins with a powerful Jupiter-Pluto square on May 2nd, highlighting the need for deep inner work and psychological exploration. This is a time to confront your shadows, release old traumas and patterns, and embrace a more authentic and empowered version of yourself. Trust that the challenges and obstacles you face are ultimately serving your highest good and leading you towards a more fulfilling and purposeful life. The Taurus New Moon on May 4th falls in your 4th house of home and family, bringing a fresh start in your personal life and emotional foundation. Use this grounded energy to create a nurturing and supportive environment for yourself, both physically and emotionally. Later in the month, the Scorpio Full Moon Total Lunar Eclipse on May 18th activates your 10th house of career and public image, bringing a major turning point or revelation in your professional life. Trust your instincts and be open to unexpected opportunities that align with your true passions and purpose. Remember that your ultimate success comes from being true to yourself and following your heart, even if it means taking a risk or charting a new course.

Love:

In matters of the heart, May 2025 is a month of deep emotional connection, vulnerability, and transformation. With Venus, the planet of love and beauty, traveling through sensitive Pisces for most of the month, you're craving a soul-level bond with your partner or love interest. This is a time to open your heart, express your feelings with authenticity and compassion, and create a safe space for love to flourish. If you're in a committed relationship, take time to connect with your partner through shared spiritual practices, such as meditation, prayer, or dream work. Explore the deeper meaning and purpose of your union, and find ways to support each other's personal and spiritual growth. If you're single, you may find yourself attracted to someone who shares your spiritual values and beliefs, and who offers emotional depth and understanding. Trust your intuition and let your heart guide you towards meaningful connections. The Scorpio Full Moon Total Lunar Eclipse on May 18th may bring a major turning point or revelation in your love life, forcing you to confront any fears or power struggles that have been holding you back. Use this intense energy to have an honest and vulnerable conversation with your partner or love interest, and be willing to let go of any patterns or dynamics that no longer serve your highest good. Remember that true intimacy requires trust, communication, and a willingness to grow and evolve together.

Career:

Aquarius, your career sector is in the spotlight this month, with a series of powerful planetary alignments activating your 10th house of professional success and public recognition. The month begins with a potent Jupiter-Pluto square on May 2nd, highlighting the need for deep transformation and renewal in your work life. This is a time to confront any fears or limiting beliefs that have been holding you back from reaching your full potential, and to embrace a more authentic and empowered approach to your career. Trust that the challenges and obstacles you face are ultimately serving your highest good and leading you towards a more fulfilling and purposeful path. Mid-month, the Sun and Mercury move through your 5th house of creativity and self-expression, inspiring you to bring more passion, innovation, and originality to your work. This is a great time to take a risk on a bold new idea or project, or to showcase your unique talents and abilities in a public way. The Scorpio Full Moon Total Lunar Eclipse on May 18th brings a major turning point or revelation in your career, perhaps in the form of a promotion, a new job offer, or a major project coming to fruition. Trust your instincts and be open to unexpected opportunities that align with your true passions and purpose. Remember that your ultimate success comes from being true to yourself and following your heart, even if it means taking a risk or charting a new course.

Finances:

In financial matters, May 2025 is a month of deep transformation and renewal for Aquarius. With Pluto, the planet of power and regeneration, forming a challenging square to expansive Jupiter on May 2nd, you're being called to confront any fears or limiting beliefs around money and abundance. This is a time to do the deep inner work of examining your relationship with wealth and prosperity, and to release any patterns or behaviors that have been keeping you stuck in a cycle of lack or scarcity. Trust that by facing your financial shadows and embracing a more empowered and abundant mindset, you will attract greater opportunities and resources into your life. The Taurus New Moon on May 4th brings a fresh start in your earned income and material resources, making it an ideal time to set intentions around financial growth and stability. Focus on creating a budget, paying off debts, and investing in your long-term security and prosperity. Remember that true wealth comes from living in alignment with your values and purpose, and that your greatest asset is your own unique talents and abilities. Later in the month, the Scorpio Full Moon Total Lunar Eclipse on May 18th may bring a sudden financial windfall or opportunity, perhaps related to your career or public image. Trust your instincts and be open to unexpected sources of income and support, even if they come from unconventional or surprising places.

Health:

When it comes to your physical and emotional well-being, May 2025 is a month of deep healing and transformation for Aquarius. With Chiron, the planet of wounding and healing, forming a supportive sextile to expansive Jupiter on May 18th, you have a powerful opportunity to confront and release any past traumas or emotional blocks that have been holding you back from optimal health and vitality. This is a time to do the deep inner work of self-love and self-care, whether through therapy, energy healing, or simply allowing yourself to feel and process your emotions in a healthy way. The Taurus New Moon on May 4th brings a fresh start in your physical body and self-care routines, making it an ideal time to start a new fitness program, healthy eating plan, or relaxation practice. Focus on nourishing your body with wholesome foods, plenty of rest and hydration, and activities that bring you joy and pleasure. Remember that true health comes from a holistic approach that addresses your mind, body, and spirit. Later in the month, the Scorpio Full Moon Total Lunar Eclipse on May 18th may bring a sudden health crisis or wake-up call, forcing you to confront any unhealthy habits or patterns that have been sabotaging your well-being. Use this intense energy to make a powerful commitment to your own healing and transformation, and trust that by taking care of yourself first, you will be better able to show up and serve others in the world.

Travel:

Aquarius, although May 2025 may not be the busiest month for long-distance travel, there are still plenty of opportunities for adventure and exploration closer to home. The Taurus New Moon on May 4th falls in your 4th house of home and family, making it a great time to plan a cozy staycation or weekend getaway with loved ones. Look for opportunities to explore your local surroundings, whether through nature walks, picnics in the park, or simply enjoying the beauty and comfort of your own backyard. This is also a great time to connect with your roots and heritage, perhaps by researching your family history, cooking traditional meals, or sharing stories and memories with relatives. Remember that adventure doesn't always have to involve grand gestures or exotic locations - sometimes the most meaningful experiences happen right in our own homes and communities, with the people we love most. Later in the month, the Scorpio Full Moon Total Lunar Eclipse on May 18th may bring a sudden opportunity for travel or expansion, perhaps related to your career or public image. Trust your instincts and be open to unexpected invitations or opportunities, even if they push you outside your comfort zone. The greatest growth and transformation often happen when we're willing to take risks and embrace the unknown.

Insights from the Stars:

May 2025 is a powerful month of deep transformation, spiritual growth, and emotional healing for Aquarius. With Jupiter and Pluto forming a challenging square on May 2nd, you're being called to confront your shadows, release old traumas and patterns, and embrace a more authentic and empowered version of yourself. This is a time to do the deep inner work of self-discovery and self-realization, trusting that the challenges and obstacles you face are ultimately serving your highest good and leading you towards a more fulfilling and purposeful life. The Taurus New Moon on May 4th brings a fresh start in your personal life and emotional foundation, urging you to create a nurturing and supportive environment for yourself, both physically and emotionally. Focus on building a strong sense of security, stability, and self-worth, knowing that your true power comes from within. Later in the month, the Scorpio Full Moon Total Lunar Eclipse on May 18th brings a major turning point or revelation in your career and public image, forcing you to confront any fears or limitations that have been holding you back from reaching your full potential. Trust your instincts and be open to unexpected opportunities that align with your true passions and purpose, even if it means taking a risk or charting a new course. Remember that your ultimate success comes from being true to yourself and following your heart, no matter what obstacles or challenges you may face along the way. Stay true to your vision, Aquarius, and keep shining your unique light in the world. The universe is conspiring in your favor, and your greatest breakthroughs and transformations are yet to come.

Best Days of the Month:

May 4th: Taurus New Moon - A powerful day for setting intentions around emotional security, material abundance, and personal growth.

May 18th: Jupiter sextile Chiron & Scorpio Full Moon Total Lunar Eclipse - A transformative alignment that brings deep healing, personal empowerment, and unexpected opportunities for success and recognition.

May 24th: Saturn enters Aries - A major shift that initiates a new cycle of self-discovery, personal responsibility, and authentic leadership in your life.

May 25th: Mercury enters Gemini - A dynamic influence that enhances your communication skills, intellectual curiosity, and social connections.

May 30th: Jupiter biquintile Pluto - A creative and transformative aspect that helps you find innovative solutions to long-standing problems and challenges..

June 2025

Overview Horoscope for the Month:

Aquarius, June 2025 is a month of significant personal growth, self-discovery, and new beginnings. The month starts with a powerful New Moon in Gemini on June 3rd, falling in your 5th house of creativity, romance, and self-expression. This lunation brings a fresh start in matters of the heart, urging you to take a risk on love and pursue your passions with courage and authenticity. Trust your unique voice and vision, and don't be afraid to stand out from the crowd. On June 9th, your traditional ruler Saturn briefly enters your sign, giving you a preview of the major life lessons and challenges you'll be working with over the next few years. Use this time to get clear on your long-term goals and commitments, and start putting in place the structures and discipline needed for lasting success. The Sagittarius Full Moon on June 17th illuminates your 11th house of friendships, community, and social activism. This is a powerful time to connect with like-minded individuals who share your vision for a better world, and to take a stand for the causes and ideals that matter most to you. Trust that your unique contributions are needed and valued, and that together, you can create positive change on a global scale.

Love:

In matters of the heart, June 2025 is a month of passion, creativity, and self-expression for Aquarius. With Venus, the planet of love and beauty, dancing through your 5th house of romance and pleasure for the first few weeks of the month, you're feeling more playful, flirtatious, and open to new experiences. If you're single, this is an ideal time to put yourself out there and take a risk on love. Attend social events, join a new club or group, or simply strike up a conversation with someone who catches your eye. Trust your natural charm and charisma to attract the right people and opportunities into your life. If you're already in a relationship, use this creative energy to bring more fun, spontaneity, and passion into your connection. Plan a surprise date, try a new hobby or activity together, or simply express your affection in a bold and authentic way. The Sagittarius Full Moon on June 17th highlights your 11th house of friendships and social connections, reminding you of the importance of community and shared ideals in your love life. If you're single, you may meet someone special through a group or organization that aligns with your values and vision. If you're partnered, this is a great time to socialize and network as a couple, connecting with other like-minded pairs who can support and inspire your growth.

Career:

Aquarius, your career sector is on fire this month, with a series of powerful planetary alignments activating your 10th house of professional success and public recognition. The month begins with a dynamic New Moon in Gemini on June 3rd, falling in your 5th house of creativity and self-expression. This is an ideal time to launch a new project, pitch an innovative idea, or showcase your unique talents and abilities in your work. Trust your natural creativity and originality to set you apart from the competition and attract the right opportunities and collaborators. On June 9th, your traditional ruler Saturn briefly enters your sign, giving you a preview of the major career lessons and challenges you'll be working with over the next few years. Use this time to get clear on your long-term professional goals and ambitions, and start putting in place the structures and discipline needed for lasting success. Focus on developing your skills, expertise, and leadership abilities, knowing that your hard work and dedication will pay off in the long run. The Sagittarius Full Moon on June 17th illuminates your 11th house of networking and social connections, highlighting the importance of collaboration and teamwork in your career. Use this energy to connect with colleagues, mentors, and industry leaders who share your values and vision, and look for opportunities to contribute your unique talents and ideas to a larger cause or movement.

Finances:

In financial matters, June 2025 is a month of opportunity and growth for Aquarius. With Venus, the planet of abundance and prosperity, moving through your 5th house of creativity and self-expression for the first few weeks of the month, you may find new sources of income and resources through your natural talents and abilities. This is an ideal time to monetize a hobby or passion project, or to invest in your own creative development and education. Trust that by following your heart and doing what you love, you will attract the right opportunities and abundance into your life. On June 9th, your traditional ruler Saturn briefly enters your sign, giving you a preview of the major financial lessons and challenges you'll be working with over the next few years. Use this time to get clear on your long-term money goals and commitments, and start putting in place the structures and discipline needed for lasting security and stability. Focus on creating a realistic budget, paying off debts, and investing in your future, knowing that your hard work and responsibility will pay off in the long run. The Sagittarius Full Moon on June 17th highlights your 11th house of community and social connections, reminding you of the importance of networking and collaboration in your financial life. Look for opportunities to partner with others who share your values and vision, and consider joining a group or organization that supports your financial goals and aspirations.

Health:

When it comes to your physical and emotional well-being, June 2025 is a month of vitality, creativity, and self-expression for Aquarius. With the Sun illuminating your 5th house of joy and pleasure for the first few weeks of the month, you're feeling more energized, playful, and connected to your body and senses. This is an ideal time to prioritize activities and experiences that bring you happiness and fulfillment, whether that's dancing, painting, spending time in nature, or simply indulging in your favorite self-care rituals. Trust that by following your bliss and expressing your true self, you'll naturally radiate health and well-being from the inside out. On June 9th, your traditional ruler Saturn briefly enters your sign, giving you a preview of the major health and wellness lessons you'll be working with over the next few years. Use this time to get clear on your long-term self-care goals and commitments, and start putting in place the structures and discipline needed for lasting vitality and resilience. Focus on developing healthy habits and routines, such as regular exercise, nutritious eating, and stress management, knowing that your dedication and consistency will pay off in the long run. The Sagittarius Full Moon on June 17th highlights your 11th house of friendships and social connections, reminding you of the importance of community and support in your wellness journey. Look for opportunities to connect with like-minded individuals who share your health and fitness goals, and consider joining a group or class that keeps you motivated and accountable.

Travel:

Aquarius, June 2025 is a month of excitement, exploration, and new horizons in your travel and adventure sector. With Venus, the planet of beauty and pleasure, moving through your 5th house of creativity and self-expression for the first few weeks of the month, you're feeling more spontaneous, curious, and open to new experiences. This is an ideal time to plan a fun and creative getaway, whether that's a weekend road trip to a nearby city, a glamping adventure in nature, or a solo retreat to explore your artistic side. Trust your natural sense of wonder and discovery to lead you to the right destinations and opportunities. On June 9th, your traditional ruler Saturn briefly enters your sign, giving you a preview of the major travel and education lessons you'll be working with over the next few years. Use this time to get clear on your long-term goals and aspirations for personal growth and expansion, and start putting in place the structures and discipline needed to make them a reality. Consider enrolling in a course or program that aligns with your interests and passions, or start saving and planning for a major bucket-list trip in the future. The Sagittarius Full Moon on June 17th illuminates your 11th house of friendship and community, highlighting the joys of group travel and shared adventures. Look for opportunities to explore new places and cultures with like-minded individuals who share your sense of curiosity and enthusiasm, and trust that the connections and memories you make will enrich your life in countless ways.

Insights from the Stars:

June 2025 is a pivotal month for Aquarius, as you stand on the brink of a major new chapter in your personal and professional life. With Saturn, your traditional ruler, briefly entering your sign on June 9th, you're getting a sneak peek of the powerful lessons and challenges you'll be working with over the next few years. This is a time to get serious about your long-term goals and commitments, and to start laying the groundwork for the life you truly want to live. Trust that the hard work and discipline you put in now will pay off in the form of greater mastery, success, and fulfillment down the road. At the same time, the Gemini New Moon on June 3rd and the Sagittarius Full Moon on June 17th remind you of the importance of joy, creativity, and connection in your journey. Don't get so caught up in your responsibilities and ambitions that you forget to have fun, express your unique self, and lean on the support of your loved ones. Ultimately, your greatest strength lies in your ability to balance structure and spontaneity, responsibility and play, independence and interdependence. Trust that by staying true to your authentic vision and values, while also remaining open to growth and change, you'll be able to navigate whatever challenges and opportunities come your way with grace, resilience, and wisdom.

Best Days of the Month:

June 1st: Jupiter semi-sextile Uranus - A day of unexpected opportunities and insights that expand your perspective and challenge you to think outside the box.

June 3rd: New Moon in Gemini - A powerful time for setting intentions around creativity, self-expression, and new beginnings in love and romance.

June 9th: Jupiter enters Cancer - The start of a new 12-year cycle of growth and expansion in your work, health, and service sector.

June 13th: Mercury trine Saturn - A day of clear communication, practical planning, and productive conversations that help you move closer to your long-term goals.

June 17th: Full Moon in Sagittarius - A culmination point in your social and community sector, highlighting the importance of shared ideals, collaboration, and global vision in your life path.

July 2025

Overview Horoscope for the Month:

Aquarius, July 2025 is a month of profound transformation, self-discovery, and new beginnings. The month kicks off with a powerful Full Moon in Capricorn on July 3rd, illuminating your 12th house of spirituality, intuition, and hidden influences. This lunation brings a culmination or turning point in your inner journey, asking you to confront any fears, doubts, or limiting beliefs that have been holding you back from living your fullest potential. Trust your inner wisdom and be willing to let go of what no longer serves you, making space for new growth and opportunities to emerge. On July 7th, Uranus, your modern ruler, shifts into Gemini for a brief stint, activating your 5th house of creativity, self-expression, and romance. This transit brings a fresh burst of inspiration, innovation, and experimentation to your personal projects and relationships. Embrace your unique voice and vision, and don't be afraid to take risks and try new things. The Leo New Moon on July 23rd falls in your 7th house of partnerships, marking a new chapter in your one-on-one connections. Whether you're starting a new relationship, taking an existing one to the next level, or collaborating with a business partner, this is a time to set intentions around balance, harmony, and mutual growth.

Love:

In matters of the heart, July 2025 is a month of excitement, creativity, and new possibilities for Aquarius. With Uranus, your modern ruler, moving into Gemini and your 5th house of romance and self-expression on July 7th, you're feeling more spontaneous, playful, and open to experimentation in your love life. If you're single, this is an ideal time to put yourself out there and explore new connections that challenge and inspire you. Attend social events, join a dating app, or simply strike up a conversation with someone who catches your eye. Trust your natural magnetism and originality to attract the right people and opportunities your way. If you're already in a relationship, use this innovative energy to bring more excitement and novelty into your partnership. Plan a surprise date, try a new hobby or activity together, or simply express your affection in a creative and authentic way. The Leo New Moon on July 23rd brings a fresh start in your 7th house of committed partnerships, marking a powerful time for setting intentions around love, harmony, and mutual growth. Whether you're deepening an existing bond or attracting a new one, focus on creating a dynamic of equality, respect, and shared purpose.

Career:

Aquarius, your career sector is undergoing a profound transformation this month, as the Capricorn Full Moon on July 3rd illuminates your 12th house of hidden influences, spirituality, and surrender. This lunation brings a culmination or turning point in your professional journey, asking you to let go of any projects, roles, or goals that no longer align with your deepest values and purpose. Trust that by releasing what's no longer serving you, you're making space for new opportunities and directions to emerge. On July 7th, Uranus, your modern ruler, shifts into Gemini and your 5th house of creativity and self-expression, bringing a fresh burst of innovation and experimentation to your work. This is an ideal time to pitch a bold new idea, launch a passion project, or showcase your unique talents and abilities in your field. Trust your natural ingenuity and originality to set you apart from the competition and attract the right collaborators and allies. Later in the month, the Leo New Moon on July 23rd activates your 7th house of partnerships and contracts, marking a powerful time for setting intentions around collaboration, teamwork, and mutual success. Look for opportunities to join forces with colleagues or mentors who share your vision and values, and trust that together, you can achieve more than you ever could alone.

Finances:

In financial matters, July 2025 is a month of inner transformation and new possibilities for Aquarius. The Capricorn Full Moon on July 3rd illuminates your 12th house of spirituality and surrender, bringing a powerful opportunity to release any limiting beliefs, fears, or patterns around money and abundance. Trust that by letting go of a scarcity mindset and aligning your financial goals with your deepest values and purpose, you're opening the door to greater prosperity and fulfillment. On July 7th, Uranus, your modern ruler, shifts into Gemini and your 5th house of creativity and self-expression, bringing a fresh burst of inspiration and innovation to your money-making ventures. This is an ideal time to explore new income streams, monetize a passion project, or invest in your own education and development. Trust your natural ingenuity and resourcefulness to attract the right opportunities and connections your way. Later in the month, the Leo New Moon on July 23rd activates your 7th house of partnerships and contracts, marking a powerful time for setting intentions around financial collaboration and shared resources. Consider joining forces with a business partner, investor, or advisor who shares your vision and values, and trust that together, you can create greater abundance and impact than you ever could alone.

Health:

When it comes to your physical and emotional well-being, July 2025 is a month of release, renewal, and inner transformation for Aquarius. The Capricorn Full Moon on July 3rd illuminates your 12th house of spirituality, intuition, and surrender, bringing a powerful opportunity to let go of any unhealthy habits, patterns, or beliefs that have been holding you back from optimal health and vitality. This is a time to turn inward, connect with your deepest needs and desires, and trust the wisdom of your body and soul. Consider practices like meditation, journaling, or energy healing to facilitate the process of release and renewal. On July 7th, Uranus, your modern ruler, shifts into Gemini and your 5th house of joy and self-expression, bringing a fresh burst of inspiration and experimentation to your wellness routine. This is an ideal time to try a new form of movement or creative activity that gets you out of your head and into your body. Dance, sing, paint, or play your way to greater vitality and aliveness. The Leo New Moon on July 23rd activates your 7th house of partnerships and balance, marking a powerful time for setting intentions around healthy boundaries, mutual support, and self-care in your relationships. Remember that taking care of yourself is not selfish, but rather a prerequisite for showing up fully and authentically in all your connections.

Travel:

Aquarius, July 2025 is a month of inner journeying and personal transformation in your travel and adventure sector. The Capricorn Full Moon on July 3rd illuminates your 12th house of spirituality, intuition, and surrender, bringing a powerful opportunity to explore the depths of your own psyche and connect with a higher purpose or calling. This is a time to turn inward, trust your inner guidance, and let go of any external expectations or pressures around where you "should" be going or what you "should" be doing. Consider a solo retreat, vision quest, or pilgrimage to a sacred site that holds personal meaning for you. On July 7th, Uranus, your modern ruler, shifts into Gemini and your 5th house of creativity and self-expression, bringing a fresh burst of curiosity and experimentation to your travel plans. This is an ideal time to explore new destinations or experiences that challenge your assumptions and expand your perspective. Consider a language immersion program, a cross-cultural exchange, or a trip that combines learning and adventure. The Leo New Moon on July 23rd activates your 7th house of partnerships and collaboration, marking a powerful time for setting intentions around shared journeys and experiences. Consider planning a trip with a loved one, friend, or group that aligns with your mutual interests and values, and trust that the memories and insights you gain will enrich your connection for years to come.

Insights from the Stars:

July 2025 is a pivotal month for Aquarius, as you navigate the powerful energies of transformation, innovation, and new beginnings. The Capricorn Full Moon on July 3rd invites you to confront your deepest fears and doubts, release what's no longer serving you, and align your life path with your soul's true purpose. Trust that by letting go of the past and surrendering to the present moment, you're making space for new growth and opportunities to emerge. On July 7th, Uranus' shift into Gemini activates your inner child, creative genius, and romantic spirit, reminding you that life is meant to be a joyful, expressive, and ever-evolving adventure. Embrace your quirks, follow your curiosity, and trust that your unique voice and vision are needed in the world. The Leo New Moon on July 23rd illuminates the importance of partnership, collaboration, and shared purpose in your journey. Remember that you don't have to go it alone, and that by joining forces with others who share your values and vision, you can achieve more than you ever could in isolation. Ultimately, this month is an invitation to trust your inner wisdom, embrace your authentic self, and open your heart to the endless possibilities of growth, connection, and transformation. You're exactly where you need to be, Aquarius, and the universe is conspiring in your favor. Keep shining your light, and know that the best is yet to come.

Best Days of the Month:

July 3rd: Full Moon in Capricorn - A powerful day for releasing the past, confronting your fears, and aligning with your soul's true purpose.

July 7th: Uranus enters Gemini - The start of a new era of creativity, innovation, and experimentation in your personal projects and relationships.

July 18th: Venus trine Saturn - A day of committed love, stable partnerships, and long-term planning in your romantic and financial life.

July 23rd: New Moon in Leo - A fresh start in your one-on-one relationships, inviting you to set intentions around balance, harmony, and shared growth.

July 30th: Mars sextile Jupiter - A day of inspired action, optimism, and expansive opportunities in your career and public life.

August 2025

Overview Horoscope for the Month:

Aquarius, August 2025 is a month of profound self-discovery, emotional healing, and spiritual growth. The month begins with a powerful Full Moon in Aquarius on August 13th, illuminating your 1st house of self, identity, and personal goals. This lunation marks a significant turning point in your journey of individuation, asking you to celebrate your unique qualities, talents, and achievements while also releasing any limiting beliefs or patterns that have been holding you back from fully expressing your authentic self. Trust your inner wisdom and be willing to make bold moves in the direction of your dreams. On August 23rd, the New Moon in Virgo activates your 8th house of intimacy, transformation, and shared resources. This is a time to set intentions around deep emotional connections, psychological healing, and financial collaboration. Be willing to vulnerably share your truth with others and trust in the power of mutual support and growth. The end of the month brings a significant shift, as Saturn, your traditional ruler, retrogrades back into Aquarius on August 31st. This transit invites you to revisit and recommit to the long-term goals, structures, and responsibilities you've been working on since Saturn first entered your sign in March 2020. Trust that the challenges and obstacles you face are ultimately serving your highest growth and mastery.

Love:

In matters of the heart, August 2025 is a month of deep emotional connection, vulnerability, and transformation for Aquarius. The Full Moon in your sign on August 13th illuminates your 1st house of self and identity, bringing a powerful opportunity to assert your needs, desires, and boundaries in your relationships. If you've been holding back or compromising your authenticity for the sake of others, this is a time to speak your truth and reclaim your power. Trust that the right people and connections will support and celebrate your unique self-expression. On August 23rd, the New Moon in Virgo activates your 8th house of intimacy and shared resources, inviting you to set intentions around deep emotional bonds, psychological healing, and financial collaboration in your partnerships. This is a time to vulnerably share your fears, hopes, and dreams with your loved ones, and to create a safe space for mutual growth and transformation. If you're single, you may find yourself attracted to someone who challenges you to confront your shadow side and evolve in meaningful ways. If you're partnered, use this energy to deepen your connection through honest communication, shared vulnerability, and a willingness to face challenges together. Saturn's retrograde back into your sign at the end of the month reminds you to take responsibility for your own happiness and fulfillment in relationships, rather than relying on others to complete you.

Career:

Aquarius, your career sector is undergoing a profound transformation this month, as the Full Moon in your sign on August 13th illuminates your 1st house of self, identity, and personal goals. This lunation brings a culmination or turning point in your professional journey, asking you to celebrate your unique talents, accomplishments, and leadership qualities while also releasing any self-doubt, imposter syndrome, or limiting beliefs that have been holding you back from fully shining in your field. Trust that your authentic self-expression is your greatest asset, and don't be afraid to take bold risks in the direction of your dreams. On August 23rd, the New Moon in Virgo activates your 8th house of shared resources, inviting you to set intentions around financial collaboration, investments, and long-term wealth-building strategies. Consider partnering with a mentor, investor, or business ally who shares your values and vision, and trust in the power of mutual support and growth. Saturn's retrograde back into your sign at the end of the month reminds you to take a disciplined, structured approach to your career goals, focusing on mastery, integrity, and long-term success rather than quick fixes or shortcuts. Trust that the challenges and obstacles you face are ultimately serving your highest professional evolution.

Finances:

In financial matters, August 2025 is a month of deep transformation, collaboration, and long-term planning for Aquarius. The Full Moon in your sign on August 13th illuminates your 1st house of self-worth and personal resources, bringing a powerful opportunity to claim your value, assert your financial needs and desires, and release any limiting beliefs or patterns around money and abundance. Trust that you are deserving of wealth, stability, and prosperity, and be willing to take bold steps in the direction of your financial goals. On August 23rd, the New Moon in Virgo activates your 8th house of shared resources and long-term investments, inviting you to set intentions around financial collaboration, estate planning, and wealth-building strategies. Consider partnering with a financial advisor, accountant, or business ally who can help you create a solid plan for the future, and be open to new sources of income and investment opportunities. Saturn's retrograde back into your sign at the end of the month reminds you to take a disciplined, responsible approach to your finances, focusing on long-term security and stability rather than short-term gains or risky ventures. Trust that by aligning your money management with your deepest values and goals, you'll create a solid foundation for lasting prosperity.

Health:

When it comes to your physical and emotional well-being, August 2025 is a month of self-care, renewal, and inner transformation for Aquarius. The Full Moon in your sign on August 13th illuminates your 1st house of body, vitality, and personal identity, bringing a powerful opportunity to celebrate your unique self and prioritize your health and happiness. This is a time to release any unhealthy habits, relationships, or beliefs that have been draining your energy, and to recommit to a self-care routine that nourishes your mind, body, and soul. Consider starting a new fitness program, healthy eating plan, or mindfulness practice that aligns with your authentic needs and desires. On August 23rd, the New Moon in Virgo activates your 8th house of deep healing and regeneration, inviting you to set intentions around emotional release, trauma resolution, and psychological wholeness. Be willing to face your shadows and vulnerably share your struggles with trusted allies, knowing that true strength comes from embracing all parts of yourself with compassion and acceptance. Saturn's retrograde back into your sign at the end of the month reminds you to take a disciplined, committed approach to your well-being, focusing on long-term vitality and resilience rather than quick fixes or band-aid solutions. Trust that by honoring your inner wisdom and consistently showing up for yourself, you'll cultivate unshakable health and happiness from the inside out.

Travel:

Aquarius, August 2025 is a month of personal transformation and spiritual growth in your travel and adventure sector. The Full Moon in your sign on August 13th illuminates your 1st house of self, identity, and personal journey, bringing a powerful opportunity to celebrate your unique path and purpose while also releasing any limiting beliefs or fears that have been holding you back from fully embracing new experiences and horizons. This is a time to trust your inner compass and take bold steps in the direction of your dreams, even if it means venturing into unknown territory. Consider planning a solo trip or retreat that allows you to connect with your deepest truth and desires, and be open to synchronicities and opportunities that align with your highest self. On August 23rd, the New Moon in Virgo activates your 8th house of deep transformation and spiritual rebirth, inviting you to set intentions around inner journeys, sacred pilgrimages, and healing adventures. Be willing to face your shadows and vulnerably share your struggles with trusted allies, knowing that true growth comes from embracing the full spectrum of your human experience. Saturn's retrograde back into your sign at the end of the month reminds you to take a disciplined, committed approach to your personal and spiritual evolution, focusing on long-term wisdom and mastery rather than quick fixes or superficial experiences. Trust that by consistently showing up for your inner work and aligning your outer journey with your deepest values and purpose, you'll create a life of profound meaning, fulfillment, and adventure.

Insights from the Stars:

August 2025 is a pivotal month for Aquarius, as you navigate the powerful energies of self-discovery, emotional healing, and spiritual transformation. The Full Moon in your sign on August 13th is a cosmic spotlight on your unique qualities, talents, and purpose, inviting you to celebrate your authenticity and release any limiting beliefs or patterns that have been holding you back from fully shining your light. Trust that your quirks, eccentricities, and innovative vision are your greatest gifts to the world, and don't be afraid to take bold risks in the direction of your dreams. On August 23rd, the New Moon in Virgo activates your 8th house of deep transformation, intimacy, and shared resources, inviting you to set intentions around emotional healing, psychological wholeness, and collaborative growth. Be willing to vulnerably share your truth with others and trust in the power of mutual support and evolution. Saturn's retrograde back into your sign at the end of the month is a reminder to take a disciplined, committed approach to your long-term goals and responsibilities, focusing on mastery, integrity, and soul-aligned success. Remember that the challenges and obstacles you face are ultimately serving your highest growth and purpose, and that by consistently showing up for yourself and your dreams, you'll create a life of profound meaning, impact, and fulfillment. Trust your journey, Aquarius, and know that the universe is conspiring in your favor. Keep shining your light, and remember that your greatest breakthroughs and transformations are yet to come.

Best Days of the Month:

August 13th: Full Moon in Aquarius - A powerful day for celebrating your unique self, releasing limiting beliefs, and taking bold steps towards your dreams.

August 18th: Venus trine Pluto - A transformative day for deep emotional connections, psychological healing, and collaborative growth in your relationships.

August 23rd: New Moon in Virgo - A potent time for setting intentions around emotional healing, shared resources, and long-term financial planning.

August 28th: Mercury trine Uranus - A day of innovative ideas, unexpected insights, and creative breakthroughs in your communication and problem-solving.

August 31st: Saturn retrograde re-enters Aquarius - A significant shift that invites you to revisit and recommit to your long-term goals, structures, and responsibilities.

September 2025

Overview Horoscope for the Month:

Aquarius, September 2025 is a month of profound transformation, spiritual awakening, and new beginnings. The month starts with Saturn, your traditional ruler, moving retrograde back into your sign on the 1st, bringing a heightened focus on your personal growth, responsibilities, and long-term goals. This transit invites you to revisit and recommit to the structures, disciplines, and aspirations you've been working on since Saturn first entered Aquarius in March 2020. Trust that the challenges and obstacles you face are ultimately serving your highest evolution and mastery. On the 7th, a powerful Full Moon in Pisces illuminates your 2nd house of values, resources, and self-worth, bringing a culmination or turning point in your relationship with money, possessions, and personal talents. This is a time to release any limiting beliefs or patterns around abundance and claim your inherent value and deserving. The New Moon in Virgo on the 21st activates your 8th house of deep transformation, intimacy, and shared resources, marking a potent new beginning in your emotional and financial collaborations. Set intentions around psychological healing, vulnerability, and mutual support in your closest bonds.

Love:

In matters of the heart, September 2025 is a month of deepening intimacy, emotional healing, and spiritual connection for Aquarius. With Saturn moving retrograde back into your sign on the 1st, you're called to take a mature, responsible approach to your relationships, focusing on long-term compatibility, shared values, and mutual growth. This is a time to get clear on your needs, boundaries, and commitments, and to have honest conversations with your partner or love interest about your hopes and fears for the future. The Full Moon in Pisces on the 7th illuminates your 2nd house of self-worth and personal resources, inviting you to release any codependent tendencies or fears of vulnerability that have been holding you back from fully showing up in your relationships. Trust that you are inherently worthy of love and respect, and be willing to assert your needs and desires with confidence. If you're single, this lunation could bring a significant romantic prospect who values your unique qualities and talents. The New Moon in Virgo on the 21st activates your 8th house of deep bonding and transformation, marking a powerful new beginning in your intimate partnerships. Set intentions around emotional transparency, psychological healing, and shared growth, and be open to new levels of vulnerability and trust with your loved ones.

Career:

Aquarius, your career sector is undergoing a profound transformation this month, as Saturn moves retrograde back into your sign on the 1st, bringing a heightened focus on your professional identity, goals, and responsibilities. This is a time to revisit and recommit to the long-term projects, roles, and aspirations you've been working on since Saturn first entered Aquarius in March 2020. Trust that the challenges and obstacles you face are ultimately serving your highest mastery and purpose, and be willing to put in the disciplined effort required for lasting success. The Full Moon in Pisces on the 7th illuminates your 2nd house of income, resources, and talents, bringing a culmination or turning point in your financial situation and sense of self-worth. This is a time to release any limiting beliefs or patterns around your earning potential and claim your inherent value and deserving in your field. Consider negotiating a raise, seeking a promotion, or exploring new income streams that align with your unique skills and passions. The New Moon in Virgo on the 21st activates your 8th house of shared resources and long-term investments, marking a potent new beginning in your professional collaborations and financial partnerships. Set intentions around mutual support, strategic planning, and sustainable growth, and be open to new alliances and opportunities that can help you achieve your goals.

Finances:

In financial matters, September 2025 is a month of deep transformation, self-reflection, and long-term planning for Aquarius. With Saturn moving retrograde back into your sign on the 1st, you're called to take a mature, responsible approach to your money management, focusing on budgeting, saving, and investing for the future. This is a time to get clear on your financial goals, values, and priorities, and to create a realistic plan for achieving lasting security and abundance. The Full Moon in Pisces on the 7th illuminates your 2nd house of income, possessions, and self-worth, bringing a culmination or turning point in your relationship with money and material resources. This is a time to release any scarcity mindset or fears of lack, and to claim your inherent deserving of prosperity and abundance. Trust that the universe will provide for your needs as you align your financial habits with your deepest values and purpose. The New Moon in Virgo on the 21st activates your 8th house of shared resources, investments, and long-term planning, marking a powerful new beginning in your financial collaborations and strategies. Set intentions around mutual support, smart investing, and sustainable growth, and be open to new partnerships and opportunities that can help you build lasting wealth and security.

Health :

When it comes to your physical and emotional well-being, September 2025 is a month of self-care, inner work, and spiritual growth for Aquarius. With Saturn moving retrograde back into your sign on the 1st, you're called to take a disciplined, committed approach to your health and wellness routines, focusing on long-term vitality, resilience, and self-mastery. This is a time to get clear on your personal boundaries, needs, and goals, and to create a realistic plan for achieving optimal mind-body-soul balance. The Full Moon in Pisces on the 7th illuminates your 2nd house of physical body and self-care, bringing a culmination or turning point in your relationship with your own well-being and self-nurturing. This is a time to release any self-neglect or martyr tendencies, and to claim your inherent deserving of rest, nourishment, and pleasure. Consider treating yourself to a spa day, massage, or other indulgent experience that helps you feel pampered and revitalized. The New Moon in Virgo on the 21st activates your 8th house of deep healing and regeneration, marking a powerful new beginning in your emotional and spiritual growth. Set intentions around shadow work, therapy, and inner child healing, and be open to new tools and practices that can help you release old traumas and patterns.

Travel:

Aquarius, September 2025 is a month of inner journeying and spiritual exploration in your travel and adventure sector. With Saturn moving retrograde back into your sign on the 1st, you're called to take a serious, intentional approach to your personal and metaphysical quests, focusing on long-term growth, wisdom, and self-discovery. This is a time to get clear on your higher purpose, beliefs, and aspirations, and to create a realistic plan for expanding your horizons and consciousness. The Full Moon in Pisces on the 7th illuminates your 2nd house of personal resources and values, bringing a culmination or turning point in your relationship with your own talents, gifts, and sense of self-worth. This is a time to release any self-doubt or limitations around your ability to manifest your dreams, and to claim your inherent deserving of adventure, abundance, and fulfillment. Consider investing in a transformative workshop, retreat, or educational program that helps you tap into your unique potential and passions. The New Moon in Virgo on the 21st activates your 8th house of deep transformation and rebirth, marking a powerful new beginning in your spiritual and psychological journeys. Set intentions around inner exploration, shamanic healing, and shadow work, and be open to new experiences and revelations that can help you shed old skin and emerge as a more authentic, integrated version of yourself.

Insights from the Stars:

September 2025 is a pivotal month for Aquarius, as you navigate the powerful energies of personal responsibility, emotional healing, and spiritual transformation. With Saturn moving retrograde back into your sign on the 1st, you're called to take a serious, mature approach to your long-term goals, commitments, and personal mastery. Trust that the challenges and obstacles you face are ultimately serving your highest evolution and purpose, and be willing to put in the disciplined effort required for lasting success and fulfillment. The Full Moon in Pisces on the 7th illuminates your 2nd house of self-worth, resources, and values, inviting you to release any limiting beliefs or patterns around your own deserving and claim your inherent abundance and potential. Remember that your unique talents and gifts are valuable and needed in the world, and don't be afraid to assert your worth and boundaries with confidence. The New Moon in Virgo on the 21st activates your 8th house of deep transformation, intimacy, and shared resources, marking a powerful new beginning in your emotional and financial collaborations. Set intentions around vulnerability, mutual support, and sustainable growth, and be open to new levels of trust and interdependence in your closest bonds. Above all, remember that you are a divine being of love and light, here to shine your authentic truth and make a positive impact on the world. Trust your journey, Aquarius, and know that the universe is conspiring in your favor. Keep showing up for yourself and your dreams, and remember that your greatest breakthroughs and awakenings are yet to come.

Best Days of the Month:

September 1st: Saturn retrograde re-enters Aquarius - A significant shift that invites you to revisit and recommit to your long-term goals, structures, and personal growth.

September 3rd: Venus trine True Node - A day of fated encounters, meaningful connections, and heart-opening experiences in your relationships.

September 7th: Full Moon in Pisces - A powerful time for releasing limiting beliefs around self-worth and abundance, and claiming your inherent deserving.

September 18th: Jupiter biquintile Chiron - A healing and expansive aspect that supports emotional breakthroughs, spiritual growth, and the embracing of your unique gifts.

September 21st: New Moon in Virgo - A potent new beginning in your emotional and financial collaborations, inviting vulnerability, mutual support, and shared growth..

October 2025

Overview Horoscope for the Month:

Aquarius, October 2025 is a month of profound self-discovery, spiritual growth, and new beginnings. The month starts with a powerful New Moon in Libra on the 1st, activating your 9th house of higher learning, travel, and personal philosophy. This lunation invites you to expand your horizons, both mentally and physically, and to embrace new experiences and perspectives that challenge and inspire you. Set intentions around education, adventure, and spiritual exploration, and be open to opportunities that align with your highest truth and purpose. On the 13th, a transformative Full Moon in Aries illuminates your 3rd house of communication, learning, and local community, bringing a culmination or turning point in your ideas, projects, and connections. This is a time to speak your truth, share your unique insights, and collaborate with like-minded individuals who support your growth and vision. The Sun's entry into Scorpio on the 22nd marks the beginning of a powerful new cycle in your 10th house of career, public image, and long-term goals. Embrace your ambition, leadership skills, and desire for success, and trust that your hard work and dedication will pay off in the long run.

Love:

In matters of the heart, October 2025 is a month of adventure, growth, and spiritual connection for Aquarius. With the New Moon in Libra on the 1st activating your 9th house of travel, philosophy, and higher learning, you may find yourself attracted to people who expand your mind, challenge your beliefs, and inspire you to grow. This is a time to seek out relationships that align with your highest values and aspirations, and to be open to new experiences and perspectives that enrich your love life. If you're single, consider joining a class, workshop, or social group that revolves around your interests and passions, as you may meet someone special who shares your curiosity and zest for life. If you're in a committed partnership, use this energy to plan a romantic getaway, take a course together, or explore new ways of connecting on a spiritual and intellectual level. The Full Moon in Aries on the 13th illuminates your 3rd house of communication and local community, highlighting the importance of clear, honest, and assertive expression in your relationships. Don't be afraid to speak your truth, set healthy boundaries, and collaborate with your partner or love interest on projects and ideas that excite you both.

Career:

Aquarius, your career sector is on fire this month, with a series of powerful cosmic events activating your 10th house of professional success, public image, and long-term goals. The month begins with a potent New Moon in Libra on the 1st, inviting you to set intentions around higher education, international connections, and philosophical or spiritual pursuits that align with your career aspirations. Consider seeking out mentors, thought leaders, or educational programs that can help you expand your knowledge, skills, and perspective in your field. On the 13th, a transformative Full Moon in Aries illuminates your 3rd house of communication, networking, and ideas, bringing a culmination or turning point in your professional projects, collaborations, and interactions. This is a time to speak up, share your unique insights and innovations, and connect with colleagues and clients who support your vision and growth. Trust your intelligence, originality, and ability to think outside the box, and don't be afraid to take calculated risks that showcase your leadership potential. The Sun's entry into Scorpio on the 22nd marks the beginning of a powerful new cycle in your 10th house, empowering you to embrace your ambition, assert your authority, and go after your long-term career goals with passion and determination.

Finances:

In financial matters, October 2025 is a month of expansion, opportunity, and spiritual alignment for Aquarius. The New Moon in Libra on the 1st activates your 9th house of abundance, prosperity, and higher purpose, inviting you to set intentions around attracting wealth and resources that align with your core values and beliefs. Consider exploring new streams of income, investment opportunities, or financial education that resonate with your philosophical and ethical principles. Trust that the universe will provide for your needs as you pursue your highest path and purpose. The Full Moon in Aries on the 13th illuminates your 3rd house of communication, commerce, and market trends, bringing a culmination or turning point in your financial ideas, strategies, and interactions. This is a time to speak up, share your unique insights and innovations, and collaborate with others who share your vision and values. Don't be afraid to negotiate, assert your worth, and take calculated risks that showcase your financial intelligence and savvy. The Sun's entry into Scorpio on the 22nd activates your 10th house of career and public success, empowering you to attract wealth, recognition, and opportunities through your professional achievements and leadership skills.

Health:

When it comes to your physical and emotional well-being, October 2025 is a month of self-discovery, spiritual growth, and holistic healing for Aquarius. The New Moon in Libra on the 1st activates your 9th house of higher learning, travel, and personal philosophy, inviting you to explore new approaches to health and wellness that align with your core beliefs and values. Consider seeking out educational resources, workshops, or retreats that focus on mind-body-spirit integration, holistic nutrition, or alternative healing modalities. Trust that by expanding your knowledge and perspective, you can find new ways to optimize your vitality and well-being. The Full Moon in Aries on the 13th illuminates your 3rd house of communication, mental activity, and daily routines, bringing a culmination or turning point in your self-care practices, thought patterns, and lifestyle choices. This is a time to speak up, assert your needs and boundaries, and make any necessary changes to your daily habits and environments that support your health and happiness. Don't be afraid to seek out the help and support of others, whether through therapy, coaching, or joining a wellness community that uplifts and inspires you.

Travel:

Aquarius, October 2025 is a month of exciting opportunities for travel, adventure, and personal growth in your expansive 9th house. The New Moon in Libra on the 1st is a powerful time to set intentions around exploring new horizons, both literally and figuratively. Consider planning a trip to a destination that has always intrigued you, or signing up for a course or workshop that expands your mind and worldview. Trust that by stepping outside your comfort zone and embracing new experiences, you can gain valuable insights, skills, and connections that enrich your life in countless ways. The Full Moon in Aries on the 13th illuminates your 3rd house of local travel, communication, and learning, bringing a culmination or turning point in your short-distance adventures, social interactions, and educational pursuits. This is a time to speak up, share your unique ideas and perspectives, and collaborate with others who share your curiosity and passion for growth. Consider taking a weekend getaway, attending a conference or networking event, or exploring a new hobby or interest that excites you. The key is to stay open, adaptable, and willing to learn from every experience that comes your way.

Insights from the Stars:

October 2025 is a pivotal month for Aquarius, as you navigate the powerful energies of self-discovery, spiritual growth, and new beginnings. The New Moon in Libra on the 1st invites you to expand your horizons, embrace new experiences and perspectives, and align your personal philosophy with your highest truth and purpose. Trust that by seeking out knowledge, adventure, and meaningful connections, you can gain valuable insights and opportunities that support your soul's evolution. The Full Moon in Aries on the 13th challenges you to speak your truth, assert your needs and boundaries, and collaborate with others who share your vision and values. Remember that your unique ideas and innovations have the power to inspire and uplift others, so don't be afraid to share them with the world. The Sun's entry into Scorpio on the 22nd marks the beginning of a powerful new cycle in your career and public image, empowering you to embrace your ambition, leadership skills, and desire for success. Trust that by staying true to your authentic self and pursuing your passions with dedication and integrity, you can achieve your long-term goals and make a positive impact on the world. Above all, remember that you are a divine being of love and light, here to shine your unique wisdom and creativity for the benefit of all. Trust your journey, Aquarius, and know that the universe is conspiring in your favor every step of the way.

Best Days of the Month:

October 1st: New Moon in Libra - A powerful time to set intentions around travel, education, and personal growth.

October 9th: Mercury trine Saturn - A day of clear communication, practical planning, and productive conversations that support your long-term goals.

October 13th: Full Moon in Aries - A transformative lunation that challenges you to speak your truth, assert your needs, and collaborate with others who share your vision.

October 18th: Jupiter biquintile Pluto - A dynamic aspect that brings opportunities for personal and spiritual transformation through the embracing of your unique talents and purpose.

October 22nd: Sun enters Scorpio - The beginning of a powerful new cycle in your career and public image, empowering you to embrace your ambition and leadership potential.

November 2025

Overview Horoscope for the Month:

Aquarius, November 2025 is a month of profound introspection, emotional healing, and spiritual growth. The month begins with the Sun in Scorpio illuminating your 10th house of career, public image, and long-term goals, empowering you to embrace your ambition, leadership skills, and desire for success. However, as the month progresses, the cosmic energy shifts towards a more introspective and transformative tone. The New Moon in Scorpio on the 20th activates your 12th house of spirituality, inner work, and emotional healing, inviting you to turn inward and explore the depths of your psyche. This is a powerful time to release old wounds, patterns, and beliefs that no longer serve you, and to connect with your inner wisdom and intuition. The Full Moon Lunar Eclipse in Taurus on the 5th brings a culmination or turning point in your 4th house of home, family, and emotional roots, highlighting the importance of creating a nurturing and supportive foundation for yourself. Trust that by doing the deep inner work and surrounding yourself with love and comfort, you can navigate any challenges or changes that arise with grace and resilience.

Love:

In matters of the heart, November 2025 is a month of deep emotional connection, vulnerability, and transformation for Aquarius. With the Sun in Scorpio activating your 10th house of public image and reputation for the first three weeks of the month, you may find yourself attracted to people who embody power, intensity, and depth. This is a time to seek out relationships that challenge you to grow, evolve, and embrace your authentic self, even if it means confronting some of your deepest fears and desires. The New Moon in Scorpio on the 20th invites you to set intentions around emotional intimacy, spiritual connection, and unconditional love in your partnerships. Trust that by being vulnerable and transparent with your loved ones, you can create a safe space for healing, growth, and transformation. The Full Moon Lunar Eclipse in Taurus on the 5th illuminates your 4th house of home and family, highlighting the importance of creating a stable and nurturing foundation in your relationships. If there are any unresolved issues or conflicts with family members or partners, this is a time to address them with honesty, compassion, and a willingness to compromise.

Career:

Aquarius, your career sector is in the spotlight for the first three weeks of November 2025, with the Sun in Scorpio illuminating your 10th house of public image, reputation, and long-term goals. This is a powerful time to embrace your ambition, assert your leadership skills, and go after your professional dreams with passion and determination. Trust that your hard work, dedication, and unique talents will be recognized and rewarded, even if it means facing some challenges or obstacles along the way. The New Moon in Scorpio on the 20th is a particularly potent time to set intentions around your career aspirations, business ventures, and public impact. Consider ways to align your professional path with your deeper purpose and values, and don't be afraid to take calculated risks that showcase your innovation and vision. The Full Moon Lunar Eclipse in Taurus on the 5th activates your 4th house of home and family, reminding you of the importance of creating a healthy work-life balance. If you've been neglecting your personal life in favor of your career, this is a time to reassess your priorities and make any necessary adjustments to ensure your long-term well-being and happiness.

Finances:

In financial matters, November 2025 is a month of deep transformation, power dynamics, and long-term planning for Aquarius. With the Sun in Scorpio activating your 10th house of career and public success for the first three weeks of the month, you may find opportunities to increase your income, negotiate a raise or promotion, or attract lucrative business deals through your professional achievements and reputation. However, it's important to be mindful of any power struggles or hidden agendas that may arise in your financial partnerships or transactions. The New Moon in Scorpio on the 20th is a powerful time to set intentions around wealth creation, investment strategies, and long-term financial security. Consider seeking the guidance of a trusted advisor or mentor who can help you navigate any complex or intense financial situations with wisdom and integrity. The Full Moon Lunar Eclipse in Taurus on the 5th illuminates your 4th house of home and family, highlighting the importance of creating a stable and secure foundation for yourself and your loved ones. If there are any financial issues or challenges related to your living situation or domestic life, this is a time to address them with practicality, patience, and a willingness to find solutions that benefit everyone involved.

Health:

When it comes to your physical and emotional well-being, November 2025 is a month of deep healing, transformation, and self-care for Aquarius. With the Sun in Scorpio activating your 10th house of public image and reputation for the first three weeks of the month, you may find yourself pushing yourself harder than usual to achieve your goals and meet external expectations. While your drive and determination can be admirable, it's important to prioritize your health and well-being along the way. The New Moon in Scorpio on the 20th is a powerful time to set intentions around emotional healing, spiritual growth, and mind-body-spirit integration. Consider incorporating practices like meditation, therapy, or energy work into your self-care routine to help you release any old traumas, patterns, or beliefs that may be holding you back from optimal vitality and happiness. The Full Moon Lunar Eclipse in Taurus on the 5th illuminates your 4th house of home and family, reminding you of the importance of creating a nurturing and supportive environment for yourself. If there are any health issues or challenges related to your living situation or domestic life, this is a time to address them with compassion, patience, and a willingness to seek help and support from loved ones or professionals.

Travel:

Aquarius, November 2025 is a month of inner journeying and spiritual exploration in your expansive 9th house. While the first three weeks of the month may be more focused on your career and public responsibilities, the New Moon in Scorpio on the 20th activates your 12th house of spirituality, solitude, and inner work, inviting you to embark on a more introspective and transformative path. This is a powerful time to set intentions around personal growth, emotional healing, and spiritual awakening, even if it means taking a step back from the outer world and turning inward. Consider planning a solo retreat, meditation course, or vision quest that allows you to connect with your deepest truth and purpose. Trust that by doing the inner work and aligning with your soul's wisdom, you can gain valuable insights and inspiration that will guide you on your next adventure. The Full Moon Lunar Eclipse in Taurus on the 5th illuminates your 4th house of home and family, reminding you of the importance of creating a stable and nurturing foundation for yourself, even as you explore new horizons and possibilities. If there are any travel plans or opportunities related to your living situation or domestic life, this is a time to approach them with practicality, patience, and a willingness to find solutions that benefit everyone involved.

Insights from the Stars:

November 2025 is a pivotal month for Aquarius, as you navigate the powerful energies of transformation, healing, and spiritual growth. With the Sun in Scorpio activating your 10th house of career and public image for the first three weeks of the month, you're being called to embrace your ambition, leadership skills, and desire for success, even as you confront any fears, challenges, or power dynamics that may arise along the way. Trust that by staying true to your authentic self and aligning your professional path with your deeper purpose and values, you can achieve your long-term goals and make a positive impact on the world. The New Moon in Scorpio on the 20th is a particularly potent time for inner work, emotional healing, and spiritual awakening, inviting you to turn inward and explore the depths of your psyche. Remember that true power comes from within, and that by doing the deep work of self-discovery and transformation, you can unlock your full potential and create a life of meaning, fulfillment, and joy. The Full Moon Lunar Eclipse in Taurus on the 5th challenges you to create a stable and nurturing foundation for yourself and your loved ones, even as you navigate any changes or challenges that arise in your personal life. Trust that by staying grounded, patient, and compassionate, you can weather any storm and emerge stronger, wiser, and more resilient than ever before. Above all, remember that you are a divine being of love and light, here to shine your unique wisdom and creativity for the benefit of all. Trust your journey, Aquarius, and know that the universe is conspiring in your favor every step of the way.

Best Days of the Month:

November 4th: Full Moon Lunar Eclipse in Taurus - A powerful lunation that challenges you to create a stable and nurturing foundation for yourself and your loved ones.

November 7th: Pluto semi-square True Node - A transformative aspect that invites you to align your personal power with your soul's purpose and evolutionary path.

November 13th: Venus trine True Node - A harmonious aspect that brings opportunities for heart-opening connections, creative collaborations, and alignment with your life purpose.

November 20th: New Moon in Scorpio - A potent time for inner work, emotional healing, and setting intentions around personal transformation and spiritual growth.

November 23rd: Jupiter quintile Chiron - A healing aspect that supports emotional breakthroughs, spiritual wisdom, and the embracing of your unique gifts and talents.

December 2025

Overview Horoscope for the Month:

Aquarius, December 2025 is a month of profound transformation, spiritual awakening, and new beginnings. The month begins with a powerful New Moon in Sagittarius on the 5th, activating your 11th house of friendships, community, and social activism. This lunation invites you to connect with like-minded individuals who share your vision for a better world, and to take action towards your dreams and ideals. Set intentions around expanding your network, collaborating on innovative projects, and making a positive impact on your community and beyond. The Full Moon in Gemini on the 19th brings a culmination or turning point in your 5th house of creativity, self-expression, and romance, encouraging you to let your unique light shine and follow your heart's desires. Trust that by embracing your authentic self and sharing your gifts with the world, you can attract joy, abundance, and meaningful connections into your life. The Winter Solstice on the 21st marks a powerful shift, as the Sun enters Capricorn and illuminates your 12th house of spirituality, inner work, and emotional healing. This is a time to turn inward, reflect on the past year, and set intentions for the new cycle ahead, focusing on your personal and spiritual growth.

Love:

In matters of the heart, December 2025 is a month of excitement, creativity, and new possibilities for Aquarius. The New Moon in Sagittarius on the 5th activates your 11th house of friendships and social connections, inviting you to expand your circle and connect with people who inspire and support your growth. If you're single, this is a powerful time to put yourself out there and meet new potential partners through group activities, online communities, or shared interests. Trust that by being open, authentic, and adventurous, you can attract a mate who aligns with your values and vision. If you're in a committed partnership, this lunation encourages you to bring more fun, spontaneity, and exploration into your relationship. Consider trying new activities, taking a trip together, or joining a class or group that allows you to learn and grow as a couple. The Full Moon in Gemini on the 19th illuminates your 5th house of romance, creativity, and self-expression, bringing a culmination or turning point in your love life. This is a time to let your heart lead the way, express your affection openly and playfully, and celebrate the magic of love in all its forms.

Career:

Aquarius, your career sector is activated by the powerful New Moon in Sagittarius on the 5th, which falls in your 11th house of networking, teamwork, and long-term goals. This lunation invites you to expand your professional connections, collaborate with like-minded colleagues, and take bold steps towards your dreams and aspirations. Trust that by aligning your work with your higher purpose and values, you can attract opportunities and success that fulfill you on a deep level. Consider joining a professional organization, attending a conference or workshop, or reaching out to mentors or influencers in your field who can support your growth and development. The Full Moon in Gemini on the 19th illuminates your 5th house of creativity, self-expression, and leadership, encouraging you to let your unique talents and ideas shine in your work. This is a time to take risks, think outside the box, and showcase your innovative spirit in your projects and presentations. Trust that by being true to yourself and sharing your gifts with confidence and enthusiasm, you can inspire and motivate others to join your vision and mission. The Winter Solstice on the 21st marks a powerful shift, as the Sun enters Capricorn and activates your 12th house of inner work, spirituality, and emotional healing. This is a time to reflect on your career path, release any limiting beliefs or patterns that may be holding you back, and set intentions for the new year ahead, focusing on your long-term goals and soul's purpose.

Finances:

In financial matters, December 2025 is a month of abundance, expansion, and new opportunities for Aquarius. The New Moon in Sagittarius on the 5th activates your 11th house of community, networking, and long-term goals, inviting you to align your money mindset with your higher values and vision. This is a powerful time to set intentions around attracting wealth and resources that support your dreams and ideals, and to collaborate with others who share your financial goals and philosophies. Consider joining a money mindset group, investing in a cause or organization that resonates with your values, or seeking out new income streams that allow you to make a positive impact on the world. The Full Moon in Gemini on the 19th illuminates your 5th house of creativity, self-expression, and entrepreneurship, encouraging you to monetize your unique talents and ideas. Trust that by following your passions and sharing your gifts with the world, you can attract abundance and success that fulfills you on a deep level. This is also a favorable time for taking calculated risks, investing in your own education and development, or launching a new business venture that aligns with your purpose and vision.

Health:

When it comes to your physical and emotional well-being, December 2025 is a month of expansion, exploration, and self-discovery for Aquarius. The New Moon in Sagittarius on the 5th activates your 11th house of friendships, community, and social connections, inviting you to seek out like-minded individuals who share your health and wellness goals. Consider joining a fitness group, attending a spiritual retreat, or connecting with a holistic practitioner who can support your journey towards optimal vitality and balance. Trust that by surrounding yourself with positive, inspiring people and environments, you can elevate your mind, body, and spirit to new heights. The Full Moon in Gemini on the 19th illuminates your 5th house of self-expression, creativity, and joy, encouraging you to prioritize activities and experiences that bring you pleasure and fulfillment. This is a powerful time to explore new forms of movement, art, or play that allow you to express yourself freely and authentically. Trust that by following your bliss and listening to your body's wisdom, you can tap into a deep well of vitality, resilience, and inner peace. The Winter Solstice on the 21st marks a powerful shift, as the Sun enters Capricorn and activates your 12th house of spirituality, inner work, and emotional healing. This is a time to turn inward, reflect on your health journey, and set intentions for the new year ahead, focusing on your personal growth and transformation.

Travel:

Aquarius, December 2025 is a month of excitement, exploration, and new horizons in your travel and adventure sector. The New Moon in Sagittarius on the 5th activates your 11th house of friendships, community, and social connections, inviting you to expand your circle and seek out new experiences and destinations with like-minded individuals. Consider planning a group trip, attending a spiritual retreat, or joining a travel community that allows you to connect with people from different cultures and backgrounds. Trust that by embracing diversity, curiosity, and open-mindedness, you can broaden your perspective and enrich your life in countless ways. The Full Moon in Gemini on the 19th illuminates your 5th house of creativity, self-expression, and joy, encouraging you to let your unique spirit shine in your adventures and explorations. This is a powerful time to take a spontaneous trip, try a new hobby or activity, or express yourself through art, music, or dance while on the road. Trust that by following your heart and embracing your authentic self, you can attract magical experiences and connections that inspire and transform you. The Winter Solstice on the 21st marks a powerful shift, as the Sun enters Capricorn and activates your 12th house of spirituality, inner work, and emotional healing. This is a time to reflect on your travel journey, release any limiting beliefs or patterns that may be holding you back, and set intentions for the new year ahead, focusing on your personal and spiritual growth.

Insights from the Stars:

December 2025 is a pivotal month for Aquarius, as you navigate the powerful energies of transformation, awakening, and new beginnings. The New Moon in Sagittarius on the 5th invites you to expand your horizons, connect with your community, and take bold steps towards your dreams and ideals. Trust that by aligning your actions with your higher purpose and values, you can attract opportunities and success that fulfill you on a deep level. The Full Moon in Gemini on the 19th encourages you to let your unique light shine, express yourself authentically, and celebrate the magic of creativity, romance, and joy in all areas of your life. Remember that your gifts and talents are needed in the world, and that by sharing them with confidence and enthusiasm, you can inspire and uplift others to do the same. The Winter Solstice on the 21st marks a powerful shift, as the Sun enters Capricorn and activates your 12th house of spirituality, inner work, and emotional healing. This is a time to turn inward, reflect on the past year, and set intentions for the new cycle ahead, focusing on your personal and spiritual growth. Trust that by doing the deep work of self-discovery and transformation, you can release any limiting beliefs or patterns that may be holding you back, and step into a new level of wholeness, wisdom, and purpose. Above all, remember that you are a divine being of love and light, here to shine your unique wisdom and creativity for the benefit of all. Trust your journey, Aquarius, and know that the universe is conspiring in your favor every step of the way.

Best Days of the Month:

December 5th: New Moon in Sagittarius - A powerful time to expand your horizons, connect with your community, and set intentions for your dreams and ideals.

December 10th: Venus trine True Node - A harmonious aspect that brings opportunities for heart-opening connections, creative collaborations, and alignment with your life purpose.

December 19th: Full Moon in Gemini - A transformative lunation that encourages you to let your unique light shine, express yourself authentically, and celebrate the magic of creativity, romance, and joy.

December 21st: Sun enters Capricorn (Winter Solstice) - A powerful shift that invites you to turn inward, reflect on the past year, and set intentions for your personal and spiritual growth in the new cycle ahead.

December 26th: Jupiter biquintile Pluto - A dynamic aspect that supports deep transformation, soul-level growth, and the embracing of your authentic power and purpose.

PISCES 2025 HOROSCOPE

Overview Pisces 2025

(February 19 - March 20)

Dear Pisces, as we embark on the transformative journey of 2025, the celestial dance promises a year of profound spiritual growth, emotional healing, and inspired creativity for you. The cosmic energies align to support your path of self-discovery and empowerment, guiding you through the ebb and flow of life with your innate intuitive wisdom and compassionate heart.

The year commences with a powerful concentration of energy in your 12th house of spirituality, dreams, and inner transformation. The Sun, Mercury, and Venus converge in this mystical sector, urging you to turn inward and connect with your subconscious mind. Embrace this opportunity to release old patterns, fears, or limiting beliefs that may have hindered your progress. Saturn's presence in this house until March 1 provides the discipline and structure necessary to build a strong spiritual foundation. Engage in practices such as meditation, journaling, or creative visualization to tap into your intuition and gain clarity on your life's purpose.

In mid-January, the True Node shifts into your sign, signaling a powerful call to step into your authentic self and embrace your unique identity. This is a time to shed any masks or roles that no longer serve you and trust the wisdom of your heart. With the South Node in your opposite sign of Virgo, strive for balance and integration between your spiritual and practical worlds. You may find fulfillment in acts of service, healing, or mentorship, as you channel your empathy and compassion into the world.

February brings a significant shift as Saturn moves into Pisces on the 1st, followed by Venus on the 2nd. Saturn's entry into your sign until May 24 marks the beginning of a new 30-year cycle of growth and maturity. Embrace the challenges and opportunities for personal development that Saturn presents. Take responsibility for your life, set clear goals and boundaries, and cultivate the discipline and perseverance needed to manifest your dreams. Venus graces your sign until March 27, enhancing your charm, creativity, and ability to attract love and abundance. Use this period to express your unique talents, nurture relationships, and find joy in the simple pleasures of life.

The Total Lunar Eclipse in your 7th house of partnerships on March 14 brings a powerful opportunity for transformation and growth in your closest relationships. This is a time to release codependent patterns, assert your needs and boundaries, and cultivate deeper intimacy and trust with your loved ones. With Saturn's influence in your sign, you may need to confront fears or insecurities that have prevented true connection and vulnerability. Communications may also be emphasized as Mercury enters your sign on March 29.

On March 30, Neptune, your ruling planet, shifts into Aries, bringing a 14-year cycle of heightened intuition, spiritual growth, and inspired creativity to your 2nd house of values and resources. This transit encourages you to align your material world with your spiritual values, trust in the flow of the universe, and attract wealth and success through your unique gifts and talents. Embrace your dreams, visions, and ideals, and trust in the magic and mystery of life.

April 4 brings the first of three Saturn-Uranus sextiles in 2025, inspiring a harmonious blend of stability and innovation in your life. Embrace change and progress while maintaining a solid foundation. The second Saturn-Uranus sextile occurs on August 11, continuing the theme of balancing structure and flexibility. These transits provide opportunities for personal growth, unconventional solutions, and the manifestation of your long-term goals.

In late April, Pluto turns retrograde in your 11th house of friendships and social groups, initiating a period of reflection and re-evaluation in your connections with others. Assess the authenticity and quality of your relationships, releasing any that may be draining or toxic. Focus on cultivating a supportive network of individuals who share your values and aspirations.

May brings a brief preview of Saturn's influence in Aries as it shifts into your 2nd house from May 24 to September 1. This transit offers a glimpse of the forthcoming growth and challenges related to your values, self-worth, and material resources. Take stock of your life, assess your strengths and weaknesses, and begin establishing the structures necessary for long-term financial and emotional security.

The second half of the year emphasizes creativity, self-expression, and personal growth. Ceres' entry into your sign on August 11 and Sun's transit through Pisces from February 18 to March 20 highlight the importance of self-care, nurturance, and emotional well-being. Prioritize activities that bring you joy, rejuvenation, and a sense of inner peace.

On September 1, Saturn retrograde re-enters your sign, providing an opportunity to revisit and refine the lessons and growth you experienced earlier in the year. Reflect on your progress, make necessary adjustments, and continue building the foundation for your long-term success and fulfillment.

The Partial Solar Eclipse in your 2nd house on September 21 marks a powerful new beginning related to your values, resources, and self-worth. This is an ideal time to set intentions, make positive changes, and embrace opportunities for financial growth and prosperity. Trust in your abilities, talents, and the abundance the universe has to offer.

October 22 brings Neptune retrograde back into your sign, amplifying your intuition, creativity, and spiritual awareness. This transit encourages introspection, dream exploration, and the release of limiting beliefs or illusions. Embrace your imagination, trust your inner guidance, and allow your creativity to flow freely.

As the year draws to a close, Saturn's direct station in your sign on November 27 and Neptune's direct station on December 10 signify a period of renewed clarity, purpose, and momentum. Trust in the growth and lessons you've experienced throughout the year, and move forward with confidence and determination. Jupiter's biquintile to Pluto on November 30 supports positive transformations and the manifestation of your deepest desires.

Throughout 2025, Chiron's presence in your 2nd house of self-worth and resources encourages healing and growth in these areas. Embrace your unique value, talents, and contributions, and release any self-doubt or feelings of unworthiness. As you navigate the challenges and opportunities of the year, remember to practice self-compassion, maintain healthy boundaries, and trust in your inherent wisdom and resilience.

In conclusion, dear Pisces, 2025 promises to be a year of profound spiritual growth, emotional healing, and inspired creativity. The cosmic energies support your journey of self-discovery and empowerment, guiding you to align with your true purpose and manifest your deepest desires. Embrace the opportunities for personal development, cultivate meaningful relationships, and trust in the wisdom of the universe. With an open heart and a willing spirit, you have the power to create a life filled with magic, love, and abundant blessings. Trust in your path, stay true to your intuition, and embrace the transformative journey ahead.

January 2025

Overview Horoscope for the Month:

Dear Pisces, January 2025 is a month of profound spiritual growth and emotional healing for you. The year begins with a powerful stellium of planets in your 12th house of spirituality, dreams, and inner transformation, including the Sun, Mercury, Venus, and Saturn. This cosmic alignment is urging you to turn inward, connect with your subconscious mind, and release any old patterns, fears, or limiting beliefs that may be holding you back.

The New Moon in Aquarius on January 29th activates your 12th house, bringing a fresh start and new opportunities for spiritual awakening and inner growth. Set intentions for emotional healing, forgiveness, and letting go of the past. Trust your intuition and allow yourself to be guided by your dreams and inner wisdom.

Love:

In love, January 2025 is a time of deep emotional connection and spiritual intimacy for you, dear Pisces. With Venus, the planet of love and relationships, traveling through your 12th house until February 2nd, you may find yourself craving a soul-level bond with your partner or seeking a relationship that transcends the physical realm.

If you're in a committed relationship, take time to connect with your partner on a deeper level through shared spiritual practices, heartfelt conversations, and acts of loving kindness. Be open and vulnerable about your feelings, fears, and dreams, and create a safe space for emotional healing and growth

If you're single, you may find yourself attracted to someone who shares your spiritual values and offers a sense of emotional depth and understanding. Trust your intuition and allow yourself to be guided towards meaningful connections that support your personal and spiritual growth.

Career:

In your career, January 2025 is a month of introspection and inner reflection for you, dear Pisces. With Saturn, the planet of responsibility and discipline, entering your 12th house on January 1st, you may find yourself questioning your current path and seeking a deeper sense of purpose and meaning in your work.

Take time to reassess your goals, values, and priorities, and make sure that your career aligns with your authentic self and soul's calling. Trust that the universe is guiding you towards your highest potential, even if the path is not always clear or easy.

If you're considering a career change or starting a new project, the New Moon in Aquarius on January 29th is a powerful time to set intentions and take inspired action towards your dreams. Trust your unique talents and abilities, and don't be afraid to think outside the box or take unconventional approaches to your work.

Finances:

In finances, January 2025 is a month of spiritual abundance and trust for you, dear Pisces. With Venus, the planet of money and resources, traveling through your 12th house until February 2nd, you are being called to release any fears or limiting beliefs around scarcity or lack, and to trust in the flow and provision of the universe.

Practice gratitude for the blessings in your life, and cultivate a mindset of abundance and generosity. Consider setting aside a portion of your income for charitable donations or acts of kindness that align with your spiritual values and beliefs.

On a deeper level, reflect on your relationship with money and any past wounds or traumas that may be blocking your financial flow. Practice forgiveness, self-love, and affirming your worthiness to receive all the good that life has to offer.

Health:

In health, January 2025 is a month of deep emotional healing and spiritual rejuvenation for you, dear Pisces. With the Sun, Mercury, and Venus all traveling through your 12th house of the subconscious mind, you may find yourself feeling more introspective, intuitive, and emotionally sensitive than usual.

Take time to rest, recharge, and connect with your inner world through practices like meditation, journaling, or creative visualization. Nourish your body with wholesome foods, plenty of water, and gentle exercise that supports your overall well-being.

On an emotional level, be gentle and compassionate with yourself as you navigate any old wounds, fears, or patterns that may arise. Seek out the support of trusted friends, therapists, or spiritual advisors who can offer guidance and a listening ear. Remember that true healing comes from within, and trust in the wisdom of your body, mind, and soul.

Travel:

In travel, January 2025 may bring opportunities for spiritual retreats, pilgrimages, or solo adventures that support your inner journey of self-discovery and growth. With Saturn entering your 12th house on January 1st, you may feel called to visit sacred sites, connect with nature, or explore new spiritual practices and traditions.

Consider taking a trip to a place that holds deep meaning and significance for you, such as a monastery, ashram, or natural wonder. Allow yourself to unplug from the distractions of daily life and immerse yourself in the beauty and wisdom of your surroundings.

If travel isn't possible or practical, find ways to create a sense of sacred space and inner retreat in your daily life. Take a nature walk, create a meditation corner in your home, or attend a local spiritual workshop or event that nourishes your soul.

Insights from the Stars:

The celestial energies of January 2025 are inviting you to dive deep into your inner world, dear Pisces, and to trust in the wisdom and guidance of your soul. With so many planets activating your 12th house of spirituality and the subconscious mind, this is a powerful time for inner growth, emotional healing, and spiritual transformation.

Embrace the journey of self-discovery and allow yourself to be guided by your intuition, dreams, and inner knowing. Trust that the universe is supporting you every step of the way, and that every challenge or obstacle is an opportunity for growth and awakening.

Remember that you are a divine being of light and love, and that your soul's purpose is to shine your unique gifts and talents in service to the world. Embrace your sensitivity, compassion, and creativity as the superpowers that they are, and trust in the magic and mystery of life.

Best Days of the Month:

January 6th: First Quarter Moon in Aries - A burst of energy and motivation to take action on your dreams and goals.

January 13th: Full Moon in Cancer - A time for emotional release, healing, and self-care.

January 21st: Last Quarter Moon in Scorpio - An opportunity to let go of old patterns and beliefs that no longer serve you.

January 29th: New Moon in Aquarius - A powerful time for setting intentions and planting seeds for the future, especially related to your spiritual growth and inner journey.

January 30th: Uranus Direct in Taurus - A shift towards greater freedom, innovation, and authentic self-expression in your communication and self-worth.

Overview Horoscope for the Month:

Dear Pisces, February 2025 promises to be a month of profound spiritual growth, emotional healing, and personal transformation. With a powerful stellium of planets in your sign, including the Sun, Mercury, Saturn, and Neptune, you are being called to dive deep into your inner world and connect with your soul's true purpose. This is a time to release old patterns, heal past wounds, and embrace your unique gifts and talents.

The New Moon in your sign on February 27 brings a powerful opportunity for new beginnings and fresh starts. Set intentions for personal growth, creative expression, and spiritual awakening, and trust that the universe is supporting you every step of the way.

Love:

In matters of the heart, February 2025 invites you to deepen your connections and cultivate greater intimacy and vulnerability. With Venus entering your sign on the 2nd, you are radiating a magnetic and alluring energy that attracts soulful connections and heartfelt exchanges.

If you're in a committed partnership, this is a beautiful time to share your dreams, fears, and desires with your loved one, and to create a safe space for emotional healing and growth. Practice active listening, empathy, and unconditional love, and be willing to let go of any patterns or dynamics that no longer serve your highest good.

If you're single and seeking love, trust that the universe is guiding you towards relationships that align with your soul's path. Focus on cultivating a loving relationship with yourself first, and know that you deserve to be cherished, respected, and adored for all that you are.

Career:

In your professional life, February 2025 encourages you to align your work with your spiritual values and soul's purpose. With Saturn and Neptune activating your 12th house of inner growth and psychic abilities, you may feel called to explore career paths that involve healing, creativity, or service to others. Trust your intuition and inner guidance, and be open to unexpected opportunities and synchronicities that lead you towards your true calling.

If you're already in a fulfilling career, this is a wonderful time to infuse more meaning, purpose, and creativity into your work. Look for ways to make a positive impact on the world around you, and to use your unique gifts and talents in service of the greater good. Remember that your work is an extension of your soul's journey, and that every challenge or obstacle is an opportunity for growth and transformation.

Finances:

In financial matters, February 2025 invites you to cultivate a mindset of abundance, gratitude, and trust. With Jupiter and Uranus activating your 2nd house of values and resources, you are being called to align your material world with your spiritual beliefs and to attract wealth and prosperity through unconventional means.

Practice affirming your worthiness to receive all the good that life has to offer, and release any limiting beliefs or fears around scarcity or lack. Trust that the universe is always providing for your needs, and that every financial challenge is an opportunity to deepen your faith and surrender.

Consider exploring alternative sources of income or investment that align with your values and passions, and be open to unexpected windfalls or opportunities that come your way. Remember that true abundance flows from a heart of generosity, service, and love.

Health:

In matters of health and well-being, February 2025 encourages you to prioritize self-care, rest, and emotional healing. With the Sun, Mercury, and Neptune activating your 12th house of spirituality and solitude, you may feel more sensitive, intuitive, and introspective than usual. Honor your body's need for rest and relaxation, and create space in your schedule for activities that nourish your soul, such as meditation, journaling, or creative expression.

Pay attention to any physical symptoms or emotional triggers that arise, as they may be pointing you towards areas of your life that need healing or release. Practice self-compassion, forgiveness, and acceptance, and seek out the support of trusted healers or therapists who can guide you on your journey of wholeness.

Remember that true health and well-being come from a place of balance, harmony, and alignment with your soul's truth. Trust in the wisdom of your body, mind, and spirit, and know that you have the power to create a life of vitality, joy, and ease.

Travel:

In the realm of travel and adventure, February 2025 invites you to explore new spiritual practices, philosophies, or traditions that expand your consciousness and deepen your connection to the divine. With Saturn and Neptune activating your 12th house of inner growth and mystical experiences, you may feel called to embark on a pilgrimage, retreat, or vision quest that allows you to unplug from the distractions of daily life and connect with your higher self.

If physical travel is not possible or practical, consider exploring virtual workshops, online communities, or foreign films and books that introduce you to new cultures and ways of being. Remember that the greatest adventure is the journey within, and that every experience - whether near or far - is an opportunity for growth, learning, and transformation.

Insights from the Stars:

The cosmic energies of February 2025 are inviting you to embrace your spiritual path and trust in the wisdom of your soul, dear Pisces. With Saturn, Neptune, and the Full Moon Total Lunar Eclipse activating your sign, you are being called to release old patterns, beliefs, and identities that no longer serve your highest good, and to step into your true power and purpose.

This is a time to connect with your inner guidance, to listen to the whispers of your heart, and to trust in the magic and mystery of the universe. Know that you are exactly where you need to be, and that every challenge or obstacle is a sacred invitation to grow, heal, and evolve.

Remember that you are a divine being of love and light, and that your presence on this planet is a precious gift to the world. Embrace your sensitivity, creativity, and compassion as the superpowers that they are, and trust that you have the strength, wisdom, and resilience to navigate any storm.

Best Days of the Month:

February 5: First Quarter Moon in Taurus - A grounding and stabilizing energy that supports practical action and manifestation.

February 12: Full Moon Total Lunar Eclipse in Leo - A powerful time for releasing old patterns and stepping into your authentic self-expression.

February 14: Mercury enters Pisces - Enhancing your intuition, creativity, and emotional intelligence.

February 18: Sun enters Pisces - Marking the beginning of a new solar cycle and fresh starts in your personal life.

February 23: Mars Direct in Cancer - Supporting forward movement and emotional clarity in your home and family life.

February 27: New Moon in Pisces - A potent time for setting intentions and planting seeds for your dreams and aspirations.

March 2025

Overview Horoscope for the Month:

March 2025 brings a powerful wave of spiritual awakening and personal transformation for you, dear Pisces. With a potent stellium of planets in your sign, including Saturn entering Pisces on March 1st, you are being called to dive deep into your inner world, confront your fears and limitations, and embrace your true path and purpose. This is a time of profound self-discovery, healing, and growth, as you release old patterns and beliefs that no longer serve you and step into a new chapter of your life.

The New Moon in Aries on March 29th falls in your 2nd house of values, finances, and self-worth, marking a fresh start in your relationship with abundance and prosperity. Set clear intentions for financial growth, positive self-talk, and aligning your resources with your spiritual values and goals.

Love:

In matters of the heart, March 2025 invites you to cultivate deeper intimacy, vulnerability, and spiritual connection with your loved ones. With Venus retrograde in Aries from March 1st to 27th, you may find yourself revisiting past relationships, healing old wounds, or gaining closure on unresolved emotional issues. Use this time to reflect on your patterns, needs, and desires in love, and to practice self-love and compassion.

When Venus re-enters your sign on March 27th, followed by the New Moon in Aries on March 29th, you may experience a renewed sense of clarity, confidence, and magnetism in your relationships. Be open to new connections or rekindled romance that align with your authentic self and highest path.

Career:

In your professional life, March 2025 marks a significant turning point, as Saturn enters your sign on March 1st, initiating a new 2.5-year cycle of career growth, responsibility, and mastery. You are being called to take a serious look at your long-term goals, develop a solid plan of action, and put in the hard work and discipline needed to achieve your dreams.

At the same time, with Mercury retrograde in your sign from March 15th to April 7th, you may need to revisit old projects, revise your communication strategies, or rethink your approach to work. Trust your intuition and allow yourself the time and space to make any necessary adjustments or course corrections.

Finances:

The New Moon in Aries on March 29th brings a powerful opportunity to set intentions and take action towards your financial goals and aspirations. With Uranus and Neptune aligning in your 2nd house of money and resources, you may experience sudden breakthroughs, unexpected windfalls, or innovative ideas for increasing your income and prosperity.

At the same time, be mindful of any tendencies towards overspending, financial risk-taking, or unrealistic expectations. Stay grounded in your values, budget wisely, and trust that the universe will provide for your needs as you align your resources with your spiritual path and purpose.

Health:

With the Sun, Mercury, Venus, Saturn, and Neptune all activating your 12th house of spirituality, solitude, and inner work, March 2025 is a deeply introspective and transformative month for your physical, emotional, and spiritual well-being. You may feel more sensitive, intuitive, and attuned to the subtler realms of your being, and may need more time alone to rest, recharge, and connect with your inner guidance.

Prioritize self-care practices that nourish your mind, body, and soul, such as meditation, dream work, energy healing, or creative expression. Be gentle with yourself as you navigate any challenges or obstacles that arise, and trust that every experience is an opportunity for growth, healing, and self-discovery.

Travel:

With so much planetary activity in your 12th house of spirituality and inner work, March 2025 may be a more inward-focused month for you, with less emphasis on physical travel or external adventures. However, this is a powerful time for inner journeys, spiritual retreats, or immersive experiences that allow you to connect with your higher self and the mysteries of the universe.

If you do feel called to travel, trust your intuition and allow yourself to be guided towards destinations or experiences that support your spiritual growth and transformation. Be open to synchronicities, divine guidance, and unexpected opportunities for healing and awakening.

Insights from the Stars:

The cosmic energies of March 2025 are inviting you to embrace your spiritual path, trust your inner wisdom, and surrender to the transformative power of love and grace. With Saturn entering your sign for the first time in 29 years, you are embarking on a profound journey of self-mastery, responsibility, and personal growth. Embrace the challenges and opportunities that arise as sacred lessons and tests of your strength, faith, and resilience.

At the same time, with the Total Lunar Eclipse in Virgo on March 14th activating your 7th house of partnerships and the Partial Solar Eclipse in Aries on March 29th igniting your 2nd house of self-worth, you are being called to release any limiting beliefs, toxic relationships, or unhealthy attachments that are holding you back from your true potential and prosperity. Trust in the power of endings and beginnings, and know that the universe is conspiring to support your highest good and evolution.

Best Days of the Month:

March 1st: Saturn enters Pisces - The beginning of a new 2.5-year cycle of personal growth, responsibility, and self-mastery.

March 14th: Full Moon Total Lunar Eclipse in Virgo - A powerful portal for releasing old patterns, healing relationships, and embracing a new level of wholeness and balance.

March 27th: Venus retrogrades back into Pisces - A time for deepening self-love, compassion, and emotional healing.

March 29th: New Moon Partial Solar Eclipse in Aries - A potent opportunity to set intentions and take action towards your financial goals and aspirations.

March 30th: Neptune enters Aries - The beginning of a new 14-year cycle of spiritual awakening, creative inspiration, and intuitive guidance.

April 2025

Overview Horoscope for the Month:

Dear Pisces, April 2025 is a month of profound spiritual growth, emotional healing, and positive transformation. The cosmic energies are supporting your journey of self-discovery and inner awakening, guiding you towards a deeper connection with your intuition, creativity, and soul's purpose.

The month begins with Mercury and Venus in your sign, enhancing your communication skills, creativity, and magnetism. This is a wonderful time to express your ideas, share your gifts, and attract positive connections and opportunities into your life.

The New Moon in Taurus on April 27 illuminates your 3rd house of learning, communication, and self-expression. Set intentions for expanding your knowledge, honing your skills, and sharing your unique perspective with the world. Trust in the power of your voice and the value of your ideas.

Love:

In matters of the heart, April 2025 invites you to deepen your emotional connections and cultivate greater intimacy and authenticity in your relationships. With Venus in your sign until the 30th, you are radiating a warm, compassionate, and attractive energy that draws others to you. Use this time to express your affection, share your desires, and create a safe space for emotional bonding and growth.

If you're in a committed partnership, the Full Moon in Libra on April 12 highlights your 8th house of deep emotional bonds and shared resources. This is a powerful time to release any fears, resentments, or blocks to intimacy, and to recommit to your love and trust for one another. Be open to vulnerable conversations and transformative experiences that bring you closer together.

If you're single, be open to new connections and synchronicities that align with your values and aspirations. Focus on cultivating a loving relationship with yourself first, and trust that the right person will come into your life at the perfect time.

Career:

In your professional life, April 2025 encourages you to align your work with your spiritual values and inner purpose. With Saturn forming a harmonious sextile to Uranus on the 4th, you may experience unexpected opportunities, innovative ideas, or breakthroughs in your career path. Trust your intuition and be open to unconventional approaches or alternative solutions that allow you to express your unique talents and perspective.

At the same time, with Mercury and Venus in your sign for most of the month, you have a powerful opportunity to communicate your ideas, collaborate with others, and attract positive attention and recognition for your work. Use your creativity, compassion, and intuition to make a meaningful impact and inspire others with your vision.

YOUR COMPLETE PERSONAL HOROSCOPE 2025· 452

Finances:

In financial matters, April 2025 invites you to cultivate a mindset of abundance, gratitude, and trust. With Jupiter and Pluto forming a harmonious aspect mid-month, you may experience unexpected windfalls, opportunities for growth, or the resolution of long-standing financial issues. Practice affirming your worthiness to receive all the good that life has to offer, and release any fears or limiting beliefs around scarcity or lack.

At the same time, be mindful of any tendencies towards overspending or financial risk-taking. Stay grounded in your values, budget wisely, and trust that the universe will provide for your needs as you align your resources with your spiritual path and purpose.

Health:

In matters of health and well-being, April 2025 encourages you to prioritize self-care, rest, and emotional healing. With the Sun and Mercury in your sign for the first part of the month, you may feel more energized, expressive, and mentally active than usual. Use this time to engage in activities that stimulate your mind, body, and soul, such as learning a new skill, trying a new form of exercise, or exploring a creative hobby.

At the same time, be mindful of any tendencies towards overextending yourself or neglecting your physical and emotional needs. Make sure to carve out time for relaxation, meditation, and introspection, especially around the Full Moon in Libra on April 12. Listen to your body's wisdom and trust your intuition when it comes to self-care and healing.

Travel:

In the realm of travel and adventure, April 2025 may bring opportunities for short trips, learning experiences, or connections with people from different backgrounds and cultures. With Mercury and Venus activating your 3rd house of communication and learning, you may feel a strong desire to expand your mind, broaden your horizons, and engage in stimulating conversations and exchanges.

If travel is not possible or practical, consider exploring online courses, workshops, or virtual communities that allow you to connect with like-minded individuals and gain new insights and perspectives. Be open to synchronicities and unexpected opportunities that align with your interests and aspirations.

Insights from the Stars:

The cosmic energies of April 2025 are inviting you to embrace your spiritual path and trust in the wisdom of your soul, dear Pisces. With Saturn forming a harmonious sextile to Uranus on the 4th, you are being called to balance structure and innovation, responsibility and freedom, in pursuit of your highest purpose and potential. Trust that the challenges and opportunities that arise are all part of your soul's journey of growth and evolution.

At the same time, with Jupiter and Pluto forming a harmonious aspect mid-month, you have a powerful opportunity to transform your beliefs, expand your consciousness, and tap into your inner power and resilience. Trust in the universe's ability to support and guide you, and know that every experience is a chance to learn, heal, and evolve.

Best Days of the Month:

April 4: Saturn sextile Uranus - A day of unexpected opportunities, innovative solutions, and breakthroughs in your career and life path.

April 7: Mercury Direct in Pisces - Clarity and forward movement in your communication, self-expression, and mental pursuits.

April 12: Full Moon in Libra - A powerful time for releasing fears, healing relationships, and cultivating balance and harmony in your emotional and financial life.

April 21: Saturn conjunct True Node - A significant alignment of your karmic path and spiritual purpose, inviting you to step into your power and leadership.

April 27: New Moon in Taurus - A potent time for setting intentions and planting seeds for growth and abundance in your communication, learning, and self-expression.

May 2025

Overview Horoscope for the Month:

Dear Pisces, May 2025 promises to be a month of personal growth, spiritual insight, and positive change. The cosmic energies are supporting your journey of self-discovery and inner transformation, encouraging you to embrace your unique talents, express your creativity, and connect with your higher purpose.

The month begins with the Sun in Taurus, illuminating your 3rd house of communication, learning, and self-expression. This is a wonderful time to explore new ideas, engage in stimulating conversations, and share your knowledge and insights with others. Trust in the power of your voice and the value of your unique perspective.

The New Moon in Gemini on May 26 activates your 4th house of home, family, and emotional foundations. Set intentions for creating a nurturing and supportive living space, strengthening your family bonds, and cultivating a deeper sense of inner peace and security. Trust that you have the resilience and adaptability to navigate any challenges or changes that arise in your personal life.

Love:

In matters of the heart, May 2025 invites you to cultivate greater harmony, balance, and mutual understanding in your relationships. With Venus moving through Aries and Taurus this month, you may feel a strong desire for both independence and stability in your connections. Take time to clarify your needs and boundaries, while also being open to compromise and cooperation with your loved ones.

If you're in a committed partnership, the Full Moon in Scorpio on May 12 illuminates your 9th house of adventure, growth, and higher learning. This is a powerful time to explore new experiences together, challenge your assumptions, and deepen your emotional and spiritual bond. Be open to transformative conversations and revelations that bring you closer to your shared truth and purpose.

If you're single, focus on cultivating a loving and accepting relationship with yourself first. Engage in activities that bring you joy, confidence, and a sense of adventure. Trust that the right person will come into your life when you're radiating your most authentic and vibrant self.

Career:

In your professional life, May 2025 encourages you to tap into your creativity, intuition, and communication skills to make progress and achieve your goals. With Mercury moving through Taurus and Gemini this month, you have a powerful opportunity to express your ideas, collaborate with others, and adapt to changing circumstances in your work environment.

At the same time, with Pluto retrograde in your 11th house of networking and future vision, you may need to reassess your long-term goals, alliances, and strategies for success. Be willing to let go of any outdated plans or associations that no longer align with your values and aspirations. Trust your inner guidance and be open to unexpected opportunities that come your way.

Finances:

In financial matters, May 2025 invites you to cultivate a mindset of abundance, gratitude, and practical planning. With the Sun and Mercury moving through your 2nd house of values and resources, you have a wonderful opportunity to reassess your priorities, create a realistic budget, and make informed decisions about your money and possessions.

At the same time, with Jupiter and Uranus forming harmonious aspects this month, you may experience unexpected windfalls, opportunities for growth, or innovative ideas for increasing your income and prosperity. Stay open to new possibilities and be willing to take calculated risks that align with your long-term vision and values.

Health:

In matters of health and well-being, May 2025 encourages you to prioritize self-care, mindfulness, and emotional healing. With the Sun and Mercury moving through grounding Taurus, you may feel a strong desire for stability, comfort, and sensory pleasure. Take time to enjoy nourishing meals, spend time in nature, and engage in activities that bring you a sense of peace and relaxation.

At the same time, be mindful of any tendencies towards overindulgence or avoidance of emotional issues. The Full Moon in Scorpio on May 12 invites you to confront any fears, resentments, or hidden wounds that may be impacting your physical and mental health. Seek the support of trusted healers, therapists, or spiritual practices to help you release and transform any heavy emotions or limiting beliefs.

Travel:

In the realm of travel and adventure, May 2025 may bring opportunities for short trips, cultural exchanges, or educational pursuits that expand your mind and broaden your horizons. With Mercury moving through your 3rd house of communication and learning, you may feel a strong curiosity and desire to explore new ideas, places, and perspectives.

If travel is not possible or practical, consider exploring online courses, virtual tours, or foreign language apps that allow you to connect with different cultures and ways of life. Be open to synchronicities and unexpected encounters that bring fresh insights and inspiration into your world.

Insights from the Stars:

The cosmic energies of May 2025 are inviting you to embrace your authentic self, trust your inner wisdom, and share your unique gifts with the world. With Saturn moving into Aries mid-month, you are entering a new 2.5-year cycle of personal growth, self-assertion, and bold action. Embrace the challenges and opportunities that arise as chances to develop your strength, confidence, and leadership skills.

At the same time, with Jupiter and Neptune forming harmonious aspects this month, you have a powerful opportunity to connect with your spiritual purpose, creative inspiration, and highest ideals. Trust in the universe's ability to guide and support you, and know that your dreams and visions have the power to manifest into reality.

Best Days of the Month:

May 4: First Quarter Moon in Leo - A day of creative self-expression, joyful play, and heartfelt connections.

May 12: Full Moon in Scorpio - A powerful time for releasing fears, transforming relationships, and embracing your inner truth and power.

May 18: Jupiter sextile Chiron - A healing and expansive aspect that supports emotional healing, spiritual growth, and the alignment of your beliefs and actions.

May 24: Saturn enters Aries - The beginning of a new cycle of personal responsibility, self-assertion, and bold leadership in your life.

May 26: New Moon in Gemini - A potent time for setting intentions and planting seeds for positive change in your home, family, and emotional foundations.

Overview Horoscope for the Month:

Dear Pisces, June 2025 brings a mix of spiritual growth, emotional healing, and new beginnings. The month starts with Venus entering your 4th house of home and family on June 6th, encouraging you to focus on creating a nurturing and harmonious living environment. This is a wonderful time to connect with loved ones, engage in family activities, and find peace and comfort in your personal space.

The Full Moon in Sagittarius on June 11th illuminates your 10th house of career and public reputation, bringing a sense of completion or culmination to your professional goals and aspirations. Trust in your abilities and the progress you've made, and be open to new opportunities for growth and recognition.

Love:

In matters of the heart, June 2025 invites you to cultivate deeper emotional intimacy and vulnerability in your relationships. With Venus in your 4th house from June 6th to July 4th, you may feel a stronger desire for security, commitment, and familial bonds. Take time to nurture your closest connections, express your affection and appreciation, and create a safe space for open and honest communication.

If you're in a committed partnership, the Full Moon in Sagittarius on June 11th may bring a significant realization or turning point in your relationship. Use this energy to have honest and expansive conversations about your shared dreams, values, and long-term goals. Be willing to compromise and adapt as needed, while staying true to your own needs and desires.

If you're single, focus on cultivating a loving and accepting relationship with yourself first. Engage in activities that bring you joy, peace, and a sense of belonging. Trust that the right person will come into your life when you're radiating your most authentic and compassionate self.

Career:

In your professional life, June 2025 encourages you to align your work with your spiritual values and inner purpose. With Mars entering Virgo on June 17th and activating your 7th house of partnerships and collaborations, you may find new opportunities for growth and success through teamwork, networking, and cooperative efforts. Trust your intuition and be open to unconventional or innovative approaches that allow you to express your unique skills and perspective.

The Full Moon in Sagittarius on June 11th may bring a culmination or breakthrough in your career path, helping you to see the bigger picture and align your goals with your higher purpose. Stay focused on your long-term vision, while also being adaptable and responsive to changing circumstances.

Finances:

In financial matters, June 2025 invites you to cultivate a mindset of abundance, gratitude, and practical planning. With Venus in your 4th house, you may find greater security and stability in your material world, especially through investments in property, home improvements, or family resources. Be mindful of your spending habits and focus on creating a solid foundation for your long-term financial goals.

At the same time, trust in the universe's ability to provide for your needs and desires, and be open to unexpected sources of income or support. Practice generosity and sharing with others, knowing that the more you give, the more you will receive in return.

Health:

In matters of health and well-being, June 2025 encourages you to prioritize self-care, rest, and emotional healing. With the Sun in Cancer from June 20th onwards, you may feel more sensitive, intuitive, and attuned to your inner world. Take time to nurture yourself through gentle activities like meditation, nature walks, or creative pursuits that allow you to express your feelings and release any stress or tension.

Pay attention to your physical health as well, especially around the Full Moon in Sagittarius on June 11th. Make sure to get enough sleep, eat nourishing foods, and engage in regular exercise or movement that helps you feel strong, flexible, and energized.

Travel:

In the realm of travel and adventure, June 2025 may bring opportunities for short trips, family vacations, or exploring new horizons close to home. With Mercury entering Cancer on June 26th, you may feel a stronger desire to connect with your roots, visit familiar places, or learn more about your ancestral heritage.

If travel is not possible or practical, consider exploring new cultures, philosophies, or belief systems through books, movies, or online resources. Be open to expanding your mind and heart through learning, dialogue, and self-reflection.

Insights from the Stars:

The cosmic energies of June 2025 are inviting you to embrace your emotional depth, intuitive wisdom, and spiritual purpose. With Neptune, your ruling planet, in harmonious aspect to Saturn and Uranus this month, you have a powerful opportunity to ground your dreams and visions into practical reality, while also staying open to divine guidance and unexpected opportunities.

Trust in the journey of your soul, and know that every challenge or obstacle is an opportunity for growth, healing, and self-discovery. Stay connected to your inner truth, your compassion for others, and your faith in the universe, and you will navigate this month with grace, resilience, and wisdom.

Best Days of the Month:

June 6th: Venus enters Cancer - A supportive influence for emotional bonding, family harmony, and creating a nurturing home environment.

June 11th: Full Moon in Sagittarius - A powerful time for expanding your vision, aligning your goals with your higher purpose, and celebrating your achievements and progress.

June 18th: Jupiter trine True Node - A fortunate aspect for spiritual growth, meaningful connections, and aligning your path with your soul's evolutionary journey.

June 25th: New Moon in Cancer - A potent time for setting intentions and planting seeds for emotional healing, family unity, and creating a secure and loving foundation for your life.

June 26th: Mercury enters Cancer - A helpful influence for heartfelt communication, emotional intelligence, and expressing your feelings with clarity and compassion.

July 2025

Overview Horoscope for the Month:

Dear Pisces, July 2025 is a month of personal growth, creative expression, and spiritual exploration. The cosmic energies are supporting your journey of self-discovery and empowering you to embrace your unique talents and desires.

The month begins with Mars entering Leo on July 22nd, igniting your 6th house of work, health, and daily routines. This transit brings a burst of energy and enthusiasm to your everyday life, encouraging you to take bold action towards your goals and prioritize your well-being.

The New Moon in Leo on July 24th further amplifies this theme, providing a powerful opportunity to set intentions and initiate new projects related to your job, self-improvement, or health regimen. Trust in your abilities and let your passion and creativity guide you forward.

Love:

In matters of the heart, July 2025 invites you to express your affection and desires with confidence and authenticity. With Venus moving through Gemini and Cancer this month, you may find yourself attracted to intelligent, emotionally attuned, and nurturing partners who appreciate your depth and sensitivity.

If you're in a committed relationship, the Full Moon in Capricorn on July 10th illuminates your 11th house of friendships and social networks, highlighting the importance of maintaining a balance between your romantic partnership and your connections with friends and community. Take time to nurture your bond with your partner while also cultivating supportive and inspiring friendships.

If you're single, focus on engaging in activities and environments that align with your interests and values. Trust that your authentic self-expression and openness to new experiences will attract compatible and meaningful connections.

Career:

In your professional life, July 2025 encourages you to bring your creativity, intuition, and dedication to your work. With Mars in Leo from July 22nd onwards, you have a powerful opportunity to showcase your unique talents, take on leadership roles, and make significant progress in your career.

However, with Mercury retrograde in Leo from July 18th to August 11th, you may need to review, revise, or reconsider certain projects or plans. Use this time to reassess your goals, refine your skills, and address any challenges or obstacles with patience and perseverance.

Finances:

In financial matters, July 2025 emphasizes the importance of balancing short-term desires with long-term security. With Venus in Gemini until July 30th, you may be tempted to indulge in impulsive purchases or risky investments. Stay mindful of your spending habits and focus on creating a stable and sustainable financial foundation.

At the same time, trust in the abundance of the universe and remain open to unexpected opportunities for growth and prosperity. Align your financial decisions with your values and aspirations, and be willing to invest in your own development and well-being.

Health:

In matters of health and well-being, July 2025 encourages you to prioritize self-care, mindfulness, and physical vitality. With Mars in Leo activating your 6th house of health and wellness, you have a strong motivation to improve your fitness, nutrition, and daily habits.

Take time to engage in activities that bring you joy, creativity, and a sense of accomplishment. Whether it's dancing, playing sports, or pursuing a passion project, find ways to express your energy and enthusiasm in a healthy and fulfilling manner.

Travel:

In the realm of travel and adventure, July 2025 may bring opportunities for short trips, cultural exploration, or learning experiences that expand your mind and broaden your horizons. With Mercury and Venus moving through curious Gemini, you may feel a strong desire to connect with new people, ideas, and environments.

If travel is not possible or practical, consider exploring your local surroundings with fresh eyes and an open mind. Engage in activities that stimulate your intellect, creativity, and sense of wonder, such as attending workshops, trying new hobbies, or connecting with people from diverse backgrounds.

Insights from the Stars:

The cosmic energies of July 2025 are inviting you to embrace your personal power, creativity, and spiritual wisdom. With Chiron retrograde in Aries from July 30th onwards, you have an opportunity to heal any wounds or insecurities related to your self-expression, leadership abilities, or pioneering spirit.

Trust in the unique gifts and perspectives you bring to the world, and don't be afraid to take risks or stand out from the crowd. Your sensitivity, compassion, and intuition are your greatest strengths, guiding you towards your highest path and purpose.

Best Days of the Month:

July 2nd: First Quarter Moon in Libra - A time for harmonizing your relationships, finding balance, and collaborating with others towards a common goal.

July 10th: Full Moon in Capricorn - An opportunity to celebrate your achievements, release limiting beliefs, and align your ambitions with your soul's purpose.

July 19th: Jupiter quintile Chiron - A transformative aspect that supports healing, growth, and the expression of your unique talents and abilities.

July 24th: New Moon in Leo - A powerful time for setting intentions, initiating creative projects, and expressing your authentic self with confidence and joy.

July 30th: Venus enters Cancer - A supportive influence for emotional connection, intuitive understanding, and nurturing your closest relationships.

August 2025

Overview Horoscope for the Month:

Dear Pisces, August 2025 is a month of emotional healing, creative inspiration, and spiritual growth. The cosmic energies are supporting your journey of self-discovery and inner transformation, encouraging you to trust your intuition, express your unique talents, and connect with your higher purpose.

The month begins with a powerful Full Moon in Aquarius on August 9th, illuminating your 12th house of spirituality, intuition, and inner growth. This lunation brings a culmination or revelation to your spiritual path, helping you to release old patterns, heal past wounds, and align with your soul's deepest truth and wisdom.

The New Moon in Virgo on August 23rd activates your 7th house of partnerships and relationships, marking a new beginning or fresh start in your connections with others. Set intentions for creating more balance, harmony, and mutual support in your relationships, and be open to new opportunities for collaboration and growth.

Love:

In matters of the heart, August 2025 invites you to deepen your emotional intimacy, vulnerability, and authenticity in your relationships. With Venus moving through Leo and Virgo this month, you may find yourself attracted to confident, expressive, and detail-oriented partners who appreciate your depth, sensitivity, and dedication.

If you're in a committed relationship, the Full Moon in Aquarius on August 9th may bring a shift or awakening in your spiritual connection with your partner. Take time to explore your shared beliefs, values, and aspirations, and be open to new ways of understanding and supporting each other's growth and evolution.

If you're single, focus on cultivating a loving and compassionate relationship with yourself first. Engage in activities that bring you joy, creativity, and a sense of purpose, and trust that your authentic self-expression will attract aligned and compatible connections.

Career:

In your professional life, August 2025 encourages you to align your work with your spiritual values and inner purpose. With the Sun and Mercury moving through Leo and Virgo this month, you have a powerful opportunity to showcase your unique talents, take on leadership roles, and make meaningful contributions to your field or community.

However, with Uranus retrograde in Gemini from August 6th onwards, you may need to navigate unexpected changes, challenges, or disruptions in your work environment. Stay flexible, adaptable, and open to new ideas and approaches, while also staying true to your core values and long-term goals.

Finances:

In financial matters, August 2025 emphasizes the importance of practical planning, organization, and wise management of your resources. With the New Moon in Virgo on August 23rd, you have an opportunity to set intentions and take action towards your financial goals, such as creating a budget, paying off debts, or investing in your future security.

At the same time, trust in the abundance of the universe and remain open to unexpected sources of income or support. Focus on aligning your financial decisions with your spiritual values and aspirations, and be willing to share your resources and talents with others in a way that feels meaningful and fulfilling.

Health:

In matters of health and well-being, August 2025 encourages you to prioritize self-care, mindfulness, and emotional healing. With the Full Moon in Aquarius on August 9th, you may experience a release or breakthrough in your mental health, helping you to let go of old patterns of stress, anxiety, or self-doubt.

Take time to engage in practices that nourish your mind, body, and soul, such as meditation, yoga, or creative expression. Pay attention to your physical health as well, especially around the New Moon in Virgo on August 23rd, which supports healthy habits, routines, and self-improvement.

Travel:

In the realm of travel and adventure, August 2025 may bring opportunities for spiritual retreats, workshops, or experiences that expand your consciousness and deepen your connection to the divine. With Venus and Mars moving through Leo, you may feel a strong desire to explore new horizons, express your creativity, and connect with like-minded individuals who share your passion for growth and transformation.

If travel is not possible or practical, consider exploring online courses, virtual events, or local communities that align with your interests and aspirations. Be open to new ideas, perspectives, and experiences that challenge and inspire you to grow beyond your comfort zone.

Insights from the Stars:

The cosmic energies of August 2025 are inviting you to embrace your spiritual path, creative power, and emotional wisdom. With Saturn retrograde in Pisces from August 1st onwards, you have an opportunity to review, refine, and recommit to your long-term goals and aspirations, while also staying open to divine guidance and unexpected opportunities.

Trust in the journey of your soul, and know that every challenge or obstacle is an opportunity for growth, healing, and self-discovery. Stay connected to your inner truth, your compassion for others, and your faith in the universe, and you will navigate this month with grace, resilience, and wisdom.

Best Days of the Month:

August 3rd: Uranus quintile True Node - A transformative aspect that supports spiritual growth, innovative solutions, and aligning your path with your soul's evolutionary journey.

August 9th: Full Moon in Aquarius - A powerful time for releasing old patterns, awakening to new insights, and connecting with your higher purpose and vision.

August 11th: Saturn sextile Uranus - A harmonious influence that supports grounded change, practical innovation, and integrating your spiritual wisdom with your everyday life.

August 23rd: New Moon in Virgo - A potent time for setting intentions and planting seeds for personal growth, healthy routines, and meaningful partnerships.

August 28th: Uranus sextile Neptune - A highly intuitive and imaginative aspect that supports creative breakthroughs, spiritual insights, and compassionate action.

September 2025

Overview Horoscope for the Month:

Dear Pisces, September 2025 is a month of profound spiritual awakening, emotional healing, and personal transformation. The cosmic energies are supporting your journey of self-discovery and inner growth, urging you to connect with your intuition, release old patterns, and align with your soul's true purpose.

The month begins with a significant shift as Saturn retrograde re-enters your sign on September 1st. This transit invites you to revisit and refine the lessons and growth you experienced earlier in the year, particularly around personal responsibility, self-discipline, and long-term goals. Embrace this opportunity to build a stronger foundation for your future and trust in the wisdom of divine timing.

The Full Moon Total Lunar Eclipse in your sign on September 7th marks a powerful culmination and release in your personal journey of self-discovery and transformation. This lunation brings heightened emotions, revelations, and a call to let go of any limiting beliefs, patterns, or relationships that no longer serve your highest good. Trust in the process of release and renewal, and have faith in the new beginnings that await you.

Love:

In matters of the heart, September 2025 emphasizes the importance of emotional authenticity, vulnerability, and spiritual connection in your relationships. With Venus entering practical and detail-oriented Virgo on September 19th, you may find yourself attracted to partners who offer stability, reliability, and a shared sense of purpose.

If you're in a committed relationship, the Partial Solar Eclipse in Virgo on September 21st activates your 7th house of partnerships, marking a significant new chapter in your relationship dynamics. Use this energetic portal to set intentions for greater harmony, equality, and mutual growth in your union. Be open to having honest conversations about your needs, desires, and shared vision for the future.

If you're single, focus on cultivating a loving relationship with yourself first. Engage in practices that nurture your self-worth, self-care, and inner peace. Trust that by radiating your authentic light and vibration, you will attract aligned and supportive connections into your life.

Career:

In your professional life, September 2025 encourages you to align your work with your spiritual values and soul's calling. With Mars entering deep and transformative Scorpio on September 22nd, you may feel a strong drive to pursue projects or roles that allow you to make a meaningful impact and facilitate positive change.

However, with Mercury stationing retrograde in Libra on September 21st, you may need to review, revise, or renegotiate certain contracts, agreements, or collaborative efforts in your work. Use this time to reassess your professional goals, communicate clearly, and make any necessary adjustments that support your long-term success and well-being.

Trust your intuition and be open to unexpected opportunities or insights that arise during this time. Remember that your work is an extension of your spiritual path, and that every challenge is an opportunity for growth and self-discovery.

Finances:

In financial matters, September 2025 emphasizes the importance of aligning your resources and investments with your values and long-term goals. The New Moon in Virgo on September 21st brings a powerful opportunity to set intentions and create practical strategies for financial growth, security, and abundance.

Trust in the universe's ability to provide for your needs and have faith in your own resourcefulness and resilience. Be open to new sources of income or innovative ways to manage your finances, but also be discerning and grounded in your choices. Focus on creating a solid foundation for your material world, while also practicing generosity and detachment.

Health:

In matters of health and well-being, September 2025 invites you to prioritize self-care, rest, and emotional processing. The Full Moon Total Lunar Eclipse in your sign on September 7th may bring intense feelings, revelations, or physical symptoms to the surface. Honor your body's wisdom and take time to nurture yourself with gentle practices like meditation, nature walks, or creative expression.

Pay attention to any persistent health issues or emotional patterns that may require professional support or targeted healing work. Trust in the power of vulnerability and ask for help when needed. Remember that true wellness involves a holistic balance of mind, body, and spirit.

Travel:

In the realm of travel and adventure, September 2025 may bring opportunities for spiritual pilgrimages, transformative workshops, or immersive experiences that expand your consciousness. With Jupiter in harmonious alignment with your North Node on September 3rd, you may feel called to explore new horizons, connect with like-minded souls, and align your path with your soul's evolutionary journey.

If physical travel is not possible, consider embarking on inner journeys through practices like shamanic journeying, lucid dreaming, or deep meditation. Seek out teachers, mentors, or wisdom traditions that resonate with your spiritual curiosity and desire for growth.

Insights from the Stars:

The cosmic energies of September 2025 are inviting you to embrace your spiritual authority, emotional authenticity, and creative power. With the Full Moon Total Lunar Eclipse in your sign on September 7th, you are being called to step into your full radiance, release the past, and claim your soul's true path forward.

Trust in the journey of your heart, even when the way seems uncertain or challenging. Know that every experience is a catalyst for your growth and that your sensitivity and intuition are your greatest allies. Stay anchored in your spiritual practice, surround yourself with loving support, and have faith in the unfolding of your divine destiny.

Best Days of the Month:

September 3rd: Jupiter trine True Node - A powerful alignment that supports spiritual growth, fated encounters, and aligning your path with your soul's evolutionary purpose.

September 7th: Full Moon Total Lunar Eclipse in Pisces - A profound portal for releasing the past, claiming your power, and birthing a new chapter in your personal journey.

September 14th: Last Quarter Moon in Gemini - A supportive influence for releasing mental clutter, integrating insights, and finding clarity in your communication and ideas.

September 21st: New Moon Partial Solar Eclipse in Virgo - A potent time for setting intentions and planting seeds for positive change in your relationships, health, and work.

September 29th: First Quarter Moon in Capricorn - A helpful energy for taking practical steps, setting realistic goals, and building a solid foundation for your dreams and aspirations.

October 2025

Overview Horoscope for the Month:

Dear Pisces, October 2025 is a month of deep emotional transformation, spiritual growth, and personal empowerment. With the Sun in Libra illuminating your 8th house of intimacy, shared resources, and psychological healing until October 22nd, you are called to confront your fears, explore your inner depths, and release old patterns that no longer serve your highest good.

The New Moon in Libra on October 21st brings a powerful opportunity to set intentions and plant seeds related to emotional healing, financial partnerships, and spiritual regeneration. Trust your intuition and be open to unexpected breakthroughs and revelations.

On October 22nd, the Sun shifts into Scorpio, followed by the ingress of Mercury and Venus later in the month. This energy activates your 9th house of higher learning, philosophy, and adventure, inviting you to expand your mind, seek new experiences, and connect with your inner truth and wisdom.

Love:

In matters of the heart, October 2025 emphasizes the importance of emotional authenticity, vulnerability, and deep soul connections. With Venus moving through Libra and Scorpio this month, you may find yourself attracted to partners who challenge you to grow, transform, and explore the deeper dimensions of love and intimacy.

If you're in a committed relationship, the Full Moon in Aries on October 6th illuminates your 2nd house of values, self-worth, and personal resources. Use this energy to have honest conversations with your partner about your needs, desires, and shared values. Be open to finding creative solutions and compromises that honor both of your individual and collective goals.

If you're single, focus on cultivating a strong sense of self-love, self-respect, and emotional resilience. Engage in activities that make you feel empowered, confident, and connected to your inner strength. Trust that by radiating your authentic light and energy, you will attract aligned and supportive connections into your life.

Career:

In your professional life, October 2025 invites you to align your work with your deepest values, passions, and purpose. With Mars moving through Libra and Scorpio this month, you may feel a strong drive to collaborate with others, take on leadership roles, and make a meaningful impact in your field or community.

However, with Mercury stationing retrograde in Scorpio on October 19th, you may need to review, revise, or reconsider certain projects, plans, or communication strategies in your work. Use this time to reassess your long-term goals, seek feedback from trusted mentors, and make any necessary adjustments to ensure that your career path is aligned with your authentic self and higher purpose.

Trust in the power of your intuition, creativity, and resilience to navigate any challenges or obstacles that arise. Remember that every setback is an opportunity for growth, learning, and self-discovery.

Finances:

In financial matters, October 2025 emphasizes the importance of deep transformation, shared resources, and aligning your investments with your values and long-term goals. The New Moon in Libra on October 21st is a powerful time to set intentions and create practical strategies for increasing your prosperity, abundance, and financial partnerships.

However, with Pluto stationing direct in Aquarius on October 13th, you may need to confront any fears, power struggles, or hidden dynamics related to money, debts, or joint financial ventures. Be willing to face the truth, take responsibility for your choices, and make any necessary changes to ensure that your financial foundation is built on integrity, transparency, and mutual trust.

Focus on cultivating a mindset of gratitude, generosity, and abundance, even in the face of challenges or limitations. Trust that by aligning your resources with your deepest values and purpose, you will attract the support and opportunities you need to thrive.

Health:

In matters of health and well-being, October 2025 invites you to embrace deep emotional healing, spiritual transformation, and holistic self-care. With the Sun, Mercury, and Venus moving through Scorpio this month, you may feel a strong desire to explore the mind-body-spirit connection, release old traumas or patterns, and connect with your inner power and resilience.

Pay attention to any physical symptoms, emotional triggers, or intuitive messages that may be guiding you towards areas of your life that need healing, release, or transformation. The Full Moon in Aries on October 6th is a powerful time for letting go of any self-defeating thoughts, behaviors, or habits that may be impacting your health and well-being.

Remember to prioritize rest, relaxation, and self-nurturing practices in your daily routines. Engage in activities that bring you a sense of peace, joy, and connection to your inner wisdom, such as meditation, yoga, or spending time in nature.

Travel:

In the realm of travel and adventure, October 2025 may bring opportunities for deep spiritual journeys, transformative retreats, or immersive experiences that challenge you to expand your mind, heart, and soul. With Mercury and Venus moving through Scorpio, you may feel a strong desire to explore the mysteries of life, death, and rebirth, and to connect with the hidden dimensions of reality.

If physical travel is not possible, consider embarking on inner journeys through practices like shadow work, shamanic journeying, or deep psychological exploration. Seek out teachers, workshops, or resources that inspire your curiosity and challenge you to grow beyond your comfort zone.

Trust in the transformative power of facing your fears, embracing change, and surrendering to the unknown. Remember that every journey, whether external or internal, is an opportunity for self-discovery, healing, and spiritual awakening.

Insights from the Stars:

The cosmic energies of October 2025 are inviting you to embrace your emotional depth, spiritual power, and transformative potential. With Saturn and Uranus forming harmonious aspects this month, you are supported in breaking free from old limitations, embracing innovative solutions, and building a stronger foundation for your dreams and aspirations.

Trust in the journey of your soul, even when the path seems dark, uncertain, or challenging. Know that your sensitivity, intuition, and compassion are your greatest strengths, guiding you towards your highest truth and purpose. Stay open to the signs, synchronicities, and miracles that surround you, and have faith in the unfolding of divine timing and grace.

Best Days of the Month:

October 6th: Full Moon in Aries - A powerful time for releasing self-limiting patterns, asserting your needs and desires, and reconnecting with your inner fire and passion.

October 13th: Pluto Direct in Aquarius - A supportive influence for transforming power dynamics, embracing social change, and aligning your actions with your highest ideals and vision.

October 21st: New Moon in Libra - A potent portal for setting intentions and planting seeds related to emotional healing, financial partnerships, and creating more balance and harmony in your life.

October 29th: Mercury enters Sagittarius - A helpful energy for expanding your mind, exploring new ideas and philosophies, and communicating your truth with optimism and faith.

October 30th: Mars enters Capricorn - A time for taking practical steps, setting realistic goals, and aligning your actions with your long-term aspirations and responsibilities.

November 2025

Overview Horoscope for the Month:

Dear Pisces, November 2025 is a month of spiritual exploration, emotional transformation, and personal growth. With the Sun in Scorpio illuminating your 9th house of higher learning, philosophy, and adventure until November 21st, you are called to expand your horizons, seek new experiences, and connect with your inner wisdom.

The New Moon in Scorpio on November 20th brings a powerful opportunity to set intentions and plant seeds related to your spiritual journey, long-distance travel, or educational pursuits. Trust your intuition and be open to unexpected opportunities for growth and self-discovery.

On November 21st, the Sun shifts into Sagittarius, activating your 10th house of career, public image, and long-term goals. This energy supports your professional aspirations and invites you to align your work with your values and vision for the future.

Love:

In matters of the heart, November 2025 emphasizes the importance of emotional depth, authenticity, and shared values in your relationships. With Venus moving through Scorpio and Sagittarius this month, you may find yourself attracted to partners who challenge you to grow, explore new ideas, and expand your understanding of love and intimacy.

If you're in a committed relationship, the Full Moon in Taurus on November 5th illuminates your 3rd house of communication and self-expression. Use this energy to have honest and heartfelt conversations with your partner about your needs, desires, and shared vision for the future. Be open to listening deeply and finding creative solutions to any challenges that arise.

If you're single, focus on cultivating a sense of adventure, curiosity, and openness in your social interactions. Engage in activities that align with your passions and values, and trust that your authentic self-expression will attract compatible and inspiring connections.

Career:

In your professional life, November 2025 invites you to take a visionary and proactive approach to your goals and aspirations. With Mars entering Sagittarius on November 4th, you may feel a strong drive to expand your skills, network, and opportunities for growth and success.

However, with Mercury stationing retrograde in Sagittarius on November 9th, you may need to review, revise, or reconsider certain projects, plans, or communication strategies in your work. Use this time to reassess your long-term objectives, gather feedback from trusted mentors, and make any necessary adjustments to align your career path with your higher purpose.

Trust in the power of positive thinking and optimism, even in the face of challenges or setbacks. Remember that your unique talents and perspective are valuable assets, and that every experience is an opportunity for learning and self-discovery.

Finances:

In financial matters, November 2025 emphasizes the importance of long-term planning, wise investments, and aligning your resources with your values and goals. With Jupiter and Neptune forming a supportive trine aspect mid-month, you may experience unexpected windfalls, opportunities for growth, or inspired ideas for increasing your prosperity and abundance.

However, with Mars in Sagittarius squaring Neptune, be mindful of any tendencies towards overspending, financial risk-taking, or unrealistic expectations. Stay grounded in your budgeting and decision-making, and seek the guidance of trusted advisors or professionals when needed.

Focus on cultivating a mindset of gratitude, generosity, and trust in the universe's ability to provide for your needs. Remember that true wealth involves a holistic balance of material, emotional, and spiritual well-being.

Health:

In matters of health and well-being, November 2025 invites you to expand your understanding of holistic healing, mind-body connection, and preventative care. With the Sun and Mercury moving through Scorpio and Sagittarius, you may feel drawn to explore new wellness practices, philosophies, or alternative therapies that support your physical, emotional, and spiritual health.

Pay attention to any areas of your life where you may be holding onto stress, tension, or unresolved emotions. The Full Moon in Taurus on November 5th is a powerful time for releasing old patterns, practicing self-care, and reconnecting with your body's natural rhythms and needs.

Remember to prioritize rest, relaxation, and joy in your daily routines. Engage in activities that bring you a sense of adventure, laughter, and connection to your inner child.

Travel:

In the realm of travel and adventure, November 2025 may bring opportunities for long-distance journeys, cultural immersions, or educational experiences that expand your mind and worldview. With the Sun and Mercury moving through Sagittarius, you may feel a strong desire to explore new horizons, connect with diverse communities, and broaden your understanding of the world.

If physical travel is not possible, consider embarking on inner journeys through practices like meditation, visualization, or shamanic journeying. Seek out teachers, workshops, or online resources that inspire your curiosity and feed your hunger for knowledge and personal growth.

Trust in the transformative power of new experiences and perspectives, even when they challenge your comfort zone or beliefs. Remember that every journey, whether external or internal, is an opportunity for self-discovery and soul evolution.

Insights from the Stars:

The cosmic energies of November 2025 are inviting you to embrace your spiritual wisdom, emotional depth, and visionary potential. With Saturn direct in your sign from November 27th onwards, you are supported in building a stronger foundation for your dreams and taking practical steps towards your long-term goals.

Trust in the journey of your soul, even when the path seems uncertain or challenging. Know that your sensitivity, compassion, and intuition are your greatest gifts, guiding you towards your highest purpose and destiny. Stay open to the signs, synchronicities, and miracles that surround you, and have faith in the unfolding of divine timing.

Best Days of the Month:

November 5th: Full Moon in Taurus - A powerful time for releasing old patterns, practicing self-care, and reconnecting with your body's wisdom and needs.

November 20th: New Moon in Scorpio - A potent portal for setting intentions and planting seeds related to your spiritual growth, higher education, and personal expansion.

November 27th: Saturn Direct in Pisces - A supportive influence for taking practical steps, building a solid foundation, and aligning your actions with your soul's purpose.

November 29th: Mercury Direct in Scorpio - A helpful energy for gaining clarity, integrating insights, and communicating your truth with depth and authenticity.

November 30th: Venus enters Sagittarius - A time for expanding your heart, exploring new forms of love and connection, and aligning your relationships with your highest ideals and aspirations.

December 2025

Overview Horoscope for the Month:

Dear Pisces, December 2025 is a month of spiritual renewal, emotional healing, and personal growth. With the Sun in Sagittarius illuminating your 10th house of career, public image, and long-term goals until December 21st, you are called to align your professional path with your higher purpose, values, and vision for the future.

The New Moon in Sagittarius on December 19th brings a powerful opportunity to set intentions and plant seeds related to your career aspirations, leadership roles, and public contributions. Trust your intuition and be open to unexpected opportunities for growth, expansion, and success.

On December 21st, the Sun shifts into Capricorn, followed by the ingress of Mercury and Venus later in the month. This energy activates your 11th house of friendships, social networks, and community involvement, inviting you to connect with like-minded individuals, collaborate on shared goals, and make a positive impact in your social circles.

Love:

In matters of the heart, December 2025 emphasizes the importance of emotional maturity, commitment, and shared values in your relationships. With Venus moving through Sagittarius and Capricorn this month, you may find yourself attracted to partners who inspire you to grow, achieve your goals, and build a strong foundation for the future.

If you're in a committed relationship, the Full Moon in Gemini on December 4th illuminates your 4th house of home, family, and emotional roots. Use this energy to have honest conversations with your partner about your needs, desires, and long-term plans for your shared life together. Be open to finding creative solutions and compromises that honor both of your individual and collective aspirations.

If you're single, focus on cultivating a strong sense of self-awareness, emotional intelligence, and personal responsibility. Engage in activities that make you feel empowered, purposeful, and connected to your inner wisdom. Trust that by radiating your authentic light and energy, you will attract aligned and supportive connections into your life.

Career:

In your professional life, December 2025 invites you to take a visionary and strategic approach to your goals and aspirations. With the Sun, Mercury, and Venus moving through Sagittarius and Capricorn this month, you may feel a strong drive to expand your skills, take on leadership roles, and make a meaningful impact in your field or community.

However, with Mercury stationing retrograde in Capricorn on December 28th, you may need to review, revise, or reconsider certain projects, plans, or communication strategies in your work. Use this time to reassess your long-term objectives, seek feedback from trusted mentors, and make any necessary adjustments to ensure that your career path is aligned with your authentic self and higher purpose.

Trust in the power of your intuition, creativity, and resilience to navigate any challenges or obstacles that arise. Remember that every setback is an opportunity for growth, learning, and self-discovery.

Finances:

In financial matters, December 2025 emphasizes the importance of long-term planning, wise investments, and aligning your resources with your values and goals. With Saturn and Neptune forming harmonious aspects this month, you may experience a sense of clarity, inspiration, and divine guidance related to your financial situation and material aspirations.

Focus on creating a solid foundation for your future security and prosperity, while also being open to unexpected opportunities for growth and abundance. Trust in the universe's ability to provide for your needs and desires, and practice gratitude and generosity in your financial dealings.

Remember that true wealth involves a holistic balance of material, emotional, and spiritual well-being, and that your inner state of abundance and contentment is the key to attracting outer prosperity and success.

Health:

In matters of health and well-being, December 2025 invites you to embrace a holistic and proactive approach to your physical, emotional, and spiritual well-being. With the Sun, Mercury, and Venus moving through Sagittarius and Capricorn this month, you may feel a strong desire to establish healthy routines, take responsibility for your choices, and align your lifestyle with your long-term goals and aspirations.

Pay attention to any areas of your life where you may be experiencing stress, imbalance, or neglect, and take practical steps to address these issues with compassion and self-care. The Full Moon in Gemini on December 4th is a powerful time for releasing mental clutter, communicating your needs and boundaries, and finding a healthy balance between work and rest.

Remember to prioritize activities that bring you joy, relaxation, and a sense of connection to your inner wisdom and divine purpose. Engage in practices like yoga, meditation, or spending time in nature to nourish your mind, body, and soul.

Travel:

In the realm of travel and adventure, December 2025 may bring opportunities for long-distance journeys, cultural exchanges, or experiences that expand your mind, broaden your horizons, and align with your spiritual path and purpose. With Jupiter forming harmonious aspects this month, you may feel a strong desire to explore new ideas, philosophies, and ways of being in the world.

If physical travel is not possible, consider embarking on inner journeys through practices like visualization, dreamwork, or studying the wisdom traditions of different cultures. Seek out teachers, workshops, or resources that inspire your curiosity and challenge you to grow beyond your comfort zone.

Trust in the transformative power of new experiences and perspectives, even when they challenge your assumptions or beliefs. Remember that every journey, whether external or internal, is an opportunity for self-discovery, learning, and spiritual evolution.

Insights from the Stars:

The cosmic energies of December 2025 are inviting you to embrace your spiritual wisdom, emotional maturity, and creative potential. With Saturn and Neptune forming harmonious aspects this month, you are supported in manifesting your dreams, aligning your actions with your higher purpose, and trusting in the divine plan for your life.

Stay open to the signs, synchronicities, and miracles that surround you, and have faith in the unfolding of divine timing and grace. Know that your sensitivity, compassion, and intuition are your greatest gifts, guiding you towards your highest truth and destiny.

Remember that you are a divine being of love and light, with a unique purpose and path to unfold in this lifetime. Trust in the wisdom of your soul, the guidance of your heart, and the support of the universe as you navigate the transformative energies of December 2025.

Best Days of the Month:

December 4th: Full Moon in Gemini - A powerful time for releasing mental clutter, communicating your truth, and finding a healthy balance between work and rest.

December 10th: Neptune Direct in Pisces - A supportive influence for spiritual awakening, creative inspiration, and aligning your actions with your highest ideals and vision.

December 19th: New Moon in Sagittarius - A potent portal for setting intentions and planting seeds related to your career aspirations, leadership roles, and public contributions.

December 26th: Sun conjunct Jupiter in Capricorn - A time for expanding your vision, embracing new opportunities, and aligning your actions with your long-term goals and aspirations.

December 29th: Mercury stations retrograde in Capricorn - A helpful energy for reviewing, revising, and refining your plans, communication strategies, and long-term objectives.

Made in the USA
Monee, IL
27 November 2024

71434403R00265